BLACK WOMANHOOD

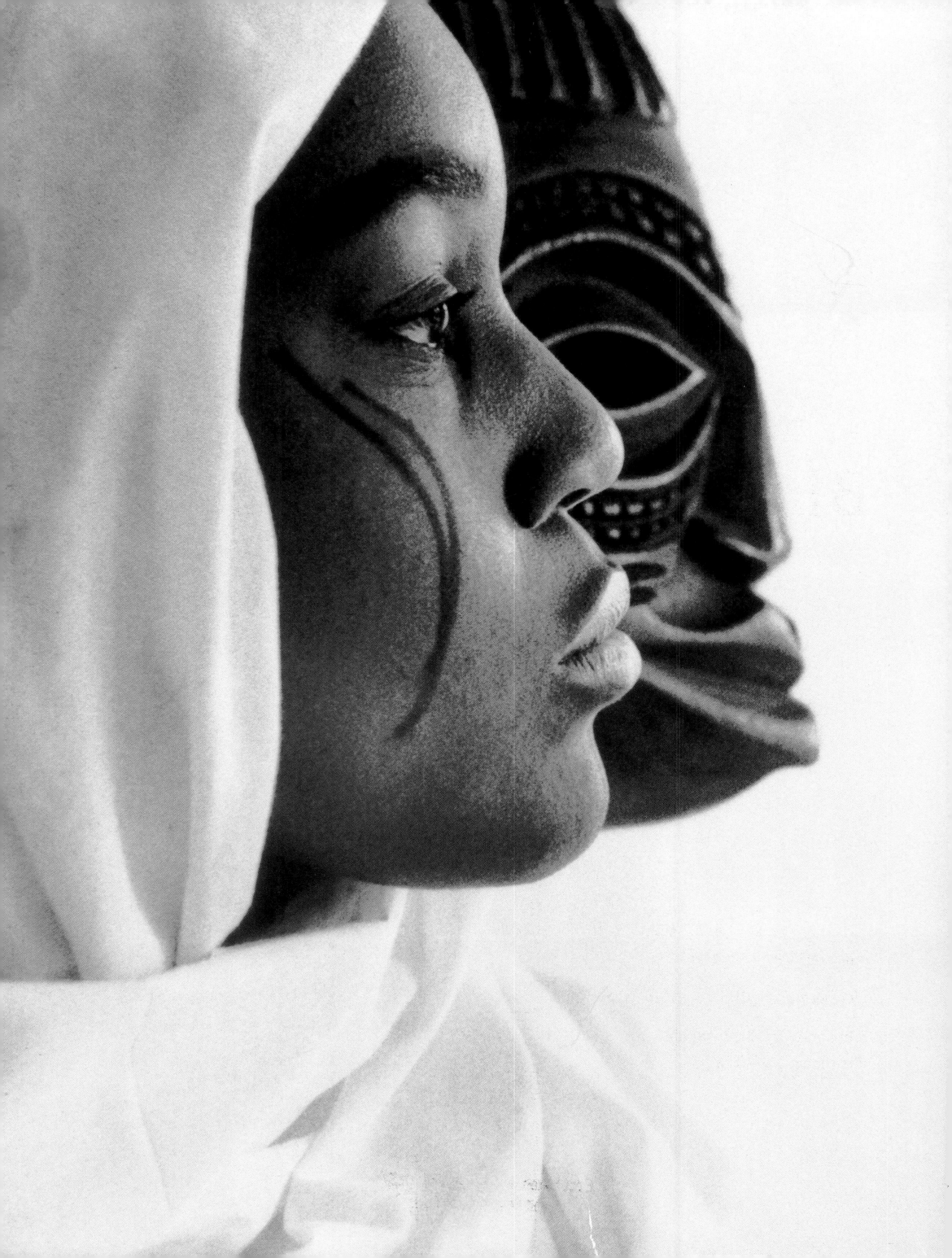

EDITED BY

Barbara Thompson

WITH ESSAYS BY

Ifi Amadiume

Ayo Abiétou Coly

Christraud Geary

Enid Schildkrout

Barbara Thompson

Kimberly Wallace-Sanders

Carla Williams

Deborah Willis

BLACK WOMANHOOD

IMAGES, ICONS, AND IDEOLOGIES OF THE AFRICAN BODY

Hood Museum of Art, Dartmouth College
Hanover, New Hampshire

in association with

University of Washington Press
Seattle and London

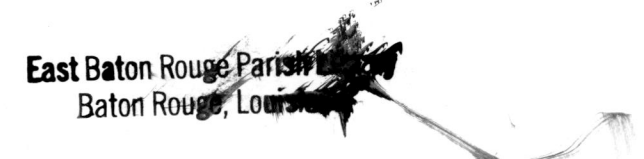

The publication and exhibition of *Black Womanhood: Images, Icons, and Ideologies of the African Body* were organized by the Hood Museum of Art, Dartmouth College, and generously funded by the William B. Jaffe and Evelyn A. Hall Fund, the Leon C. 1927, Charles L. 1955, and Andrew J. 1984 Greenbaum Fund, the Hanson Family Fund, and the William Chase Grant 1919 Memorial Fund. Additional support has been provided by The Andy Warhol Foundation for the Visual Arts.

EXHIBITION DATES

Hood Museum of Art, Dartmouth College, Hanover, New Hampshire
April 1–August 10, 2008

Davis Museum and Cultural Center, Wellesley College, Wellesley, Massachusetts
September 10, 2008–December 10, 2008

San Diego Museum of Art, San Diego, California
January 31–April 26, 2009

University of Washington Press
P.O. Box 50096, Seattle, WA 98145 U.S.A.
www.washington.edu/uwpress

Hood Museum of Art
Dartmouth College, Hanover, NH 03755
www.hoodmuseum.dartmouth.edu

Edited by Suzanne G. Fox
Designed by Carol Beehler

Typeset in Scala and Scala Sans by General Imaging, Washington, D.C.

Printed by C&C Offset Printing Co., Ltd.

LIBRARY OF CONGRESS
CATALOGING-IN-PUBLICATION DATA
Black womanhood: images, icons, and ideologies of the African body / edited by Barbara Thompson; with essays by Ifi Amadiume . . . [et al.]. – 1st ed.
          p. cm.
Issued in connection with an exhibition held at Hood Museum of Art, Dartmouth College, Hanover, New Hampshire, and at later dates, Davis Museum, Wellesley College, Wellesley, Massachusetts, and San Diego Museum of Art, San Diego, California.
Includes bibliographical references and index.
ISBN-13: 978-0-295-98770-5 (hardback : alk. paper)
ISBN-13: 978-0-295-98771-2 (pbk. : alk. paper)
1. Women, Black, in art–Exhibitions.
1. Thompson, Barbara, 1960–
11. Amadiume, Ifi, 1947–
111. Hood Museum of Art.
1V. Davis Museum and Cultural Center.
v. San Diego Museum of Art.
N8232.B55 2008
704.9'42408996–dc22   2007041938

The paper used in this publication meets the minimum requirements of American National Standard for Information Sciences— Permanence of Paper for Printed Library Materials, ANSI z39.48-1984.

PHOTO CREDITS
Unless otherwise stated, all photographs appear by permission of the photographers listed in the captions. Many of the images in this publication are protected by copyright and may not be available for further reproduction without the permission of the photographer, lending institution, or copyright holder. Every effort has been made to contact copyright holders for all reproductions.

Front cover: Maud Sulter, *Terpsichore* (detail), 1989. Photograph courtesy of Maud Sulter and the Arts Council Collection, London.

Back cover: Jonathan A. Green, *Native wedding dress*, c. 1890, before 1905. Courtesy of Christraud Geary.

I am writing. I am writing on me, I am writing on her. The story began to be written the moment the present began. I am asking, how can I be simultaneously inside and outside? I didn't even know this world existed, I thought it existed only in my head, in my dreams. And now here I am, an open book: Inside the book cover, chapters are chaotic and confusing. The cover says more than the book. Chapter One is in fact the ending. Chapter Two is missing. Chapter Three builds a reference to the unknown, and the rest of the book is still in progress. Some paragraphs are written and re-written and some are completely erased with the hope that they will never be read. Some are boldly typed to stand out. Some pages are ripped out, some freshly cut. Paper cuts make the reader bleed at times, reflecting the persona inside. Some chapters are written for me, by authors known and unknown.

Take a person out of her cocoon and watch her quiver in confusion.

Holding onto ideas, sleeping (sometimes not) with a vision so real, so defined, a vision of a perfect world. In the stress of confusion: an unnumbered chapter begins, and ends.

A dialogue between reality and dreams. Arguing, fighting, hope comes creeping in silence, but forceful. The more you read, the more I recollect, the more I understand that expectancy is a sharp blade tearing the pages and disrobing the soul. Sometimes it is troublesome and painful. A chapter is obscured by absence and nothing could make it radiant. Words written on paper thick enough for me to feel the blood flowing under the skin, under the paper. Reading, I wonder, whether this is birth or suicide? Here I might raise the question. Am I independent or not? Or am I just autonomous enough to dream? I feel almost shameless confronting my nakedness.

—LALLA ESSAYDI*

* Artist's translation of the henna painted texts in her photography, personal e-mail communication with Barbara Thompson, October 27, 2006.

Contents

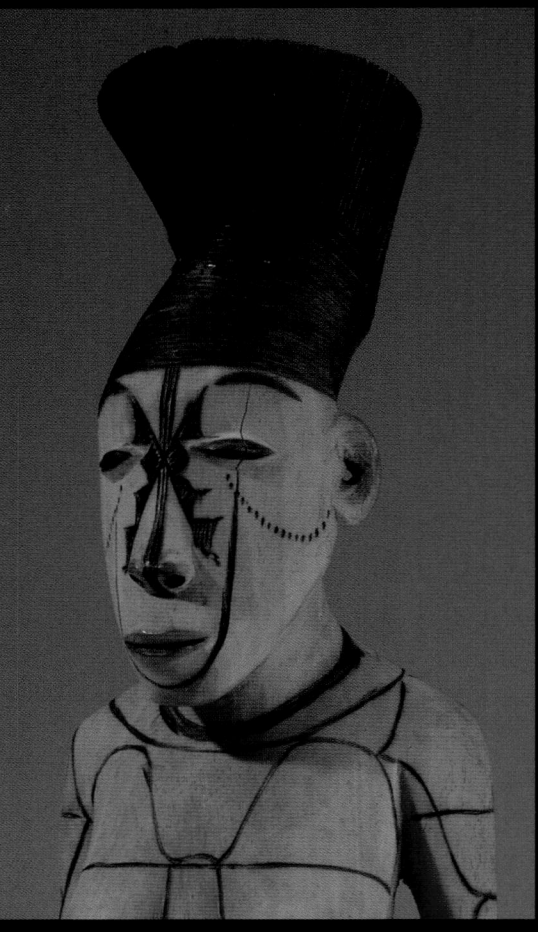
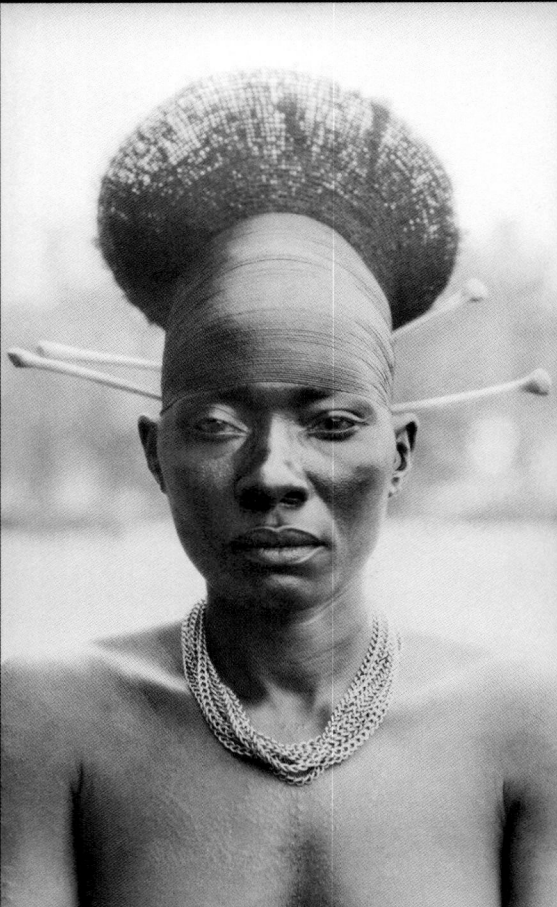
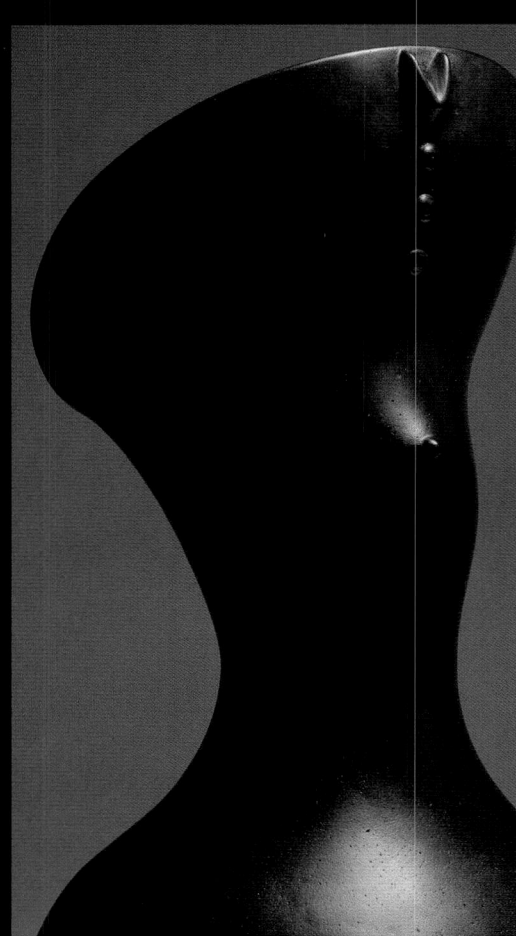

Lenders to the Exhibition

American Museum of Natural History
Arts Council Collection, London
Axis Gallery, New York
The Baltimore Museum of Art
Bernice Steinbaum Gallery, Miami
Cliché Bibliothèque nationale de France, Paris
Maria Magdalena Campos-Pons
Citigroup Private Bank
Christraud Geary
Howard Yezerski Gallery, Boston
Jack Shainman Gallery, New York
Johannesburg Art Gallery, Johannesburg
Olivia Lahs-Gonzales
Senzeni Marasela
Hassan Musa
IngridMwangiRobertHutter
National Anthropological Archives and Human Studies Film Archives,
    Smithsonian Institution
National Museum of African Art, Smithsonian Institution
His Royal Highness, Duke Franz of Bavaria
Bonnie Rabin
Robert Miller Gallery, New York
Angela Rosenthal
Berni Searle
Schomburg Center for Research in Black Culture, Art and Artifacts Division,
    New York Public Library, Astor, Lenox and Tilden Foundations
Bill and Gale Simmons
Penny Siopis
Jerome Stern
Deborah Willis

Foreword

The Hood Museum of Art, opened in 1985, was founded on one of the oldest museum collections in America. Dartmouth College began collecting classifiable examples of the "natural and moral world" as early as 1772. The college was founded to provide "for the education and instruction of youth of the Indian tribes in this land . . . and also of the English youth and any others." Building upon the few Native American students admitted under the college's original charter, racial diversity began on the Dartmouth campus in 1824, when students and faculty successfully petitioned the college to admit Edward Mitchell, from Martinique in the West Indies. Among the earliest African works to enter the Dartmouth College Museum were forty-eight "Zulu" objects, still in the collection today, including a wooden headdress and a beaded snuff container gifted in 1885 by Josiah Tyler, son of Bennett Tyler, who was president of Dartmouth College from 1822 to 1828.[1] Throughout its history, the museum has continued to display its firm commitment to the arts of Africa.

In recent years, museums showing contemporary art have increasingly focused on issues of identity and race. Few have sought to organize an exhibition that investigates these themes within a framework both historical and contemporary in scope. The Hood Museum of Art's ambitious traveling exhibition *Black Womanhood: Images, Icons, and Ideologies of the African Body* looks at the historical roots of a charged icon in contemporary art: the black female body. Only through an examination of the origins of the prevalent stereotypes of black womanhood can we begin to shed new light on the powerful revisionism occupying contemporary artists working with these themes today. This innovative and scholarly art project presents in a single exhibition three separate but intersecting perspectives: the traditional African, the colonial, and the contemporary global.

The unconventional method of juxtaposing historic and contemporary representations of the black female body enables us to peel back the layers of social, cultural, and political realities that have influenced the emergence and transformation of stereotypes of black womanhood from the nineteenth century to the present. *Black Womanhood* therefore promotes a deeper understanding of the ideologies of race, gender, and sexuality that inform contemporary responses—both the viewer's and the artists'—to images of the black female body by encouraging viewers to challenge their own preconceived notions. Over the last two centuries, representations of the black female body, especially unclothed, have evolved into obstinate stereotypes, leaving behind a trail of romanticized, exoticized, and sexualized icons. *Black Womanhood* examines the different ways in which cultural imaginations from the nineteenth century to the present have become embedded into these images.

Critically approaching this controversial subject is not new to some circles of artists, curators, scholars, or critics. The subject does *not* offer, however, the comfortable grounds most often associated with or expected from museum art exhibitions. Images of the black female body are certainly familiar to the general public. In fact, today—as in the past—we are bombarded with and consume representations of black womanhood on a daily basis—on television and in the movies, in music videos, in news programs, and in popular magazines. Despite the ubiquity of such imagery in contemporary popular culture, museum visitors to *Black Womanhood* may yet be variously overcome with a sense of empowerment, discomfort, or pain when looking at these works. Some may be seized by a wave of nostalgia, others appalled, yet others aroused. Some will question; others will accept.

The display and contemplation of such images inevitably evokes issues concerning the complex and often competing definitions and virtues of self-representation and the representation of others. Not surprisingly, many African and African-descended artists are directly confronting these issues and striving to usurp damaging ideologies that have contributed to the perpetuation of stereotypes. The exhibition *Black Womanhood,* as well as the contemporary artists featured therein, acknowledges the role that this image history has played in our own lives. The exhibition is not an attempt to present a survey of images of the black woman throughout human history. Rather, it offers a focused examination of a selection of iconic representations of black womanhood that reveals how these images have affected African and African-descended artists. In this manner, *Black Womanhood* hopes to promote and encourage a deeper understanding of the various processes in which ideologies and responses—including the viewer's— have been shaped as much by past histories as by contemporary experiences.

Since her appointment in 2002 as the Hood Museum of Art's Curator of African, Oceanic, and Native American Collections, Barbara Thompson has organized a series of thoughtful, diverse, and beautifully presented permanent collection displays and temporary exhibitions. *Black Womanhood* represents a project on an altogether different scale, and she has applied her intellectual vigor, hard work, and great flair to her collaborative interactions with artists, lenders, colleagues, staff, and curators at the Hood and many other institutions, and her fellow contributors of essays for this catalogue. Barbara Thompson's important and provocative show will, we are sure, along with this catalogue, add considerably to scholarship and knowledge about the black female body as an icon of contemporary art. 🐚

BRIAN P. KENNEDY, *Director*
Hood Museum of Art
Dartmouth College

1 Barbara Thompson, "The African Collection at the Hood Museum of Art," *African Arts* 37, no. 2 (Summer 2004): 14–33, 93n.

Acknowledgments

The exhibition *Black Womanhood: Images, Icons, and Ideologies of the African Body,* with this accompanying catalogue, has been an incredible professional and personal experience that brought together the energy, support, and encouragement of many people. This project could not have happened without support from the William B. Jaffe and Evelyn A. Hall Fund, the Leon C. 1927, Charles L. 1955, and Andrew J. 1984 Greenbaum Fund, the Hanson Family Fund, and the William Chase Grant 1919 Memorial Fund. Thanks are due also to The Andy Warhol Foundation for the Visual Arts and to Pamela Clapp for their generous support of this exhibition and catalogue.

My deepest gratitude goes to the artists in this exhibition, whose creativity, support, friendship, encouragement, and participation made it a truly collaborative experience: Sokari Douglas Camp, Maria Magdalena Campos-Pons, Renée Cox, Angèle Etoundi Essamba, Lalla Essaydi, Emile Guebehi, Senzeni Marasela, Nandipha Mntambo, Zanele Muholi, Hassan Musa, Wangechi Mutu, IngridMwangiRobertHutter, Magdalene Odundo, Etiyé Dimma Poulsen, Alison Saar, Joyce J. Scott, Berni Searle, Fazal Sheikh, Malick Sidibé, Penny Siopis, Maud Sulter, Kara Walker, Carrie Mae Weems, and Carla Williams. For their expertise, scholarship, and critical guidance, I thank my colleagues who contributed essays to this multidisciplinary publication: Ifi Amadiume, Ayo Abiétou Coly, Christraud Geary, Enid Schildkrout, Kimberly Wallace-Sanders, Carla Williams, and Deborah Willis. Thanks are also due to my colleagues at Dartmouth College—Judith Byfield, Deborah King, Celia Naylor, and especially Angela Rosenthal—for their support, critical assessment, and advice in the conceptual stages of the project.

For their generosity and willingness to part with their treasures, I thank the lenders of artwork and photography to *Black Womanhood,* and those who facilitated the loans and reproductions for this catalogue: Stephanie Carson, Naomi Goodman, Mark Katzman, Barry Landua, Kirsten Mable, Barbara Mathé, and Charles S. Spencer at the American Museum of Natural History; Jill Constantine and Marianne Mulvey at the Arts Council Collection, London; Robert Leopold and Daisy Njoku at the National Anthropological Archives and Human Studies Film Archives, Smithsonian Institution; Clarissa Fostel, Bryna Freyer, Julie Haifley, Chris Mullen Kreamer, Sharon Patton, and Amy Staples at the National Museum for African Art, Smithsonian Institution; Mandy Bartram, Briana Bedigan, and Karen Milbourne at the Baltimore Museum of Art; Sandra Abbott at the Indianapolis Museum of Art; Lizanne Garrett at the National Portrait Gallery; Bonnie Coles and Barbara Moore at the Library of Congress; Jacklyn Burns at the J. Paul Getty Museum; Stefan Eisenhofer and Dorothee Schaefer at the Staatliches Museum für Völkerkunde, Munich; Brigitte Schuhbauer and Beata Sigrist at the Verwaltung des Herzogs von Bayern; Michèle Lenoir and Philippe Mennecier at the Musée National d'Histoire Naturelle; the Boston Anthenæum; Wendy Hurlock Baker and Susan Cary at the Smithsonian Institution Archives of American Art; Catherine Goeres, Rudolf Issorat, Jean-Noël Jeanneney, and Nathalie Léman at the Cliché Bibliothèque nationale de France; Thierry Devynck at the Bibliothèque Forney, Paris; Susan Snyder at the Bancroft Library, University of California, Berkeley; Tammi Lawson at the Schomburg Center for Research in Black Culture; Dianne Nilsen at the Center for Creative Photography, University of Arizona; Gail Miller DeLoach and Steven W. Engerrand at the Georgia Archives; Nina Johnson and Bernice Steinbaum at Bernice Steinbaum Gallery, Miami; Lisa Brittan and Gary Van Wyk at Axis Gallery, New York; Ron L. Jagger, Phyllis Kind, and Jamie Sterns at Phyllis Kind Gallery, New York; Alexis Dunfree and Howard Yezerski at Howard Yezerski Gallery, Boston; Andrea Wood at the Citigroup Private Bank, New York; Judy Sagal and Jack Shainman at Jack Shainman Gallery, New York; Alix du Serech at Skoto Gallery, New York; Ellie Bronson at Sikkema Jenkins & Co. Gallery; Jeannine Howse and Clive Kellner at the Johannesburg Art Gallery, Johannesburg; Joost Bosland and Sophie Perryer at the Michael Stevenson Gallery, Cape Town; Jennifer Brennan, Royce Howes, and Amy Young at Robert Miller Gallery, New York; Claire Fortune at Condé Nast Publications, Inc.; Adam Hirschberg at Cambridge University Press Rights & Permissions; Helen Sanders and Amy Woods at Thomson Publishing Services; Cristin O'Keefe Aptowicz and Janet Hicks at the Artist's Rights Society; Routledge Rights & Permissions; and Getty Images. I also thank Arthe Anthony, His Royal Highness, Duke Franz of Bavaria, Cynthia Becker, Marla Berns, Herbert Cole, Henry Drewal, Tina Dunkley, Christraud Geary, Sabine Jell-Bahlsen, William Katz, Olivia Lahs-Gonzales, Bernardo Lecci, Hassan Musa, Ingrid Mwangi and Robert Hutter, Liz Peri, Bonnie Rabin, Angela Rosenthal, Joyce J. Scott, Bill and Gale Simmons, Jerome Stern, Oliviero Toscani, Donna Van Der Zee, Kimberley Wallace-Sanders, Bruce White, Kathleen Wicker, Deborah Willis, and Min-An Wu.

I wish to thank James Wright, President of Dartmouth College, Barry Scherr, Provost, Mary Gorman, Associate Provost, and the Hood Museum of Art Board of Overseers for their support of this large-scale project. The exhibition and this publication would not have been possible without the support of Derrick Cartwright, former Director of the Hood Museum of Art, who embraced the idea.

Present Director Brian Kennedy's immediate commitment to the work-in-progress enabled the project to reach fruition. With respect and admiration I wish to thank the staff at the Hood Museum of Art for their continual show of excellence, especially Kathy Hart, Associate Director, and Juliette Bianco, Assistant Director, for their guidance and assistance with grants, logistics, and organization; Nils Nadeau, Publications and Web Manager, for facilitating all stages of this publication; Exhibition Designer Patrick Dunfey and Exhibition Preparators John Reynolds and Matt Zayatz; Lesley Wellman, Amy Driscoll, Kristin Berquist, and Adrienne Kermond in the museum's Education Department; Kristin Garcia; Nancy McLain, Christine MacDonald, Roberta Shin, and Sharon Greene for their budgetary and administrative assistance; Mary Ann Hankel and Sharon Reed for their support in the exhibition's planning, public relations, and marketing; Kellen Haak, Kathleen O'Malley, Cynthia Gilliland, Deborah Haynes, and Rebecca Fawcett for their assistance with registrarial needs; Jeff Nintzel for his beautiful photography; Gary Alafat and the museum's security staff; Mary Ellen Rigby in the museum store; and all the museum volunteers.

I owe special thanks and recognition to my Dartmouth curatorial interns, the often unsung heroes who kept the energy fresh during this project: Mercedes Duff '03, Class of 1954 Curatorial Intern; Risa Needleman '04, Curatorial Intern; Alexis Ettinger '05, The Homma Family Curatorial Intern; Cody Harjo '05, Special Project Intern; Meghan Rice '06, The Erbe/Mellon Intern, Curatorial Special Project; Sophia Hutson '06, Kathryn and Caroline Conroy Curatorial Intern; and Alexandra Franco '07, The Homma Family Curatorial Intern. To Catherine "Cat" Roberts '05, first my Special Project Intern and then my Curatorial Assistant on *Black Womanhood* through the busiest phases of research, writing, and organization, I owe my profound thanks for her marvelous ability to keep things organized and for writing the artist biographies. Thanks also to the volunteers on this project: Sean VanDerVliet, Bates College; Elizabeth Bouton, Wheaton College; Chase Delaney; and Emily Shubert, University of Connecticut.

I am most grateful for the unconditional support, patience, and encouragement of mentors and colleagues whose scholarship, fieldwork, and inquisitive minds have helped me along. I particularly thank Professors Robin Poynor, University of Florida; Christopher D. Roy, University of Iowa; and Allen F. Roberts, University of California, Los Angeles, for introducing me to African art and instilling in me a great respect for the people and cultures of the continent. I also thank Tamara Northern for her encouragement and steadfast counsel, and for shaping the foundations of the Hood's African art collection. My gratitude goes also to my dear friend, co-conspirator, and treasured sounding board, Susan Cooksey, Curator of African Art at the Samuel P. Harn Museum of Art.

I wish to thank, for their participation in presenting this exhibition, our colleagues at the Davis Museum and Cultural Center, Wellesley College, and the San Diego Museum of Art. At the Davis, our appreciation goes to David Mickenberg, Ruth Gordon Shapiro '37 Director, as well as Nancy Gunn, Dennis McFadden, Bo Mompho, Jim Olson, Connie Willard, Elizabeth Wyckoff, Rebecca Dolloff, Anja

Chavez, Andrew Daubar, Elaine Mehalakes, Alexa Miller, and John Rossetti. In San Diego, we wish to thank Derrick R. Cartwright, The Maruja Baldwin Director, and Betti-Sue Hertz, Curator of Contemporary Art, as well as Julianne Markow, Scott Atkinson, Vanessa Cobera, Tiffany Lee, Sonya Quintanilla, Paul Brewin, Scot Jaffe, Marya Villarin, Tammie Bennett, John Digesare, Sarah Beckman, Katy McDonald, Golda Akhgarnia, Carrie Spaniol, Christianne Penunuri, Vas Prabhu, and Gwen Gomez.

With devotion I thank my son, Dorian Thompson, for tolerating my preoccupation with this project during his teenage years. Finally, I thank John Malcolm Nyberg III for his love, sensibility, and constant support and patience with our uninvited houseguest, named *Black Womanhood.*

BARBARA THOMPSON
Curator of African, Oceanic, and Native American Collections
Hood Museum of Art
Dartmouth College

Introduction

The black body has, of course, been demonized in Western culture;
represented as ogreish, coarse, and highly menacingly sexualized.
But the black body has also been valorized, represented as darkly alluring—
still highly menacingly sexualized but, well, in a good way. And this,
historically, is its ambiguous role in the Western imagination.

—HENRY LOUIS GATES JR.[1]

While conceiving *Black Womanhood,* I was asked, "Why this, why now?" and *especially* why the combination of traditional African, colonial, and contemporary representations of the black—mostly unclothed—female body? As an Africanist, the question seemed naïve to me. For more than a decade, I had been examining the development of contemporary African and Diaspora arts and the emergence of black feminist voices from Africa who have been attempting to free their art from long-standing cultural, racial, and gender politics. But as a museum curator, I knew that many visitors to the exhibition would be walking into completely new, and possibly difficult, territory. For some visitors, they might be familiar only with African art through exhibitions of or books about objects created in the traditional cultural milieu. Other visitors may never have questioned the fact or fiction of colonial and postcolonial representations of Africa and Africans. For yet others, the very notion of combining "contemporary" with "traditional" art in an exhibition may seem contradictory, as seldom do these two categories share the same space. And yet as a deeper understanding of cultural constructions and mechanisms reveals, it is not uncommon that "traditional" and "contemporary" contexts often overlap, merge, or co-exist.

As with all cultural production, the art works in *Black Womanhood* are as much grounded in and intersect with tradition and history and art and ethnography as they do with modernity and contemporaneity. This exhibition reflects upon and critically examines these multiple—and also contested—forces that have shaped Western constructions of stereotypical representations of the black female body. As South African curator and scholar Rory Bester has noted,

> From art to ethnography and back again, the unclothed black subject has consistently been the focus of voyeurism and science. But as much as such gazing has "disarmed" women, so too have women used their nakedness to disarming effect, to claim or reclaim a power that is threatened or lost.[2]

Black Womanhood uses the opportunity of contemporary interests in self-reflection to reconsider our own past and present role in creating or perpetuating stereotypes and to examine how artists today are "disarming" the dominant histories/histories of dominance embedded in these stereotypes, thereby reclaiming dignity and power through the black female body.

As a curator of traditional and contemporary arts from Africa and the Diaspora, I have felt a deep need to understand the individual histories and circumstances of each artist and each culture to fully appreciate the forging of meanings and identities through art. Yet no single project could ever present the whole range of images, icons, and ideologies of black womanhood. Through the presentation of art works created within different cultural, social, and chronological contexts, however, this exhibition can reveal the simultaneous existence of multiple and often contradictory ideologies. Indeed, the very nature of diversity in the construction of "truths" in "histories" of black womanhood—regardless of their origins or intentions—begins to emerge in such an endeavor. I stress here *begins to emerge,* as this project must be seen as a point of departure for many more conversations and examinations.

This catalogue exposes not only the multiplicity of art forms presented in the exhibition *Black Womanhood* but also a multiplicity of perspectives expressed through the authors' and artists' viewpoints. Both are critically reflecting upon the impact of objectivity and subjectivity in constructions of black womanhood and developing new methods of investigating and debunking mythologies and stereotypes through art. This engagement insists upon inclusivity of multiple voices—even when these may conflict with each other or with other existing theories. Rather than attempting to simplify the histories behind ideologies and stereotypes of black womanhood, this project attempts to expose their complex nature. It is therefore not only the art that will generate further questions and provoke thought and discussion but also the participating authors and contemporary artists, who have seized the opportunity offered by an academic museum to investigate—in fact, crack open—this complex subject as it manifests itself in current artistic trends. Consequently, this exhibition and catalogue divulge the various strategies that contemporary scholars and artists currently use to deconstruct, re-examine, and renegotiate this difficult terrain. For many artists in this exhibition, as also other members of the communities and cultures to which they belong, they still feel and battle the very real constraints of past ideologies of black womanhood in their everyday lives. For this reason, as sculptor Joyce J. Scott so poignantly has stated, we "can't be complacent about the world [we] live in. . . . It's important . . . to use art in a manner that incites people to look and then carry something home—even if it's subliminal—that might make a change in them."[3]

OPPORTUNITIES AND OBSTACLES: FROM THE FRINGES TO THE CENTER

Although feminism has had a firm grip in the Western art world since the 1970s, the development of feminist approaches in contemporary African arts is still in its infancy. With the limited (although slowly increasing) participation of female artists from Africa and its Diaspora in large international art venues, the complex relationships between race, gender, and sexuality have yet to be fully explored. For many African artists, participation in the global art world has been possible only through the outward flow of their artistic talent—a kind of "right-brain" drain from Africa to the West, which inevitably limits further development of feminist aesthetics within Africa. And yet it is precisely this transnational flow of ideas and experiences that has contributed to the beginnings of feminist approaches in contemporary arts in African nations. With both male and female artists showing interest in examining meanings inscribed upon colonized bodies, the subversion of racialized and gendered stereotypes is now becoming a reality among African and African-descended artists living both in and away from Africa.

Especially since the rise of international biennials in the early 1990s, contemporary African and African-descended artists have begun to leave their mark in the global and ever-diversifying art world. Art journals such as *Nka: Journal of Contemporary African Art, Revue Noire, Art South Africa,* and *Third Text* have played a particularly important role in introducing the names of newly emerging contemporary African artists into larger artistic discourses. New avenues are being paved for their contributions to and participation in these venues, such as the Venice Biennale, Documenta, the Havana Biennial, Dak'art, and Miami/Basel, providing African-based artists especially with much-needed access to influential circles of contemporary art critics, curators, and collectors.

At the same time, large traveling museum exhibitions, such as *Africa Explores: 20th Century African Art* (Museum for African Art, New York, 1991), *In/Sight: African Photographers from 1940 to the Present* (Guggenheim Museum, New York, 1996), *The Short Century: Independence and Liberation in Africa, 1945–1994* (Villa Stuck Museum, Munich, 2001), *Looking Both Ways: Art of the Contemporary African Diaspora* (Museum for African Art, New York, 2003), and *Africa Remix* (Museum Kunst Palast, Dusseldorf, 2004), have introduced the broader public to the vast diversity of contemporary art made by African nationals and transnationals.

Together, these initiatives have helped relocate African and African-descended artists from the fringes of the contemporary art world to the center. And although one could argue that some of these artists, such as Ouattara Watts, Chris Ofili, Yinka Shonibare, and William Kentridge, have become "household" names in contemporary art discourses, one must also acknowledge that they are seldom discussed without debates around the "authenticity" of their "African" identity or artistic style—issues that never seem to matter in deliberations about Western artists who migrate elsewhere in the world.

In the exhibition *A Fiction of Authenticity: Contemporary Africa Abroad* (Contemporary Art Museum, St. Louis, 2003), curators Shannon Fitzgerald and Tumelo Mosaka directly confronted the debates about authenticity and identity in contemporary art by Africans living abroad. As Fitzgerald noted, the exhibition sought to analyze constructs of perceptions (fictions) about what constitutes an authentic Africa—within that continent and abroad . . . and consider how these fictions have skewed what it means to be African and to what extent Africanness is expressed, understood, exploited, and relevant in contemporary global culture.[4]

Along with a small selection of other exhibitions of African transnational artists, *A Fiction of Authenticity* has shown that many artists of African descent have had to move across local, national, and international boundaries to participate in the global art world. Such movement inevitably challenges fixed notions of cultural identity, regardless of the artists' place of birth or ethnic origins.

Confounding as it may be that questions of authenticity of "Africanness" or "blackness" *still* permeate discussions about contemporary arts by African and African-descended nationals and transnationals (as is also the case in contemporary arts from Asia, the Pacific, the Middle East, and Latin America), such debates have opened up important forums of critical discussion pertaining to race, politics, sex, and gender. And although in some contemporary art circles the jury is still out on the debate over African "authenticity" in art, the continuation of these critical discourses exposes the forces impacting the placement, meaning, and future of contemporary arts from around the world.

Until more recent years, African and African-descended artists usually made their entrance into the international art venues as a consequence of working and living in the West, as most African nationals faced numerous obstacles by remaining in Africa. Except for isolated cases during the last decade of colonial occupation, these obstacles were deeply entrenched in colonial practices and ideologies, particularly in European-dominated governments that saw little advantage in the education of Africans, much less the need for their artistic education.[5] During the era of independence from the 1960s to the 1970s, the newly independent African national governments were profoundly absorbed with the devastating challenges of political, social, and economic emergencies, often in the face of ongoing attempts to meet their populations' basic needs. Again, art education played a minor, if any, role.

Today, most African nations continue to grapple with the long-term ramifications of colonialism now further challenged by postcolonialism, globalization, and rising global political instability. Few of these countries—with the exceptions of perhaps South Africa, Ghana, and Nigeria—have been privileged with sufficient financial or academic resources to develop strong national and internationally connected art institutions. And in those countries where larger art infrastructures have developed in recent years, such as Mali and Tanzania,[6] rarely can they align themselves with international art partners because of their limited resources. Consequently, for contemporary artists still living on the African continent, participation in the larger global art world presents almost insurmountable financial and logistic challenges.[7] And since the international art market in Europe only began to develop a serious interest in contemporary African artists living *in*

Africa over the past decade or so (America lags egregiously behind), steadfast partnerships are still in the making.

When African-based artists have successfully entered the highly politicized international art market, the majority have been male. One of the most pervasive obstacles facing female contemporary artists living in Africa is that they generally have had fewer opportunities and means than men to study art at reputable institutions, whether in Africa or abroad. Consequently, they have even less exposure to international curators, large exhibitions organizers, and international art brokers. Moreover, cultural restrictions and social expectations often discourage African women from seeking careers in contemporary art practices that go beyond local, national, or regional levels. Young women who pursue careers in contemporary media often do so at the risk of breaking family ties and/or cultural norms.

For example, as the young Malian artist Fatoumata Diabaté explains, her father rejected her for pursuing a career in photography rather than marriage or a culturally acceptable "woman's" art form, such as textile-making or pottery. "In Mali," she explained, "photography is still widely viewed as man's work. Nevertheless, persevering in my career as a photographer was a sacrifice worth making. After I won the AFAA *Afrique en Création* award at the *Rencontres Africaines de la Photographie* in Bamako in 2005 my father accepted me back, realizing that photography can be a serious and laudable profession—even for a woman."[8] For new generations of African women pursuing contemporary art careers, such as Diabaté, the cultural and social restrictions are further compounded by the fact that most of the artists teaching in major African art institutions are male. Many were trained in the West prior to the feminist art movement and thus teach their students about male-dominated art movements, forms, and aesthetics. Except for South Africa, where feminist art developed along with resistance art in the late Apartheid era, art institutions on the continent generally continue to experience a palpable void of outspoken feminist voices or aesthetics to guide their young female students. The importance of these male art professors in African art institutions, nevertheless, cannot be denied. Their international training and the contacts they have maintained in the West help place their young female students in residency programs and small group shows in Europe and the United States, where interaction with artists from other parts of the world encourages them to broaden their self-expression and self-representation.

DIS/ARMING AND DE/SCRIBING BLACK WOMANHOOD TODAY

Although larger group exhibitions of contemporary arts from Africa have dealt with the marginalization of these artists in the global context, they have been less concerned with gender issues that affect young aspiring female artists in Africa. This is also the case in some areas of the Diaspora, such as the Caribbean. Consequently, smaller exhibitions at commercial galleries and academic-based museums in Europe and the United States have been the primary means for these female artists to move beyond the otherwise male-dominated contemporary art scene in Africa. And despite the obvious drawbacks of the tendency toward ghettoization in exhibitions featuring, for example, exclusively "black artists," "female artists," or "African artists," many of these projects have brought together artistic voices from Africa, Europe, and America to reveal blended influences and interests that emerge out of common conceptual, ideological, or experiential threads, even as superficial as those based on race, gender, or geography. It is within this larger setting that crucial exhibitions such as *Gendered Visions: The Art of Contemporary African Women Artists* (Herbert F. Johnson Museum of Art, Cornell University, 1997) and *Africaine* (The Studio Museum, Harlem, 2002) stand out with their focus on female artists from Africa and the Diaspora, thereby setting the stage in the United States for the emergence of counternarratives to the dominant voices occupying the center stage of the contemporary global art world.

The exhibition *Gendered Visions* focused specifically on the works of six African female artists,[9] revealing their shared concerns as African and African-descended women working within the international art milieu. Similarly, the exhibition *Africaine* focused on the mutual interests of four African female artists[10] in feminist deconstructions of the black female body in popular European, American, and African imagery. While a few of the artists in these two exhibitions were already well known in the European or American contemporary art world, most were just emerging. Both exhibitions exposed the Africana artists' struggles with issues of identity, displacement, and transnationalism—some of the same issues experienced by African male artists. However, the exhibitions revealed also that the female artists are challenged additionally with the task of finding new forms of self-representation that can counteract the iconic and stereotypical images of the black female body that have dominated the Western cultural imagination.

The exhibition *Black Womanhood* builds upon the foundations laid by *Gendered Visions* and *Africaine* by inserting and juxtaposing both male and female artistic perspectives, from the past as well as from the present. As such, the exhibition reveals the dynamics and diversity of these artists' responses to the histories contributing to and embedded in stereotypes of black womanhood. Over the past two decades, both male and female artists have been appropriating, recasting, and critically re-exposing historical images and icons of the black female body in an effort to disarm persistent stereotypes. By challenging preconceived ideas about black female identity and diversifying representations of difference from within *and* between cultures, these artists are faced with the formidable task of confronting some of the most pernicious ideologies of womanhood, which, for the most part, others have constructed for them.

This is, no doubt, a difficult and controversial endeavor and one that Mieke Bal argues only serves to perpetuate the stereotype while also exposing the represented subjects once again to the violence of subjugation.[11] As the contemporary artists in this exhibition and the essayists contributing to this catalogue contend, however, one cannot create a new and unfettered visual language about the black female body without first decolonizing, diversifying, and rewriting its history. Particularly important to the process is this deconstruction of notions born from the ideological frameworks of conquest, colonialism, enslavement, and voyeurism. The complex historiographies behind each perspective on or stereotype of black womanhood easily could have been conceived as a focused exhibition. Indeed, each carries its own biases that deserve further investigation and therefore also its own vulnerability toward controversy and criticism about the continued misrepresentation and re-exploitation of the black female body. Brought together, however, the different perspectives, ideologies, and stereotypes expose a much larger issue: the insidious nature of rigid ideological terrains and the potential risks inherent in negotiating new paradigms. Just as some works in this exhibition directly confront disputable territories in art, feminism, and museum practices, so too do the polemics presented in this catalogue. Like many such difficult, painful, and controversial endeavors, the risk is worthwhile if it bears the fruit of liberation from fettered and erroneous colonial fixations on race and sexuality, thereby clearing the path toward empowerment and freedom of self-expression and self-representation.

For this reason, *Black Womanhood* takes the alternative route—certainly not without risks—of presenting ideologies of black womanhood from three different perspectives: the traditional African, the colonial, and the contemporary global. Although the means of expression, media, circumstances, or original intentions differ in many ways, each perspective carries a preoccupation with sub-narratives about ideals of beauty, fertility and sexuality, maternity and nurturance, and women's social roles and identities. The exhibition's clearly delineated tripartite organization allows each moment in time and each cultural milieu to tell its own story. Yet, as when one looks through a prism, the overlap and synthesis of iconic themes and images across perspectives disclose the complex and interwoven relationships between Africa and the West, male and female, and past and present, all of which have contributed to the inscription of meaning onto the black female body.

Like the exhibition, the catalogue is divided into three parts, each offering a different lens through which we can (re)read images of black womanhood. The essays in this publication build upon important studies of representations of black womanhood conducted over the last few decades in art history, anthropology, history, science, literature, and women and gender studies.[12] They reveal the cogent and often disturbing historical evidence of the ideological and visual manipulation of representations of black womanhood. They also demonstrate how contemporary artists are using similar means of manipulation to decolonize and de/scribe, indeed to "disarm," historical narratives about black womanhood to create a new visual language of the empowered black female body.

Opening part 1 of this catalogue, *Iconic Ideologies of Womanhood: African Cultural Perspectives,* I examine the complementary nature of gendered technologies and practices in representations of womanhood in traditional African arts. Ifi Amadiume follows with a comparison of how empowerment and agency are negotiated through the female body in both the traditional and contemporary African cultural milieus. Enid Schildkrout ends the section with a case study that discusses local agency in the fashioning of Mangbetu female identity during the nineteenth and early twentieth century in response to the colonial fascination with the "exotic" beauty of Mangbetu women. In part II of the catalogue, *Colonizing Black Women: The Western Imaginary*,[13] Christraud Geary examines how the photographic gaze in colonial era postcards contributed to Western stereotypes of African womanhood, while evidence of African agency in the creation of some of these images can be re-evaluated as counternarratives to colonial racist and voyeuristic ideologies. Kimberly Wallace-Sanders then discusses the association between literary and artistic representations of "Mammy" in American literature and visual arts. In part III, *Meaning and Identity: Personal Journeys into Black Womanhood*, Deborah Willis examines the emergence of counternarratives to American stereotypes of black women through portrait photography of the New Negro movement. Building upon Willis's essay, Carla Williams considers the modeling careers of Maudelle Bass and Florence "Flo" Allen, who anticipated contemporary black women's nude self-portraiture through their alternative performances of modern black womanhood. Ayo Abiétou Coly then compares different artistic strategies in appropriating stereotypes of black womanhood to expose and disrupt the continuation of colonial fixations on the racialized female body. Finally, the catalogue closes with my examination of the cultural, historical, social, and gender boundaries crossed and the artistic tactics used by contemporary artists in their attempts to decolonize the black female body. Interleafs of artists' commentaries, called "exchanges," are dispersed throughout the catalogue and delineate the artists' personal thoughts about and responses to the histories of cultural, racial, and gender politics, which have shaped their own responses to icons of the black female body. Like the selection of works in the exhibition, each essay and exchange teases out the interplay between the past and the present, between male and female, and between history and contemporaneity. Together these narratives divulge the tangled forces that have created ideologies of black womanhood, many of which continue to shape our world. 🐾

1 Henry Louis Gates Jr., "The Body Politic," in *Thirteen Ways of Looking at a Black Man* (New York: Random House, 1997), 61.

2 Rory Bester, "Floating Free" in *Berni Searle* (Cape Town: Bell-Roberts Publishing), 9.

3 See Thompson, "Decolonizing Black Bodies: Personal Journeys in the Contemporary Voice," in this volume.

4 Shannon Fitzgerald and Tumelo Mosaka, eds., *A Fiction of Authenticity: Contemporary Africa Abroad* (St. Louis: Contemporary Art Museum, 2003), 2.

5 See N'Goné Fall and Jean Loup Pivin, eds., *An Anthology of African Art: The Twentieth Century* (New York: Distributed Art Publishers, Inc., and Paris: Revue Noire Éditions, African Contemporary Art, 2002), for a general survey of African art movements of the twentieth century.

6 In recent years, Bamako, the capital of Mali, has become an important center for the development of African photography through the African photography biennial. The House of Photography and the newly established Centre de Formation en Photographie have played a vital role in supporting and promoting the work of emerging photographers, while the new Conservatory of Art in Bamako provides formal education for Malian students in the visual, media, and performing arts. Similarly, Dar es Salaam, the capital of Tanzania, now hosts the East African Art Biennale, which began in 2003 and brings together artists from across the East African region. Each year the Zanzibar International Film Festival (ZIFF) promotes also the development of film, performance, and the visual arts in the greater East African region.

7 In a foreword to the exhibition catalogue *Looking Both Ways: Art of the Contemporary African Diaspora*, South African artist Sue Williamson provides an effective personal account of the difficulties of being—and remaining—an artist in Africa and the challenges that African artists encounter when they leave the continent for the "established art world centers" in the "old world." Sue Williamson, "Should I Stay or Should I Go: The Ceaseless Dilemma of the Artists of Island Africa," in *Looking Both Ways: Art of the Contemporary African Diaspora*, ed. Laurie Ann Farrell (New York: Museum for African Art, and Gent: Snoeck Publishers, 2003), 10–11.

8 Fatoumata Diabaté, personal communication with Barbara Thompson, 2006.

9 These included Elsabeth Tariqua Atnafu, Xenobia Bailey, Renée Cox, Angèle Etoundi Essamba, Houria Niati, and Etiyé Dimma Poulsen.

10 These included Candice Breitz, Wangechi Mutu, Tracey Rose, and Fatimah Tuggar.

11 Mieke Bal, *Double Exposure: The Subject of Cultural Analysis* (London: Routledge, 1996).

12 These include Sanders Gilman's seminal examination *Difference and Pathology* (Ithaca: Cornell University Press, 1985); Zola Maseko's film *Life and Times of Sara Baartman* (New York: First Run/Icarus Films, 1998); T. Denean Sharpley-Whiting's *Black Venus: Sexualized Savages, Primal Fears, and Primitive Narratives in French* (Durham: Duke University Press, 1999); Deborah Willis's and Carla Williams's *The Black Female Body: A Photographic History* (Philadelphia: Temple University Press, 2000) and *They Called Her Hottentot: The Art, Science and Fiction of Sarah Baartman* (Philadelphia: Temple University Press, 2006).

13 I use the term "imaginary" here as a noun in reference to the Lacanian term—which is also called the social imaginary—and to connotations of illusion, seduction, and fascination. In Lacanian philosophy and critical theory, the term is often used to define the dual relationship between the ego and the specular image. Jacques Lacan, *The Four Fundamental Concepts of Psycho-Analysis*, ed. Jacques Alain Miller, translated from the French by Alan Sheridan (New York: Norton 1978). I find this concept particularly relevant to the mirroring of African culture through the lens of Western eyes.

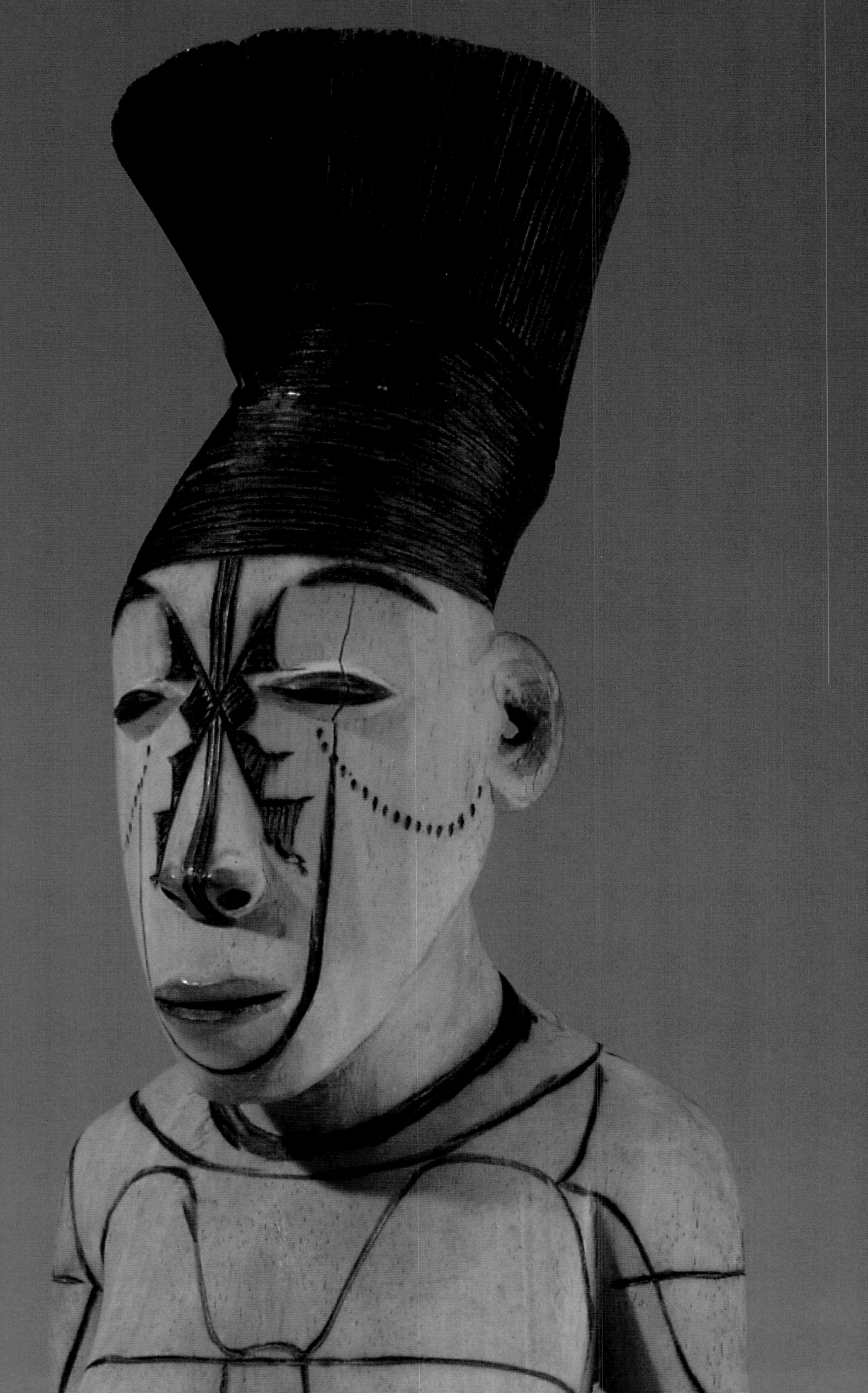

PART I | ICONIC IDEOLOGIES OF WOMANHOOD: AFRICAN CULTURAL PERSPECTIVES

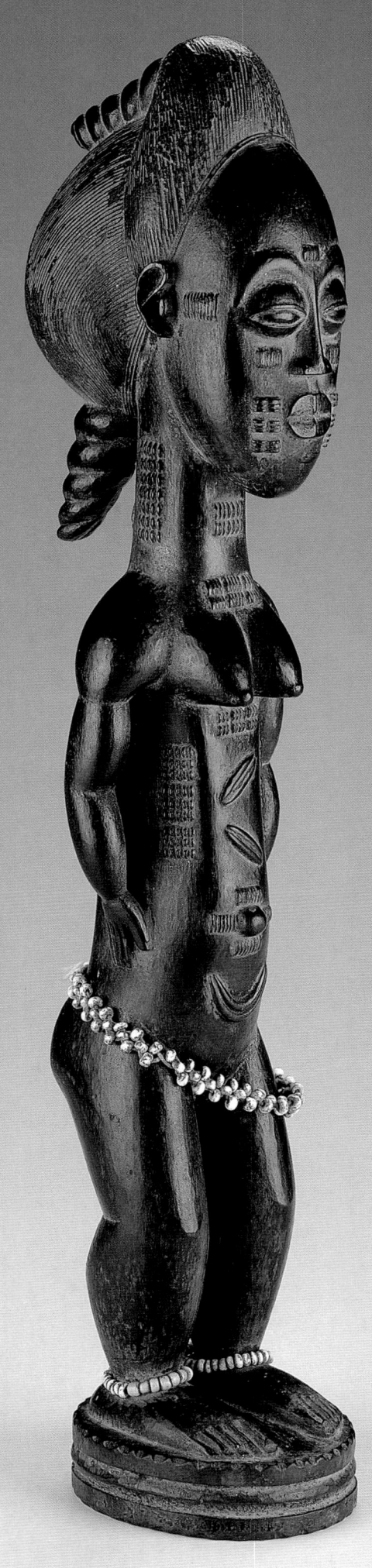

1 The African Female Body in the Cultural Imagination

Tradition . . . involves a perception, not only of the pastness of the past, but of its presence.

—THOMAS STEARNS ELIOT[1]

THE AFRICAN FEMALE BODY ON DISPLAY

When Europeans first encountered indigenous peoples from beyond their shores in the fifteenth century, nonwhite bodies became curiosities to Western societies. So began a long history of placing indigenous peoples and their cultures on display.[2] A growing appetite for the exotic led to the display of indigenous bodies, cultural artifacts, and images of the exotic "Other" from around the world.[3] Initially this occurred in the private salons of the European nobility and social elite, but over time such activities began to serve larger political, scientific, and public entertainment purposes.

From the beginning of the nineteenth until the mid-twentieth centuries in Europe and America, the display of indigenous bodies increasingly occurred in circuses, zoos, and museums. World expositions especially were popular forums for human spectacles toward the end of the nineteenth century, when "native villages" were reconstructed and populated with indigenous men, women, and children who performed their daily routines and rituals for Western audiences.[4] The spectacle of cultural otherness did not stop at live human displays. The dissected and embalmed remains of "native" bodies, particularly their skulls and sexual organs, provided further attraction and entertainment in public displays and exhibitions conducted in the name of "science."[5] For Western nations interested in the exploitation of Africa and its human and natural resources, world expositions were especially useful in justifying colonization. In fact, exhibition organizers openly promoted notions of Western racial, economic, technological, and artistic superiority over African cultures, infantilizing them as needy recipients of Western discipline, religion, civilization, and industry.

Typically, the display of African peoples in the Western arena featured nude or semi-nude men and women, the latter serving as potent counterpoints to Western ideologies of white female beauty, womanhood, morality, and civilization. One of the best-known examples of the indiscriminate display of an African

oppposite Unknown artist, Baule peoples, Côte d'Ivoire, female figure (*blolo bla*), mid-twentieth century, wood, glass beads, plant fiber. National Museum of African Art: Gift from the collection of Toby and Barry Hecht; 2000-26-1. Photograph by Franko Khoury, courtesy of National Museum of African Art, Smithsonian Institution.

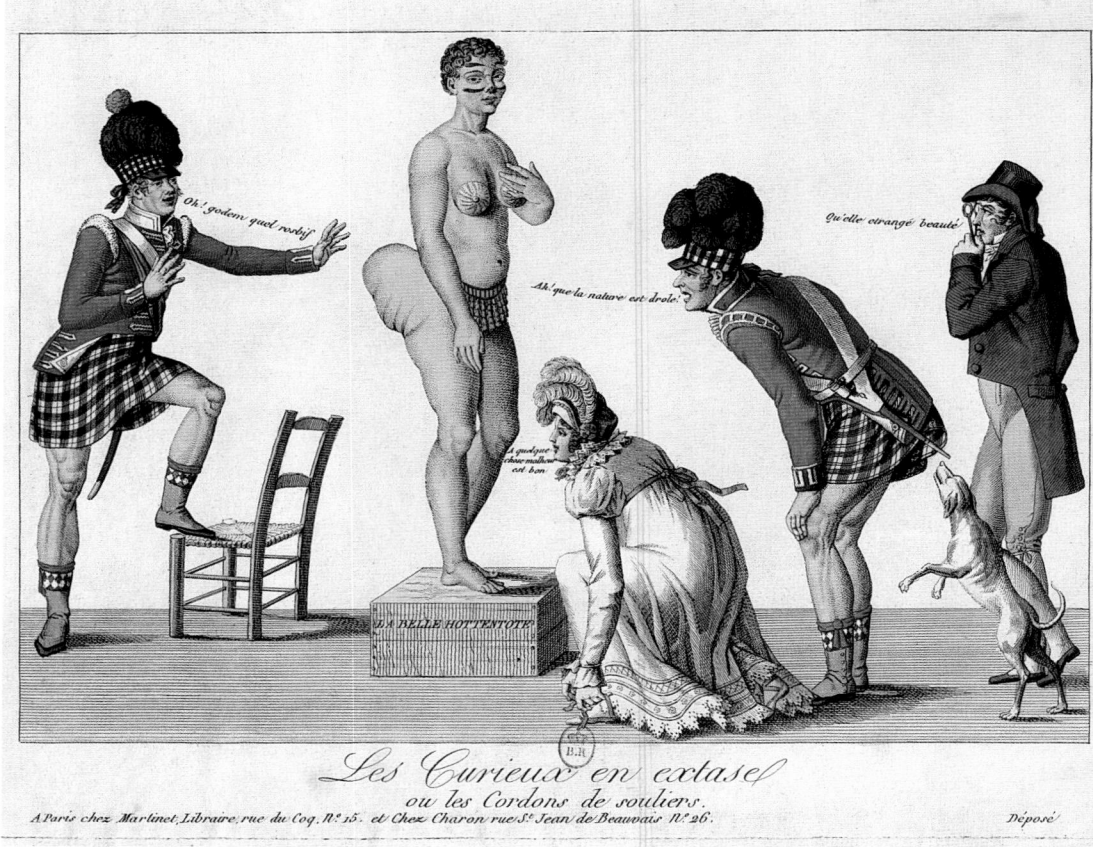

woman as the polar opposite to European ideals of womanhood began in 1810, when an English ship's surgeon brought a young Khoi-San woman, Saartjie Baartman,[6] from South Africa to London. Born in 1789 in what is now the Eastern Cape, Baartman was publicly exhibited throughout England as a sexual oddity in sideshow attractions. As contemporary accounts describe, she was paraded on a "stage two feet high, along which she was led by her keeper and exhibited like a wild beast, being obliged to walk, stand or sit as he ordered."[7] During Baartman's London appearances, she

> was dragged out to squat before the mob at 225 Piccadilly, the show's promoters billed her genitals as resembling the skin that hangs from a turkey's throat. For several years, working-class Londoners crowded in to shout vulgarities at the protruding buttocks and large vulva of the unfortunate woman made famous across Europe as the "Hottentot Venus." The aristocracy were no less fascinated at what they saw as a sexual freak, but they had private showings.[8]

In 1814, Baartman was sold to a circus owner in France where, in the light of increased protest against human displays, she became a scientific specimen for anatomists and naturalists to study. Her nude figure, ridiculed throughout the European media (figure 1.1), became an iconic stereotype of the evolutionary inferiority of Africans in general and of African and black women's sexual deviance more specifically.[9] Baartman died in 1816, after which the French anatomist Georges Cuvier dissected her body. Her brains, skeleton, and genitals were placed on public display in the Musée de l'Homme in Paris, where they remained until 1974. Twenty years later, President Nelson Mandela demanded the repatriation of Baartman's remains to South Africa, but it took the French government another eight years to finally oblige.

Throughout nineteenth-century Europe and America, black womanhood and sexuality were studied and defined in the context of anthropometry or physiognomy, categorizing a person's evolutionary status and intelligence according to the measurements of his or her physical characteristics.[10] The nineteenth-century invention of photography, *cartes des visites,* and postcards—with their promise of cheap reproduction and dissemination—provided "evidence" of the African racial inferiority defined by these pseudo-sciences, which served both the popular and scientific worlds, further solidifying European racist perceptions of Africa's "primitive" and "promiscuous" women.

The "discovery" of African sculpture by Western audiences in the early twentieth century not only reinforced prejudicial notions about African primitivism but also introduced a new fascination for and fetishization of African "arts."[11] At that time, Western viewers of these "exotic" sculptures, which often featured the nude female figure, lacked any understanding of or cultural context for the specific symbolism, function, or ideologies embedded in these works. Consequently, the widespread African artistic convention of physically exaggerating sexual body parts of the female figure as metaphors for human and agricultural fertility, maternity, and nurturance was repeatedly interpreted through the lens of dominant European theories about the pathological sexuality of black women.[12] These sculptural representations fed into the Western cultural imagination, further conjuring up notions of the sexually conflated image of the African woman and aligning them with the ever-popular image of the black Venus.[13] I would argue further that as the display of real indigenous bodies was increasingly challenged in Europe and America, African artistic renditions of black womanhood—along with colonial-era photographs and postcards—became a convenient substitute for owning and consuming the exotic African female body.

CHALLENGING THE CANON: GENDER COMPLEMENTARITY IN AFRICAN ART AND WOMANHOOD

The Western sexualization and pathologizing of the African female body sharply contrasts with traditional African ideologies of womanhood, in which women were[14]—and in many cultures today continue to be—honored and depicted in the visual and performing arts as the givers of life, as guardians of moral integrity, and as cornerstones of family continuity and communal unity. Because European and American museum exhibitions of African art did not provide contexts for greater understanding of these sculptures until the 1970s, however, many late nineteenth- and early twentieth-century Western assumptions about black

womanhood remained largely unchallenged in mainstream society. As art historical and anthropological research began to reveal from the 1970s onward, the female
body occupied—and continues to occupy—a fundamental place in African art
and society *not* as an object of sexual deviance or desire, as perceived in the West,
but as a symbol of ideal female beauty; as an icon of nascent fertility and procre-
ativity; as a representation of maternal and communal nurturance; and as a metaphoric embodiment of socially, politically, and religiously important powers.

Until recently, the dominant approach of presenting icons of African womanhood in public exhibitions in the West has been through the analysis of the
female form and its function in African figurative sculpture.[15] Western museums,
with their proclivity for figurative art, have created many exhibitions that take
refuge in the now tried-and-true, yet ever more murky, paradigm of "classic" and
"canonical" figurative sculpture, many including outstanding cultural renditions
of the "ideal" African female body. This particular method of examining and displaying what are often referred to as "masterpieces" of African sculpture had its
advantages in the first half of the twentieth century, since it promoted a better
understanding of African sculpture as "art" in the Western sense of the word. It
also promoted connoisseurship and greater awareness of the enormous skill and
creativity of African carvers and metalsmiths.

However, given that African figurative sculpture is primarily made and used
by and for men, this paradigm has left little room for locating women's arts within
the broader traditional cultural milieu, much less for discussions of how ideologies of African womanhood have been constructed and visually expressed *by and
for* women. And despite the increasing number of important academic studies
and fieldwork on African women's arts and power since the 1980s,[16] these topics
continue to be marginalized in most museum exhibitions, adding yet another
layer in the construction of ideologies of black womanhood in the Western cultural imagination.

The bias of exhibitions of traditional African art toward men's artistic
expression undoubtedly has shaped the way we think about black womanhood in
Africa, creating a unilateral understanding that fails to reveal the true diversity
and depth of how gender and culture are embedded in different forms of representation and self-representation. If we are to gain a more balanced understanding of African ideologies of womanhood as they have been—and in many cases
still are—communicated in traditional African art and life, it is imperative that
museum exhibitions begin to examine *both* male and female artistic expressions.
Indeed, the prevalence of male perspectives and the limited presence of women's
artistic voices in museum exhibitions raise a number of important questions.
How did/do women in the traditional African cultural context represent themselves in the arts? How did/do men and women learn about ideologies of womanhood through the arts? How did/do men's and women's representations of
womanhood differ? How were/are they the same? To which visual precedents or
cultural traditions can contemporary artists turn for inspiration in developing
their own visual language?

To answer these vital questions, one must take into account that in most traditional African cultural contexts, principles of gender division govern what kinds of media, technology, and forms of artistic expression men and women are allowed to use. Gender complementarity plays a key role in underscoring and balancing power as well as the social and economic roles of men and women in society. For example, throughout Africa, wood sculpture is predominately a male art form, whereas pottery is often—though not exclusively—women's. Even a single art form can be governed by gendered technologies. In West Africa, for instance, men create narrow strip-woven cloths on horizontal looms while women use vertical looms. In some cultures, both men and women are involved in specific aspects of an object's creation, such as in some forms of figurative pottery, in which a female molds the body of the clay vessel while a man adds the figurative portions.[17]

The rules and conventions of gendered technologies in traditional African art are highly specific to the culture, the kind or function of the object, and, at times, the artist's age or status in life. These conventions are not always cut and dried. Among the Yoruba peoples of Nigeria, women traditionally are prohibited from creating figurative sculpture. This is not the case, however, in the production of sacred figurative pottery, such as *awo otun Eyinle* (plate 39). The Yoruba potter Abatan Odefunke Ayinke Iga of Oke-Odan, for example, began to make these sacred vessels for the God Eyinle only after she had spent many years perfecting non-figurative domestic pottery.[18] These vessels are placed in a shrine and used to hold stones and water in the worship of Eyinle, who is reputed to be an androgynous deity of unearthly beauty. In the Yoruba pantheon of gods, Eyinle represents cosmic duality, is the patron deity of river waters, fisherman, hunters, and doctors, and symbolizes also human sustenance as the provider of food from the waters. Eyinle also heals human ills.

Awo otun Eyinle are particularly notable for their symbolic design, featuring a lid in the form of a woman's upper body—most likely a female devotee or one of the deity's royal wives. The figure's body is surrounded by strap-like projections that can be perceived as a crown and refer to her royal status. Characteristically she holds a bowl to contain spiritual offerings of kola nuts and cowries for Eyinle during worship. Like Yoruba sculptures of female figures made by male carvers, such as the ritual bowl (plate 29) and staff (plate 43) for the Yoruba thunder god Shango, who helps women in issues of fertility and childbearing, the figure on the *awo otun Eyinle* has full and outward jutting breasts, representing the Yoruba ideals of female beauty embodied by the image of the fertile woman.

ICONS OF BEAUTY AND GENDERED IDENTITIES

Expressions of female beauty are among the most ubiquitous aspects of inscribing womanhood onto the African female body or onto objects that metaphorically represent the female form. Throughout Africa, carved masks and figures are the most common forms of male expressions and celebrations of ideal physical—

and, by extension, spiritual—female beauty. In the case of masks, which are usually worn during elaborate ritual masquerades, male dancers not only perform and evoke but also embody the grace, beauty, and nurturing power of women, female spirits, or female deities. Among the Mende peoples of Sierra Leone, the women's Sande or Bondo Society commissions male carvers to create helmet masks, called *sowei* (plate 1), worn by Sande Society members during girls' initiation masquerades. The Sande Society masquerade is one of the few examples of women's masked dancing in Africa and serves as a means of portraying the physical, intellectual, and spiritual attributes of female beauty. The *sowei* mask and the symbolically choreographed dance emulate the qualities of wisdom, grace, and self-control that girls learn during their initiation into womanhood and that women will need in the multigenerational, polygamous households of their future husbands.[19]

Among the Punu peoples of southern and south-central Gabon, male carvers create masks, called *mukudj* (plate 4),[20] which male masqueraders traditionally wear and perform during funeral celebrations.[21] During the colonial era, these masks served also as commemorative portraits of ancestors and were used as a ritual instrument to represent an idealized Punu woman. According to art historian and curator Alisa Lagamma,

> The creator of a mukudj mask would attempt to capture the likeness of the most beautiful woman in his community. The subject of this particular idealized and stylized portrait was embellished in classic nineteenth-century fashion with a coiffure composed of a central lobe and two lateral tresses and with cicatrisation motifs on the forehead and temples. Kaolin taken from riverbeds, which was associated with healing and with a spiritual, ancestral realm of existence, was applied to the surface of the face. By using this material the artist both celebrated the beauty of a mortal woman and transformed her into a transcendent being.[22]

The masks' rounded contours, naturalistic proportions, narrow slit eyes and swollen lids, thin, high arched eyebrows, fleshy lips, ornate coiffure, and formations of keloidal scarification all illustrate Punu ideals of female beauty. During the *mukudj* masquerade, the male dancer wears the female mask and a full body costume while performing incredible acrobatic feats and complexly choreographed dances upon stilts, which are concealed under the fiber costumes. The elegant, controlled, and beautiful movements of the stilt dancer reflect his extraordinary skill and emulate Punu ideals of female beauty.

Throughout Africa, male carvers have conveyed their visual interpretations of womanhood through figures with outward physical features that echo their cultures' ideals of female beauty. Such carved female figures can represent spirit beings (plate 5), deities, or female ancestors (plate 7), as well as portraits of actual people, such as queens or chiefly mothers (plate 30). As many of these figures illustrate, in those cultures where women adorned their bodies with symbolic scarification patterns and elaborate hairstyles, male carvers also adorned the bodies of their female sculptures with physical characteristics that mimic a woman's own outward expression of beauty and her public declaration of Self as a social and sexually mature being. In many cases, endowing these figures with idealized physical features, elaborate hairstyles, body scarification, and references to culture-specific personal adornment served also to mirror the woman's inward beauty, particularly her strength of character.

Throughout Africa, hair and hairstyling—especially the preparation of elaborate coiffures—play an important role as a form of body art. As Roy Sieber illustrated in the exhibition *Hair in African Art and Life* in 2000, hair and the dressing of hair was—and continues to be—a vital social activity (as hairdressing occurs primarily in gender divided social groups) as well as a means of expressing beauty, ethnic identity, clan identity, age, and social status.[23] For this reason, exquisite and complex hairstyles commonly are found throughout Africa in personal adornment practices and also are incorporated into sculptural depictions of ideal female beauty (plates 1, 3, 4, 5, 12, 14, 15, and 20).

During the first part of the twentieth century, Fulani women distinguished themselves from their neighbors in West Africa by their beautiful hairstyles (plate 52), which consisted of high crests arched over the head, sculptural braids, and coiled tufts of hair. The particular style was determined not only by the fashion of the times but also by a woman's age. Sieber, for example, describes in great detail the different hairstyles that Peul women (a subgroup of the Fulani) wore according to age and rank:

> Peul girls wear very tight longitudinal braids going from forehead to nape and falling down the shoulders and the back, while transversal braids emerge from the sides of the head. An adolescent girl has tight braids separated by symmetrical partings and a coiled tuft on either side of her head. Adult women of lower rank have two raised transversal braids and also small parallel braids on either side and separated by a part down the middle. High ranking women may have their own hairstyle, an intricate combination of braids interpolated with more or less thick coils distributed in front, in back and on the sides of the head.[24]

The elaborate coiffures of these women were a vivid reminder of the leisure and wealth of their elite cattle-herding culture.

One of the distinguishing characteristics of Fulani culture is the careful cultivation of physical beauty, not only through hairstyles but also through dress, jewelry, body adornment, facial tattooing, and comportment (figure 1.2).[25] A Fulani woman's body adornment, including massive gold earrings, often reflects her lineage and hereditary occupation, accentuating her attractiveness while literally displaying her family's wealth on her body and ensuring its safe-keeping. Fulani expressions of both ideal female and male beauty also acknowledge the importance of sensuality and sexual appeal, not just for personal pleasure but also for the desire to attract a spouse with whom one can conceive healthy and beautiful children.[26]

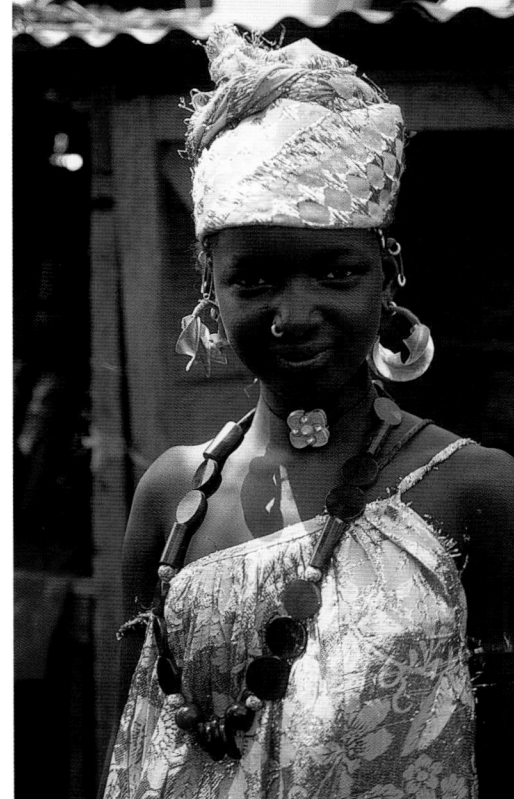

FIGURE 1.2 *Fulani woman in Mopti, Mali*, photograph by Eliot Elisofon, 1970. Image no. EEPA EECL 2618. Photograph courtesy of Eliot Elisofon Photographic Archives, National Museum of African Art, Smithsonian Institution.

FIGURE 1.3 *Dogon stilt dancer in Fulani woman mask, Sangha, Mali,* photograph by Eliot Elisofon, 1972. Image no. EEPA EECL 3624. Photograph courtesy of Eliot Elisofon Photographic Archives, National Museum of African Art, Smithsonian Institution.

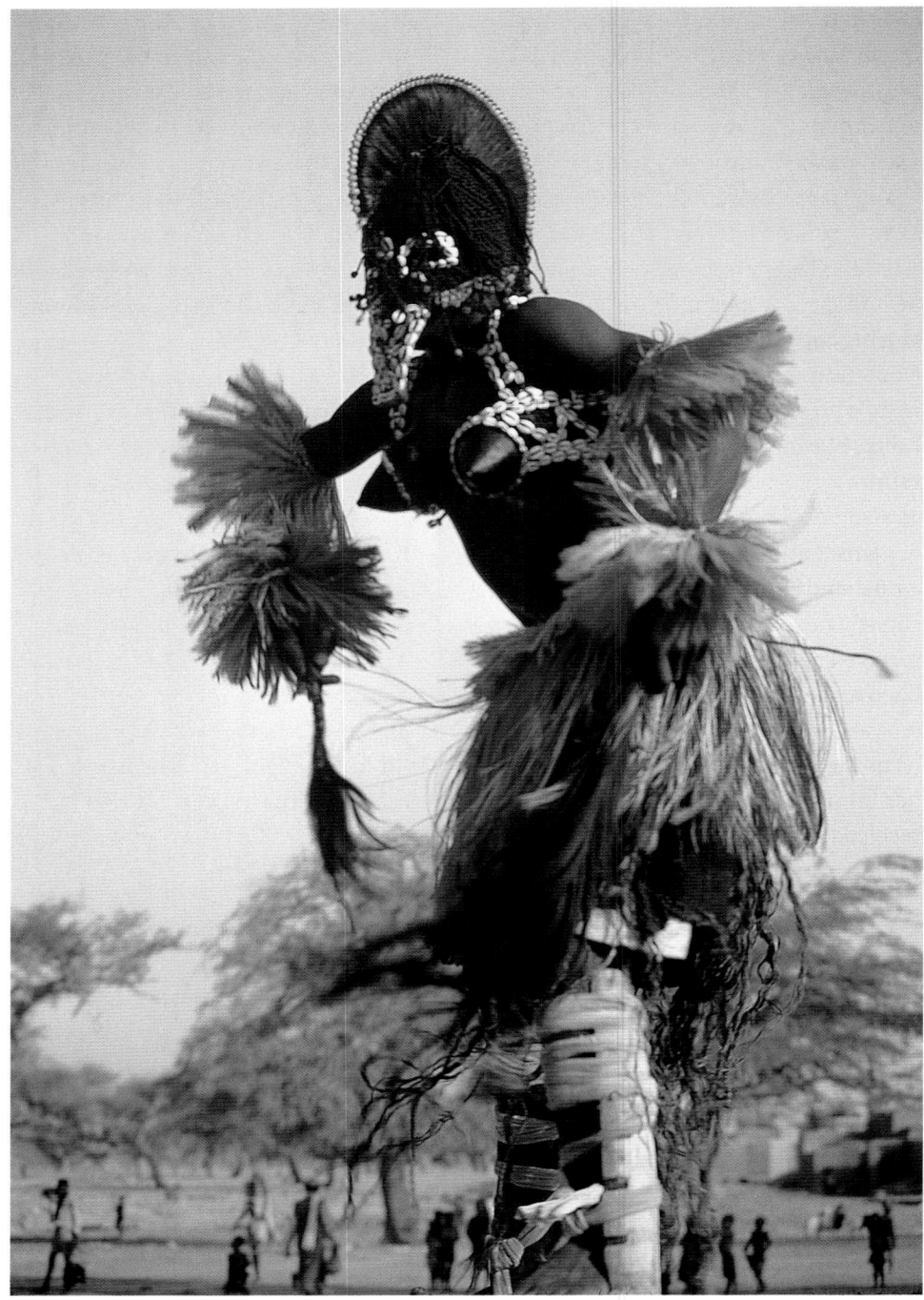

The dramatic beauty of the Fulani women is widely reputed throughout West Africa but is a subject of mockery for male masqueraders of the Dogon culture of Mali. The Fulani inhabit a vast territory from the west of Dogon lands to northern Nigeria. For centuries, the Dogon have viewed the Fulani as enemies who forced them away from their original lands. Although Fulani women sell milk from their cattle herds in Dogon markets and are greatly admired for their beauty and femininity, male Dogon masqueraders impersonate Fulani maidens during funerary activities by wearing false breasts and head-conforming masks, called *bede* (plate 3), made of fiber and cowrie shells that mimic the characteristic Fulani hairstyle. Both the costume and dance performance represent exaggerated femininity (figure 1.3) but according to Barbara DeMott, Dogon dancers also use such masks representing foreigners to affirm their culture and to gain protection against the malevolent spirit forces believed to have been introduced by these same foreign populations.[27]

Perhaps the most ubiquitous form of women's own expressions of female beauty is accomplished through the painful process of facial and body scarification. During the colonial period in the Gongola River area of Nigeria, girls and young women in the Ga'anda culture inscribed the skin of their bodies, forehead, and neck with complex, extensive, and very specific patterns of scarification markings called *hleeta*.[28] The markings served as an important means of transmitting and reinforcing socio-cultural values. This process began when a girl was about five or six years old, was carried out by an elderly woman guided by the creative spirit N'gamsa, and was prepared in six biennial stages during her lengthy betrothal to a husband. The patterns consisted of rows of closely placed cuts that formed slightly raised "dots" or nodules. With each new set of markings, the girl's parents received a gift from her fiancé and his family, with whom the girl's marriage had been arranged in her infancy.

Hence, there was a direct correlation between the sequence of *hleeta* patterns cut into a woman's skin and the number of bride wealth payments given to her family. A young woman could not consummate her marriage until she had received her final marks and the groom had fulfilled his obligations to her family. Completion of the intricate markings on a young woman's body therefore publicly announced her arrival at sexual maturity, adulthood, and marriagability, but declared also that obtaining these rights had been paid for in pain.[29] A woman's endurance of this experience demonstrated her endorsement of community values and her alliance with spirit-guardians that would provide protection essential for procreation.[30]

Ga'anda potters, who were predominately women (although older men sometimes produced sacred pottery), created tall and elegantly decorated terracotta vessels for both ritual and secular purposes. The Ga'anda used elaborately decorated vessels, such as the ritual beer pot (*lekleke*) in plate 34, to contain spirit powers that protected and sustained Ga'anda prosperity. The decoration of these ritual vessels mimicked the female body transformed by scarifying (*hleeta*), linking the spirit contained within the vessel with the positive human characteristic of social responsibility, thereby enhancing the spirits' ability to influence the positive forces governing human survival and wellbeing. The spherical shape of these vessels also referred to a woman's body—regardless of the gender of the spirit power contained within—to which were added references to sexual body parts and a projecting umbilicus. The vessel's "torso" was intricately decorated with bands of pelletted ridges and lozenges or zigzag-shaped designs that created single, double, or triple outlines of geometric forms, like the *hleeta* designs worn by

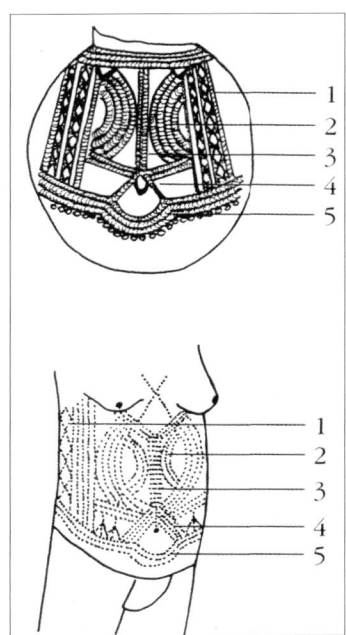

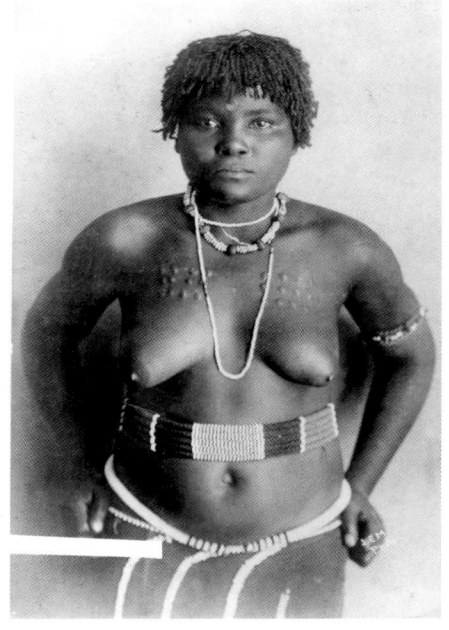

FIGURE 1.4 *Hleeta* designs on a Ga'anda woman's body, 1986, drawing by Marla Berns. Photograph courtesy of Marla Berns and the Fowler Museum at the University of California — Los Angeles.

FIGURE 1.5 Unknown photographer, *Zulu woman*, before May 1910, black and white photograph. Photograph courtesy of the American Museum of Natural History, negative no. 014081.

Ga'anda women (figure 1.4). As Marla Berns suggests, the intentional incorporation of the *hleeta* scarification designs as markers of social transition onto Ga'anda ritual vessels—as also onto other Ga'anda objects—may have signified the deceased's transition from a human to an ancestral status, thereby encouraging the spirits to display a similar commitment to social responsibility as that avowed by young women undergoing the *hleeta* ordeal.[31]

The Kurumba storage vessel in plate 6 is also embellished with applied curvilinear patterns, which in this case represent the scarification patterns applied to the abdomen of married Kurumba women who have given birth. The application of breasts on the vessel's upper "torso" and a projecting navel on its "belly" further links the vessel's symbolism to human and agricultural fertility. Both are vital to survival in this farming culture, located in the extremely dry northern regions of Burkina Faso at the edge of the Sahel desert. Similarly, pots from the Mambila culture (plate 24) are decorated with blatant references to women's bodies, including breasts, genitalia, and body scarification.

The practice of decorating objects that mimic the female body and body arts often help to associate such objects more generally to the female principle. Among the Zulu peoples of South Africa, female potters decorate ritual beer pots (plate 10) with nodules, called *amasumpha*, in graphic designs that emulate some forms of Zulu women's body scarification worn during the colonial era (figure 1.5).[32] More important, however, is the association of these glossy black and symmetrically rounded beer vessels to the female principle, which is underscored by Zulu mythology in which Earth is regarded as the female twin of the male entity, Sky. Earth (and therefore also clay as a product of Earth) is perceived as the provider of nourishment for the people and helps to maintain a spiritual connection to the ancestors, who are in turn closely involved with human conception and childbirth. In most Zulu families, beer made from maize and sorghum has great social and ritual significance and is associated with crop fertility. In some Zulu regions, however, the process of brewing the beer is equated with human pregnancy.

The *amasumpha* patterns on these vessels—as also on other Zulu art objects—are said to be directly associated with references to herds of cattle, which in the past (and still in some areas) were the measure of a man's wealth. The Zulu peoples traditionally raised cattle and farmed, the former being men's work and the latter being women's work.[33] After brewing beer for ritual offerings to the ancestors, the senior woman in a household stacked beer vessels at the rear of her home, where her husband or son would come to pour libations of beer to their forefathers. Placing symbolic references to cattle on these beer vessels indicated the interdependence of men's and women's domains while helping to invoke the guidance and blessings of human and agricultural fertility from the ancestors.[34]

Zulu women have been noted also for their highly accomplished beadwork. Applied to clothing and objects of personal adornment in complexly encoded designs, Zulu beadwork conveys information about the wearer's identity, gender, and stage of life from childhood to adulthood (especially through the amount and types of beaded items worn), as well as about a man and woman's personal relationship to each other.[35] During the nineteenth century, young unmarried women wore several beaded squares or bands of beads around their neck, waist, arms, and ankles, as well as short leather aprons, leaving their breasts and thighs exposed as represented in the colonial-era postcards in plate 49. The beauty of their youthful bodies was believed to reflect the beauty of their inner character, which helped them secure husbands. Young men and women (figure 4.3) wore the most lavish beadwork during courtship, while married men and women wore minimal beadwork, except for special occasions.

In the early nineteenth century, married Zulu women were noted also for a hairstyle, called *isicholo,* created by shaving the head of all but a tuft of hair on the crown, which was then smeared with a mixture of fat and ochre. This hairstyle evolved at the end of the nineteenth century with longer tufts of hair being interwoven with grass or false hair to create a shape that resembled a truncated cone. Women also wore a woven fiber headband around the forehead as a sign of respect for adult men of their husband's family. At the turn of the century, however, a detachable disk-shaped woven red hat replaced this hairstyle and headband, which married women wore—and on some important occasions still wear—to signify their marital status (figure 1.6).

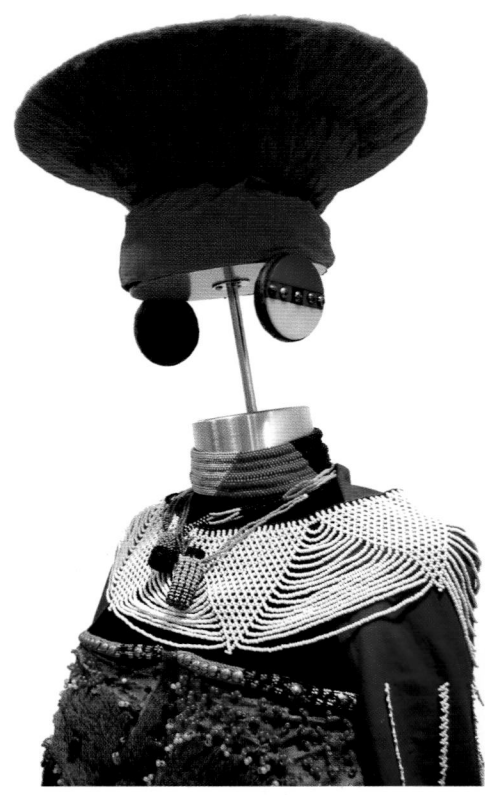

FIGURE 1.6 Unknown artist, Msinga-Zulu peoples, South Africa, married woman's dress (detail), late nineteenth to mid-twentieth century, cloth, leather, beads, metal. Axis Gallery. Photograph courtesy of Axis Gallery.

THE INITIATED BODY: FERTILITY, SEXUALITY, AND SOCIALIZATION INTO WOMANHOOD

To create a more balanced view of the ways in which gendered technologies and gender complementarity are learned within traditional African cultures, one must consider how ideologies of womanhood are taught to both men and women during their initiation into adulthood. Throughout Africa, undergoing initiation into adulthood is an important tool in socializing adolescents. Although initiation rites and processes differ from one culture to another, and in some cultures can encompass undergoing various phases throughout a person's lifetime, initiation rites commonly share the fundamental purpose of teaching young men and women about their future gender roles and the challenges they will face as adults. Vital to such processes are learning culturally specific ideologies about the adolescent's impending fertility and sexuality, and about the social roles they are expected to meet as functioning members of the adult community, all of which are connected to or communicated through the body.

During the colonial era, for example, Makonde men and women in Tanzania and Mozambique inscribed complex geometric designs on their faces and bodies[36] during initiation rites to pronounce their ethnicity. The scarification designs included combinations of chevrons, angles, zigzags, straight lines, circles, diamonds, and dots, as well as abstractions of plants and animals. But the designs communicated more than just ethnic identity, as scarification patterns on a woman's pubic area, for example, were believed to have the power to attract a husband. Other designs on her thighs and buttocks were considered erotic as well as having spiritual powers. In some areas of Mozambique, women from the Makonde and Makua (cultural relatives of the Makonde) cultures also painted their faces with a white clay substance as a sign of beauty.[37]

Like that of Ga'anda scarification, the Makonde process of inscribing a woman's body with symbolic designs was slow and painful. But undergoing the arduous process was important to a woman's identity, for it taught her to be strong, prepared her for the physical pains of pregnancy, labor, and childbirth, and publicly proclaimed her acquired knowledge, endurance, and tolerance—all of which would help her in her future married life.[38] Emulating these scarification designs, Makonde potters, who are women, produce large terracotta water and storage vessels (plate 9) decorated with incised geometric designs similar to those traditionally cut into Makonde women's skin. After firing the vessels, the potters rub a white clay substance—similar to that once used in facial painting—into the inscribed designs.

The woman's body and related body arts in Makonde culture play an important role also in the men's domain of visual culture, especially in initiation masquerades, where boys and young men learn about their upcoming responsibilities in adult life. The Makonde art of masquerade serves as a common didactic means of communicating ideologies of manhood *and* womanhood. For example, in an initiation dance that celebrates the coming-out of male initiates and their entrance into adulthood, a male performer wears a carved wooden mask of a woman over his face and a female breastplate, or *njorowe* (plate 26), depicting a swollen belly with scarification markings over the abdomen. Together the facial mask and breastplate represent a pregnant woman. Another masked performer, dressed as a male, accompanies the dancer masquerading as a pregnant woman. Together they move slowly and laboriously, imitating the difficulties of pregnancy and childbirth, teaching the emergent male celebrants about the pains of a woman's labor.[39]

The didactic role of this Makonde dance echoes the kind of female symbolism often found on the superstructure of cap masks made by Yaka artists from the Democratic Republic of Congo (plate 28). Such masks are associated with initiation rituals surrounding male circumcision, or *nkanda,* and are worn by leaders of the initiates during choreographed masquerades that evoke the appearance of male ancestors and cultural heroes who promote life, growth, and healing. The spirit beings also welcome the new generation of men during these dances. The masks used in *nkanda* dances are particularly known for the representation of explicit sexual imagery, which is embedded with a coded system of references to male and female sexuality, to the fertility of the earth, and to the cycles of the sun and the moon. The superstructure of the mask in plate 28 represents a woman receiving assistance while giving birth, no doubt a lesson about the ordeal of welcoming new life into the community—be it the newborn child that comes from procreation learned during initiation or the boy now transformed into and emerging as a man through the arduous processes involved in initiation.[40]

Throughout Africa, gender and sexual symbolism play a vital role in initiation rites for pubescent boys and girls, who are separated from society and secluded from their villages or communities during the learning process. This seclusion gives adolescents time to learn about the physical changes occurring in their bodies, their emerging fertility, and their future procreative roles. It is a time when adolescents also learn about appropriate sexual, domestic, and social behaviors, cultural histories, and spiritual responsibilities. In northeastern Tanzania, for example, young men and women learn the layered meanings behind ritual objects, songs, and dances while secluded during the initiation process. Carved female figures are particularly common in initiation arts among the Kwere, Zaramo, Luguru, and Gogo peoples and serve both as instructional devices and as protection against malevolent spirit forces. While blatant visual references to the female figure openly suggest the embodiment of the female principle, the male element is also present—though visually less obvious—through phallic forms and by virtue of metaphorical associations with manhood and womanhood.

In northeastern Tanzania during the colonial era, at the onset of her first menstruation, a young girl was secluded from society for many years, generally until the day of her wedding, to undergo initiation into womanhood. Girl's initiation is still practiced among some of the northeastern Tanzanian cultural groups, though on a much smaller scale than in the colonial era. As I found during brief fieldwork in Luguru and Kwere initiation practices in 2006, for example, most girls undergo a shortened version of initiation that accommodates school schedules. In a few cases, though, girls indeed can spend up to a year or more in seclusion.[41] During an initiate's (*mwali*) seclusion, her paternal aunt gives her a carved female figurine (*mwana hiti*) or an anthropomorphized gourd containing many seeds to enhance fertility (*mwana sesere*) (figure 1.7). The figure or gourd, which is passed down through generations of women from within the initiate's clan, is returned to her clan once she has consummated her marriage. The image of *mwana hiti* represents the image of the initiate, or *mwali,* but is also a signifier for the matriclan, since most northeastern Tanzanian cultures are matrilineal, with inheritance passing through the senior maternal uncle.

These *mwana hiti* or *mwana sesere* figures kept the initiate company during her seclusion, but they also served as a surrogate child, which could be male or female, regardless of the female form of the figure itself. The initiate was expected to lavish great care and attention upon the figure in mock motherhood to ensure her own fertility and to protect her reproductive powers after seclusion was complete. When used in initiation rites, the figures represented and enhanced the initiate's budding fertility and reproductive powers. Hence, the *mwana hiti* figure was incorporated into various objects used in the context of initiation during the colonial era, including large abstractly rendered wooden posts (plate 16), stools, musical instruments, staff finials (plate 17), fly-whisks, and figurative stoppers for medicine gourds, or *tunguli* (plate 18). Many of these objects embodied the inchoate physical attributes of the *mwali,* including a pair of breasts and a crest designed like the clefted hairstyle typically worn by female initiates, said by some

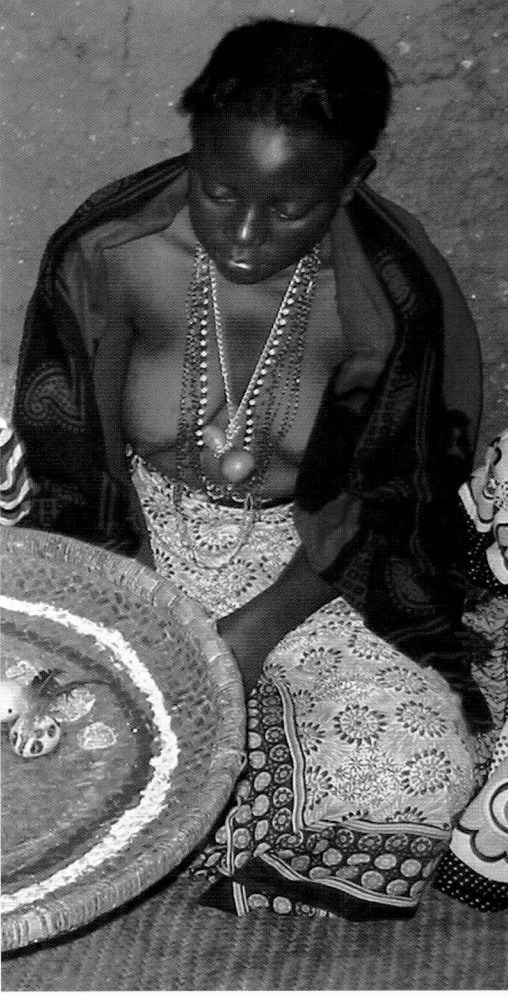

FIGURE 1.7 A young Kwere initiate (*mwali*) wears a fertility gourd (*mwana sesere*) and beadwork around her neck while learning about symbolism of the female body embedded in ritual colors and objects (left, bottom corner), Chalize, Tanzania, 2006. Photograph by and courtesy of Barbara Thompson.

to represent the vagina. More broadly speaking, the figures also signified the unity and continuation of the clan through procreation, as the desire to have children was vital to the perpetuation and strengthening of the clan's name. Hence, having many children was regarded as a sign of wealth and power.

Historically, the *mwali* rite underscored and reinforced various teachings including the position of women in the community and their involvement with economic production at both the family and community level. The seclusion of the *mwali* from the community served to teach her about feminine hygiene and about respect for family members. It was also a time to fatten her and increase her health, strength, and fertility, but also to protect her from sexual contact before marriage. Toward the end of seclusion, she was also instructed in sexual matters, particularly how to please a husband and how to associate with her potential spouse, relatives, co-wives, and children in her future role as wife and mother. Of utmost importance to the *mwali's* education was the acquisition of ideal qualities of womanhood, which included hard work, generosity, discretion, and a strong caring and nurturing consciousness.[42]

True to a widespread Tanzanian philosophy, the female and male initiation rites emphasized the complementarity of women and men in everyday life. Together, the symbolism and metaphoric associations that were played out in initiation through visual and performing arts largely communicated ideologies about the balance of the opposite elements and characteristics embodied by men and women. Often ideologies of manhood and womanhood were communicated metaphorically through references to gendered objects and concepts such as mortar/pestle, home/wilderness, hot/cool, wellness/illness, order/chaos, west/east, down/up, etc. As such, they created a symbolic system that taught emerging adults not only about their future role as sexual beings but more importantly how to meet their social and cultural obligations to each other and to their communities.

As in the northeast, young women from the Iraqw culture of northern Tanzania underwent a period of seclusion during which they too performed a series of rituals aimed at preparing for marriage and procreation. When going into seclusion (*marmo*), young girls brought with them a large undecorated piece of leather, upon which they embroidered intricate beaded designs. The finished design of these leather skirts (plate 19) was divided vertically and horizontally into three sections for a total of nine, each decorated differently, each worn on specific areas of the woman's body, and each corresponding most likely to specific areas of Iraqw life.[43]

As curator and scholar Marie-Louise Labelle suggests, the beaded motifs and their spatial location on strategic places on the female body played an important role in representing a young girl's fertility and future roles as a mother and caretaker, and as an active adult member of the community.[44] The motifs of circles, lines, crosses, squares, zigzags, wavy lines, and crenellations created positive and negative spaces, which corresponded to known symbols of spatial, religious, and domestic elements in the Iraqw universe. Consequently, Labelle suggests, these skirts can be read as an aerial view that maps out the living space of the future married woman and locates and correlates her house, the neighborhood, and the fields within the Iraqw social and cosmological world. For example, the circles, sometimes depicted with rays or divided into three or six sections, could evoke the sun, but could also visually represent the Iraqw spirit *Lo'a* or the traditional Iraqw round house. Wavy lines could represent actual rivers as well as the subterranean *Netlaang* spirits, which are depicted in Iraqw symbolism as streams. Lines, often crenellated, define open and closed spaces, which represent communal spaces, such as the courtyards surrounding the houses, or other nearby spaces, such as fields. As Labelle suggests, the young Iraqw girl arrives into ritual seclusion with an empty map: the undecorated leather skin. But after being transformed into a woman, she leaves with a "detailed plan of her future life."[45]

Emerging from seclusion in spectacular coming-out celebrations and wearing these heavily beaded skirts, the young Iraqw initiates celebrated their transformation into womanhood. When the wearer walked or danced in these brightly colored, fringed skirts, she communicated the visual power of her grace, beauty, and poise, signaling knowledge about her physical, sexual, spiritual, and cultural transformation, as well as her readiness for taking on the responsibilities of an Iraqw woman, marriage, and motherhood. Once a young woman was married, she resumed wearing her elaborate leather skirt in everyday life.

The colors used to create the designs of the Iraqw skirts, particularly red, white, and black or dark blue, were also emblematic, as this color triad played an important role in conveying knowledge to young girls during their initiation. This is also the case in women's initiation rites among the Kwere peoples,[46] where the color white can signify male semen and female vaginal discharge. It can also symbolize purity, cleanliness, and the spirit of the benevolent ancestors. Red can represent the commencement of menstruation as well as the family bloodline, which underscores the woman's role in continuing her lineage through successful conception and childbirth. In the context of traditional medicine in northeastern Tanzania, the color red is used frequently in conjunction with women's gynecological issues, particularly problems with menstruation, fertility, conception, and difficulties during delivery. Black or dark blue represents the new growth of pubic hair at the onset of puberty and menstruation, which is an important sign of impending womanhood. But black denotes also impurity, for once a young woman begins to menstruate, her body, menstrual blood, pubic hair, and anything stained with her menstrual blood are regarded as unclean and ritually dangerous. After the beginning of menses, a girl must therefore remove all of her pubic hair on a regular basis through a painful process using ashes. She must also adhere to strict rules in the proper disposal of menstrual blood and pads. An initiate learns these important steps of menstrual hygiene during seclusion, as she will use them to re-establish her sexual "cleanliness" following each menstruation period, to maintain her desirability to her husband, and to ensure the blessing of successful conception and the birth of a healthy child.

Fertility is an all-important concept in African initiation rites, as is the role of woman as wife and mother. Motherhood is a pervasive concern in the traditional cultural milieu, given that the continuity of the family, community, and clan is dependent upon a woman's ability to successfully conceive and have healthy children. A woman's sense of social identity, however, is also underscored by her role as a mother, since her adult children will provide social security for the elders and proper burial rites for the deceased, ensuring thereby their proper integration into the ancestral world. In the case of a woman's barrenness, the whole community—both the human and the ancestral—will suffer. As John Mbiti writes,

> Unhappy is the woman who fails to get children, for whatever other qualities she might possess, her failure to bear children is worse than community genocide: she has become the dead end of human life, not only for the genealogical line but also for herself . . . the childless wife bears a scar which nothing can erase. She will suffer for this, her own relatives will suffer for this; and it will be an irreparable humiliation for which there is no source of comfort in traditional life.[47]

Despite the importance of pregnancy and birth in African life and culture, in figurative sculpture, direct representations of pregnancy, birth, and infancy are rare; instead they are usually implied in representations of fertility and parenting or, more generally, expressed through gender symbolism and visual references to the emerging fertility and sexual maturity of young female initiates. There are, of course, exceptions to this, as in the examples of a seated Senufo figure (plate 20) and an Agni figure (plate 21), both represented with swollen abdomens denoting pregnancy. One of the most expressive examples of pregnancy in African sculptural arts can be found in pre-colonial kingdoms of the Cameroonian grasslands, such as the exceptional life-size portrait of a Bamileke queen mother in the throes of labor (figure 1.8). The Bamileke, as also other grassland cultures, have portrait figures carved for new kings (*fon*) and the wife who bears his first child. According to royal practices, an heir to the throne could not rule until he had proven his fertility through the birth of a child. Once this was established, portraits of the king and the nursing or pregnant queen mother were created and used in the rites of installation of the successor. They were placed permanently outside the palace and served as symbols of the king's fertility and the queen's maternity, the continuity of the royal line, and as a temporary embodiment for the souls of deceased rulers. Given the natural and symbolic likeness of ceramic vessels to the pregnant belly, the more common reference to pregnancy is found in pottery, in which the addition of breasts, arms, and sometimes female heads to a vessel's heavily rounded form, as evident in plate 25, creates a blatant mirroring of the pregnant body.

In the traditional African cultural milieu—both in the past as in the present—no other icon is as powerful as the actual woman as a mother, going about

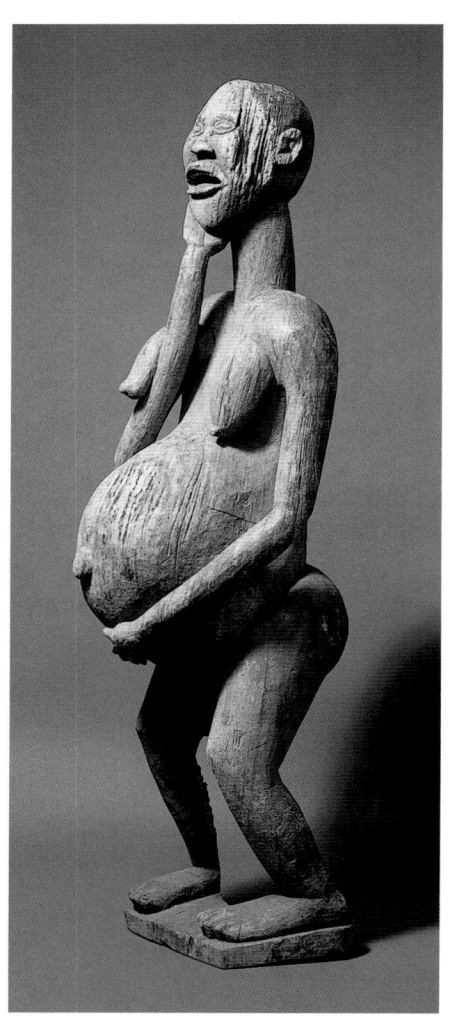

FIGURE 1.8 Unknown artist, Bamileke peoples, Pápit, Grasslands, Cameroon, pregnant queen mother with child, nineteenth to twentieth century, wood. Staatliches Museum für Völkerkunde, Munich; 79-300 913. Photograph by S. Autrium-Mulzer and courtesy of Staatliches Museum für Völkerkunde, Munich.

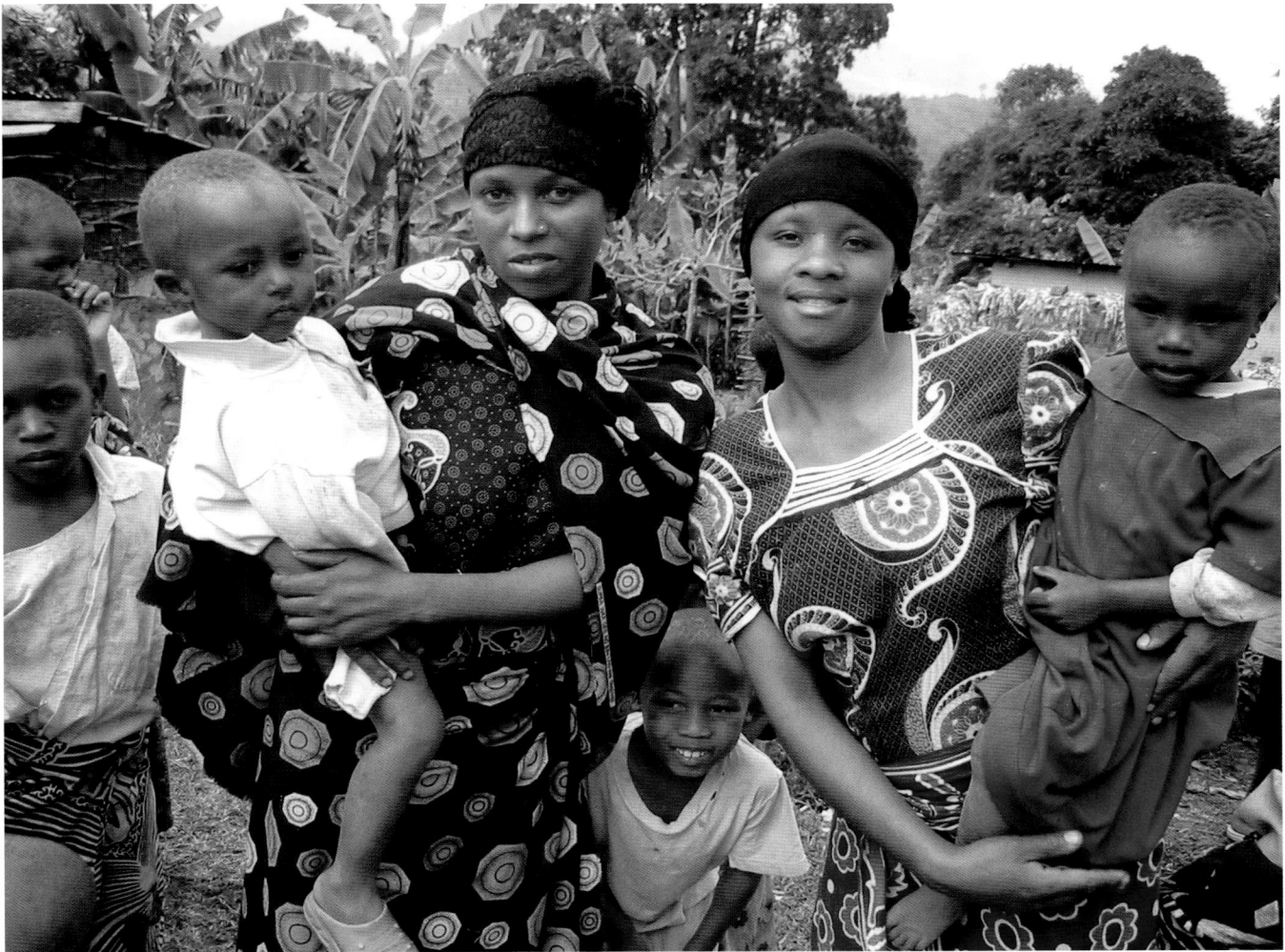

FIGURE 1.9 Two young Shambaa mothers with their children, nieces, and nephews, Irente Juu, Lushoto District, Tanzania, 2006. Photograph by and courtesy of Barbara Thompson.

her daily social and ritual life, her children on her body or to her side (figure 1.9). Whether she is pounding maize for the evening meal, fetching water or firewood, tending to the family or local shrine, transporting pots or goods on her head, or sitting at market conducting business, a married woman with her child or children is, in fact, the living model for artistic renditions of all that encompasses traditional African ideals of womanhood. In African arts, the most pervasive depiction of motherhood takes form as a depiction of a mother and child(ren). These figures, most frequently made by male artists, epitomize the accumulated embodiment of ideals of womanhood. The ideal image of motherhood is a woman of calm repose, of childbearing age, in the bloom of her youthful beauty. She may have a slight bulge to her abdomen denoting her fertility. Full or projecting breasts indicate lactation, while flat pendulant breasts identify her as a mother who has nursed many children. Often she is depicted holding and/or with children (plate 29)—sometimes nursing (plates 30 and 37), sometimes carrying a child on her back (plates 31 and 32). Along with clothing and other forms of personal adornment that identify the female figure as a mother, she is often also marked with scarification patterns that identify her status as a wife and mother (see the markings above the female figure's breasts in plate 30). The important social, religious, or political roles that women—particularly mothers—play in traditional societies are often symbolized through the female figure seated on a stool (plates 17 and 20) or as a caryatid figure (plate 44), indicating her status as a pillar of the community and the vital link to future generations.

Since African women in the traditional milieu are generally prohibited from creating figurative sculpture, body arts such as scarification, personal adornment, clothing, or hairstyle are commonly used to declare pregnancy or maternity. For example, when a Zulu woman was pregnant or lactating, she wore a beaded leather apron to cover and protect her abdomen. She decorated the surface of the leather apron (plate 27) with designs executed in patterns made up of *amasumpha* type clusters, which are symbolically associated with cattle. The leather for the apron was taken from a cow slaughtered by the expectant mother's husband as an offering to his ancestors, which underscored the role of cattle and cattle symbolism in his marriage and in the blessings for successful procreation sought from the ancestors.

In traditional Zulu life, a marriage was negotiated through gifts of cattle to a bride's family as bride price. If the ancestors approved of the union, the successful birth of a child was granted. If the child was male, he inherited his forefather's herds of cattle, which supplied his family with meat and milk, staples of Zulu diet. Cattle also provided hides for shields used in warfare and for dress, including the pregnancy apron. Thus, the symbolism of cattle was an important means of communicating ideologies of womanhood and motherhood, and manhood and fatherhood.[48] In other parts of Africa, such as in West Africa, the different and yet complementary social roles of women and men are symbolized in the arts through the incorporation of both female and male iconography on the same object (plates 33 and 40a and b).

CONCLUSION

Despite gendered restrictions and divisions in the traditional African cultural milieu that have limited women from creating figurative arts, they have found numerous ways to artistically express and represent themselves. One of the most common ways for African women and men to express ideologies of womanhood historically has been through the inscription of meaning into and upon objects that metaphorically stand in for the female body. For women, however, their own bodies have served as the primary means for self-expression and self-representation, whether through clothing, personal adornment, coiffure, or body scarification and painting. While scarification practices have diminished drastically—if not disappeared altogether—in many cultures, the decoration of the female body in more ephemeral means continues to play an important role in defining womanhood both publicly and privately.

Indeed, the body and skin have been the canvas upon which African women have inscribed abstract and complexly encoded symbols of womanhood since at least 8000–6000 B.C.E.[49] The continuing pervasiveness of the role of African women's bodies—and skin—in self-expression and self-representation continues in ever-changing ways in Africa both in rural and urban areas. As an important form of female self-expression, inscribing meaning onto the female body has not evaded contemporary artists in Africa and the Diaspora. As we will see, in the contemporary and transnational context of artistic expression in Africa and the Diaspora—with its growing number of artists concerned with feminist issues and aesthetics—the limitations of culturally specific gendered technologies are more easily crossed by both men and women, who celebrate, challenge, reject, and rewrite such historic boundaries. For many female African artists, this process of change has given them a means of reclaiming their lost power and voice in a male-dominated world. For those who lost the power of self-expression and empowerment during the colonial era, art has become a means of regaining the choice to imagine and represent themselves and others on their own terms. 🪶

1 Thomas Stearns Eliot, "Tradition and the Individual Talent" in *The Sacred Wood* (London: Methune, 1920; Bartleby.com, 1996. www.bartleby.com/200/sw4.html, printed out November 10, 2006), 18.

2 For example, in 1493, Columbus brought back several Arawaks from the Caribbean to Queen Isabella's court, where one of them remained on display for two years until he died, reputedly of sadness.

3 See Oliver Impy and Arthur MacGregor, eds., *The Origins of Museums: The Cabinets of Curiosities in Sixteenth- and Seventeenth-Century Europe,* second ed. (London: House of Stratus, 2001), for discussions of the history of curiosity cabinets, museums, and the display of cultural otherness.

4 See Robert William Rydell, *All the World's a Fair: America's International Expositions, 1876–1916* (Chicago: University of Chicago Press, 1984); Rydell, *World of Fairs: The Century-of-Progress Expositions* (Chicago: University of Chicago Press, 1993); Rydell and Nancy E. Gwinn, eds., *Fair Representations: World's Fairs and the Modern World Century-of-Progress Expositions* (Amsterdam: VU University Press, 1994); and Pieter van Wesemael, *Architecture of Instruction and Delight: A Socio-historical Analysis of World Exhibitions as a Didactic Phenomenon (1798–1851–1970)* (Rotterdam: Uitgeverij, 2001), for a history of world expositions in Europe and America.

5 The public display of dissected human bodies in the name of "science" is not solely a phenomenon of the voyeuristic past, as recently evidenced by the controversial anatomical exhibitions *Body Worlds* and *The Amazing Human Body.*

6 Please note that Baartman's name has been spelled in various ways throughout this publication, which reflects the diverse spellings found in the literature on her history.

7 Richard Altick, *The Shows of London* (Cambridge: Harvard University Press, 1978), and Robert Chambers, ed., *The Book of Days: A Miscellany of Popular Antiquities,* 2 vols. (London and Edinburgh: W. & R. Chambers, 1864), ii, 621.

8 Chris McGreal, "Coming Home," *The Guardian,* 21/02/2002 (London: Guardian News and Media Limited, 2002), http://education.guardian.co.uk/print/0,,436008 2-110555,00.html.

9 See Londa Schiebinger, *Nature's Body: Gender in the Making of Modern Science* (Boston: Beacon Press, 1993), for a discussion of Baartman's role in definitions of race and gender. For more on the image of Saartjie Baartman, see also Yvette Abrahams, "Images of Sara Bartman: Sexuality, Race and Gender in Early Nineteenth-Century Britain," in *Nation, Empire, Colony: Historicizing Gender and Race,* eds. Ruth Roach Pierson and Nupur Chaudhuri (Bloomington and Indianapolis: Indiana University Press, 1998), 220–236.

10 The proportions of the African female body—especially genitalia such as that seen on the body of Saartjie Baartman—were used as "evidence" of and justification for prejudicial notions about African women's deviant sexuality.

11 Although exhibitions of African sculpture had been on display in Paris since 1878 as ethnographic manifestations of "primitive" cultures, when European artists such as Picasso, Matisse, Derain, and Vlaminck first saw and started to collect these sculptures at the beginning of the twentieth century, they were promoted from ethnographic specimen to masterpieces of great artistic achievement.

12 See Sanders Gilman, *Difference and Pathology: Stereotypes of Sexuality, Race, and Madness* (Ithaca: Cornell University Press, 1985), for a seminal study on European notions about the pathology of the black female body.

13 Although the nineteenth century gave birth to a plethora of sexually conflated imagery of black women, depictions of the black temptress had appeared in European biblical narratives already as early as the fifteenth century, embedded into images of the Libyan Sibyl; the Ethiopian wife of Moses and daughter of the King Tarshish; the black bride of the Song of Songs, who is depicted in the Krumlov Compilation (Bohemia, about 1420); and the Queen of Sheba, who put Solomon's virtues to the test, as depicted in Hans Vintler's *Die Blumen der Tugend* (Tyrol, 1411) and the *Speculum humanae salvationis* (Lübeck, circa 1430).

14 I use the term "tradition" here in reference to long-established practices and beliefs that are handed down from one generation to another and are greatly valued as a vital part of a particular culture. The term does *not* intend in any way to imply cultural stasis, as change and adaptation are integral to all cultures. In many cases, traditional practices mentioned in this text continue to play a role in contemporary African culture and society, especially in rural areas. In some cases, however, certain traditions are no longer practiced and are therefore referred to in the past tense.

15 Some examples of exhibitions following this paradigm are *African Women/African Art* (Rosalyn A. Walker, The African-American Institute, New York, 1976); *She: Images of the Woman in Black African Art* (Alfred Scheinberg, Germans Van Eck Gallery, New York, 1983); *Mother and Child in African Sculpture* (Kate Ezra, The African American Institute, New York, 1986); *Women and Power: The Feminine Spirit in African Art, Selections from the Museum of Art and Archaeology* (Museum of Art and Archaeology, University of Missouri-Columbia, Columbia, 1990); *Woman Eternal: The Female Image in African Art* (Allen Wardwell, Alfred L. Scheinberg, Maureen A. Zarember, and Tambaran Gallery, Tambaran Gallery, New York, 1991), and *Mistress of the House, Mistress of Heaven: Women in Ancient Egypt* (Anne K. Capel and Glenn E. Markoe, Cincinnati Art Museum, Cincinnati, 1996).

16 Lisa Aronson ("African Women in the Visual Arts," *Signs: Journal of Woman in Culture and Society* 16, no. 3 [1991]: 550–574) summarized the emerging state of research in women's arts of Africa in the 1980s and early '90s, many of which laid the foundations for further studies too numerous to mention here. Many have been published in *African Arts.* See also Flora S. Kaplan, ed., *Queens, Queen Mothers, Priestesses, and Power: Case Studies in African Gender* (New York: New York Academy of Sciences, 1997), an anthology of essays on the history of women's power in Africa.

17 See, for example, Schildkrout's discussion of Mangbetu figurative pottery in this volume.

18 See Robert Farris Thompson, "Abatan: A Master Potter of the Egbado Yoruba," in *Tradition and Creativity,* ed. Daniel Biebuyck (Berkeley: University of California Press, 1969), 120–182, for a detailed study of the life and pottery of Abatan, who is regarded as one of the best makers of the sacred Eyinle vessels.

19 See Ruth B. Phillips, *Representing Women: Sande Masquerades of the Mende of Sierra Leone* (Los Angeles: UCLA Fowler Museum of Cultural History, 1995), for a complete treatise on the exceptional practice of women's masquerades of the Sande Society.

20 The names used for these masks varied according to geographical location, such as *mukuyi* or *okuyi*.

21 Today, the Punu peoples also display these masks in their homes as a sign of ethnic identity and wear *mukudj* masks made specifically for other types of performances that celebrate a number of events. See Alisa Lagamma, "The Metropolitan Museum of Art, New York," *African Arts* 34, no. 2 (Summer 2001).

22 Lagamma, "The Metropolitan Museum of Art, New York," 74.

23 See Roy Sieber, *Hair in African Art and Culture* (Munich: Prestel Verlag, 2000).

24 Sieber, *Hair in African Art and Culture*, 27.

25 See Thomas MacDonald Shaw, "Beauty and Art," in *Fulani Matrix of Beauty and Art in the Djolof Region of Senegal* (Lewiston: Edwin Mellen Press, 1994), 47–84, for a discussion of art and concepts of beauty among the Fulani of Senegal.

26 See Mette Bovin, *Nomads Who Cultivate Beauty: Wodaabe Dances and Visual Arts in Niger* (Uppsala: Nordiska Afrikainstitutet, 2001), for an in-depth study of the concepts of beauty among the Wodaabe, a subgroup of the Fulani of Niger.

27 Barbara DeMott, *Dogon Masks: A Structural Study of Form and Meaning* (Ann Arbor: UMI Research Press, 1982), 98.

28 The *hleeta* ordeal was officially outlawed in 1978 after over twenty years of protest by the Christian church.

29 See Marla Berns, "Ga'anda Scarification: A Model for Art and Identity," in *Marks of Civilization*, ed. Arnold Rubin (Los Angeles: UCLA Museum of Cultural History, 1988), 57–76, for a full description of Ga'anda scarification art.

30 Boys underwent separate initial ordeals called *sapta*, which did not involve body scarification but did include intense physical and psychological challenges.

31 Marla Berns, "Ceramic Clues: Art History in the Gongola Valley," *African Arts* 22, no. 2 (February 1989): 48–59, 102–103. See Berns 1989 for a study of Ga'anda pottery.

32 In the past, these designs might have replicated the keloidal patterns of the vessel's female owner.

33 In traditional Zulu culture, women were not allowed to have anything to do with cattle or any operations connected with cattle, as this was believed to cause the cattle to cease giving milk.

34 See Brendan Bell and Ian Calder, eds., *Ubumba: Aspects of Indigenous Ceramics in KwaZulu-Natal* (Pietermaritzburg: Tatham Art Gallery, 1998), for a study of Zulu ceramics, and Patricia Davison, "South Africa Beer Pots," *African Arts* 18, no. 3 (May 1985): 74–77, 98, for a discussion of beer pots and beer brewing among the Zulu.

35 Young women would make beaded adornment that youths would exchange as a token of their affection for each other.

36 Men and women wore different scarification patterns.

37 See Betty Sneider, "Body Decorations in Mozambique," *African Arts* 6, no. 2 (Winter 1973): 26–31, 92, for a description of Makonde body decorations.

38 Although Makonde women no longer practice body scarification, one can still see elderly women whose faces bear the markings of this now-defunct practice.

39 J. A. R. Wembah-Rashid ("Isinyago and Midimu: Masked Dancers of Tanzania and Mozambique," *African Arts* 4, no. 2 [Winter 1971]: 38–44) asserts that the origin of this dance is commonly believed to relate to the legend of the first created man, who carved a figure from wood, that then came to life and became his wife.

40 See Arthur P. Bourgeois, "Yaka Masks and Sexual Imagery," *African Arts* 15, no. 2 (February 1982): 47–50, 87, for a discussion of the sexual imagery of Yaka masks.

41 In 2006, I conducted brief research among the Kwere of Chalinze, where a young girl had been in seclusion for a year.

42 See Fadhili S. Mshana, "Art and Identity Among the Zaramo of Tanzania" (Ph.D. dissertation, State University of New York, Art History Department), chapter 2, for an in-depth discussion of the *mwana hiti* figures in Zaramo initiation rites.

43 As Marie-Louise Labelle has noted, the *marmo* seclusion period has been abolished since the 1930s; consequently the exact meaning of the symbolism on these skirts can only be inferred according to broader Iraqw symbolic ideologies. *Beads of Life: Eastern and Southern African Beadwork from Canadian Collections* (Gatineau: Canadian Museum of Civilization, 2005), 88.

44 Labelle, *Beads of Life*, 84–88.

45 Ibid., 87–88.

46 The following information about Kwere color symbolism in girl's initiation was shared with me by a group of women and a young girl undergoing initiation in a secluded compound outside the town of Chalinze in September of 2006. According to the senior officiant, knowing the meanings of the colors within the context of initiation without undergoing proper initiation rites can be ritually dangerous to people from that culture. Consequently, she warns Kwere readers of the possible dangers of this knowledge. See also Marja-Liisa Swantz, *Ritual and Symbol in Transitional Zaramo Society* (Uppsala: Scandinavian Institute of African Studies, 1986), for similar references to Zaramo initiation and color symbolism.

47 John S. Mbiti, *African Religions and Philosophy* (New York: Praeger, 1969), 110–11.

48 Cattle symbolism is also used in Zulu symbolism in conjunction with references to male sexuality. For example, appreciative wives would compare their husband's virility to the sexual appetite of a bull.

49 The rock paintings of the Tassili n'Ajjer region of Algeria illustrate a horned woman covered with body art and adornment, possibly representing a predecessor of the Egyptian cattle-headed goddess Hathor.

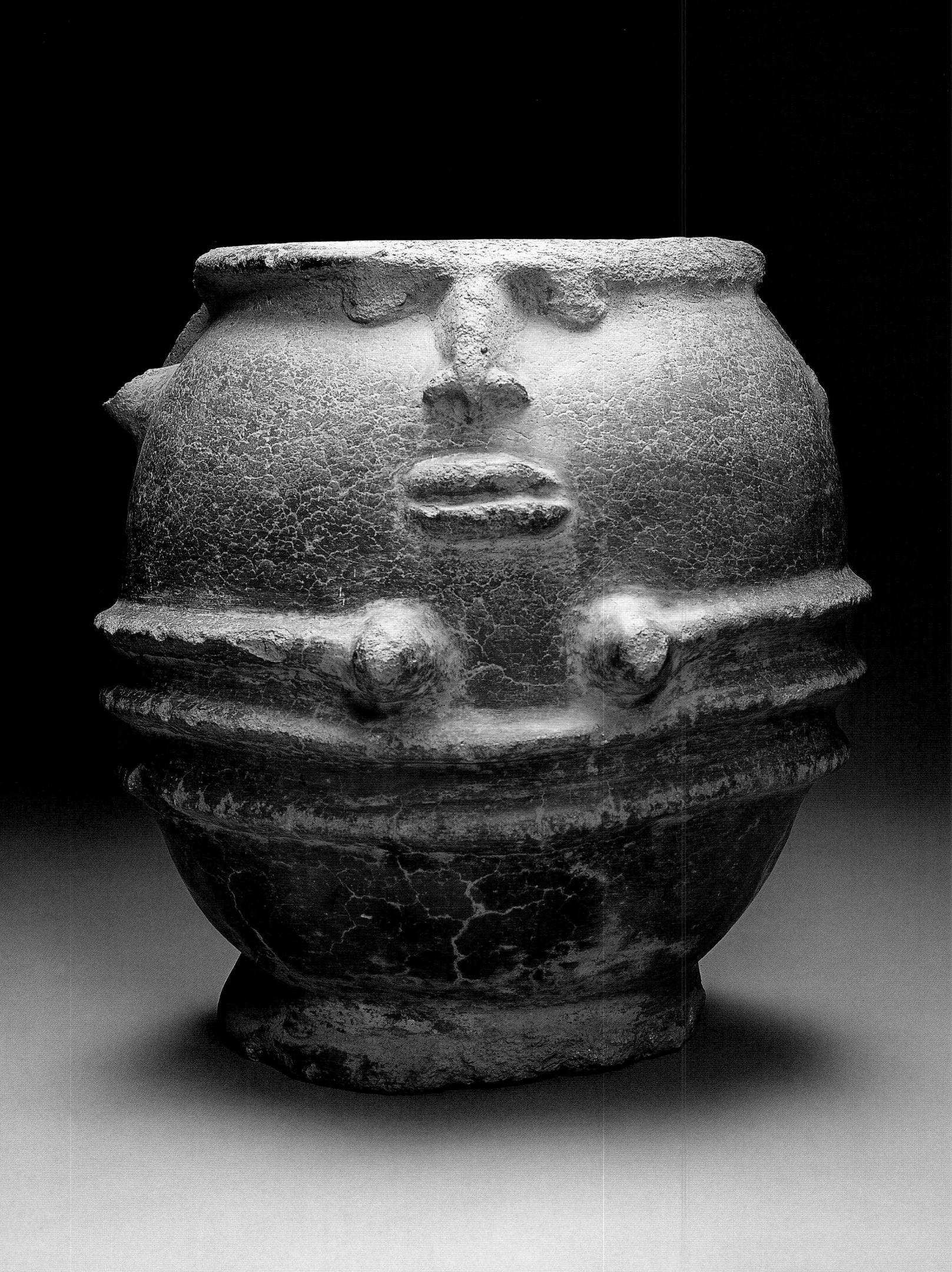

2 African Women's Body Images in Postcolonial Discourse and Resistance to Neo-Crusaders

In traditional African systems of power, inscribing signs and meaning onto the female body through art has served as a significant and time-honored tool in maintaining women's solidarity movements, women's matriarchal cultures, and rituals. These art forms, which honored women and their bodies, ensured also the well-being of women and the community as a whole, despite the objectifying and civilizing agenda of colonialism and missionaries. Under the postcolonial setting, however, new inscriptions of meaning upon the African female body serve as a means of subduing the power of enduring traditional matriarchy, particularly through the mandatory re-conversion from traditional cultural practices into patriarchal orthodox Christian and new fundamentalist Christian values. This damaging process imposes a new form of patriarchal control over women and their body images. In this essay, I will first examine traditional African art practices that use representations of the female form to convey the place, power, and role of women in social, cultural, and religious institutions. I will then present case studies that reveal specifically how Igbo and other women in West Africa continue to use their bodies to convey important messages about matriarchal ideals of womanhood, despite forces that attempt to block access to women's freedom of expression through their bodies.

BODIES OF POWER AND ICONS OF WOMANHOOD IN TRADITIONAL AFRICAN ART

In the traditional setting, institutions of female solidarity over which African matriarchs presided—such as women's organizations and initiation societies— served as a means of self-representation and empowerment. Often these organizations and societies used the female body and art forms to communicate their ideologies. Under the critical gaze of neo-Christian crusaders, however, indigenous institutions of female power have been marginalized, if not directly

opposite Unknown artist, Bozo peoples, Burkina Faso, vessel with Janus head, early to mid-twentieth century, terracotta. Collection of Bill and Gale Simmons, New York. Photograph by Bruce White.

suppressed. By covering up the African female body and erasing its artistic, symbolic, and cultural significance, these women are being re-objectified once again.

Ideologies of womanhood are strongly represented both physically and metaphorically in traditional African sculptural arts, deriving their variety from the many ways in which women themselves have power and are visible in society. In the traditional setting, the image of woman as mother, daughter, leader, goddess, and queen is depicted in the arts of both male and female domains of life. The image of woman and her body feature prominently not only in matriarchal sacred objects but also as larger symbols of beauty given form on masks, figures, and vessels (plates 1–15) that emulate women's scarification markings and ephemeral designs of beauty. These carved and painted representations allow for individual creativity in the embodiment and depiction of ideologies of womanhood, but demonstrate also a deep concern for matriarchal collective norms embedded in social, cultural, religious, and political ideals.

Among the Mano and Vai peoples of Liberia and the Mende, Sherbro, and Temne of Sierra Leone, for example, the Sande Women's Society prepares young girls for transition into adult womanhood. The Sande Society teaches young girls social and economic skills, instills notions of morality, appropriate social comportment, and sexual behavior, and passes on knowledge of herbal medicine. It also supports the female members throughout their lives by maintaining social and political interests that promote women's solidarity in the face of the men's initiation society, called Poro.

During Mende girls' initiation rituals, high-ranking members and leaders of the Sande Society wear helmet masks (plates 1 and 65), called *sowei,* during dances that teach about women's roles and power. The mask embodies the spirit *sowo* (or *bondo*) and is encoded with visual symbols of Sande ideals of feminine perfection and sexuality, which carry different meanings according to the contexts of its use. The high, full forehead of the female mask can symbolically stand for wisdom, intelligence, or achievement, while the downcast eyes for modesty or sexual allure. The polished, glossy black finish of the mask relates the origin of Sande knowledge from the depths of the rivers but also emulates the oiled skin of the emerging initiate as she is transformed into a beautiful young woman. The elaborate hairstyle, possible only through collaborative effort, reveals close ties within the community of women. The neck rings indicate the initiate's health but also her prosperity, while cowrie shells denote the hopes for wealth and abundance. Antelope horns and amulets refer to good medicine but also to the spiritual protection needed by the young initiates during their ritually vulnerable passage from girlhood into womanhood.[1] Allen Wardwell describes the *sowei* mask:

> They are worn with a costume of raffia, black cloth with the sleeves sewn together, and black stockings that completely obscures the bearer from view so that the spirit evoked by the mask can only enter from within. This apparition symbolizes bondo, the primordial ancestress who was the first to nurture the young and is guardian spirit of the Sande Society. Those who wear this awe-inspiring costume

pronounce judgments, execute laws, and otherwise instill respect for the traditions of the group among both initiates and adults.[2]

Representing one of Africa's rare forms of masquerading that is controlled and performed exclusively by women,[3] these Sande Society dances highlight the vital position of women *vis-a-vis* men. Consequently, the *sowei* masquerade is performed also publicly during civic events to emphasize the unity and strength of the female corporate body and the political significance of the Sande Society within the larger community. Among the Temne peoples, female figures (plate 42) are similarly created as reflections of the Sande ideals of womanhood.

Ideals of female beauty are apparent in Baule "spirit spouse" figures, or *blolo bla* (plate 5), with their intricate hairstyles, smoothly polished surfaces, and exquisite body scarification. According to Baule sources, before birth all human beings had spouses while existing in another world (*blolo*) where spirits originate. These spirit spouses follow their human partners into this world and therefore require carved figures to visually manifest themselves; through the carved form, the spirit can interact with its human partner and bestow prosperity on those dwelling in this world. The figures usually belong to one individual, who places the figure in a private shrine, often hidden within the bedroom. The perfect physical form of the figure attracts the spirit into it but also represents the spirit spouse's inward social, moral, and intellectual achievement.[4]

African sculptures frequently deal with themes of fertility and sexuality. For example, Agni women in Côte d'Ivoire and Akan and Asante women in Ghana traditionally used small, carved wooden figures to represent, induce, protect, or enhance a woman's fertility (plates 21 and 22). The origin of the figures called *akua'ba* is traced to the Akan legend of Akua, an infertile woman who nurtured a small wooden child as if it were a real baby as instructed by a priest. She did this for so long that she eventually was able to conceive and give birth to a beautiful, healthy daughter. The fertility doll became generally known as Akua's child, or *akua'ba,* in the Akan language.[5] Subsequently, other women who experienced difficulty conceiving or bearing healthy children turned to the instruction of priests and the aid of *akua'ba* figures that visually emulate local ideals of female health, fertility, and beauty.

Even within the practices of men's associations and initiation societies, women were honored as vital members of larger cultural institutions, such as the Poro Men's Society (the male parallel of the Sande Women's Society), which has a Poro Mother. As in other men's organizations throughout Africa, the theme of fertility plays an important role in the Poro Society. In the Senufo culture of Côte d'Ivoire, for example, carved wooden staff finials (plate 20) depict seated women who embody the grace and seductive beauty of idealized Senufo womanhood. Each year, these staffs were awarded to junior members of the Poro Men's Society who were named as champion cultivators in a yearly hoeing competition that was part of their ritual initiation into manhood. The swollen bellies of the female figures on these finials evoke pregnancy and symbolize the power of humans to reproduce and the fertility of the soil upon which the Senufo agriculturalists rely.[6]

In the southwestern regions of Yoruba country in Nigeria and Benin, men honor women's power and authority (*ashe*) through the *gelede* dance, which is put on by the Gelede Society, an organization made up of men and women and led by an elderly woman. This sumptuous masquerade publicly commemorates the deified Great Mother, Iya Nla, who dwells at the bottom of the ocean. The dance attempts to persuade her to use her great powers for the communal good—not its destruction. During *gelede* performances, male dancers pay tribute particularly to mature women and mothers, who are hailed in *gelede* songs as "the gods of society" and the "owners of the world." Emulating their patience, control, reverence, and achievements, *gelede* dancers appease the potential wrath of the all-powerful mothers, female ancestors, and female deities.[7] During the dance, male *gelede* masqueraders wear a female mask (plate 2) and full body costume (figure 2.1), sometimes incorporating layers of textiles, stomach and breastplates, and back plates with representations of babies attached to emphasize the female form and woman's maternal and nurturing role. The London-based artist Sokari Douglas Camp, who is originally from Nigeria's Delta region, captures the spectacle of the *gelede* masquerade in her life-size sculpture *Gelede from Top to Toe* (plate 96). She commits her own form of gender reversal by creating these large female figures of metal and wood—a medium associated with "male" art forms—that centralize the female perspective as an observer and critic.

Gelede performances are staged at local markets—the domain of Yoruba women—which are often run under the leadership of powerful women. Since the main occupation of Yoruba women was trading, high status was often accomplished through their reputation in trade, their craftsmanship, and their wealth rather than through their husband's standing or importance. Consequently, Yoruba *gelede* masks also depict and celebrate these market women, who are economically independent and can earn more money than their husbands through trade.

Given the importance of women in markets and local economies, it is not surprising that icons of women's productivity are commonly depicted in African traditional art. Most often women's economic roles are represented through the image of the working woman, carrying a load on her head, including pottery (plates 36 and 37) or bundles (plate 38), pounding maize (plate 35), or working at a combination of these activities. Similarly, caryatid female figures (plate 44) reflect the ability of women to carry heavy loads of work and responsibility with grace, strength, wisdom, and agility. These figures also pay homage to the important role of women in traditional society in bearing children, who will continue the family lineage and become the social security system for elders in their advanced years.

Iconic images of the mother and child reflect one of the most powerful and celebrated roles of womanhood in both secular and sacred life. The very conditions of maternity and motherhood are greatly honored and widely depicted in traditional African art representing ordinary women to queens as mothers (plates 25–32 and 37).

In Yoruba culture, mother figures are often characterized as symbolic vessels of life. For example, a carved wooden offering bowl from the Oyo state in Nigeria depicts a mother with her children (plate 29). The female figure, in this case, is a devotee of the Yoruba thunder god Shango and embodies the ideals of fertility, motherhood, and abundance, as symbolized by her full breasts and the children surrounding her. Such figurative bowls were placed on shrines and used to raise concerns about fertility and seek the help of this powerful deity.[8] In Yoruba villages and cities, women sometimes carry these bowls as well as other female figures through the streets during religious ceremonies that honor the various patron deities who concern themselves with issues of womanhood.

Among the many forms of sacred arts representing female devotees are ritual vessels for the river god Eyinle (*awo otun Eyinle*) (plate 39), patron deity of hunting and medicine; ivory divination tappers for Ifa, the god of divination; and wooden staffs for Shango (*oshe Shango*), who helps women conceive (plate 43). The woman's pose on the Shango staff, with hands to breasts, is a widespread traditional gesture of obeisance. This pose is often depicted in both secular and ritual arts throughout Africa, symbolizing women's respect of and attention to the spirit world, as in a Bozo ceramic vessel from Mali (plate 40a) and Kamba spoon from Kenya (plate 41; see also plates 42–44).

Colonial-era photography and postcards (plates 62a and 63a) have often misrepresented the respectability of this pose, which through uninformed Western readings mistakenly can be taken for sexual invitation, which California-based artist Alison Saar addresses in her mixed media work *Sable Venus* (plate 109). In Saar's work, she juxtaposes the Western veneration of the "white Venus" epitomized in Botticelli's *Birth of Venus* (c. 1485) as a Western symbol of purity, beauty, and fertility with the "black Venus" of Thomas Stothard's *The Voyage of the Sable Venus from Angola to the West Indies* (1793). Stothard's depiction of the Sable Venus is rife with references to eroticism and empire and reduces the terror and abject abuse endured by black women during the Middle Passage journey into a benign, harmless, and leisurely voyage leading to their eventual procurement by white men. Saar's *Sable Venus,* with her piercing hollow eyes, tackles the disturbing contradictions embedded in these early iconic references, which she superimposes with African symbolism of piety and purity. Saar's Venus holds her breast with one hand, like the reverential pose depicted in traditional African carvings of female devotees in attendance to the gods. With her other hand, she covers her pudendum in a gesture reminiscent of Eve's shame. Floating around her body are fragments of objects from or representing the sea, such as shells, corals, crustaceans, Dürer's *Eve* (from *Adam and Eve*, 1507), a Minoan octopus vase, and Mary Cassatt's *La Toilette* (1891), among others, whose Western symbolism coincides with African cosmological associations with water, purity, and cleanliness. Saar's *Sable Venus* stands in total opposition to and defiance of the Sable Venus depicted in the eighteenth century, which later gave birth to colonial imagery of the African female body as a justification for the imperialist agenda of the Western colonial powers.

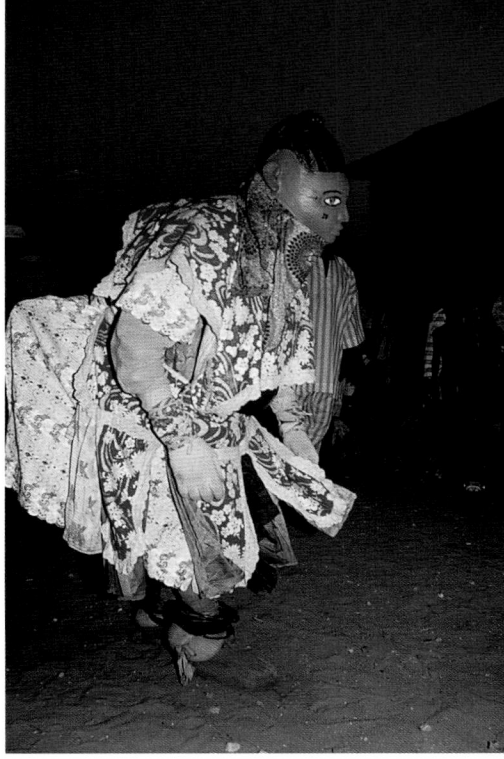

FIGURE 2.1 *Gelede* dancing, Isale-Eko, Lagos, Nigeria, 1978. Photograph by and courtesy of Henry Drewal.

In the Grasslands region of Cameroon, queen mothers are symbols of great fertility and are often represented in sculptural form.[9] The Bamileke peoples of the Grasslands, for example, permanently display life-size mother-and-child figures of the queen mother outside of the royal palace as an important signifier for the abundance of the kingdom.[10] A Bamileke figure in the collection of the Völkerkunde Museum in Munich, which depicts a pregnant queen mother in the midst of excruciating labor pains, is a very rare and unique example (figure 1.8).[11]

As Benjamin Ray writes, "African ritual art is iconic in the sense that it portrays the invisible spiritual world in a symbolic and abstract manner, using some of the features of the natural world."[12] Art speaks from and to the culture in which it is produced, but it is at the same time open to general appreciation as well as to appropriation, beginning more journeys of being localized in a specific culture or generalized in popular aesthetics. Like any art form, these objects that embody ideologies of African womanhood have their localized aesthetic quality and layers of cultural meanings—both inside and outside of their original context. The meeting of these traditional images and objects with contemporary African cultural and religious practices adds a rich narrative layer and exposes new ways in which women negotiate power and self-representation today, despite postcolonial cultural transformations.

AFRICAN TRADITIONS VERSUS CHRISTO-CENTRIC MODERNITY

African women have made a unique contribution to world civilizations through traditional women's organizations, women's councils, and matriarchal institutions.[13] In traditional African societies, women often were organized on the basis of kinship and lineage, age-sets, and through girls' and women's initiation societies and women's political, prestigious, or religious associations, many of which honored the highest achieving women. This became a topic of great interest to me during my fieldwork in Nnobi, a rural village of Igbo-speaking peoples in Nigeria's Anambra State, formerly known as the Southeastern Region.[14] I was drawn to the research of Nnobi women's institutions because that work had not been done. Although women's presence was minimal in social anthropological data, in the field one could not overlook the presence and importance of women in all aspects of social life.

When I was working in the field in 1982, the notion of the body as art and the use of the body to make a statement was first conveyed to me by the famous Nwajiuba Ojukwuisiana na Nnobi (figure 2.2), a traditional Igbo woman in Nnobi society. She is the woman I have described as a "male daughter" in my monograph, *Male Daughters, Female Husbands*,[15] in which I show how the Nnobi traditional descent-based society used gender-flexibility in Igbo language and culture. For example, in the Igbo language, there is no gender distinction in subject and object pronouns. In cultural practices, if biological gender might constrain women in economic and political positions, gender-flexibility allowed for restrictions in marriage and political office to be lifted. Nwajiuba's place in the Nnobi

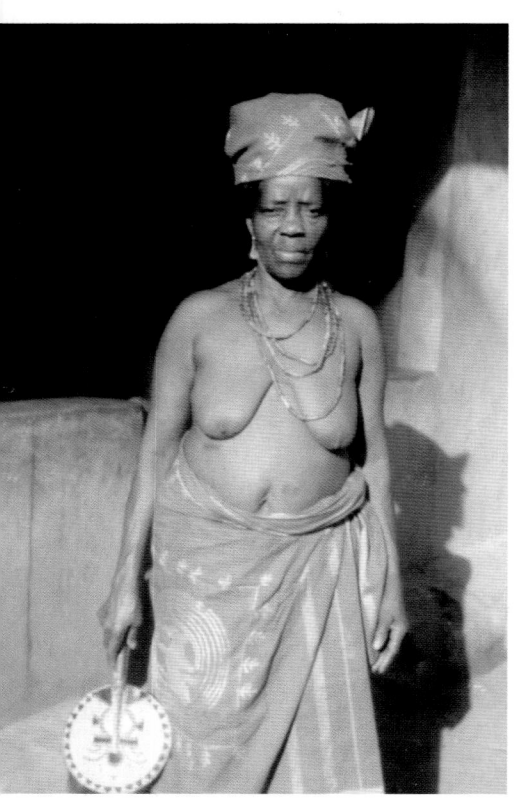

Figure 2.2 Nwajiuba Ojukwuisiana na Nnobi, Nnobi, Anambra State, Nigeria, 1981. Photograph by and courtesy of Ifi Amadiume.

political hierarchy is important for illustrating this type of system in Igbo societies. In the Nnobi system of patrilineal succession to political office, first sons replace their fathers as heads of an *obi,* the ancestral house. If there is no male heir to this position, a daughter can officially succeed her father and head an *obi.* She can also marry a woman and perpetuate the family line through offspring from woman and woman marriage. The incoming wife's children belong to the family of the "male" spouse through completing required marriage rituals. In this case, women get pregnant from visiting male lovers, which I have described as "invisible" lovers since they have no claims to the children. This was what happened with Nwajiuba, who became officially a male-daughter in the most senior political *obi* in Nnobi, where she held the position of priest of the Land/Earth spirit of Nnobi.

During my research with Nwajiuba, I found her to be very knowledgeable in Nnobi-Igbo tradition. She was an impressive woman with an aura of authority expressed in a gentle and likeable manner. I knew that we liked each other and I was eager for images that would capture our wonderful encounter. As I normally did in my fieldwork, I asked Nwajiuba's permission to take her photograph. Since she had been very hospitable to me in the past, I was surprised when she declined. With a smile, she told me that she was not dressed; that she was barebodied! I found this puzzling since I could see that she was fully dressed wearing a blouse and wrapper. She suggested that we do it during my next visit and that she would be ready.

To my surprise, on the appointed day, Nwajiuba came out posing topless, radiating confidence, pride, and dignity through her poise. I needed to quickly make sense of our differing understandings of the meaning of nakedness, plainness, and being dressed. Nwajiuba immediately took charge of the situation and instructed me on the significance of her different stance and poses. She pointed also to her body, which was decorated with a line of short horizontal scarification markings (barely visible in figure 2.2), which ran vertically from the base of her throat down her chest and stomach. Such scarification markings are made up of pearl or berry-shaped keloidal patterns, called *mbubu* or *ebubu,* which are inscribed onto the bodies of young Igbo girls in preparation for marriage (figure 2.3). *Mbubu* or *ebubu* designs are cut directly into the skin of the torso as a permanent expression of the ultimate beauty of women. Nwajiuba also wore painted designs on her body, which are referred to by the Igbo peoples as *uli* and are a creative, ephemeral expression of artistic motifs and, in some cases, serve as a coded communication system. Nwajiuba called *uli* an Igbo women's traditional art as only women could paint and draw *uli* designs (figure 2.4). In traditional Igbo societies, women were the painters and usually used this form of vegetable-dye drawing and painting to beautify both the walls of their houses and their bodies. They could also draw these designs onto the bodies of their men.

Nwajiuba's insistence on completing the ethnographic narrative that I was compiling through her body art and physical comportment later made perfect sense to me, but not quite at the time. In the context of my collecting empirical

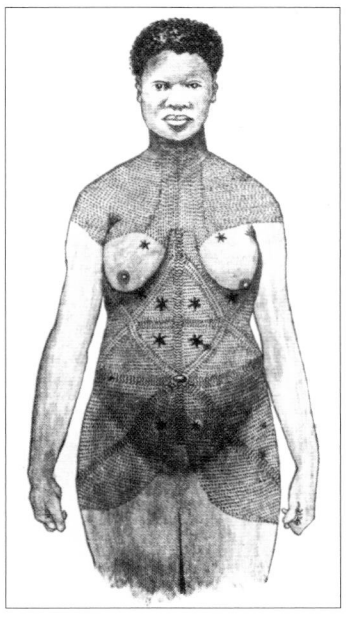

FIGURE 2.3 A cicatrized woman, from *Niger Ibos*, George Thomas Basden, London: Frank Cass & Co. Ltd., 1966 [1938], p. 336. Photograph courtesy of Taylor and Francis.

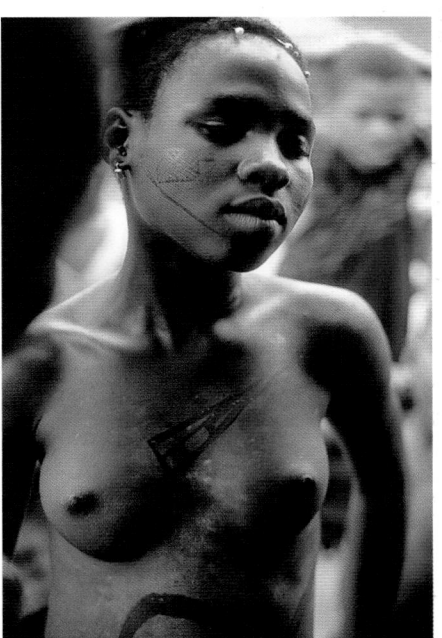

FIGURE 2.4 Igbo *uli* painting, Ugbene, Nigeria, 1983. Photograph by and courtesy of Herbert Cole.

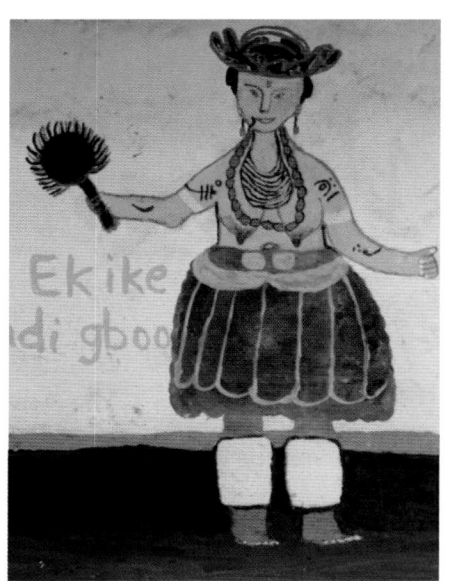

FIGURE 2.5 Illustration of a traditionally dressed woman on Nwajiuba's wall, from Willis 1988–1989: 16, no. 10. Photograph by and courtesy of Liz (Willis) Peri.

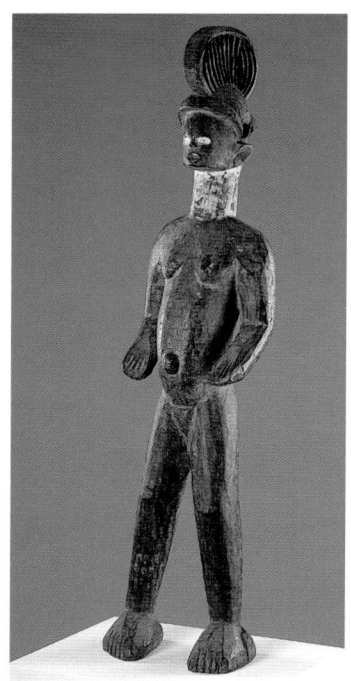

FIGURE 2.6 Unknown artist, Igbo peoples, Nigeria, female figure (alusi), nineteenth century, wood, pigment. The Baltimore Museum of Art: Gift of Dr. and Mrs. Bernard Berk; BMA 1973.77. Photograph courtesy of The Baltimore Museum of Art.

data, Nwajiuba's traditional pose—topless but covered in traditional body art— seemed logical. It was one more illustrative story that she used to teach me about traditional Nnobi ways. While I was taking photographs of Nwajiuba in her traditional attire, everyone around us supported her, helping to fetch one item or the other, or reminding her of a missing piece of traditional ornament that they knew she usually added to the decoration of her body. This demonstration of attire, decoration, and stance illustrated how she comported herself and dressed in an appropriately "traditional" fashion for an Igbo woman of her status and age when the occasion called for it, which is illustrated also in a drawing on Nwajiuba's wall titled *"Ekike ndi gboo"* or "traditional way of dressing" (figure 2.5).[16] Large figures of female tutelary deities (*alusi*) (figure 2.6) can be decorated with the permanent *mbubu* scarification patterns and with ephemeral painted *uli* designs reapplied in annual renewal rites.

In this context of ethnographic monograph, tradition retained its wholesomeness, pride, and dignity. It was—and still is—the dominant focus of attention and narrative. Nwajiuba, like many Nnobi elders including my father, had come to realize the importance of recorded history. Consequently, they were willing and eager for me to record as much as I could of Nnobi traditional culture. During these narratives, it seemed as though time stood still and there was only tradition, but that was not the case. Even in 1982, Nnobi traditions, social institutions, and culture continued to be affected by the long-lasting effects of colonialism and postcolonial transformations. Nwajiuba was fully aware of the tensions between "tradition" and "modernity," yet she still chose to cling to and insist on her rightful and traditional place of high status in Nnobi society. Bringing the empirical data and narratives that I collected in Nnobi into gender theoretical discourses enabled me to better understand Nwajiuba's use of her body art as a statement of resistance that can be understood in terms of culture, gender, history, and politics.

In traditional Nnobi philosophy and cultural institutions—into which Nwajiuba was born in 1896, before British colonialism reached the village—she is considered to be a matriarch and a male-daughter, who occupies the first-son political position in all of Nnobi.[17] We can understand her position as a sort of queen-king, a woman's role that the Nnobi community recognized and respected. In these roles, which she took seriously during her lifetime and for which she respected traditional customs, she remained one of the last adherents to traditional Nnobi religion and political protocol. Throughout her life, however, Nwajiuba chose how and when to appear in public, and in what particular mode of dressing—whether "traditional" (wearing body art) or "modern" (wearing Western-style clothing). For example, in an undated photograph (figure 2.7, top), Nwajiuba appears with a group of other traditionalists, including the late Eze Agba, the former priest of the Goddess Idemili of Nnobi and his wife. On a different occasion, she appears wearing modern Igbo-style clothing in a photo from June 1988, posing with members of the Nnobi Women's Council, which was comprised of both Christian and traditional practitioners (figure 2.8).

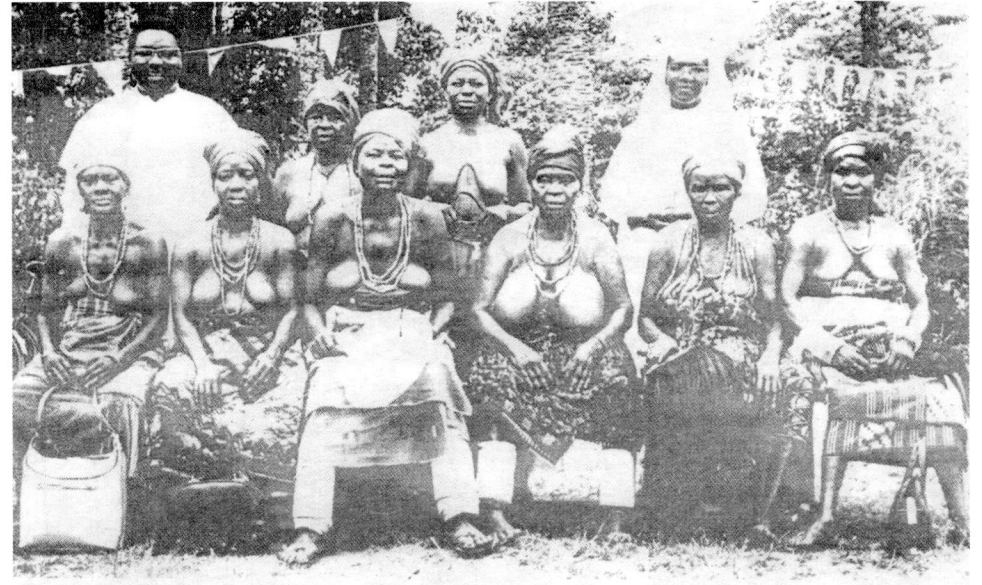

Mama as a Traditionalist

FIGURE 2.7 Top: "Mama as a Traditionalist" (front row, second from the left), undated photograph. Bottom: "Nwajiuba with the Traditionalists" (front row, second from right), from Nwajiuba's Memorial Service program pamphlet, 2003, p. 19. Photograph courtesy of Ifi Amadiume.

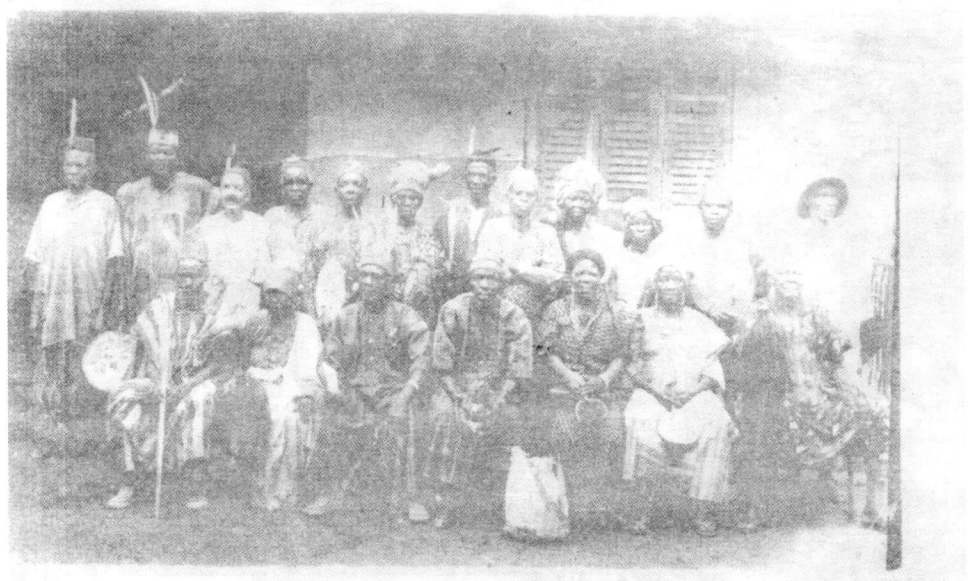

Mama with the Traditionalists

When she died in 2002, Nwajiuba's status as both a modern Christian and a traditionalist created controversy in the Nnobi community. Activities, statements, publications, and films concerning her funeral services provide particularly interesting sources that illustrate some of the gender, religious, cultural, and political conflicts involving Eurocentric Christianity.[18] More specifically, these sources inform my argument about neo-Christian articulations over and control of Nnobi Igbo women's body images.

FIGURE 2.8 Nwajiuba (front row, far right) with the Nnobi Women's Council, June 1988. Photograph by and courtesy of Ifi Amadiume.

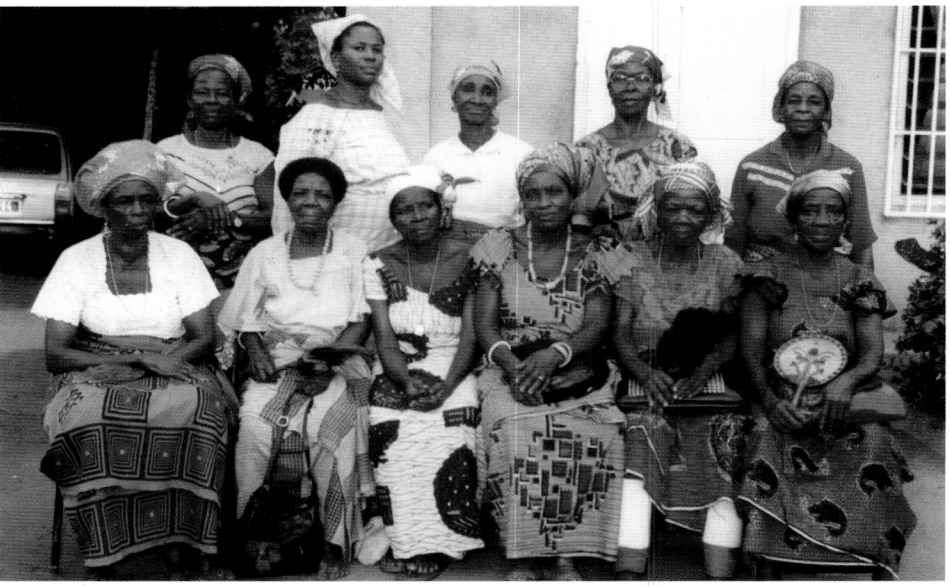

Before Nwajiuba died, she had converted to Christianity. A team of about ten Catholic priests therefore led her memorial service. In their sermon, the priests condemned and made a mockery of Nwajiuba's life as a traditionalist, pointing to a photograph on page nineteen of her memorial service program booklet (see figure 2.7, bottom). The priests used this image of Nwajiuba in traditional dress and posing with other traditionalists to strengthen their rebuke of indigenous practices. Then proudly pointing to photos of Nwajiuba dressed for baptism and standing next to a priest in church on page twenty-two of the program, the priests sang praises of her late conversion to Christianity! According to the Catholic priests, Mary Rose, as she was renamed after her conversion to Christianity, was superior to Nwajiuba as a traditionalist.[19]

It is not just the conflict of images that is in contention here, but also a contest of culture from within. In this case, the contestation is articulated through gender, politics, and class, but not race, for these are black African Catholic priests from the same Nnobi culture as Nwajiuba, who speak the same Igbo language, and who might even be her blood relatives. Their claim of religious and aesthetic superiority, enacted through Christian modernization and dress code, denies traditional values and worth. It also rejects indigenous processes toward and negotiations with modernity. In its rigid rejection of traditional Nnobi religion as "heathenism," this case of orthodox Catholicism is no different from the orthodox Protestant Churches (Anglicans, Baptists, Methodists, and Episcopalians in the U.S.A.). In Nigeria, and Africa more broadly, Evangelical Pentecostal churches are even more hostile to traditional religions, attacking the "evil" and "devils" that they imagine are embedded in traditional African practices and religions. Initially received through missionary and colonial encounters, these anti-traditionalist motives are perpetuated today in the postcolonial climate of extreme class inequality, individualism, poverty, corruption, and violence.[20] This anti-traditionalism demonstrates de-Africanization and re-conversion into an objectifying Eurocentric neocolonial situation, one that denies African cultural identities. This is a process, I argue, that negates arguments for African liberation from colonized cultures and minds as a condition of independence and freedom. I contend that re-Africanization and decolonization of *both* culture and gender are necessary.

DECOLONIZING, RE-AFRICANIZING AFRICAN WOMANHOOD

Similar to the contemporary artistic voices featured in *Black Womanhood: Images, Icons, and Ideologies of the African Body,* Ngozi Onwurah's film *And Still I Rise* documents the voices of women of African descent who critically examine and comment on historical and media images of women of African heritage. The film details distorted images of African womanhood dating back from Atlantic slavery in the Americas to misrepresentations in contemporary Hollywood film and mass media. They argue that false images and myths of the supposed black woman's "ugliness" and her animal-like rabid sexuality are used to justify economic exploitation in the logic and metaphor of rape. As the film attempts to illustrate, African expressiveness of body and sexuality—in all its spontaneity and loudness—is a body culture of celebration. Hence, Onwurah borrows a phrase from Maya Angelou's poem, "Still I Rise," for the title of her film, whose spirit is captured in verse seven and two lines from verse eight:

> Does my sexiness upset you?
> Does it come as a surprise
> That I dance like I've got diamonds
> At the meeting of my thighs?
>
> Out of the huts of history's shame
> I rise
> Up from a past that's rooted in pain
> I rise[21]

In the cultures, religions, and art of the European colonizers, African women have had to struggle against imposed forms of patriarchal domination to find creative spaces to express themselves and their own choice of womanhood. Many African women are still struggling to own their bodies. This was not the case for Nwajiuba in traditional Nnobi society, where women were artists and painters who "clothed" their naked bodies in signifying patterns and designs.

In a comparative and illustrated study of *uli* body and wall painting in different Igbo societies, Liz Willis notes that motifs may be general, but styles are distinctive and localized. Nature motifs of *uli* relate to the Igbo worldview and ideas about women and womanhood.

> Women are the appropriate mediators of *uli* aesthetic because of their special relationship with Ala, goddess of the earth, with whom they share many qualities and concerns. Ala ensures the land's fertility and nurtures crops to fruition; women too have procreative power and are a life-sustaining force.[22]

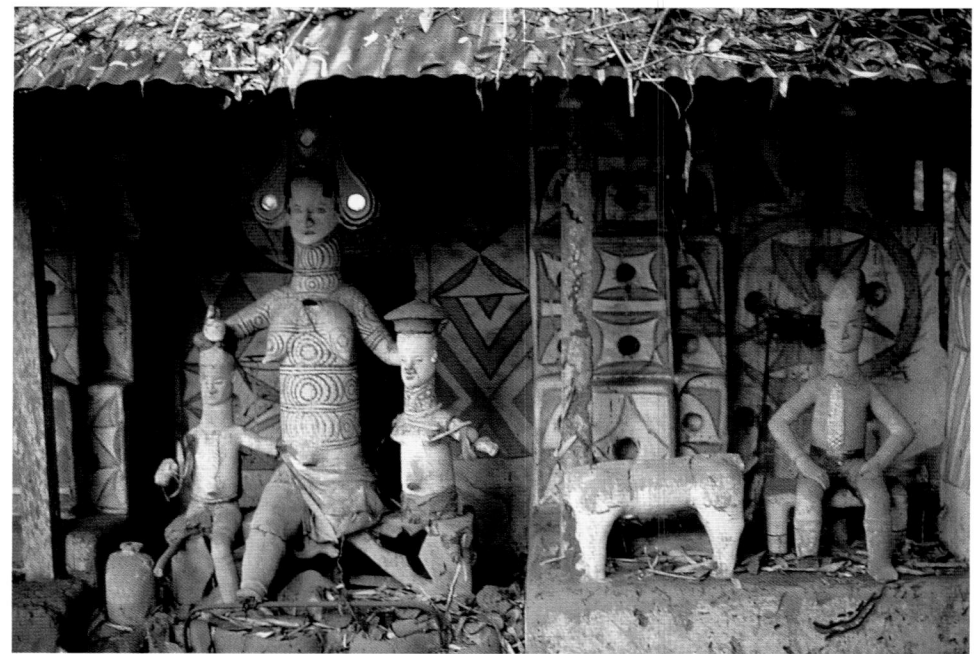

Uli painting is believed to be a gift of artistry given directly to Igbo women by Ala, who is honored in communal Igbo shrines depicted with her children (figure 2.9). Considered a major fertility spirit and a moral force in Igbo society, she is both revered and feared for her many powers.[23] *Uli* is an art of beauty and goodness that passes from woman to woman, generation to generation, and is learned during the young women's coming-of-age ritual. *Ide uli* usually takes place at the end of the *nkpu* ritual confinement for the girls' outing ceremony, while the *mbubu* or *ebubu* cuts are done just before marriage and certainly before conception.

Before colonialism and conversion to Christianity, all the constituting wards that make up the village of Nnobi worshipped the River Goddess Idemili. Ideologies and theories from the Goddess Idemili were at the center of Nnobi social structure. The mythology of this goddess provided an integrating economic philosophy of hard work and prosperity for Nnobi people in general, but more especially for Nnobi women. Nnobi people were mostly farmers and traders; women spent a good portion of their time in the marketplace selling farm produce, especially perishable commodities such as vegetables. During the year, the climatic season around Nnobi is divided between a rainy and a dry season. The latter was considered a time of scarcity and hunger until the rains came again. As Nnobi women told me during an interview in January 1982, however, they always had vegetables available to them, even during times of extreme dry weather. On such occasions, the women would go to the Idemili River where the goddess dwelled and she would let them pick vegetables from the riverbanks. According to my sources, there were vegetables at the riverbanks even when nothing should be growing there. In the quarrel between the Goddess Idemili and the Deity Aho, she had caused all the other rivers to dry up, except her own. This thinking is associated with Nnobi belief that the Goddess Idemili is supportive of women's subsistence, hard work, and economic ventures.[24]

In Nnobi mythological narrative, the goddess Idemili is the mother of all of Nnobi people. Like Nnobi women, she gave her daughter Edo the pot of medicine (a metaphor for herbal knowledge and wisdom) and the pot of prosperity. Edo became a goddess in her own right, founding her own town, and repeating her mother's fame in wealth and popularity. In addition to the gift of prosperity, Idemili rewarded achieving women with the prestigious title of *ekwe*. In this decentralized, relatively undifferentiated society, symbolic distinctions such as hairstyles, neck beads, strings of coral beads, arm and leg adornments made of elephant tusk (figure 2.10), special string anklets, and special fans were all worn or carried as prestigious markers that distinguished titled women from the rest. Titled women, or *ekwe,* associated their economic success with the Goddess Idemili and became not only representatives and models of the Goddess herself, but also of the ideal image of Nnobi womanhood. *Ekwe* were the most respected and honored women in their lineages and villages. They became the leaders of Nnobi women's organizations and of women in the broader community, and presided over the powerful village Women's Councils that ruled on women's affairs and managed the marketplaces. Local women supported these matriarchs, recognizing their leadership qualities, enthroning them, and economically sustaining the *ekwe* as their leaders.[25] The Goddess Idemili of Nnobi—and her human representatives in the form of titled women—was therefore a subversive phenomenon in gender and power relations that were at the center of Igbo sociocultural constructions of patriarchal power. Consequently, in traditional Nnobi society, titled matriarchs were just as actively and consciously involved in ensuring cultural continuity and social renewal as were Nnobi titled men, as opposed to the male-focused patriarchal political system imposed by colonialism and the inherited postcolonial state where women are struggling for representation and participation.

Igbo women's body art played a major role not only in the lives of the titled *ekwe* and high-ranking women, such as Nwajiuba, but also in women's rituals in general, especially in girls' puberty rites, women's initiation rituals, and marriage rituals, where *ekwe* held the highest authority as wise and knowledgeable women to teach and bless the conclusion of important rituals. Through the painted *uli* images and motifs, Igbo women invented a system of representation and communication. Women in societies along the Delta of the Niger River practice similar art traditions to Igbo *uli* painting. For example, the Ijaw-speaking peoples of Okrika in Rivers State call this women's body art *burumo,* which like *uli* is described as an intimate woman-to-woman art. In their films, Judith Gleason and Elisa Mereghetti Tesser (*Becoming a Woman in Okrika,* 1990) and Ngozi Onwurah (*Monday's Girls,* 1993) describe and illustrate the details of the preparation and application of this body art, which is used in *iria* (similar to Igbo *nkpu*), the girls' and young women's coming-of-age ritual practiced in the Rivers and Cross River States of Nigeria. These films, and most academic texts on *iria,*

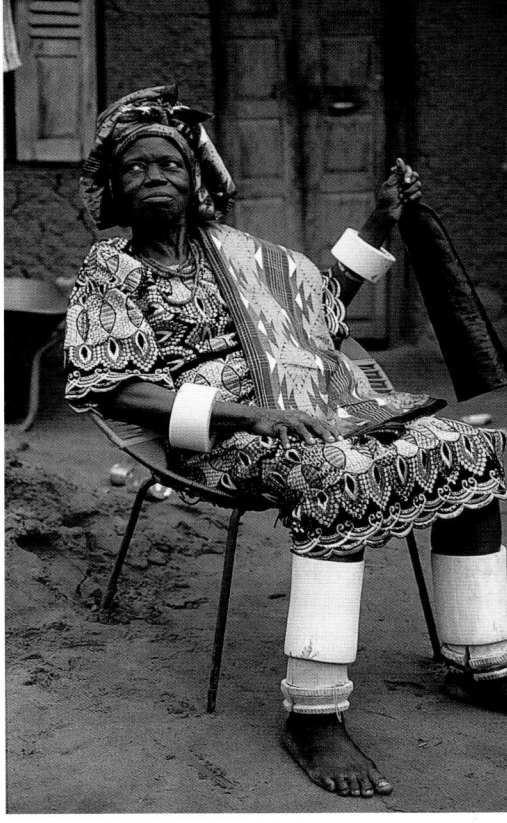

FIGURE 2.10 Titled woman (*ekwe*) wearing ivory bracelets and leglets, Ugbene, Nigeria, 1983. Photograph by and courtesy of Herbert Cole.

describe how girl celebrants or initiates are separated from the general community and placed in "fatting" or "fattening" rooms. The accounts describing this ritual suggest to me, however, that "beauty rooms" or "beauty and healthcare rooms" is a more appropriate description for our understanding of the *iria* process. In *iria* ritual, the celebrant girls and young women are beautified, pampered, and over-fed by their mothers and female relatives to prepare and lead them into adult womanhood. At the end of this period of intensified health and beauty treatment, the young women come out looking glossy and healthy, of marriageable and childbearing age.

There is a question, however, about how images and symbolism of *iria* should be interpreted. Some of the normative reasons for *iria* emphasize objectives such as chastity and marriage, which led some researchers like Judith Gleason to accept a patriarchal interpretation; she writes, "To perform *Iria* is, in effect, to assent to a traditional, patriarchal definition of womanhood. It is a bodily definition."[26] Rejecting Gleason's notion that it serves traditional patriarchy, I have reassessed *iria* from a matriarchal gender perspective, as an institution driven by and serving the female-based power structure. It is important to distinguish and compare between what we receive through patriarchal versus matriarchal thought, theory, and scholarship. One needs to build up a matriarchal scholarship, however, for this comparison even to be possible.

In Igbo society, it is not only patriarchy that dictates the writing, reading, and constructing of women's bodies, womanhood, and spirituality. Women themselves are also involved in processes of social and cultural construction, and particularly in the reconstruction of notions and images of African womanhood. For example, when Gleason writes of the Dawn Songs that the girls sing early in the mornings of the *iria* ritual and the *burumo* body painting as traditions that were passed through generations of women, she recognizes the presence and voicing of a women's subjective reality. Indeed, Gleason sees the deep symbolism in and connection between the *burumo* designs and phases of the ritual process that link them to water ecosystems, enchanting water spirits, pulverization of plant extract, matting processes of body painting, paint lines from women's paint sticks, women's songs full of innuendo, and most importantly, the connection between "Grandmother's ground camwood," a "good body rub," and the spreading of "good knowledge."[27]

In traditional Igbo, Ijaw, and Cross River cultures, among others, rituals of songs, stories, and body art were vital to the construction of women's cultures, organizations, and institutional leadership structures. They were also important for talking about and teaching about sexual pleasure or restriction.[28] These were matriarchal alternatives that were based on the women's knowledge and wisdom passed down through generations, which contributed both to the solidarity of women within a community and to the greater well-being of that community. In other words, an organized women's system was quite distinct from traditional and postcolonial patriarchal systems. Women as an organized entity had—and still have—a voice in the claims and counterclaims of ideas and values shaping the social structure of their society through their input in rituals, songs about gender roles, folktales, and other creative and artistic expressions, of which body art is just one.

In traditional Igbo culture, women seemed quite comfortable with their bodies. Postcolonial discomfort and bodily shyness—and even shame—are obviously a carryover from Africa's encounter with the religions of the European colonizers. Gleason confirms the modern rejection of native bodies, as in the case of the Catholic priests condemning the so-called "traditional" Nwajiuba in Nnobi. According to Gleason in Okrika,

> To perform *Iria* properly one has to go back in time and dress the way girls dressed before the arrival of the missionaries. (For a while the Anglican Church offered an alternative *Iria* in blouses. The girls carried parasols. This practice did not become popular and was eventually discontinued.)[29]

In Ngozi Onwurah's film about *iria* among the Wakirike peoples, the matriarch Monday Moses gives her view on art versus clothes on her girls participating in *iria* by saying, "Indigo dyes are more beautiful than the clothes she might wear."[30] Then someone else responds to the girls, "Iriabos, how beautiful you are in such a scruffy crowd!"[31] This seems to me a statement that recalls Nwajiuba's decision to be photographed in her traditional Nnobi fashion. It also subverts the stance of the Catholic priests in Nnobi and their vilification of Nnobi traditionalists.

In *iria* ritual, all that is Wakirike nation (in the case of Onwurah's film) or Okrika (in Gleason's) is represented through the girls for one day in the gathering of the entire nation in the village square, re-enacting and recreating ritual, music, art, history, religion, and politics, all the while decolonizing their African culture, even if in a limited way. The national community interest is achieved and, at the same time, there is a joyful sense of heroism, triumph, and accomplishment in these young women. Women's art in this experience is visual, expressive, and participatory. It creates a body image that empowers women in their Africanness, as opposed to contemporary situations where women might not even have a voice in men's choices of women's fashion and body look. While imported religions like Christianity and Islam struggle against African women's freedom of body expression, creative thought asserts local images and symbolism into modernity through popular art and religions—if and when they are allowed their own organic development. In some instances, old images and symbols acquire new meaning, while in others, new imported images and symbols are Africanized.

AFRICANIZATION AND RE-AFRICANIZATION OF MAMMY WATER

Modern and contemporary prejudices against indigenous Africans and their cultures often lead to a misrepresentation of traditional practices as unchanging and lacking complexity and space for difference. An examination of the emergence of the "Mammy Water" figure in traditional African art and religions, however, reveals the creativity, sophistication, and complexity of traditional ideologies.

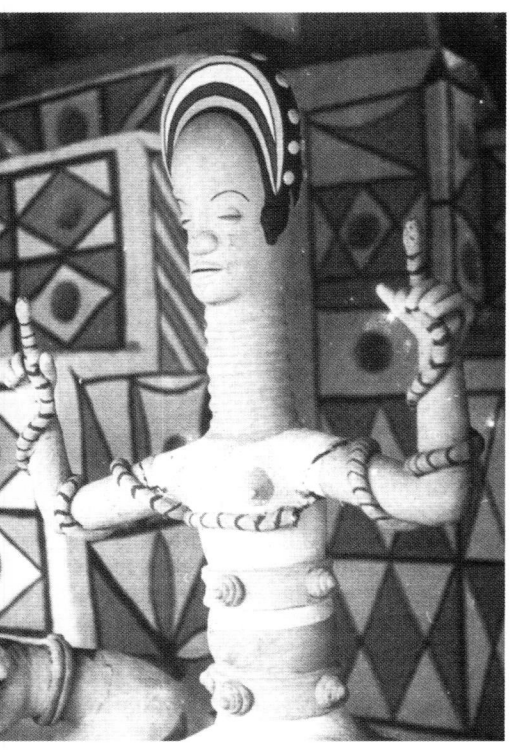

FIGURE 2.11 *Mbari* shrine for Mammywater, from *The Art of Eastern Nigeria*, G. I. Jones, Cambridge: Cambridge Press, 1984, no. 19. Photograph courtesy of Cambridge Press.

More importantly, it exposes continuity in the acceptance of the female body as a fluid medium for expressing ideologies of African womanhood in whatever ways this may change over time.

As she is conceived throughout Africa, Mammy Water is a water spirit who speaks to environmental awareness, economic gain, and sexual liberation.[32] Like the nature motifs of painted *uli* and *burumo* designs that synchronize themselves with the environment, the iconography of Mammy Water also reflects the natural ecosystem of water. In West and Central Africa, belief in this water spirit is widespread in communities along rivers, creeks, lagoons, oceans, and lakes, but it also persists in African cities. Mammy Water is usually depicted as a fish-tailed woman, resembling the European mythological siren or mermaid, with lots of hair, often looking into a mirror, and holding snakes wrapped around her shoulders and arms (figure 2.11). Like Idemili, Mammy Water rewards Igbo women with economic success, but unlike Idemili, who was a central goddess in Nnobi, Mammy Water is worshipped as a peripheral goddess. Consequently, Mammy Water is in my view a subversive goddess that relates more to the individual rather than the communal perspective.

In contemporary scholarship, Mammy Water is celebrated as an icon, a concept, and an object and is hence a particularly popular subject of art, aesthetic, and art historical discourses. Scholars have questioned whether Mammy Water is indigenous to Africa or a result of colonial contact with European or Asian cultures. Many writers have traced the prototype of the Mammy Water iconography to figureheads of women on the prows of colonial ships as well as to a popular postcard image commonly found in African markets and stores, where I was also able to purchase one.[33]

In African practices, she is an object of worship, particularly in possession religions based on water spirits found in both rural villages and urban cities. In many grassroots practices, particularly in urban shrines, Mammy Water followers also employ motifs and ideas from Hindu, African, European, Christian, American, occult, and astrological imagery for their representations of this goddess.[34] Rosalind Hackett describes Mammy Water as a seductive water spirit, who derives her characteristics from the aquatic environment. Hackett attributes the widespread art of Mammy Water throughout Africa to the popularity of a postcard reproduction of a German chromolithograph of a female Indian snake charmer with "lighter skin complexion denoting watery and/or foreign origins"[35] (figure 2.12). According to Hackett, "Sometimes the priestess herself or paintings on the walls [of temples] recreate the image of the snake-charmer which derives from the nineteenth century European chromolith and which has become one of the key images of Mami wata."[36]

Many African communities have had beliefs in water spirits; therefore, the new concept of Mammy Water was incorporated into an already existing belief system. Hence, it is not unusual for African cultures to appropriate and use foreign objects in their religious practices in "the quest for additional knowledge and meaningful rites to promote wealth and well-being."[37] Whether or not

Mammy Water is about mimicry or local agency in religious innovation, the practice involves predominantly desiring or appropriating foreign and capitalist representations of power.[38]

In 1994, while researching Pentecostalism in Nigeria, I came upon a large billboard of Mammy Water on the junction between Igbariam Street and Agbani Road in Achala Layout Enugu (figure 2.13). Although retaining some resemblance to the postcard image of the snake charmer, the Agbani Road billboard version of Mammy Water was more Africanized and localized, which is apparent if we compare their waists and curves. The image of Mammy Water on Agbani Road depicts a woman who exhibits vanity and poise, two common characteristic of this water goddess, along with her snakes and makeup.[39] Although grounded in local figurative conventions of shape and curvature, the sign reveals its own sense and knowledge of modernity, invention, and borrowing. As figure 2.13 illustrates, Dr. Ezenwoke, a Knight Spirit Member of India High Temple, announces his transcultural and transnational practice in this street sign, also asserting to be deeply invested in occult sciences. Using the icon of Mammy Water to advertise his business, he claims, "Trial will convince you." At these crossroads, Mammy Water stands her ground also in the intense competition of signboards and posters that clutter the side roads of this African city.[40] It is Mammy Water who speaks for women in this tough market called capitalism! Contextualized as she usually is in the center of capitalist materialism, this water goddess is enchanting and seductive, but also a temptress who demands a high price. As art historian Henry Drewal writes of Mammy Water,

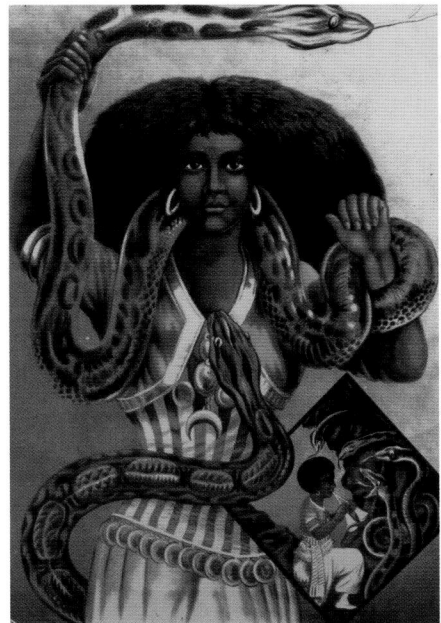

FIGURE 2.12 Color postcard of Mammy Water. Photograph courtesy of Ifi Amadiume.

> She personifies unattainable, exquisite beauty, vanity, jealousy, sexuality, romantic not maternal love, limitless good fortune—not health, long life or progeny, but riches, material and monetary. She is thus very much part of international trading systems between Africa and Europe commencing in the late fifteenth century and now including other regions of the world as well.[41]

There are many Mammy Waters, both in image and thought in Africa and the African Diaspora. Just as with other images of black womanhood, we cannot so easily categorize Mammy Water within a single perspective. Not all believers in Mammy Water see her as lacking in maternal love. In Kathleen O'Brien Wicker and Kofi Asare Opoku's film *Priesthood and Ritual in Ghana: Abidjan Mami Water Shrine* (1994), Mammy Water is portrayed in the Abidjan Mami Water village shrine on the banks of the Volta River in the Eastern Region of Ghana. In this study, Mammy Water is represented as more culturally local and African—like her village followers. In the Abidjan shrine she is kneeling and looks like a young African woman holding a snake (figure 2.14); she is black and resembles the Agbani Road Mammy Water in curvature and sitting position. She takes her place among other village deities and ancestors. It is not surprising that in this case, her followers consider Mammy Water to be their mother. Although Mammy Water does not have a child herself, her followers say that they are her children and that their prayers to her are always for peace, good health, and prosperity.

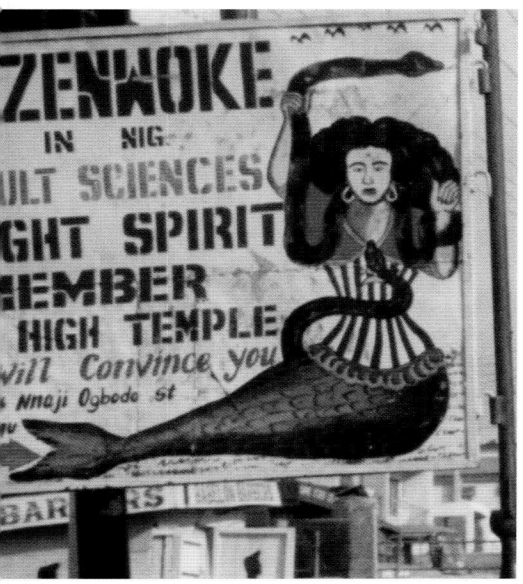

FIGURE 2.13 A roadside sign of Mammy Water, junction of Igbariam Street and Agbani Road in Achala Layout Enugu, Nigeria, 1994. Photograph by and courtesy of Ifi Amadiume.

Mammy Water is similarly incorporated into Moree shrines in Ghana, as portrayed in *Priesthood and Ritual in Ghana: Moree Maame Water* (1996), another film by Kathleen O'Brien Wicker and Kofi Asare Opoku.[42] This Mammy Water is situated with other divinities who all have their own specific iconographic symbols. In these contexts, Mammy Water is not presented as a purely individualistic spirit but takes her place alongside the seventy-seven other Moree deities. She is subjected to local traditional kinship beliefs and representations. It is said that her father is Osanfo Mensa and her mother is Osanfo, Mother of the Sea, so that Mammy Water still has the youthfulness of her categorization as a daughter (for example, Mammy Water images do not usually have drooping or fallen breasts) who is viewed as being like a mother to her followers. Thus, Mammy Water retains her free spirit of individual self-embodiment, which radically contrasts with divine Mother Goddesses and mother and child fertility images that represent the solidarity of women or the community as a whole in traditional African religions and their art iconography.[43]

In her multiplicity in Africa and elsewhere, Mammy Water provides a model for some normative continuity, and also non-conformist innovative characters and characteristics.[44] She enables a negotiation between perceived contradictions of tradition and modernity with her many images, which provide black women's art an African matriarchal continuity and new possibilities for radical and creative departures. As an afflicting spirit, Mammy Water's call either to her priesthood or as a follower is most commonly experienced through spirit possession. Women called into her service become priestesses and healers,[45] who often address the paradoxes of tradition and modernity that impact women's lives, afflictions, and misfortunes, as well as their successes and personal achievements. As such, Mammy Water helps women overcome social stigmatization through economic and professional success. She gives them the ability to *choose* individual lives outside of marriage, to pursue self-representation and self-determination. Through Mammy Water, there is a counter-cultural creativity for criticism and the opening of new possibilities. We have this continuing narrative in the Water Goddess Mammy Water, whose controversial sea waves disturb the waters of norms and expectations of "traditional" and "modern" womanhood. As a model standing in for the educated Nigerian "lady"—that is, an elite model in fashion, skin color, and lifestyle—Mammy Water raises questions of class. As a hybrid icon, however, she also raises questions about race, especially with the emergence of a biracial and multiracial class in Africa and its Diaspora. Equally so, she complicates notions of motherhood, as some of her devotees see her as the childless mother, yet still powerful—in direct contradiction to traditional notions of ideal womanhood.

CONCLUSION

Viewed together, these cases of female objectification and struggle between African traditions and Christo-centric modernity over women's body image reveal

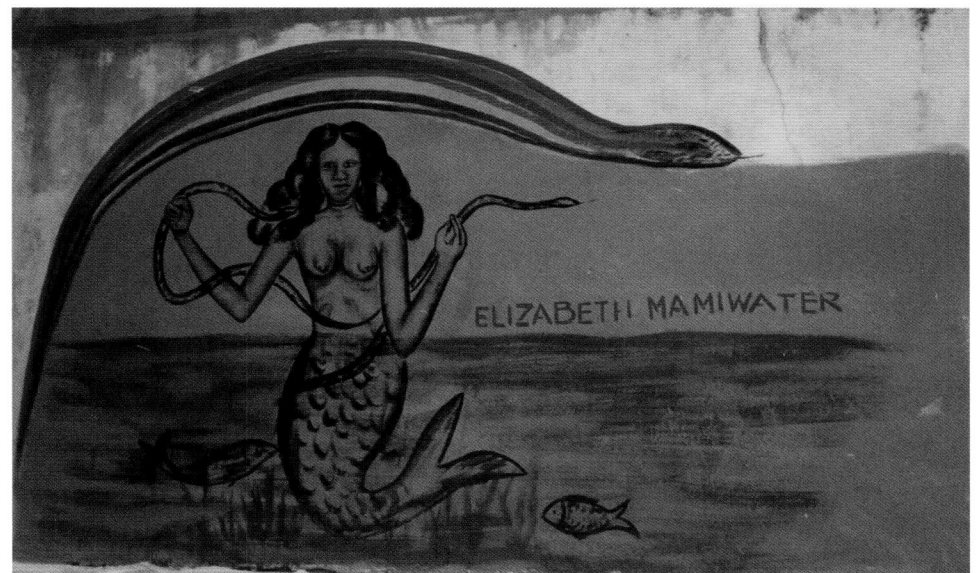

FIGURE 2.14 Elizabeth Mamiwater, wall painting at Abidjan Mamiwater Shrine, Eastern Region, Ghana, by A. A. Ofori. In Kofi Asare Opoku and Kathleen O'Brien Wicker, "Abidjan Mamiwater and Aba Yaba: Two Profiles of Mami/Maame Water Priesthood in Ghana," in *Sacred Waters: Arts of Mami Wata and Other Water Divinities in Africa and the African Atlantic World,* ed. Henry John Drewal (Bloomington: Indiana University Press, forthcoming 2008). Photograph by Allan W. Wicker and courtesy of Kathleen O'Brien Wicker.

that African matriarchy and cultures are the losers when change is forced from without against traditional local gender power systems. But when change is organic from within, Africans can adapt new images, such as Mammy Water, and new ideas in ways that ensure forms of positive cultural continuity that retains familiar notions of women's power.

Irrespective of misrepresentations and the condemning voices of colonizing religions and more recent neo-Christian crusaders, traditional African women's organizations, rituals, and art enable women and girls to enter the supportive system of a women's society in a dual-gender system. There is an empowering visual aesthetic and creative energy for women and society in individual experience. Yet there is also collective empowerment through creativity that builds upon social and cultural institutions of women's solidarity through the body, art, and performance of ritual. Women's cultures and creativity in turn contribute to the balance and well-being of the community as a whole. I have used an interdisciplinary approach in presenting these illustrations to capture the variety of icons, narratives, and aesthetics that speak to the empowerment of African women both from the past and in the present. Contrary to what some might argue, African traditions and modernity are *not* organically dichotomous. There is therefore no need for this new imperialism of body violations and the loss of traditional African women's body art within the postcolonial setting. As the examples demonstrate, the enormous legacy of continuity, re-Africanization, and creative departure in images, icons, and ideologies of womanhood rely upon both comfort with and freedom of expression through the African female body. ❧

1 See Ruth B. Phillips, *Representing Women: Sande Masquerades of the Mende of Sierra Leone* (Los Angeles: UCLA Fowler Museum of Cultural History, 1995), for discussion of meanings and symbolism of *sowei* masks.

2 Allen Wardwell, *African Sculpture* (Philadelphia: University of Pennsylvania Press, 1986), 42–43.

3 Throughout Africa, masquerading is predominantly a male art form.

4 See also Susan Mullin Vogel, "Baule Scarification: The Mark of Civilization," in *Marks of Civilization: Artistic Transformations of the Human Body*, ed. Arnold Rubin (Los Angeles: Museum of Cultural History, University of California—Los Angeles, 1988), 97–106, for a discussion of Baule scarification on the human body and on figures.

5 Doran H. Ross and Timothy F. Garrard, *Akan Transformations* (Los Angeles: Regents of the University of California, 1983), 87.

6 Larger seated female figures with similar scarification markings and symbols of fertility are used by the Sandogo Women's Society, a powerful women's institution among the Senufo peoples of Côte d'Ivoire. See Anita Glaze, "Woman Power and Art in a Senufo Village," *African Arts* 8, no. 3 (Spring 1975): 24–29, 64–68, 90–91, for a detailed discussion of women's power in Senufo culture.

7 See Henry John Drewal and Margaret Thompson Drewal, *Gelede: Art and Female Power Among the Yoruba* (Bloomington: Indiana University Press, 1983), for a detailed discussion of *gelede* as a celebration of female power.

8 William Fagg, *Yoruba Sculpture of West Africa* (New York: Alfred A. Knopf, 1982), 99.

9 See Elsy Leusinger, *The Art of Black Africa* (Graphic Society Ltd: New York, 1972), plate 1.

10 Roy Sieber and Roslyn Adele Walker, *African Art in the Cycle of Life* (Washington, D.C.: Smithsonian Institution Press, 1988), 40.

11 In a personal communication with Barbara Thompson, Tamara Northern noted that the Munich sculpture exhibits an extraordinary level of artistic license in its deviation away from canonical representations, which usually depict a self-possessed queen mother, often carrying or nursing a child.

12 Benjamin C. Ray, *African Religions: Symbol, Ritual, and Community*, 2nd ed. (Upper Saddle River: Prentice Hall, 2000), 141.

13 Ifi Amadiume, *Reinventing Africa: Matriarchy, Religion and Culture* (London: Zed Books, 1997), chapter 4.

14 Nnobi is my father's village; hence I have both an academic and kinship relationship with the Nnobi community. Between 1980 and 1982, I conducted fieldwork in Nnobi as part of my training for a Ph.D. qualification in social anthropology from the University of London. "The mouth that spoke a falsehood will later speak the truth: going home to the field in Eastern Nigeria," in *Gendered Fields: Women, Men & Ethnography*, ed. Diana Bell, Patricia Caplan, Wazir Jahan, and Abdul Karim (London: Routledge, 1993), 182–198.

15 Amadiume, *Male Daughters, Female Husbands: Gender and Sex in an African Society* (London: Zed Books, 1987), 32–33.

16 Willis's caption to this drawing reads, "Mural showing a woman in traditional dress and decorated with *uli* motifs in the compound of Nwajiuba Ojukwa[u] Nnobi 1987" (1988–1989: 16, no. 10).

17 Amadiume, *Male Daughters, Female Husbands*, 52.

18 Africanized Christianity originated as a reaction against and challenge to the rigid orthodox form of European Christianity that gained ground in Africa due to its association with colonialism and colonial powers, which were based on European cultural values and notions of white superiority. African converts were forced to denounce and reject their traditional customary practices, especially their religions that incorporated many gods and goddesses who resemble themselves, and to accept a patriarchal monotheistic faith originating elsewhere. Representation and images are therefore a major difference between orthodox Christianity and Africanized Christianity both on the African continent and in the African Diaspora with their syncretic religious mixing of African deities and Catholic saints.

19 According to one of the priests, when Nwajiuba was asked why she picked the name "Mary," she retorted, "Is Mary not the mother of God?" Nnobi matriarchy and Christianity, however, would have a very different understanding of Mary's status as the mother of God. In his description of Fon (Republic of Benin) metal sculptures called *asen*, Benjamin Ray demonstrates the ease with which African imagery and philosophy—and by extension declarative statements such as Nwajiuba's—can be misunderstood: "The Fon say that the cross that often appears on the *asen* is not a sign of the Christian god but of Mawau, the Fon female creator goddess to whom everyone owes his or her life" (*African Religions*, 135). This quote might be used to better understand the powerful beliefs about goddesses in African traditional religions, so that when for example Nwajiuba refers to Mary as the mother of God, if she is thinking in her knowledge of the Igbo Goddess Idemili or in a knowledge of the Fon Goddess Mawau, Mary would take on a characteristic and representation that is more Africanized, and hence also very different from Mary as she is understood in Euro-Christian perspectives.

20 Brian Larkin and Birgit Meyer, "Pentecostalism, Islam & Culture: New Religious Movements in West Africa," in *Themes in West Africa's History*, ed. Emmanuel Kwaku Akyeampong (Athens: Ohio University; Oxford: James Currey; and Accra: Woeli Pub. Services, 2006), 286–312.

21 Maya Angelou, *And Still I Rise* (1978). Reprinted by permission of Random House, Inc. (http://www.poets.org).

22 Liz Willis, "*Uli* Painting and the Igbo World View," *African Arts* 22 (1988–89): 63.

23 Fagg, *Yoruba Sculpture of West Africa*, 135.

24 Amadiume, *Male Daughters, Female Husbands*, 110, note 19.

25 As I have argued elsewhere, this ability to construct, affect, and lead a women's system empowered them structurally against dualistic and monologic patriarchy (that is, seeing power only through a patriarchal perspective) and worked in conjunction and co-operation with the existing traditional patriarchal system. "Bodies, Choices, Globalizing NeoColonial Enchantments: African Matriarchs and Mammy Water," *Meridians: Feminism, Race, Transnationalism* 2, no. 2 (2002): 41–66.

26 Judith Gleason and Chief Allison Ibubuya, "My Year Reached, We Heard Ourselves Singing: Dawn Songs of Girls Becoming Women in Ogbogbo, Okrika, Rivers State," Nigeria, January 1990, *Research in African Literatures* 22, no. 3 (Fall 1991): 138.

27 Ibid., 141.

28 Amadiume, "Sexuality, African Religio-Cultural Traditions and Modernity: Expanding the Lens," Africa Regional Sexuality Resource Center, 2006 (http://www.arsrc.org/index.htm).

29 Gleason and Ibubuya, "My Year Reached," 138.

30 Ngozi Onwurah, *Monday's Girls* (film) (San Francisco: California Newsreel, 1993).

31 Ibid.

32 Given the wide distribution of Mammy Water worship in Africa and the Diaspora, her name is spelled differently depending on locality.

33 See also Sabine Jell-Bahlsen, "Eze Mmiri di Egwu, The Water Monarch Is Awesome: Reconsidering the Mammy Water Myths," in *Queens, Queen Mothers, Priestesses and Power: Case Studies in African Gender*, ed. Flora S. Kaplan (New York: New York Academy of Sciences, 1997), 105; and John Henry Drewal, "Mami Wata Shrines: Exotica and the Construction of Self," in *African Material Culture*, ed. Mary Jo Arnoldi, Christraud M. Geary, and Kris L. Hardin (Bloomington and Indianapolis: Indiana University Press, 1996), 312, for additional images.

34 Rosalind Hackett, *Art and Religion in Africa* (Leicester: Leicester University Press, 1996), 195.

35 Hackett, *Art and Religion in Africa*, 63.

36 Ibid., 147. Jill Salmons also reproduces and examines the copying of the imported postcard print, looking at the variations of the Mammy Water carving styles in areas of the Cross River state, now Akwa Ibom State ("Mammy Wata," *African Arts* 10, no. 3 [April 1977]: 11). Salmons has noted also that Mammy Water carvings in the Cross River state are used in entertainment masquerades and in possession rituals in which the spirit is believed to be fair-skinned and long-haired who gives riches to her followers but not children ("Mammy Wata," *African Arts* 10, no. 3 [April 1977]: 8).

37 Hackett, *Art and Religion in Africa*, 149.

38 Drewal, "Mami Wata Shrines," and Charles Gore and Joseph Nevadomsky, "Practice and Agency in Mammy Wata Worship in Southern Nigeria," *African Arts* 30, no. 2 (Spring 1997): 60–69, 95. In this essay, I am focusing more on images, icons, representation, and current practice. Therefore, I will not address the question of origin of Mammy Water beliefs and practices, the issue of foreign images, ideas and their local significance, and experiences of possession, which I have examined elsewhere in relation to women's power; women's collective cultures and movements; matriarchy and leadership; and the perspective of power through individual subjectivity (see Amadiume, "Bodies, Choices, Globalizing Neo-Colonial Enchantments: African Matriarchs and Mammy Water").

39 Traditionally snakes symbolized fertility and abundance, but if the snake is a python, it can represent the spirit messenger or totemic messenger of the Goddess Idemili, as the snake symbolizes water. The Western style of makeup is associated with Western modernity as opposed to *uli* representing tradition.

40 The advertisements, which include Eagle Stout, the Church of God Mission Int. Inc., Miracle Revival Center, Tristar Copy Center, a records and videos store, a ladies shoe store, Deeper Life Bible Church, the Pentecostal Assemblies of God Church, and St Anthony's Hospital Center, show this modern crossroads as a marketplace where all parties, religions, and commerce sell their wares in a hot competitive atmosphere.

41 Drewal, "Mami Wata Shrines," 311.

42 The film includes an interview with Aba Yaba, who discusses her work as a *Maame Water* priestess, and an interview with Kwesi Kaya, a Moree fisherman who is a devotee of *Maame Water*. Aba Yaba has been a Mammy Water priestess for fifty years after training for three years. She is an herbalist, a spirit medium for the community, and a spiritual advisor to chiefs. She also participates in rituals and ceremonies for other divinities. In this film, we see Aba Yaba going into possession, during which she kisses the pictures of Mammy Water and pays homage to her shrine at the bridge of the Emfa Lagoon in Moree in the Central Region of Ghana.

43 Amadiume "Bodies, Choices, Globalizing."

44 Like the syncretic constructions of Mammy Water as a religious icon in many African cultures, in the contemporary pluralistic societies of the African Diaspora, especially in South America and the Caribbean, Mammy Water cuts across class, race, and ethnicity, also borrowing elements from African, Catholic, and Indian religions. In the Haitian religion of Vodou, for example, African continuity in local perceptions of Mammy Water as the powerful mother figure is found in the spirit Ezili (or Erzulie). As Karen McCarthy Brown describes, Haiti is a patrifocal culture in which Vodou empowers women ("Mama Lola and the Ezilis: Themes of Mothering and Loving in Haitian Vodou," in *Unspoken Worlds: Women's Religious Lives*, eds., Nancy Falk and Rita Gross, 2nd ed. [Belmont: Wadsworth, 1989], 235–245). This empowerment of women derives from the particular aspect of Vodou practice linking women and female spirits like Ezili with her Mammy Water and other African influences.

45 Jell-Bahlsen, "Eze Mmiri di Egwu, The Water Monarch is Awesome," and Flora Nwapa, "Priestesses and Power Among the Riverine Igbo" in *Queens, Queen Mothers, Priestesses and Power: Case Studies in African Gender*, ed. Flora S. Kaplan (New York: New York Academy of Sciences, 1997), 415–424.

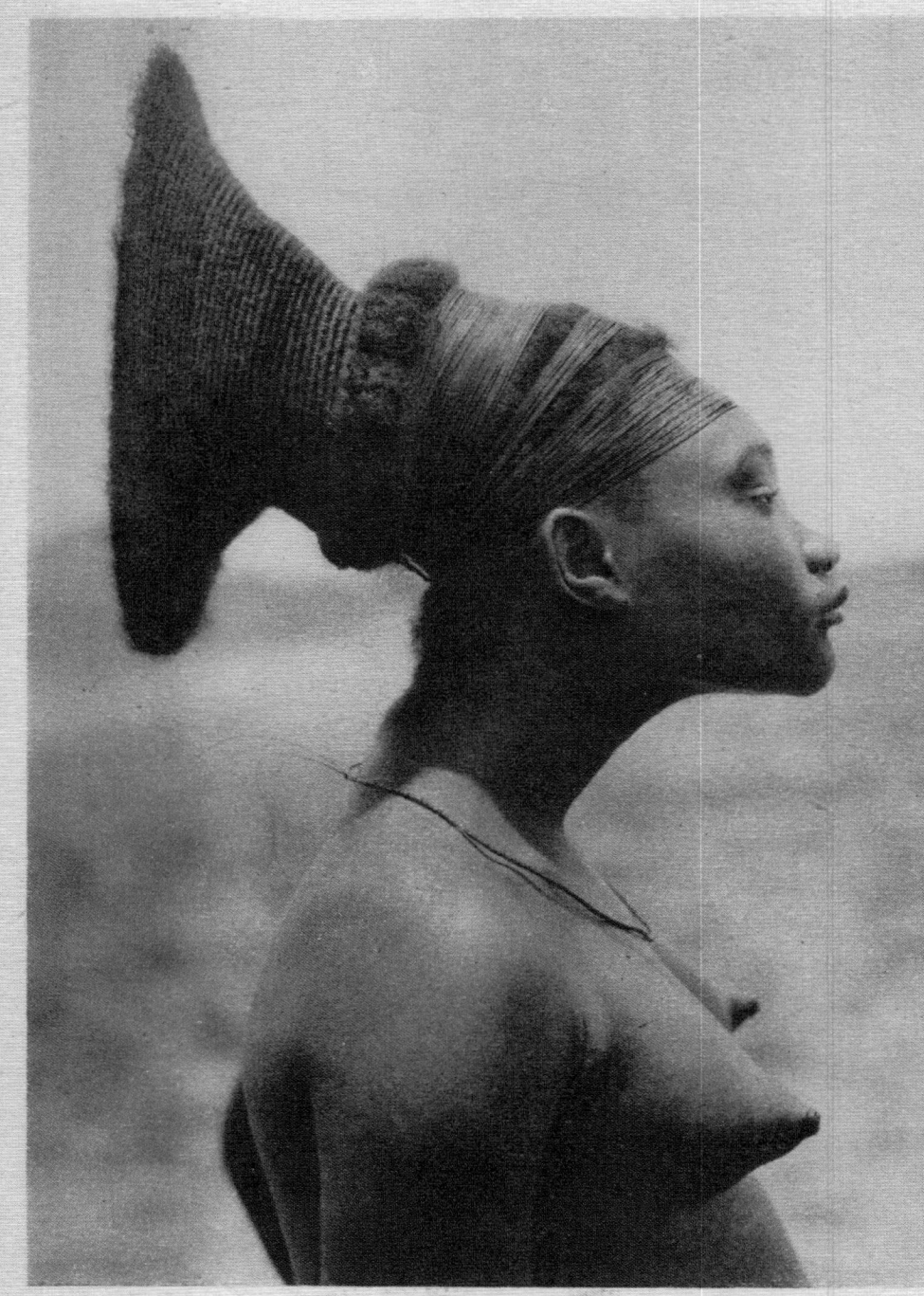

LA CROISIÈRE NOIRE
Femme d'un chef Mangbetu (Congo belge)

3 *Les Parisiens d'Afrique:* Mangbetu Women as Works of Art

Seated in a hierarchical formation on small ebony stools, the Mangbetu women were arranged in a line like figures in an Egyptian fresco. They suddenly evoke in our minds a precise picture linking across the centuries the present to the civilization of the Pharaohs.

—GEORGES-MARIE HAARDT and LOUIS AUDOUIN-DUBREUIL[1]

This description of the scene awaiting the team of European researchers and explorers who participated in the Citroën Central African expedition in 1924 could easily have served as a caption for the famous drawing made by Georg Schweinfurth (1836–1925) half a century earlier. Schweinfurth's depiction of King Munza (Mbunza) dancing before his wives (figure 3.1), first published in German in 1871, is the starting point for one of the most powerful and enduring images of African womanhood. In the original drawing and in hundreds of representations, the Mangbetu woman, with her deliberately elongated head, majestic halo-like coiffure, and semi-nude painted body, has come to represent one of the most enticing, exotic, yet ambivalent images of African womanhood.

By the second decade of the twentieth century, this image was widely disseminated throughout the Western world in every possible medium—paintings, photographs, and prints on postcards, calendars, movie posters, and postage stamps. To this day, the image of the Mangbetu woman inspires designers, artists, and writers. She embodies an idealized image of African beauty, yet at the same time captures the ambivalence of the colonial attitude to African women. In description after description, the African woman is beautiful, yet "deformed"; she comes from a wild place, yet she is not part of nature; she is a work of art and a product of civilization.

But whose civilization? While the Mangbetu woman encapsulates the Western idea of the seductive but forbiddingly exotic African beauty, she was not entirely a Western invention. Besides scores of European drawings, photographs, and souvenirs representing her, there is also a large corpus of African sculpture and graphic art that depicts this idealized image of African female beauty. In a subtle collaboration between voyeuristic Westerners and innovative African artists, this iconic image of black womanhood was sculpted in wood, ivory, and

opposite Léon Poirier, French (1884–1968) & Georges Specht, French (active 1909–1931), *Wife of Mangbetu Chief (Belgian Congo)* [Nobosodrou, Wife of Mangbetu King Touba], 1925, halftone print, postcard, publisher unidentified. Courtesy of Christraud Geary.

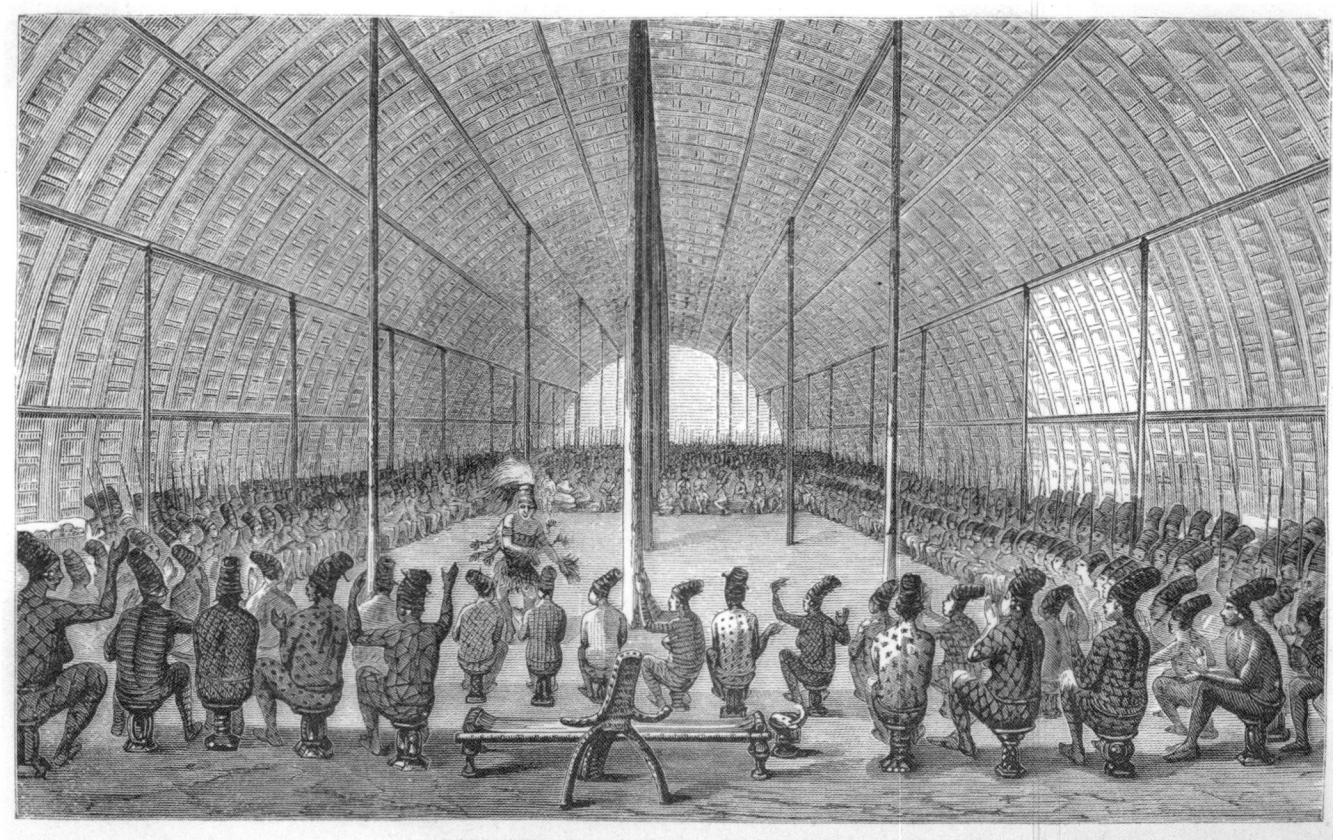

KING MUNZA DANCING BEFORE HIS WIVES.

FIGURE 3.1 King Mbunza dancing before his wives, illustration by Georg Schweinfurth, 1871. From *The Heart of Africa: Three Years' Travel and Adventures in the Unexplored Regions of Central Africa from 1868 to 1871*, 1874. Vol. 2, facing p. 74.

clay; incised and painted on gourds, walls, and musical instruments; and recreated for several decades in the dress and deportment of Mangbetu women themselves. As they posed on their wooden stools to welcome visitors, both Africans and Europeans, the wives of prominent Mangbetu chiefs re-enacted for almost a century the scene Schweinfurth had described.

EARLY DESCRIPTIONS OF MANGBETU WOMEN

The idea that the Mangbetu represented survivals of ancient Egypt comes directly from the writing of Georg Schweinfurth, the German botanist who was the first European to visit and publish a firsthand account of these people. In *The Heart of Africa: Three Years' Travel and Adventures in the Unexplored Regions of Central Africa from 1868 to 1871* Schweinfurth describes his month-long visit to the court of King Mbunza.[2] Unlike later visitors who entered the area from the West via the Congo River, Schweinfurth traveled south, following the Nile. While he did not claim to be able to trace direct connections to ancient Egypt, he and others who followed felt that they had enough visual evidence to at least make such a comparison. Such claims have to be seen in light of the fascination with Egypt that had raged in Europe from the time of Napoleon's campaign in 1798 well into the nineteenth century. This was the period of Egyptomania, of the Grand Tour, of wealthy travelers climbing pyramids, not to mention looting tombs whenever possible. The Egyptian connection, however hypothetical, led the way for the Mangbetu to claim a place in the Western imagination and eventually to become part of Modernism and Art Deco style.

Stunned by the spectacle of the dancing king surrounded by more than 180 beautifully painted and coiffed women, all described as the king's wives, Schweinfurth extolled and exaggerated the power of the Mangbetu chieftaincy. The practice of head-binding, by then associated with the Mangbetu ruling class, and the addition of elaborate halo-like coiffures, produced a silhouette that seemed to Europeans to be unquestionably Egyptian.[3] Seeing Mbunza holding court in a spectacular and enormous rectangular building[4] made of carved wooden columns and wickerwork walls reinforced Schweinfurth's impression of a highly centralized political system akin to pharaonic Egypt.[5] And finally, the fact that Mangbetu material culture—especially the beautiful pottery made by women— was characterized by symmetry suggested that here in "darkest Africa" was a higher order of civilization. But this depiction was only one side of the story. Every reference to the refinement, intelligence, beauty, and order of Mangbetu people, artwork, and villages was countered by a description of antithetical characteristics: the cruelty of chiefs, the lasciviousness of women, and the supposed propensity for cannibalism on the part of the entire population.[6]

Schweinfurth's writings became the basis of virtually all subsequent descriptions of the Mangbetu. In addition to the Egyptian connection, Schweinfurth described the deportment of Mangbetu women, their role in society, and their physical appearance. He even noted that women were wood carvers—an observation never confirmed by subsequent observers. In *Artes Africanae: Illustrations and Descriptions of Productions of the Industrial Arts of Central African Tribes* (1875), the very first European book to describe African material culture as art, Schweinfurth praised the architectural skill of the Mangbetu, noted the fine workmanship of their ceramics and iron work, and described the tools they used to carve ivory and wood. In *The Heart of Africa*, however, Schweinfurth wrote:

> Polygamy is unlimited. The daily witness of the Nubians only too plainly testified that fidelity to the obligations of marriage was little known. Not a few of the women were openly obscene. Their general demeanor surprised me very much when I considered the comparative advance of their race in the arts of civilization. Their immodesty far surpassed anything that I had observed in the very lowest of the negro tribes, and contrasted most unfavourably with the sobriety of the Bongo women, who are submissive to their husbands and yet not servile. The very scantiness of the clothing of the Monbouttoo women has no excuse.[7]

Following Schweinfurth, many explorers, collectors, and traders visited the region. These travelers described the villages they visited as royal capitals, reiterating Schweinfurth's somewhat misguided perception of a highly centralized state.[8] Subsequent observers slightly modified Schweinfurth's image, sometimes turning the idea of immodesty into the idea that Mangbetu women were outspoken and independent. Schweinfurth himself noted that Mangbetu women owned property,[9] and a number of others contrasted the deportment of the Mangbetu with the more timid nature of Zande women.

The conclusion one reaches from these writings is that if Mangbetu women had less power, fewer prerogatives, and worked harder than men, they nevertheless were exceptional in the region for their high social status. Many early Western observers commented that in neighboring villages of other cultural groups, such as the Azande, women hid when strangers arrived, but in Mangbetu villages the women approached foreigners and even talked openly with them. In 1881, for example, Willhelm Junker (1840–92) wrote,

> The Mangbetu woman, much more independent, takes part in men's meetings. The Mangbetu princes who I went to see were surrounded by their favorite wives, even in the grand assemblies of their advisors. In the evening, the women often brought their stools and sat beside my fire, laughing and joking without embarrassment.[10]

In 1897, the Belgian Commandant Christiaens wrote that women could be seen discussing politics and community events with men, both African and European:

> The European is received [by the chief] . . . surrounded by important advisors and his principle wives. These are much less shy than their Zande sisters, far from avoiding the gaze of the white man, they are very flattered when they see that they have attracted attention and they do not hesitate, far from it, from making conversation. They attend the preceedings, receive presents, and on their own behalf actively take part in discussions.[11]

The longest and most extensive visits by Westerners occurred in the early years of Belgian rule.[12] In 1909, when King Okondo welcomed the scientists Herbert Lang and James Chapin from the American Museum of Natural History in New York, the number of wives the chiefs accumulated and the role of women in the court also impressed them. Lang photographed Okondo dancing before his wives (figure 3.2) in virtually the same tableau as in Schweinfurth's drawing; Mbunza's great hall had by then disappeared, but for them Okondo painstakingly commissioned workers to recreate the great building. Staying in the region for almost six years, however, Lang soon realized that Okondo was one of many leaders vying for control of people and villages in the area, making alliances through marriage, seeking Belgian support, and jockeying for the attention of visitors.

Lang too confirmed the independence and assertiveness of Mangbetu women: "Mangbetu women make and receive [presents] absolutely independent[ly] from their husbands . . . sell and buy objects, but they always answer, when questioned to whom an object belongs, 'to Okondo.'"[13] Thus, although Mangbetu women did not usually hold formal leadership positions, most observers agreed that they greatly influenced village and kingdom affairs. The most important wives of Mangbetu kings regularly judged court cases involving women.[14]

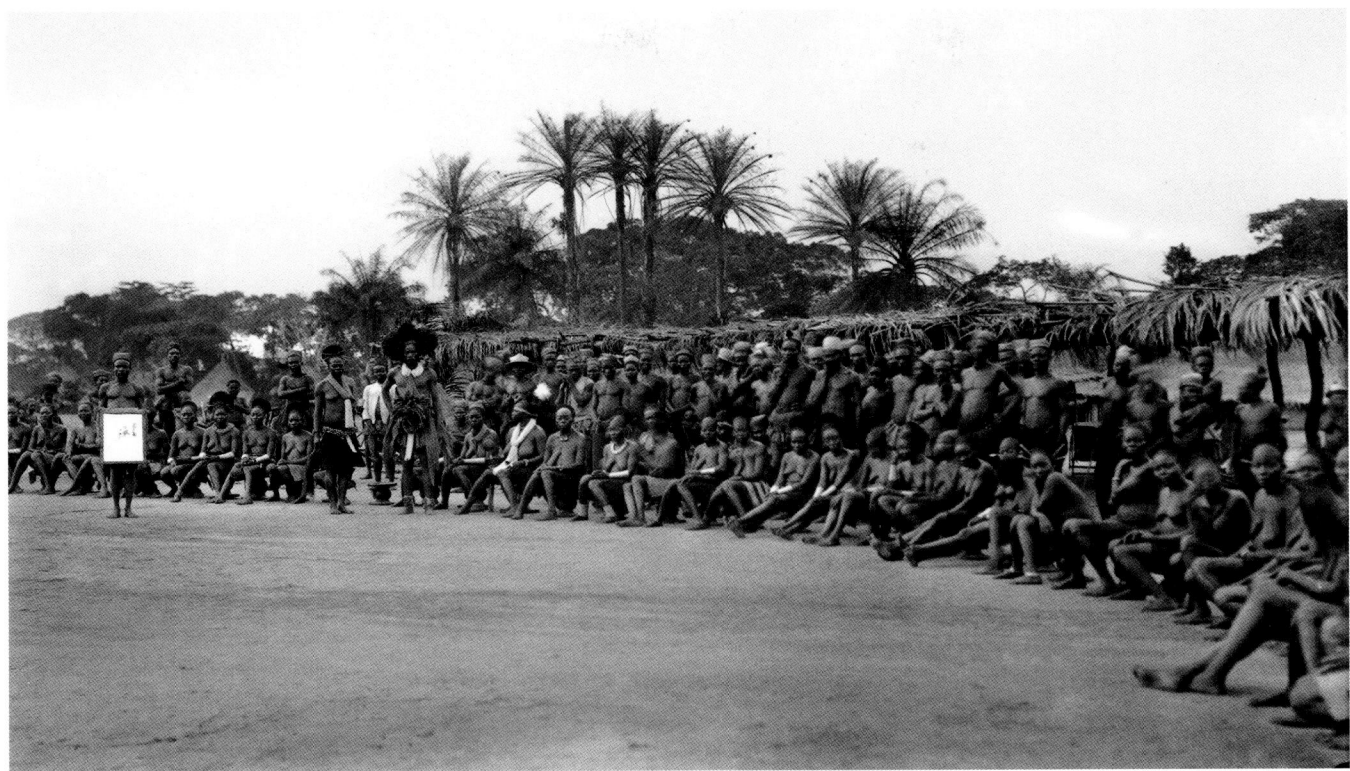

FIGURE 3.2 Okondo dancing before his wives, Okondo's village, Belgian Congo, black and white photograph by Herbert Lang, from the Lang Congo Expedition, 1909–1915. Photograph courtesy of American Museum of Natural History, negative no. 111886.

One of the governing goals of a Mangbetu lineage and its "House" was to maintain and increase village populations to perpetuate the lineage, produce the necessities of life, and defend the village. Thus women were valued because they reproduced the lineage through childbearing, because they produced material wealth, and because they linked the lineage to people beyond the village. The acquisition of women was at the foundation of house survival and prosperity. From the point of view of most men, having as many wives as possible was the best way to be assured of having children who would become producers, defenders, caregivers, and heirs. From the Mangbetu woman's perspective, having many children was desirable, but the benefits of many co-wives were less obvious, as bickering was common in polygynous families (usually co-wives only tolerated their positions). Women without children were at a disadvantage, but not despised. While childbearing conferred status, the Mangbetu also recognized that women—especially a first wife (*nedjombine*), who always remained in charge of a household—could make other contributions. In cases where there were many wives, the first wife became an administrator, allocating work and resolving disputes among her co-wives.

There are documented instances when women played crucial roles in Mangbetu history.[15] Schweinfurth told of Nalengbe, a heroic sister of the great king Mbunza, who "had once arrayed herself in a man's dress and entered into personal conflict with the Nubians."[16] Even better known is Nalengbe's sister, Nenzima (figure 3.3), who is reputed to have had no children and who from about 1875 to 1926 was chief adviser to four successive kings. In 1896, it was reported

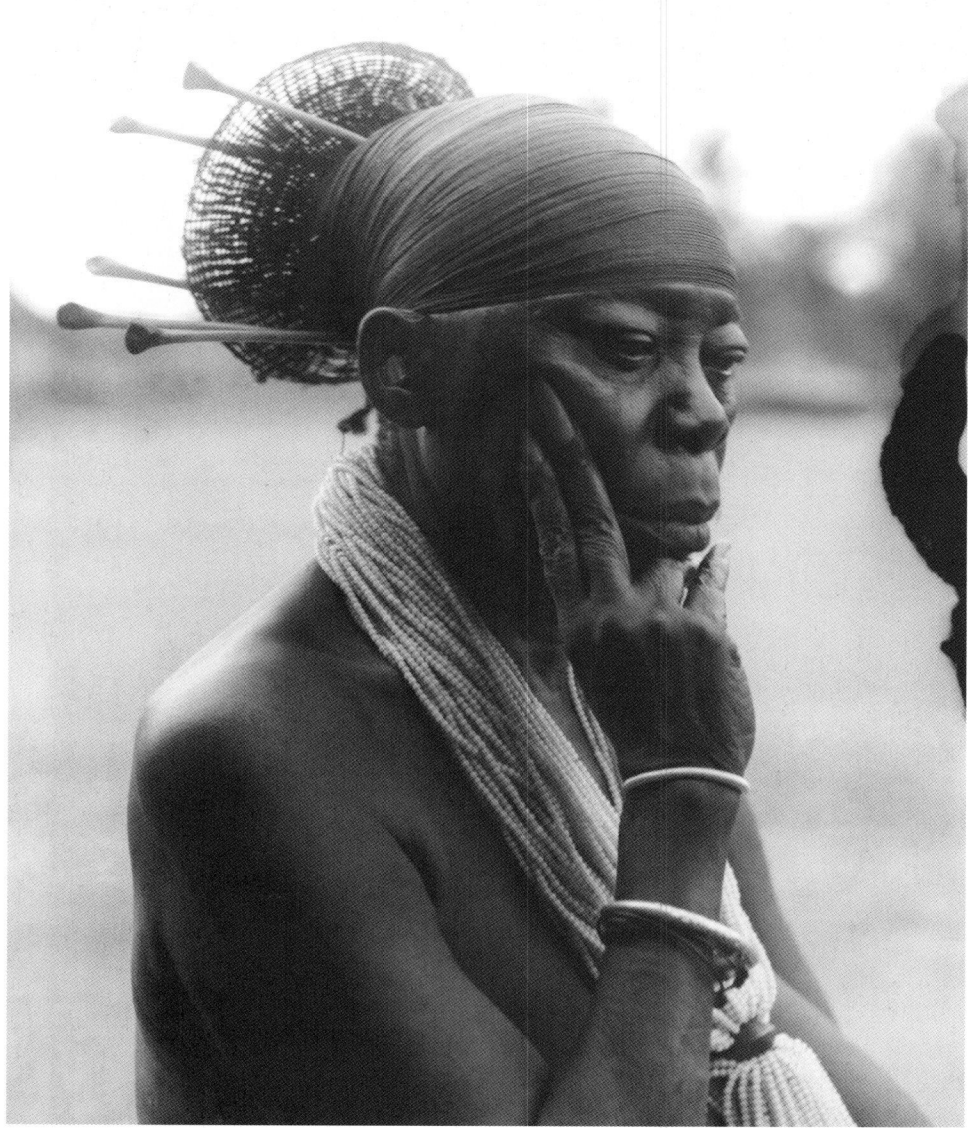

that Nenzima "holds the fate of many individuals in her hands and inspires a certain fear, but her wisdom is universally recognized."[17] Armand Hutereau, the Belgian ethnographer who made a vast collection for the Belgian government (now in the Musée de l'Afrique Centrale in Tervuren), wrote that Nenzima was so powerful that "she was considered by everyone as a true Mangbetu chief."[18]

The physical appearance of Mangbetu men and women was another major topic in early writings. Head elongation, hairstyles, and body decoration were mentioned in virtually every text written before 1909. Authors noted the elaborate hairstyles of men and women, described head binding and grooming, and discussed how women spent hours painting designs on their bodies (figure 3.4) with

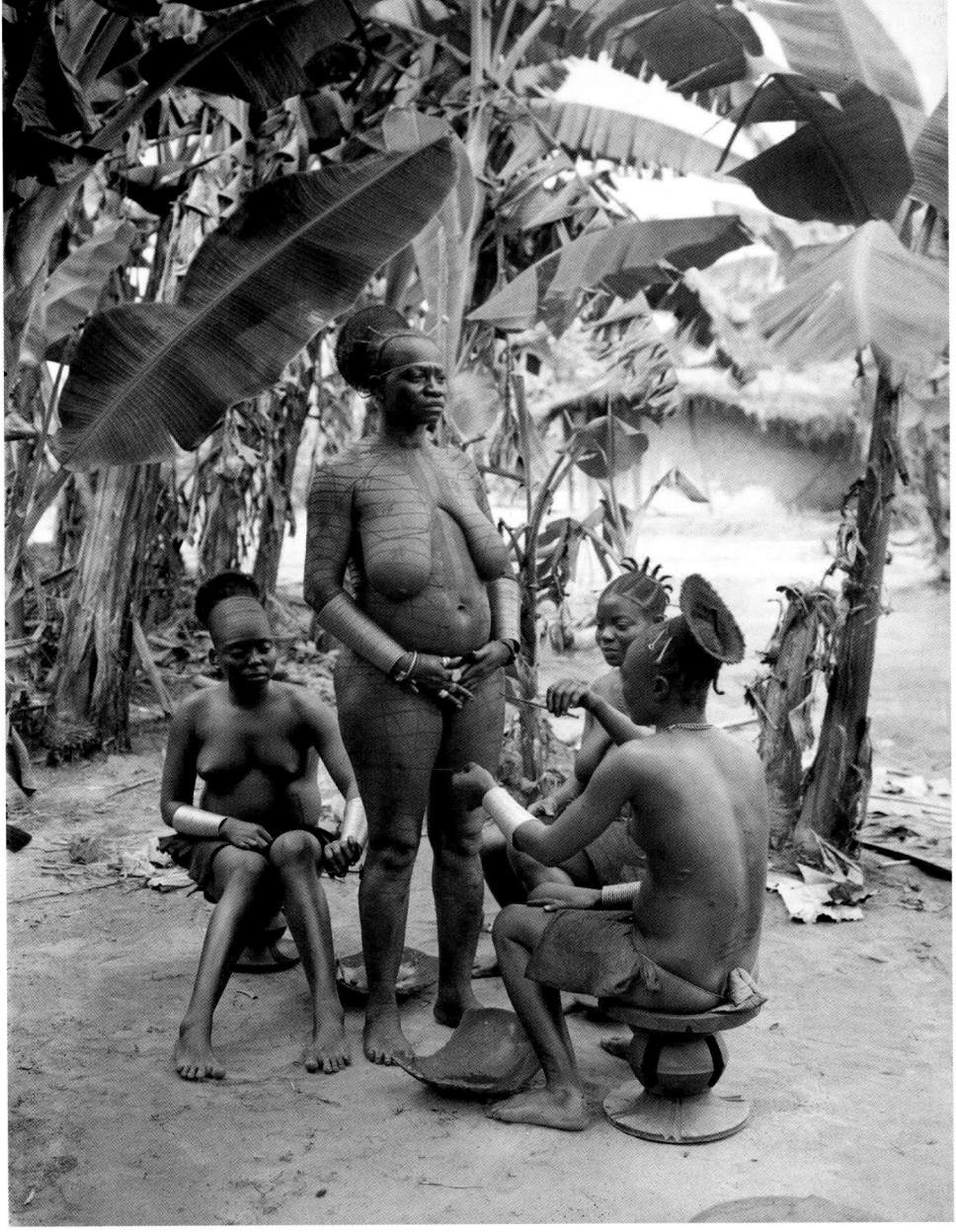

FIGURE 3.4 Matubani undergoing body painting, Belgian Congo, black and white photograph by Herbert Lang, from the Lang Congo Expedition, 1909–1915. Photograph courtesy of American Museum of Natural History, negative no. 111920.

the juice of the gardenia plant. In many of these descriptions it is clear that the body is being described as an object, indeed as a work of art.

Commandant Christiaens, for example, wrote that

> Mangbetu women are generally very well endowed by nature. . . . Many have regular features, a sympathetic face, and firm gracefully modeled breasts; add to that a torso with a gracefully arched back, elegantly modeled limbs, small and delicate extremities, tied together with feline suppleness, you will then have a portrait of the Mangbeto Venus, at the same time tinged with provocative seductiveness.[19]

But, he continues,

> If you are even a bit sentimental and think you can get through the glacial impassivity, guard yourself against going too far with your admiration! Because you will soon discover that this envelope of multiple seductions covers a soul that has difficulty responding to the beats of love. Dare we say, however, that this reserve, this impassible coolness is only an appearance, because the Mangbetu woman that one meets has one child in her hand, another sucking on her breast, and another . . . on the way.[20]

Head elongation was a common practice among the Mangbetu at the beginning of this century.[21] Babies' heads were bound with braided cord made of human hair or plant fibers. In addition to describing the labor-intensive process of making the string,[22] Herbert Lang described head binding as follows:

> The band is put on the very day of the child's birth after the first bath with lukewarm water has been given. It is often taken off at irregular intervals. . . . The mothers I asked told me if the child strampels [sic] much and becomes restless the bandage is taken off. The children very often sleep with it. The bandage is seldom left longer than 48 hours. The child's head is always well oiled before putting the bandage on and also after taking it off. Usually the bandage is left off a day. . . . They always stated that it was very pleasing to have such a long head.[23]

The Mangbetu spent a great deal of time on their personal appearance, and the head was clearly the focus of Mangbetu personal aesthetics. The shape of the head, the hairstyle, and ornaments for the head, including hairpins, hatpins, hats, and combs worn by both men and women, were of paramount importance. Mangbetu hairstyles varied considerably according to the class of the wearer and the occasion.

Wealthier people could afford the time to prepare elaborate coiffures. Schweinfurth noted in 1871 that at Mbunza's court both men and women wove their hair at the top and back of the head over an arrangement of reeds and they twisted the front hair into thin rows across the forehead. Hair taken from war victims or purchased from others was used to supplement a woman's hair and to make the arrangement larger. By 1910, when Lang visited, new hairstyles had developed. Men no longer dressed their hair to enhance the impression of head elongation, and women now added a halo-shaped basketry frame covered with hair, either their own braided into it, or in the form of a hairpiece.[24] Lang wrote that this new style for women was very common and was considered especially pleasing by the Mangbetu: "The Mangbetu women very often change their style of hairdressing according to their moods. The basketlike type, however, if once adopted is seldom abandoned. It needs rather long hair and women are proud of it."[25] In 1970 when Eliot Elisofon visited the Mangbetu, he photographed a woman braiding hair into such a basketry frame, although by then many older women can be seen in his images without any headdresses whatsoever.

Early observers also described how Mangbetu women took great care in covering their bodies with painting as well as scarification. Lang noted that the Mangbetu liked to rub their bodies with scented and colored oils, which were stored in pots. For dances and special events, women painted geometric designs on their bodies with a black pigment made from the gardenia plant. Some designs were painted freehand and some were applied with stamps or small carved cylinders of wood similar to those used on pottery. According to Schweinfurth, the variety of patterns was "unlimited" and included stars, Maltese crosses, bees, flowers, stripes, and irregular spots. He wrote that he saw "women streaked with veins like marble, and even covered with squares like a chess-board."[26] The designs lasted for about two days and then were rubbed off and replaced by new designs. Most observers noted how Mangbetu men and women rubbed their bodies with a mixture of pulverized redwood and oil from palm kernels to give the skin a coppery gloss.

In terms of clothing, in the nineteenth and early twentieth centuries the Mangbetu manufactured and wore barkcloth, sometimes decorated with alternating bands of light and dark cloth (the dark was achieved by soaking the cloth in a specific type of mud). Men wore large cloths draped and pleated in folds over a belt. Women carried and also wore small pieces in front of the pubic area. In back, they wore a palm fiber apron called a *negbe,* decorated by overlaid and appliqued patterns of light and dark fiber, as represented in plate 15.

LA CROISIÈRE NOIRE

In 1924 the French motorcar company Citroën sponsored a series of expeditions across Africa called collectively "La Croisière Noire." Ethnographers, filmmakers, and photographers drove across Africa, accompanied by drivers, hunters, mechanics, and representatives of the company, demonstrating the style and fortitude not only of the Citroën motorcar but also of the French colonial project. Through subsequent newspaper and magazine articles, movie screenings, and exhibitions, the European public would come to appreciate the beauty and wonder of African scenery, wildlife, and culture, not to mention the potential for spreading French civilization and commerce. Works of art and images from Dakar to Djibouti were widely disseminated and incorporated into the visual vocabulary of pre-war Europe.

After a two-day stop in the northeastern part of the Congo, in the village of Chief Ekibondo, the expedition leaders Georges-Marie Haardt (1884–1932) and Louis Audouin-Dubreuil (1887–1960), the filmmaker Léon Poirier (1884–1968), and the artist Alexandre Iacovleff (1887–1938) raved about the advanced state of Mangbetu art. The painted houses, the carefully swept clearings, and the hospitality of Chief Ekibondo—who by then, with his fifty-three wives, had created a veritable tourist village—convinced them that the Mangbetu undisputedly had art.[27] The art made by Africans they previously encountered was merely "a crude copy of natural forms." Mangbetu artists, on the other hand, could reproduce human features in a lifelike way. Mangbetu pottery, basketry, house painting, and

women, they said, reminded them, like their predecessors, of the wonders of the ancient world.[28]

The Mangbetu, wrote Haardt and Audouin-Dubreuil,

> seem to bear the imprint of ancient civilizations in which the passage of time envelops them like the ghostly tombs enclosing the mummies of pharaohs. Brought into daylight by modern expeditions, just as one has excavated the treasures of the Valley of the Kings, the Mangbetu do not have the bitter roughness of something new but rather the decadent charm of ancient drawings.[29]

Like his predecessors, Ekibondo knew how to impress visitors with the physical appearance of his village as well as with the reception he organized. The visitors believed that the women who swept the grounds did so as punishment for adultery. Musicians and dancers were on call to perform and Ekibondo did the obligatory dance before the assembled crowd. Iacovleff and Poirier were so impressed that they remained behind for an extra day while their colleagues went hunting. Iacovleff mounted an exhibition of his drawings that "astonished" the Mangbetu,[30] while his colleague Poirier struggled to resist the charms proffered by one of the local women at the behest of the Chief.

Haardt and Audouin-Dubreuil, who wrote the account of La Croisière Noire, also described Mangbetu women as works of art, albeit highly eroticized works. After they left the Mangbetu and moved on to visit the Logo people, they pined, "Gone are the elegant women, the fine hands, the courts of Negro kings, the painted houses, sculpted ivories, ebony drums, music, dance, finished the reign of art."[31] The Logo had retained nothing of the ancient Egyptians and their graceless women, according to Iacovleff, were "beauties a bit Cubist."[32] In contrast, he described the Mangbetu beauty named Ourou as someone "with skin a golden ochre color, and features defined by the deformation of her head. Her eyes shaped like almonds have the fixed expression of an Egyptian sculpture: the whites of inlaid quartz, the pupils of agate."[33]

THE DISSEMINATION OF IMAGES

In addition to these widely circulated texts, a growing body of artwork and photography circulating in Europe represented Mangbetu women.[34] In the Van Overbergh and de Jonge 1909 compendium of references to the Mangbetu, eight of nine unattributed photographs at the end of the book show women. There were two genres of photographs: the anthropological photographs which showed males and females in static views that could be used for purposes of "scientific" measurement (plates 53a–c), and the "art" photographs that showed women doing things or more often posed to show off their bodies, body scarification and painting, and adornments, particularly hairstyles (plates 48 and 52). In either genre, the image of the long-headed Mangbetu woman became a standard European expression of the exotic and erotic beauty of Africa.

Beginning with the visits of the Belgian ethnographer Armand Hutereau and the German zoologist Herbert Lang around 1910, images of the Mangbetu began appearing in newspapers, magazines, posters, advertisements, and even eventually on a Belgian Congo postage stamp (figure 3.5). Photography, painting, and drawing all contributed to an iconography of the Mangbetu that was strongly, although by no means exclusively, focused on women. While Hutereau and Lang saw themselves as scientists, and their photographs primarily as documentation, as images of Mangbetu women became more prominent in the public print media, the Mangbetu woman as exotic and erotic beauty became the dominant image. By the 1930s, the image of the "long-headed Mangbetu" woman was virtually a logo of Belgian colonialism, featured in images at the 1931 and 1937 French expositions and on postcards, posters, guidebooks, and in art galleries. This image was simultaneously exotic, erotic, and easily aestheticized, for in the 1920s and 1930s, the statuesque elongated figure fit nicely with some of the emerging preoccupations with Art Deco style.

In addition to artists' firsthand renditions of the Mangbetu, photography was important in the production and dissemination of this imagery. Photography among the Mangbetu has a long history that I can only summarize here. Herbert Lang, the leader of the American Museum of Natural History Congo Expedition (1909–15), lived among the Mangbetu for several years and took over 10,000 photographs of the fauna, flora, and people of northeastern Congo. Lang took three types of photographs of people: posed photographs taken for the purposes of anthropometric measurement, portraits of individual men and women showing hairstyles and headdresses, and pictures showing different kinds of activities. In addition, there were a few informal images, rarely (if ever) reprinted, that more often showed men and women wearing imported cotton clothing rather than bark cloth skirts and with nude torsos. Lang's formal photographs of women

FIGURE 3.6 A woman nursing her child, Belgian Congo, black and white photograph by Herbert Lang, Lang Congo Expedition, 1909–1915. Photograph courtesy of the American Museum of Natural History, negative no. 111837.

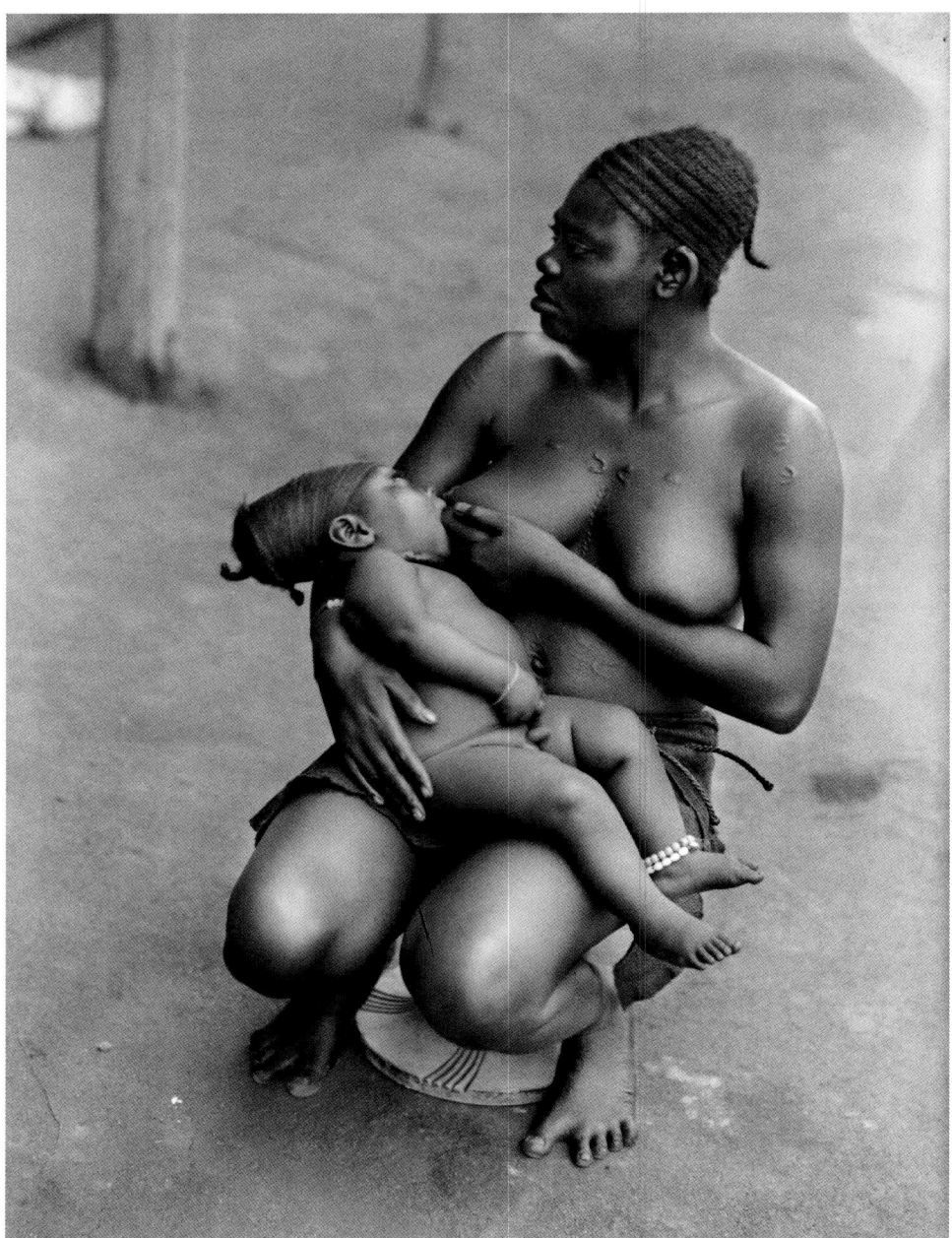

highlighted head elongation, hair styles, body scarification and painting, and activities including dance, body painting, agricultural labor, pottery making, head binding, beer brewing, and maternity—the ubiquitous mother and child (figure 3.6), which had its counterparts elsewhere in European photography in the same period. These images were exhibited and printed in journals and newspapers and surely would have been seen by the participants in the Citroën expedition before they set out for the land of the Mangbetu.

After 1915, other photographers visited the region and focused their lenses even more exclusively on women. Many close-ups, shot at interesting angles that exaggerated the elongated heads, were reprinted on postcards and in magazines.

Casimir Zagourski's images, for example, were issued in several series of post cards, including one of 216 images printed on photographic paper, called *L'Afrique qui disparait*. A number of filmmakers also focused on women, including a National Geographic crew that accompanied James Chapin on a visit in the 1920s.

By far the largest public impact of visual images occurred in Paris after the return of Iacovleff and Poirier from Central Africa. Poirier's film ran for ten weeks starting in April 1926, while Iacovleff's drawings drew huge crowds at La Galerie Jean Charpentier, 76 Fauborg Saint-Honoré, and the next year in Brussels. Rave reviews compared him to Ingres and Jacques Louis David, the artist who documented Napoleon's Egyptian campaigns. One reviewer noted that Iacovleff "gave the Negro magnificent style, a savage and nervous grace. Doing what Josephine Baker did for fashion, he created a 'Central African' style in art. . . ."[35] Nobosodrou (plate 46), the Mangbetu woman filmed by Poirier, became an emblem of the whole expedition and may have inspired the radiator ornament that graced one of the Citroëns in Audouin-Debreuil's collection.

An exhibition about La Croisière Noire opened for a ten-week show at the Louvre in October 1926 and was so successful its run was extended until February 1927. The museum entrance on rue Rivoli was decorated with bold black and red Mangbetu geometric patterns that fit perfectly into the sensibility of Art Deco design. That style had reached its apogee in 1925 with the International Exhibition of Decorative and Industrial Modern Art, but the fashion designer Paul Poiret was still designing his African- and Asian-inspired garments, and furniture designers and decorators were using geometric designs with exotic materials like ebony, rosewood, and ivory.

Many more European and American painters, sculptors, and photographers visited the northeastern Congo in the 1920s and 1930s. The American painter Paul Travis, whose work is now at the Cleveland Museum of Art, visited the village of Ekibondo in the 1920s and continued to paint scenes of Mangbetu life for many years after his return to America. A portfolio of engravings by the Belgian artist Henri Kerels (1896–1956) was issued for the Belgian Pavilion of the 1937 Paris exposition and includes a woodcut of a Mangbetu woman playing a harp (Mangbetu women did not play harps!), kneeling beside a ceramic pot whose head is, as these pots were, a reflection of the woman's head.[36] In 1930, the African American sculptor Malvina Hoffman (1887–1966) created a bust of a Mangbetu woman for her "Races of Mankind" project commissioned by the Field Museum.

In 1929, following the Citroën expedition, Grace Flandrau, a writer and filmmaker, went to Congo to make a film. Her film has not survived, but the book describing her trip can still be found. She described how the village of Ekibondo was becoming a magnet for tourists, photographers, and filmmakers, with the Mangbetu collaborating in the construction of images of themselves. She explained how she directed Mangbetu women to act in her film: "There were shots of ladies approaching a cannibal village, close-ups of ladies looking into boiling pot and of human bones boiling in pot, shots of ladies rescuing natives about to be buried alive."[37] Flandrau, however, was well aware that all this was fiction and was disappointed in the end when the buyers of her now-lost film, *Up the Congo,* changed the story to focus on the adventures of the European female explorers, portraying them as alone and isolated in Africa, which was hardly the case.

Ten year's later, Martin Birnbaum traveled to Ekibondo's village and described how Chief Ekibondo was presenting his village and its women to tourists:

> But when I met Chief Ekibondo, dressed in white duck and wearing a wristwatch, I began to suspect that all this charming grouping of forest giants and ornamental huts was done with a keen eye for business. He encourages women to show how they dress their hair, to pound manioc and other foodstuffs in the open, to pose for photographs and sell their negbes and neatly woven hats without crowns. . . .
>
> I felt that Ekibondo was as enthusiastic about "tourisme" as Mussolini himself, and I was tempted to give him a bitter account of white exploitation of primitive paradises. Fortunately, perhaps, there was no time. At any rate, he has not yet built a hotel or rest house for whites.[38]

When one looks at these images, it is important to remember that the camera, particularly the box camera of the early twentieth century, was far from unobtrusive. The subjects always knew they were being photographed and sometimes were given prints of the images. The act of posing and the circulation of the subsequent images inevitably influenced how the Mangbetu perceived themselves and their relationship to the gaze of foreigners. Lang, for one, developed his photographs in the field and prints were given to the subjects. Iacovleff mounted an exhibition in the Mangbetu town of Niangara and described the reactions of the Mangbetu to his images. Many others, including Eliot Elisofon, whose Mangbetu photographs are now in the collection of the Smithsonian Museum of African Art, shared their work with their subjects and encouraged the collaboration that was a pre-condition of their work.

There are many consequences of this, not all easily documented. It is clear, however, that the African artists of the region began to produce objects that represented the same images that were being captured in European drawings, photographs, and film. This was especially the case in the first half of the twentieth century, but even in the 1980s one visitor came upon a painting of Queen Nenzima, the wife of Chief Okondo, made by a Congolese artist who seems to have copied the image from a Lang photograph. The painting may have been done decades after Lang's departure. As Christraud Geary has noted, there was a constant practice of copying going on between photography, lithography, and painting.[39] Once printing developed as a medium for reproducing images, the transfer of ideas and images from one medium to another was continuous. Often shown seated on a stool, the Mangbetu woman, with her elongated head, halo-coiffure, bare breasts, barkcloth and back apron, body painting, and scarification, was a major trope in the industry of inventing Africa. It not only influenced the

Western image of Africa, but also the work that African artists were producing to represent themselves.

THE MANGBETU IMAGE IN AFRICAN ART

While figurative art was rare in the northeast Congo before the twentieth century, anthropomorphic art became the defining characteristic of Mangbetu style right after Europeans began visiting and working in the area. Elsewhere Curtis Keim and I have explored how Western tastes influenced the art of this region in the early colonial period.[40] Art was a major factor in defining ethnic boundaries, but this was not so much because each group had its own style, but rather because artists created naturalistic work in many different media that represented real local differences in material culture and body adornment. Artists and objects circulated in the region, as they had in the years before the colonial period, but in the early twentieth century, new patrons and clients—namely Europeans— began to influence art production and encourage this naturalistic tendency. From the time of Schweinfurth's publication to the photographs taken in the 1970s by Eliot Elisofon, there was a close synergy between how Mangbetu people presented themselves, in both art and life, and how outsiders represented them. Given this relationship between art and life, it is not surprising that in both art works and photography—by Africans and Westerners—depictions of women came to define this classic Mangbetu style.

One way of looking at Mangbetu art is as a discourse, written in objects made by Africans and in images made by Westerners, on the topics of power and sexuality. The brief chapter on the Mangbetu culture in *La Croisière Noire* suggests that this is an appropriate way to understand the encounter between the participants in the Citroën expedition and the Mangbetu. The development of this discourse produced a certain amount of anxiety among both Europeans and Africans. According to most observers in the first half of the twentieth century, for all their beauty and charm, Mangbetu women were not to be trusted. Chief Ekibondo himself, wrote Haardt and Audouin-Dubreuil, worried about what was happening to women: "Our host worries about the future because the women, Mangbetu women that is, have showed for some time a regrettable spirit of independence."[41] The dialogue on sexuality takes place for the most part between African and Western men; women's voices mainly remain silent, unless one considers the act of modeling or posing as an assertion of agency. Most of the time, men made the art, just as men consumed it. In many areas of artistic production, from pottery to hairstyling to body painting, there is evidence that women were transformed from being artisans to models; colonialism recast the status of women from subject to object.

Pottery manufacturing is a case in point: certainly before the turn of the century, and probably up until the early 1920s, women were the main producers of basketry and pottery among the Mangbetu. They made all of the household pottery, wove most of the baskets, and probably did most of the house painting.

Men made woven hats and did metalwork and wood and ivory carving. When Schweinfurth described Mangbetu pottery in the 1870s, he noted the fine pots made by women. His drawings are similar to pots collected by Lang forty years later—delicate jars with imaginative geometric forms and fine incised decorations.[42] By Lang's time, however, the situation had begun to change. Women continued to produce pottery for domestic use (plate 12), but once anthropomorphic pottery became a commodity, men began doing ceramics and women were unable to take advantage of the new opportunities. They became the subject of the art of pottery and lost their stake in its production.

This gender shift may have involved input from the northern neighbors of the Mangbetu, the Azande, among whom men were traditionally potters.[43] When pottery with female heads (plate 13) began to be produced among the Mangbetu, men sculpted the heads. Herbert Lang photographed a male potter—the same man who made a pot with a protruding phallus—and also noted that men made the "art pottery," which he distinguished from utilitarian pottery. The latter often was made in complicated forms with wonderful fine decoration but, being non-representational, was not considered "art." Lang did not say that all the male potters were Azande, leaving us to ponder whether Zande men were making Mangbetu-style pots, or whether Mangbetu men were taking up pottery in addition to wood carving, ivory carving, and ironwork. The answer is most certainly both. In a series of photographs taken in the 1940s, in the collection of the Musée Royal de l'Afrique Centrale, a woman can be seen making a coiled pot. When she reached the neck of the pot, a man came over and sculpted the head.

But Mangbetu artists in the early colonial period also sculpted and drew men. These representations were satirical portraits that mocked the foreigners who commissioned the art that objectified the Mangbetu as women. These objects incorporate exaggerated representations of sexuality. In the American Museum of Natural History collection assembled by Lang between 1909 and 1915, for example, there is a wood carving of a military "messenger" holding a gun taller than himself. The man wears only a cap and a cartridge belt and has a large erect penis sticking out under the belt.[44] There is also the ceramic pot with a handle representing a man with a penis longer than the man's head protruding from one side of the pot (figure 3.7).[45] Drawings on ivory horns, boxes, and gourds show copulating couples. These examples have a pornographic intent—they were made to shock and amuse the audience, both European and African.

Around 1900, then, representations of Mangbetu women began to appear on a great variety of functional objects: on the necks of ceramic jars, on the wooden covers for bark boxes, on the arms and backs of wooden steamer chairs, on handles of metal knives, on the ends of many kinds of musical instruments (plate 14), and on ivory hair pins. Many objects were made with multiple heads: double-headed pots, hair pins with six or seven heads, chairs with heads protruding from every possible piece of wood, harps with heads on the neck and on the tuning keys. With the exception of folding chairs based on a Western model, all of these object forms existed within the repertoire of Mangbetu material culture

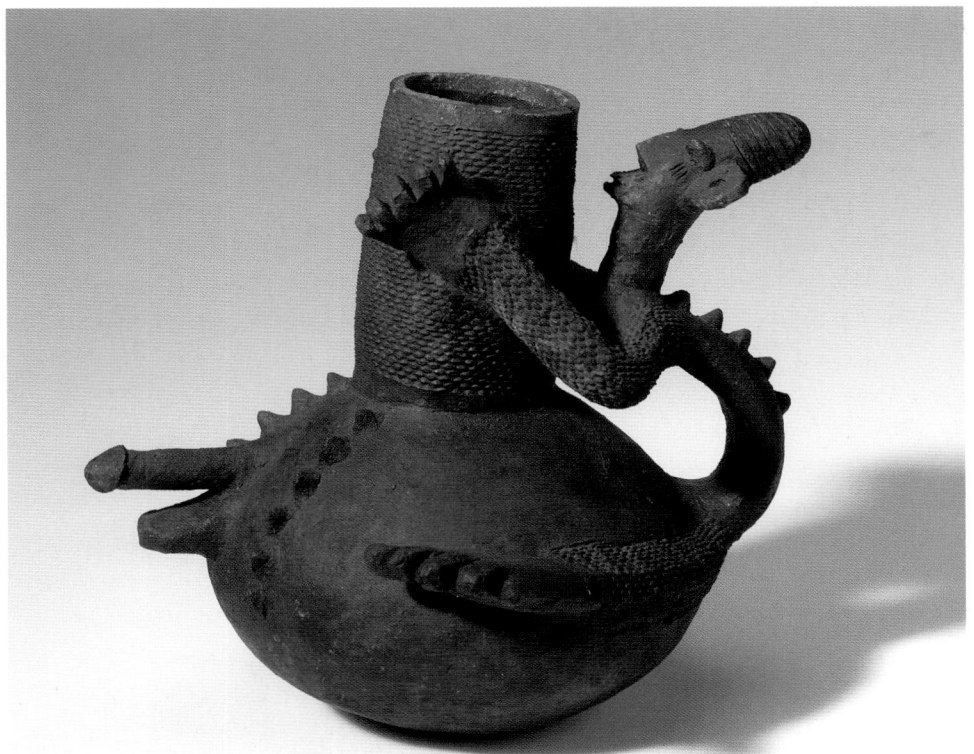

FIGURE 3.7 Unknown artist, Mangbetu peoples (?), Niangara, Democratic Republic of Congo (former Belgian Congo), figurative jar, late nineteenth to early twentieth century, terracotta. Photograph courtesy of American Museum of Natural History, 90.1/ 4703.

before contact with Westerners. The fascination with this Mangbetu style of body adornment, however, led to the commoditization and embellishment of what were hitherto objects of daily use.

Although Mangbetu people themselves did not have a tradition of anthropomorphic art before the end of the nineteenth century, the idea of adorning functional objects with heads was present in the region before the arrival of Europeans. I am not arguing, by any means, that figurative art *per se* was a colonial import, since the Barambo, the Bongo, and other neighboring people adorned functional objects like harps and knives with heads. European visitors collected these kinds of objects as early as the 1850s.[46] The Bongo in the southern Sudan made trumpets and funerary sculpture decorated with heads, described by Schweinfurth in the 1870s, while the Nzakara, the Ngbaka, and possibly the Azande, then known as the Niam-Niam, may have made harps with heads.[47] Some of the earliest known anthropomorphic objects—for example, an ivory dagger in the collection of the American Museum of Natural History, collected by agents of King Leopold around the turn of the nineteenth century—seem to be gender neutral. Many of the heads sculpted on nineteenth-century harps are generic human heads, with coiffures that can be either male or female, while others are long-eared animals, probably bats. Representations of European men and women were also incorporated into the colonial iconography of the larger region (figure 3.8).

Objects of beauty were valued and exchanged across ethnic boundaries before Europeans began to collect objects. African rulers commissioned and exchanged fine knives, musical instruments, and pottery. Gifts of artwork such as carved knives were used in diplomatic exchanges and as a form of tribute before Europeans ever set foot in the region.[48] Evans-Pritchard reports that among the Azande "it was a common practice for those who journeyed to the south to collect oracle-poison to bring back with them also Mangbetu artifacts, carefully bound in leaves, to present to their princes."[49] Schweinfurth described a harp representing a Mangbetu head as being Niam-Niam, or Zande, but it is clear that even in his day, objects and artists moved around and artists from one group often portrayed members of other groups. Thus while the origin of the anthropomorphic style in the region is still not totally clear, what is clear is that in the early colonial period there was a new tendency to naturalism and towards representation of a particular group of people: the Mangbetu.

There is no question that during this period Mangbetu women, and men for that matter, spent a lot of time on personal beauty. The focus on body adornment was not something imposed by Europeans: women spent hours braiding the fine thread that they used to bind babies heads, carefully bathed babies, and rubbed their skins with oils. They painted designs on their bodies that replicated the designs on bark cloth and spent hours and hours applying the same aesthetic to functional household objects: baskets, incised pottery, floor mats, aprons, and barkcloth. The body was one among many surfaces that people decorated with care. They took great care of their villages and carefully planned and decorated the surfaces of their buildings, shields, and receptacles.[50]

The increased production of anthropomorphic art in the Mangbetu style, however, was unquestionably associated with a shift in patrons and audience from other Africans to Westerners. In northeastern Congo, European collecting began on a large scale in the first decade of the twentieth century. King Leopold, and subsequently the Belgian government, sponsored major collecting expeditions. The American Museum of Natural History in New York sent scientists to study and collect. The Germans, Swedish, and French sponsored expeditions to the area. Inevitably, the perceptions and misperceptions of taste and the stereotyping of African life by both Africans and Europeans led to the commoditization of what came to be known as Mangbetu art. The paradox here, of course, is that even though this art came to stand for an archetype of African reality, it was in fact an innovation that emerged in the crucible of colonial contact. It drew on the reality of Mangbetu fashion as it existed at the turn of the twentieth century and in the half-century following, but indeed it was highly innovative, as much a response to the gaze of foreigners as to the aesthetic preferences of Mangbetu artists themselves.

One of the reasons that African artists in the region may have found it easy to respond to the desire of foreigners for highly naturalistic figurative sculpture (plate 15) is that it had no place in traditional Mangbetu culture. Unlike many African societies in which figure carvings, often highly abstract, have important religious roles, this does not seem to have been the case among the Mangbetu. Both Armand Hutereau and Herbert Lang wrote in their notes that the Mangbetu

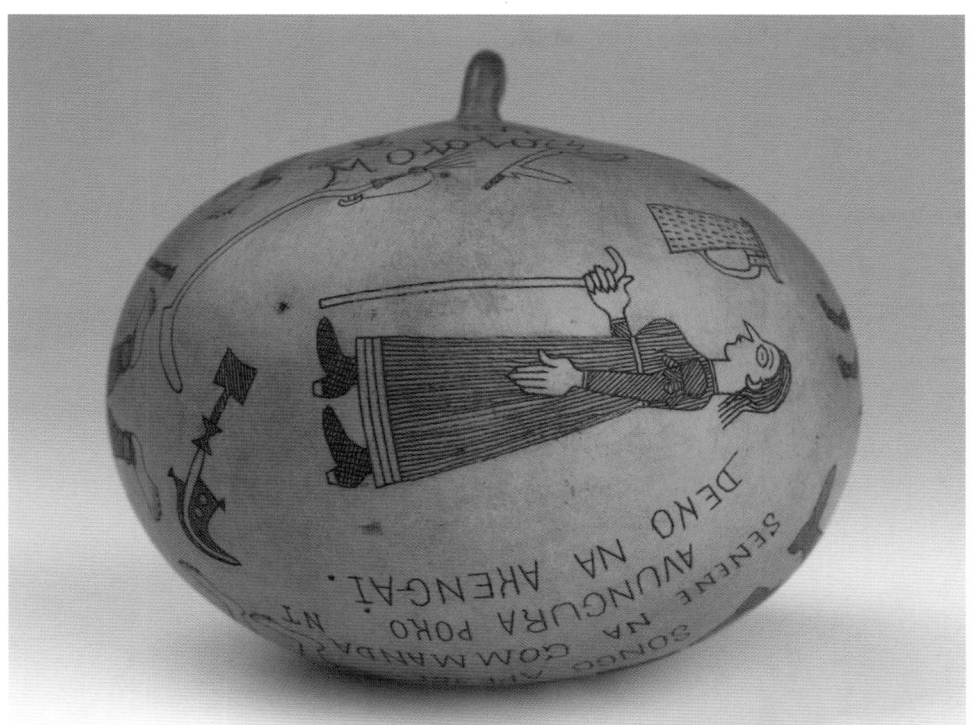

FIGURE 3.8 Unknown artist, Zande peoples, near Poko, Democratic Republic of Congo (former Belgian Congo), cup, gourd, pigment, Lang Congo Expedition, 1909–1915. Photograph courtesy of the American Museum of Natural History, 90.1/4313.

did not use figure sculpture for religious rituals and that carvings of animals or humans were seen by the Mangbetu simply as embellishments, as what we would call "art for art's sake." Contrary to the use of what they described as "fetishes" elsewhere in the Congo, the early collectors in the northeast Congo noted explicitly that figurative carvings had no religious meaning to the Mangbetu.

This secular attitude towards art—often dismissed in discussions of non-Western art—was surely one of the factors that allowed the Mangbetu and some neighboring artists to respond so readily to foreign tastes. In this case, the taste was clearly for highly naturalistic representations of the body, though this was not just any body, but rather the highly adorned and carefully coiffed Mangbetu, and predominately female, form. In the eyes of the members of the Citroën expedition, this naturalism was what distanced the Mangbetu artists from their neighbors and elevated their works from the status of fetish to that of art. Ironically, however, as the understanding of African art and authenticity has changed in the West, and many of these works have been "refetishized" by Westerners, they are sometimes described as royal ancestor figures, which they clearly were not.

The image of the Mangbetu woman has continued to have a presence in Western iconography of Africa, taking on new forms and meanings. In Magdalene Odundo's *Untitled* (plate 101), she has reduced the basic female body into a sensuous dialogue between positive and negative space. A closer look at its abstract form, however, reveals the sculpture's reference to the Mangbetu female head. Odundo's sleek and magnificent coil-built pottery moves away from Mangbetu naturalism, but clearly evokes the elongated head and halo coiffure perpetuated by the "classic" images of Mangbetu women. Odundo, who is interested in the ways that the female body has been defined and reshaped to conform to specific cultural ideals of beauty, celebrates the regal elegance of Mangbetu women—as portrayed in life, in colonial photography, and in Mangbetu arts. Despite the apparent influences of Mangbetu pottery and body arts in her art, Odundo equally pays tribute to Nigerian, Kenyan, Ugandan, South African, and Native America pottery traditions, as well as ancient Egyptian, Jomon, Chinese, Minoan, Mediterranean, and Mesopotamian ceramics, and modernist sculpture. As seen in ceramic traditions worldwide, Odundo anthropomorphizes her vessels with surface decorations and molded applications that echo the female form and body arts. In particular, the blackened surface and patterns of nodules evoke the tactile and seductive quality of scarification marks worn by Mangbetu—and other African—women to mark their passage through the various stages of female life: the onset of menstruation, conception, childbirth, nursing, and motherhood.

Like Odundo, Carrie Mae Weems re-appropriates Mangbetu imagery, specifically Poirier's portrait of Nobosodrou (plate 46). In *From Here I Saw What Happened And I Cried* (1995–1996) (plate 127),[51] Weems reproduced two indigo-dyed mirror images of Nobosodrou, whose profile serves as a visual parenthesis around a series of red-tinted, mostly anthropological-type photographs of African Americans. Each is framed in circular black mats that emulate the focus of a lens on a specimen and each has its own epithet—Weem's personal commentaries sandblasted into the glass mounts. Together, the texts read like a poem:

YOU BECAME A SCIENTIFIC SUBJECT PROFILE
A NEGROID TYPE
AN ANTHROPOLOGICAL DEBATE
& A PHOTOGRAPHIC SUBJECT
YOU BECAME MAMMIE, MAMA, MOTHER & THEN, YES, CONFIDANT—HA
DESCENDING THE THRONE YOU BECAME FOOT SOLDIER AND COOK [. . .]

Originally comprised of thirty-two photographs, Weems created the installation so that individual sets could be combined into smaller groups to disclose a whole new set of counterpoint narratives. The group of images in the exhibition *Black Womanhood* combines four historic portraits of African American women, each branded by a single definitive word—"FIELD," "HOUSE," "KITCHEN," and "YARD"—to which the inward facing Nobosodrou laments, "FROM HERE I SAW WHAT HAPPENED" "AND I CRIED." The combination of images creates a powerful and jolting commentary on the re-identification and displacement of the African female body and its colonized transformation into categories within the American hierarchy of enslavement—as anonymous workers in the field, house, kitchen, and yard, representing the ancestors of enslaved Africans brought to America. These women, including Nobosodrou, represent African womanhood transformed by colonialism and the Atlantic slave trade, while painfully acknowledging also the debasement of black people in America. Therefore, the details of place and of origin are not germane to this work. As curator Thomas Piché notes,

By examining the myths, the stereotypes, and the popular and media sources, Weems sets out to explore the more encompassing issues of power relationships, gender, identity, and class, as well as race.[52]

Weems's combination of photographic image and text in this work not only disrupts the "objectifying, dispassionate gaze of the camera,"[53] but forces the viewer to attend to the human dimension and to re-imagine the silencing, subjugation, and renegotiation of voices and power.

CONCLUSION

The art known today as Mangbetu was forged in the furnace of colonial contact. For over a century, Europeans have perceived the Mangbetu, as they have perceived Africa as a whole, through the lenses of their own cultural concerns. In the case of the Mangbetu, the images that Western artists brought back and that African artists created resonated with ideas about beauty, design, gender relationships, and the structure of society. Rulers like Okondo and Ekibondo were not passive in these circumstances, nor were Mangbetu women and artists. They understood the texts that the Europeans created, if not through the written word, then through paintings, photographs, and the art market. They developed and invented their own traditions in accord with these images, thus joining the foreigners in the creation of Africa and visions of African womanhood embedded in the imagined beauty and allure of nineteenth-century Mangbetu women. ❧

1 "Assises dans une pose hiératique sur des petits tabourets d'ébène, les femmes Mangbetou sont rangées en file comme les figures d'une fresque égyptienne. Évocation d'une precision documentaire qui, subitement dans la pensée, relie par-dessus les siècles les temps presents et la civilization des Pharaons." Georges-Marie Haardt and Louis Audouin-Dubreuil, *La Croisière noire. Expédition Citroën Centre-Afrique* (Paris: Librarie Plon, 1927), 15.

2 The book was published in English in 1874.

3 See Enid Schildkrout and Curtis A. Keim, *African Reflections: Art from Northeastern Zaire* (New York and Seattle: American Museum of Natural History and University of Washington Press, 1990), 124–125, on head binding. This practice was common in the region and did not originate with Mangbetu rulers, even though local traditions and European writers make this claim.

4 The building was 150 feet long by sixty feet wide by fifty feet high.

5 Despite early colonial perceptions, the Mangbetu were never as centralized as Schweinfurth thought, and by the late nineteenth century a series of wars and chieftancy disputes, as well as the ravages of the Arab slave trade, had taken their toll. One ruler after another was propelled into relative prominence and subsequent obscurity, and whatever incipient centralization there was in Mangbetu country disappeared with the onset of Belgian rule. The Mangbetu were organized into local groups or "Houses" ranging in size from one hundred to as many as two thousand people. These lineage-based groups consisted of a male head and his many wives and children as well as other relatives, servants (formerly captives), and allies from neighboring groups.

6 See Schildkrout and Keim, *African Reflections*, chapter 2, for a discussion of the Mangbetu myth.

7 Georg A. Schweinfurth, *The Heart of Africa: Three Years' Travels and Adventures in the Unexplored Regions of Central Africa from 1868 to 1871* (New York: Harper and Bros., 1874), vol. 2, 91.

8 In fact, each Mangbetu Big Man made his own village a center of government. He did not rule over a state as the Europeans understood it in the nineteenth century, but was rather the head of a "House" that more closely resembled the "Houses" of Renaissance princes and feudal lords.

Upon the death of a chief, the capital would move, and successive leaders would recreate the accoutrements of leadership. Jan Vansina, "Reconstructing the Past" in *African Reflections*, pp. 69–88; Curtis A. Keim, "Precolonial Mangbetu Rule: Political and Economic Factors in Nineteenth-Century Mangbetu History (Northeast Zaire)," Ph.D. dissertation, Indiana University, 1979.

9 Mangbetu women could in fact own property, not only household utensils like pots, brooms, and baskets but also the produce of their own plantations. Keim, "Precolonial Mangbetu Rule: Political and Economic Factors in Nineteenth-Century Mangbetu History (Northeast Zaire)," 169.

10 "La femme Mangbetu, beaucoup plus indépendante, prend part aux réunions des hommes. Les Princes Mangbetu, qui j'allais voir, étaient entourés de leurs femmes favorites, même dans les grandes assemblées du Conseil. Le soir, elles portaient souvent leurs tabouret à côté de mon feu et se mettaient à rire et à badiner sans gène" (in Cyrille Van Overbergh and Eduard De Jonghe, *Les Mangbetu* [Brussels: Institut international de bibliographie, Albert de Wit, 1909], 518).

11 "L'European y est reçu . . . par le chef, entouré de quelques notables, ses conseillers et de ses principales femmes. Celles-ci beaucoup moins farouche que leurs soeurs Azande, loin d'éviter le regard de l'homme blanc, sont très flattés de s'apercevoir qu'elles attirent l'attention et ne dédaignent pas, loin de là de faire avec lui un bout de conversation. Elles assist à la palabre, reçoivent des présents, et en font en leur nom personnel prennent une part active à la discussion." Christiaens quoted in Van Overbergh and de Jonghe, *Les Mangbetu*, 344.

12 The partition of Africa by European powers in 1894 gave Leopold II, King of the Belgians, control over the area that is now the Democratic Republic of the Congo. In 1908 the Belgian government took control of the Congo until its independence in 1960.

13 Herbert Lang, *Fieldnotes, Department of Anthropology* (New York: American Museum of Natural History, December 19, 1910), fieldnote 1147.

14 De Renette, a Belgian colonial officer of the late nineteenth century, noted of the Mangbetu woman that "Elle est entourée de considération; son avis compte; elle ne un être agissant et pensant dans la famille et non un objet, comme chez les Azande et les Ababua" (her opinion counts; she is an acting and thinking being in the family and not an object). Quoted in van Overbergh and de Jonghe, *Les Mangbetu*, 330.

15 Guillaume-François van Kerckhoven, "L'expédition Vankerckhoven," *Belgique coloniale* 2 (1896): 39.

16 Schweinfurth, *The Heart of Africa*, vol. 2, 58.

17 Van Kerckhoven, "L'expédition Vankerckhoven," 1896: 39.

18 Armand Hutereau, *Notes sur la vie familiale et juridique de quelques populations du Congo belge* (Tervuren: Musée du Congo Belge, 1909), 71.

19 "Les femmes Mangbetu sont généralement assez biens douées par la nature au point de vue physique. Beaucoup d'entres elles ont des traits assez réeguliers, la physionomie sympathique et la gorge aux fermes appas est souvent gracieusement modelée; ajoutée à cela une taille hardiment cambrée, des membres aux lignes élégantes, aux extrémités petites et fines, aux attaches félinement souples et flexibles; vous aurez ainsi le portrait de la Vénus mangbetu, à la demarche empreinte d'une provocante coquetterie." Christiaens in van Overbergh and de Jonghe, *Les Mangbetu*, 119.

20 "Mais, si vous êtes quelque peu sentimental et que vois craignez l'atteinte glaciale de la désillusion, garder-vous bien de pousser plus loin votre admiraton! Car vous apprendriez bientôt que cette enveloppe aux multiples séductions couvre une âme vibrant difficilement aux accents de l'amour. Hâtons-nous de dire, cependant, que cette réserve, cette froide impassibilité n'est que apparente, car les femmes manbetu quo l'on rencontre ont généralement un enfant par la main, un nourrisoon attaché à la hanche au moyen d'une lanière en écorce et un autre . . . en expectative" (ibid.).

21 Children's heads are no longer bound, but elongated heads can still be seen on older people.

22 Schildkrout and Keim, *African Reflections*, 125.

23 Lang, *Fieldnotes*, fieldnote 573.

24 There are several examples of such hairpieces in the collection of the American Museum of Natural History. Two are catalogued as Mangbetu (90.1/1447, 90.1/1448) and two as Azande (90.1/4815, 90.1/4816).

See the Anthropology Collections Database at http://anthro.amnh.org.

25 Lang, *Fieldnotes*, fieldnote 56.

26 Schweinfurth, *The Heart of Africa*, vol. 2, 105.

27 See Schildkrout, "L'art Mangbetu: l'invention d'une tradition," in *Du Musée Colonial au Musée des Cultures du Monde. Actes du colloque organise par le Musée National des Arts d'Afrique et d'Oceanie et le Centre Georges Pompidou, 3–6 juin 1998*, ed. Dominique Taffin (Paris: Maisonneuve et Larose, 2000), 109–125.

28 "Nous pensons, avec Iacovleff, qu'il y a indiscutablement un art Mangbetou . . . L'art primitif n'est jamais qu'une copie grossière des formes de la nature. Chez les Mangbetou, au contraire, la stylisation est manifeste. Les décorations murales sont de simples jeux de lignes gometriques et de coueurs vives, purement ornementales et n'ayant à aucun moment le caractère enfantin des dessins que nous avons remarqués sur les cases de l'Oubanghi; de même pour les travaux de vannerie ou de poterie, les harpes et les trompes d'ivoire.

"Lorsequ'un artiste Mangbetou reproduit les traits humains, il accentue l'allongement du crâne, déforme les traits du visage, de façon à composer un véritable motif décoratif, qui tire son harmonie du rapport des lignes et des volumes. Ne sont-pas là les principes d'un grand art?" (Haardt and Audouin-Debreuil, *La Croisière noire*, 226–227).

29 "Ils [the Mangbetu] sembles porter l'empreinte des civilisations antiques dont l' écroulement a laissé le temps se refermer sur eux comme les pierres sépulcrales se sont refermées sur les momies des Pharaons. Remis au grand jour par les explorations modernes, ainsi que l'ont été par les fouilles les trésors de la Vallée des Rois, les Mangbetou n'ont pas l'âpre rudesse des êtres neufs mais le charme décadent des silhouettes anciennes" (Haardt and Audouin-Debreuil, *La Croisière noire*, 227).

30 Haardt and Audouin-Debreuil, *La Croisière noire*, 237.

31 "Finis les femmes élégantes, les mains fines, les cours de rois nègres, les cases peintes, les ivoires sculptés, les tabourets d'ébène, la musique, la danse; fini le règne de l'art" (Haardt and Audouin-Debreuil, *La Croisière noire*, 252–253).

32 "Des beautés un peu cubistes" (Haardt and Audouin-Debreuil, *La Croisière noire*, 254).

33 "La bell Ourou, à la peau couleur ocre d'or, aux traits tirés par la déformation du crâne. Ses yeux fendus en amande ont l'expression fixe des sculptures égyptiennes: le blanc incrusté de quartz, les pupilles d'agate" (Haardt and Audouin-Debreuil, *La Croisière noire*, 227).

34 Christraud M. Geary, "Different Visions? Postcards from Africa by European and African Photographers and Sponsors," in *Delivering Views: Distant Cultures in Early Postcards*, ed. Christraud M. Geary and Virginia-Lee Webb (Washington, D.C.: Smithsonian Institution Press, 1998), 147–177; Schildkrout, "The Spectacle of Africa through the Lens of Herbert Lang," *African Arts* 24, no. 4 (1991): 70–85, 100. Male chiefs were the main counterpoint to this, often shown dancing before their wives, or otherwise surrounded by women.

35 "Son dessin sobre et précis, un dessin qui fait penser à Cranach, est arrivé à donner au type nègre un style magnifique, une grâce sauvage et merveuse, celle que Joséphine Baker a mise à la mode. Bref, il a créé dans l'art le style 'Afrique Centrale' qui lui manquait." "Les Trois Moustiquaires: 'Le Peintre Alexandre Iakovleff,'" in *Pourquoi pas? gazette hebdomadaire belge*, 6 mai 1927. Quoted in Caroline Haardt de la Baume, *Alexandre Iacovleff, L'Artiste Voyageur* (Paris: Flammarion, 2000), 86.

36 Henri Kerels, *Arts et métiers Congolais: douze gravures originales en couleurs* (Brussels: Les Editions de Belgique, 1937).

37 Grace Flandrau, *Then I Saw the Congo* (New York: Harcourt, Brace, and Co., 1929), 98–99.

38 Martin Birnbaum, "The Long-Headed Mangbetus," *Natural History* 43 (1939): 73–83.

39 Geary, "Different Visions?"

40 Schildkrout and Keim, *African Reflections*.

41 "Notre hôte n'est pas sans inquietude sur l'avenir, car les femmes—les femmes Mangbetou bien entendu—montrent depuis quelque temps un facheux esprit d'indépendence" (Haardt and Audouin-Debreuil, *La Croisière noire*, 231).

42 Enid Schildkrout, Jill Hellman, and Curtis A. Keim, "Mangbetu Pottery: Tradition and Innovation in Northeast Zaire," *African Arts* 22, no. 2 (1989): 38–47.

43 See E. E. Evans-Pritchard's essays: "A Contribution to the Study of Zande Culture," *Africa* 30 (1960): 309–324; "A Further Contribution to the Study of Zande Culture," *Africa* 33 (1963): 183–197; and "A Final Contribution to the Study of Zande Culture," *Africa* 35 (1965): 21–29.

44 Schildkrout and Keim, *African Reflections*, 87; Schildkrout, "Gender and Sexuality in Mangbetu Art," in *Unpacking Culture: Art and Commodity in Colonial and Postcolonial Worlds*, ed. Ruth Phillips and Christopher B. Steiner (Berkeley: University of California Press, 1999), 197–213.

45 Schildkrout and Keim, *African Reflections*, 242.

46 These visitors include the Italians Giovanni Miani and Romolo Gessi and the English travelers Mr. and Mrs. James Petherick and Alexandrine Tinne.

47 While Schweinfurth described a harp with a head as being "Niam-Niam" (Azande), it is significant that Evans Pritchard later wrote that the Azande did not make anthropomorphic art but rather adopted the practice from the Mangbetu. E. E. Evans-Pritchard, *The Azande: History and Political Institutions* (Oxford: Clarendon Press, 1971), 96–99.

48 John Mack, "Art, Culture and Tribute Among the Azande," in *African Reflections*, Schildkrout and Curtis A. Keim, 217–233.

49 Evans-Pritchard, *The Azande*, 97–98.

50 This care applied to all materials—ivory, metal work, woodcarving, basketry, and pottery—and both artists and ordinary people seem to have participated in an aesthetic preoccupation that extended to the entire material world.

51 This piece was originally commissioned by the Getty Museum as a response to their exhibition of rare photographs of African Americans dating from the 1840s to 1860s, entitled *Hidden Witness: African Americans in Early Photography*. In Weems's provocative response to the Getty, she created her own counternarrative—as an alternate history of slavery and racism in America—that, as curator Thelma Golden writes, "simultaneously embraced and rejected what the museum's photographs represented." Thelma Golden, "Some Thoughts on Carrie Mae Weems," in *Carrie Mae Weems: Recent Works, 1992–1998* (New York: George Brazilier Publisher, in association with Everson Museum of Art, Syracuse, New York, 1998), 29–30.

52 Thomas J. Piché, "Reading Carrie Mae Weems," in *Carrie Mae Weems: Recent Works, 1992–1998*, 11.

53 Ibid., 14.

PLATES

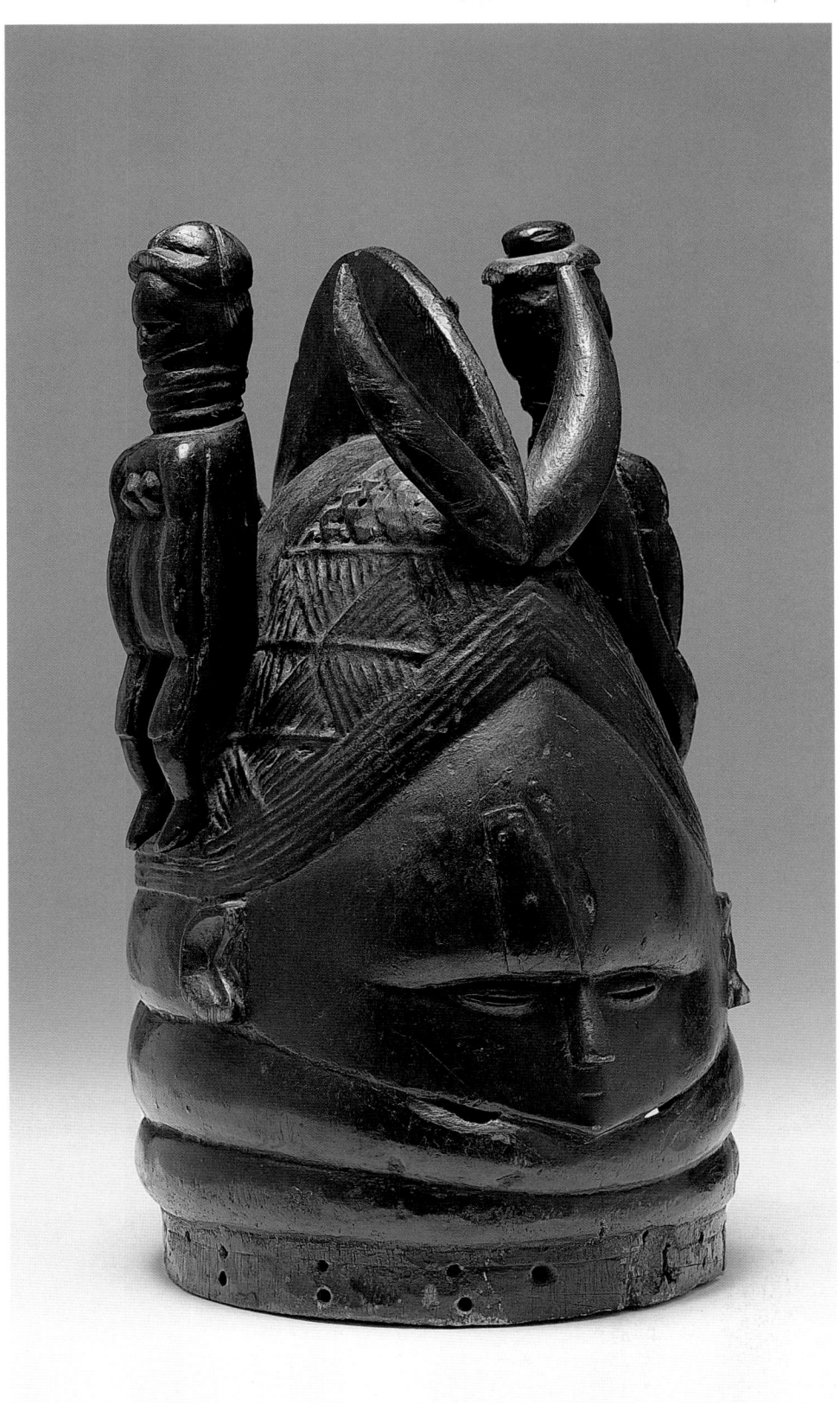

PLATE 1
Unknown artist, Mende peoples, Sierra Leone
Initiation mask (*sowei*), mid-twentieth century
Wood
Hood Museum of Art: Gift of Burton Elliott,
Class of 1948; 992.42.29086
Photograph by Jeffrey Nintzel

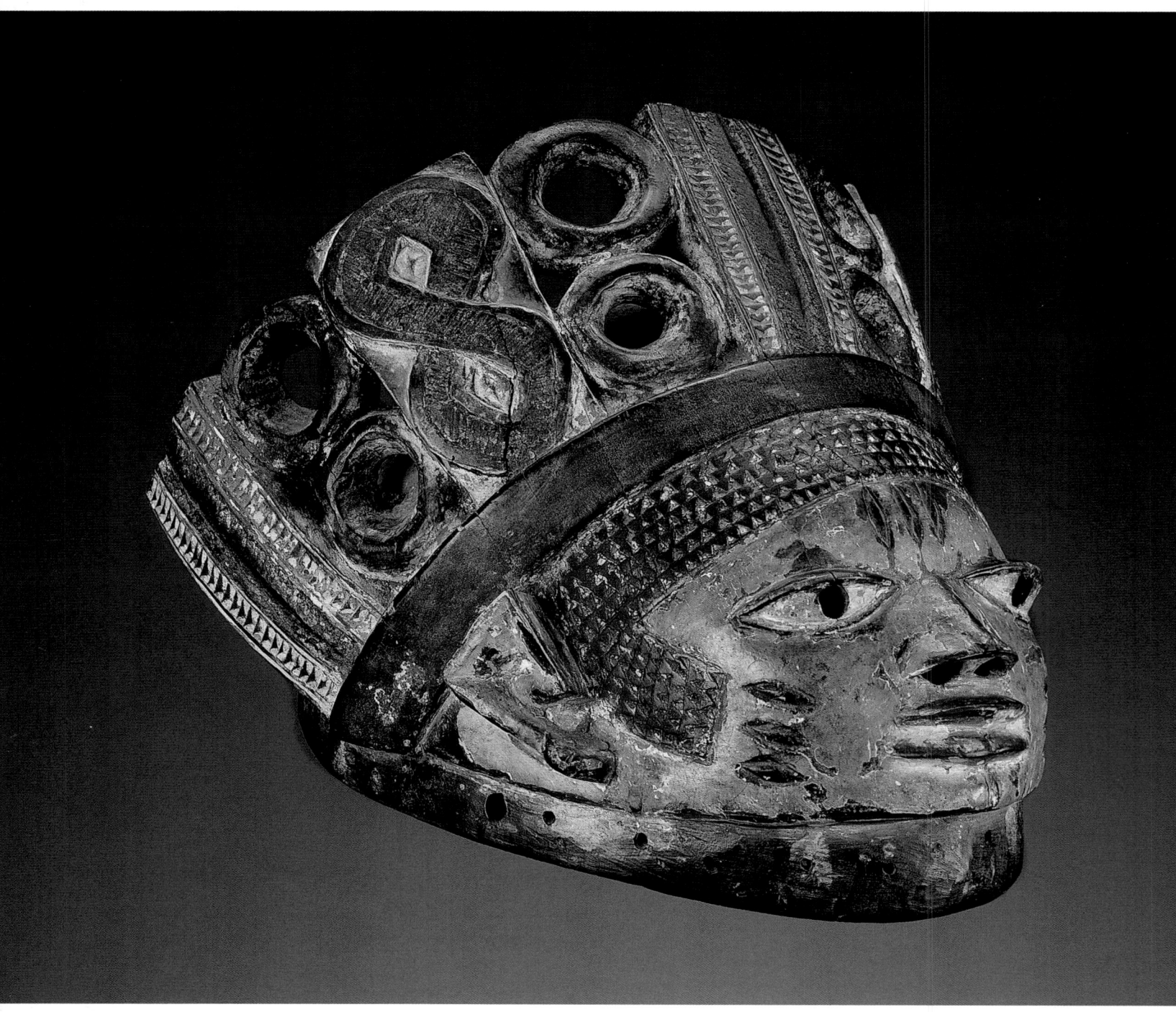

PLATE 2
Unknown artist, Anago Master, Yoruba peoples, Benin
Cap mask (*gelede*), nineteenth century
Wood, pigment
National Museum of African Art: Museum purchase;
97-11-1 Photograph by Franko Khoury, courtesy of
National Museum of African Art, Smithsonian
Institution

EXCHANGES: SOKARI DOUGLAS CAMP I*

Gelede from Top to Toe (plate 96) was made as a reaction to the way that [African] objects in museums are shown out of context. *Gelede* (opposite) masks are part of prized collections in Europe, but collectors I met could not describe the full costume that accompanied the mask. From conversations with London-based Yoruba people who had seen *gelede* in Lagos, I discovered what the full masquerade might look like, as I have never seen a live performance. I loved their stories that the masquerade was played (designed and created) by the sons of female market traders. They would try to copy their mothers by wearing a frame to exaggerate the bottom, the costume had breastplates with erect breasts, dropping breasts, or some had breasts with a child attached. The songs and poetry used by the masqueraders commented on the politics of the day. Different-colored strips of cloth were also used to decorate the costume.

The traditional *gelede* mask is enticing (which is why there are so many in collections). The smooth placid faces, with elaborate carvings swimming out of the head, are like thought bubbles, depicting people on bicycles, forests, or animals. This was an artist's reaction to the *gele* head tie that Nigerian women wear. I have used this format for a series of sculptures. One example was showing the placid face of the *gelede* mask with London council housing and a plane flying overhead. This was my version of a *gele*.

The aim of *Gelede from Top to Toe* was to make a lifesize figure to combat the bodiless portrayal of this vibrant masquerade in museums. My work is influenced by traditional African art in museums and by traditions (performances) in the Delta region in Nigeria where I see masks in action. What I have seen in museums in the West, I would not have been able to have a good look at in my hometown in Nigeria. Representations of women that I have seen in the Delta are performed by men; it is only when I listen to the praise songs in the masquerades that I realize it is a female masquerade. But then there is a bigger concern: the masquerade—whether representing a female or male—is a spirit. The representation of women in a masquerade performance is poor; they seem to play a secondary shadowy role. And when women perform with men, they have to have passed the age of menstruation. And yet our traditional God in Kalabari is female. All these factors play a part in my view of women.

* Sokari Douglas Camp, personal communication with Barbara Thompson, January 14, 2007.

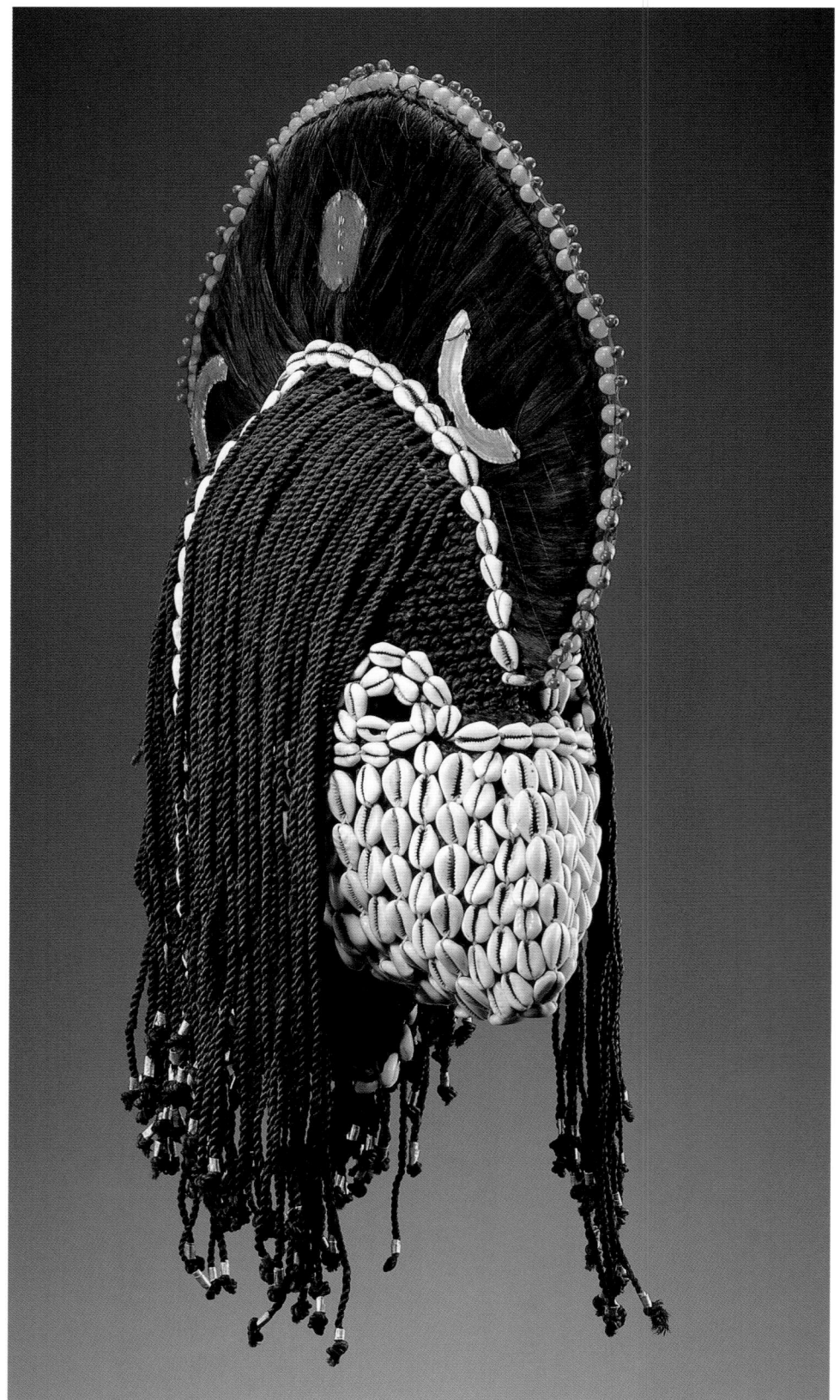

PLATE 3
Unknown artist, Dogon peoples, Mali
Fiber mask (*bede*), c. 1968
Fiber, cowrie shells, plastic beads, metal, cloth
National Museum of African Art:
Gift of Dr. William H. Stewart; 84-9-1
Photograph by Franko Khoury, courtesy
of National Museum of African Art,
Smithsonian Institution

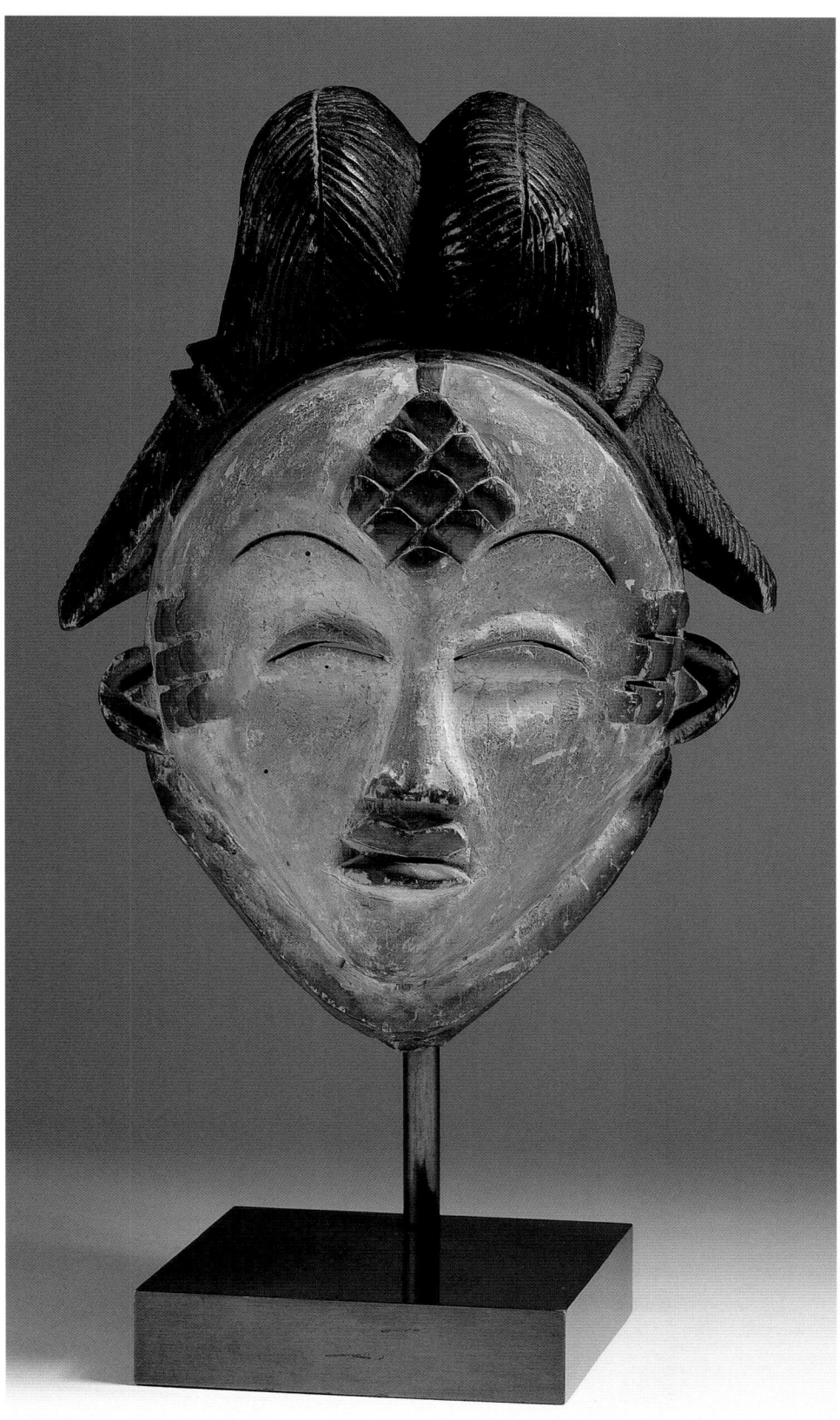

PLATE 4
Unknown artist, Punu peoples, Gabon
Female mask (*mukudj*), nineteenth to
twentieth century
Wood, kaolin
Hood Museum of Art: Purchased through
the Mrs. Harvey P. Hood W'18 Fund;
2004.17.35574
Photograph by Jeffrey Nintzel

PLATE 5
Unknown artist, Baule peoples, Côte d'Ivoire
Female figure (*blolo bla*), mid-twentieth century
Wood, glass beads, plant fiber
National Museum of African Art: Gift from the
collection of Toby and Barry Hecht; 2000-26-1
Photograph by Franko Khoury, courtesy
of National Museum of African Art,
Smithsonian Institution

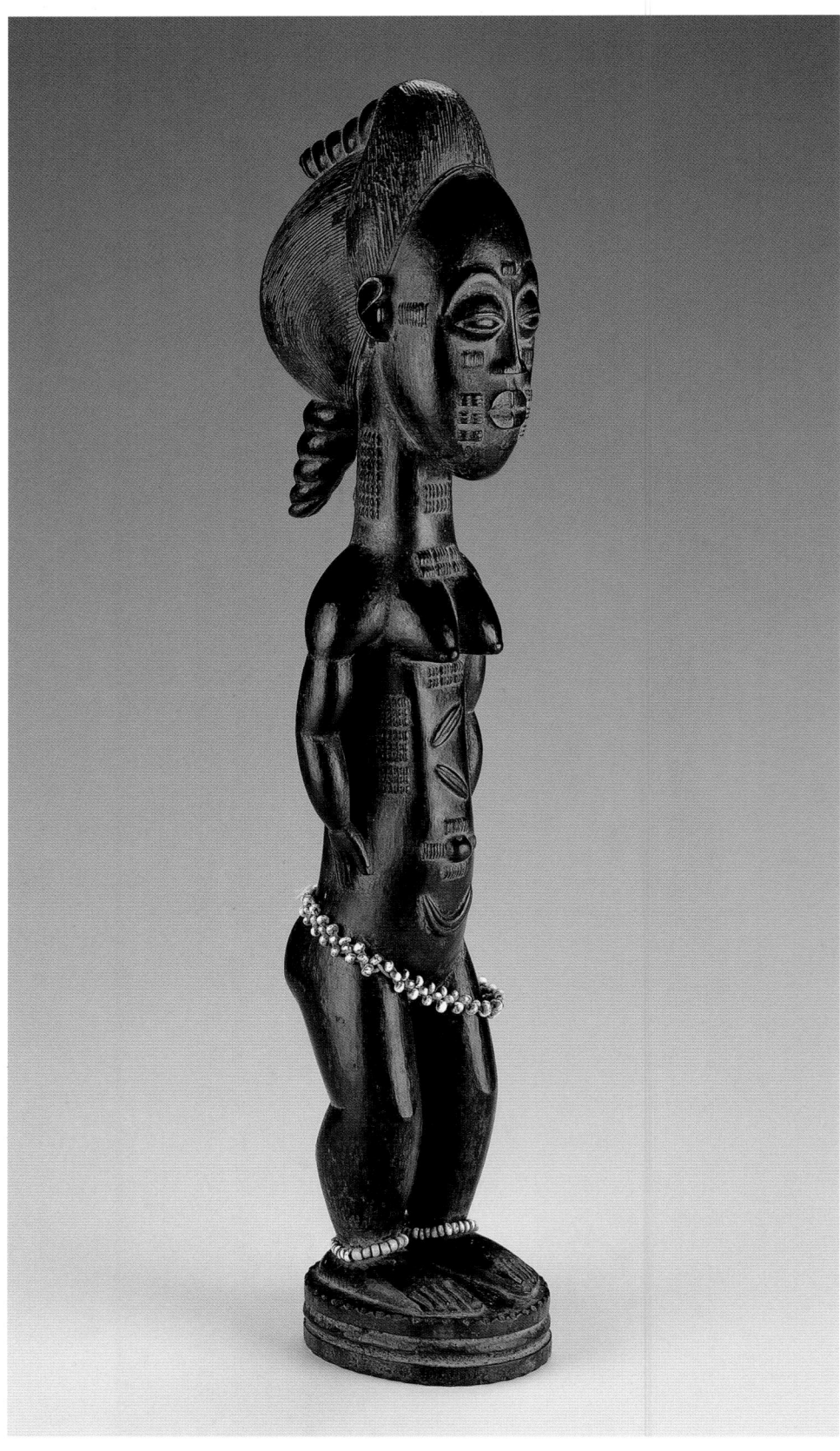

opposite PLATE 6
Unknown artist, Kurumba peoples, Burkina Faso
Storage vessel, mid-twentieth century
Terracotta
Collection of Bill and Gale Simmons, New York
Photograph by Bruce White

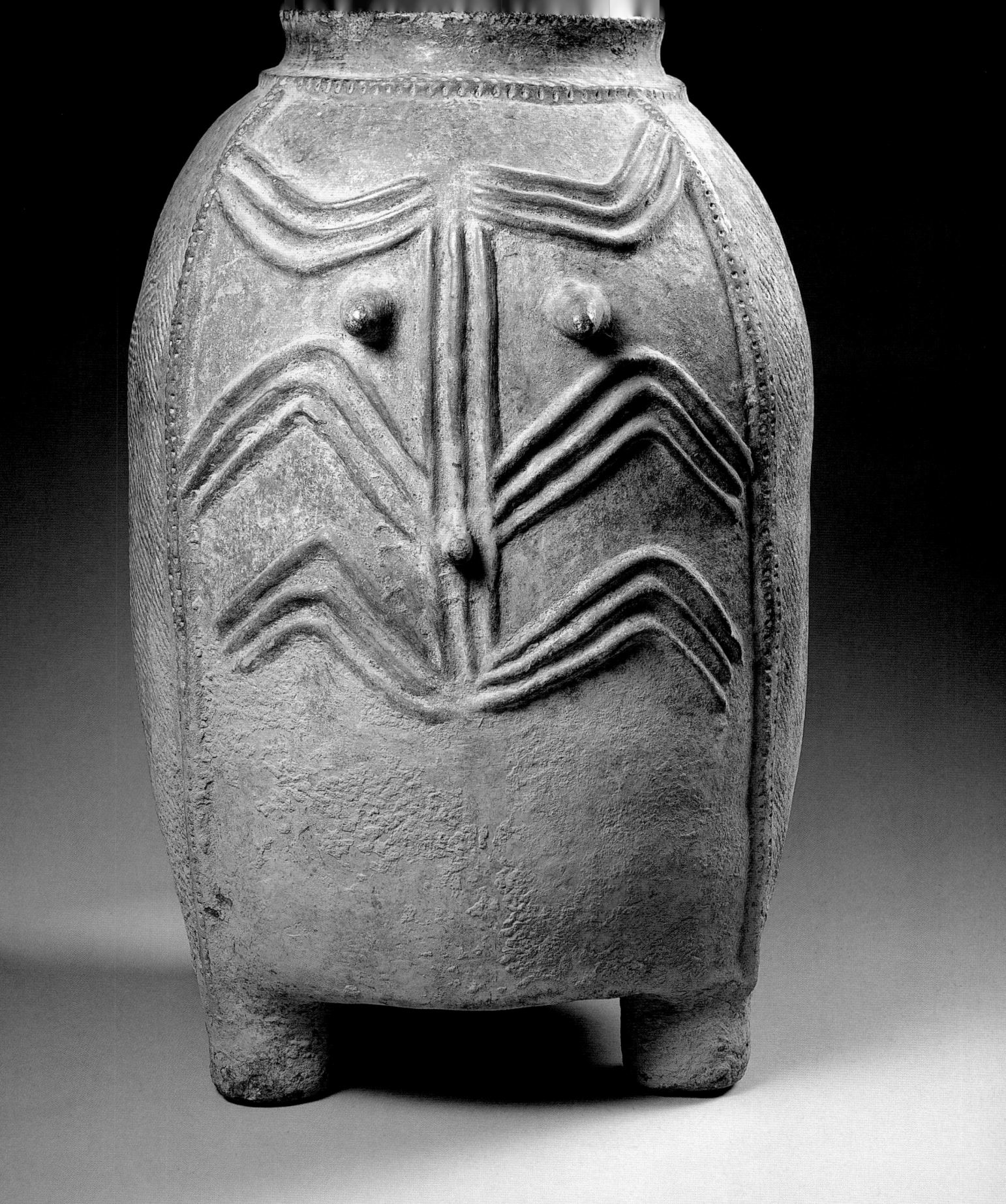

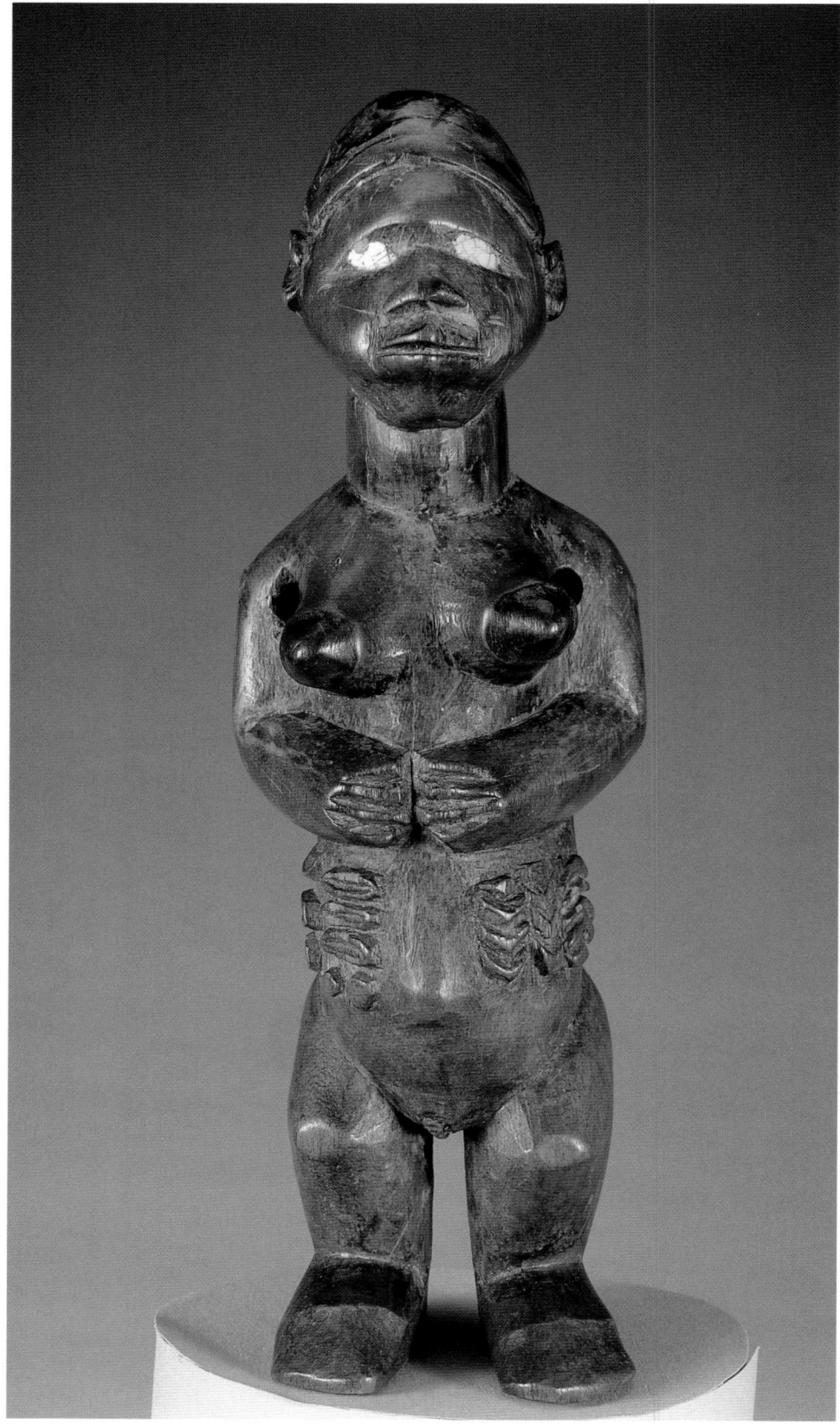

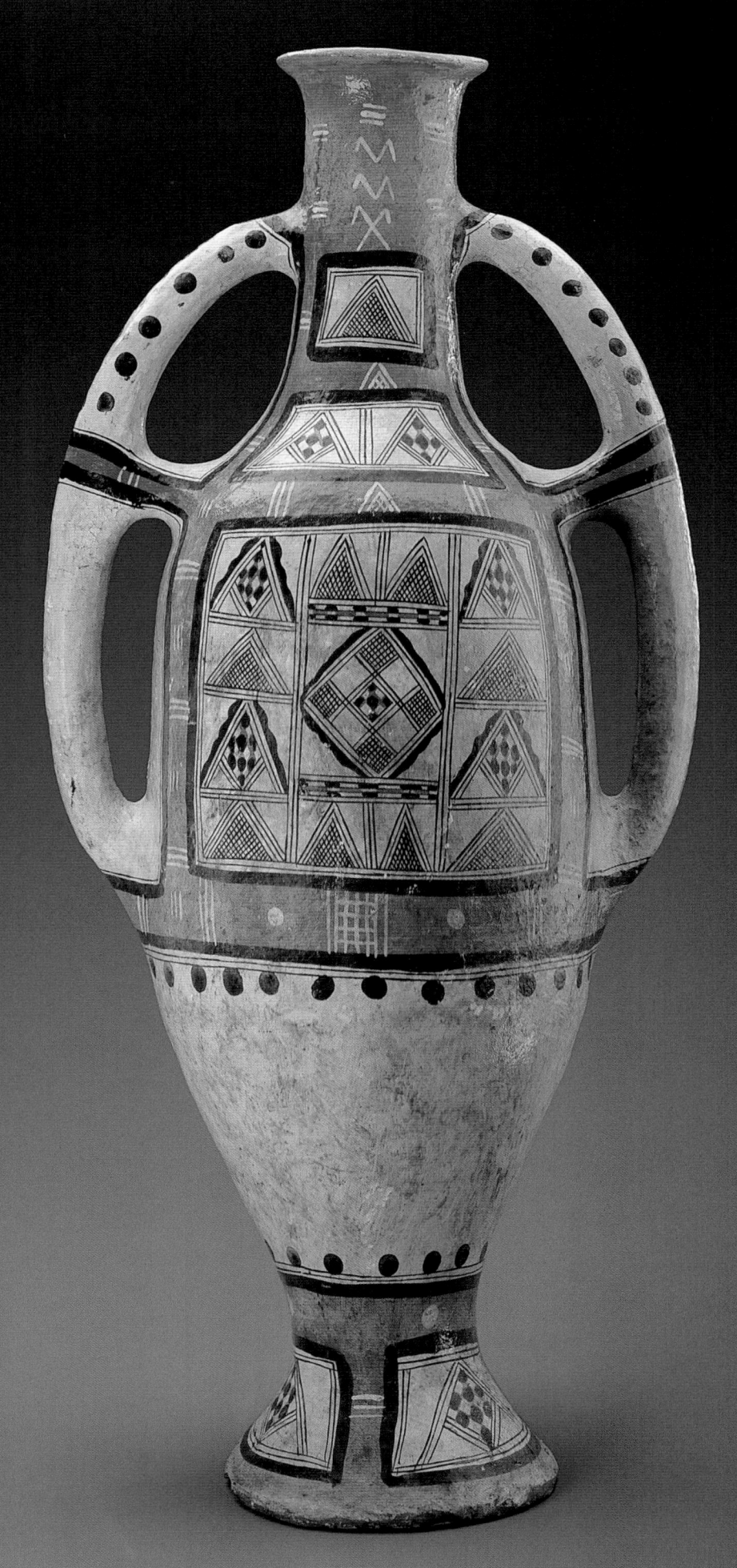

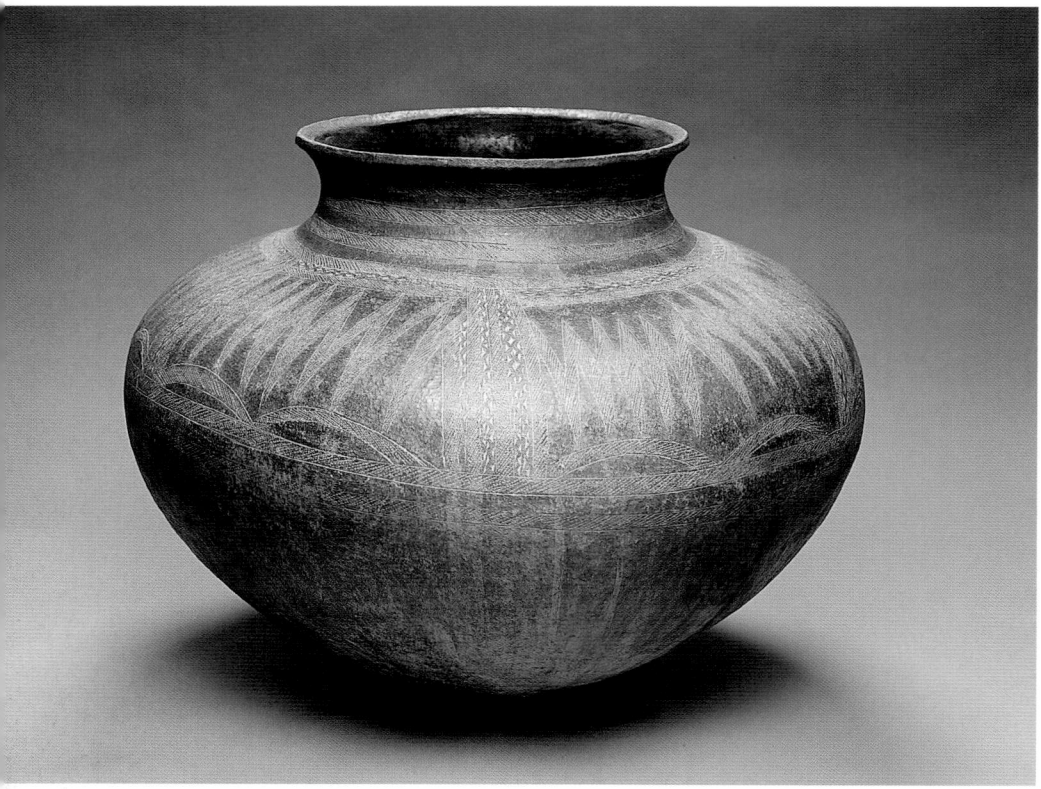

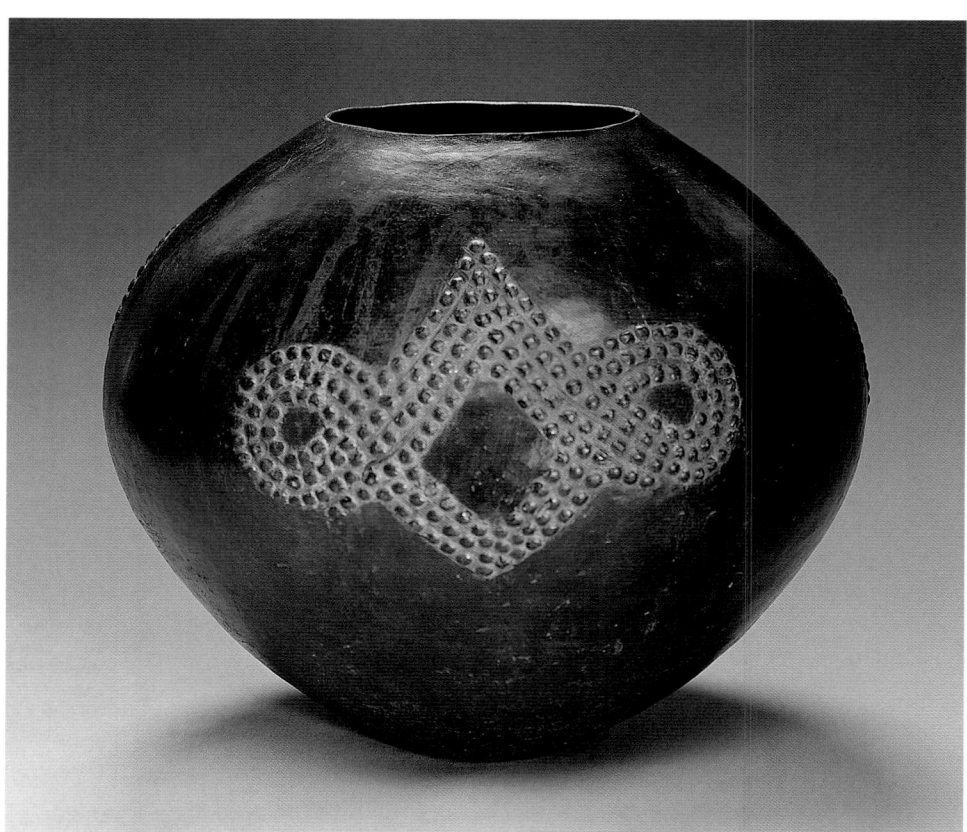

PLATE 11
Unknown artist, Fulani peoples, Chad
Bowl, 1970–1973
Gourd, pigment
National Museum of African Art:
Gift of Ellen Patterson Brown; 94-2-1
Photograph by Franko Khoury, courtesy
of National Museum of African Art,
Smithsonian Institution

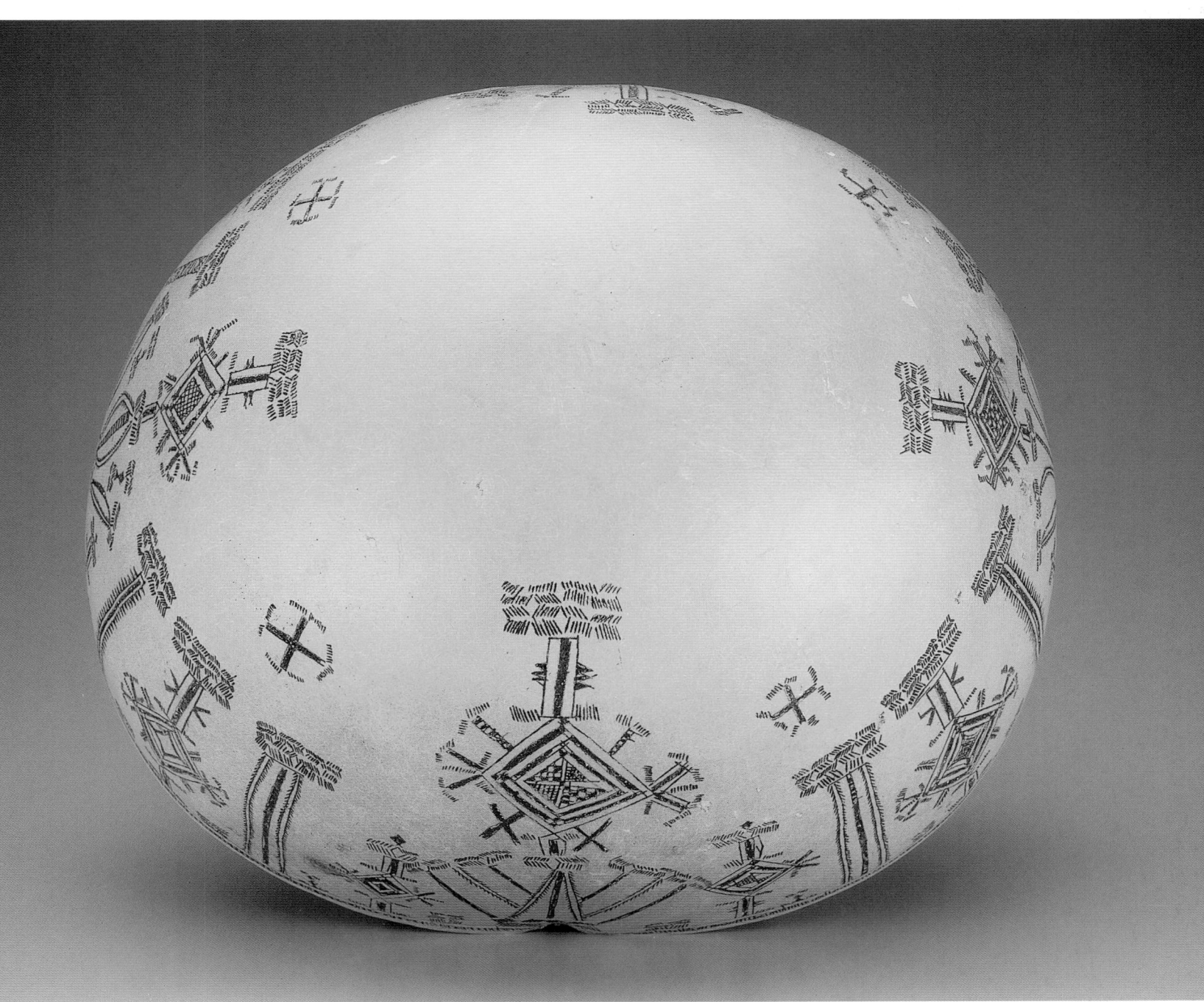

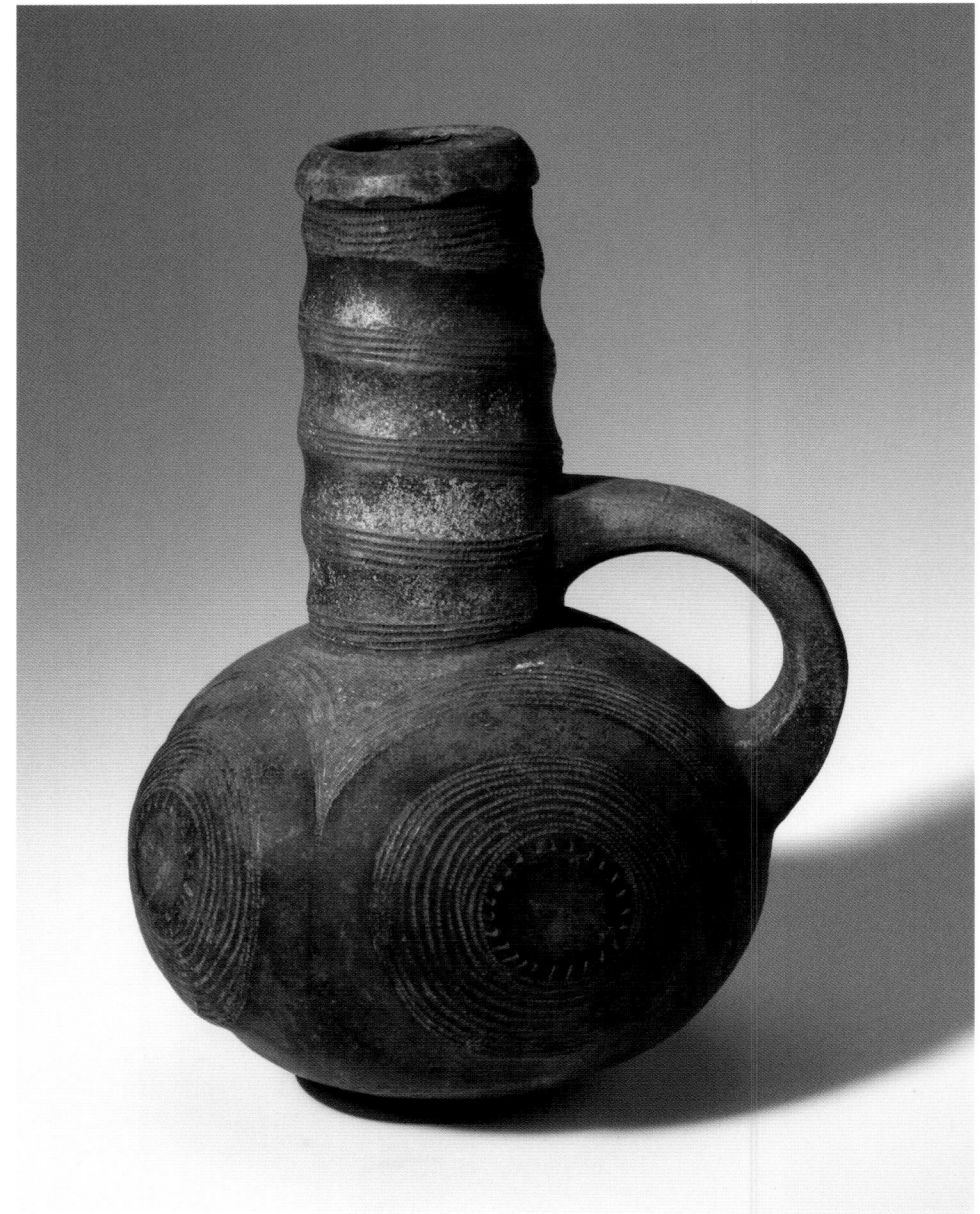

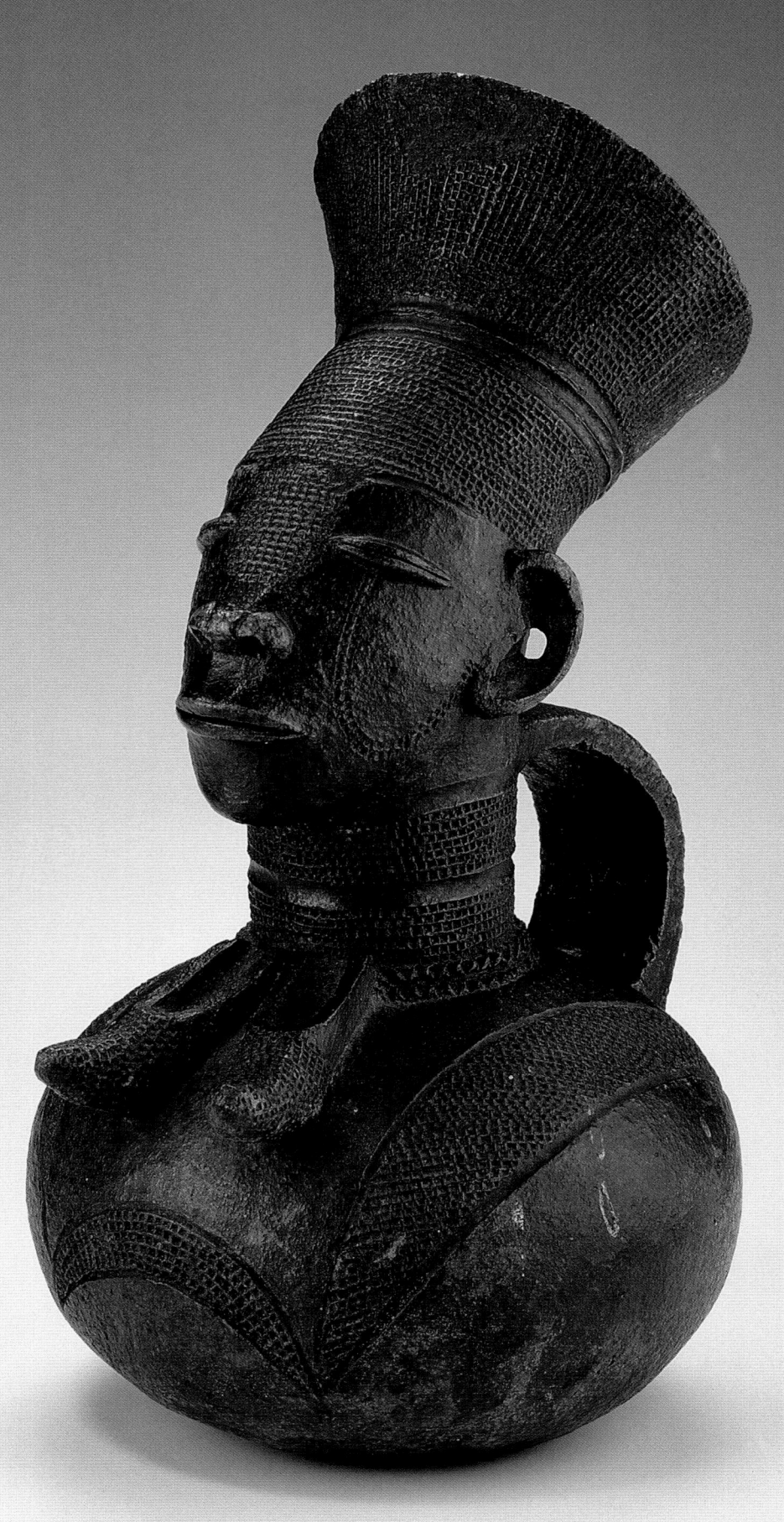

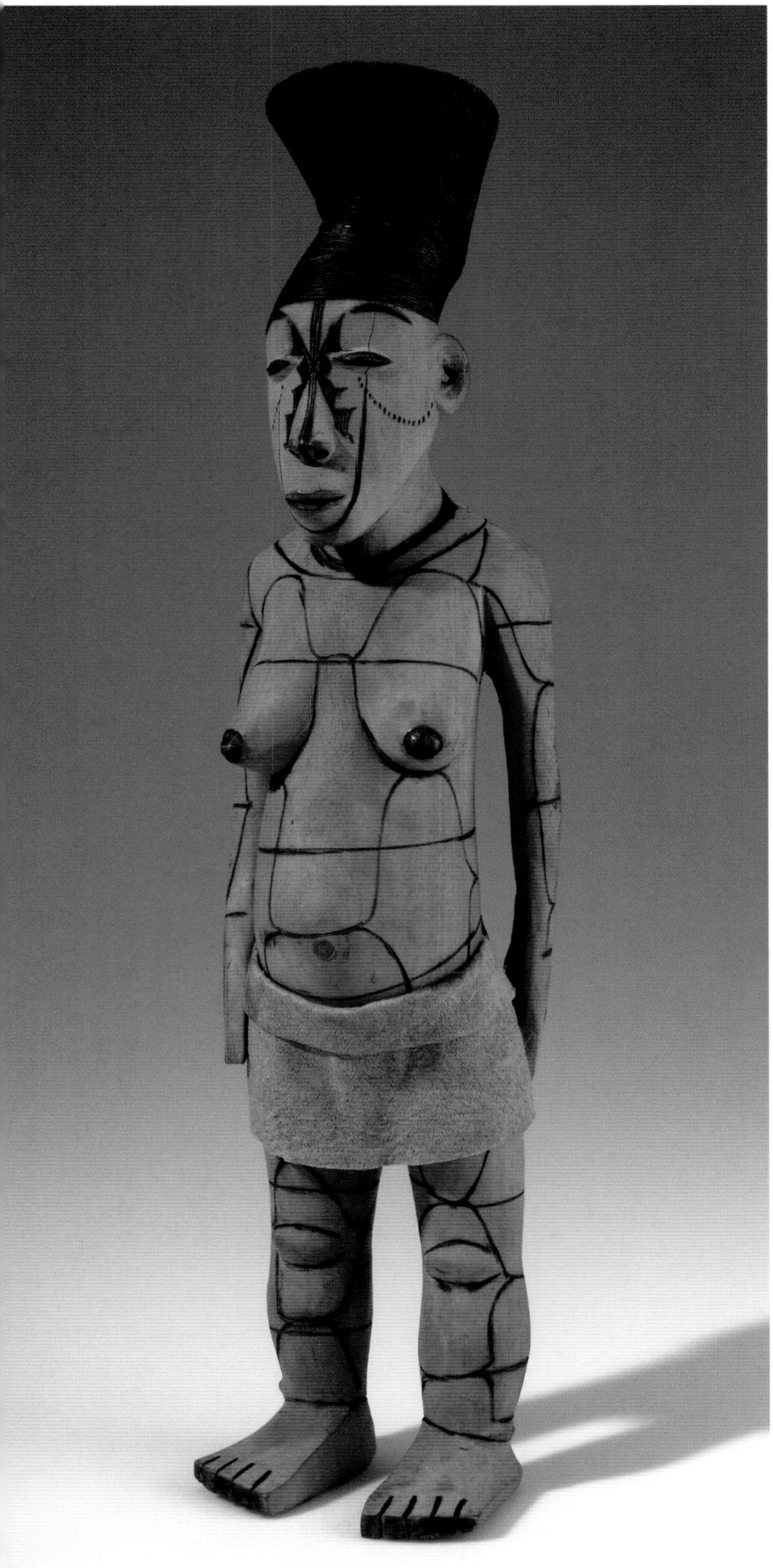

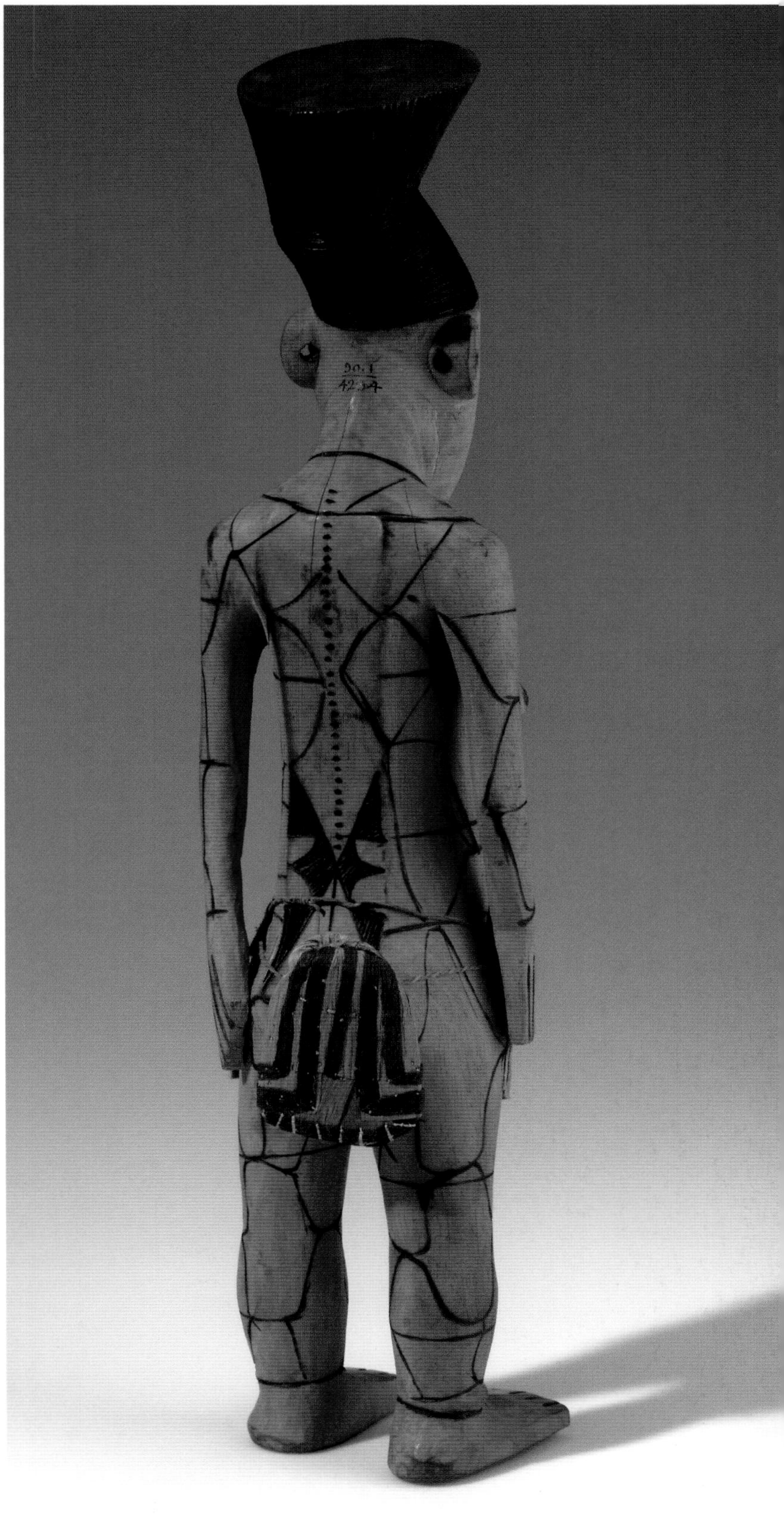

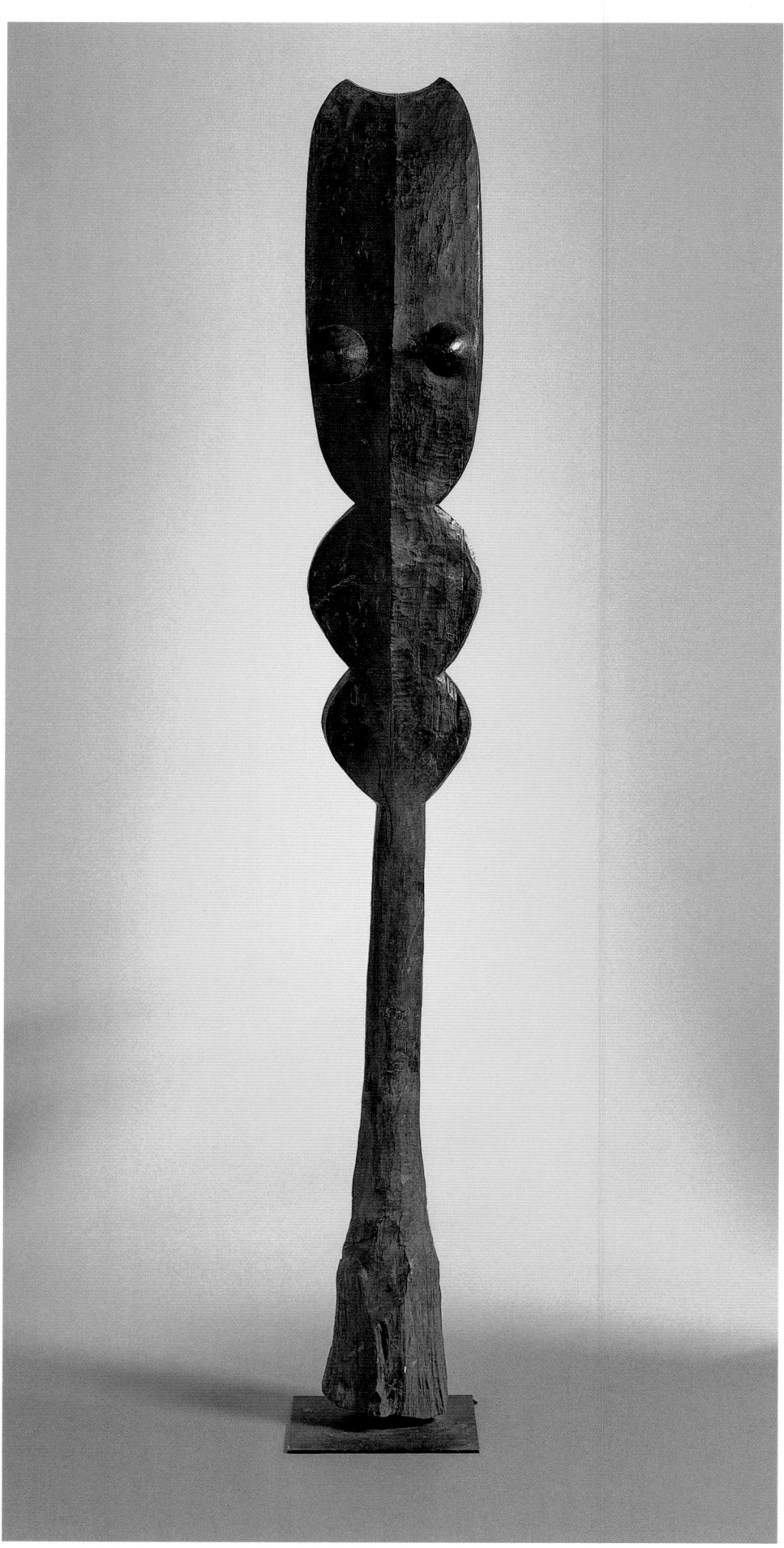

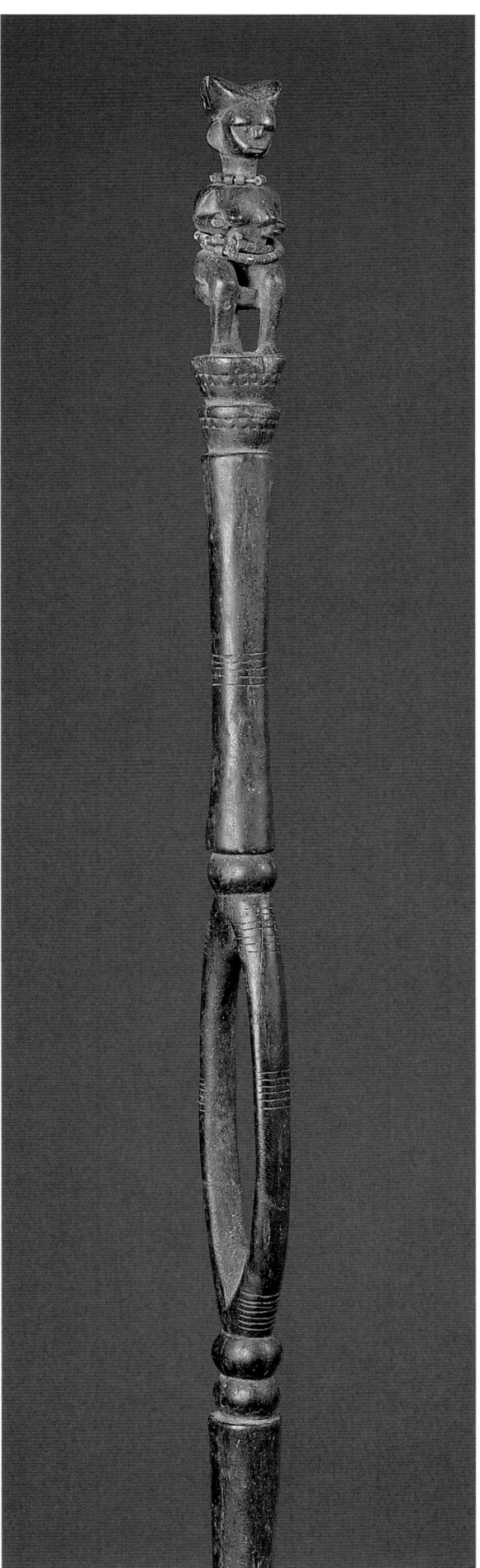

PLATE 17
Unknown artist, Kwere peoples, Tanzania
Initiation staff, twentieth century
Wood, glass beads
Hood Museum of Art: Purchased through the
Phyllis and Bertram Geller 1937 Memorial
Fund; 2006.41
Photograph by Jeffrey Nintzel

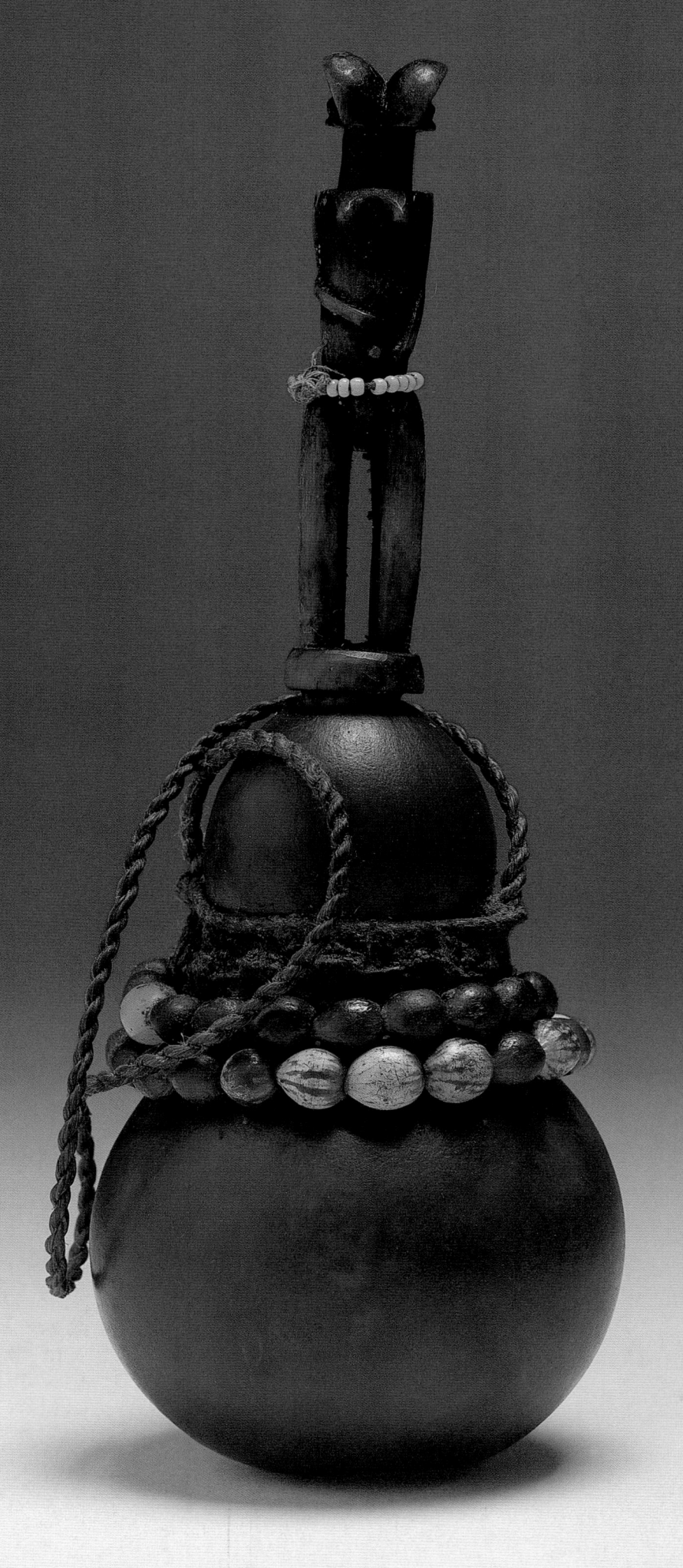

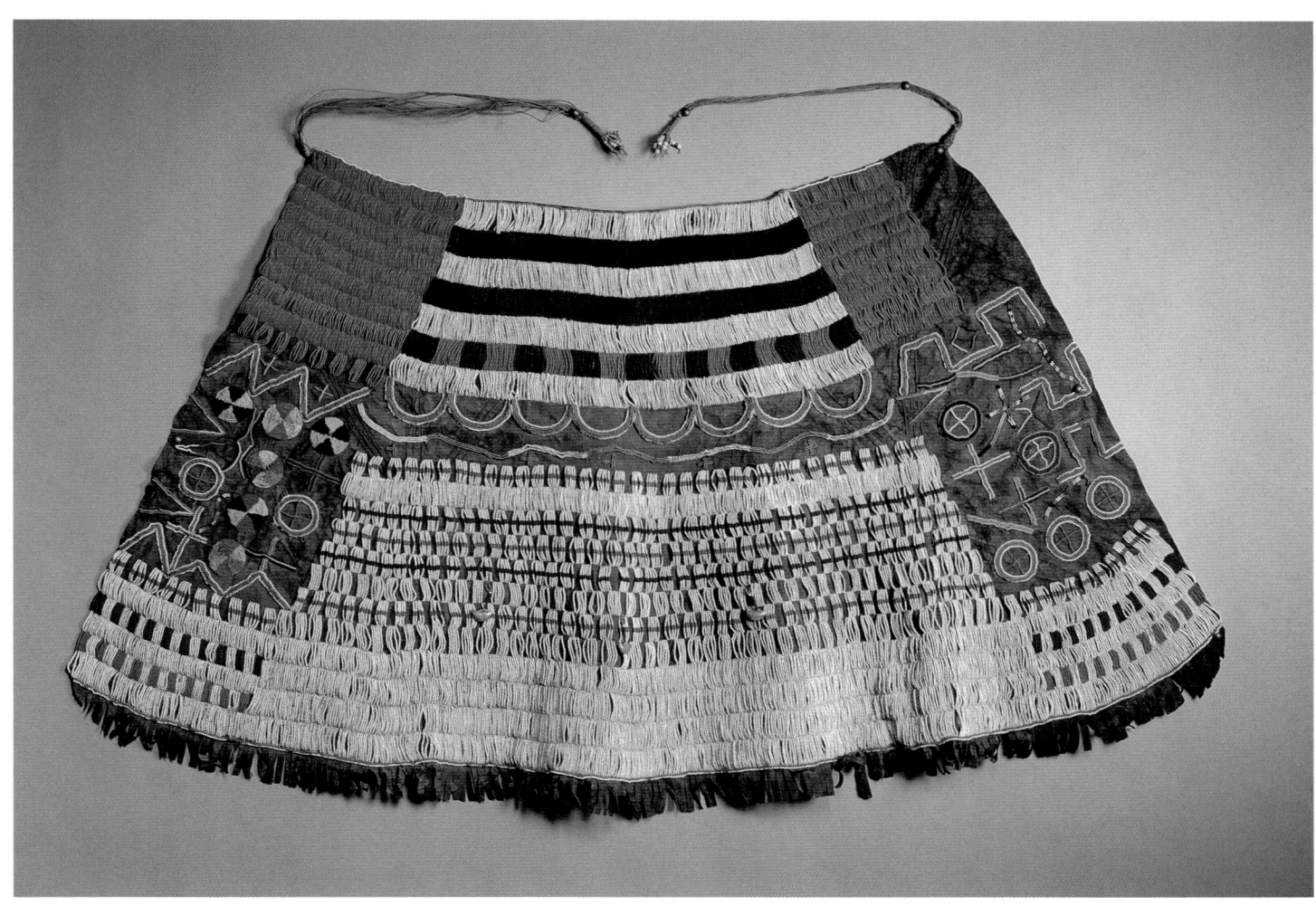

opposite

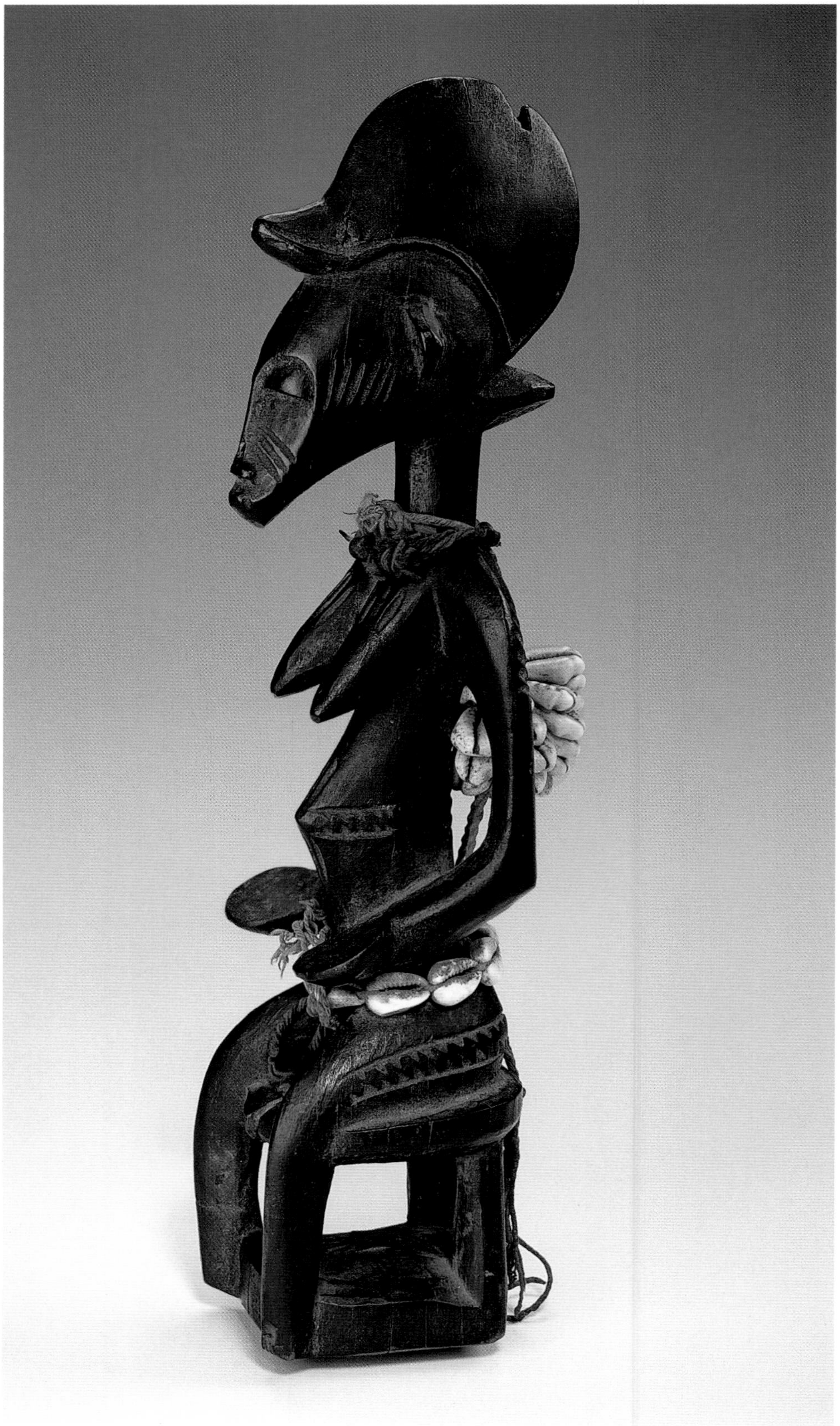

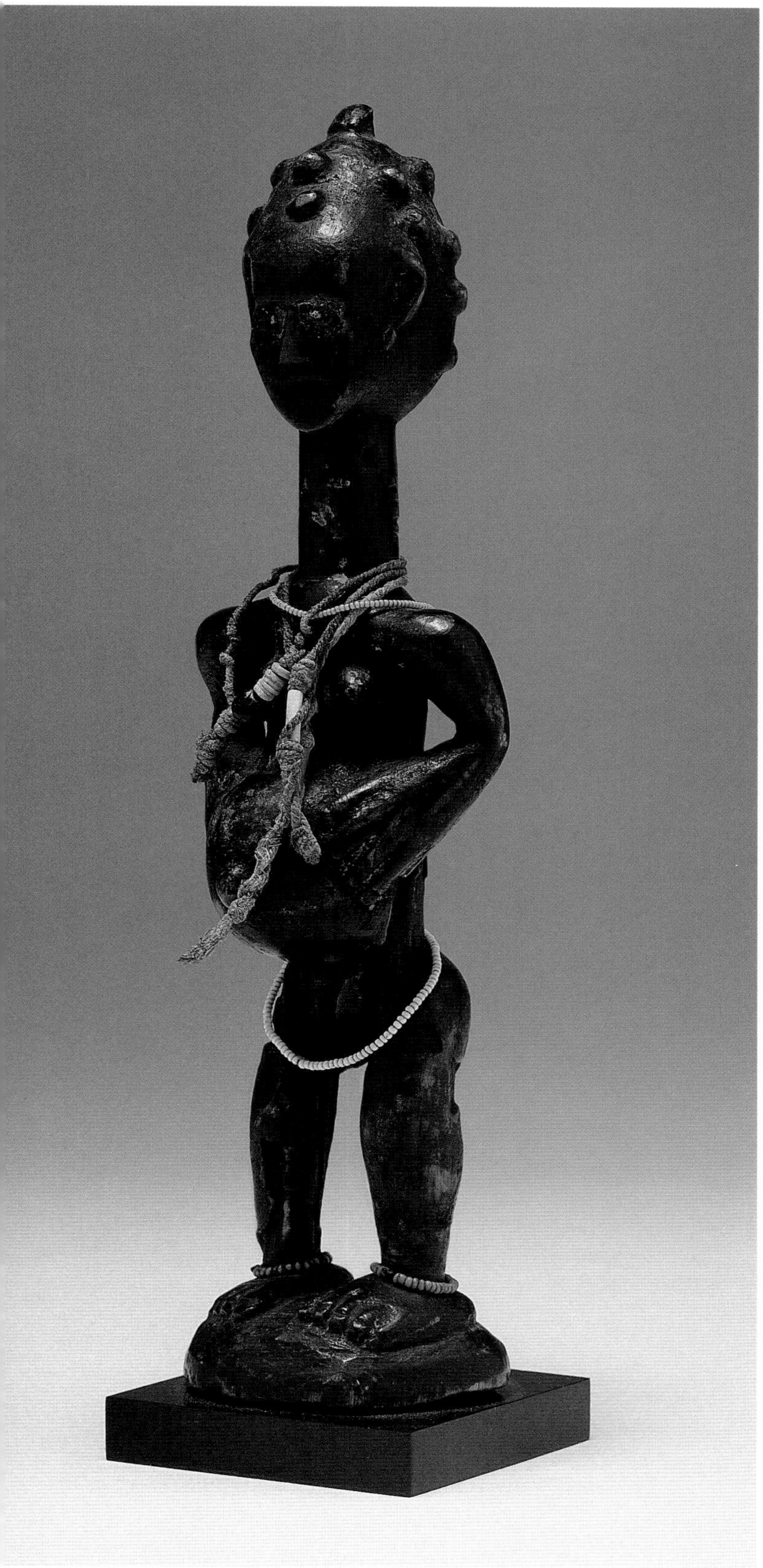

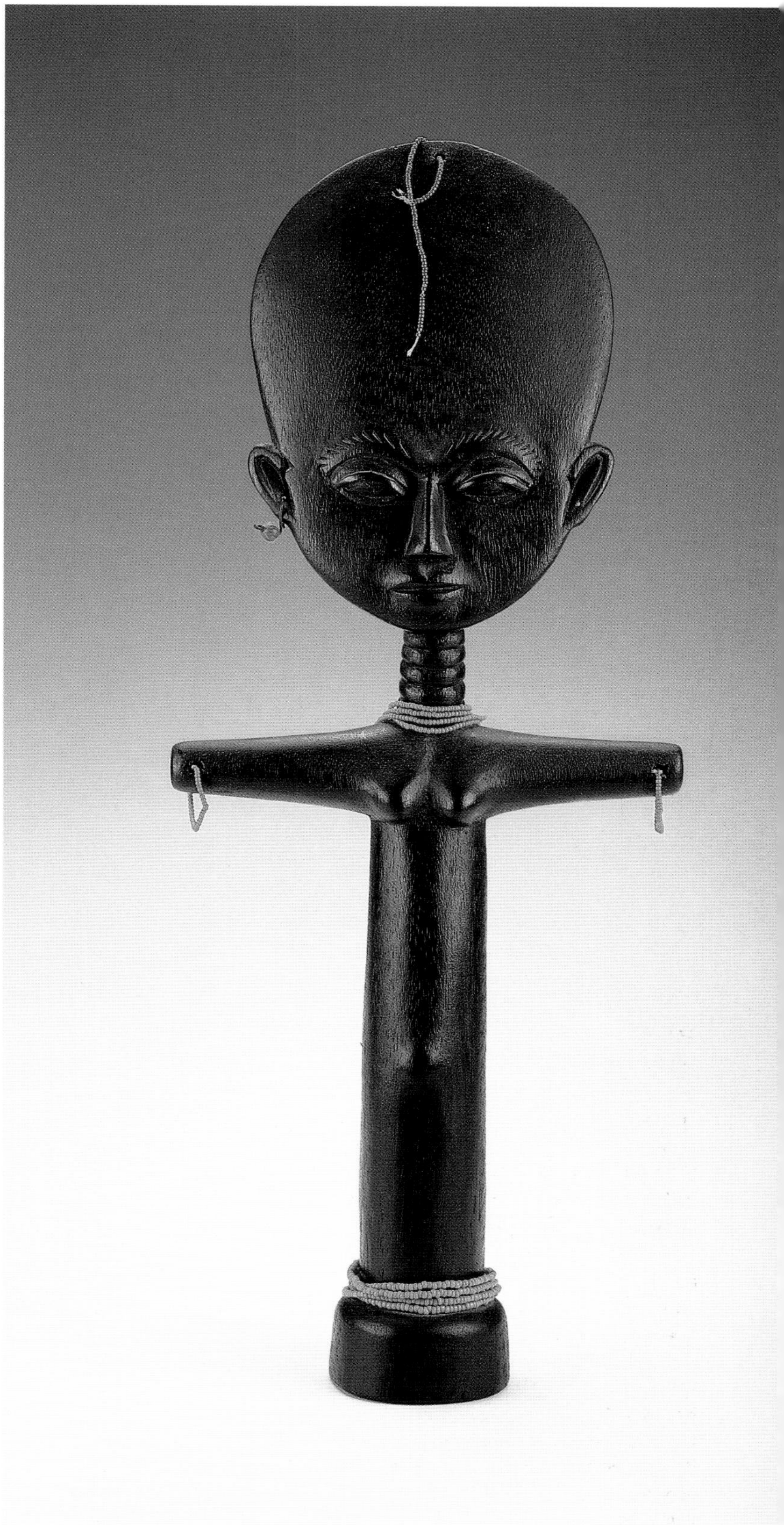

PLATE 23
Unknown artist, Nupe peoples, Nigeria
Vessel, nineteenth to twentieth century
Terracotta
Collection of Bill and Gale Simmons, New York
Photograph by Bruce White

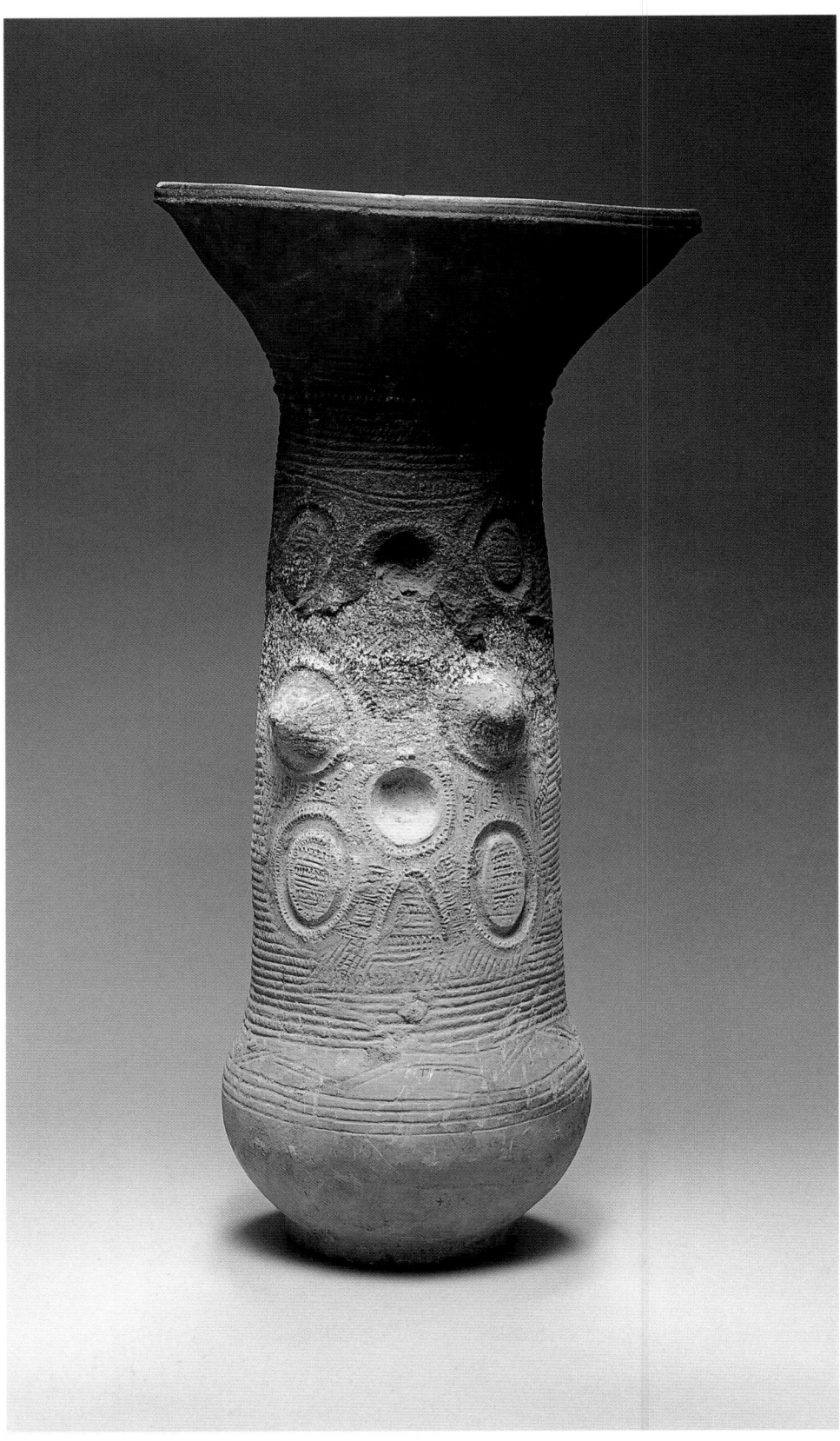

opposite PLATE 24
Unknown artist, Mambila peoples, Nigeria
Vessel, nineteenth to twentieth century
Terracotta
Collection of Bill and Gale Simmons, New York
Photograph by Bruce White

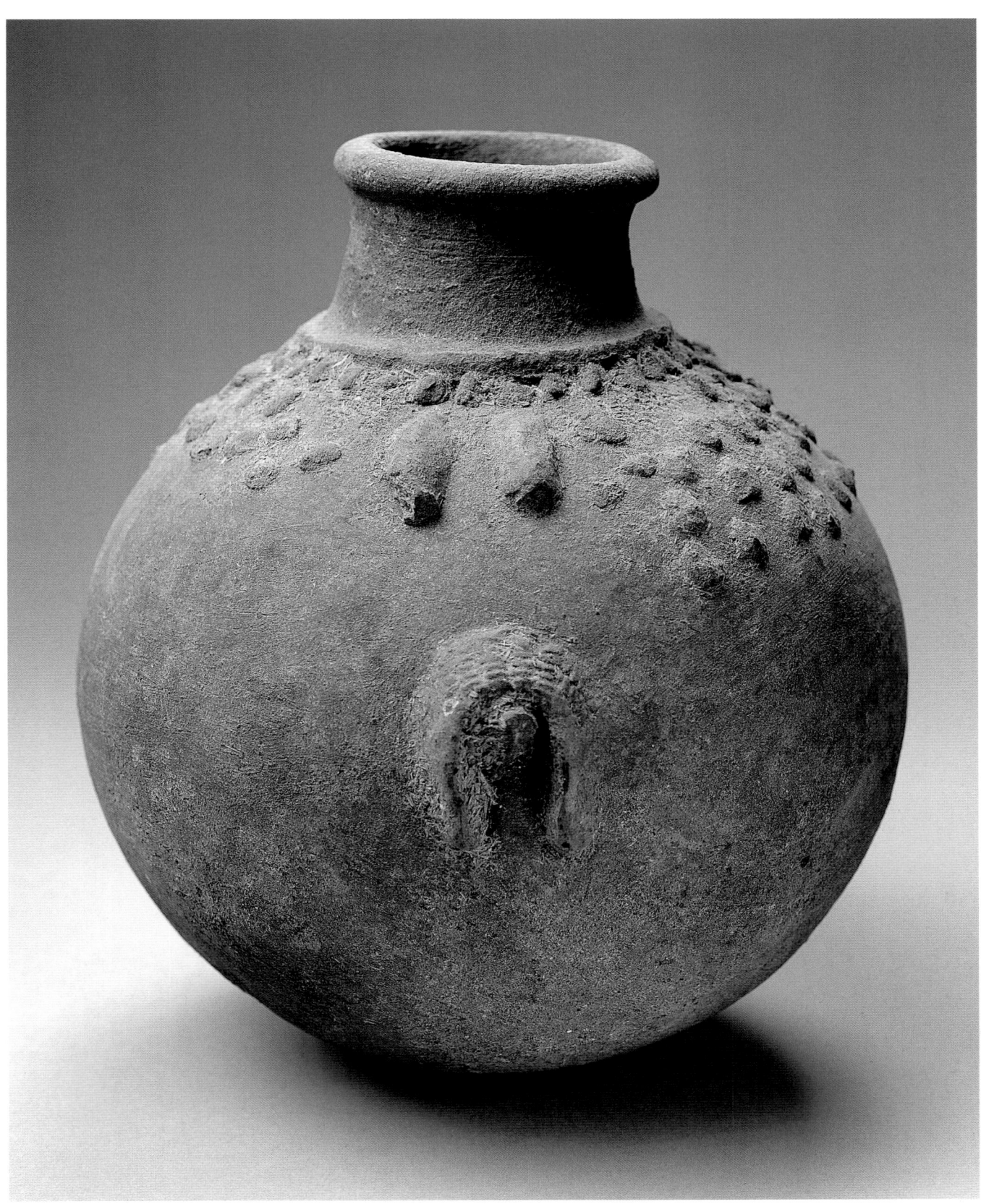

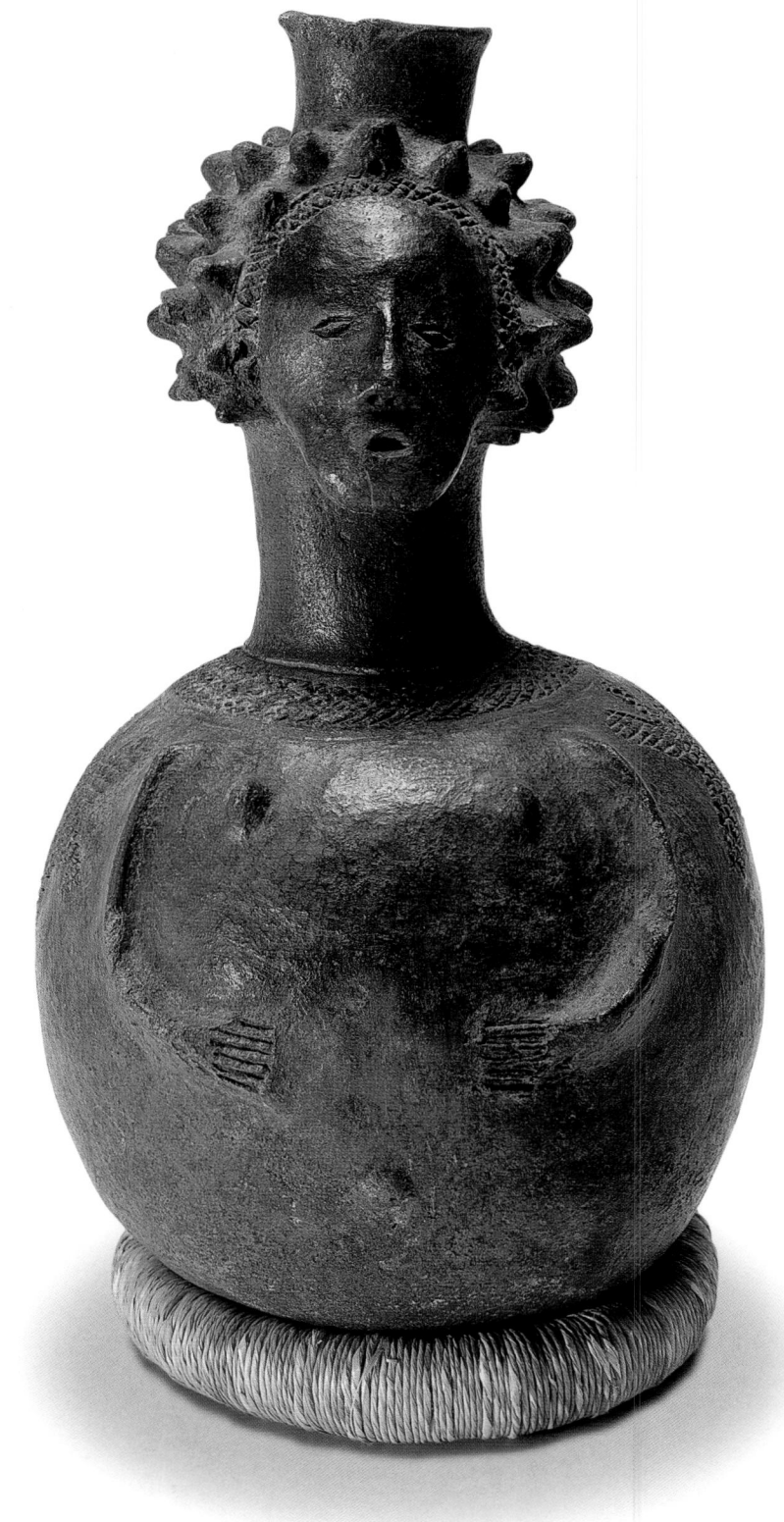

PLATE 25
Unknown artist, Mangbele peoples,
Democratic Republic of Congo
Vessel in female form, nineteenth to
twentieth century
Terracotta
His Royal Highness, Duke Franz of Bavaria;
FVB1101
Photograph by Min-An Wu

opposite PLATE 26
Unknown artist, Makonde peoples, Tanzania
Breastplate (*njorowe*), nineteenth to
twentieth century
Wood, beeswax, iron, fiber, pigment
Hood Museum of Art: Purchased through
the Julia L. Whittier Fund; 2005.69
Photograph by Jeffrey Nintzel

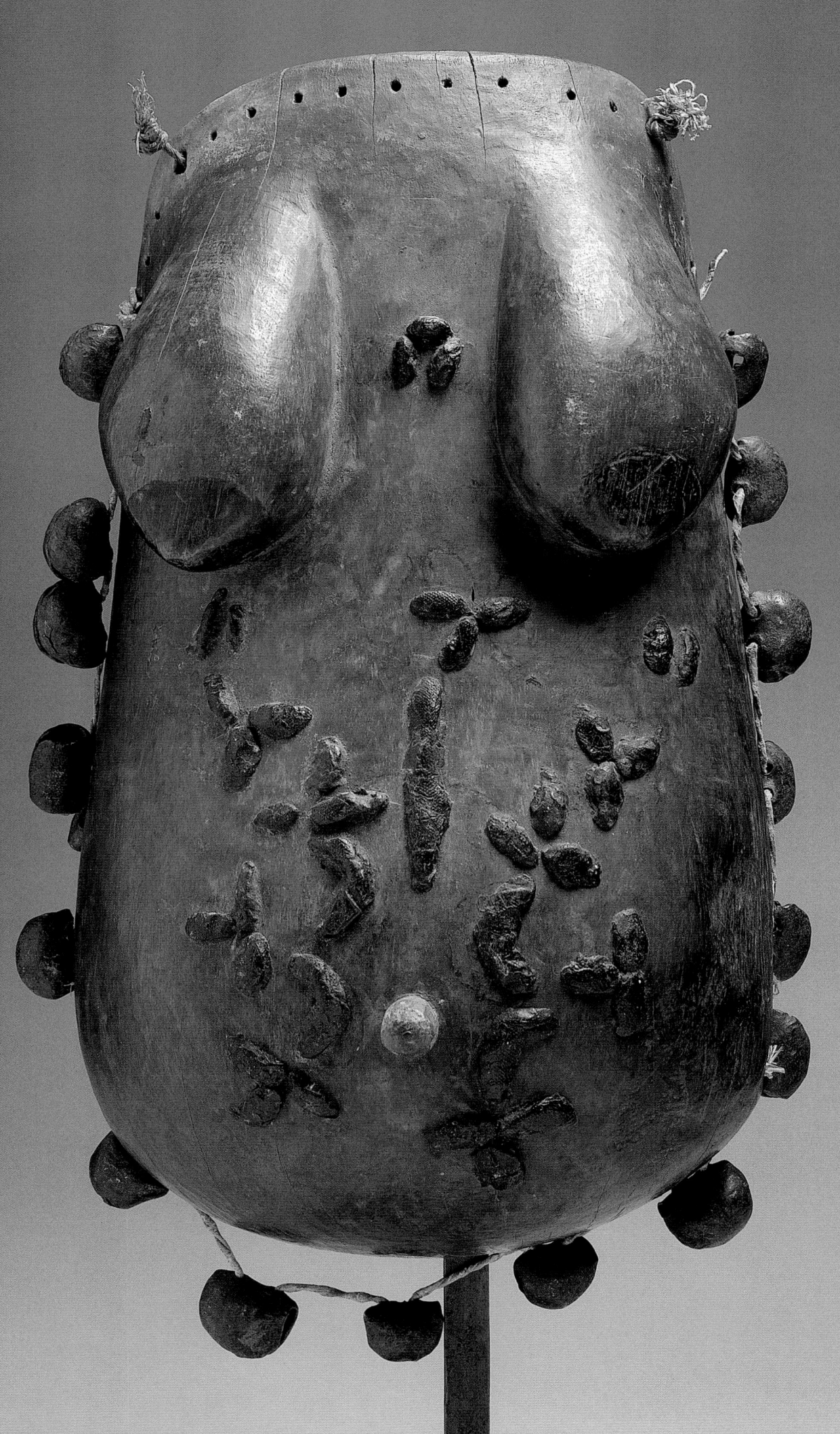

EXCHANGES: NANDIPHA MNTAMBO*

My work (plate 97) has been an investigation into the subjective nature of the things that I experience in my conscious state and how these relate into the dreams that influence my artistic creation. I create work in a material that historically has specific associations and is linked to my cultural background in certain ways but exists within a context also that is removed from these aspects. Subjective views of the significance of [cowhide], drawn from the past but with reference to the present, are particularly interesting to me. The cultural and historical memory of this material is a continuous element in the interpretation and experience of my work. It has increasingly become important to begin accepting past thoughts on the material and uncovering new/contemporary thoughts and how these could influence my own understanding of this material.

The mixed reactions I have received in response to my work have made it clear that some see this process as "'taboo," *something not done.* I have recently become aware that some viewers of my work [in South Africa] were under the assumption that I was a male artist because of the material [cowhide] I have chosen to use. These viewers, from various cultural groups and ages but all male, were unaware of my name or background but thought that I had to be a man because according to them, working with hide is "'hard work, only for men to do." These men were interested, repelled, attracted, and confused both by me (my actual appearance versus what they were expecting) and my artwork (material and subject matter).

* Artist statement for master's thesis "Locating me in order to see you," Capetown University, Michaelis School of Fine Arts, 2006.

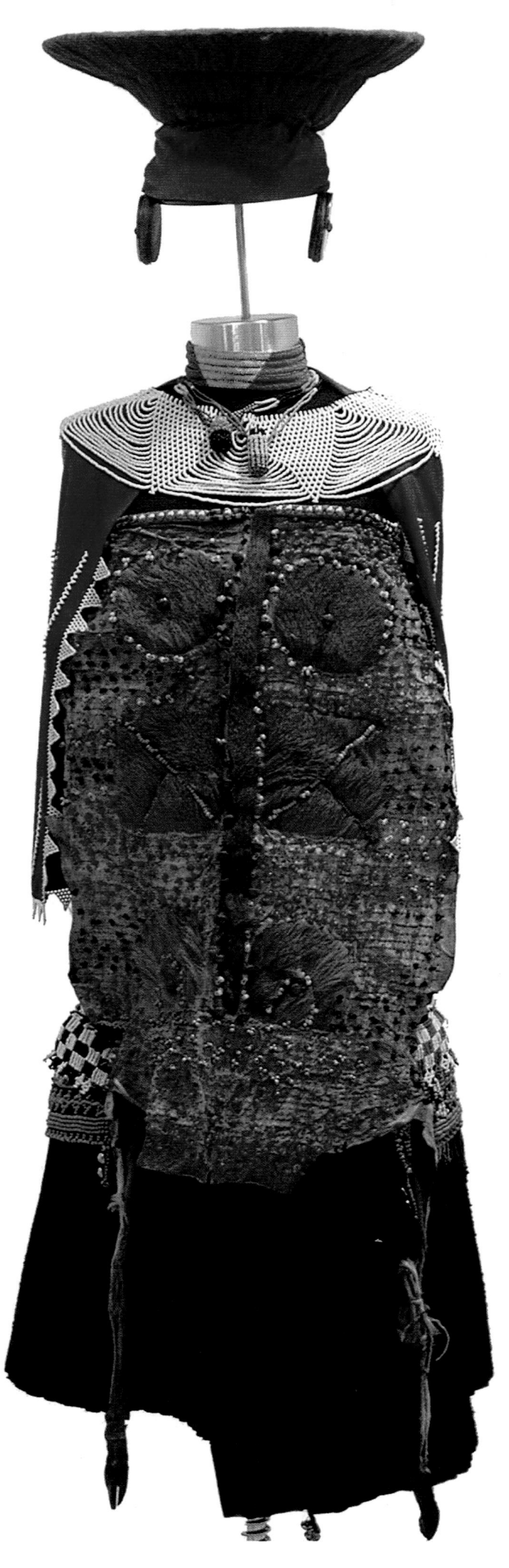

PLATE 27
Unknown artist, Msinga-Zulu peoples,
South Africa
Married woman's dress, late nineteenth to
mid-twentieth century
Cloth, leather, beads, metal
Axis Gallery
Photograph courtesy of Axis Gallery

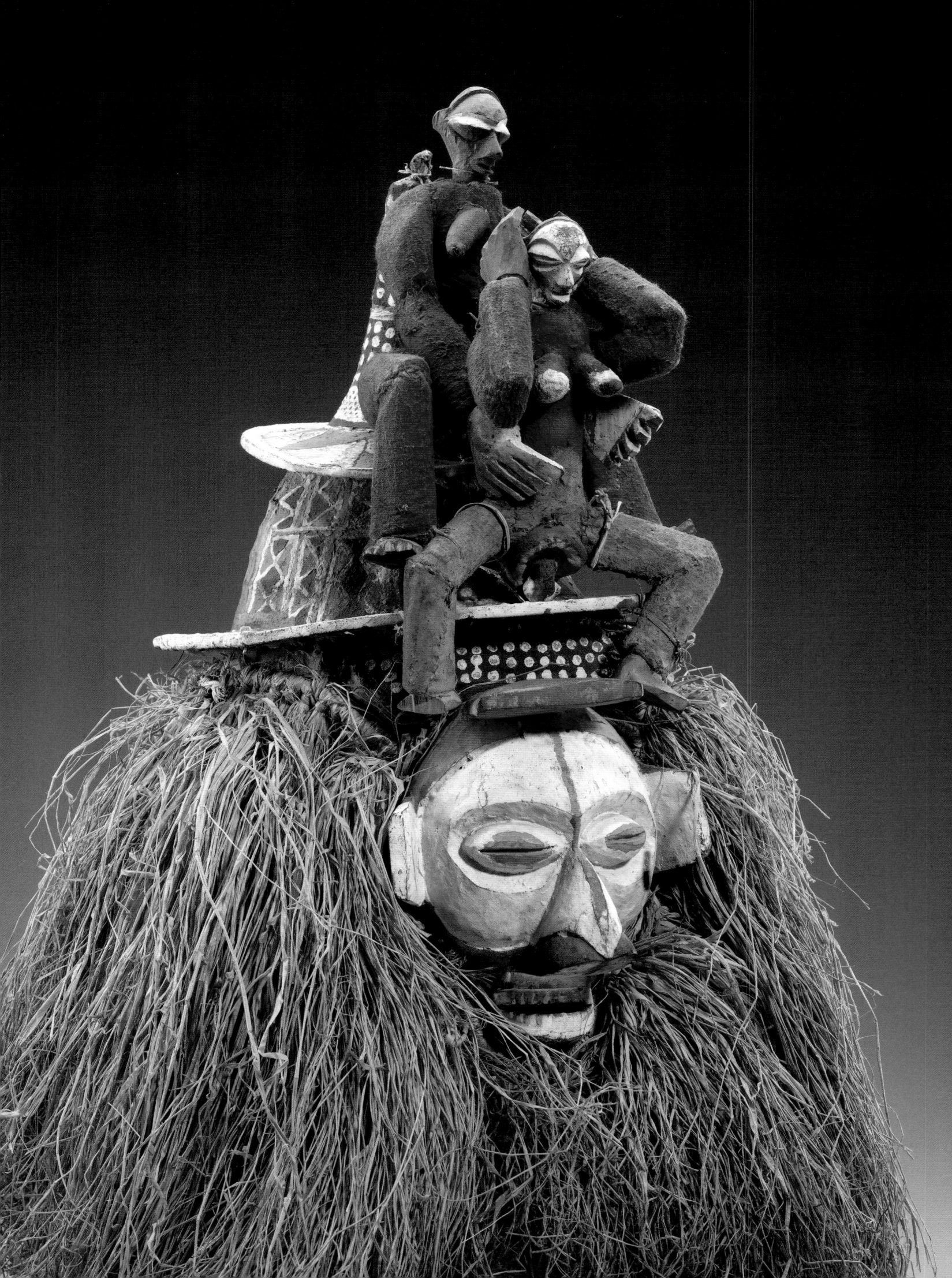

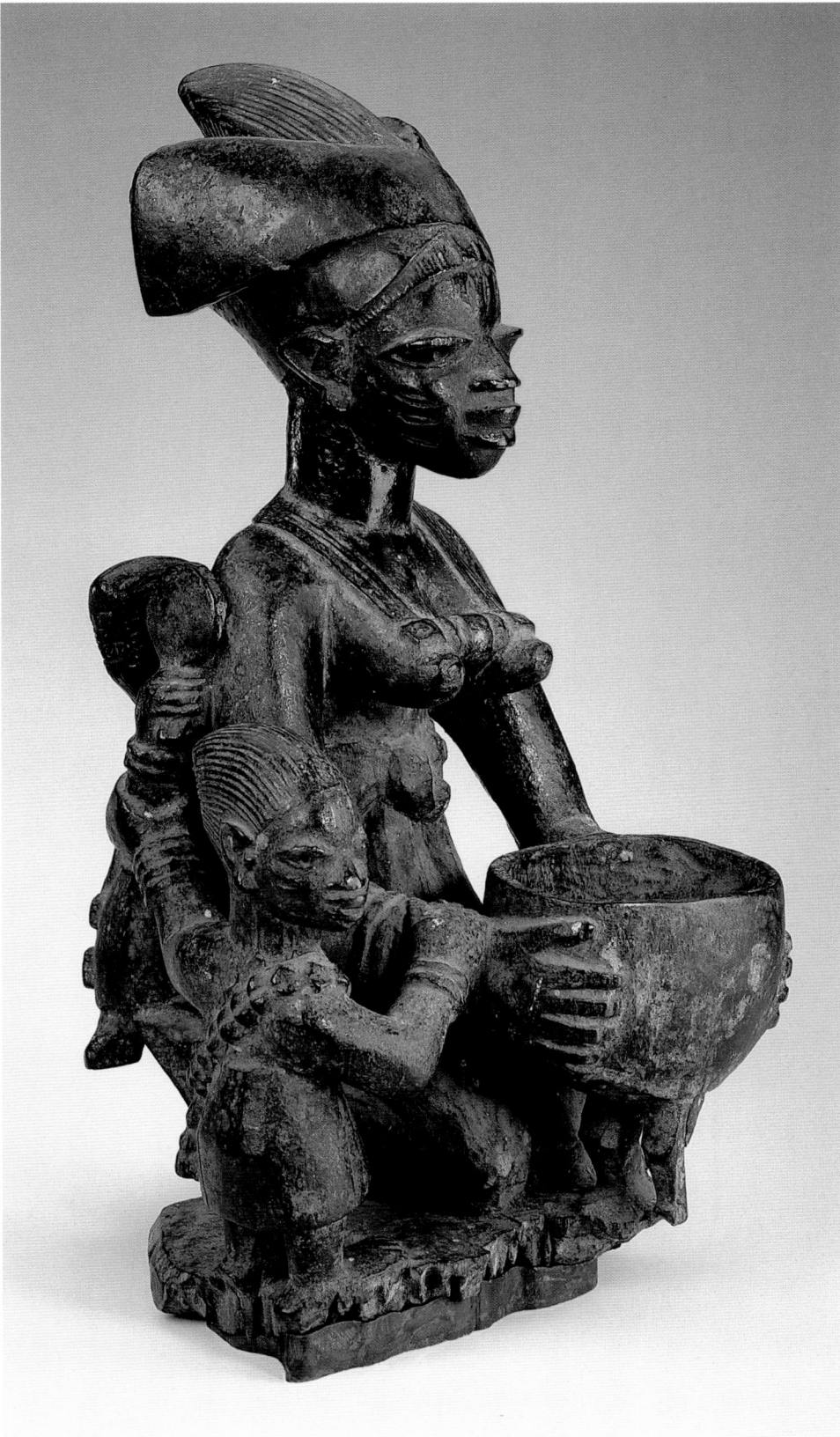

opposite PLATE 28
Unknown artist, Yaka peoples,
Democratic Republic of Congo
Cap mask, mid-twentieth century
Wood, raffia, cloth, pigment, paint
National Museum of African Art;
Bequest of Eliot Elisofon; 73-7-366
Photograph by Franko Khoury, courtesy of
National Museum of African Art,
Smithsonian Institution

PLATE 29
Unknown artist, Yoruba peoples, Nigeria
Female figure with children, early to
mid-twentieth century
Wood, indigo pigment
National Museum of African Art:
Museum purchase; 85-1-11
Photograph by Franko Khoury, courtesy
of National Museum of African Art,
Smithsonian Institution

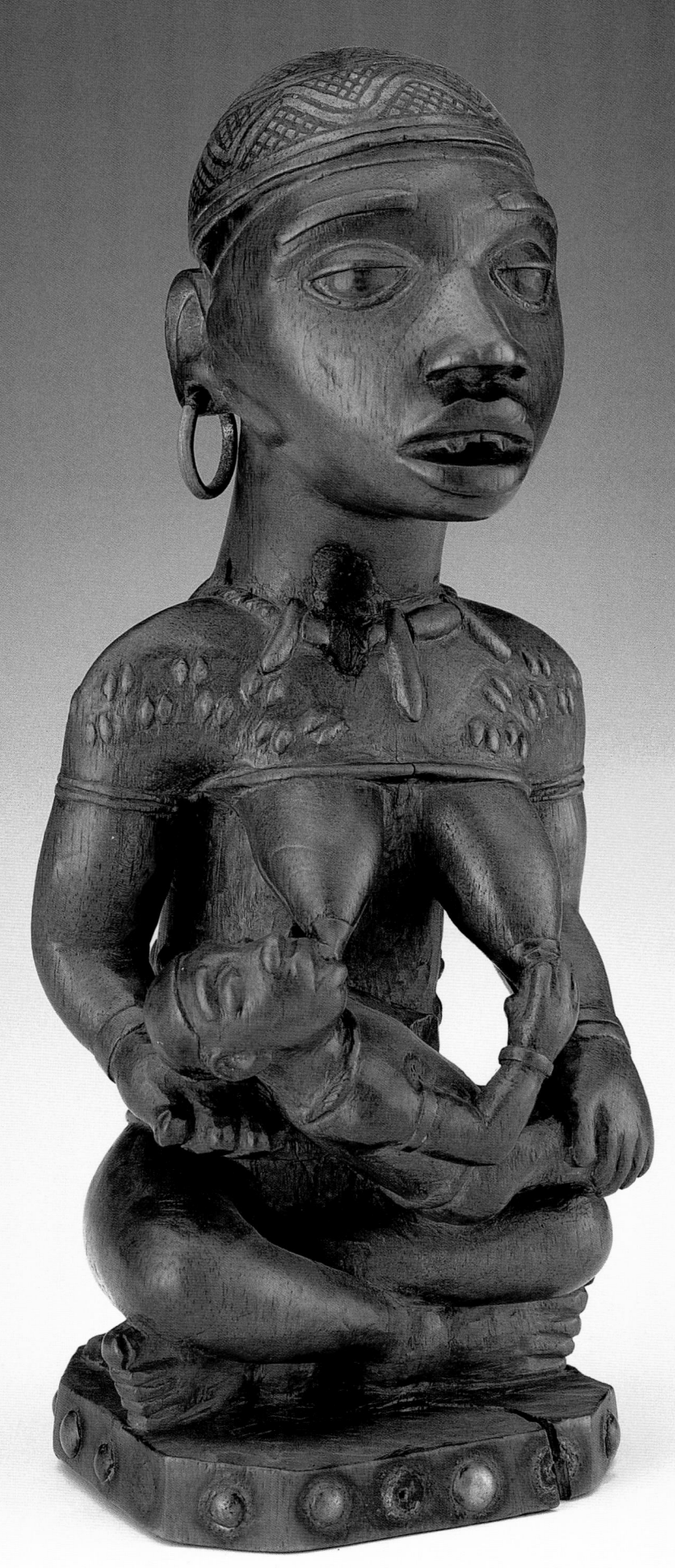

EXCHANGES: MARIA MAGDALENA CAMPOS-PONS*

I was born in a very strong family of black women. Being a woman and being black has something to do with how I am perceived in the world and how I am treated, how I am accepted, and what my opportunities are. Earlier in my work, I focused a lot on issues of sexuality regarding the female body and the representation of femininity through different historical and cultural periods. So early in my career I questioned: what is the history and code of representation of the body, of sexuality in the Mesoamerican aspects of that culture, of the Cuban/Latin American aspects of that culture, in Hispanic aspects of that culture, in the African aspect of that culture? Through that line of inquiry, I came across [the idea] of trying to portray my own view and the view that I wanted to propose to my audience [was] to really reconsider the idea of the female body as a martyr (plate 115), but a martyr to whom, of what, and representing what? [It was] important to me, to really propose some idea of representing femininity, blackness, and womanhood, of Africanness, Cubanness, and Latin Americaness.

* Maria Magdalena Campos-Pons, personal communication with Barbara Thompson, December 8, 2006.

opposite PLATE 30
Artist unknown, Kongo peoples, Mayombe region, Democratic Republic of the Congo
Female figure with child, late nineteenth to early twentieth century
Wood, metal, brass tacks, resin, pigment
National Museum of African Art:
Museum Purchase; 86-12-12
Photograph by Franko Khoury, courtesy of National Museum of African Art, Smithsonian Institution

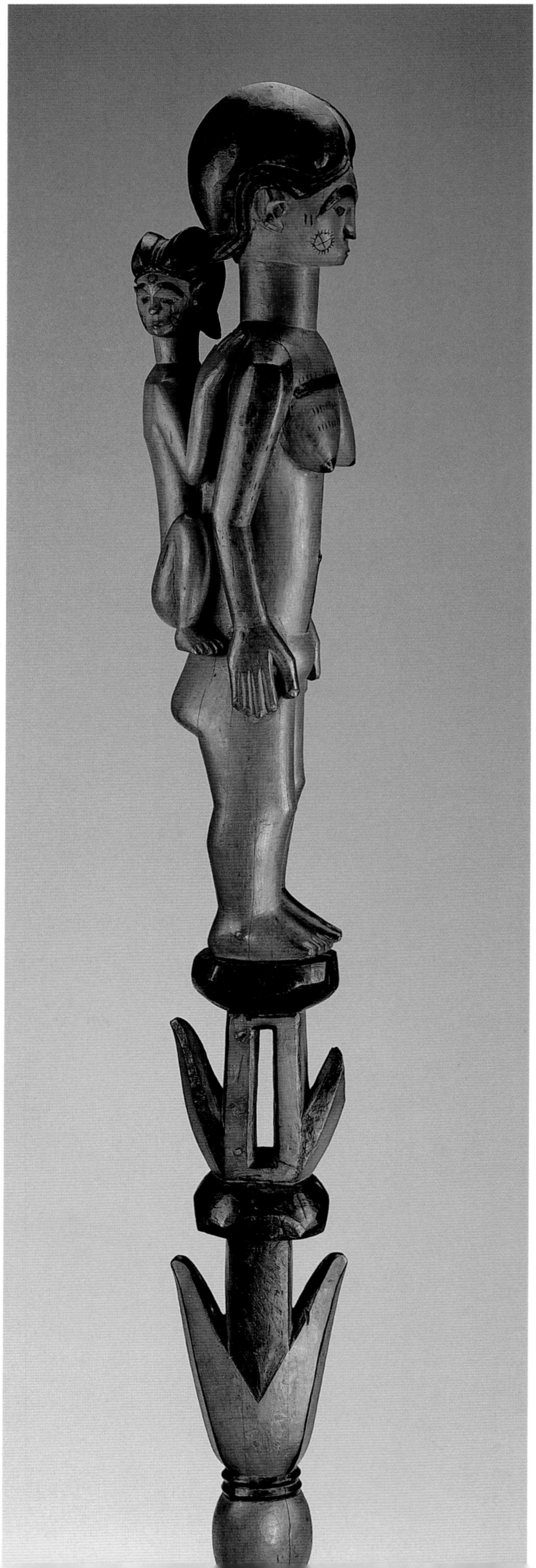

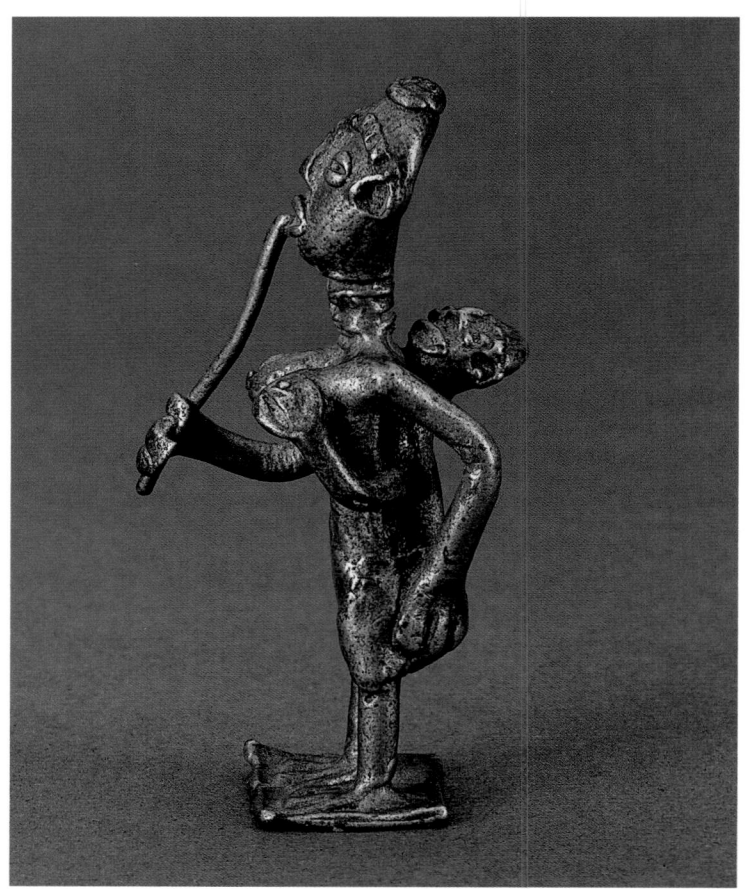

From the point of view of many African artists, there is an understandable need to speak about problems and pains, which in part probably arise from the history of colonialism. Some artists reflect and artistically document crimes of war and atrocities of violence, which have happened or are going on in their countries. I too have dealt in my work with the topics of discrimination and violence against black people in history and now. At this point, I feel the need to search for images that could speak about hope, strength, and continuity. With the video installation *Dressed Like Queens* (plate 114), I am attempting a strategy of artistic defense.

The work concentrates on depicting the strength, creativity, and potential power of African people and especially of the African woman symbolizing motherhood and creation. To learn and borrow from the power of tradition and the rituals of my African ancestors and relations, it was necessary to research on the values and customs of my tribe as well as of other tribes in Africa, in the past and today. The general approach to life, music, dance, creativity, but also to illness and death, including topics such as communal behavior, the stages of maturity, and the various ceremonies concerned with initiation were of interest to me.

Working with myself and another woman of color on articulating our personal histories and experiences through gestures and individual movement, I was intent on revealing strong presence and expression of pride. In the resulting installation, videos are projected in large dimensions onto a triptych of colorful hand-dyed fabrics. The central figure is a pregnant woman, observantly recorded by the camera as she sits, stands, and moves in a slow majestic manner. Flanking her, on the complementary colors red and green are projections of myself, gesturing expressively while speaking a poetical text of my own. The narration tells about women, my metaphorical queens, whose clothes have been taken away from them, and how, after difficulties and troubled times, they finally reclaim their rightful property.

* Excerpt from artist statement in Ingrid Mwangi and Robert Hutter, "Redressing," *Dressed Like Queens*, 2003. http://www.ingridmwangi.de/mh/text_Statments1.html.

PLATE 33
Unknown artist, Frafra peoples, Burkina Faso
Vessel, nineteenth to twentieth century
Terracotta
Collection of Bill and Gale Simmons, New York
Photograph by Bruce White

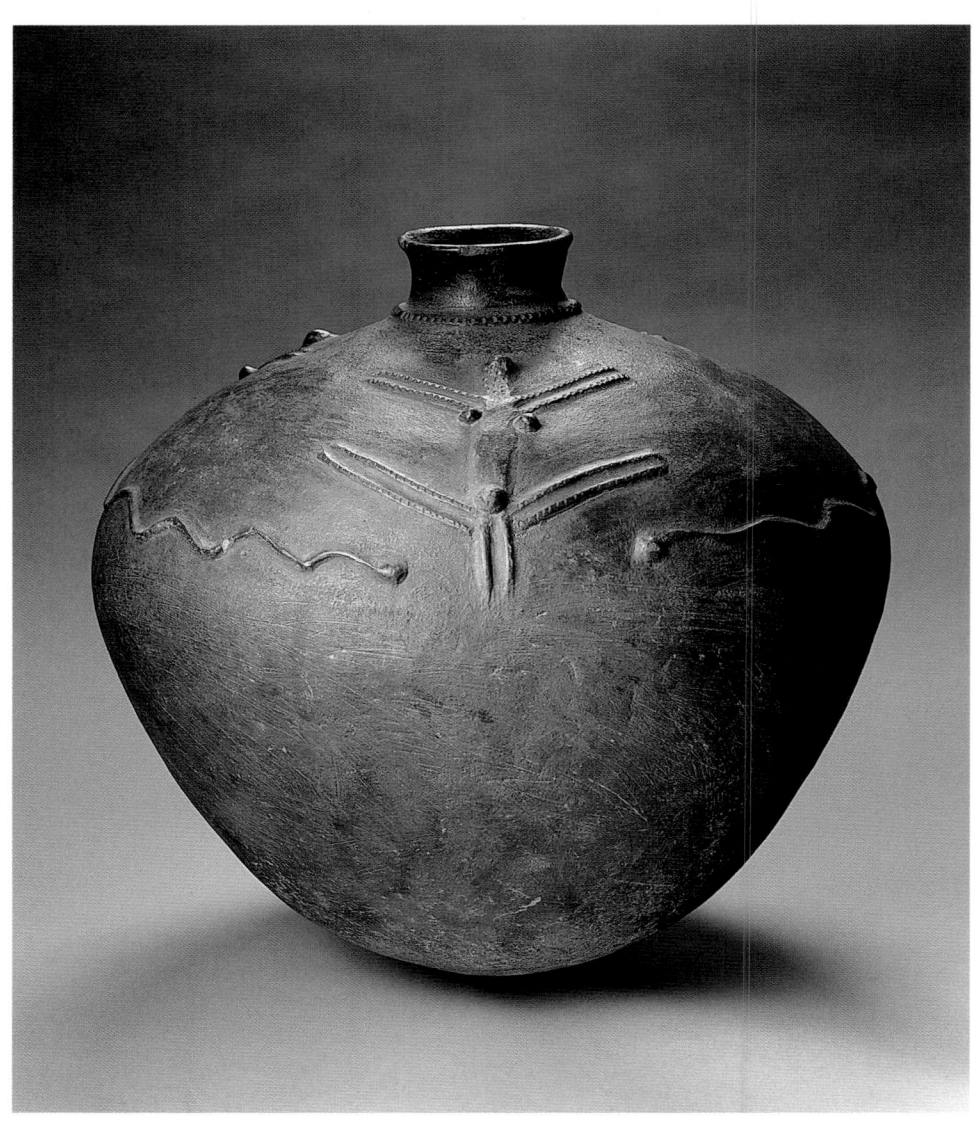

opposite PLATE 34
Unknown artist, Ga'anda peoples, Nigeria
Ritual beer pot (*lekleke*), nineteenth to
twentieth century
Terracotta
Collection of Bill and Gale Simmons,
New York
Photograph by Bruce White

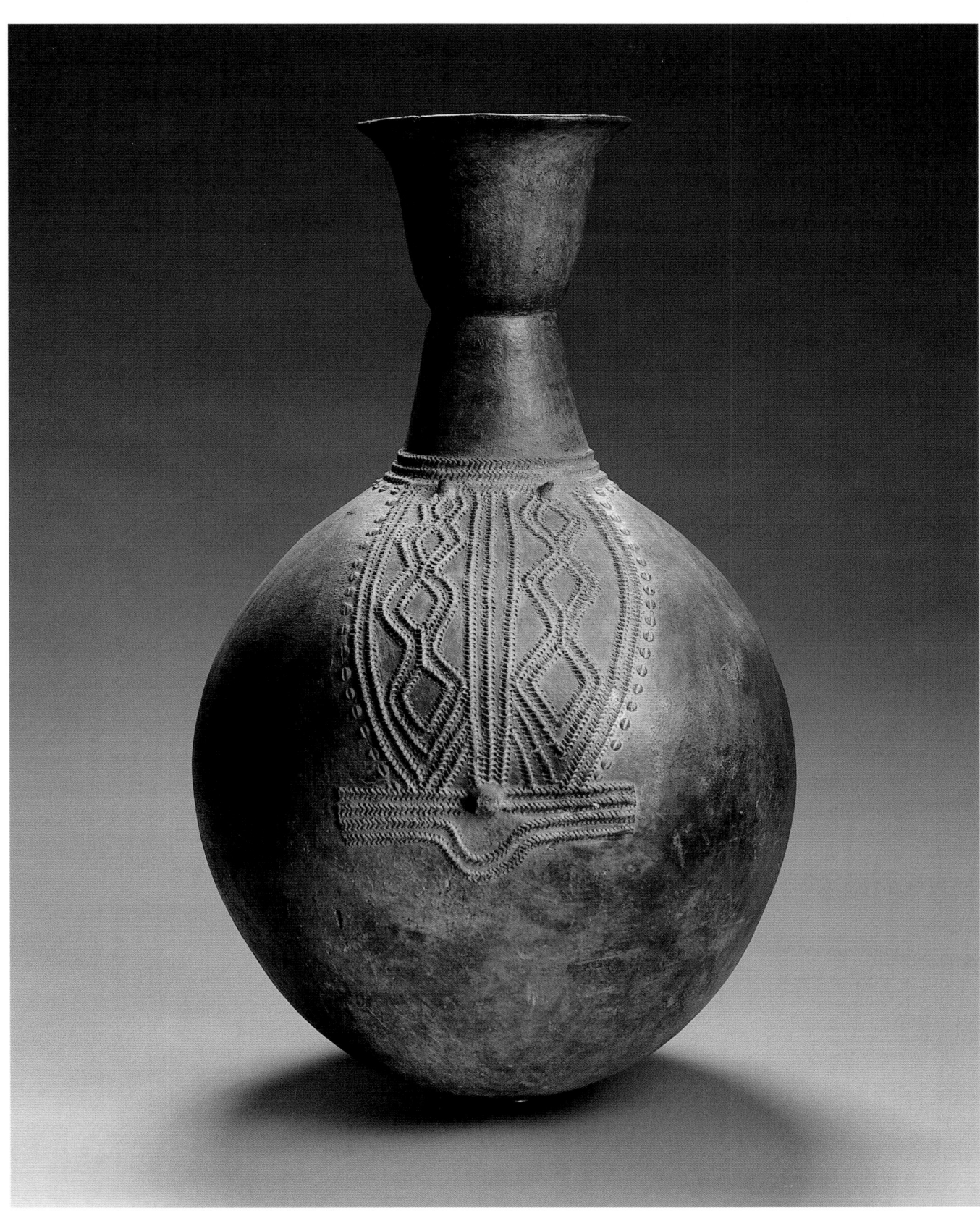

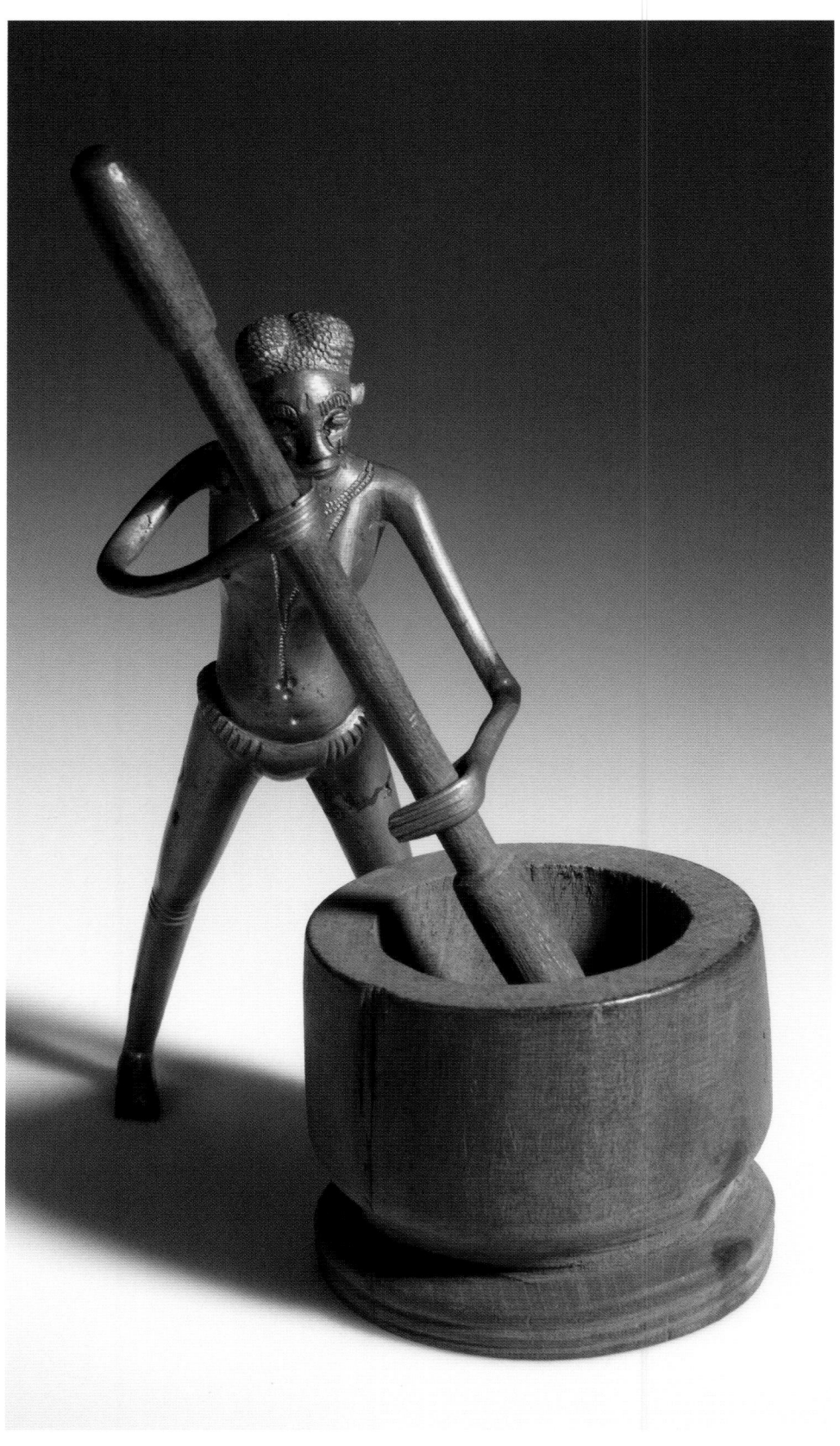

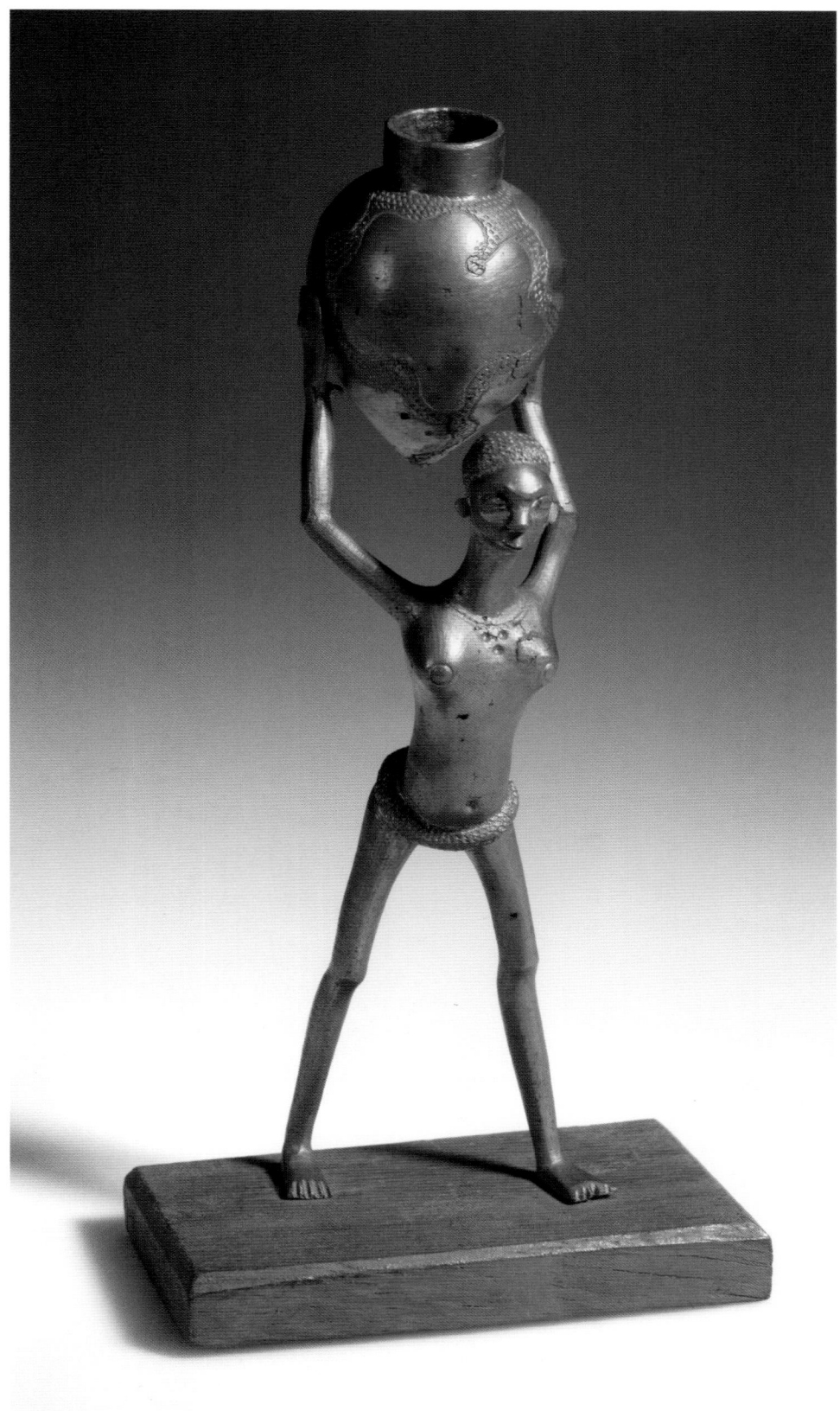

PLATE 36
Unknown artist, Fon peoples, Benin
Female with pot, twentieth century
Brass
American Museum of Natural History;
90.2/ 3564
Photograph courtesy of American Museum
of Natural History

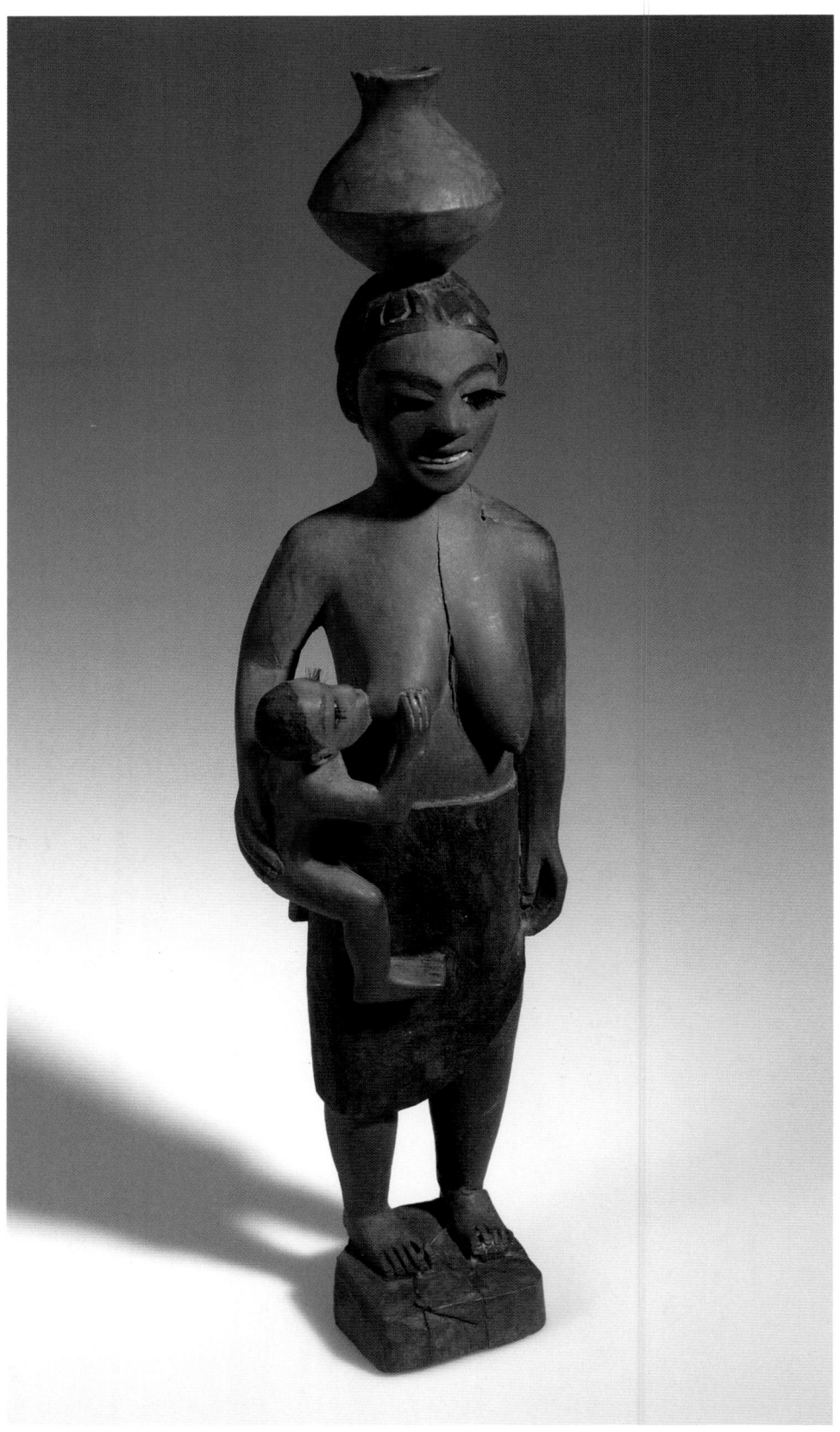

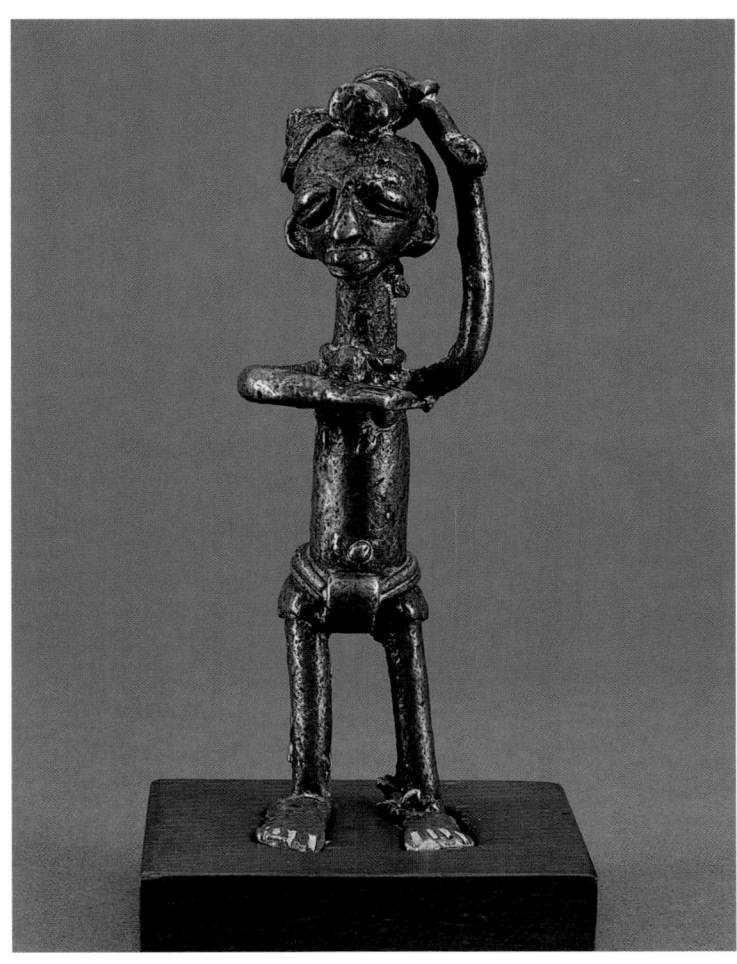

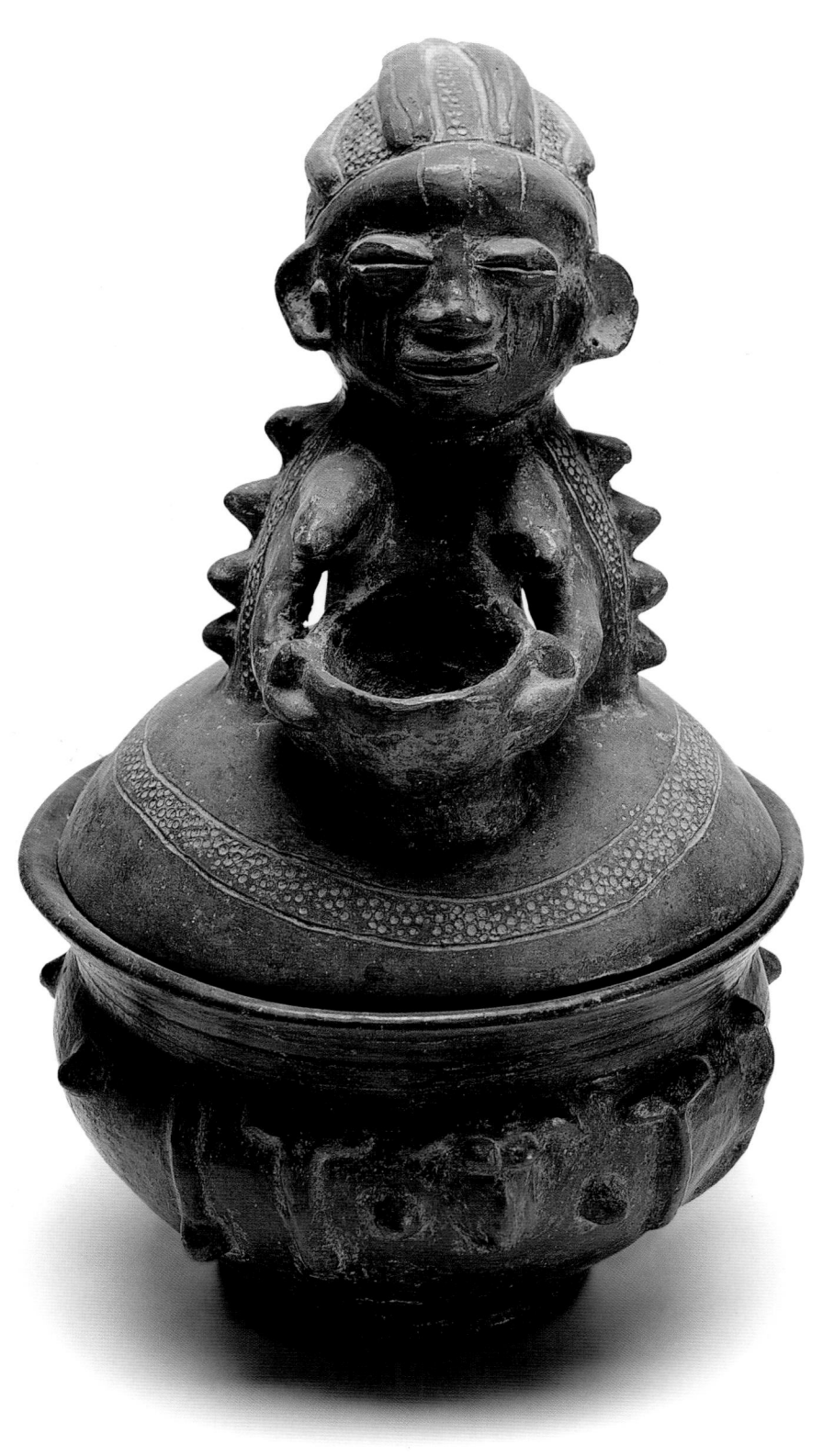

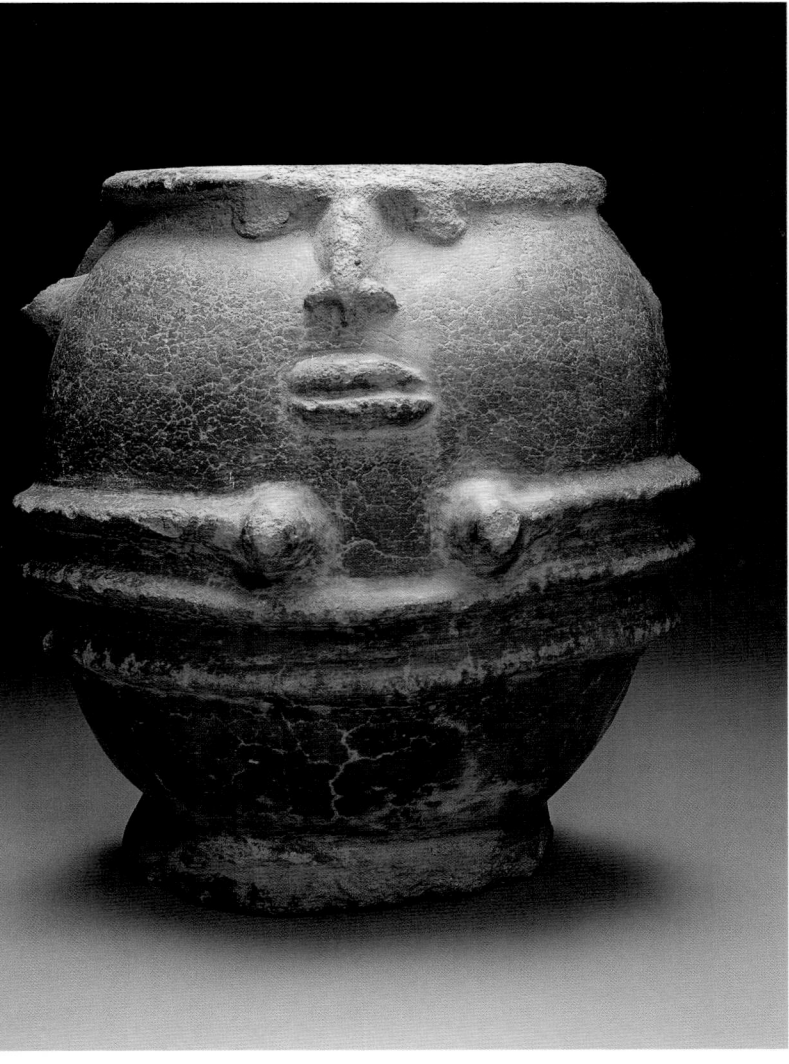
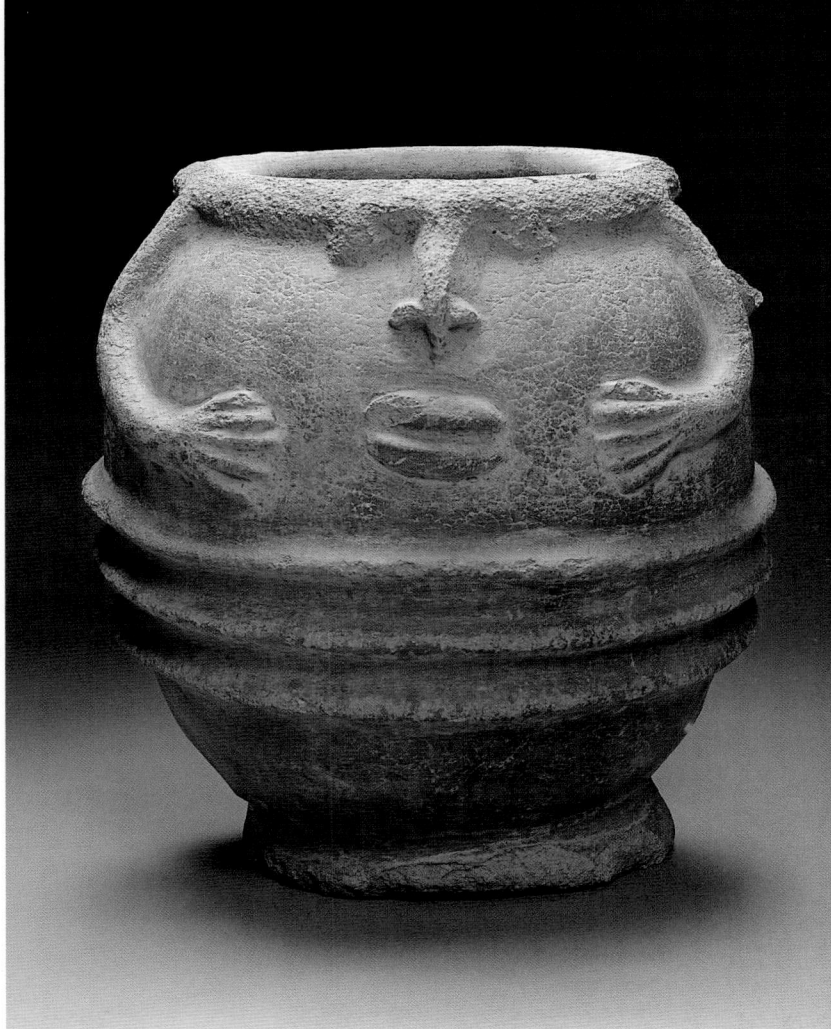

PLATE 40
Unknown artist, Bozo peoples, Burkina Faso
Vessel with Janus head, early to mid-twentieth century
Terracotta
a. Female view
b. male view
Collection of Bill and Gale Simmons, New York
Photograph by Bruce White

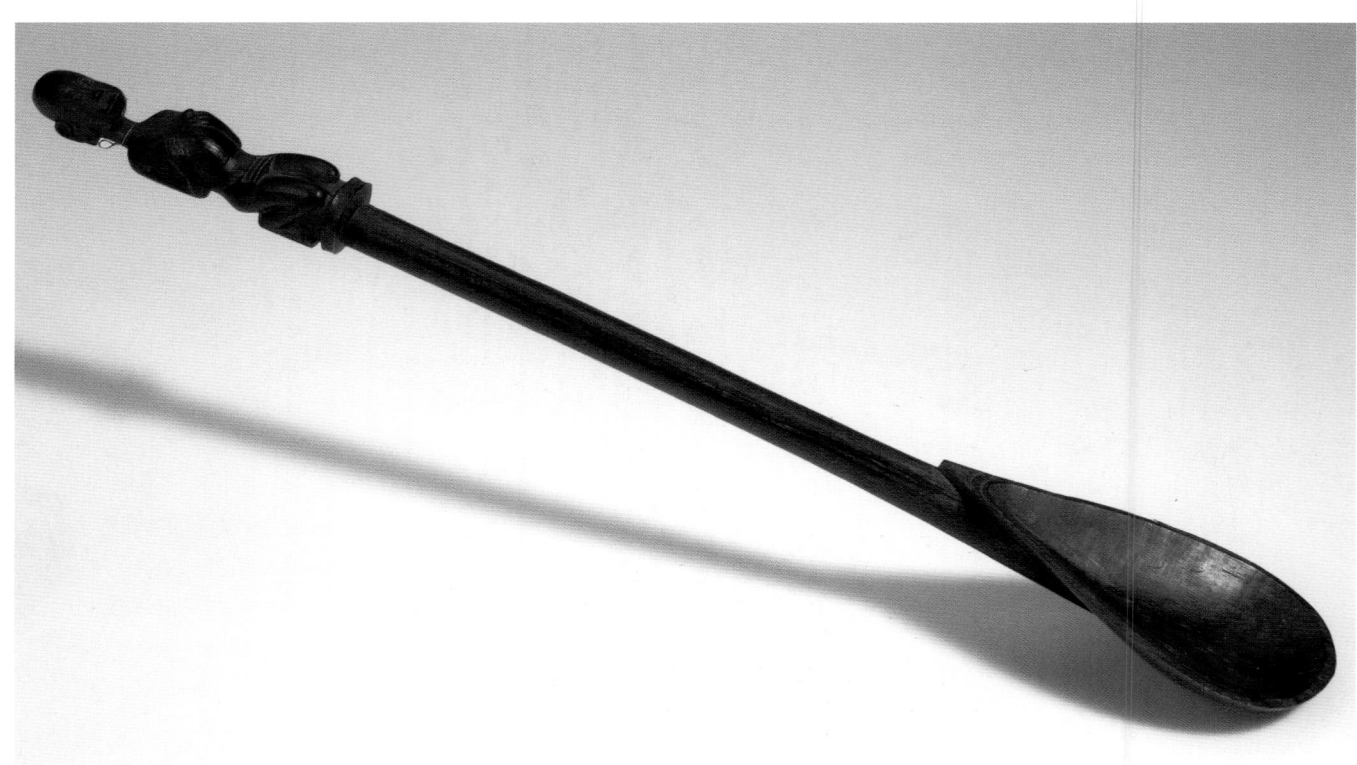

PLATE 41
Unknown artist, Kamba peoples, Kenya
Spoon of female, eighteenth to
twentieth century
Wood, metal
American Museum of Natural History;
90.1/8768
Photograph courtesy of American Museum
of Natural History

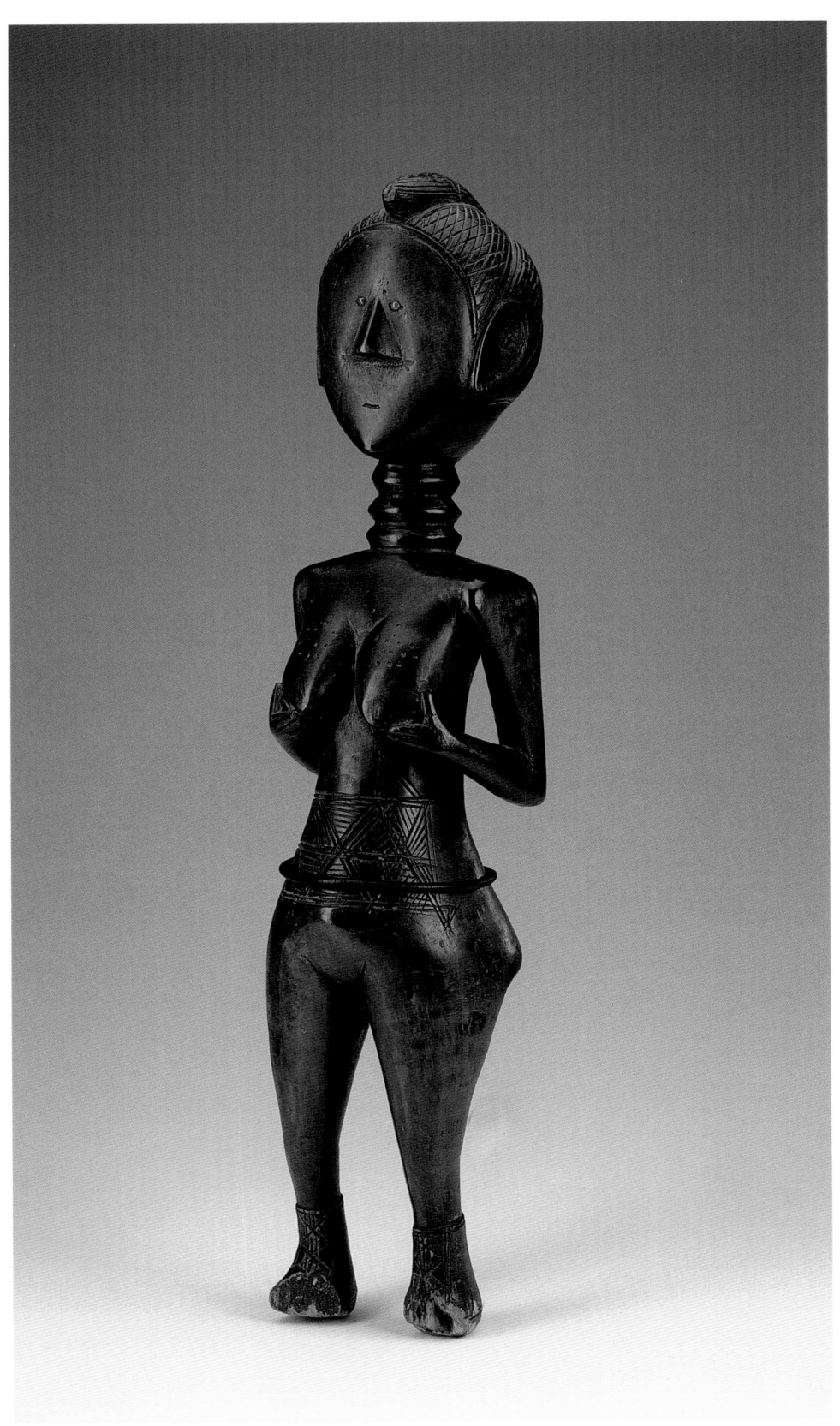

PLATE 42
Unknown artist, Temne peoples, Sierra Leone
Female figure, late nineteenth to
mid-twentieth century
Wood, glass beads, plastic beads
National Museum of African Art:
Museum purchase; 94-6-1
Photograph by Franko Khoury, courtesy
of National Museum of African Art
Smithsonian Institution

PLATE 43
Unknown artist, Yoruba peoples, Nigeria
Staff for Shango (*oshe Shango*),
nineteenth century
Wood
Hood Museum of Art: Gift of Evelyn A. and
William B. Jaffe, Class of 1964H; S.972.20
Photograph by Jeffrey Nintzel

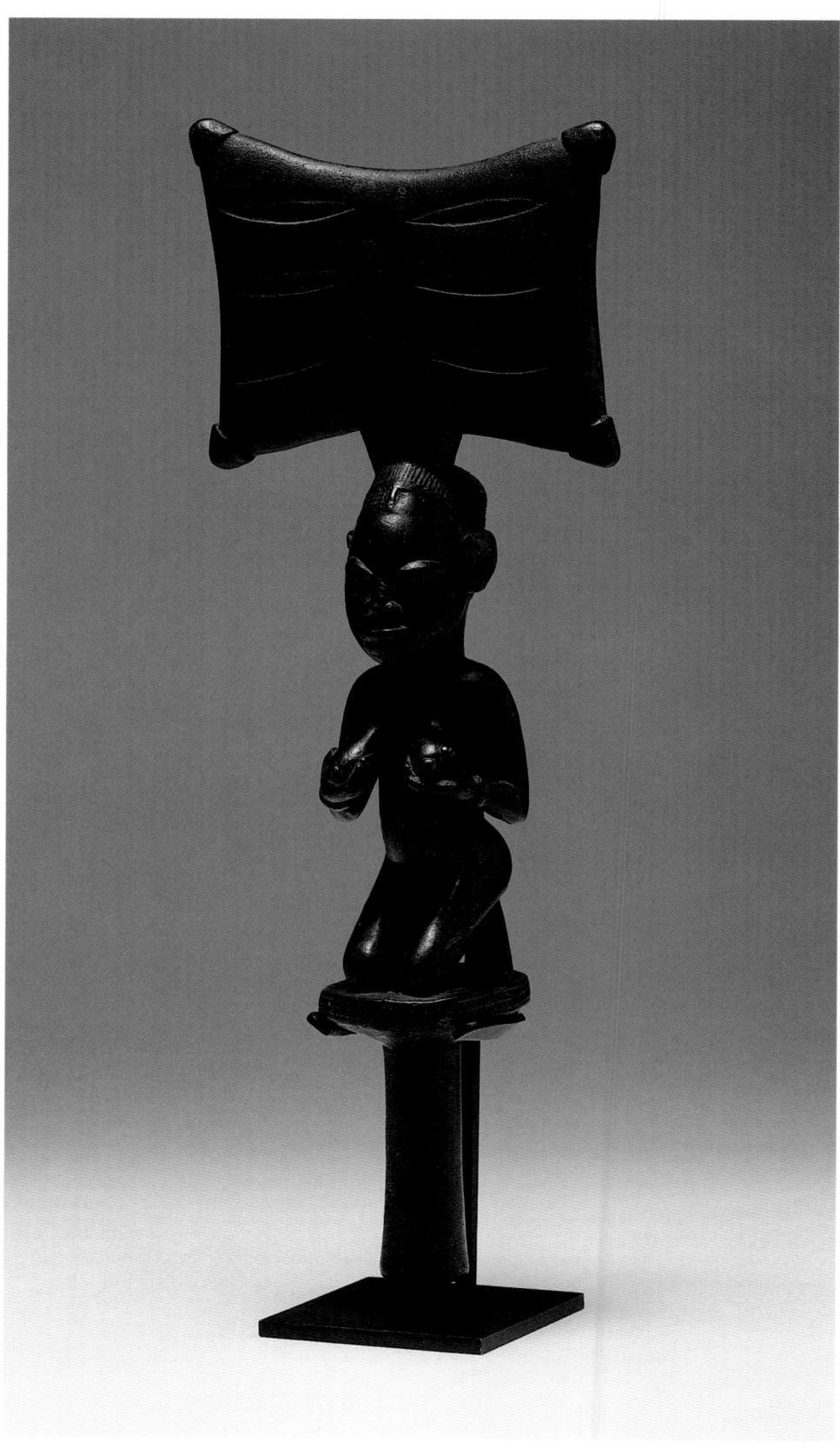

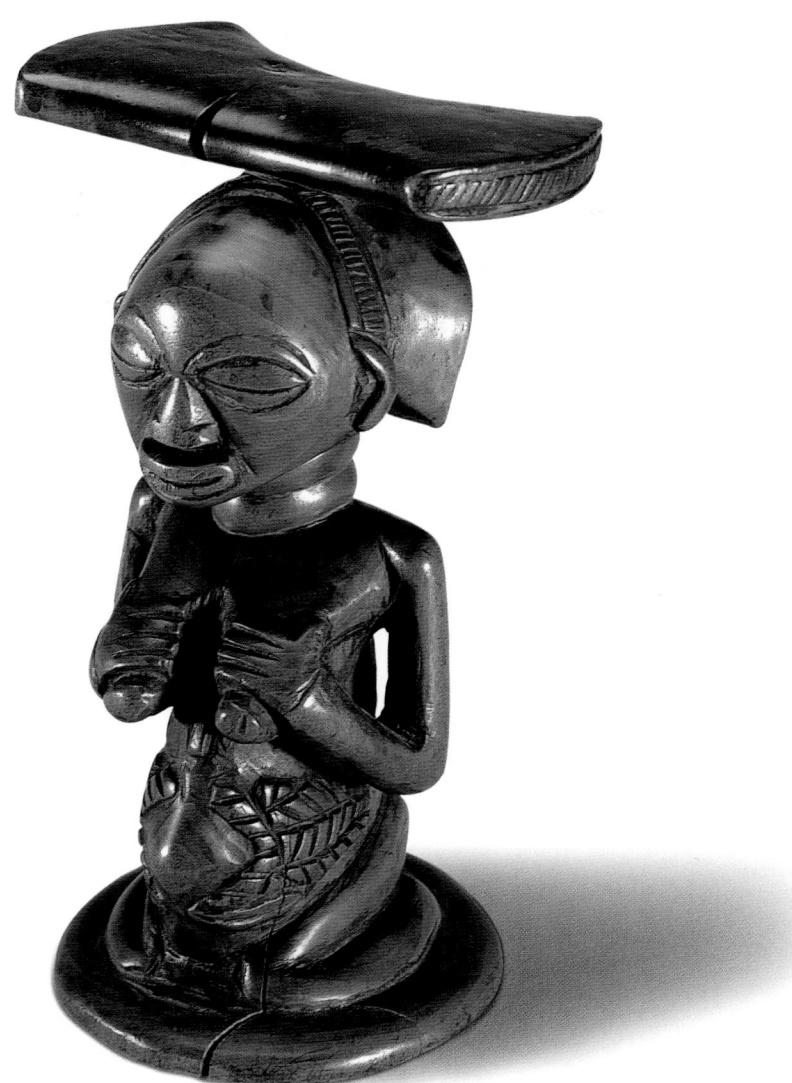

PLATE 44
Unknown artist, Luba peoples,
Democratic Republic of Congo
Caryatid headrest, nineteenth to
twentieth century
Wood
The Baltimore Museum of Art: Gift of
Alan Wurtzburger; BMA 1954.145.91
Photograph courtesy of The Baltimore
Museum of Art.

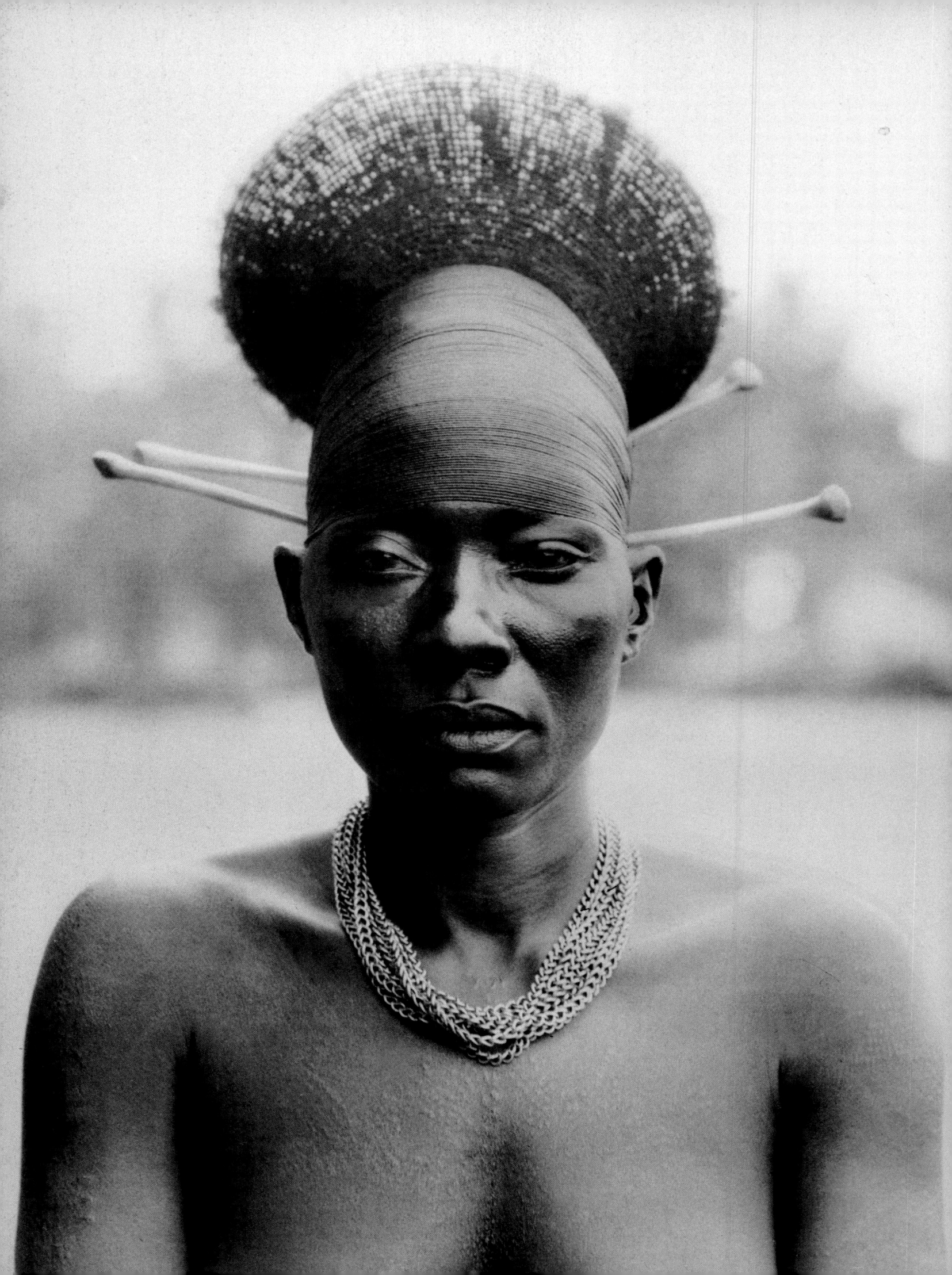

PART II | COLONIZING BLACK WOMEN: THE WESTERN IMAGINARY

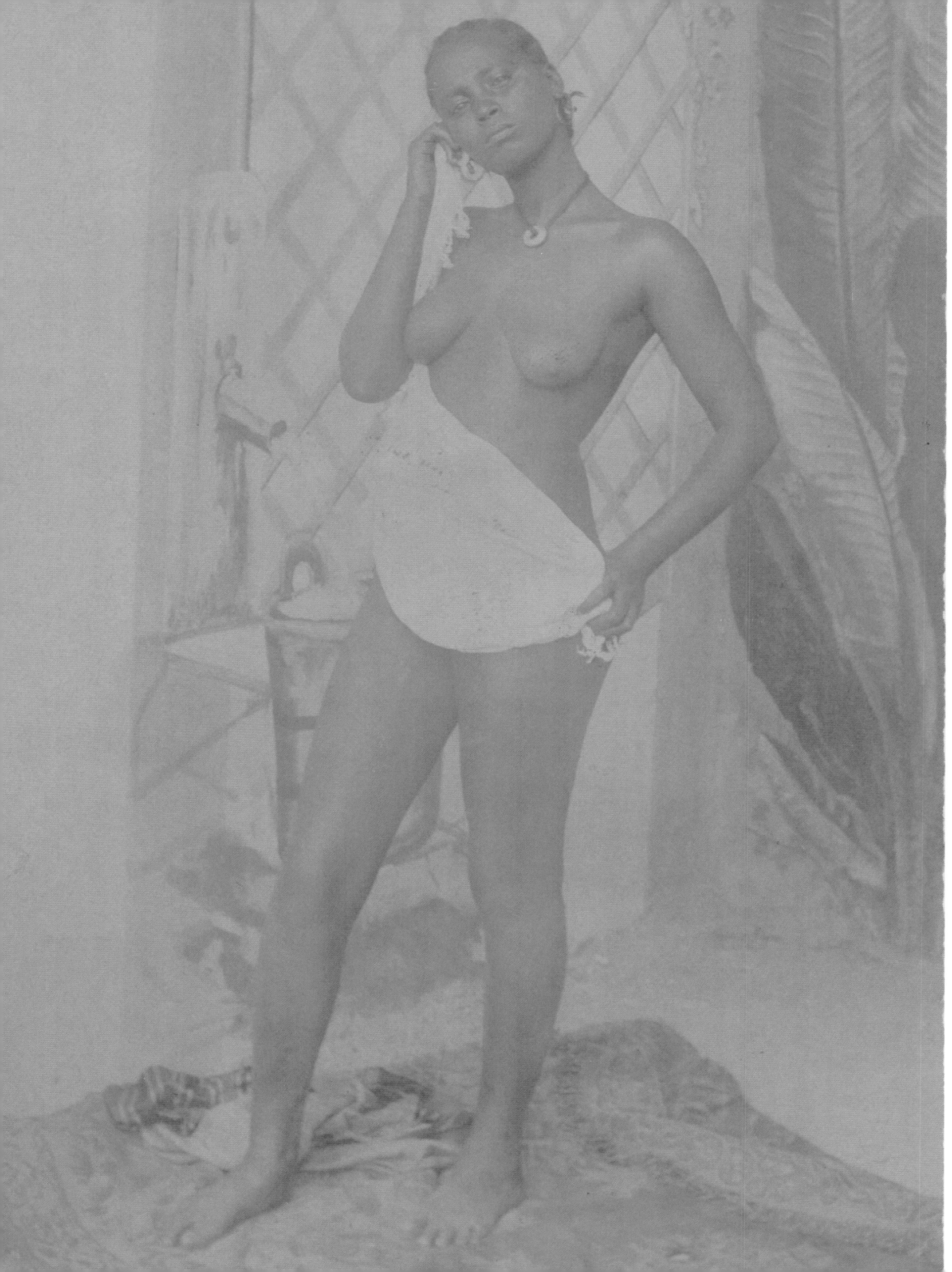

4 The Black Female Body, the Postcard, and the Archives[1]

The legacies of decades of colonial rule and of powerful racist regimes on the African continent work in both obvious and subtle ways. Until recently, one of the less apparent legacies with tremendous impact has largely gone unnoticed— the hundreds of thousands of postcards produced by and for colonizers, settlers, travelers, and collectors. These images of the colonies circulated widely and created and promulgated narratives about the colonized and colonial achievement. They form a huge archive with regional and thematic subsections covering all of Africa and can be found in public repositories as well as private holdings. Increasingly, these collections appear on internet websites, where they are widely accessible.[2] The narratives about Africans and Africa constructed and reinforced in the West through these pictures have had staying power and have shaped popular imagination to this day. This continuous influence derives from the haunting beauty and patina of age of many of these images, which beguile the viewer's senses. Furthermore, nostalgic books, scholarly examinations, and exhibitions continue to disseminate these pictures well into the present.[3]

One type of imagery in particular has drawn attention and been republished more than any other: pictures of the black female body, both unclothed and clothed.[4] Some of these depictions border on the erotic, even the pornographic.[5] Books, among them Monti's *Africa Then* or Baschet's *Africa 1900: A Continent Emerges*, revel in provocative images of African women, so-called "colonial nudes," such as this image of a young Somali woman in a suggestive pose, with her clothes dropped behind her (figure 4.1).[6] This preoccupation with studying and re-publishing these images raises important issues, among them the question of which place they occupy in the vast archives of colonialism. Were they as common as current publications, discussions, and critiques suggest, or did this recent emphasis give them disproportionate weight? Do images of the black female body, in particular when nude, remain racist and deeply disturbing when re-published today—even if accompanied by a critical assessment? Does their

opposite FIGURE 4.1 Unknown photographer, Somalian nude woman with cloth, c. 1915, silver gelatin print, postcard, publisher unidentified. Courtesy of Christraud Geary.

repetitive use and consumption not perpetuate stereotypes held about black women—many derogatory, others celebratory, but most of them misleading, wrong, and painful?

Artists, scholars, and curators have begun to address these stereotypical and damaging pictures in different ways. Artists seek to undermine and re-interrogate them by appropriating, manipulating, and re-writing them in their creations, thus attempting to counter the racist and sexist narratives of such imagery. Some of these works appear in this exhibition and catalogue. Scholars who study representation have published critical books, and curators have begun to mount exhibitions. But all these efforts encounter a major dilemma: how does one successfully break the hold of this imagery, which seems to extend into the present, without re-victimizing the victims? Scholars, curators, and artists have come under scrutiny for not accomplishing their goals and for ultimately perpetuating the very representational practices that they seek to overturn.

I will address a few issues linked to depicting and "disseminating" the black female body both in the past, when the images first circulated, and in the present through recycling older imagery. Focusing on the picture postcard, I begin with a brief history of the postcard medium. Images of black women, often unclothed, on postcards, which appear demeaning and painful to the contemporary viewer, are the theme of the second part of this essay. There are, however, other, overlooked postcards offering a different view of the female body. These are photographs obviously commissioned by the women themselves, showing them in dignified poses and in ways they wanted to present themselves. In the third part of this essay, I propose that these portraits, which migrated into the postcard medium as well, can be used to construct a counternarrative to that of the exploitation, oppression, and overt sexualization of the black woman's body. Finally, I return to the critics' questions concerning representational practices and the issues that arise from re-publishing such imagery today.

A BRIEF HISTORY OF THE POSTCARD

At the end of the nineteenth century, the establishment of colonial rule over most of the African continent coincided with the ascendance of photography as a medium for bringing images of distant regions of the world to the public. In addition, printing technology had evolved so that photographic images could be duplicated easily and disseminated in many forms. When photographs of Africa and Africans first appeared in large quantities in Europe, the public consumed them as illustrations in books and magazines, stereographs,[7] posters, advertisements, and postcards. Indeed, postcards were among the most prominent means of moving imagery around the globe.

In the heyday of postcard production before the First World War (1914–1918), postcards were akin to newspapers and covered all kinds of topics, ranging from recent events such as natural disasters or official government visits, to portraits of important personalities. When Western powers implemented their rule over the

African continent, postcards documented the process both for the foreign residents in the colonies and for the audience at home. Postcards were one of the few means to visualize these faraway places. They included depictions of the growing colonial infrastructure, architecture, colonial activities and personalities, landscapes, flora, and fauna, which constituted the bulk of the production, and the Western "discovery" of Africa and achievements in self-congratulatory ways. Renderings of African peoples who had come under domination were also common and, akin to those of European populations, thought picturesque. Among these were craftsmen (the "petit métier" genre in France), herdsmen in the Alps, and maidens in ethnic costumes from different regions of Europe. In North America, Native Americans were the focus of postcards, just as peoples in India, Japan, Mexico, and other places became postcard staples. The postcard medium thus created an entire universe and taxonomies of peoples for inspection and consumption by the viewers in Europe and the United States.[8] As part of this wave, postcard images of Africans reached a wide public and etched views of Africa and Africans indelibly into the Western imagination.[9]

Postcards are multi-authored artifacts, combining image, caption, and—in many instances—text by the sender. Stamps may also contain depictions, which often repeated iconic images that enjoyed great popularity, and thus took on narrative qualities of their own, adding to the impact (figure 4.2). The production of a postcard began with taking the actual photograph. At the turn of the twentieth century, photographers came from many different backgrounds. Some were amateurs, others professionals who operated studios in major cities and traveled the countryside. On the African continent, the French, Germans, British, Portuguese, Italians, and other Europeans supplied images for postcard production. African photographers followed suit, as did practitioners from India in the eastern and southern regions of the continent. Once they had taken their photographs, they fed them into the "pipeline" of postcard publishing, which—with the exception of South Africa, which developed its own postcard industry—took place in European countries.[10] In the European printing houses, where the images were reproduced most often as black and white collotypes and later on as halftones on postcard stock, colorists subsequently hand-colored many cards. These workers had never been to Africa and used their imagination to develop color schemes (plates 65, 80, and 85).

Cards also carried captions, ranging from short descriptive statements, such as *Afrique Occidentale; Jeunes Foulahs* in plate 52 to *Her Country Cousins*, the caption of a card juxtaposing a "civilized" woman in Western dress with what then

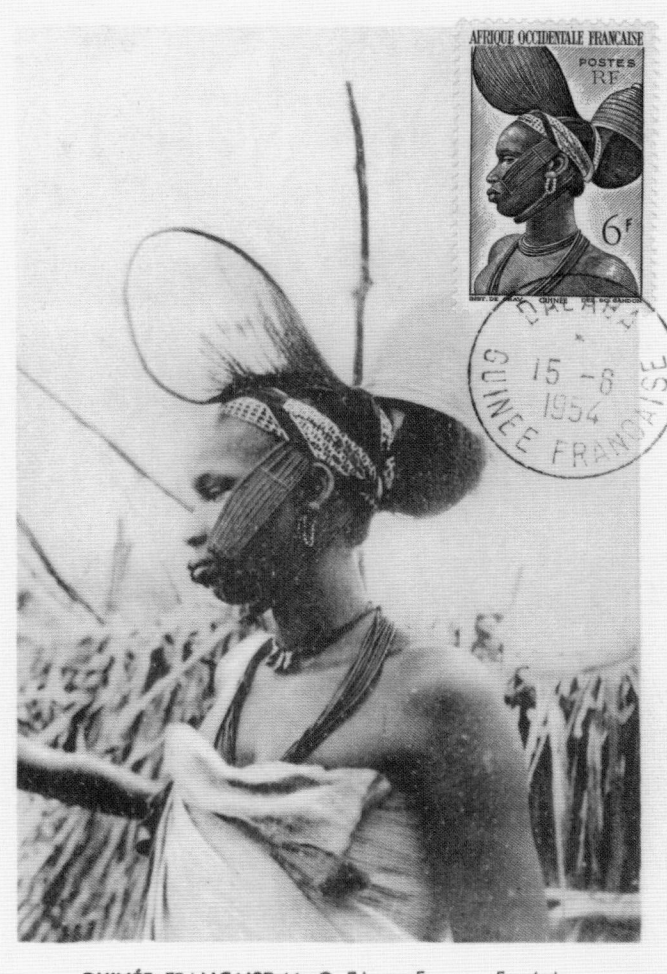

GUINÉE FRANÇAISE (A. O. F.) — Femme Foulah

FIGURE 4.2 Unknown photographer, *Guinée française (A.O.F) — Femme Foulah* [French Guinea (A.O.F.) Fulbe woman], c. 1940, collotype, postcard, published by Agence Photographique de la France d'Outre-Mer, c. 1950, cancellation June 15, 1954. Courtesy of Christraud Geary.

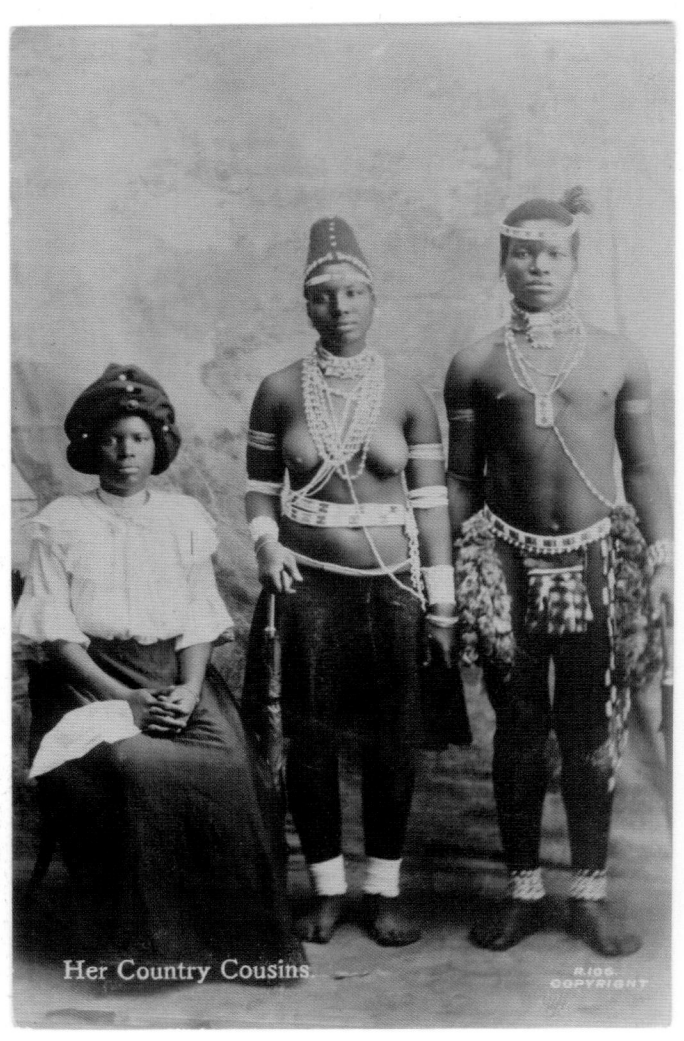

FIGURE 4.3 Unknown photographer, *Her Country Cousins*, c. 1900, silver gelatin print, postcard, published by "SAPSCO" Real Photo, Box 5792, Johannesburg, South Africa, c. 1910. Courtesy of Christraud Geary.

would have been perceived as "primitive peoples"—her so-called "cousins" in their traditional attire (figure 4.3). Postcards frequently depict this contrast, in an effort to demonstrate the Western "success" in civilizing African subjects (plates 58, 86, and 87). The photographers provided these captions or the European publishers/editors assigned them, even though they had never been to Africa, thus inserting their own clichés and stereotypes.

Captions, which directed and shaped meaning-making, could change over the production cycle of cards, especially if a postcard was commercially successful and re-edited to satisfy demand. One of the most fascinating of such examples is a provocative card photographed and published by the Creole photographers Arthur and Alfonso Lisk-Carew, who worked in Freetown, Sierra Leone. In circa 1910, an image of a seductive young woman, captioned *Timnie* [Temne] *Girl, Sierra Leone*, appeared among the many postcards by these two prolific photographers (figure 4.4). In the 1920s, the same card, now republished and retouched so that the young woman's lap is covered with a loin cloth, carries the caption "Just you and me, Sierra Leone" (plate 66). While the image has been toned down, the caption now makes up for this lack of suggestiveness. Too little attention has been paid to multiple levels of inscribing and meaning-making in postcards, for most studies to date focused on the postcard image and consequently on the creator of the photographs and on the circumstances of photographic production.[11]

Print runs for one single card may have been as high as three thousand and successful images were reprinted in many subsequent editions.[12] Three numbers allow us to gauge the impact postcards must have had in shaping the visual landscape and public perception: in 1889, French printers turned out eight million postcards; about sixty million cards in 1902; and 123 million by 1910.[13] Even though their numbers declined thereafter, postcards enjoyed continued popularity between the two world wars and to this day remain an important commercial product, which can be found in all tourist destinations around the world.

When printing in Europe was completed, the cards were shipped back to Africa to be sold to travelers, residents, and collectors in fancy good stores, photo studios, and other sales outlets. Many cards were then mailed from Africa back to Europe and America and often contained messages by the senders. Only occasionally did a sender refer to the actual picture on the card. The comments may range from descriptive statements to racist remarks. A South African card posted in 1906 shows two Zulu women with babies on their backs. The publisher's caption neutrally describes them as *Zulu Mothers* (plate 79) but the sender's added remark, "Are these not horrid looking creatures?" (plate 80), betrays blatantly racist attitudes. Transformed through the private processes of selecting, inscribing, postmarking, and sending, the cards found their way back to parts of the world as far away as Japan and India, where they were thrown out or became part of private collections.

Throughout their history, postcards have been open to multiple interpretations, last but not least by contemporary scholars, artists, and curators. Their fascinating migration and openness to meaning-making, I suggest, is at the core of the postcards' recent ascent as a key artifact in addressing issues of representation of Africans, particularly African women. Postcards, with their multilayered histories of production and consumption, provide an apt metaphor for the complexities in the way Western imagination constructed and disseminated ideas about the foreign. They were and remain one of the most influential media in the "invention of Africa,"[14] and rightfully deserve attention.

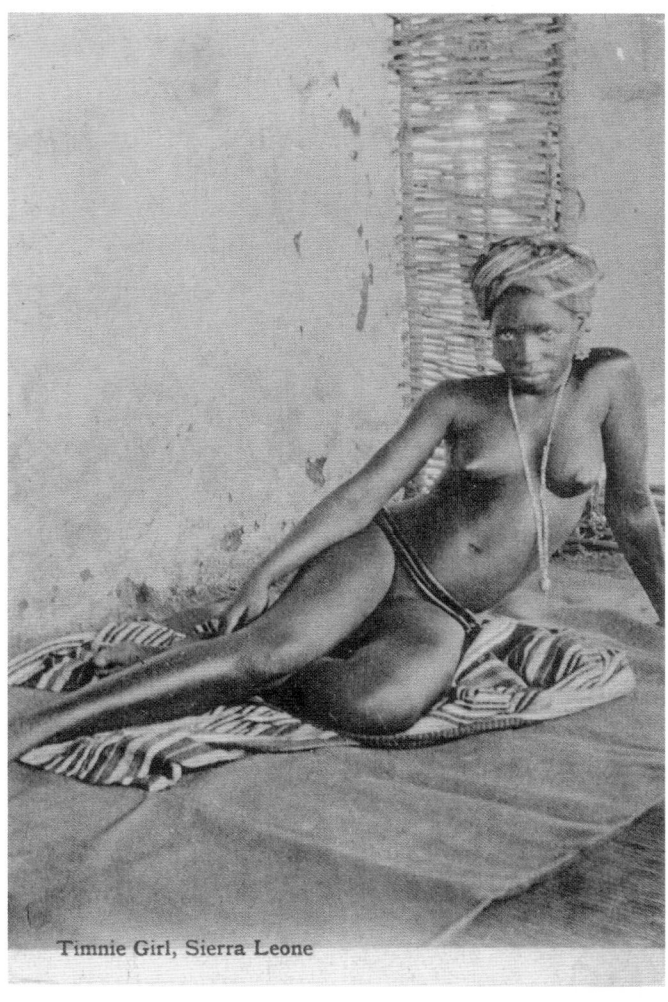

Timnie Girl, Sierra Leone

ETHNOGRAPHIC AND ANTHROPOMETRIC POSTCARDS OF THE BLACK FEMALE BODY

Postcards of the black female body form a subsection of the visual archive of colonialism. They are relatively small in number, for the majority of postcards produced during the colonial period focuses on everyday aspects of life in the colonies/territories, the new infrastructure, missionary activities, general ethnography, architecture, and landscapes. The relevance given to cards of the black female body is partly the result of the preoccupations of collectors and interpreters of images. Initially, photographs of the black female body came in the guise of "ethnographic" and "anthropometric" images, a distinction that might be helpful as an analytical tool. "Anthropometric" refers to the study of the human body and its parts as practiced in scientific circles in the late nineteenth century, which helped to delineate "race," while the term "ethnographic" denotes the description of social life and cultural practices, such as body adornment and coiffures.[15] Anthropometric images single out the individual as a physical "type" representative of his or her "race" and present him or her in prescribed frontal and profile views,[16] while ethnographic images illustrate human activities. The distinction between the two kinds of imagery blurs, because a picture might contain elements of both. A group photograph taken in Angola is a good case in point (figure 4.5). Captioned *Huilla. Typos e penteados* [Huila. Types and Hairstyles], the postcard combines the "type" photography approach, showing men and women in arranged frontal and profile poses, with ethnographic information about their coiffures. The distinction between the two modes of photography

FIGURE 4.4 Alphonso and Arthur Lisk-Carew, Sierra Leonians (active c. 1905–c. 1959), *Timnie* [Temne] *girl, Sierra Leone*, c. 1910, collotype, postcard, publisher unidentified, c. 1910. Courtesy of Christraud Geary.

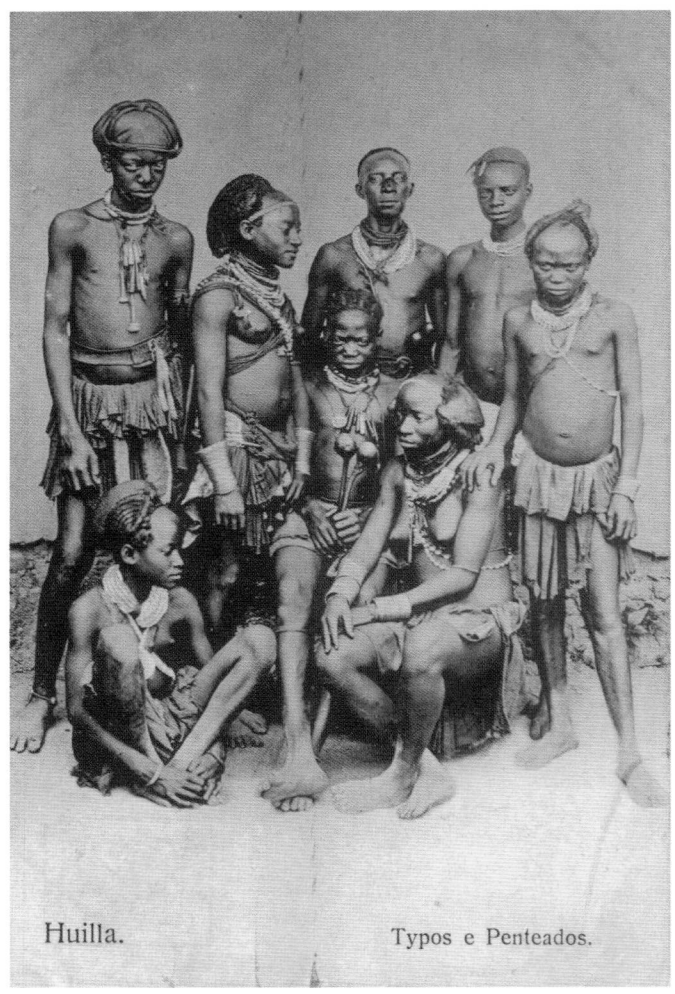

Huilla.   Typos e Penteados.

FIGURE 4.5 Unknown photographer, *Huilla — Typos e Penteados* [Huila — Types and Hairstyles], c. 1900, collotype, postcard, published by Ferreira, Riberao & Osoria, Loanda, Angola, c. 1910. Courtesy of Christraud Geary.

nevertheless provides a helpful heuristic device to examine postcards devoted to the black body.

Ethnographic postcards depict Africans going about their daily routines, including economic pursuits such as hunting as well as ceremonies and rituals, among them coming-of-age celebrations (plate 64), masquerades (plate 65), and dance, all of which are associated in Western photographers' and consumers' imagination with Africans' "typical" ways of life. Floating in an ahistorical space outside time and fixing an imaginary "tribal" Africa through image and captions, these postcards are often picturesque mises-en-scène, for they are mostly staged[17] or even fabricated. In their totality, such cards present a primordial, "traditional" landscape of African ways of life, constructed through the lenses of both African and foreign photographers. Even though most of the foreign photographers—administrators, missionaries, professional photographers, and travelers, among others—had no scholarly agendas and were not trained in ethnography, they aptly followed the conventions of ethnographic photography, as did their African counterparts. Handbooks both of photography and anthropology/ethnography popularized these rules for the amateur, and successful, widely distributed images set precedents for ethnographic image capture.

One genre of ethnographic postcards focused on women engaged in domestic tasks, such as visiting (plate 72), bathing their children, sweeping (plate 90), braiding hair, trading (plate 91), and cooking. Here, the Western viewers could recognize the familiar in the foreign, for it was the woman who also carried out household and nurturing activities in the West. There are countless pictures from all over Africa of women pounding grain (plates 92 and 93). These *"pileuses,"* to use the French term in numerous captions of French postcards of this subject, form a theme that is part and parcel of any visual depiction of Africa and pervasive in photography books well into the present. Its popularity derives from the visual aspects of pounding, since several women worked the pestles in rhythmic fashion. In most of these carefully staged postcards, the women wore traditional attire and, depending on the region of Africa, were thus bare-breasted. More importantly, some of these cards had an erotic subtext as they presented the nude black female body in movement. In the case of women preparing or grinding grain, their posture (often on all fours) alludes to animalistic qualities associated with Africans in the Western mind. Cooking over open fires with clay pots is another domestic theme. Again there are subtexts. In "cooking or eating" postcards from South Africa, for example, I suggest that one finds a blurring of domestic activity with stereotypes about African savagery, especially if men and women surround these pots and have their meal. In the Western popular imaginary of the nineteenth and early twentieth centuries, this type of round cooking pot was often associated with invented "cannibalistic" practices.

These postcards of domestic scenes evoked a sense of the "primitive" and the "primordial." Yet they also need to be understood in connection with another narrative—that of the civilizing mission. After Western intervention, the black female body of alleged unbridled and uncomfortable sexuality became clothed and tamed. At times, the before and after was juxtaposed in the same image, as in a South African postcard captioned *Zulu Maidens, the difference* (plate 85). At times this complementary narrative, often promulgated by missionary societies, came to life in the images of fully clothed women, now engaged in activities such as sewing (figure 4.6), knitting, and laundry, expected also of women in the West. In some instances, the women's dress followed indigenous fashions and design, which evolved over time and integrated many foreign elements; in others, it was clearly of missionary origin. Clad in smocks introduced by the missionaries, which resembled children's and lower class girls' outfits in Europe, the women now exuded decency and epitomized civility. The black female body had been colonized, domesticated, and infantilized (figure 4.7).

Another sub-genre of postcards depicted mother and child. The attraction of these images for Western viewers derived on the one hand from the fact that they represented a universal theme. On the other hand, they were exotic, for the women carried the children on their backs (see plates 79, 80, and 90) and were at times bare-breasted. In some instances, the husband joined the two, an image that promoted the ideal of the nuclear family. Moving women visually out of the polygamous household, which according to Western misconceptions favored uncontrollable sexuality and conjured up notions of the harem, provided another avenue for demonstrating the progress of "civilization" (plate 87).

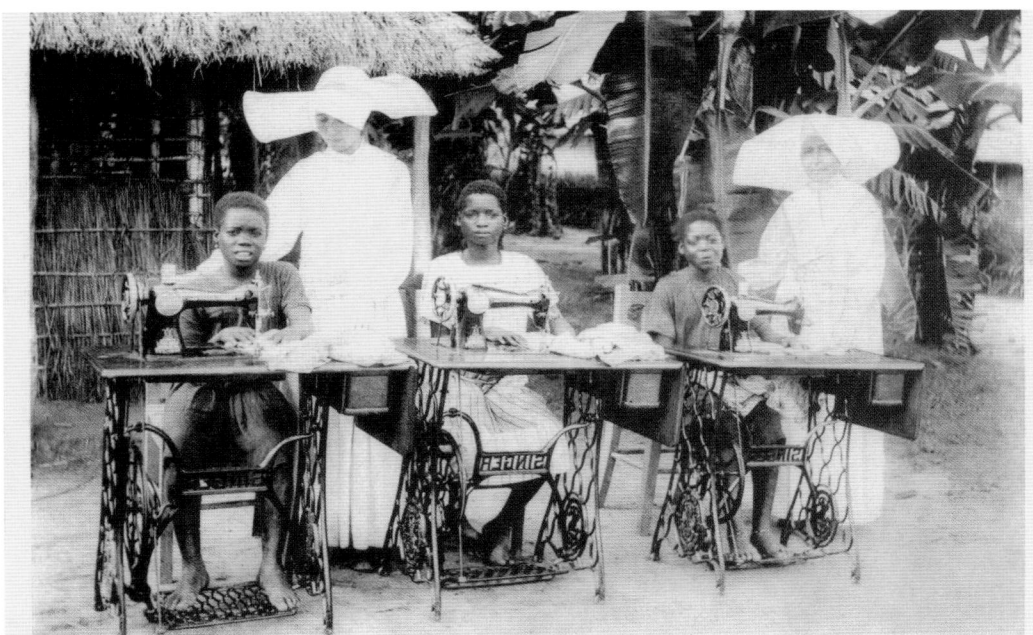

FIGURE 4.6 Unknown photographer, women with Singer sewing machines and two nuns, c. 1910, collotype, postcard, published for the Mission des filles de la Charité à Nsona-Mbata by Ern. Thill, Brussels, Belgium, c. 1915. Courtesy of Christraud Geary.

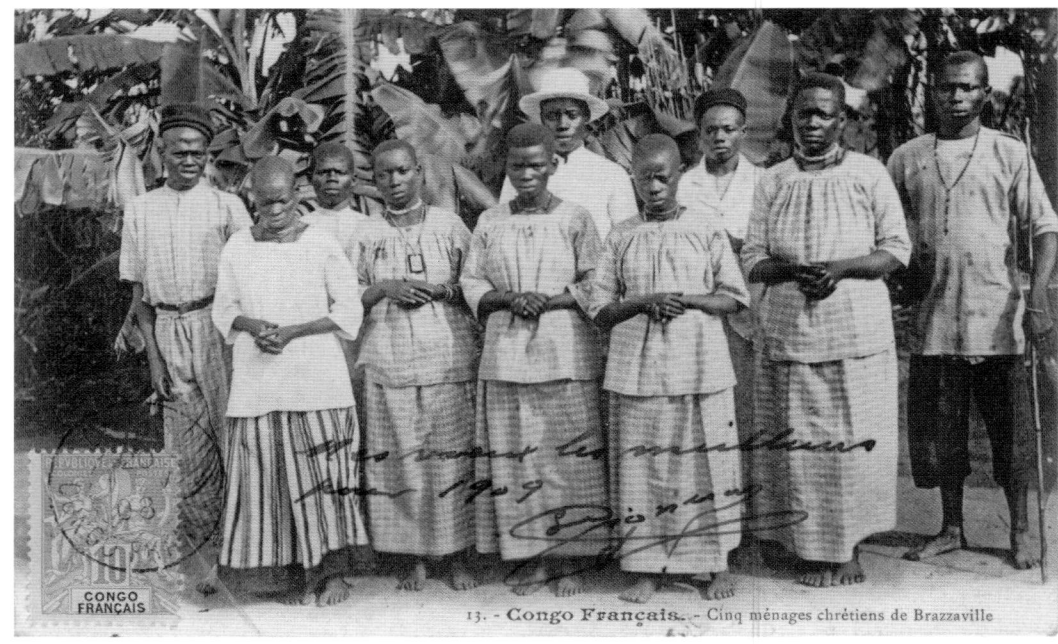

FIGURE 4.7 Unknown photographer, *13. Congo Français—Cinq ménages chrétiens de Brazzaville* [French Congo—Five Christian households of Brazzaville], c. 1900, collotype, publisher unidentified, c. 1904, cancellation November 20, 1908. Courtesy of Christraud Geary.

13. - Congo Français. - Cinq ménages chrétiens de Brazzaville

Anthropometric photography, a category of images of the unclothed black body and close-up prescribed views of the face, focused on the racial characteristics of Africans as delineated by Western scientists. In the nineteenth century, Darwin's theories became influential, postulating that human physical and cultural forms were end products of a long chain of evolution and that physical characteristics allowed Europeans to place humans in an evolutionary hierarchy. In this misleading schema, Caucasians occupied the highest level, while Africans were at the lowest rung of the ladder—not far removed from apes, which were thought the antecedents of man.[18] Scientists who practiced anthropometry, that is, measuring the human body for classificatory purposes, looked for the presence or absence of selected physical characteristics to determine "race" and to place individual "specimens" in the evolutionary scheme. This effort led to the creation of the "type," an individual that exemplified his or her "race" by displaying all characteristics established by the scientists.

Photography, which came into its own at the time when these theories gained popular acceptance, was a convenient means to document "types." Based on instructions widely discussed in photographic and anthropological handbooks, photographers of all backgrounds began to capture "types" in the last decade of the nineteenth century. They photographed representatives of the races of mankind, which included Caucasians, in rigid frontal, semi-profile, and profile poses, so that the outcome was an authoritative image, useful for scientific purposes.[19] There are hundreds of images of Africans—many of which became postcards—that had been created for this purpose. Other related anthropometric images focused on the physiognomy of Africans, presenting close-ups of facial characteristics in frontal and profile views (plate 53a–c). Images of this nature were associated with phrenology, the study of the shape of the skull, and the examination of human physiognomy, which wrongly sought to associate facial features with character and intellect.[20] In many instances, the lines between the anthropometric image and the ethnographic depiction of bodily practices, such as scarification and coiffure, which formed an important subsection of the visual record of Africans, are difficult to draw (plates 46, 47, 48, and 52; see also figure 4.2).

Anthropometric postcards of the black body demonstrate that most photographers failed to follow the detailed requirements for such photography. Rather, they singled out individuals and depicted them in various poses, which often bore little resemblance to scientific "type" images. Many of these vulgarized postcard images, however, were subsequently inserted into the discourse on race through their captions, which designated the subject as such-and-such "type" (plates 59, 68, 82, 84, 94, and 95) or "race" (plate 60). The "type" or "race" was a mainstay of postcards of Africans published before World War II. Postcards from all different regions of Africa created an imaginary, neatly ordered universe of African racial "types," thereby achieving the visual control of the black body.

"Type" postcards of women took on yet another dimension, for erotic and pornographic images often masqueraded as anthropometric depictions (plates 48 and 51). A postcard distributed by François-Edmond Fortier (1862–1928), a Dakar-based French photographer and postcard producer,[21] shows a young woman in a studio setting (figure 4.8). One of several "models" that appear in his cards, she has been partly and seductively undressed by the photographer (her clothes can be seen behind her on the floor) and assumes an uneasy pose. The caption describes her as *Jeune fille, type Lébou* [young girl, Lebou type], but in reality this pseudo-scientific caption masks a crass erotic depiction. Inspired by Orientalist imagery, Fortier had young nubile women pose—often in pairs—and accentuated their availability and sexuality. One of the mainstays of Orientalist imagery was the reclining nude that evokes the iconography of earlier Western depictions of eroticized women (plate 76) and thus appeals to the Western imagination (plates 73 and 74). Fortier depicted two young Arab women in this pose (plate 75), one of which reappears in the postcards in plates 68 and 69. The aesthetic quality of Fortier's beautifully composed cards contributed to their popularity and wide dissemination.

Fortier was perhaps the most prolific and important producer/distributor of postcards of the black female body, but there were other contemporaries whose works had a large impact as well. Jean François Audema (1864–1936), a French colonial administrator who worked in the French Congo from 1894 to 1905, produced a fascinating series of postcards, many of which depict so-called "types," including women in the

FIGURE 4.8 François-Edmond Fortier? French (1862–1928), *Afrique occidentale Française, 1045. Sénégal. Jeune Fille, type Lébou* [French West Africa. Senegal. Young girl, Lebou type], c. 1900, collotype, postcard, published by Collection Fortier, Dakar, Senegal, c. 1910. Courtesy of Christraud Geary.

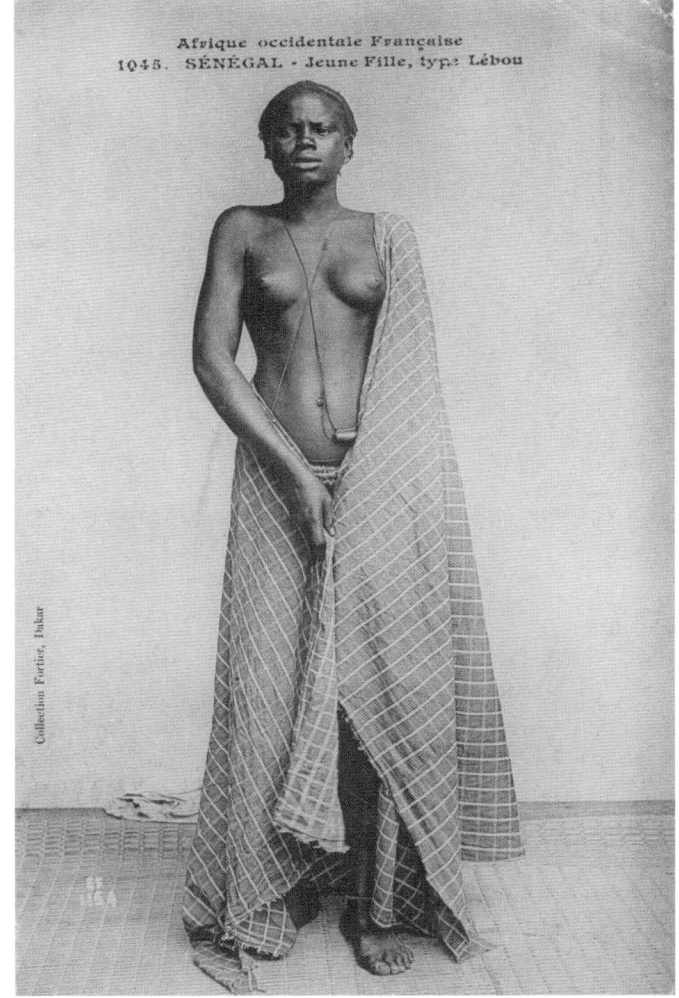

nude.[22] Many South African photographers also produced photographs of nudes, often in studio settings that evoked the notion of the wild and untamed Africa, conflating indigenous peoples and savagery (plate 49). Laid open to the Western gaze, the black female body—in the guise of ethnographic or anthropometric depictions—was thus legitimately brought to the salons of the European and American middle-class consumer/viewer who had never been to Africa, while depictions of the white female body remained hidden, relegated to backrooms— an illicit pleasure for voyeurs.

IMAGES OF PRIDE AND CONFIDENCE

Among the postcards of black women are certain images that seem to stand apart from these ethnographic and anthropometric depictions—portraits in carefully crafted settings, clearly collaborative efforts by both the sitter and photographer. They share many characteristics, such as the poses of the portrayed, the arrangement and furnishings of the space in which the photograph was taken, and the props surrounding the sitter. Many of them depict particular African modernities of the time and location in which they were made. The similarities between such images taken in Senegal and in the Congo or in Nigeria and in Angola are striking. Were there somehow connections between the photographers who created the pictures? How did similar conventions of portraiture become established over such a large area?

Among the most puzzling postcards are several photographs that appear under Fortier's imprint but are distinct from his output of erotic pictures of nude women. When examining Fortier's thousands of postcards, it becomes obvious that he published photographs he had not taken himself and acted as a conduit for other local photographers to the printing houses in France. Putting "Collection Fortier" on their images was actually not as predatory as it might seem, because copyright did not yet exist. Moreover, photographers took over entire collections of images when they bought a colleagues' studio, for instance, and often published them as their own.[23] One popular Fortier card is an image of two women and a child, which, judging by the poses and setting, seems to be the product of a local (perhaps Senegalese) photographer who was attuned to his sitters desires (figure 4.9). The two women, wearing outfits typical for well-to-do married Senegalese matrons and adorned with

FIGURE 4.9 François-Edmond Fortier? French (1862–1928), *1303.—Afrique Occidentale.—Femmes Ouolofs* [West Africa.—Wolof Women], Collection Générale Fortier, Dakar, Senegal, c. 1900, hand-tinted collotype, postcard, published by Collection Générale Fortier, Dakar, Senegal, c. 1905. Courtesy of Christraud Geary.

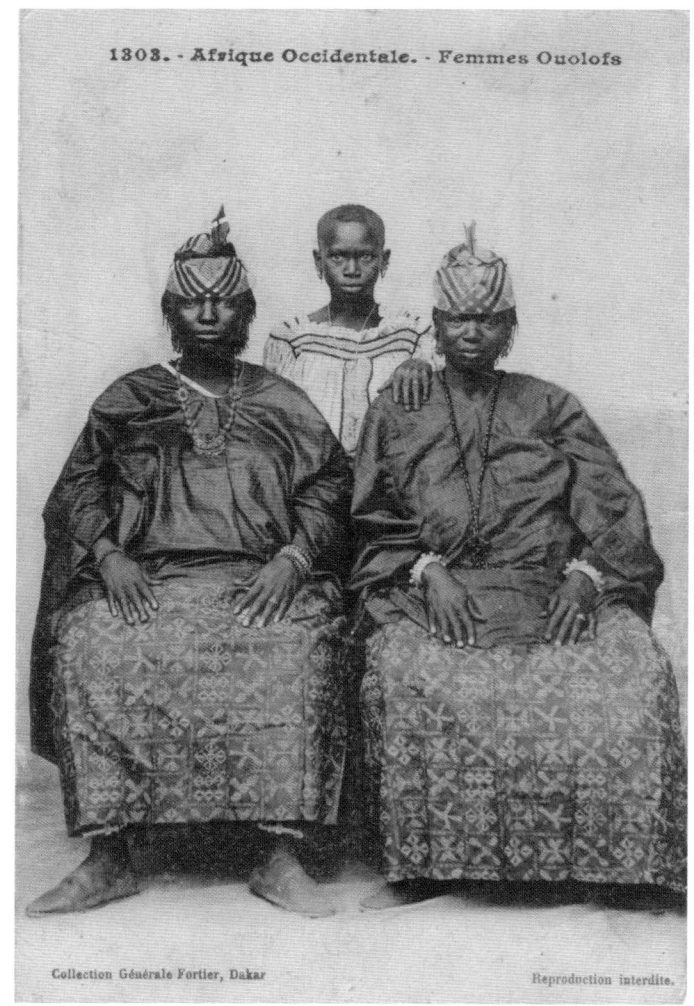

1303. - Afrique Occidentale. - Femmes Ouolofs

Collection Générale Fortier, Dakar   Reproduction interdite.

necklaces and gold bracelets, serenely face the camera. The pattern of their *pagnes*, or wrappers, seems almost identical. Their hands with all fingers visible rest in their laps and they place their legs solidly on the floor of the studio, which seems to fade away. A young girl stands behind them with her left hand on one of the women's shoulders, a gesture perhaps indicating that they are mother and daughter. We do not know what the two women's relationship might have been. Were they sisters or friends? The way the women present themselves in this image echoes similar poses of friends, relatives, and women belonging to the same associations in many African studio photographs up and down the coasts from the late nineteenth century until the 1960s and 1970s.

When this image—commissioned by the sitters and created in collaboration with the photographer—migrated onto postcards, however, it moved from the private into the public realm and metamorphosed from a personal memento into a depiction for public consumption. The caption facilitated that transformation. The text, *1303.—Afrique Occidentale.—Femmes Ouolofs* [1303.—West Africa.—Wolof Women], places the picture into the numbered series of Fortier's ethnic and "type" postcards and turns the women into representatives of their ethnic group/race, the Wolof. Judging by the fact that this image appeared in several editions, including a much more garish rendering with a different caption, it must have enjoyed commercial success (figure 4.10).[24]

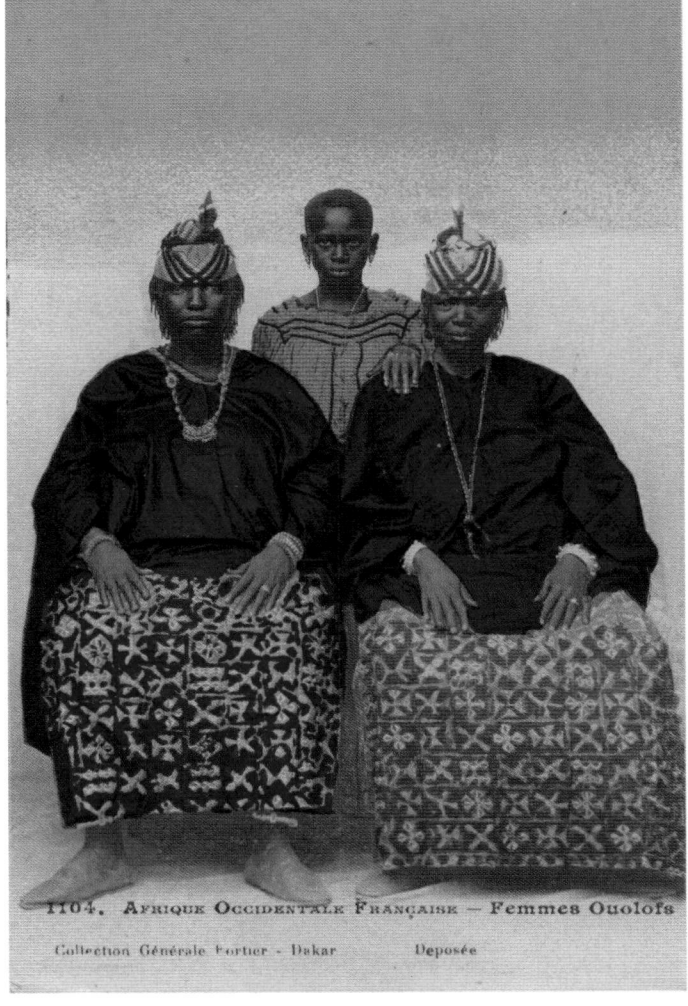

FIGURE 4.10 François-Edmond Fortier? French (1862–1928), *1104. Afrique Occidentale Française.—Femmes Ouolofs* [French West Africa—Wolof Women], Collection Générale Fortier—Dakar, Senegal, c. 1900, hand-tinted collotype, postcard, published by Collection Générale Fortier—Dakar, Senegal, c. 1915, dated July 7, 1919. Courtesy of Christraud Geary.

Similar postcards from other parts of West and Central Africa, which migrated from the private into the public domain, resonated with Western purchasers and collectors because they were both familiar and exotic. They rendered the photographic studio—a place Westerners frequented as well. The studio set-up, which was outdoors because of the lack of electricity in Africa, often included a painted backdrop, a carpet or mat, and props. Since photographs of the sitter were taken up close, the images create the illusion of an interior, demarcated space. At times, however, postcards reveal the particular arrangement, as in a card photographed by Khalilou, most likely a Senegalese photographer, and distributed by his countryman Demba Ndiaye, who was a merchant in Libreville in the French Congo (figure 4.11). Behind the backdrop, held in place by a piece of wood, we see a clothesline, a common sight in residences all over Africa. Painted backdrops provided the sitter with proper decorum and evoked bucolic and architectural scenes. Many of them, such as the backdrop in Khalilou's image, were imported from Europe, while others sported local

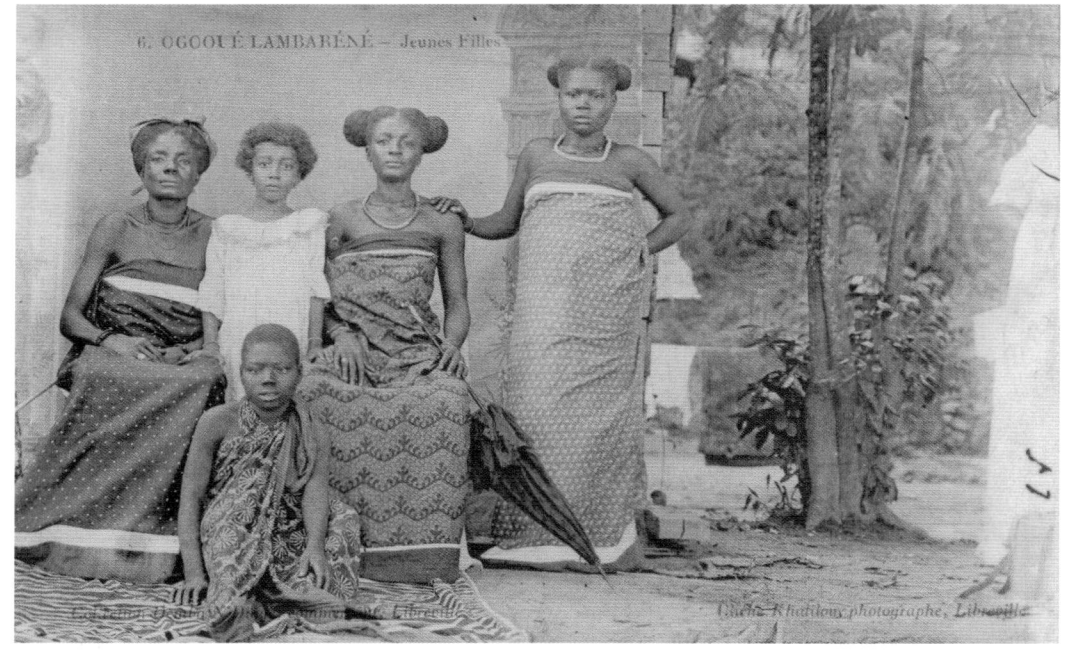

left FIGURE 4.11 Khalilou, photographer, Libreville, Senegalese (active 1900–1930), *6. Ogooué Lambaréné—Jeunes Filles* [Ogowe Lambarene—young girls], collotype, postcard, c. 1905, published by Demba Ndiaye, Senegalese, Libreville, Gabon, c. 1910. Courtesy of Christraud Geary.

lower left FIGURE 4.12 Reveyron, photographer, à Dakar (Sénégal), (active c. 1900–1920), *30. — Jeune Filles de Dakar (Sénégal), en Costume national* [Young women of Dakar (Senegal) in national costume], c. 1905, collotype, postcard, publisher unidentified, c. 1907, cancellation 1909. Courtesy of Christraud Geary.

lower right FIGURE 4.13 J. Benyoumoff (active c. 1900–1920), *Dakar—Jeune Fille Wolof* [Dakar—young Wolof girl], c. 1900, hand-tinted collotype, postcard, c. 1910, publisher unidentified. Courtesy of Christraud Geary.

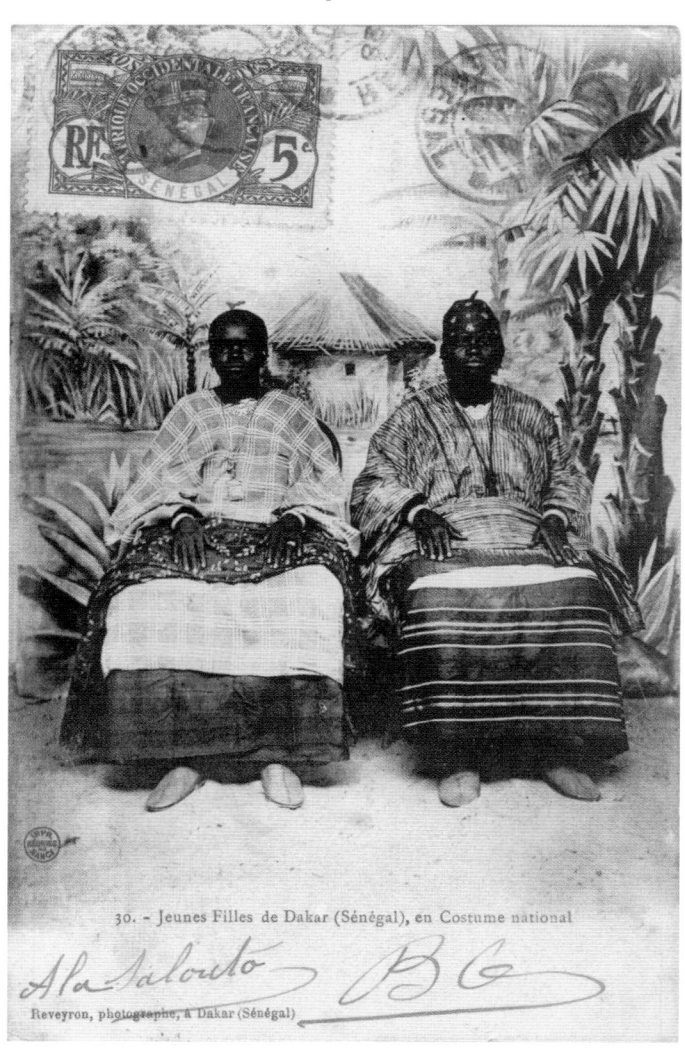

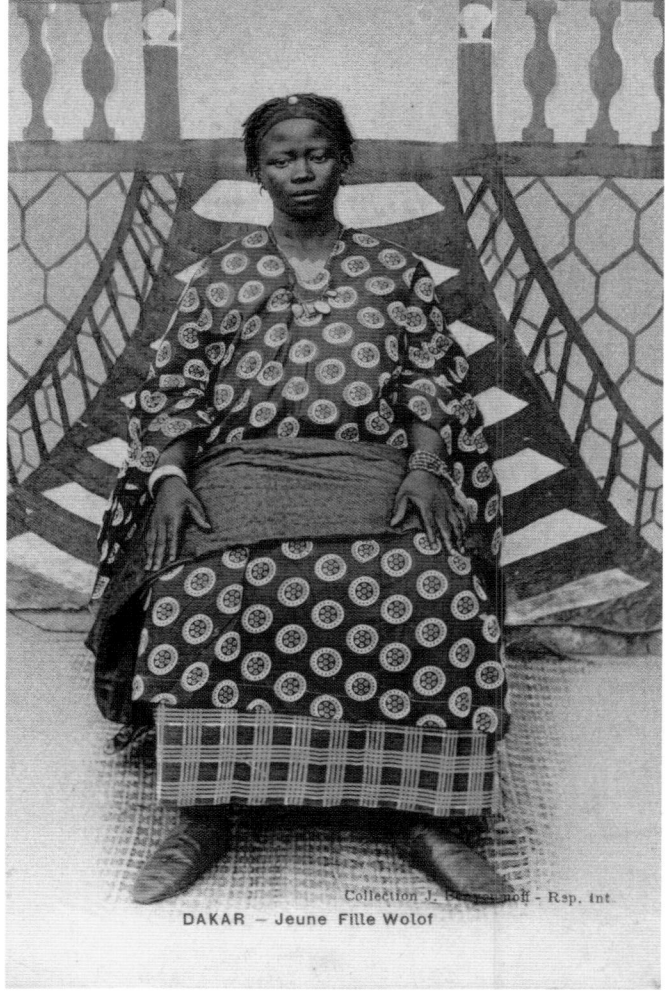

motifs, most likely created by local painters (plates 55, 56, 60, 61, 64, 81, 84, 85, and 91).[25] In some of these, the backdrop recreates African scenes with indigenous houses and palm trees (figure 4.12). A portrait taken by J. Benyoumoff, a photographer of unknown origins[26] who was active in Dakar during the first decades of the twentieth century, shows such a locally produced backdrop, depicting the typical winding staircases found in the houses of rich Senegalese merchants (figure 4.13).

Studio props ranged from chairs to side tables, vases to pedestals, and flowers (plates 57–63, 67, 84, 94, and 95). The sitters surrounded themselves with icons of modernity, most likely provided by the studio: books, glasses, glass bottles, and letters, all indicating that they wanted to be seen as learned and cosmopolitan people. They held bowler hats, fans, flowers, umbrellas, walking sticks, and pocketbooks (figure 4.14, see also plates 57, 58, 61, and 81). Their poses were constrained and conventional—legs planted on the ground as behooves an important person, hands in the lap or the right hand holding the left arm, the eyes directly focused on the camera and thus the viewer. In these studio settings, the women exude self-confidence and do not appear pressured, embarrassed, or ill at ease.

We do not always know whether the photographers of these portraits commissioned by the sitters were African practitioners. Most likely they were, but a few may have been from Europe or from yet another part of the world. Suffice it to say that all of them were professionals subjected to the forces of the marketplace, for they needed to make a living. The African clients portrayed in these images were eager to create their representation and to appear as they wanted to be seen. They had choices, for they could wear particular dress and adornment for the occasion, select one photographer over another, and accept or reject the result of the studio session. With every small act, they shaped the photographic landscape, assured that local conventions were maintained, or accepted a photographer's slight innovations.

These observations lead us back to considering the striking similarities of poses and settings in studio portraits taken along the West and Central African coasts. As research slowly unearths the history of African photography, we gain a clearer picture of how photography spread and who initially commissioned portraits. Late nineteenth-century African photographers were highly mobile, traveling up and down the coast on ships and steamers that connected the major ports. They were among the many African men and women searching for economic opportunities. The bustling harbor towns and their hinterlands were magnets for entrepreneurs. Thus, Sierra Leonians settled in many major African ports and commercial centers; Vai and Kru peoples from Liberia arrived in the service of

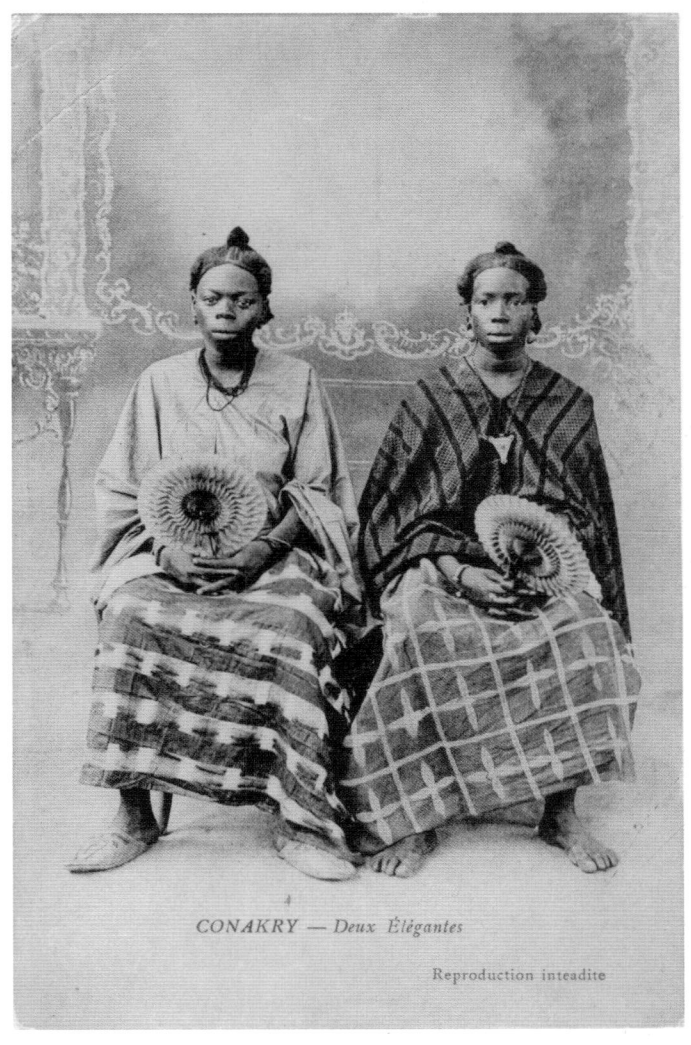

CONAKRY — Deux Élégantes

Reproduction inteadite

FIGURE 4.14 A. James, Sierra Leonian? Guinean? (active c. 1900–1930), *Conakry—Deux Élégantes* [Conakry—two elegant women], c. 1905, collotype, postcard, publisher unidentified, c. 1910, cancellation 1910. Courtesy of Christraud Geary.

shipping lines and as preferred soldiers and porters for European colonial armies; and Senegalese and Nigerians worked in the Congo.[27] Many early photographers, men who enjoyed innovation and technical challenges, relocated frequently along the coast, establishing studios in one town and then moving on to another if the business opportunities seemed more promising.

Not only the photographers traveled—the images themselves journeyed as well and were seen by many. They were displayed in family homes, exchanged, carried along as people traveled and moved to distant places. Did African sitters see postcards such as the ones presented here? Most likely they did, for many cards were published in large quantities and sold locally. Thus the constant movement of people and postcards may have fostered the development of similar photographic styles and conventions in portraits commissioned by African sitters along the coastlines of the continent.

CHALLENGING THE LEGACY

Although the role of the postcard medium in constructing views of Africa was of great importance, until recently its impact did not receive much attention. Before the 1980s, few writings on postcards of Africa and Africans went beyond reference for postcard collectors. Then two major types of scholarly studies emerged. One focused on postcards as historical sources. From the 1980s onward, museums and cultural centers increasingly supported exhibitions of postcards as historical documents—often promulgating nostalgic and romanticized views of a colonial past that seems benign.[28] Postcards as contextual images were also included in exhibitions devoted to other subjects. The second type of examination advanced the critical analysis of postcards in studies of representation, a field that became preoccupied with the examination of images of the black female body. Among such studies of representation were Alloula's *The Colonial Harem* (1986) and Corbey's *Wildheid en beschaving: De Europese verbeelding van Afrika* (1989).[29]

These writers, whose work critiques the postcard medium for its past representational practices, agree that depictions of the black female body are among the most painful legacies of colonial image-making, for they captured the black female body and laid it open to the Western desire to create taxonomies, to establish control, and to find pleasure. They also concur that such images in general helped to construct, reflect, and enact colonial ideologies of race and of innate superiority and inferiority, reinforcing Western perceptions of Africans. Their well-illustrated exposés (a term understood here in the double meaning of "to lay open for examination" and "to exhibit") go to great lengths to demonstrate these processes. They intended to challenge paradigms and point to the racist and sexist nature of these images. But do they succeed in disempowering this imagery or, more to the point, *can* they succeed?

Most of these authors—scholars, writers, and/or collectors—are male. This gendered nature of the interpretive enterprise in and of itself brings up a relevant issue. "Who does the looking?" asks feminist Mieke Bal, who examined this literature in 1998 in a seminal essay titled "A Postcard from the Edge" about the practice of exhibiting and publishing postcards of the black female body.[30] Answering her own provocative question, Bal suggested that no matter who looks and how well-intentioned these publications may be, these writers and curators ultimately *expose* these images/women again to the voyeuristic gaze, a practice she condemned as repeat victimization. Bal also questioned whether the (male) authors' extensive critiques of this colonial visual practice are in fact a pretense, legitimizing their re-looking and republishing of these images. Indeed, the beautifully printed images singled out in these books remain visually powerful and do not lose their effect to denigrate those depicted in them, even as critical texts accompany them.[31] Through republishing, these postcards appear to gain an additional layer of power—the patina of age, which evokes nostalgic and to a certain extent romantic sentiments in the viewer. This effect is particularly pronounced in Alloula's work, for the postcard images—although mostly black-and-white in their original version—are enlarged and tinted in quaint sepia tone throughout the book.

If the question "who does the looking" interrogates the legitimacy of this enterprise, the question "who does the speaking" equally deserves attention. This question might be expanded particularly in reference to Alloula's work—he is Algerian—and phrased as "who may speak for whom?" May Alloula speak for Algerian women? The answers to these questions need further attention and debate beyond the scope of this essay. Deborah Willis and Carla Williams's book *The Black Female Body: A Photographic History* (2002), an elaborately produced photographic history of depictions of the black female body, however, addresses this dilemma head-on. Both scholars, themselves African American (and photographers), are conscious of what they perceive as "doubly objectifying black woman by re-presenting exploitive and derogatory images created in another time and historical context."[32] Their strategy relies on countering these deeply painful misrepresentations through exploring also the agency of the African and African American subjects in the image-making process and by presenting black women photographers' depictions of their own bodies and the bodies of other black women, a topic that Willis and Williams explore even further in this book.

In 2002, in my exhibition *In and Out of Focus: Images from Central Africa, 1885–1960* and its accompanying catalogue, I took a similar approach and looked at the full spectrum of photographic practice, including that of African photographers.[33] This approach seems to be one way to counter this imagery, setting it in a different context—one of agency and self-representation. At that time, I chose not to publish or exhibit any blatantly sexual depictions of the "colonial nude," so as to not invite voyeurs. Here, however, I have included sexualized images of African womanhood because this exhibition and book seek to critique and contextualize such renderings in many subtle and direct ways. This raises another question, which needs to be carefully considered: "where and how does one speak?" Both questions were among the issues that came into focus during a heated debate about the practice of several South African artists, who "sometimes almost

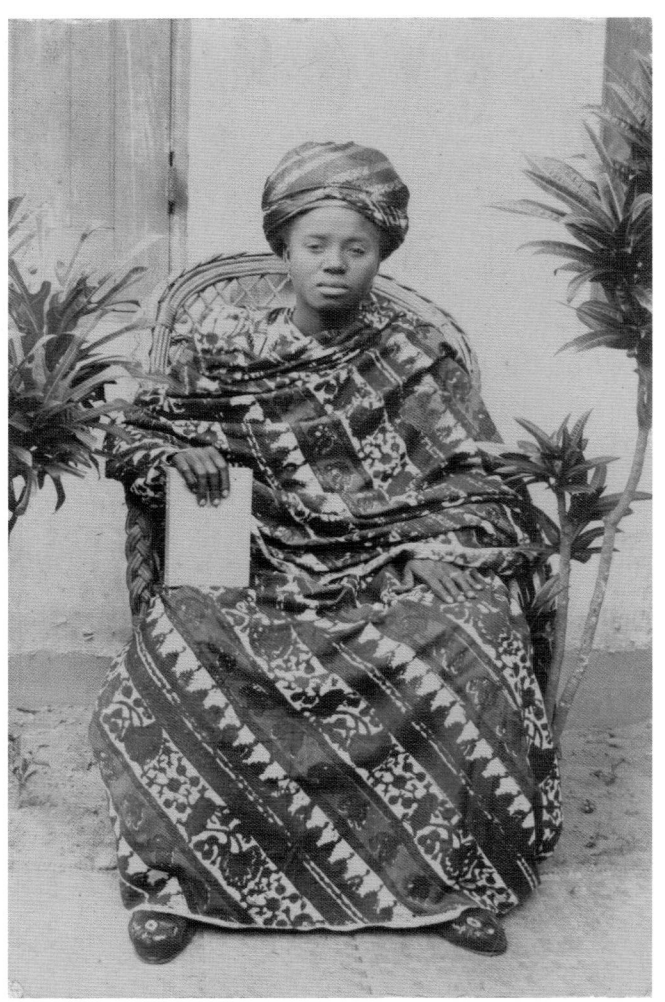

FIGURE 4.15 Unknown photographer, seated woman with book, Nigeria, c. 1910, silver gelatin print, postcard, publisher unidentified, c. 1912, dated February 26, 1913. Courtesy of Christraud Geary.

routinely plunged into the past and accessioned 'tribal' imagery . . . into the 'archival bank of the new South African Nation,'" as Colin Richards, a professor in the Department of Fine Arts at the University of Witwatersrand, observed in an essay commenting on the origins of the controversy. It began with a provocative 1997 exposé by Nigerian art critic and promoter Okwui Enwezor, titled "Reframing the Black Subject: Ideology and Fantasy in South African Representation."[34] In this essay, initially published in conjunction with a less-than-memorable exhibition of South African contemporary art in Norway,[35] and later reprinted in the journal *Third Text*, Enwezor comments on the "resurgence of the black subject as a popular form of image in all forms of representation in contemporary South Africa."[36] He critiqued the artists' practice of appropriating historical imagery from various sources, among them postcards, illustrations in textbooks, and iconic images. It so happens that the artists he challenged were white, which introduced the element of race into the polemic. Enwezor lamented the "anxious repetition" of stereotypes, which "finds itself inscribed again and again in the almost obsessive usage of old photographic images of Africans or in the ethnographic, tourist postcards depicting near-naked African women in a state of colonial arrest."[37] Artists, among them Penny Siopis[38] and Candice Breitz, both white South Africans, manipulated postcard images of the nude black female body (plate 98). Breitz created photomontages, which joined pornographic images of the white female body with anthropometric/ethnographic ones of the black female body, drawing a parallel between the colonial representational and contemporary pornographic practices that violate the female body. It is beyond this short essay to delve deeper into this provocative exchange with racial overtones, which is far from concluded and may never be resolved.[39] But it is worth mentioning that the same questions of race that pertained to the authors, who wrote about the imagery in their books, were at the core of this debate about artistic expression.

Bal's caution about the power of the visual reminds us, however, that the critic may become the expository agent and contribute to this legacies' continuous impact and exploitation, even though intending the opposite. Who then may legitimately challenge this powerful and painful legacy? Cultural critics, among them Bal and Enwezor, caution that all scholars, artists, and curators who engage in these analyses, critiques, and displays—that is, the re-representation—of colonial imagery should heed their concerns and take pause. In an address to participants in a conference on colonial images in 1993, Achille Mbembe, an eminent Cameroonian scholar, pointed to the heightened impact of colonial imagery due to contemporary repetition, its density and power to re-enact stories—even lies.[40] He then describes his personal reaction—anger and the feeling of impotence—

when he faced the image that producers and viewers fabricated of Africans who remain voiceless. Bal, Enwezor, and Mbembe thus warn that images might never lose their power to perpetuate fabrications, stereotypes, and racist ideologies unless challenged in ways clearly understood by multiple audiences. Ultimately, then, clarity of intent *and* execution are the goals that any writer, artist, or curator who addresses this legacy through re-presenting such imagery (no matter his or her origin and background) needs to achieve.

One might consider here that meaning-making is not only directed by the intent of the writers/critics—in other words, by our agenda—but also by the mode and forum of re-presentation. In this case, *Black Womanhood* unfolds in a university art museum setting, which attracts both academic and general audiences and fosters critical thinking, debate, and multi-platform discussions. Additional programming held in conjunction with the exhibition helps explain and contextualize the complex issues for the viewers and contribute to a nuanced understanding of the issues at hand. In this essay and exhibition, one of the modes to redress this painful visual legacy beyond critical words about exploitation and victimization has been to juxtapose it with images that show African and (African-descended) women as they represented themselves and as they wanted to be seen. Having begun this essay with an erotic/exotic postcard to address the subject of exploitation of the black female body, I now end with the picture of an anonymous Nigerian woman created by an unknown photographer around 1900. Seated in an outside studio space, she looks straight at us, holding a book in her right hand and placing the other hand on her thigh (figure 4.15). She is self-confident, strong, and in command of her own image. This postcard, as also others in this essay, clearly demonstrates African women's agency and control over their own bodies, thus recalling Willis and Williams's approach in presenting counternarratives to one-sided discussions about victimization. It is my sincere hope that this essay—and the larger project of *Black Womanhood*—will provide some traction in this difficult terrain; that it will teach and raise broader awareness about the contested nature of the imagery in these historical postcards; and that it will succeed in fostering constructive discussions where others have come up short, rather than victimize women of color again. 🐏

1 I thank Barbara Thompson, Rory Bester, and Amanda Carlson for their constructive comments and careful editing, which helped shape this essay.

2 The Eliot Elisofon Photographic Archives, National Museum of African Art, Smithsonian Institution, has more than 16,000 images posted on the internet (www.si.siris.edu). Other archives such as the Mission 21 (formerly Basel Mission) Archive also are available on the web (www.bmpix.org), and many archives plan to follow suit.

3 Several contributors to this catalogue have previously published books and essays containing such photographs.

4 I use the term "black" in reference to the body of "all women of African descent," thus including North African women, as Deborah Willis and Carla Williams did in *The Black Female Body: A Photographic History* (Philadelphia: Temple University Press), 2002, x.

5 The term "erotic" commonly refers to depictions that may create sexual desire in the viewer, while the term "pornographic" describes sexually explicit, obscene materials. Pornographic images have not been included in this essay or, for that matter, in the exhibition. The lines between those two categories of images, however, are fluid, and the perceptions of what constitutes erotic or pornographic images have fluctuated over time. To complicate matters even more, cultural and historical circumstances deeply affect a viewer's interpretation of such images.

6 In the strictest sense, "nude" implies the deliberate act of undressing and posing the female model/subject by an artist/photographer. For an image to be considered a nude, it needs to comply with conventions established in the visual arts and taught in academic settings. John Berger, *Ways of Seeing* (London: British Broadcasting Corporations and Penguin Books, 1977; 1st ed., 1972), 53.

7 Stereographs are side-by-side, nearly identical photographic prints mounted on cardboard. Seen through a stereopticon, they merge into one image, which appears three-dimensional. Companies such as Underwood and Underwood and Keystone marketed large sets to private buyers and educational institutions.

8 See Christraud M. Geary and Virginia-Lee Webb, eds., *Delivering Views: Distant Cultures in Early Postcards* (Washington, D.C.: Smithsonian Institution Press, 1998).

9 See Christraud Geary, "Different Visions? Postcards from Africa by European and African Photographers and Sponsors," in *Delivering Views: Distant Cultures in Early Postcards*, 147–177.

10 Some European countries had major postcard industries that serviced postcard needs worldwide, among them Germany and France.

11 This also pertains to my own research, which—originating in the examination of photography in Africa as historical documentation—has emphasized the image over the other meaning-making parts of the postcards. See also Max Quanchi and Max Shekleton, "Disorderly Categories in Picture Postcards from Colonial Papua and New Guinea," *History of Photography* 25, no. 4 (Winter 2001): 315–333.

12 David MacDougall, *The Corporeal Image: Film, Ethnography, and the Senses* (Princeton and Oxford: Princeton University Press, 2006), 195–196.

13 David Prochaska, "The Archive of *Algérie Imaginaire*," *History and Anthropology* 4 (1990): 373–420.

14 In his book *The Invention of Africa: Gnosis, Philosophy, and the Order of Knowledge*, Mudimbe argues that European colonial science created misleading information about Africa and Africans based on misperceptions and fascination with the otherness, thus in the guise of science "invented" an imaginary Africa (Bloomington: Indiana University Press, 1988).

15 The term "ethnographic" is used in the original sense of the Greek word (*graphein* means to write and *ethnos* means a people), which stresses the descriptive element in analysis.

16 See Elisabeth Edwards, "Photographic 'Types': The Pursuit of Method," in *Picturing Cultures: Historical Photographs in Anthropological Inquiry*, Joanna Cohan Scherer, ed., *Visual Anthropology* 3, nos. 2–3 (1990): 235–258.

17 It should be noted here that due to long exposure times, early cameras could not capture movement. Even after the technology improved, the conventions of the staged, static image remained common in ethnographic depictions.

18 George W. Stocking, ed., *Bones, Bodies, Behavior* (Madison: University of Wisconsin Press, 1988), 11.

19 See Edwards, "Photographic 'Types.'"

20 Physiognomy was a science claiming that one could judge a person's character through the analysis of facial features, while phrenology sought to achieve similar results through the analysis of the shape of the skull.

21 See Philippe David, *Inventaire générale des cartes postales Fortier*, 3 vols. (Saint-Julien-du-Sault: Fostier, 1986–1988).

22 MacDougall, *The Corporeal Image*. In an excellent, in-depth study of his oeuvre, MacDougall analyzed Audema's personal style and comes to the conclusion that his images of African men and women, which at first glance appear to be anthropometric renderings, were often collaborative efforts and marked by a refreshing directness, setting them apart from other such imagery.

23 See the discussion of Fortier's appropriation of images by Louis Hostalier and the Noal Frères who were based in St. Louis, Senegal, in Philippe David's, "Hostalier—Noal. Un duel de photographes au *Journal Officiel* du Sénégal, il y a cent ans," *Images & Mémoires* 14 (2006): 7–13.

24 The caption now reads 1104. *Afrique Occidentale Française—Femmes Ouolofs* [1104. French West Africa—Wolof women].

25 For backdrops in Ghana, see Tobias Wendl, "'Observers are Worried': Fotokulissen aus Ghana," in *Snap me one: Studiofotografen in Afrika*, ed. Tobias Wendl and Heike Behrend (München: Prestel Verlag, 1998), pp. 29–35.

26 With the ongoing research on early photography in Africa, Benyoumoff's biography may well be reconstructed. The keys lie in French archives and possibly with his descendants, if they can be traced.

27 There are several studies underway that will cast light on early African photographers. The recent edited volume *Fotofieber* focuses on the link of photography and travel both by European and African photographers; see Jürg Schneider, Ute Röschenthaler, and Berhard Gardi, eds., *Fotofieber: Bilder aus West- und Zentralafrika, Die Reisen von Carl Passavant 1883–1885* (Basel: Christoph Merian Verlag, 2005).

28 Several of these exhibitions were held in African countries, such as an exhibition on postcards from Guinea in 1991, which was a fine examination of Guinea's colonial history through the postcard medium. See P. Dürr, Steven Grant, B. Sivan, and E. Tompapa, *Images de Guinée* (Conakry: Editions Imprimerie Mission Catholique, 1991).

29 Malek Alloula's *The Colonial Harem* (Minneapolis: University of Minnesota Press, 1986), and Raymond Corbey's *Wildheid en beschaving: De Europese ver-beelding van Afrika* (Baarn: Ambo, 1989), in translation "Savagery and civilization: The European representation of Africa." The collection, on which Corbey's book is based, is now part of the Eliot Elisofon Photographic Archives at the National Museum of African Art, Smithsonian Institution (accession 2002–0006).

30 Mieke Bal, *Double Exposure: The Subject of Cultural Analysis* (London: Routledge, 1996). The essay is one of the chapters in this book (Bal, 195–224).

31 Bal, *Double Exposure*, 195–197.

32 Willis and Williams, *The Black Female Body*, ix.

33 Christraud M. Geary, *In and Out of Focus: Images from Central Africa, 1885–1960* (London: Philip Wilson, 2002).

34 Okwui Enwezor, "Reframing the Black Subject: Ideology and Fantasy in Contemporary South African Art," in *Contemporary Art from South Africa*, ed. Hope Marith (Oslo: Riksutstillinger, 1997), and "Reframing the Black Subject: Ideology and Fantasy in Contemporary South African Representation," *Third Text* 40 (Autumn 1997): 21–40.

35 This led to a fascinating discussion of "foreign curating" of exhibitions, which revolved around the ability of foreigners to understand the parameters and nuances of the history of representation and representational practices in South Africa. See Brenda Atkinson and Candice Breitz, eds., *Grey Areas: Representation, Identity and Politics in Contemporary South African Art* (Johannesburg: Chalkham Hill Press, 1999).

36 Enwezor, "Reframing the Black Subject," *Third Text*, 24.

37 Ibid., 28.

38 See Thompson, "Decolonizing Black Bodies: Personal Journeys in the Contemporary Voice," in this volume, for a discussion of Siopis's work.

39 See the Atkinson and Breitz book *Grey Areas*, which is devoted entirely to this debate. See also Colin Richards, "About Face: Aspects of Art History and Identity in South African Visual Culture," *Third Text* 16/17 (Autumn/Winter 1991): 101–133.

40 "Regard d'Afrique sur l'image et imaginaire coloniale," in *Images et colonies*, eds. Pascal Blanchard and Armelle Chatelier (Paris: ACHAC and SYROS, 1993), 136.

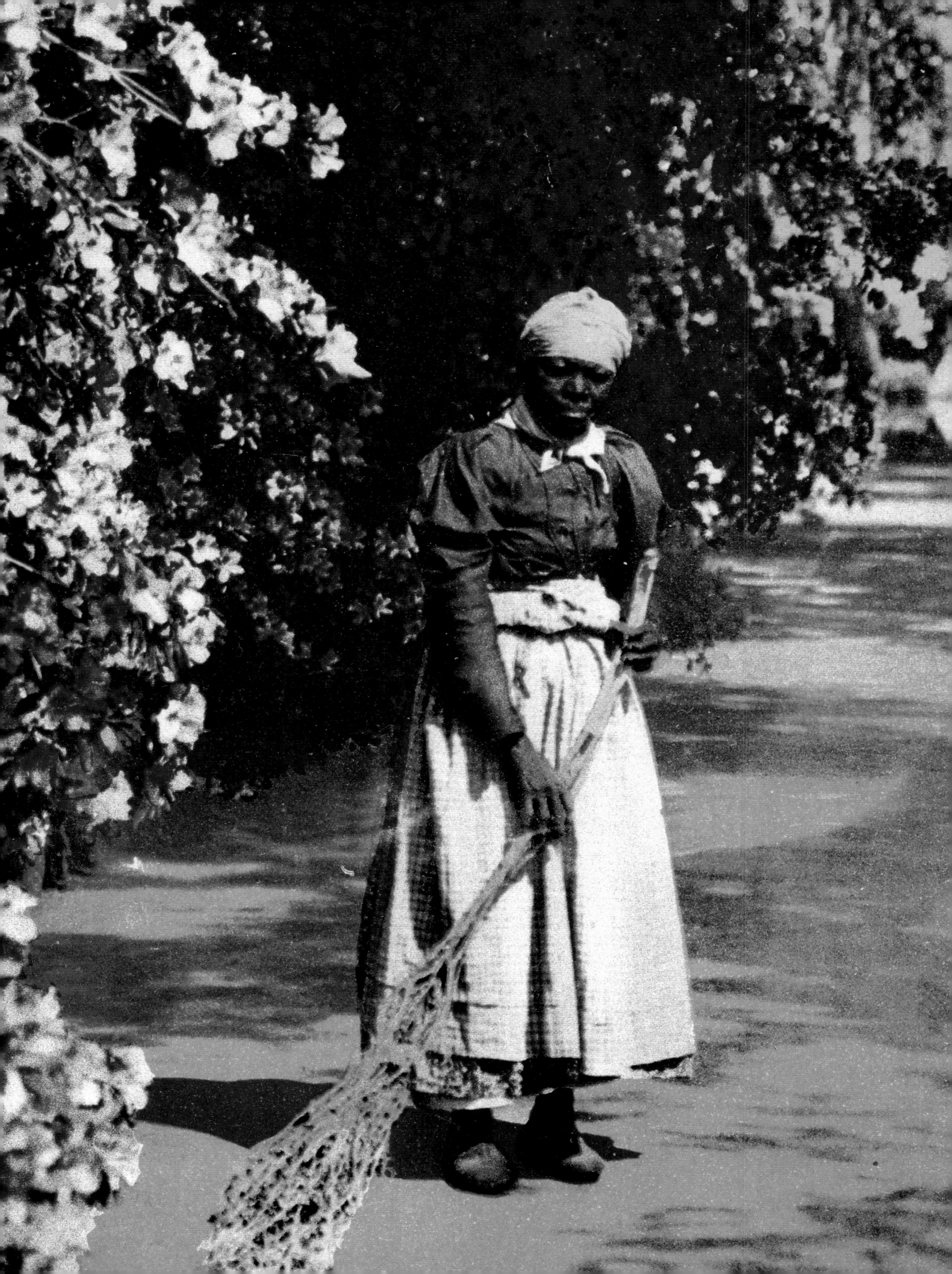

5   The Body of a Myth: Embodying the
Black Mammy Figure in Visual Culture

*The use of the Negro woman as an embodiment of myth and fantasies that
have little to do with her and much to do with the troubled and repressed
conscience of the country . . . has reached so far down in the national psyche
that not even the best of the white writers have escaped it.*

—PAULE MARSHALL[1]

In American culture, images of "Mammy" seem to tower over our imaginations
to such an extent that more accurate representations of African American women
wither in her shadow. This stereotype continues to have a tenacious, provocative,
and troubling hold on our national imagination. The word "Mammy"—or
"Auntie," "Negro Nurse," and "Colored Nurse"—is originally part of the nineteenth-century lexicon of antebellum plantation literature and folklore. It is a
term that describes both a role and a person serving as baby nurse, cook, and
all-around domestic help within the plantation home. Primarily through well-
established physical attributes—large dark body, substantial bosom, ever-expand-
ing lap, and round face marked with a permanent smile—representations of
Mammy point to a long-lasting and troubled marriage of racial and gender essen-
tialism, mythology, and a presupposition of the black female body as ultimately
maternal.

Mammy is arguably the most recognizable stereotype of the black female
body in America and has shaped and influenced a wide range of perceptions
about black womanhood, particularly black motherhood. Here I examine some of
the most intriguing visual representations of the "black mammy" figure as a way
to better understand how the embodiment of this myth is linked to concepts and
misconceptions about African American women that extend far beyond the
stereotype. The first section of this essay explores questions about how the black
mammy's maternity, body size and shape, and skin color work together to
influence our understanding of this iconic figure as an ultimate representation of
maternal devotion. I will then consider the idea that in American visual and popular culture black women are frequently reduced to body parts, often with an
exaggerated emphasis placed on their breasts. Finally, the essay points to new
directions in creating representations of African American motherhood by evoking the mammy figure and introducing some unexpected features that add complexity and depth to a flat stereotype.

opposite Unknown photographer, *5779
Aunt Phoebe, Magnolia-on-the-Ashley*,
early twentieth century, hand-tinted
collotype, postcard. Hood Museum
of Art: Anonymous gift; 2007.20.1

Fat Aunt Bess is older than Time

But her eyes still shine like a bright, new dime,
Though two generations have gone to rest
On the sleepy mountain of her breast

She has had children of her own,
But the white skinned ones are bone of her bone

—Stephen Vincent Benet[2]

Before the phenomenal success of *Uncle Tom's Cabin*,[3] pro-slavery authors used images of African American women with a white child as a symbol of racial harmony within the slave system. In addition to the vivid physical descriptions of mammy characters, illustrations accompanied many of these characterizations. These particular depictions of African American motherhood are consistent with the ones popularized through literature, travel narratives, and religious propaganda during the early and mid-nineteenth century. They also indicate how black motherhood became defined and shaped as part of the mythology of a benevolent slave system.

Although the popular figures of Mammy and Aunt Jemima often are used interchangeably today, it is significant to note that Mammy predates Aunt Jemima by almost a century. Aunt Jemima, whose domain was the kitchen, was introduced to the public at the 1893 Chicago World's Fair as a Reconstruction-era alter ego to Mammy, whose domain was the nursery. Aunt Jemima offered Northerners the Southern antebellum experience of having a mammy without actually participating in slavery. In this way, Aunt Jemima's popularity bolstered the romantic mythology of the Southern plantation.

I define the standard, most recognizable mammy character in American literature as a creative combination of extreme behavior and exaggerated features. Mammy's body is grotesquely marked by excess: she is usually extremely overweight, very tall, and broad-shouldered, and her skin is very dark. She manages to be a jolly presence—she often sings or tells stories while she works—and a strict disciplinarian at the same time. First as a slave, then as a free woman, Mammy is largely associated with the care of white children or depicted with noticeable attachment to white children. Her alleged unprecedented devotion to her white family is used to reflect her racial inferiority. "Mammy" is often both her title and the only name she has ever been given by her white family and charges. She may also be a cook or personal maid to her mistress—a classic Southern Belle— whom she infantilizes. Her clothes are typical of a domestic servant, headscarf and apron, but she is especially attracted to brightly colored, elaborately tied scarves. Mammy speaks with the same ungrammatical "plantation dialect" made famous in the United States in the 1890s by popular white southern authors like Joel Chandler Harris and subsequent minstrel shows featuring white actors portraying "plantation darkies."[4]

Her children are usually dirty and ill mannered, yet they serve as suitable playmates for her white charges. Typically, she is depicted as impatient or brusque (sometimes even violent or abusive) with her own children in contrast to her lavish, affectionate patience for her white charges. Mammy wields considerable authority within the plantation household and subsequently retains a measure of dubious, unreliable respect in the slave quarters. Many slaves consider her untrustworthy because she allegedly identifies so completely with the culture that oppresses them.

The most fundamental elements of the standard mammy type fall into two categories: appearance and behavior. Her identity as a mother supplies rich nuances that have not been adequately addressed, which focus on her role as domestic; hence, her maternal status constitutes a third category. Mammy's relationship to and interaction with her biological children is therefore crucial to this examination.[5] In particular, I base my analysis upon the character's relationship with both black and white children, isolating indications that the mammy character prefers the latter. I also examine the constants and variables in the patterns of her appearance.

Scholars have speculated that the term "Black Mammy" was developed in the nineteenth century to draw boundaries between the various maternal figures on the plantation. One scholar writes, "She is referred to as the 'Black Mammy,' a name probably given to distinguish her from the real mother and also from the elderly slave woman, 'Mammy,' who took care of slave children while their mothers worked in the fields or in master's home."[6] The term "Black Mammy" appears in both historic and fictional accounts of plantation life, often as a uniquely southern term of endearment. More often it served as a generic name for all slave women who served as a wet nurse or baby nurse for white children. Historian Deborah Gray White writes that Mammy was the "perfect slave for the antebellum south."[7] She became the center of a white southern perception of the perfectly organized society. The word "mammy"—an alteration of the expression "mamma"—eventually replaced the black nanny's own given name. Although it is not unusual for white southerners to write that this woman was the most influential force in their childhood, they typically do not know her real name. This is true, for example, of the well-known literary characters of Little Eva's "Mammy" in *Uncle Tom's Cabin* and Scarlett's "Mammy" in the best-selling novel *Gone with the Wind*.[8] Mitchell's domineering "Mammy" is a composite character with almost all of the stereotypical qualities I define elsewhere,[9] each trait exaggerated until Mammy is reduced to a comical caricature. She is not just fat; she is grossly obese. She is not just subservient to her master's family; she has adopted their entire belief system, which insists on her inferiority.

Mammy is not a biological mother in this epic novel; her familial ties have been sacrificed so that she may belong more fully to the O'Haras. We learn early in the novel that Mammy was raised "in the bedroom of Solange Robillard, Ellen O'Hara's mother,"[10] removing her so completely from contact with her own race that we understand that her behavior, attitudes, and values are the result of her

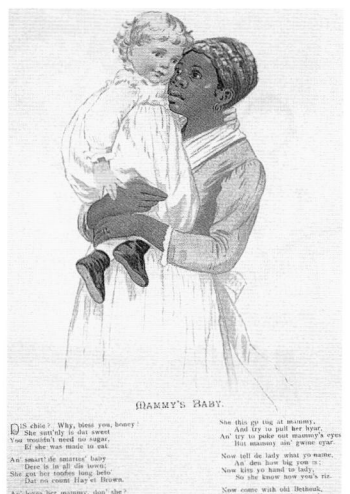

MAMMY'S BABY.

FIGURE 5.1 Ida Waugh, American (d. 1919), *Mammy's Baby*, 1890, illustration, from the book of children's verses *Mammy's Baby* by Amy Ella Blanchard, 1890. Photograph courtesy of Kimberly Wallace-Sanders.

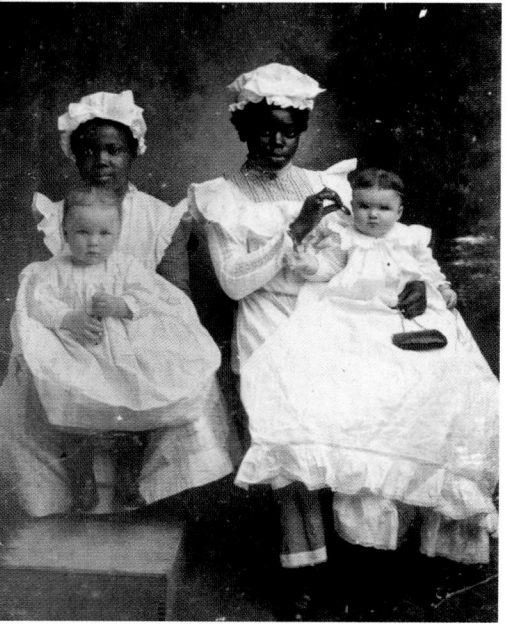

FIGURE 5.2 Unknown photographer, young African American girls in white caps, 1903, black and white photograph documented as "Unidentified black nurses." The babies' names are John and Allie Lamon. Photograph courtesy of Georgia Archives, Vanishing Georgia Collection, LOW010.

completely isolated existence as a black servant for three generations of O'Hara women. In this one line, Mitchell carefully detaches Mammy from the historic black community and the mythic Slave Quarters of Joel Chandler Harris's Uncle Remus stories.[11] Like Topsy's, Mammy's parentage is erased so that she comes to her white owners as a *tabula rasa*, making her the perfect mammy—the product of such specialized upbringing that her loyalty, indeed her heart and soul, belong to the O'Haras—because she has never belonged to her own family or to herself in any way.

When Mitchell formally introduces Mammy, she creates an improbable sense of mutuality, insisting, "Mammy felt that she owned the O'Haras, body and soul," and that Mammy was "devoted to her last drop of blood to the O'Haras."[12] Mammy "owns" the O'Hara's only in her obsessive need to run their lives and to hold Scarlett to ridiculous codes of Southern propriety. The length to which she has internalized white Southern values and codes of behavior is so extreme that Mammy's world consists only of "quality" (meaning wealthy) white folks, white trash, and "wuthless nigguhs," her general category for nearly all blacks. Mammy has no concept of any positive black qualities because she exists in a vacuum; she does not even have a name for herself other than "Mammy." Mammy affirms Trudier Harris's argument that the "true southern maid is the mammy whose ineffective compromise in the home of the white mistresses causes her to identify completely with the status quo; she believes within her heart in the rightness of the established order of which see is a part. She has lost her black cultural identity (if she ever had one) and all sense of spiritual identification with black people."[13]

In *Gone with the Wind*, there seems to be an endless supply of mammies at Tara. Along with the indomitable Mammy, there are two other black mammy characters: Dilcey, brought in solely as a wet nurse for Melanie's baby, and her daughter Prissy, the mammy-in-training, whose famous line about birthing babies is one of the three best known and most widely repeated lines from the film *Gone with the Wind*.

In Dilcey's physical description, her body and even her ethnicity are compared—and compared more favorably—with Mammy's body:

> Dilcey was tall and bore herself erectly. She might have been any age from thirty to sixty, so unlined was her immobile bronze face. Indian blood was plain in her feature, overbalancing the Negroid characteristics. She was self-possessed and walked with a dignity that surpassed even Mammy's, for Mammy had acquired her dignity and Dilcey's was in her blood.[14]

In other nineteenth-century literature, author Isabel Drysdale writes in glowing terms about the pious Negro nurse "Aunt Chloe" in *Scenes in Georgia*. Her small book is an unusual blend of children's prayers and travel narratives. Drysdale assumed that the mammy figure is a well-known type especially recognizable to children as early as 1827, when she wrote her book. In describing Aunt Chloe's physical characterization, Drysdale uses Chloe to play upon racial and cultural differences between white and black southerners, "her sawed teeth and curiously branded cheek bespeak her a native of Africa."[15] Her "sawed teeth" and culturally marked cheeks are typical signs of beauty in West Africa, but Drysdale probably intends to exoticize Chloe, not to convey her beauty, as it would have been perceived in Africa. Like the standard mammy figure in later American literature, this African Old Chloe is very dark skinned and energetic, but she is much smaller in stature than the stereotypical mammy. Drysdale describes her in this way: "She was a little, brisk, old woman with the wrinkles and gray hairs of sixty, combined with all the lively alertness of twenty-one."[16] Chloe's dark skin also serves a specific purpose for Drysdale, who writes, "Perhaps a more interesting picture is seldom seen, than that which was often exhibited by Old Chloe and her little nursling, its fair face pillowed in her faithful bosom, contrasting the sable but loving countenance bent above it."[17] Here an aesthetic value is introduced with the image of a dark-skinned woman holding a fair-skinned child. Chloe hardly seems to be a slave at all, but rather a dark-skinned Madonna, holding her precious Savior to her breast.

When Harriet Beecher Stowe describes her own "Aunt Chloe," who is "Uncle Tom's" wife, in 1852, she makes her mammy sound almost edible. "A round, black, shining face is hers, so glossy as to suggest the idea that she might have been washed over with white of eggs, like one of her own tea rusks."[18] As for her body, Aunt Chloe is the quintessential fat and happy slave. "Her whole plump countenance beams with satisfaction and contentment from under her well-starched checked turban."[19]

From Aunt Chloe's perspective white women's bodies seem to be naturally superior to black women's bodies, explaining that her mistress has "beautiful white hands with long fingers" resembling "white lilies." She describes her own hands as "great, black and stumping."[20] Her conclusion is that she is meant to make piecrust and that delicate white women are meant to stay in the parlor.

By comparing visual culture with literary characterizations, we can see how the mammy figure in fiction was blended with nostalgic images of African American women as domestic servants and caretakers for white children. This figure eventually became the stereotypical black mammy (plates 88 and 89). Such depictions include illustrations of romanticized drawings of black women with white children (figure 5.1) and photographs of young African American girls posing with white children (figure 5.2) and of African American women with white children (figure 5.3). In many such photographs, the white children are named, whereas the nurses' names usually are stripped from their forms in an effort to deny their individuality and create a subgenre of African American womanhood. It was also not unusual for a novel or memoir about plantation life to incorporate photographs and drawings of Mammy in the same book, such as in *Social Life in Old Virginia* (1897) by Thomas Nelson Page (figures 5.4 and 5.5). The illustration by Genevieve Cowles shows a black mammy with a white child in her arms with the caption: "She was never anything but tender with the others." Known for her murals and stain-glass windows, Genevieve Cowles was also a painter whose

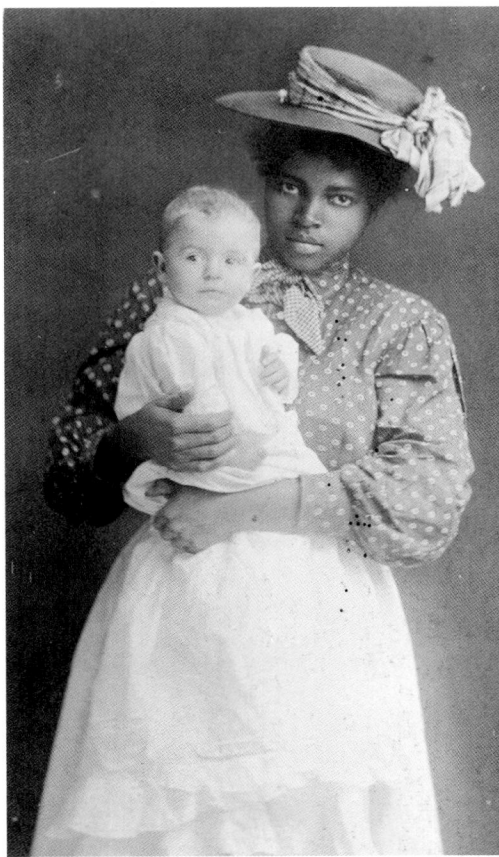

FIGURE 5.3 Unknown photographer, *Bessie Morse Holding Earle Sinclair McKay Jr.*, 1908, black and white photograph. Photograph courtesy of Georgia Archives, Vanishing Georgia Collection, LOW010.

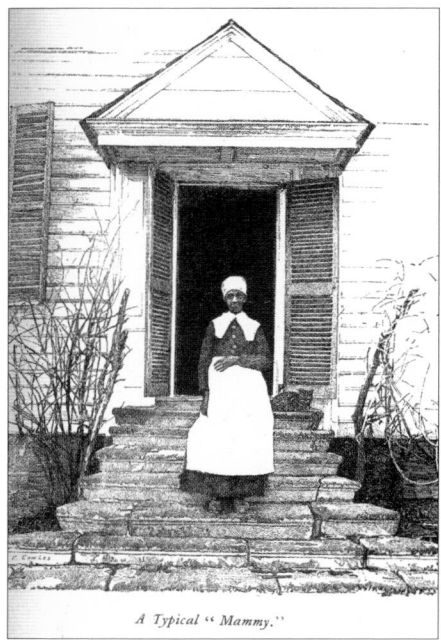

FIGURE 5.4 Unknown photographer, *A Typical "Mammy,"* before 1897, photograph from *Social Life in Old Virginia Before the War* by Thomas Nelson Page, 1897. Photograph courtesy of Kimberly Wallace-Sanders.

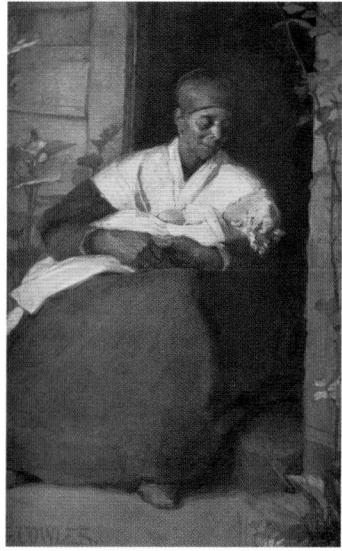

FIGURE 5.5 Genevieve Cowles, American, (1871–after 1929), *She Was Never Anything But Tender With Others*, 1897, illustration from *Social Life in Old Virginia Before the War*, Thomas Nelson Page, 1897. Photograph courtesy of Kimberly Wallace-Sanders.

illustrations appeared in Hawthorne's *House of the Seven Gables* and in *Scribner's* and *McClure's* magazines.

INCREDIBLE, EDIBLE WOMAN: BLACK FEMALE BREASTS AND PUBLIC CONSUMPTION

In visual culture, black women are frequently reduced to body parts, with an exaggerated emphasis on their breasts or buttocks. This corporeal fragmentation results in more than "T and A" in blackface—it deters an audience from acknowledging and accepting black women's normal, healthy sexuality and their existence as whole—and sexual—human beings. One of the more striking aspects of the *Black Womanhood* exhibition checklist is the large number of representations figuring black women's exposed breasts. What are we to make of so many portraits of exposed black female breasts? What is it about black women's breasts that seem to be so universally fascinating?

For years, black women's breasts were served up for public consumption in ways that simply did not occur for white women before the 1950s. Each illustration is a reminder that black women have historically been devalued and dehumanized. For example, in 1861, the Clerk's Office of the District Court for the Eastern District of Pennsylvania produced a number of patriotic decorative envelopes. Patriotic Cover #8944 shows an African American woman with one breast fully exposed so that she can nurse the enormous white baby on her lap (figure 5.6). Her exposed breast serves as an actual "return address" for the envelope. Her body is arranged to hold this enormous white baby as a sarcastic reminder that the south has grown fat on slave labor. In the 1920s, rubber bottle nipples were painted black and made into diminutive black mammy "nipple dolls" posed with tiny white baby dolls cradled in their arms (figure 5.7). These "black nipples" became toys for white children. Today they are considered both a "well-kept secret" and an excellent investment among collectors of southern Americana.[21]

Black feminist Patricia Hill Collins draws historical connections between "the display of Sarah Baartman as a sexual 'freak' of nature in the early nineteenth century (figure 1.1 and plate 45) to Josephine Baker dancing bare-breasted for Parisian society (plate 77 and 78) to the animal-skin bikinis worn by the group Destiny's Child to the fascination with Jennifer Lopez's buttocks. . . ." She argues that "women of African descent have been associated with an animalistic, wild sexuality."[22] Along with this "wild sexuality" we see the fragmentation of black women's bodies into compartments of commodity that sanction their corporeal fragmentation. Deborah Willis and Carla Williams's extraordinary book *The Black Female Body: A Photographic History* chronicles a long and deeply troubling history of black women's bodies used as a disruptive force in American culture.[23] Their book offers both proof of and redemption from this kind of racist, misogynist hyper-fragmentation. The examples included in the section titled "The Cultural Body" start with their observation that "Beginning with Saartjie

Baartman, some famous black female bodies became a bona fide part of the popular culture, their images engraved on the public conscience."[24] Mammy's body has been inscribed into both an American and an international memory in a similar manner. For example, Baartman and Mammy each reflect a projection of excess—excess sexuality or excess maternity—onto the black female body.

Black feminist author and critic bell hooks invites us to draw a connection between a national nostalgia for the black mammy figure and a chocolate breast-shaped cake. At the beginning of her seminal essay "Selling Hot Pussy," bell hooks relates an anecdote of walking into a restaurant with her white colleagues and seeing a display of breast-shaped chocolate cakes. hooks immediately saw a connection between the cake and the black mammy figure. She writes that the deserts were shaped like "gigantic chocolate breasts with nipples—huge edible tits"[25] and that her colleagues found the display entertaining instead of offensive. For hooks, the chocolate breasts are a "sign of displaced longing for a racist past,"[26] specifically for the black mammy figure so prevalent in American culture and consciousness.

Consider now hooks's statement and the appearance of "Janet Jackson breast cupcakes" on the internet after the 2004 Super Bowl halftime show, when the singer's exposed breast launched a national scandal, an event dubbed "nipple-gate" by the media.[27] Clearly, whatever Janet Jackson's success amounted to before her right breast was exposed during the Super Bowl, we knew that her breast and the accompanying nipple piercing has now become a "bona fide part of the popular culture . . . engraved on the public conscience,"[28] essentially eclipsing the rest of her artistic career.

This insight is blended with feminist Iris Marion Young's theory that it is the exposed nipple that is taboo "[because it is] quite literally, physically and functionally, *undecidable* in the split between motherhood and sexuality. One of the most subversive things feminism can do is affirm this *undecidability* of motherhood and sexuality."[29] There is nothing "*undecidable*" about Jackson's pierced nipple; it was clearly sexualized—and sexualized for her pleasure. The pierced nipple may be the most obvious example of a "non-maternal" black breast. Perhaps this is what was so shocking to the viewing audience: an African American woman's breast that clearly announced itself as more sexual than maternal.

An Institution of the "O. S. A."
—COTTON STATES ARISTOCRACY.—

Though now unconscious on Ma Ma's breast,
  Glorious destiny awaits the *high born* babe;
A Knight, A Baron, A Duke. A Royal crest
  May yet upon his diadem wave.

FIGURE 5.6 Unknown artist, Patriotic Cover #8944, 1861, illustration showing an African American woman nursing a European American child. Photograph courtesy of the Boston Athenaeum.

FIGURE 5.7 Unknown artists, black mammy rubber bottle "nipple dolls," 1920s, mixed media. Photograph courtesy of Kimberly Wallace-Sanders.

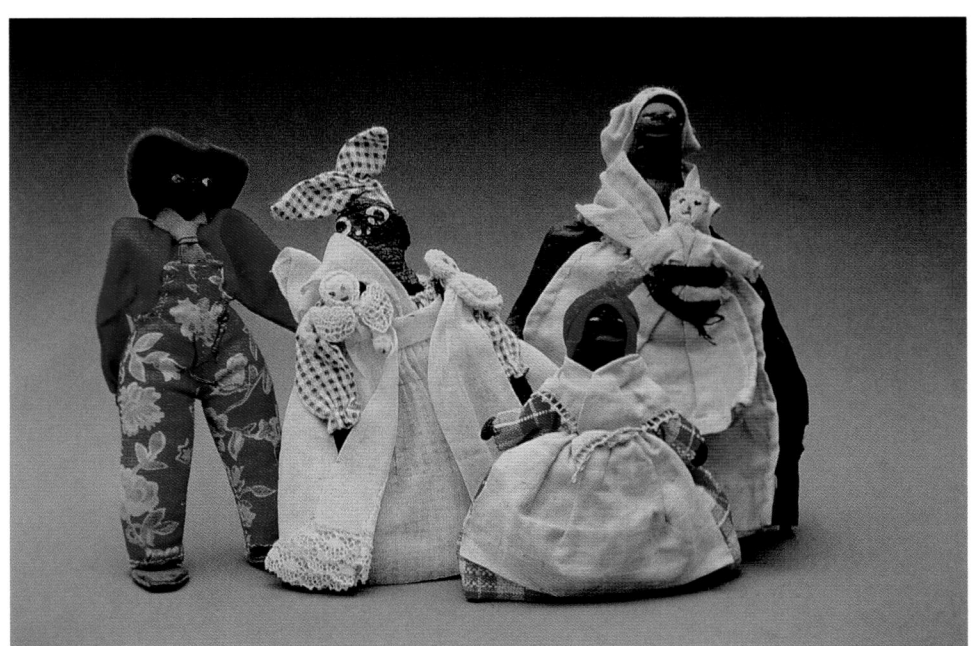

In what I would call a "perversely perfect echo" of hooks's example, shortly after the halftime show when Janet Jackson's breast was exposed, either inadvertently or on purpose, an Emory University Law School student named "Adam" launched a website entitled "Janet Jackson Breast Cupcakes." The author admits that his mission was simple; he wanted to turn a close-up photograph of Janet Jackson's breast "into a work of edible art." Adam worried about "creating the perfect breast color" for his edible art, so he enlisted the help of a friend, who emailed him this message: "Janet is more latte than bittersweet, I'd say. You could flavor the icing with coffee actually, and that would be yummy." Using a Hershey's kiss for the nipple and white icing to duplicate what he called "the nipple shield that boggled so many viewers the night of the Superbowl," Adam's edible black breasts are complete.[30]

Iris Young argues that our "phallocentric culture tends to think of a woman's breasts as belonging to her husband, her lover, her baby, it's hard to image a woman's breasts as being her own."[31] Young may be surprised to find her observation affirmed by African American comedian Chris Rock in his 2004 live performance "Never Scared." Early in his performance Rock shouts, "Janet Jackson showed her titty on national television! And a forty-year-old titty at that! You're not supposed to show that! Twenty year old titty, that's *community* titty, forty year old titty: that's *your man's* titty!" Rock's categories of "breast possession" emphasize the notion that black women's breasts usually belong to someone else, especially given the history of African American women as wet nurses for white children.

I want to look more closely at a postcard of a black nursemaid and a white child by G. Mizrahi, which we can assume was taken in Adana, Turkey, and compare it to other historical and contemporary images, which can be read against one another for new insights on the differences between these historic and contemporary representations of the black mammy figure. In Mizrahi's postcard 46. *Type of Negresse d'ADANA* (plate 84), he depicts a beautiful African woman whose face and decorated hair are completely overshadowed by her engorged breasts and the white toddler attached to her left breast. It looks as though milk is dripping from the right breast. The top of her dress is open and her legs are spread apart to accommodate the child. She is wearing rings, her feet rest on a fur rug, and she is sitting on a decorative chair, her hair pulled back with a scarf and artificial flowers. The photo is clearly staged and shot in a studio; this is not a moment of childcare/intimacy captured by the photographer. It appears as though everything about the photograph has been artificially arranged. Her dress is opened to *showcase* both milk-laden breasts. The word that comes to mind is "ample," as her breasts are literally spilling out of her clothes, milk is spilling from her breasts, and the white toddler is spilling out of her lap.

Why is the child "spilling" from her lap? *Because she is not really holding the baby at all.* Instead of embracing the baby, she is nourishing it, allowing the child to simply lie across her lap and left arm. There is no emotional bond between this woman and the child. Compare her posture with a postcard of a mother and child

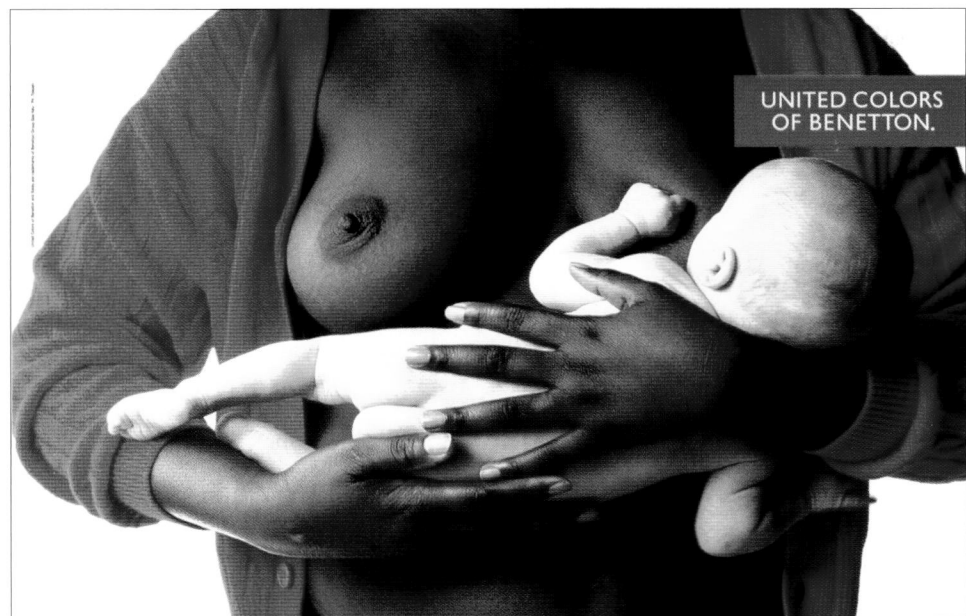

UNITED COLORS
OF BENETTON.

FIGURE 5.8 Oliviero Toscani, Italian (born 1942), *Breastfeeding*, 1987, printed advertisement. Photograph courtesy of Benetton Group, S.p.A.

with the caption *Femme Soussou* (plate 81). There is a dramatic difference in the posture of this nursing mother, who is holding her baby with both hands. Her back is supported (the way it must be to nurse comfortably) and her legs are not spread wide but modestly posed to accommodate her baby.

In Mizrahi's "Negresse" of Adana, the black woman's breasts compose the centerpiece of the photograph; they are as large as the baby's head. This image surely evokes the black mammy stereotype, but it also leaves the viewer in awe of the woman's body and her ability to provide so much nourishment to such a large child. Her abundant lactation is the sign and symbol of a previously pregnant body. Perhaps she is a professional wet nurse for several white children, but we also know that she must have or have had children of her own. Where are her children?

Unlike the mother and child image depicted in *Femme Soussou*, Mizrahi's postcard actually has a cancelled postal marking. Numbered photographs like this one smack of anthropological cataloging. In this case, however, the photographer —or postcard publisher—thought that this black woman represented a particular "type" of black woman in Adana, Turkey. Compare this postcard with the decorative envelope issued by the Clerk's Office of the District Court for the Eastern District of Pennsylvania (see figure 5.6). Postcards and envelopes are considered ephemera that does not usually have a long life span. Yet both the postcards and the envelopes were collected, providing an invaluable insight about the archetypal power of this kind of tableau.

In this context, we must consider also a close-up photograph of the breast of a headless black woman holding a much smaller, thinner (hungrier?) white baby to her breast (figure 5.8). The Italian fashion photographer Olivero Toscani created this photograph in the late 1980s as an advertisement for a red Shetland sweater made by Benetton, a major chain of retail stores. The woman's right breast, including the nipple, is completely exposed. The advertisement was met with unbridled criticism from African Americans, yet it won more advertising awards than any other image in Benetton's advertising history.[32] In Toscani's photograph, it is impossible to miss the difference in the size and shape of the model's breasts compared with the previous two images discussed. In these three instances, the black female breast "belongs" to a child who is not her own. Her breast is then being consumed by both the white children and the viewer.

When we introduce into this discussion Maria Magdalena Campos-Pons, a Cuban artist of Nigerian ancestry artistically trained in Havana and Boston, we know that her use of black female breasts, specifically her own breasts, will be markedly different from the three previous examples. In one panel of her work *When I Am Not Here/Estoy Allá* (1994) (plate 115), Campos-Pons strings twin milk bottles with plastic tubing around her neck so that the bottles hang *over* her breasts. I wonder if this is a comment on women choosing—or being forced to use—*bottles over breast-feeding*? The milk bottles drip down into a boat-shaped wooden bowl, reminiscent of a slave ship, while the headless body is painted blue with white "waves" from neck to waist, including arms and hands. In this rendition combining a black woman's fragmented body, black breasts, and milk, the wooden vessel seems to be held at her waist as an offering of milk as a sacrament. The title of this work is reminiscent of the beginning of the sentence, or a poem, or a song that might be completed: "when I am not here/carry my milk in something precious for my children/even if you have to go across the water." Or "When I am not here—keep this gift from my body/Don't waste a single drop."

One of the reasons that I was so moved by *When I Am Not Here/Estoy Allá* is because the milk bottles reminded me of pumping milk for my infant son Isaiah while I was away at work. Like so many working mothers, I was so appreciative of the small miracle of breast-pumps, which allowed my son to have my milk even when I was away from him. What is key for me here is that for Campos-Pons, *the milk is an offering—not her breasts*. This artistic evocation of the black mammy manages to create an effective and powerful distinction between a black woman disappearing behind her breasts as in Mizrahi's "Negress" and Campos-Pons's self-possessed and self-constructed woman in *When I Am Not Here/Estoy Allá*.

In response to the "Nipplegate" incident, Campos-Pons created a multimedia piece ironically entitled *A Reason Why Janet Jackson Should Move to the Veneto Region: A Wardrobe Malfunction Early on Go* (sic) *Unnoticed*, 2006 (figure 5.9). Here is a shapely black woman, in a yellow sundress and matching sandals. One hand on her hip announces her self-confidence; the other hand easily holds up the globe. As she reaches up, her dress has slipped down over one shoulder, as though she is too busy holding up the world to notice or mind that her breast is exposed. The narrow blocks of color invoke multi-national flags and the twisting vine with leaves symbolizes growth and life. This is a woman who will not be stopped by a "wardrobe malfunction."

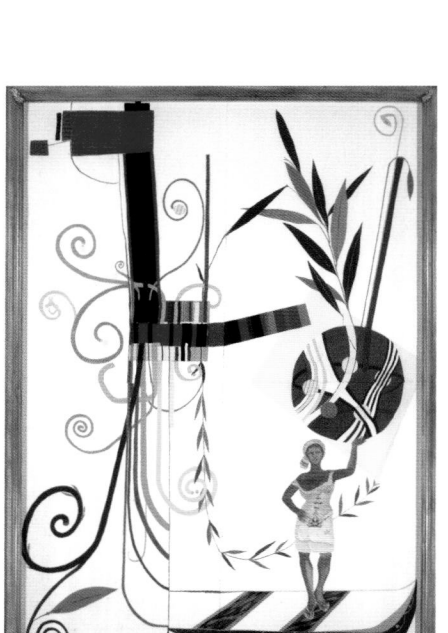

FIGURE 5.9 Maria Magdalena Campos-Pons, Cuban (born 1959), *A Reason Why Janet Jackson Should Move to the Veneto Region: A Wardrobe Malfunction Early on Go Unnoticed*, gouache, watercolor pencil, and cloth on paper, 2006. Photograph courtesy of Maria Magdalena Campos-Pons and Galleria Pack, Milan, Italy.

The representation of Mammy comprises a unique layering of artistic images and material culture and is just one example of how myth, biography, fiction, history, and visual culture merge in a dispute about race, motherhood, and southern nostalgia in American culture. But while I was writing my book *Mammy, A Century of Race, Gender and Southern Memory*, I learned that the subject matter was much more controversial than I had originally imagined.[33] Everyone has an opinion about Mammy, about who she was, what she meant, and why her image seems so pervasive and enduring. Most of what we know about the women who have been called "Mammy" over the years has been based upon an incomplete and very one-sided written history. Yet there is an intriguing attraction/repulsion with the black mammy figure, precisely because of its blending and blurring of stereotype and archetype.

In my book, I decided to focus on cultural representations of the stereotypical black mammy *instead* of collecting biographies and personal narratives of African American women working as domestics and childcare workers. I wanted to better understand the curious power behind the particular image of a large black woman with a small white child. Just as historic representations of the black female body have immediate and far-reaching implications, so do contemporary renditions. It is unwise for us to ignore them or dismiss them without appropriate analyses, an analysis that has formed the basis of contemporary artistic revisions of Mammy by four African American artists: Raymond Wallace, Tina Dunkley, Joyce J. Scott, and Kara Walker; works by the last two are featured in the exhibition *Black Womanhood*.

Before publishing my book, I asked Raymond Wallace, an artist from Pennsylvania, to suggest some of his art works for possible use on the cover. In one of these works, *Faceless Mammy with Baby and Cooking Spoon* (2006) (figure 5.10), Wallace shows how a few images—headscarf knotted at the top of her head, round, dark, featureless face, large bosom, white baby—have become symbols that we immediately associate with the mammy body and with the myth of what she represented as a maternal figure.

Wallace's "faceless mammy" reminds us of the many portraits of anonymous African American women with white children, often called only "nursemaid and child." This white "charge" could be any white child, a child that is often as easily exchanged as the mammy herself. What we notice most about Wallace's red, white, and black mammy placed against a background of blue sky is that she does not have the requisite wide grin that invokes Aunt Jemima. There are no gleaming white teeth to break up the dark circle of her face. With her spoon in one hand and the howling baby in the other, the double role of Mammy as both nursemaid and cook are made plain. The baby's mouth is a black hole of endless demands. The similarity of pattern of white points in her headscarf and in her neckerchief prompt the viewer to see that one face is as good as another—even if you turn this mammy's head upside down, nothing would change.

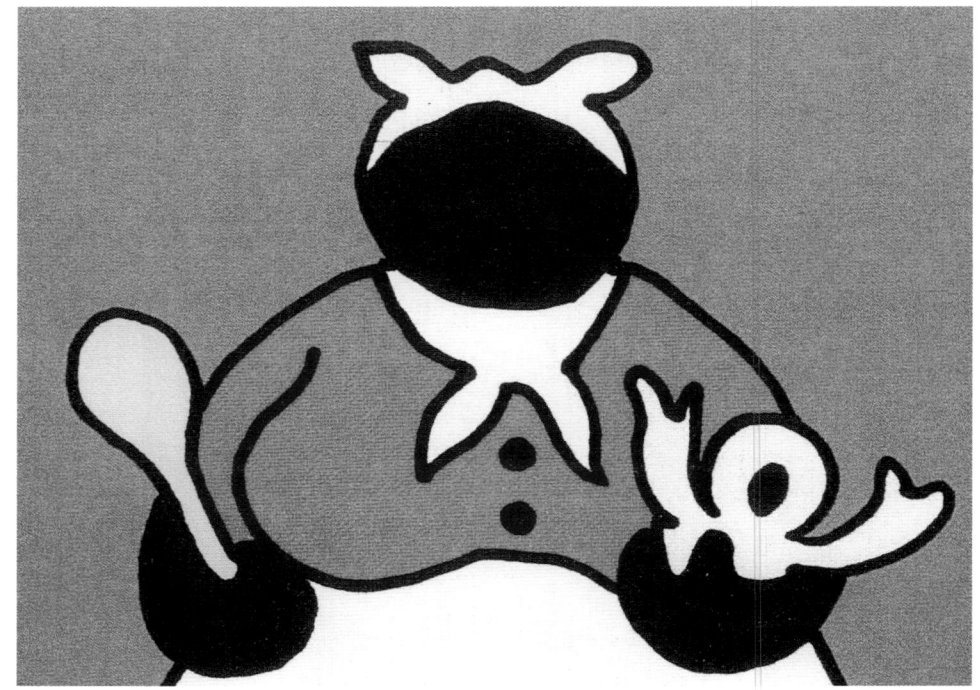

Joyce J. Scott, another contemporary artist, takes on the icon of Mammy in sculptural compositions that depict African American women whose own biological children are neglected as a result of their role as caretaker of white children. Scott, who specializes in weaving, quilting, beadwork, and glass, was born in 1948 in Baltimore, where she still resides, sharing a home with her mother, textile artist Elizabeth Talford Scott. In her *Mammy/Nanny* series, Scott creates soft sculptured three-dimensional figures made of black leather and beadwork that depict the multi-dimensional persona of Mammy. In this series, Mammy is a tall, slim, and menacing character who towers over her black and white children, who are competing for her attention. While Scott's mammy figures resemble large dolls, providing an echo of the mammy dolls, their innovative placement in confrontational scenes reflects perhaps more accurately the real-life struggles between black mammies and their two sets of children: one black and one white. Through her *Mammy/Nanny* series (figure 5.11 and plate 116), Scott gives a voice to both Mammy and her often-invisible biological children.

Scott notes that she was interested in investigating the notion of the mammy image as "black monolith . . . a big, black mask."[34] Feminist art critic Terry Gips writes that "Scott confronts the viewer with the contradictions and hypocrisies embedded in the historical and continuing culture surrounding the Black women who served as nannies for white America."[35] In June 2004, I interviewed Scott in Atlanta, Georgia, during which she spoke at length about the art she produced during the 1980s and 1990s and how her childhood experiences inspired her art. I learned that Scott's mother told her about her experiences working as a childcare provider for white families, a job she took at an early age in South Carolina.[36]

Born in 1916, Elizabeth Scott picked cotton before moving to Baltimore in 1940. She worked in factories, cleaned houses, and served as a nanny, somehow always managing to continue the sewing and craftwork she had learned as a child. Scott says, "My mother told me how offended she was when the white children she took care of began to call her by pejorative names."[37] In more than one instance Scott's mother recalls the parents of her wards teaching them that their nanny was a "nigger." The last time this happened, she was so hurt that she left to live with another family, with whom she stayed extremely close over the years. This incident inspired Scott to create the seventeen-inch piece called *Nanny Now, Nigger Later,* with her black leather nanny holding a white beaded baby against her front while the child sucks its thumb.

When asked if she thought her mother loved the children she took care of, Scott said, "Yes, and sometimes I was jealous of them. I was friendly with those children. We played together but sometimes I felt like asking her to stay home with me. That's what the piece *No Mommy, Me* was about."[38] *No Mommy, Me* is a two-part series and includes a black female figure made of black leather and iridescent black beads resembling a large mammy doll, complete with turban and apron. In *No Mommy Me I* (figure 5.11), the figure holds a white baby made of pink beads up to her face as if she is cooing her, while a black child made of black beads clutches the mammy/nanny's long skirt, howling in jealousy. Scott shows that being the caretaker in this kind of mother and child relationship often means comforting her white charge while her own black child may feel abandoned. In the second piece, *No Mommy Me II,* a similar black mammy/nanny holds out a white child at arm's length while a small black girl sits crying on the floor, her arms wide open and empty. In this piece, the mammy/nanny's mouth is twisted in a grimace—like "the mask" that Scott describes. Instead of wearing a tidy turban, this Mammy's hair is loose, perhaps in braids or dreadlocks. In *Nanny Gone Wrong,* the leather nanny wears her headscarf tied in a knot at the front of her head. She dangles a beaded white baby by the hair while a tiny, black baby is at her feet.

The sculpture that I find most evocative is *Chainsaw Nanny,* in which Scott shows us a topless mammy/nanny with a beaded white baby chained to her waist. This piece speaks to the unrelenting quality of mammy's day—being chained to a baby of another race. Or perhaps the chainsaw is cutting the nanny in half so there will be enough of her to go around. As Terry Gips explains, "these sculptures also remind us that the Black children of nannies often seem to take a back seat to the white children their mothers care for. Perhaps there aren't enough arms or hours to go around. . . . While the days of wet nurse's need to short her own child to feed her master's are behind us, the tug-of-war over her body still exists."[39]

Black feminist historian Darlene Clark Hine writes,

> Creating and disseminating a visual history is perhaps more important with
> Black women than with any other single segment of the American population.

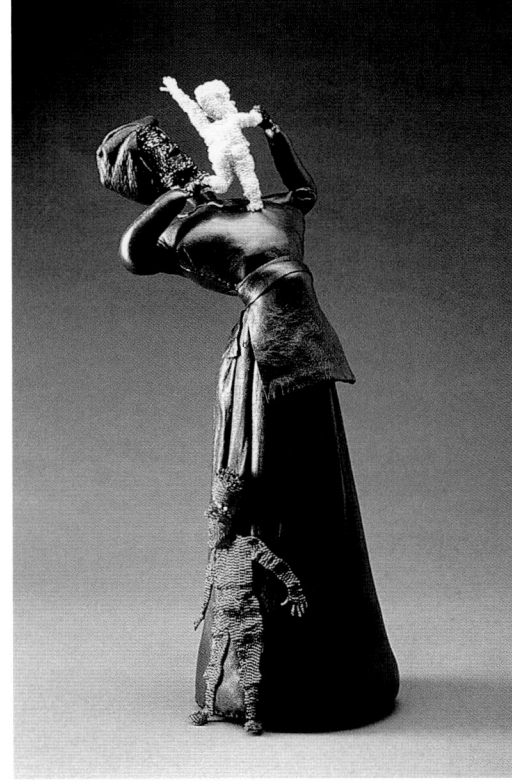

FIGURE 5.11 Joyce J. Scott, American (born 1948), *No Mommy Me I,* 1991, leather, beads, and thread. Photograph courtesy of Joyce C. Scott and Kimberley Wallace-Sanders.

We know all too well what this society believes Black women look like. . . . What we have not seen nearly enough is the simple truth of our complex and multidimensional lives.[40]

Scott accomplishes this by integrating many of the unspoken aspects of mammy into her work without relying on the Aunt Jemima trope.

Another response to the tug-of-war over Mammy's body is Kara Walker's book *Freedom: A Fable; A Curious Interpretation of the Wit of a Negress in Troubled Times* (plate 118) and the tableau installation called *The End of Uncle Tom and the Grand Allegorical Tableau of Eva in Heaven* (1995) (figure 5.12). Walker, who is often identified as notable and controversial, creates her tableaus from black cutout figures placed on white canvases or on blank walls, similar to the traditional Swiss-German technique called *scherenschnitte*, which the Pennsylvania-Dutch brought to the United States in the eighteenth century. During the nineteenth century, silhouette portraits became a popular craft, especially for portraits of American children.

Art historian Michael D. Harris writes that Walker's "work has the haunting spectacle of a fatal three car automobile accident with its routine depiction of the unspeakable, the perverse, and the supposedly dark secrets of racist histories in the United States. Often it is grisly, but you are compelled to look at it . . . [there is a] text lurking behind the American dream that no one wants to talk about. . . ."[41] The body of Walker's mammy in *Freedom: A Fable; A Curious Interpretation of the Wit of a Negress in Troubled Times* is one manifestation of a "text lurking" behind or beneath the American dream, as she represents maternity, loyalty, and servitude, specifically as they were configured within the plantation genre of nineteenth-century America. As Harris also writes, however, "Walker's identifiably black figures tend to fulfill and extend all the wildest fears and fantasies whites have had about blacks as she seems to ask, 'Is *this* what you think? Is *this* what you believe [about us]?'"[42] This leads us to ask, what is Walker questioning about the mammy mythology in these works?

Harris finds that, "In a sense, Walker is recycling and exaggerating antebellum thought and imagery as she pulls down curtains and reveals the darkest implications behind racist thinking." Harris calls the ring of African American women in *The End of Uncle Tom* "a sucking circle,"[43] which may be intended to evoke the tradition of "circle jerks," where men stand in a circle masturbating and then compare ejaculations. How do these three African American women and one baby girl constitute "the end of Uncle Tom"? Does "the end of Uncle Tom" refer to the end of sentimentalized narratives of slavery? How and why does this involve breast-feeding, wet nursing, the mammy mythology, and the mammy body?

The three women cast shadows so intriguing that I went out of my way to get a picture that I could turn upside down and sideways. I wanted to see this from every possible angle so that I wouldn't miss any partially hidden detail or obscured perspective. Inspired by the long-standing legend that vinyl records could be played backwards to reveal hidden secret messages, eventually I was

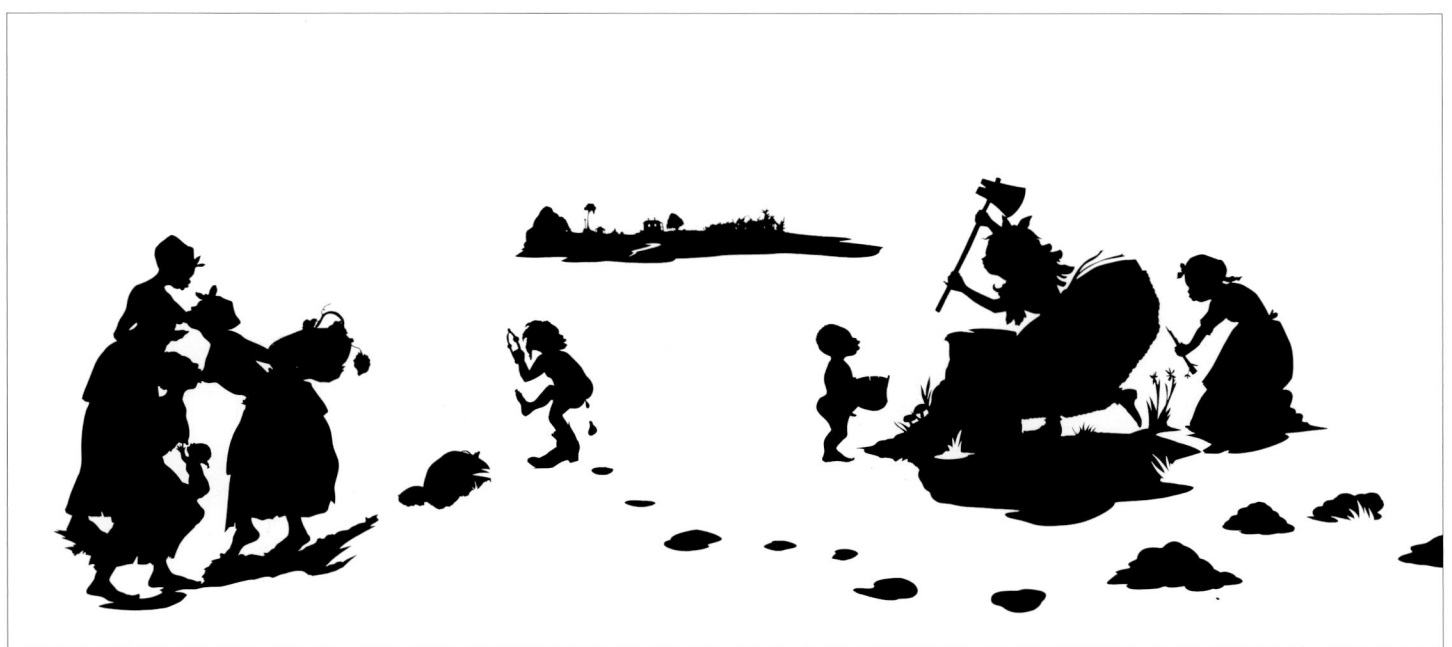

driven to hold this image up to a mirror. I was that desperate to understand this piece and that convinced that there was more to Walker's version of the mammy mythology. *The End of Uncle Tom and the Grand Allegorical Tableau of Eva in Heaven* became a kind of Rorschach test for me—I wanted an interpretation of this tableau to reveal something that could only be coaxed to the surface through art. And what did I finally see? Myself. There I was, squinting into the mirror, looking at this image from every possible position, peering into a mirror for answers.

Recalling Paule Marshall's words ("The use of the Negro woman as an embodiment of myth and fantasies that have little to do with her"), I want to consider a wonderful piece by Atlanta artist and curator Tina Dunkley. Her work *Ain't Cha Mama Yemanja?* (figure 5.13) invites us to draw a connection between Yemanja, the Santeria goddess of creation, and Aunt Jemima. Dunkley uses an international and multilayered approach combining representations of African, Caribbean, and African American women wearing elaborately tied headscarves. The intricate wrapping of beautiful fabric as turbans, *geles*, and bandannas by black women around the globe seems to connect these women in a powerful way. Dunkley says she was moved to do this piece after traveling throughout the African Diaspora, seeing black women in African *geles*, and then considering a possible connection with Aunt Jemima. She says, "I realized that this is who Aunt Jemima might have become had she been left in Nigeria."[44] Here she is also playing on the phonetic similarities between Jemima and Yemanja, the Yoruba deity representing motherhood in the Santeria pantheon of goddesses.

By using mammy-images on currency, Dunkley reminds us how black women's bodies functioned as part of a peculiar kind of currency. In her excellent analysis of Mammy's role in visual culture, "Mammy the Huckster," JoAnn

FIGURE 5.12 Kara Walker, American (born 1969), *The End of Uncle Tom and the Grand Allegorical Tableau of Eva in Heaven*, 1995, paper. Photograph courtesy of Kara Walker and Sikkema Jenkins & Co.

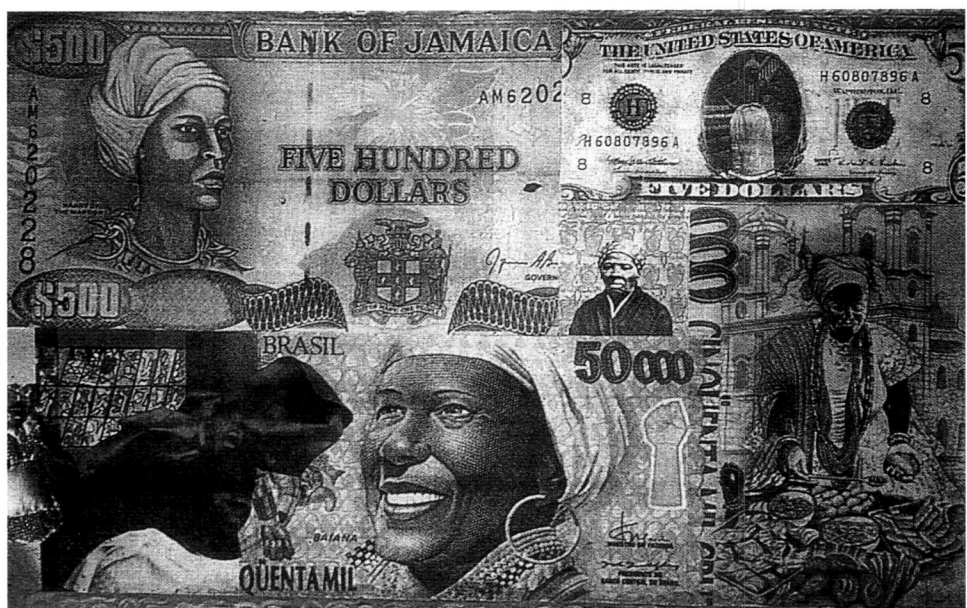

Morgan explains, "Not only did Mammy and scores like her promote consumer goods but more importantly, they sold the public a bill of goods about the old south."[45] Besides serving as a symbol of reconciliation and redemption, mammy became a "requisite fantasy for any southerner seeking to establish his or her pedigree."[46] By extension, one way to interpret the body of the black mammy figure is to consider how it has been used to reify racial purity for white southerners. Like the one drop of "black dope"—the chemical that makes the white paint "whiter than white" in Ralph Ellison's *Invisible Man*—the mammy body produced the milk that made white southerners more purely white, and therefore more purely southern, than their less affluent counterparts.

CONCLUSION

The works of these contemporary artists seem to provide an extraordinary example of what Darlene Clark Hine calls for when she says that it is time to honor "the simple truth of the complex and multidimensional lives of Black women."[47] A true understanding of African American women's identity, both self-imposed and externally constructed, requires us to pay greater attention to this kind of creative work because it provides us with more than new words about an old image, indeed, with a new language altogether. This new visual language is extremely crucial for expressing and processing the difficult emotions related to this country's past and the ways that our history and our national consciousness has been influenced by representations of Mammy as a symbol of mythologies of black maternity. The works in the exhibition *Black Womanhood* challenge us to reconsider and re-imagine what we believe we know well, and to search with renewed enthusiasm for what we have missed. ❦

1 Paule Marshall, "The Negro Woman in Literature," *Freedomways* 6 (1966): 21.

2 Excerpt from Stephan Vincent Benet, *John Brown's Body* (New York: Rhinehart and Company, 1927), 152.

3 Harriet Beecher Stowe, *Uncle Tom's Cabin, or, Life among the Lowly* (Boston: John P. Jewett & Company, and Cleveland: Jewett, Proctor & Worthington, 1852).

4 Readers may be familiar with Harris's character Aunt Minervy Ann from *The Chronicles of Aunt Minervy Ann* (New York: Scribner, 1899). See also Lucinda MacKethan's "Plantation Fiction," in *The History of Southern Literature*, ed. Louis Rubin with Blyden Jackson, Rayburn S. Moore, Lewis P. Simpson, and Thomas Daniel Young (Baton Rouge: Louisiana University Press, 1985), 204–218.

5 See also Bonnie Thornton Dill, "Across the Boundaries of Race and Class: An Exploration of the Relationship Between Work and Family among Black Female Domestic Servants," Ph.D diss., New York University, 1979; Judith Rollins, *Between Women* (Philadelphia: Temple University Press, 1985); Trudier Harris, *From Mammies to Militants* (Philadelphia: Temple University Press, 1982), 24–25; Patricia Morton, *Distorted Images: The Historical Assault on Afro-American Women* (Westport: Praeger, 1991); and Patricia Turner, *Ceramic Uncles and Celluloid Mammies* (New York: Anchor Books, 1994).

6 Jesse Parkhurst, "The Role of the Black Mammy in the Plantation Household," *Journal of Negro History* 23 (1938): 25.

7 Deborah Gray White, *Aren't I a Woman?* (New York: W. W. Norton & Co. Books, 1985), 49.

8 Margaret Mitchell, *Gone with the Wind* (New York: Macmillan Company, 1935).

9 Kimberly Wallace-Sanders, "A Peculiar Motherhood: The Black Mammy Figure in American Literature and Popular Iconography," Ph.D diss., Boston University, 1995.

10 Mitchell, *Gone with the Wind*, 25.

11 Joel Chandler Harris, *Uncle Remus, His Songs and His Sayings: The Folk-lore of the Old Plantation* (New York: D. Appleton and Company, 1881).

12 Mitchell, *Gone with the Wind*, 24–25.

13 Trudier Harris, *From Mammies to Militants* (Philadelphia: Temple University Press, 1982), 24–25.

14 Mitchell, *Gone with the Wind*, 65.

15 Isabel Drysdale, *Scenes in Georgia* (Philadelphia: American Sunday School Union, 1827), 30.

16 Ibid., 4.

17 Ibid., 31.

18 Stowe, *Uncle Tom's Cabin*, 17.

19 Ibid.

20 Ibid.

21 Wendy Lavitt, *America Folk Dolls* (New York: Knopf, 1982), 40–42. Lavitt notes that "rubber nipple dolls were popular in the 1920s and 1930s and were always Black. Many hold white babies" (Knopf Collectors Guide to American Antiques: Dolls [New York: Knopf, 1983], 13). See also Evelyn Coleman, *The Collector's Encyclopedia of Dolls* (New York: Crown, 1971), 237 and 464–470.

22 Patricia Hill Collins, *Black Sexual Politics: African Americans, Gender, and the New Racism* (New York: Routledge, 2004), 27.

23 Deborah Willis and Carla Williams, *The Black Female Body: A Photographic History* (Philadelphia: Temple University Press, 2002).

24 Willis and Williams, *The Black Female Body*, 84.

25 bell hooks, "Selling Hot Pussy: Representations of Black Female Sexuality in the Cultural Marketplace," in *The Politics of Women's Bodies*, ed. Rose Weitz (New York: Oxford University Press, 1998), 118.

26 Ibid.

27 Peg Tyre, "Shocking the Jocks," *Newsweek*, March 8, 2004 (http://msnbc.msn.com/id/4409142/).

28 Willis and Williams, *The Black Female Body*, 84.

29 Iris Marion Young, "Breasted Experience: The Look and the Feeling," in *The Politics of Women's Bodies*, ed. Rose Weitz (New York: Oxford University Press, 1998), 127.

30 See the Amateur Gourmet (www.amateur-gourmet.com/the_amateur_gourmet/2004/02/janet_jackson_b.html).

31 Young, "Breasted Experience," 125.

32 Willis and Williams, *The Black Female Body*, 133–134.

33 Kimberly Wallace-Sanders, *Mammy: A Century of Race, Gender and Southern Memory* (Ann Arbor: University of Michigan Press, 2006).

34 Terry Gips, "Joyce Scott's Mammy/Nanny Series," *Feminist Studies* 22, no. 2 (Summer 1996): 312–13.

35 Gips, "Joyce Scott's Mammy/Nanny Series," 312.

36 Joyce J. Scott, personal communication with Kimberly Wallace-Sanders, June 15, 2004. See also Joyce J. Scott, *Fearless Beadwork: Handwriting and Drawings from Hell* (Rochester, New York: Visual Studies Workshop, 1994).

37 Joyce J. Scott, personal communication with Kimberly Wallace-Sanders, June 15, 2004.

38 Ibid.

39 Gips, "Joyce Scott's Mammy/Nanny Series," 312.

40 Darlene Clark Hine, "Introduction" in *The Face of Our Past*, ed. Kathleen Thompson and Hilary Mac Austin (Bloomington: University of Indiana Press, 1999), xi.

41 Michael D. Harris, *Colored Pictures: Race and Visual Representation* (Chapel Hill: University of North Carolina Press, 2003), 210.

42 Harris, *Colored Pictures*, 211.

43 Ibid.

44 Taken from comment made by the artist during a Women's Studies event at Emory University in October 2002.

45 Jo Ann Morgan, "Mammy the Huckster," *American Art* (Spring 1995): 90.

46 Ibid., 96.

47 Hine, "Introduction," xi.

PLATES

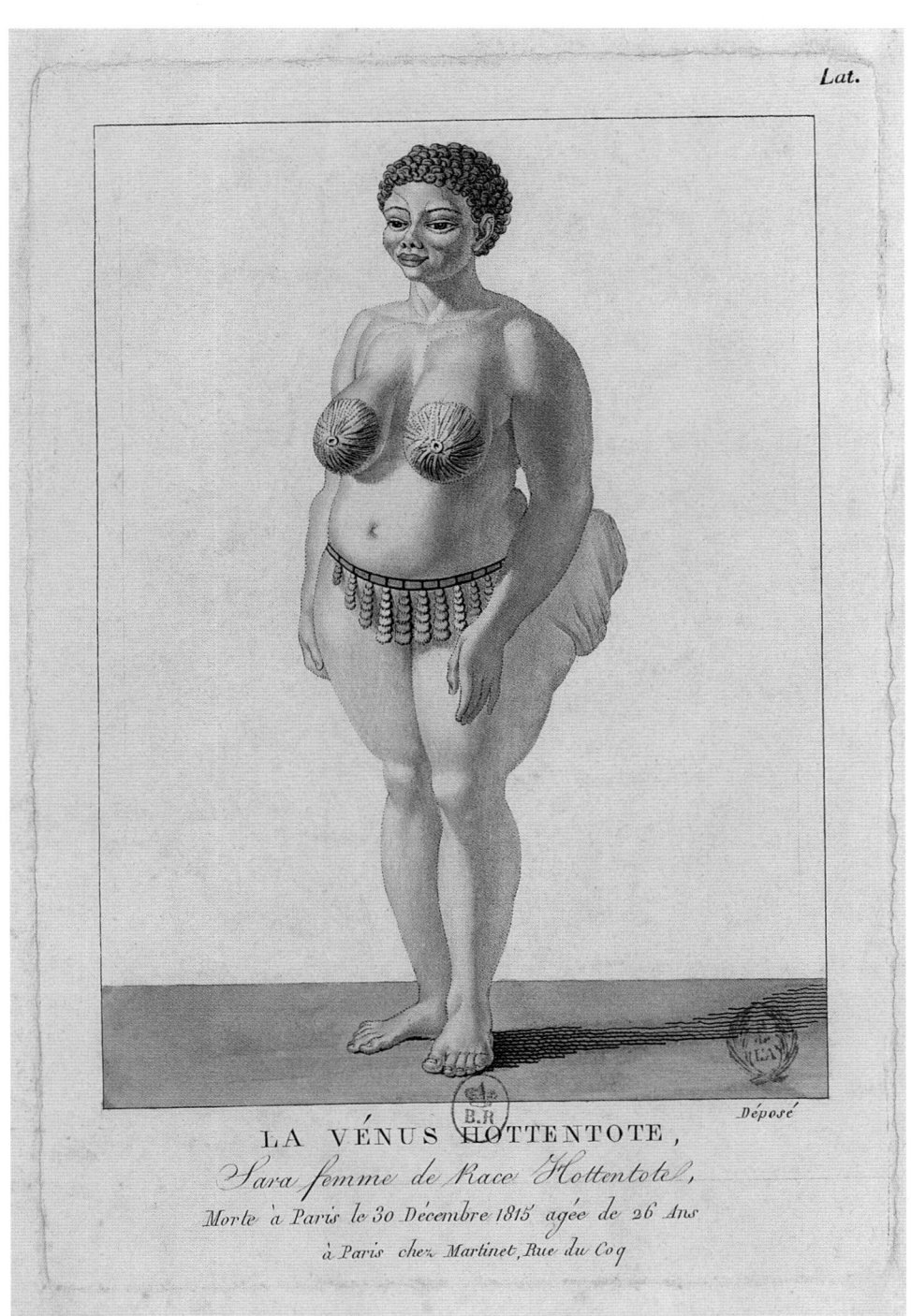

LA VÉNUS HOTTENTOTE,

Sara femme de Race Hottentote,

Morte à Paris le 30 Décembre 1815 agée de 26 Ans

à Paris chez Martinet, Rue du Coq

PLATE 45
Unknown artist
Le vénus Hottentote, C. 1815
Engraving
Cliché Bibliothèque nationale de France,
Paris, EST-223
Photograph courtesy of
Cliché Bibliothèque nationale de France

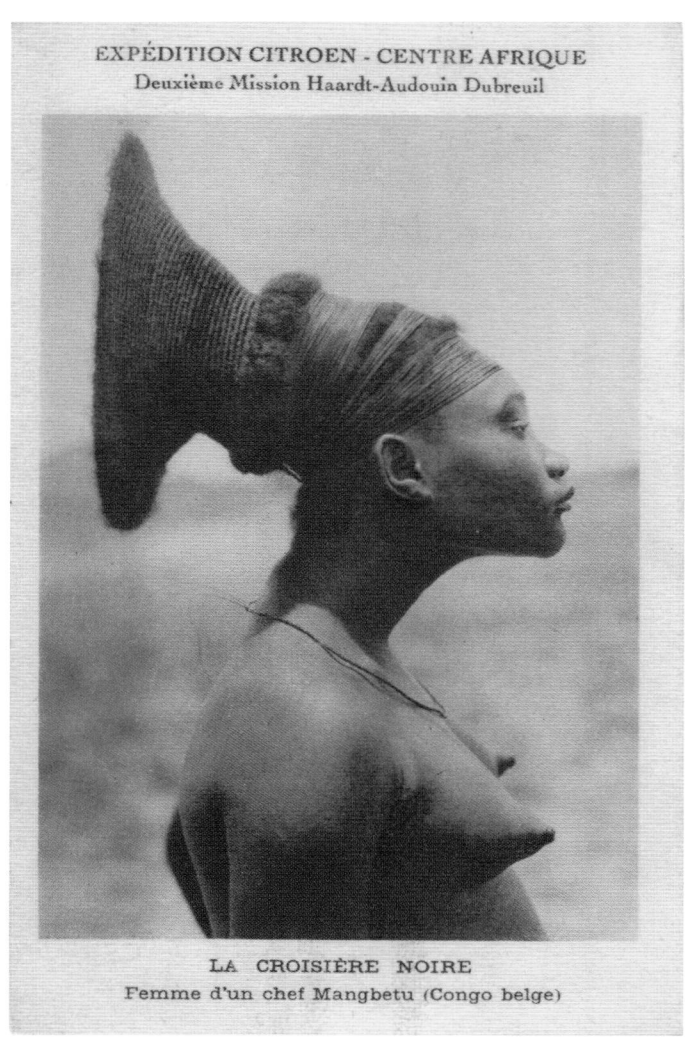

EXPÉDITION CITROEN - CENTRE AFRIQUE
Deuxième Mission Haardt-Audouin Dubreuil

LA CROISIÈRE NOIRE
Femme d'un chef Mangbetu (Congo belge)

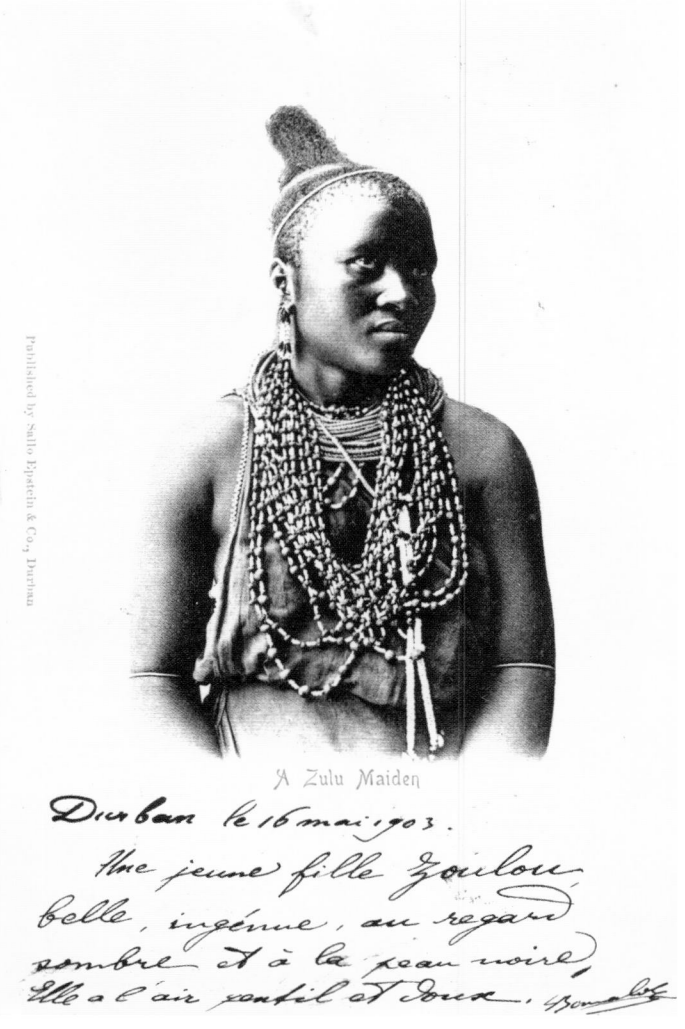

A Zulu Maiden

Durban le 16 mai 1903.
Une jeune fille Zoulou
belle, ingénue, au regard
sombre et à la peau noire,
Elle a l'air gentil et doux.

PLATE 46
Léon Poirier, French (1884–1968), and
Georges Specht, French (active 1909–1931)
Femme d'un chef Mangbetu (Congo belge)
[Wife of Mangbetu Chief (Belgian Congo)]
[Nobosodrou, Wife of Mangbetu King Touba], 1925
Publisher unidentified
Halftone print, postcard
Courtesy of Christraud Geary

PLATE 47
Unknown photographer
A Zulu Maiden
Published by Sallo Epstein & Co., Durban,
South Africa, early twentieth century
Collotype, postcard, cancellation date illegible
Hood Museum of Art: Purchased through
the Hood Museum of Art Acquisitions Fund;
2006.18.30

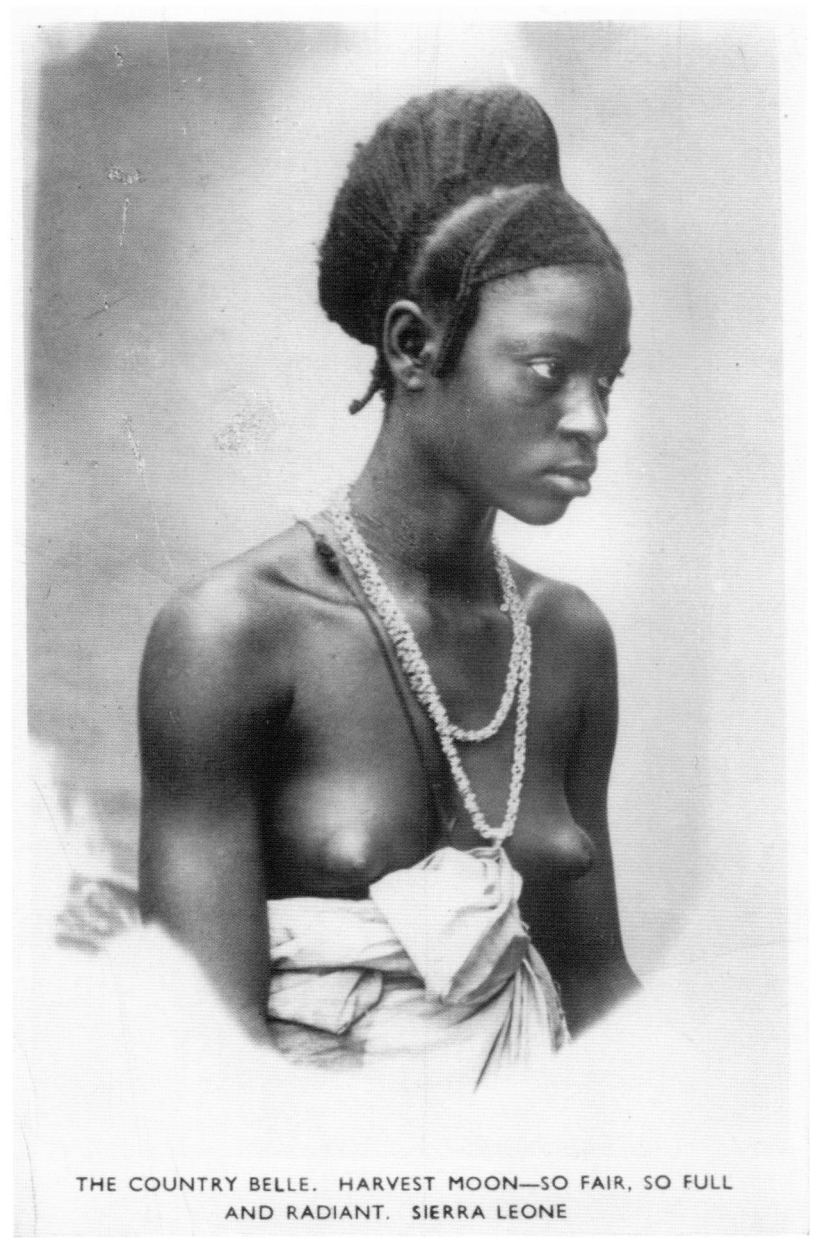

THE COUNTRY BELLE. HARVEST MOON—SO FAIR, SO FULL
AND RADIANT. SIERRA LEONE

PLATE 48
Arthur and Alphonso Lisk-Carew,
Freetown, Sierra Leone, Sierra Leonians
(active c. 1905–c. 1959)
*THE COUNTRY BELLE. HARVEST MOON—SO FAIR,
SO FULL AND RADIANT. Sierra Leone*, c. 1910
Published by Arthur and Alphonso Lisk-Carew,
c. 1920
Toned silver gelatin print, postcard
Courtesy of Christraud Geary

EXCHANGES: PENNY SIOPIS*

South African Postcard 3 (plate 100) was one of a series I made in 1994, the year of our first democratic elections. It was part of a larger series of works in which I drew on imagery from mechanically reproduced images—photocopies, photographs (pubic, public, and personal), etc. I manipulated and sometimes interfered with these ready-made images with oil paint, found objects, and other material. My choice of medium or objects lay largely in the associative and symbolic weight offered by these, as each seemed embedded in its own distinctive set of visual codes and emotions. This series follows on from my ironical history paintings of the 1980s in which I used illustrations from South African secondary school history textbooks to make collaged paintings that sought to critique apartheid and colonialism. Important in these works was to reveal how the pictorial conventions of representation—in (mostly) engraved form—were and remain powerful in shaping our colonial imaginary.

In 1994 the transition from apartheid to democracy was not a clean break and signs of apartheid persisted in the new dispensation. Ethnographic postcards of indigenous people that seemed exploitative and racist to many of us were typical of this situation as they remained on the shelves of local bookshops and were sold at tourist venues. This phenomenon continues today. Initially there was much anxiety about these postcards on account of how they perpetuated negative stereotypes of black people. However, as time passed and the political power shifted and other positive representations of indigenous black people populated the media, a certain pride developed about such images. Or, more accurately, these images were re-appropriated and co-opted for positive self-assertion by recently liberated South Africans. This is a complex phenomenon, but partly it has to do with the fact that "tribal" culture was no longer simply a negative category involving subjugation and control. At any rate, such images are now seen differently.

My work, *South African Postcard 3,* references an example of one such postcard. It shows a Zulu woman in traditional beaded dress. The reverse side of the postcard titles the image "Zulu tribe—South Africa." The extended caption reads "Beautiful picture of Zulu woman in her tribal ceremonial Cele dress showing Cele bead-work and beaded dancing stick." I enlarged the image through the black and white laser print process. I then laminated the print, applying oil paint and small plastic medical objects on selected parts of the laminated surface. I especially worked with very thick oil paint in the areas where the beadwork was rendered "white" or absent through the photocopy process. In other words, I painted into the erased or negative spaces. Oil paint has its obvious cultural freight but for me the painstaking filling-in of tiny parts of the image was as much about the effort to identify with the image through embodying what I saw as a kind of historical and psychic absence; something missing or lost.

I also placed multicolored plastic medical instruments at intervals across the field of the whole image. Sometimes these work with the image-ground, at other times they seem brutally applied with no recognition of that ground. All sorts of anxious associations linked to ethnographic images, material technology, and more generally science are invoked in my placing of these objects over the image. These are not simply "symbolic," but part of the formal rupturing that occurs between the objects, the oil paint, and the smooth reflective surface of the reprographic image. That surface also implicates the viewer in what can be a disconcerting process of looking.

* Artist statement for *Black Womanhood: Images, Icons, and Ideologies of the African Body*, received by e-mail, May 14, 2007.

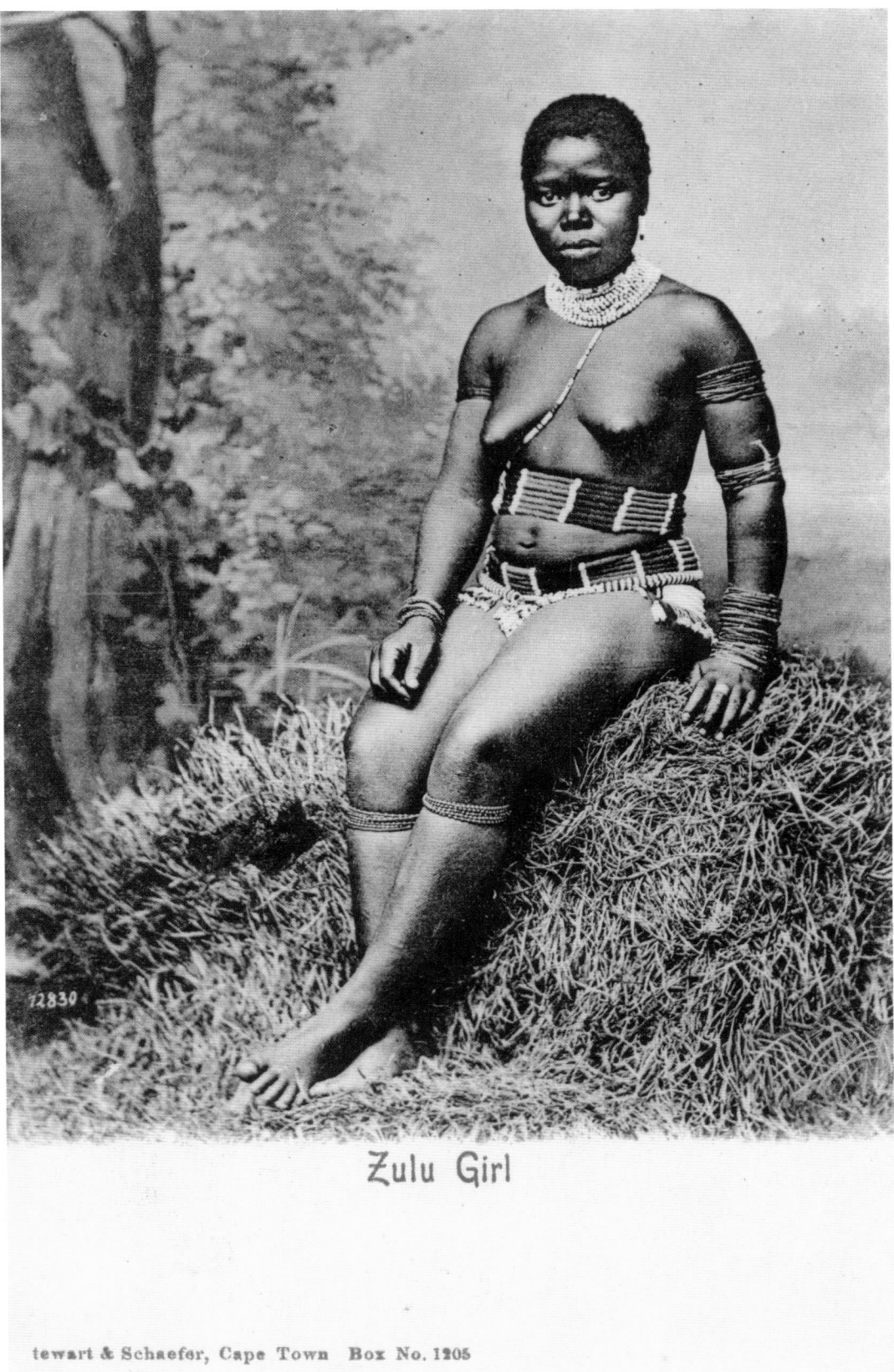

Zulu Girl

tewart & Schaefer, Cape Town   Box No. 1205

PLATE 49
Unknown photographer
Zulu Girl
Published by Stewart & Schaefer,
Cape Town, South Africa,
early twentieth century
Collotype, postcard
Hood Museum of Art: Purchased
through the Hood Museum of Art
Acquisitions Fund; 2006.18.29

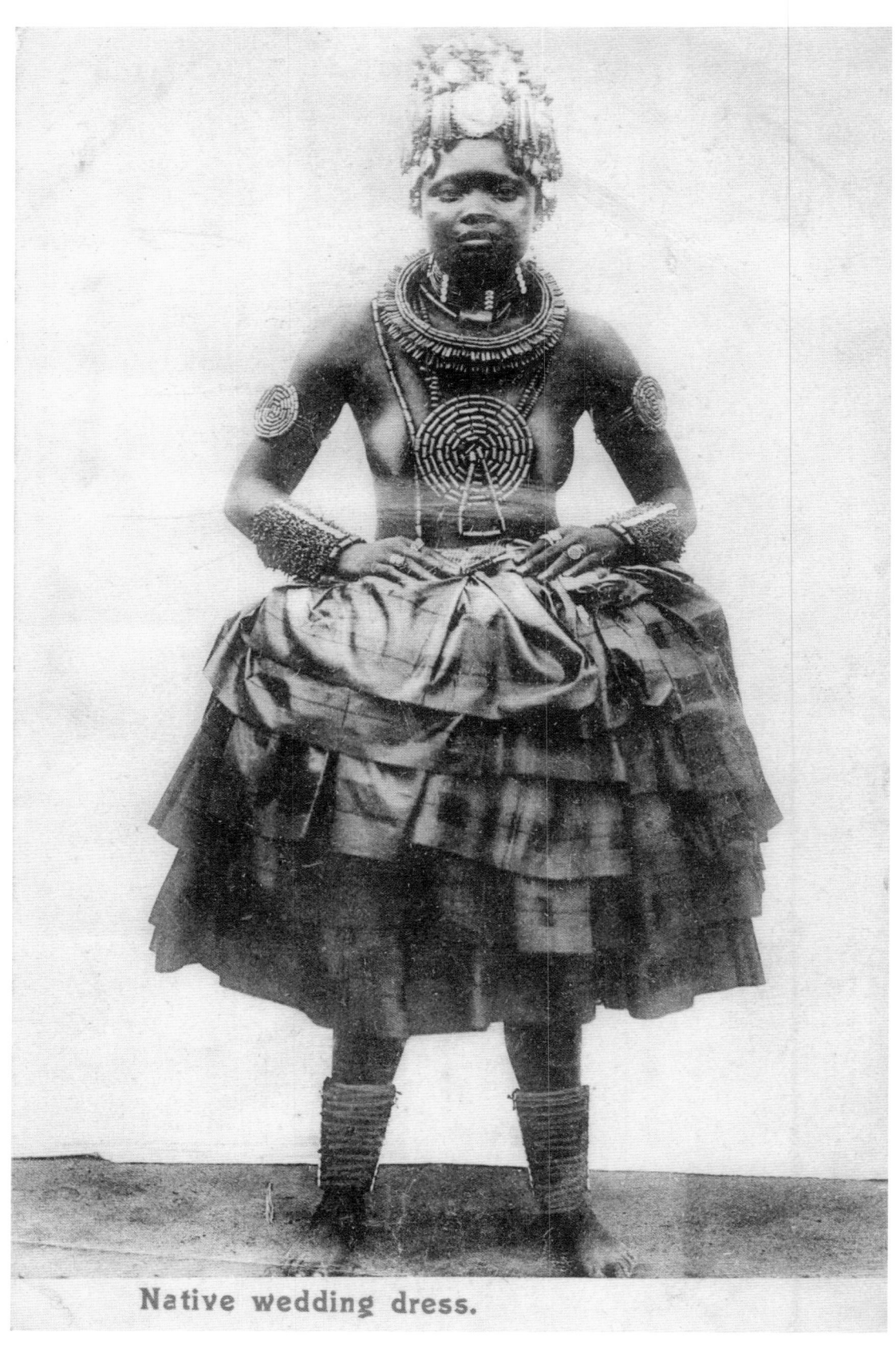

Native wedding dress.

PLATE 50
Jonathan A. Green, Nigerian
(active c. 1890–c. 1930)
Native wedding dress, c. 1890
Publisher unidentified, before 1905,
cancellation October 26, 1910
Collotype, postcard
Courtesy of Christraud Geary

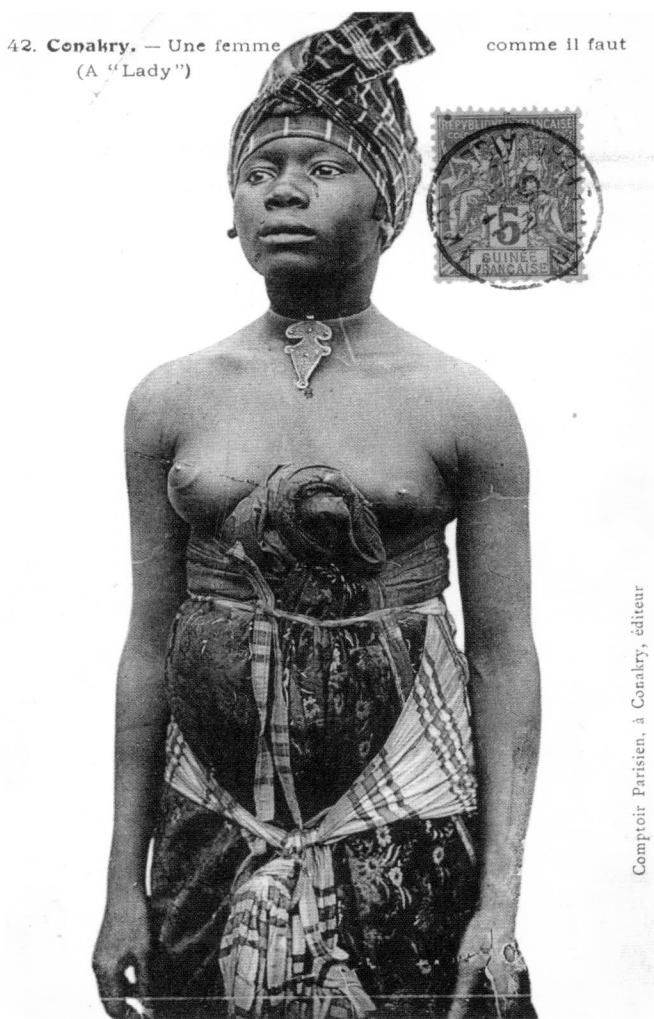

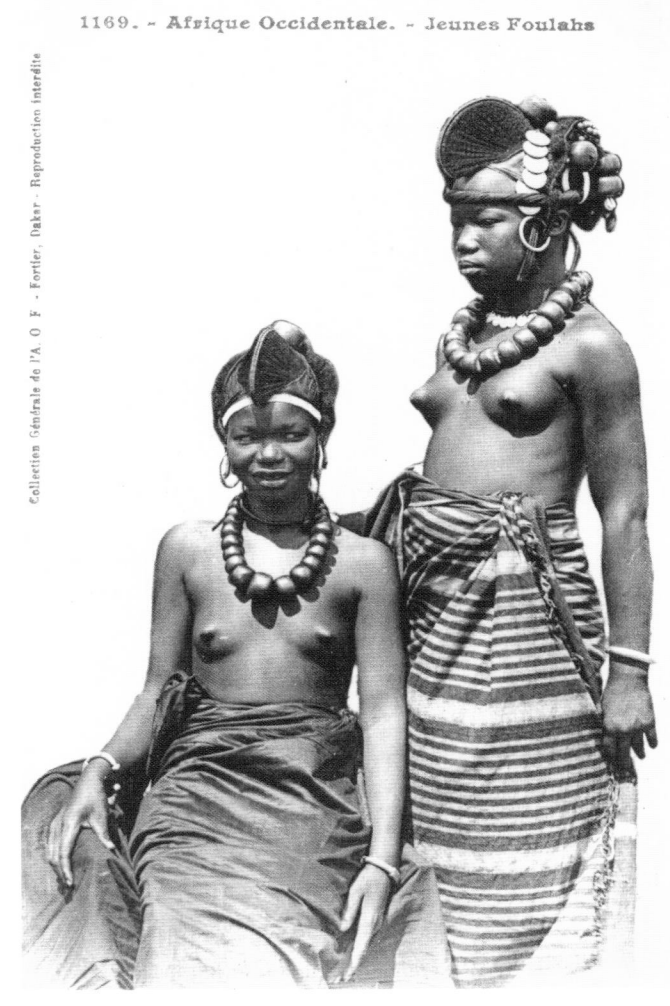

PLATE 51
Unknown photographer
*42. Conakry—Une Femme comme il faut
(A "Lady")* [42. Conakry—A proper woman
(A Lady)], before 1906
Published by Comptoir Parisien,
Conakry, Guinea, cancellation May 11, 1906
collotype, postcard
Hood Museum of Art: Purchased through
the Hood Museum of Art Acquisitions Fund;
2006.18.8

PLATE 52
François-Edmond Fortier?, French (1862–1928)
1169.—Afrique Occidentale.—Jeunes Foulahs
[1169.—West Africa.—Young Fulah girls]
Published by Collection Générale de l'A.O.F.—
Fortier, Dakar, Senegal, early twentieth century
Collotype, postcard
Hood Museum of Art: Purchased through
the Hood Museum of Art Acquisitions Fund;
2006.18.12

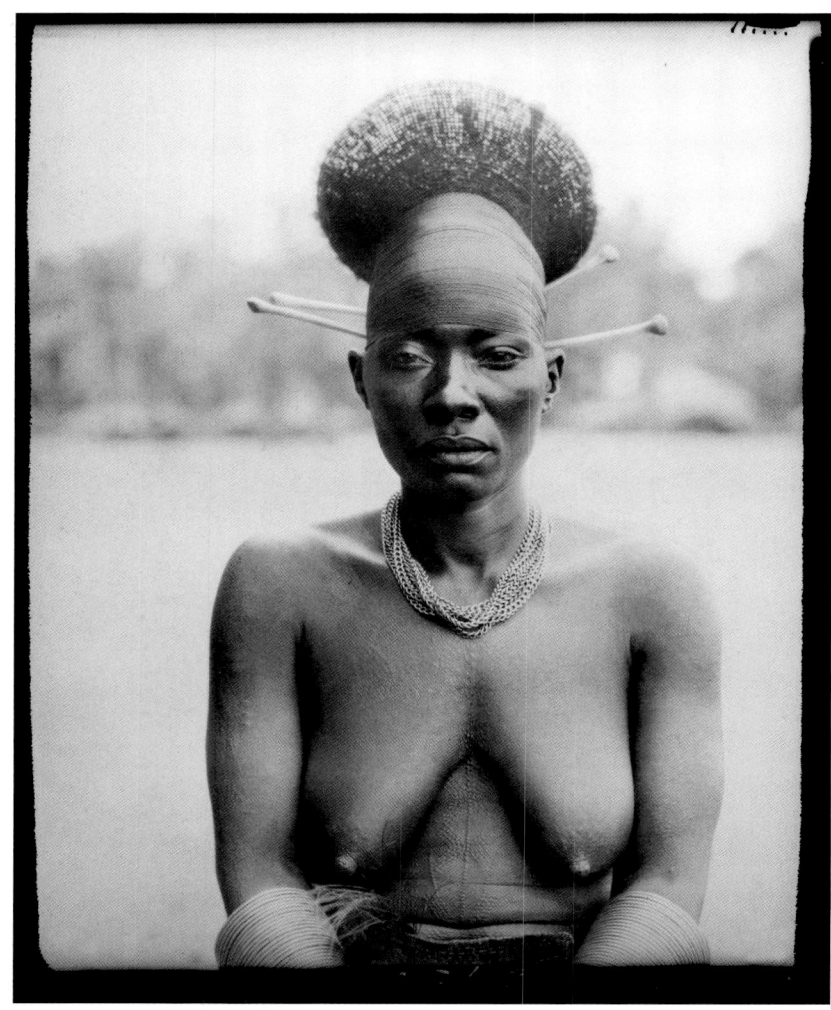

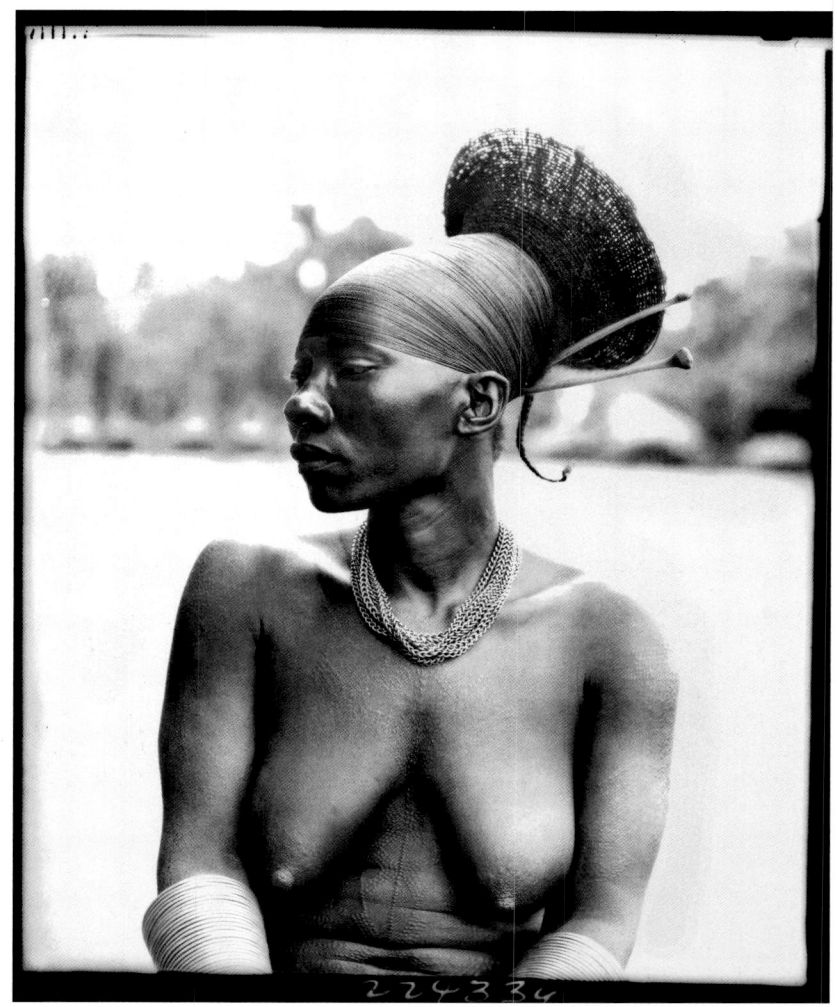

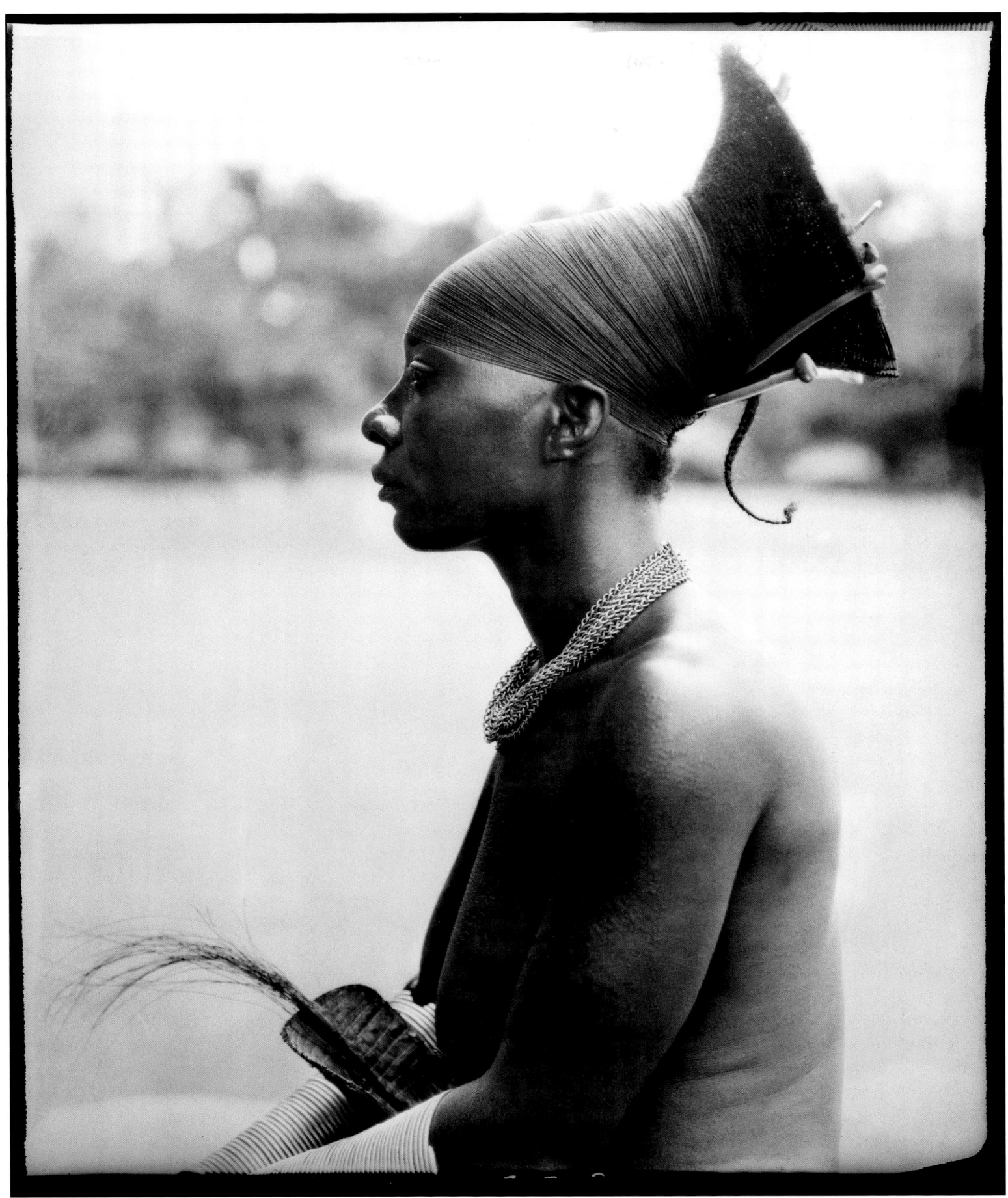

PLATE 53 a–c
Unknown photographer
Mangbetu Woman, early twentieth century
Black and white photograph
American Museum of Natural History; 224337-339
Photograph courtesy of American Museum of Natural History

Photography has a universal language, which crosses all barriers. It is for me a need to express, to communicate, to question, and to protest. As long as the need will exist, I will create. Living as an African woman in a Western world has developed in me a strong need to consistently focus on the African self-image. My images (plate 113 and figure 9.5) express a part of myself; they develop a personal view free from all anthropological, ethnographic, exotic, and romantic blemishes of the colonial era and media that are embedded in the Western consciousness. The different cultural backgrounds in which I grew up have considerably influenced my life and my vision. I get my inspiration inside this cultural mix mainly dominated by my African heritage. People fascinate me and so the human being, the body, became central in my work. Being black, African, and a woman—born in Cameroon, growing up in Paris, and now living in the Netherlands—[do not] remain without incidence in my work.

In the mystery that the body in general represents—and the black body, in particular, with its own codes—I am using stereotypical images and clichés in my work to give back the bodies and faces their independence, freedom, strength, and pride—and their awareness too. It is a need, a call to immortalize the black woman, and to celebrate her inner and outer beauty. There is no body without a soul, and beyond the black woman herself, it is the black soul—in its entirety—that I intend to celebrate. Aesthetics is my instrument to attract attention and enable the viewer to see beyond [stereotypical] forms and familiar references.

* Artist statement, personal e-mail communication with Barbara Thompson, November 16, 2006.

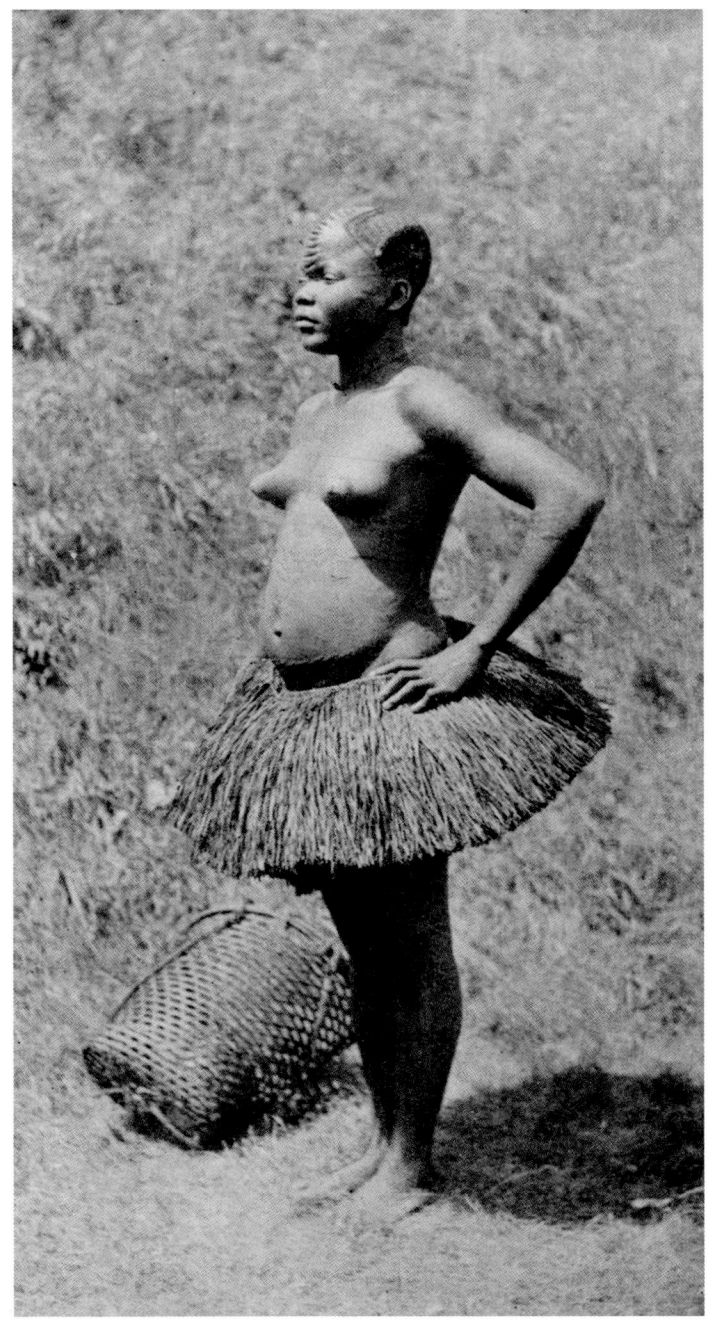

PLATE 54
Photographer unknown
A Congo woman, early twentieth century
Black and white photograph reproduced
from newspaper
American Museum of Natural History; 276935
Photograph courtesy of American Museum
of Natural History.

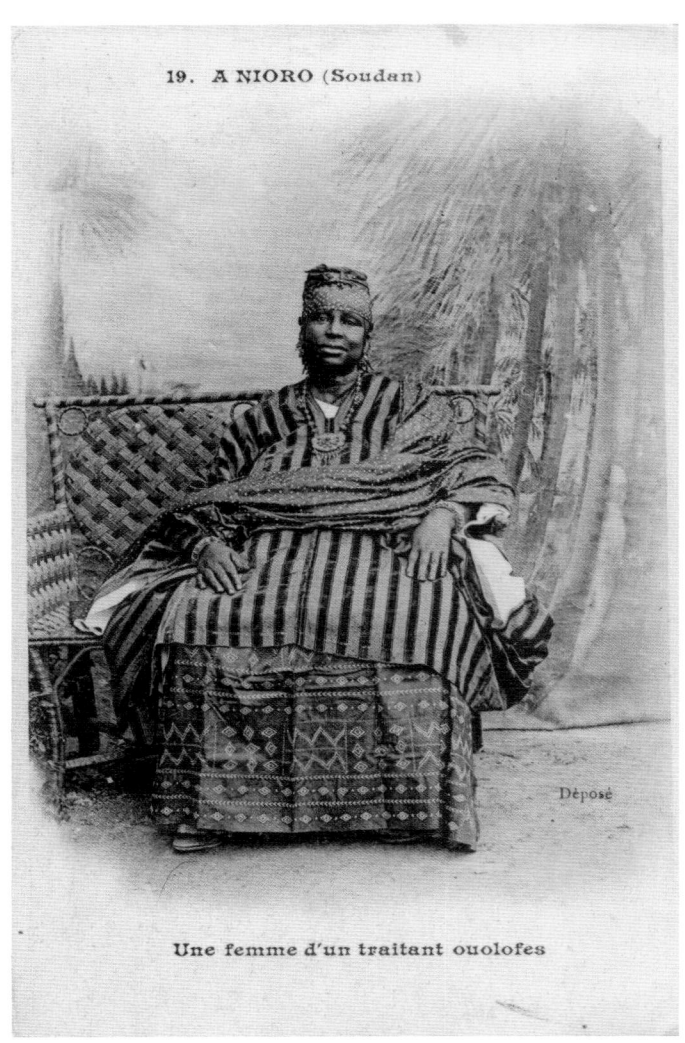

19. A NIORO (Soudan)

Déposé

Une femme d'un traitant ouolofes

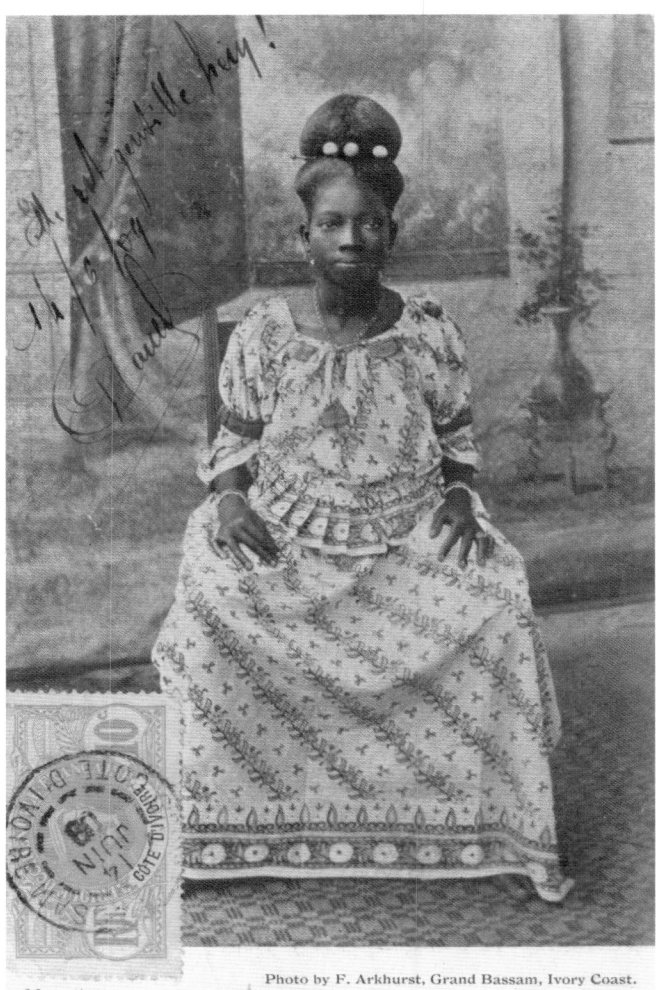

Photo by F. Arkhurst, Grand Bassam, Ivory Coast.

NO. 1. GOLD COAST NATIVE WOMAN, STYLE OF HAIR.

PLATE 55
Louis Hostalier, St. Louis, Senegal
(active 1890–1905)
19. A NIORO (Soudan) — *Une femme d'un traitant ouolofes*
[At Nioro (Sudan). Wife of a Wolof merchant], c. 1900
Publisher unidentified, c. 1905
Collotype, postcard
Courtesy of Christraud Geary

PLATE 56
F. Arkhurst, Grand Bassam, Ivory Coast, Ghanaian
(active c. 1900–1930)
NO. 1. GOLD COAST NATIVE WOMAN, STYLE OF HAIR,
c. 1910
Publisher unidentified
Halftone print, postcard
Courtesy of Christraud Geary

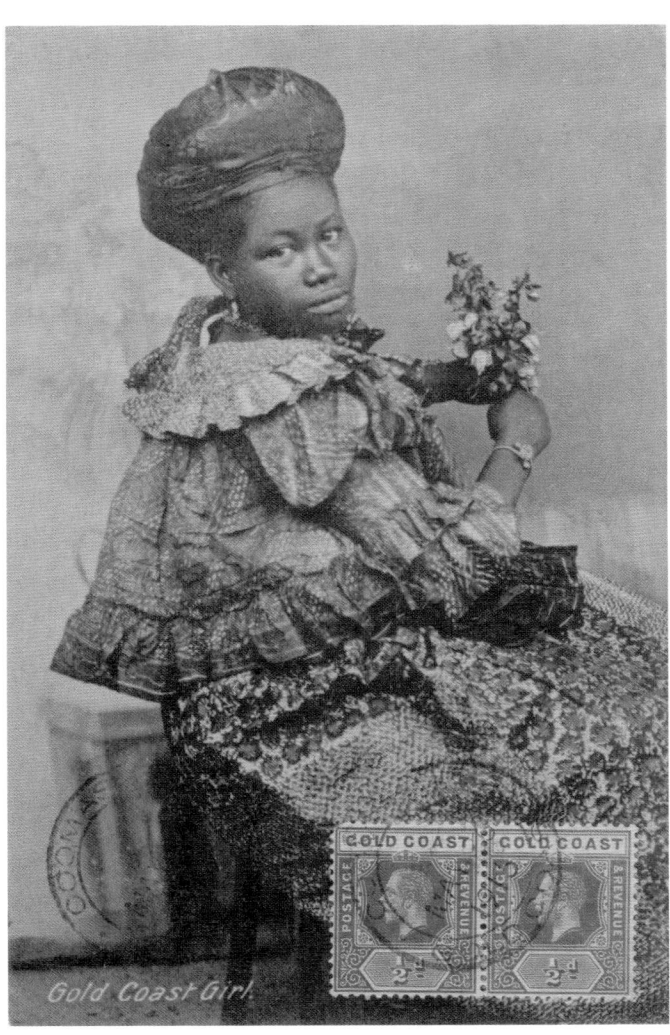

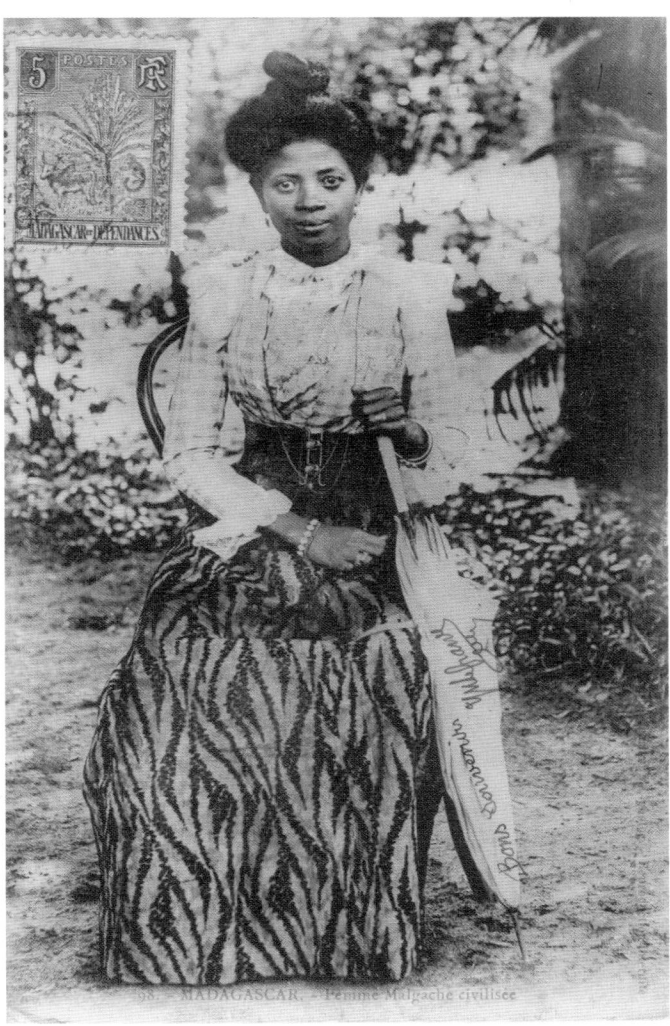

PLATE 57
J. Vitta, Tarquah, West Africa (Tarkwa, Ghana)
(active c. 1900)
Gold Coast girl, c. 1910
Published by J. Vitta, Tarquah, West Africa,
cancellation May 1915
Collotype, postcard
Courtesy of Christraud Geary

PLATE 58
Charifou fils (active c. 1900–1930)
98. MADAGASCAR—Femme Malgache civilisée
[Madagascar, civilized Malagasy woman], c. 1900
Publisher unidentified, before 1905,
cancellation May 7, 1906
Collotype, postcard
Courtesy of Christraud Geary

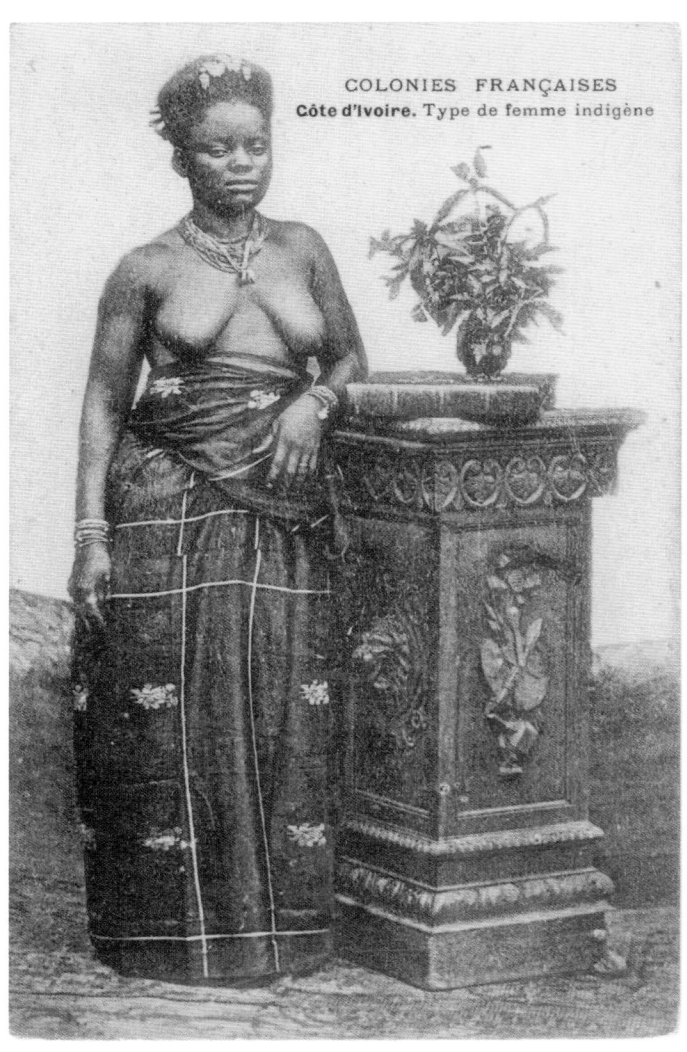

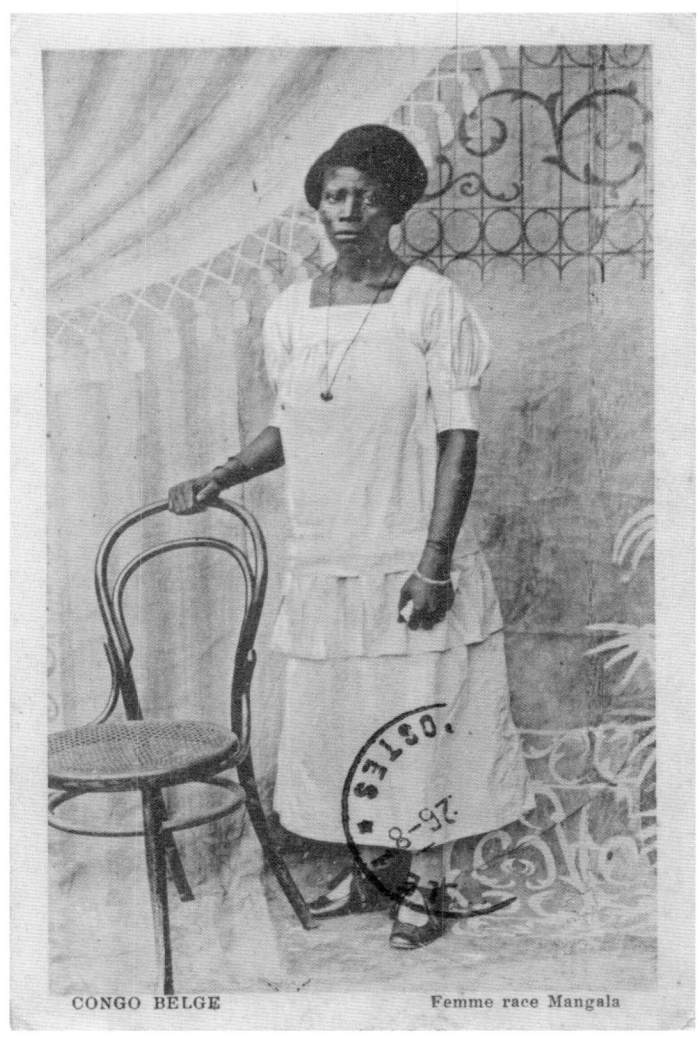

PLATE 59
Unknown photographer
COLONIES-FRANÇAISES, Côte d'Ivoire. Type de femme indigène [French Colonies, Côte d'Ivoire. Type of indigenous woman], c. 1910
Publisher unidentified
Collotype, postcard
Courtesy of Christraud Geary

PLATE 60
Unknown photographer
CONGO BELGE—Femme race Mangala [Belgian Congo—Woman of the Mangala race]
Published by Peter Frères, Antwerp, Belgium-Kinshasa, Democratic Republic of Congo (formerly Belgian Congo), c. 1925
Collotype, postcard
Courtesy of Christraud Geary

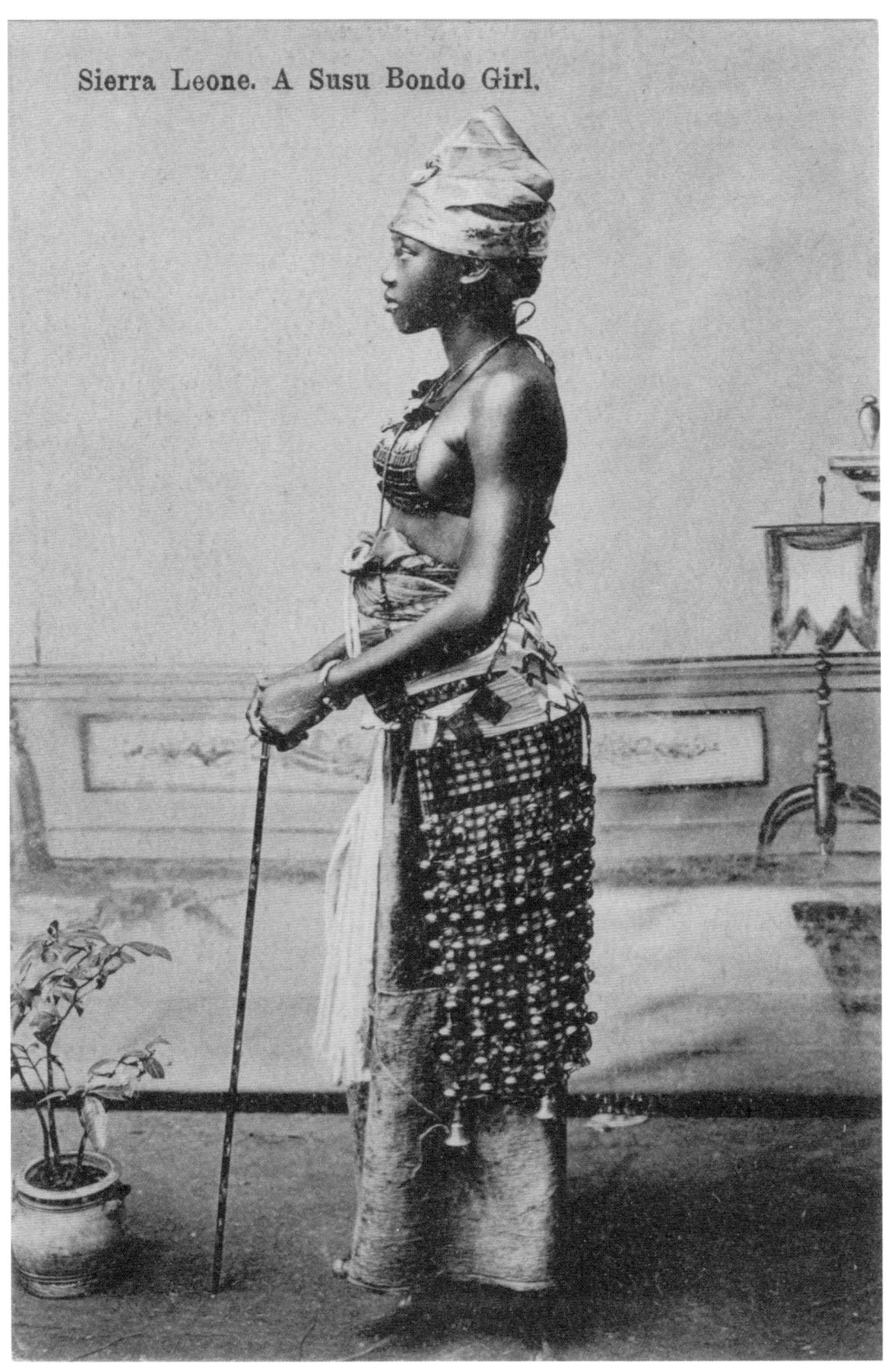

Sierra Leone. A Susu Bondo Girl.

PLATE 61
W. S. Johnston & Sons, Art Photographers,
Freetown, Sierra Leone, Sierra Leonians
(active c. 1900–c. 1950)
Sierra Leone. A Susu Bondo Girl, c. 1910
Publisher unidentified
Collotype, postcard
Courtesy of Christraud Geary

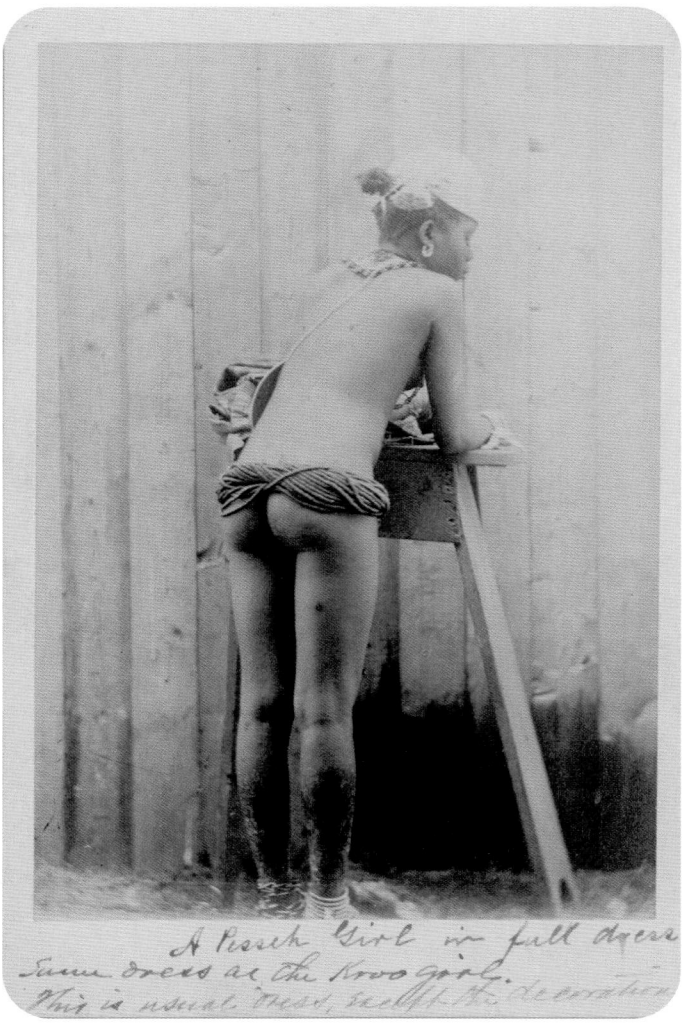

A Pesseh Girl in full dress
Same dress as the Kroo girl.
This is usual dress, see all the decoration

06014400 USNM

and compensation. Polygamy
prevails. There is no restraint as
to the number of wives. Marriage
by capture does not exist except
in case of war when captive
women are made wives.
Slavery does not exist, except that
in case of captives taken in war
who are required to pay or work out
a ransom.

EXHIBIT,

WORLD'S FAIR.

Chicago, Ill., U. S. A.

1893.

MAIN OFFICES,
149 S. FRONT STREET,
PHILADELPHIA, PA., U. S. A.

Copy Neg. # 98-10144

PLATE 62

a. Unknown photographer
Portrait of Young Pesseh Woman from Near Monrovia with Body Paint and in Costume
Published by Liberian Art Publishing Co., 1893
Black and white photoprint on standard card
National Anthropological Archives; Inv. 06014500
Photograph courtesy of National Anthropological Archives © 1999–2007 by the Smithsonian Institution. All rights reserved

b. Back view of the same card
National Anthropological Archives; Inv. 06014500.
Photograph courtesy of National Anthropological Archives © 1999–2007 by the Smithsonian Institution. All rights reserved

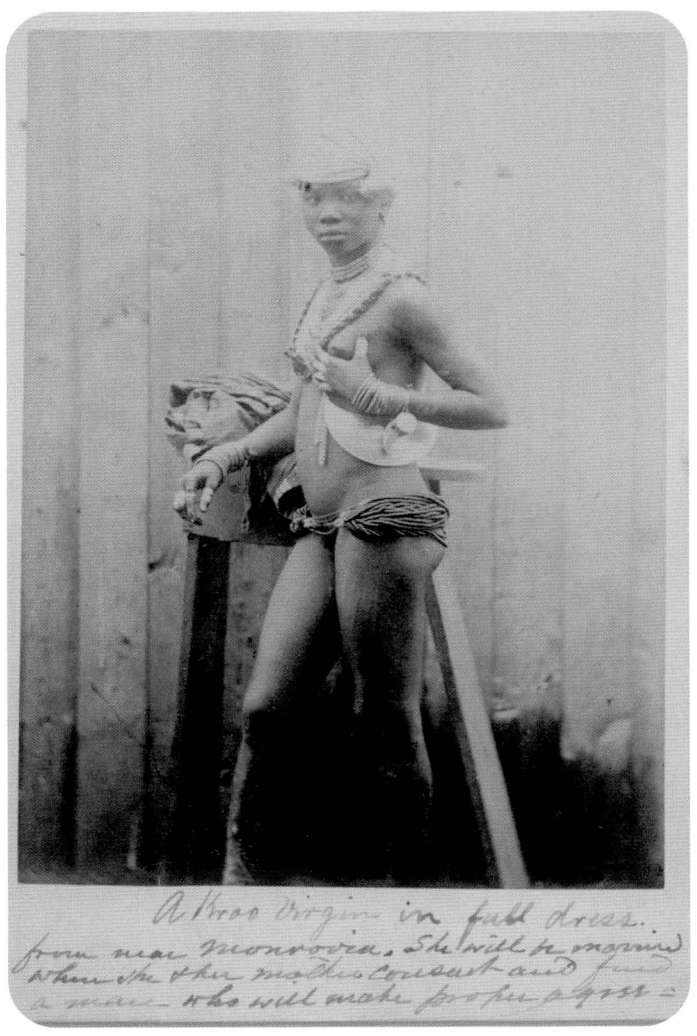

A Kroo Virgin in full dress. from near Monrovia. She will be married when she & her mother consent and find a man who will make proper dress=

PLATE 63
a. Unknown photographer
Portrait of Young Kru Woman from Village Near Monrovia with Body Paint and in Costume
Published by Liberian Art Publishing Co., 1893
Black and white photoprint on standard card
National Anthropological Archives; Inv. 06014400
Photograph courtesy of National Anthropological Archives © 1999–2007 by the Smithsonian Institution. All rights reserved.

b. Back view of the same card
National Anthropological Archives; Inv. 06014400
Photograph courtesy of National Anthropological Archives © 1999–2007 by the Smithsonian Institution. All rights reserved.

and compensation. Polygamy prevail. There is no restraint as to the number of wives. Marriage by capture does not exist except in case of war when captive woman are made wives. Slavery does not exist except that in case of captives taken in war

Liberian Art Publishing Co.

who are required to pay or work out a ransome.

EXHIBIT,
WORLD'S FAIR.
Chicago, Ill., U. S. A.
1893.
MAIN OFFICES,
149 S. FRONT STREET,
PHILADELPHIA, PA., U. S. A.

06014400 USNM

Copis NPg # 98-10144

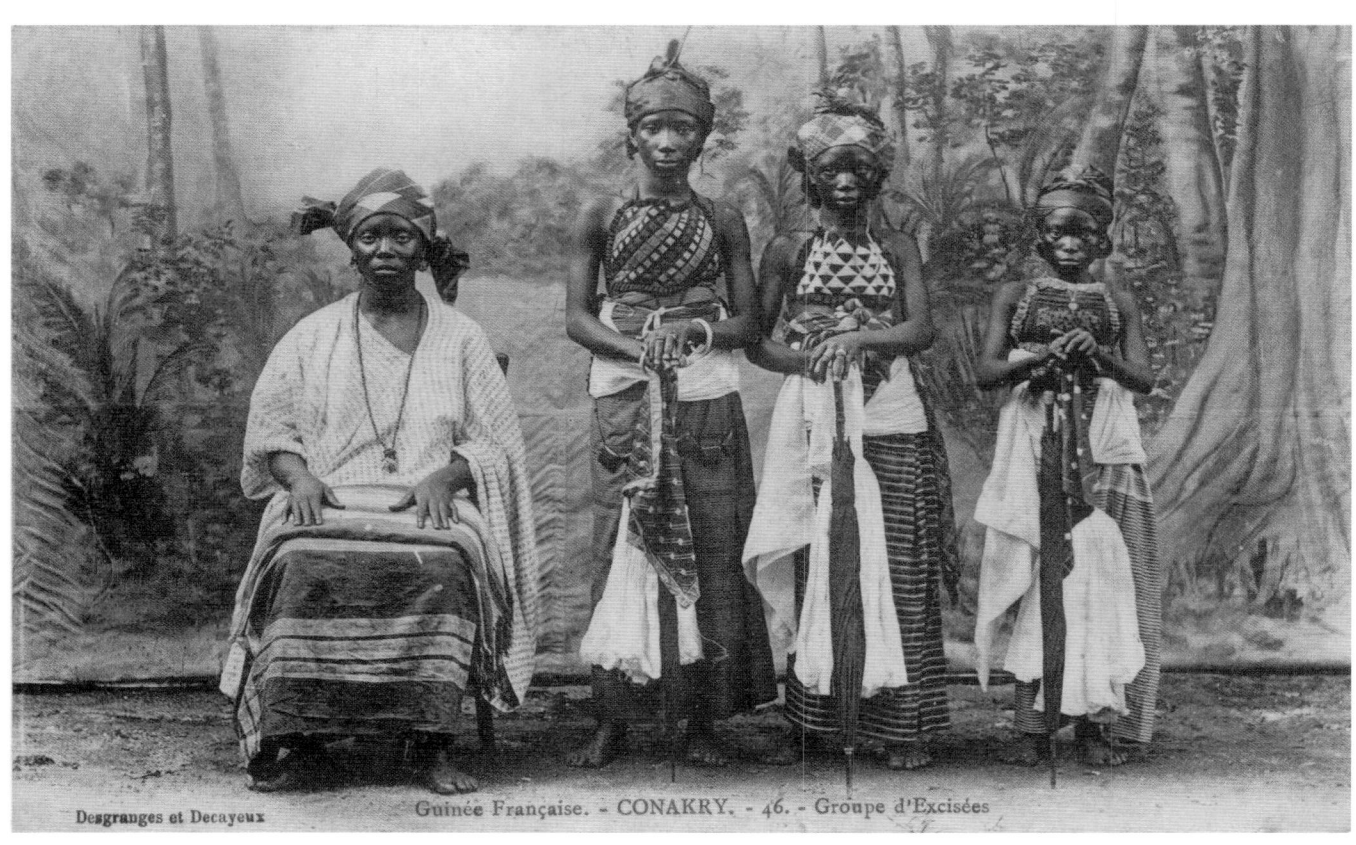

Desgranges et Decayeux   Guinée Française. - CONAKRY. - 46. - Groupe d'Excisées

PLATE 64
A. Albaret, Dakar, French (active c. 1900–1930)
47. Guinée Française—CONAKRY—46.—Groupe d'Exicées
[47. French Guinea—Conakry—46.—Group of excised
women], c. 1912
Published by Desgranges et Decayoux
Collotype, postcard
Courtesy of Christraud Geary

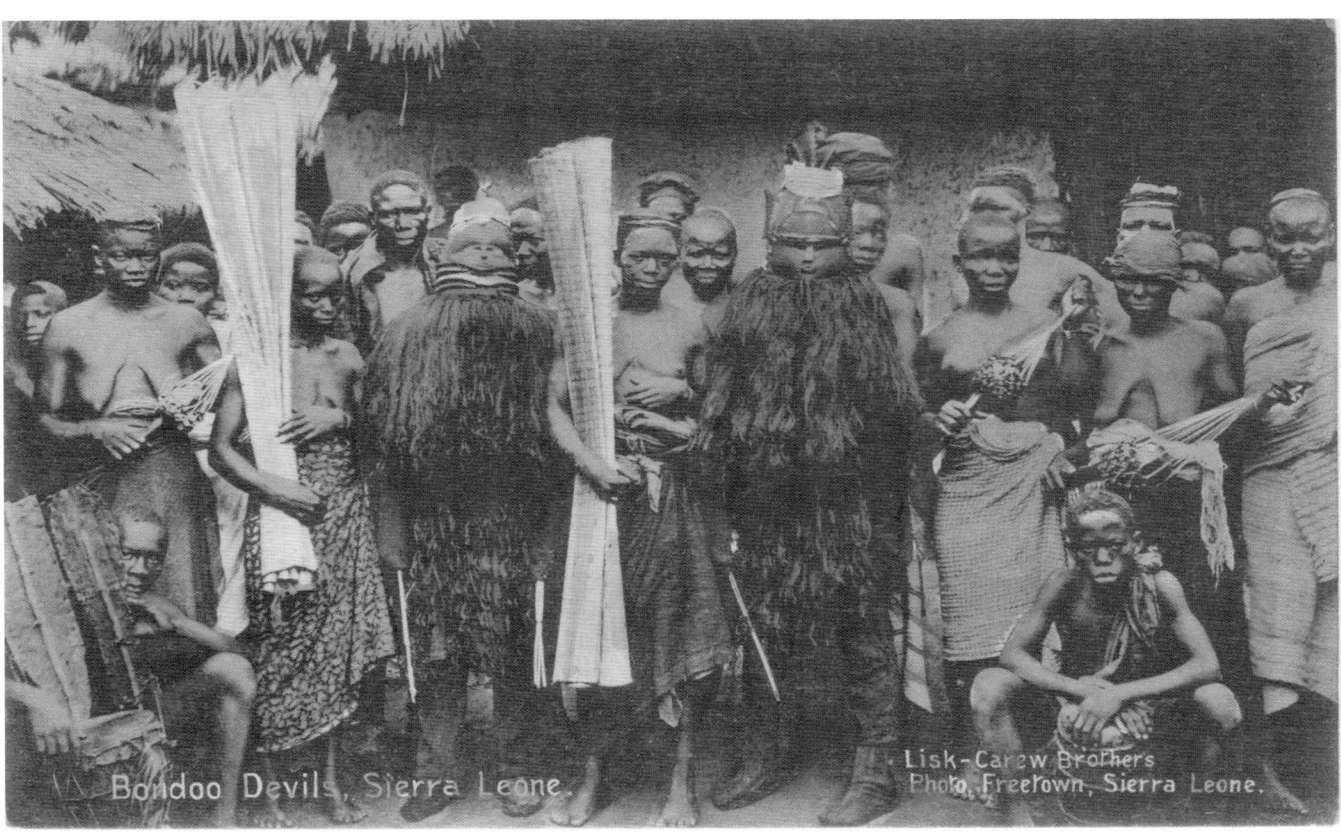

PLATE 65
Arthur and Alphonso Lisk-Carew, Freetown, Sierra Leone
Sierra Leonians (active c. 1905–c. 1959)
Bondoo Devils, Sierra Leone, c. 1910
Publisher unknown
Hand-tinted collotype, postcard
Courtesy of Christraud Geary

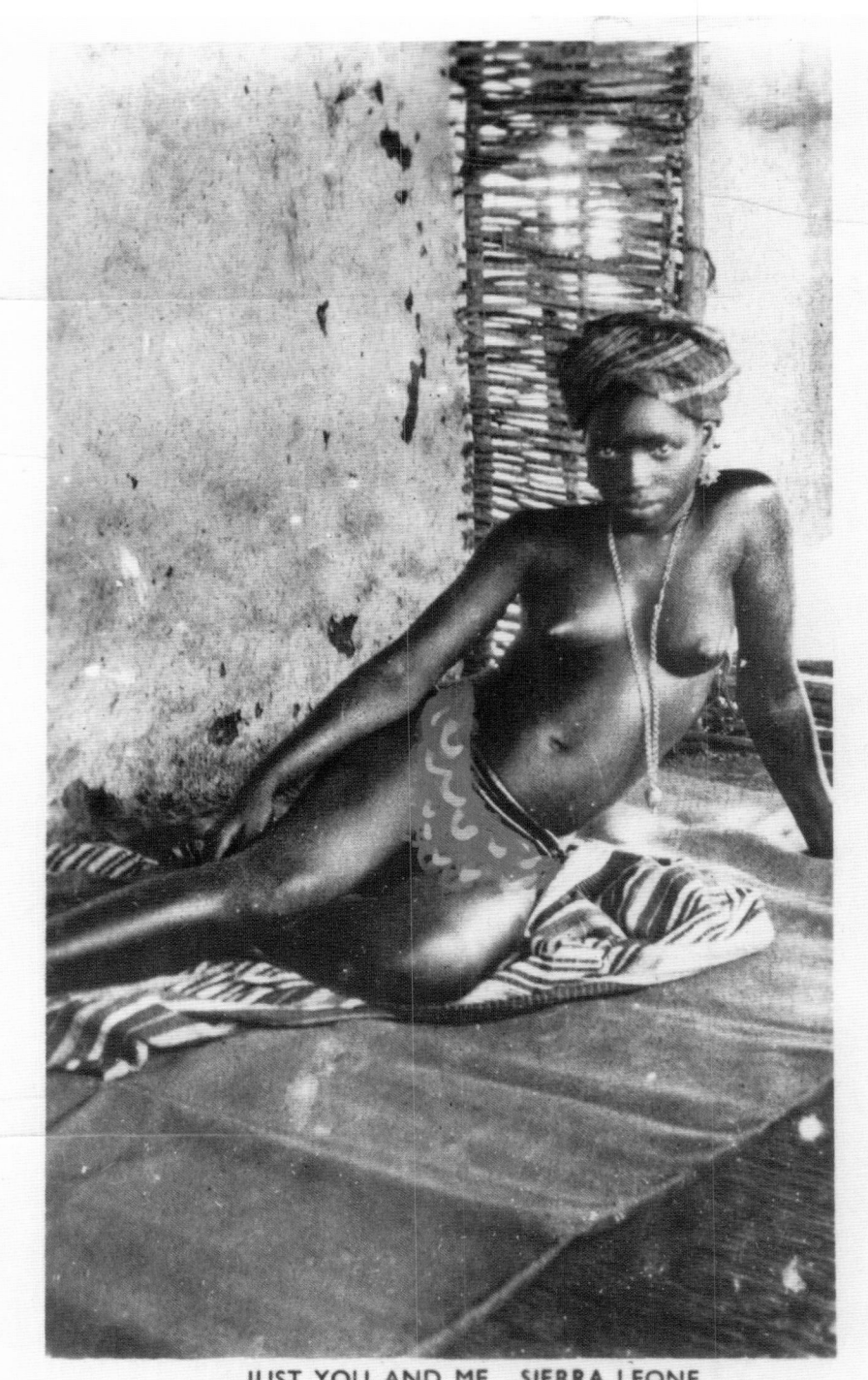

JUST YOU AND ME. SIERRA LEONE

PLATE 66
Arthur and Alphonso Lisk-Carew,
Freetown, Sierra Leone, Sierra Leonians
(active c. 1905–c. 1959)
JUST YOU AND ME. SIERRA LEONE, C. 1920
Publisher unidentified
Toned silver gelatin print, postcard
Courtesy of Christraud Geary

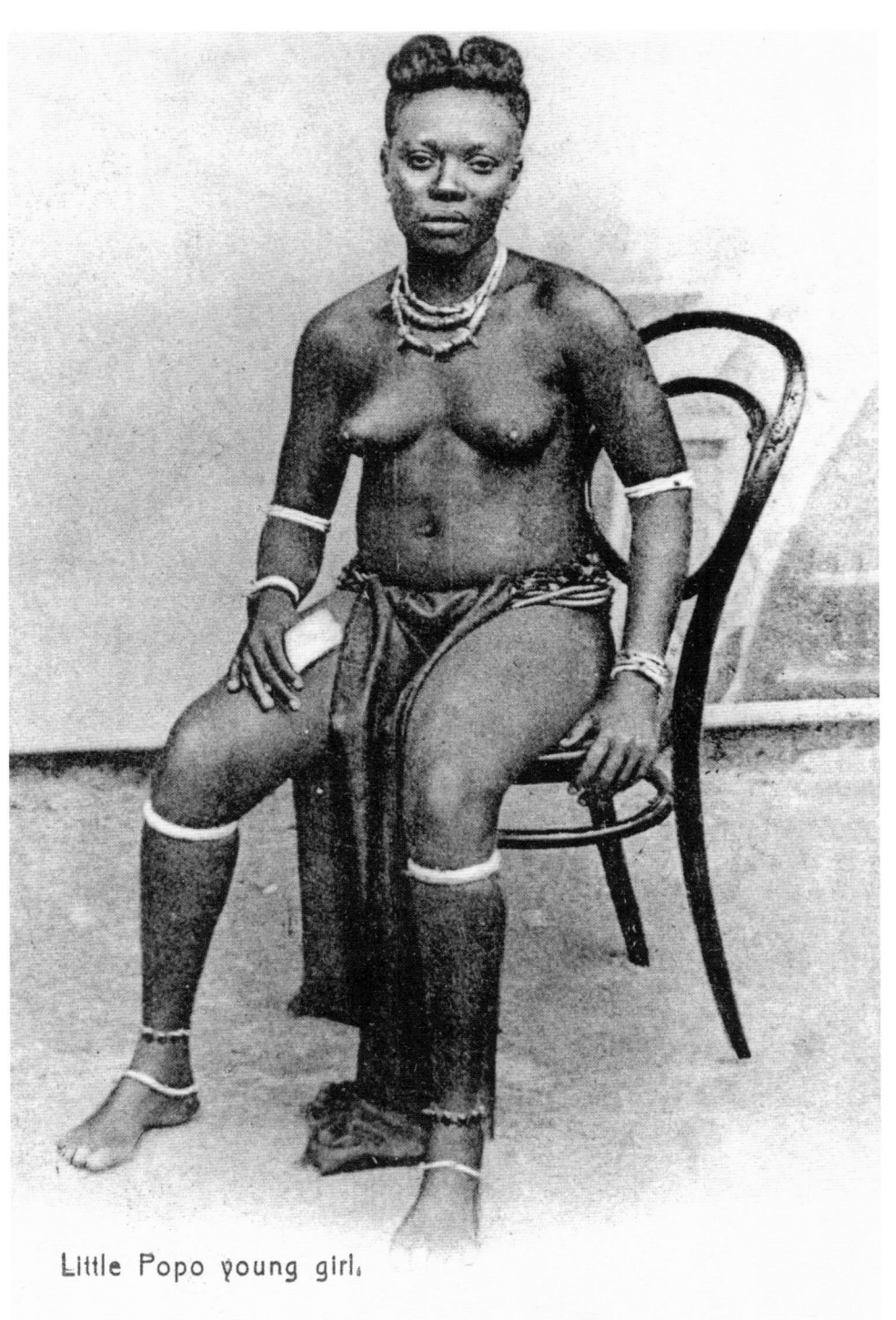

Little Popo young girl.

PLATE 67
Arthur and Alphonso Lisk-Carew, Freetown,
Sierra Leone, Sierra Leonians
(active c. 1905–c. 1959)
Little Popo young girl
Published by Lisk-Carew Brothers Photography,
Freetown, Sierra Leone, early twentieth century
Collotype, postcard
Hood Museum of Art: Purchased through
the Hood Museum of Art Acquisitions Fund;
2006.18.7

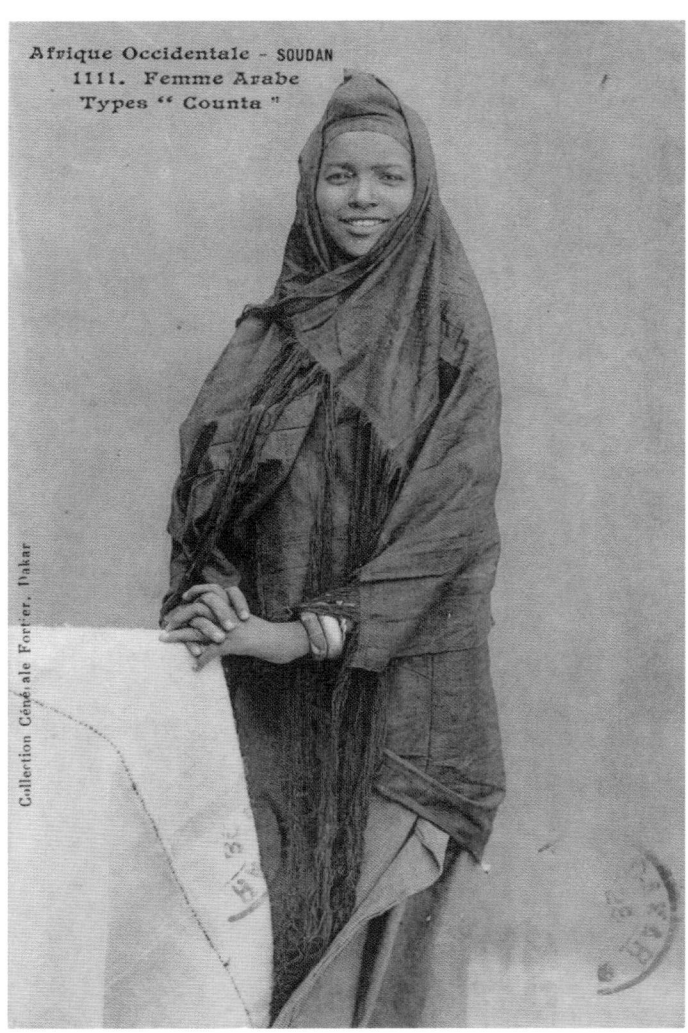

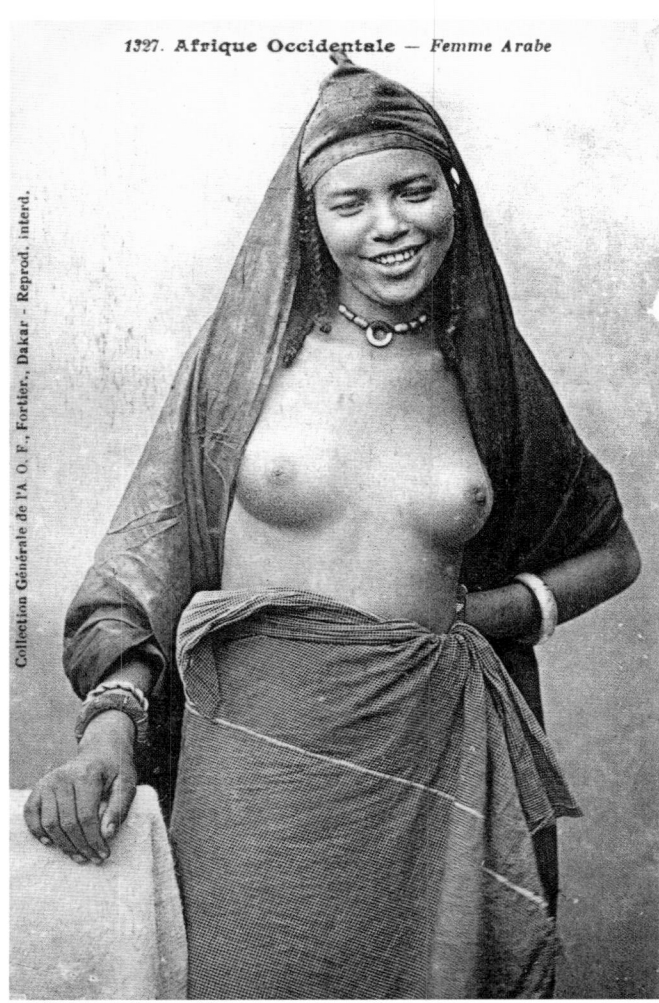

PLATE 68
François-Edmond Fortier?, French (1862–1928)
Afrique Occidentale—SOUDAN, 1111. Femme
Arabe Type "Counta" [West Africa—Sudan,
1111. Arab woman, "Counta type"], c. 1906
Published by Collection Générale Fortier, Dakar,
Senegal, cancellation September 6, 1907
Collotype, postcard
Courtesy of Christraud Geary

PLATE 69
François-Edmond Fortier?, French (1862–1928)
1327. Afrique Occidentale—Femme Arabe
[1327. West Africa—Arab Woman]
Published by Collection Générale de l'A.O.F.
Fortier, Dakar, Senegal, early twentieth century
Collotype, postcard
Hood Museum of Art: Purchased through the
Hood Museum of Art Acquisitions Fund;
2006.18.10

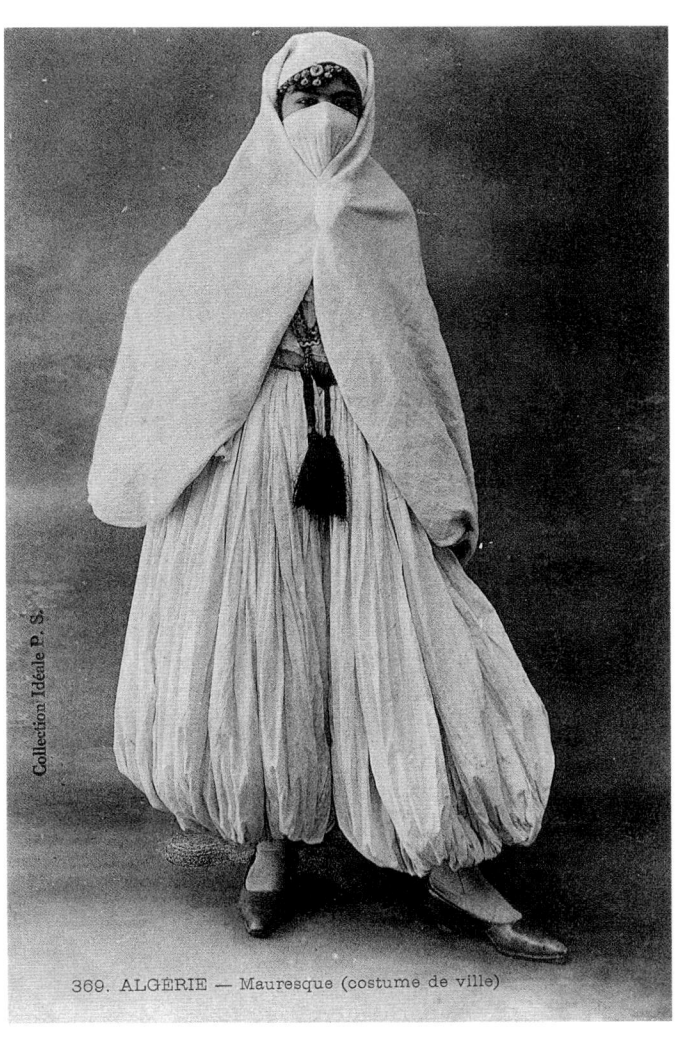

369. ALGÉRIE — Mauresque (costume de ville)

2. NU ACADÉMIQUE MAROCAIN

PLATE 70
Unknown photographer
369. ALGERIA—Mauresque (costume de ville)
[369. Algeria—Moorish woman (city outfit)]
Printed by Collections Idéale, c. 1905
Collotype, postcard
EEPA Postcard collection, AE 1995-0020-42,
Eliot Elisofon Photographic Archives, National
Museum of African Art, Smithsonian Institution
Photograph courtesy of National Museum of
African Art

PLATE 71
Unknown photographer
2. NU ACADÉMIQUE MAROCAIN [2. Academic
nude of a Moroccan] ,early twentieth century
Handwritten dating August 21, 1922
(no cancellation)
Collotype, postcard
Hood Museum of Art: Purchased through
the Hood Museum of Art Acquisitions Fund;
2006.18.14

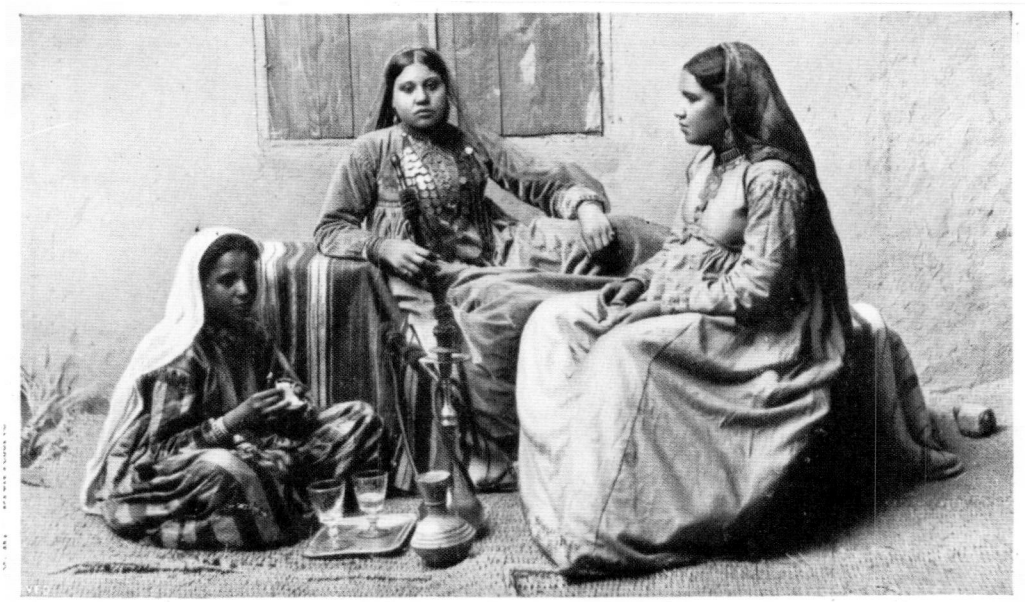

1026   EGYPTE. — Femmes arabes en visite.

PLATE 72
Unknown photographer
*1026. EGYPTE. — Femmes arabes en
visite* [1026. Egypt.— Arab women
visiting]
Published by G.K.,
early twentieth century
Collotype, postcard
Hood Museum of Art: Purchased
through the Hood Museum of Art
Acquisitions Fund; 2006.18.19

PLATE 73
Unknown photographer
*Scènes et Types 15. HENNA dans
son intérieur* [Scenes and types
15. Henna indoors]
Published by N. Boumendil,
early twentieth century
Collotype, postcard
Hood Museum of Art: Purchased
through the Hood Museum of Art
Acquisitions Fund; 2006.18.36

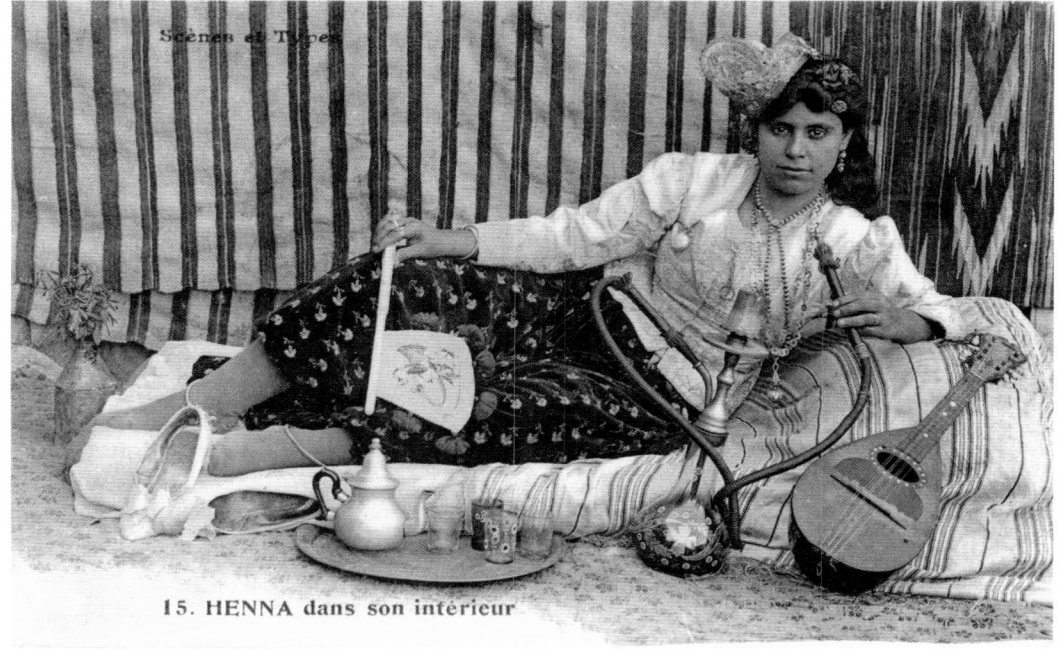

15. HENNA dans son intérieur

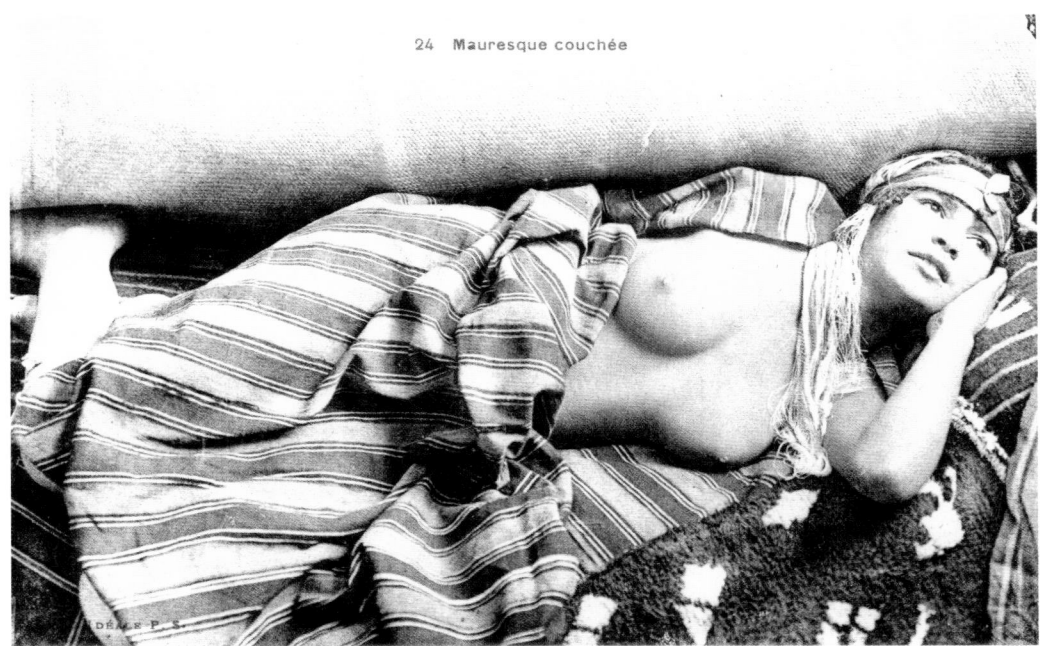

24 Mauresque couchée

PLATE 74
Unknown photographer
24. Mauresque couchée
[24. reclining Moor], early twentieth
century
Published by Collection Idéale P.S.
Collotype, postcard
Hood Museum of Art: Purchased
through the Hood Museum of Art
Acquisitions Fund; 2006.18.16

PLATE 75
François-Edmond Fortier?, French
(1862–1928)
*1087.—Afrique Occidentale—Sudan. Jeunes
Femmes Arabes* [1087.—West Africa—
Sudan. Young Arab women], c. 1905
Published by Collection Générale, Fortier,
Dakar, Senegal, c. 1920
Collotype, postcard
Courtesy of Christraud Geary

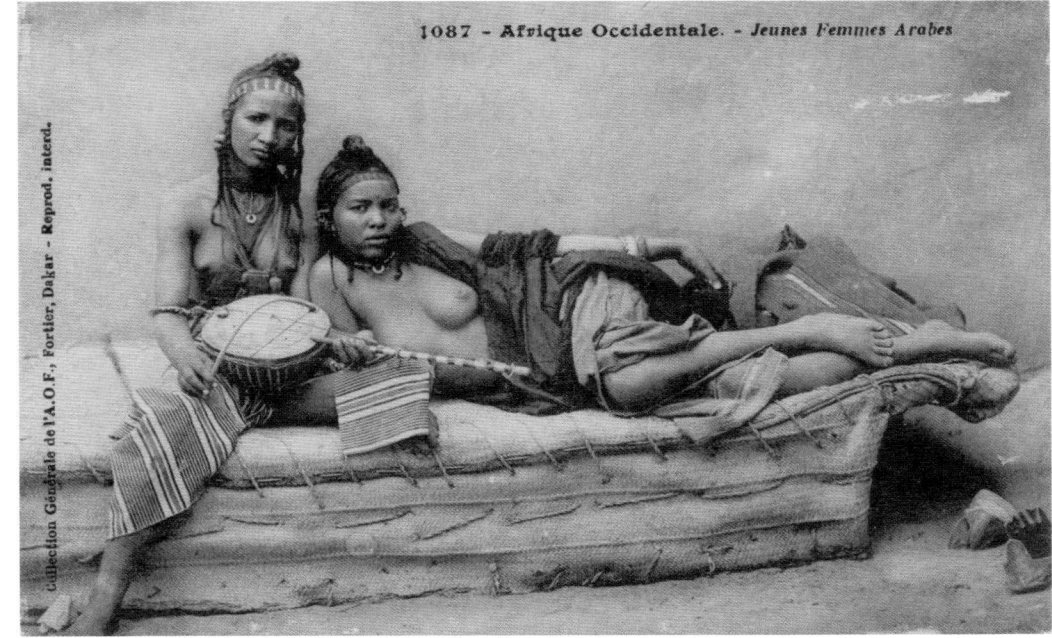

1087 - Afrique Occidentale. - Jeunes Femmes Arabes

Collection Générale de l'A.O.F., Fortier, Dakar - Reprod. interd.

EXCHANGES: LALLA ESSAYDI*

[*Black Womanhood* raises questions about] the difference between how one presents oneself; that is, how one identifies oneself versus how one is represented by others. Being Moroccan, I identify myself first with the land, which gave me birth: Africa. I, therefore, identify myself as an African. Yet at the same time, I also identify myself as an Arab since Morocco is considered part of the Maghrib, representing the fusion of the civilizations of Africa and Arabia since the seventh century. My faith makes me a member of a global community. As a woman and an artist, I find myself part of a community that since the nineteenth century began to assert its historical and artistic presence and confront the (mis)representations by others (plate 126). Colonial depictions of women have bequeathed an artist legacy to the "West," which has only made visible the types of images that fill museums and art books. It is only in the second half of the twentieth century that these images have been critiqued in the social sciences and humanities. In the twenty-first century, the voices of women artists have also joined in insisting on their multiple identities. I insist on my multiple identities and demand that all of my identities be respected—be they geographic, cultural, faith-based, or artistic—since they demonstrate that I am part of a cosmopolitan world with its joyous and sorrowful aspects.

* Lalla Essaydi, personal e-mail communication with Barbara Thompson, November 13, 2006.

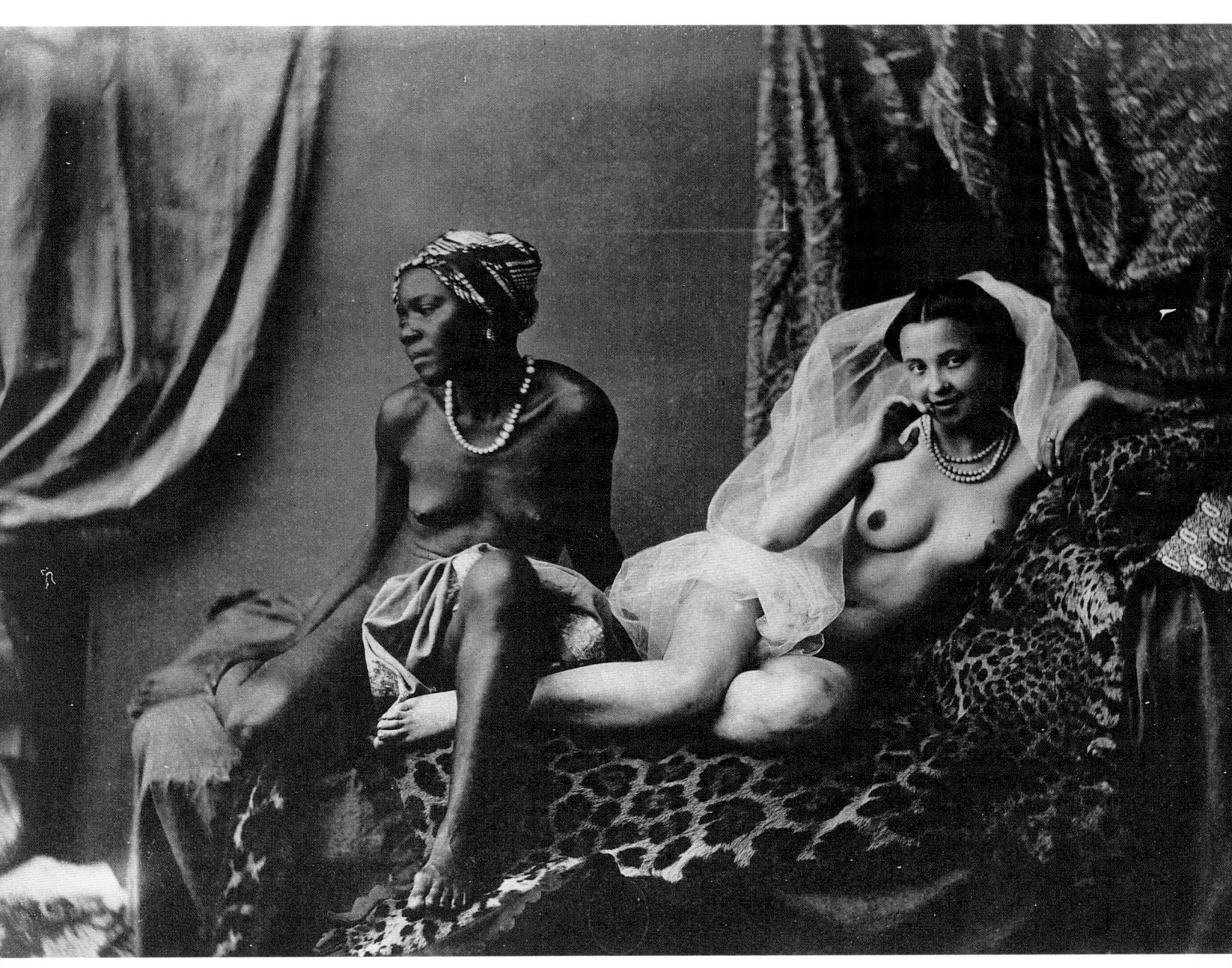

PLATE 76
Félix Jacques Antoine Moulin, French (1802–1875)
Untitled (Boudoir scene), from *Etudes Photographiques*
[Photographic Studies], 1850s
Albumen silver print
Cliché Bibliothèque nationale de France; R.CA 85655. Photograph
courtesy of Cliché Bibliothèque nationale de France

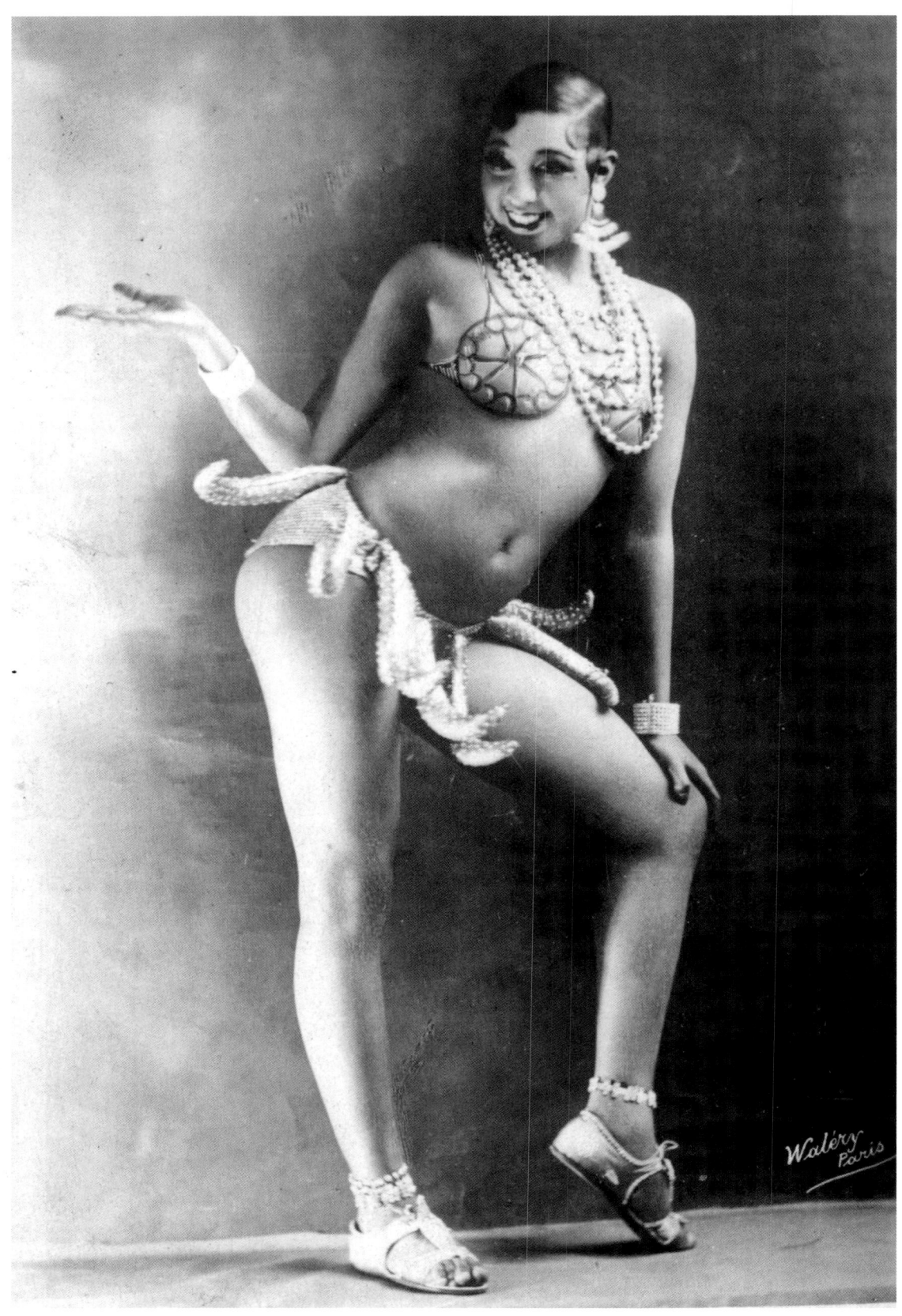

PLATE 77
Stanislaw Julian Ignacy, Count Ostrorog,
known as Walery, British (1863–1935)
Josephine Baker, La Folie du Jour, Paris, April 1926
Collotype, postcard
Olivia Lahs-Gonzales Collection
Photograph courtesy of Getty Images, Inc

I think the first time I saw an image of Josephine Baker was toward the end of the fifties. It was a fascinating sequence in a black and white film about a black woman singing in a cage. At that time, I think I was eight years old but I was already a serious movie-goer. I had no idea who that woman was but I was intrigued by the fact that the cage was not really a cage that could keep anybody in and that the woman could leave if she wanted. In fact, I wished secretly that she would walk out of the cage and be free. But the woman seemed to enjoy being in that cage.

Later I started to know more about Josephine Baker but never managed to make the connection between the singer in the cage and the dancer with the banana skirt until a few years ago when I reviewed that sequence of the cage singer while watching a French TV documentary on Josephine Baker. The fact that the singer was happy with her cage seemed to me referable to these biblical figures like Jesus or St. Sebastian who seem to enjoy their pain so much that they metamorphose into extra-humans. There is something biblical about the experience of Josephine Baker—the way that she accepted (and enjoyed) the role of the typical African female for the benefit of the European colonial male society. This biblical dimension is absent in the experience of Saartje Baartman, who was captured, transported to Europe, and forced to play the savage African female in a real cage where no escape is possible.

If the career of Baartman was so short compared to the long career of Baker, it is because of the miserable material conditions of life that her "owners" offered her. What is common in the Baker and Baartman experience is that both of them were put on a stage in front of a European male audience. The difference between the two women might be in the attitude that each showed towards the fact of being perceived as black females. It seems to me that Josephine Baker was raised as a black person. Her education as a black American made her internalize the identity of a black being, whereas Baartman, who was uprooted from the traditional African context, might have found it difficult to assimilate the version of identity that Europeans reserved for black beings. I think Africans living in the traditional pre-capitalist societies never identified themselves according to the color of skin. Africans started to identify themselves as black when Europeans, who define themselves as "white," came and called them "blacks."

The term "African" itself is a European idea. During my childhood in the western part of Sudan, I remember we used to meet with foreign people from the neighboring countries. There were some Egyptians, a few Ethiopians, and a lot of people from West African countries. West Africans were generally Muslim pilgrims walking their way to Mecca. Like everybody else, I used to identify these people by reference to their countries. The idea of including all of them in the category of "Africans" seemed rather incongruous to me during the middle of the fifties. To internalize the concept of "Africans," we had to assimilate all the "Panafricanist" propaganda of the Cold War period in order to give existence to this strange idea of belonging to a continent called "Africa." The Panafricanism, which was a political tool that the African nationalists used to fight colonialism, is not easy to understand outside of the geopolitical context of the Cold War.

You may ask about the connection between the situation of black womanhood in the Baker/Baartman perspective and what I am saying about the invention of "Africans" as a false category. I think the connection is in the fallacy of these two categories: Blackhood and Africanhood. Africans never had the opportunity to choose being "black" or being "African." Both identities were imposed upon them from the outside by dominating colonial forces. Nevertheless, the falsehood of black and African categories is imposed as an accomplished fact. That said, one has to face the second question: What can the African and black person do with this real-false status? The reality of an African falsehood as an attractive practical option—or maybe the only real option *allowed*—is in the heart of all the conceptual debates about images related to African cultures.

This is where I try to work as an imagemaker (plates 106 and 107), manipulating the levers of art and exclusion in this specific zone of contemporary art called "contemporary African art." This is where I also differentiate between the destiny of Saartje Baartman and the destiny of Josephine Baker. I feel a great compassion—and a great anger—for the terrible moral and physical sufferings of Saartje Baartman but it is not the same kind of compassion that I have for Josephine Baker, who is different. She positioned herself as an artist; art offered her not only the means to escape the condition of excluded persons, but also a shortcut to recognition and glory. Nevertheless, the artist she was allowed to be in Paris was conditioned by the colonial and racial considerations of French society at that time. The complexity of her attitude as a black person, a woman, *and* an artist deserves much more attention than the usual commemoration of *la Revue Négre*. As such, Josephine Baker stands as a central figure in the problematic question of Africanist aesthetics when instrumentalized as a lever for exclusion.

In some of her music-hall performances, Josephine Baker used to cover her "white" skin with black paint so as to look and conform more to white audience expectations of the "African" image. In such an attitude, Josephine Baker, the artist, is taking a "security distance" from the risk of being African. She knows she is not African; she is just playing the role. Africanhood is just one icon, among others, that she was able to use. Other persons—like Michel Leiris (another African icon)—helped her to assume the role of the African female. I think researchers on contemporary art of African nationals should pay more attention to the role of Michel Leiris in the invention of an art defined today as "African." In a book about the artist Wifredo Lam, the French art historian Jean-Luis Paudrat reported how Picasso once asked Leiris to "teach Lam l'art nègre."** I think that most of the Parisian intelligentsia around Josephine Baker were trying to "teach" her *l'art nègre*. I also think that Baker was happy to learn and to perform *l'art nègre* for her Parisian audience. The film sequences of the black singer enjoying the cage condition is a fine illustration of the state of *complaisance* affecting Baker's artistic career.

* Hassan Musa, personal e-mail communication with Barbara Thompson, November 25, 2006.

** Wilfredo Lam and Musée Dapper, *Lam Métis* (Paris: Edition Dapper, 2001), 75.

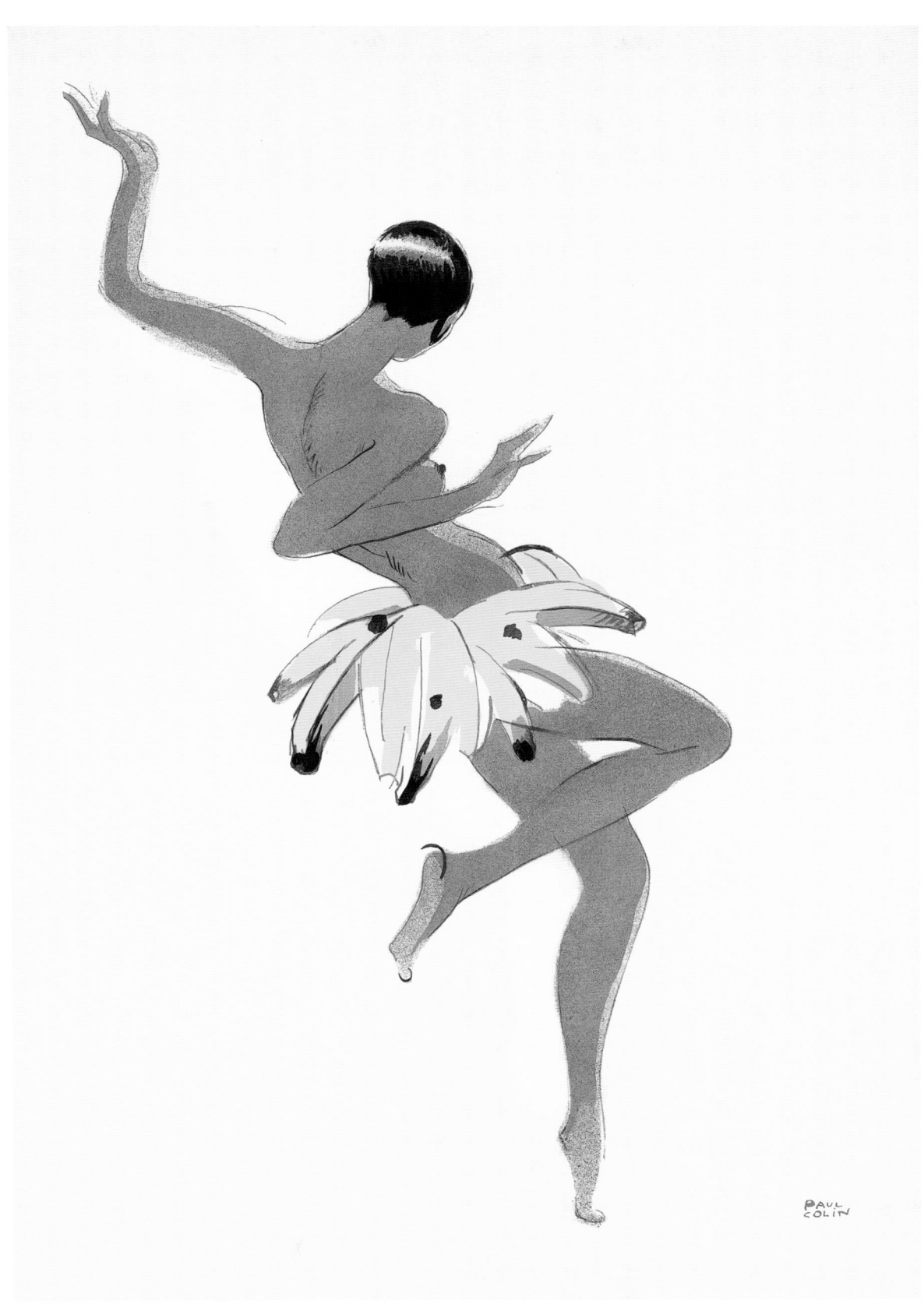

PLATE 78
Paul Colin (1892—1985), French
Josephine Baker in Banana Skirt, from *Le Tumulte Noir*, 1929
Lithograph
Schomburg Center for Research in Black Culture, Art and Artifacts
Division, New York Public Library, Astor, Lenox and Tilden Foundations
Photograph courtesy of National Portrait Gallery © 2007 Estate of
Paul Colin/Artists Rights Society (ARS), New York/ADAGP, Paris

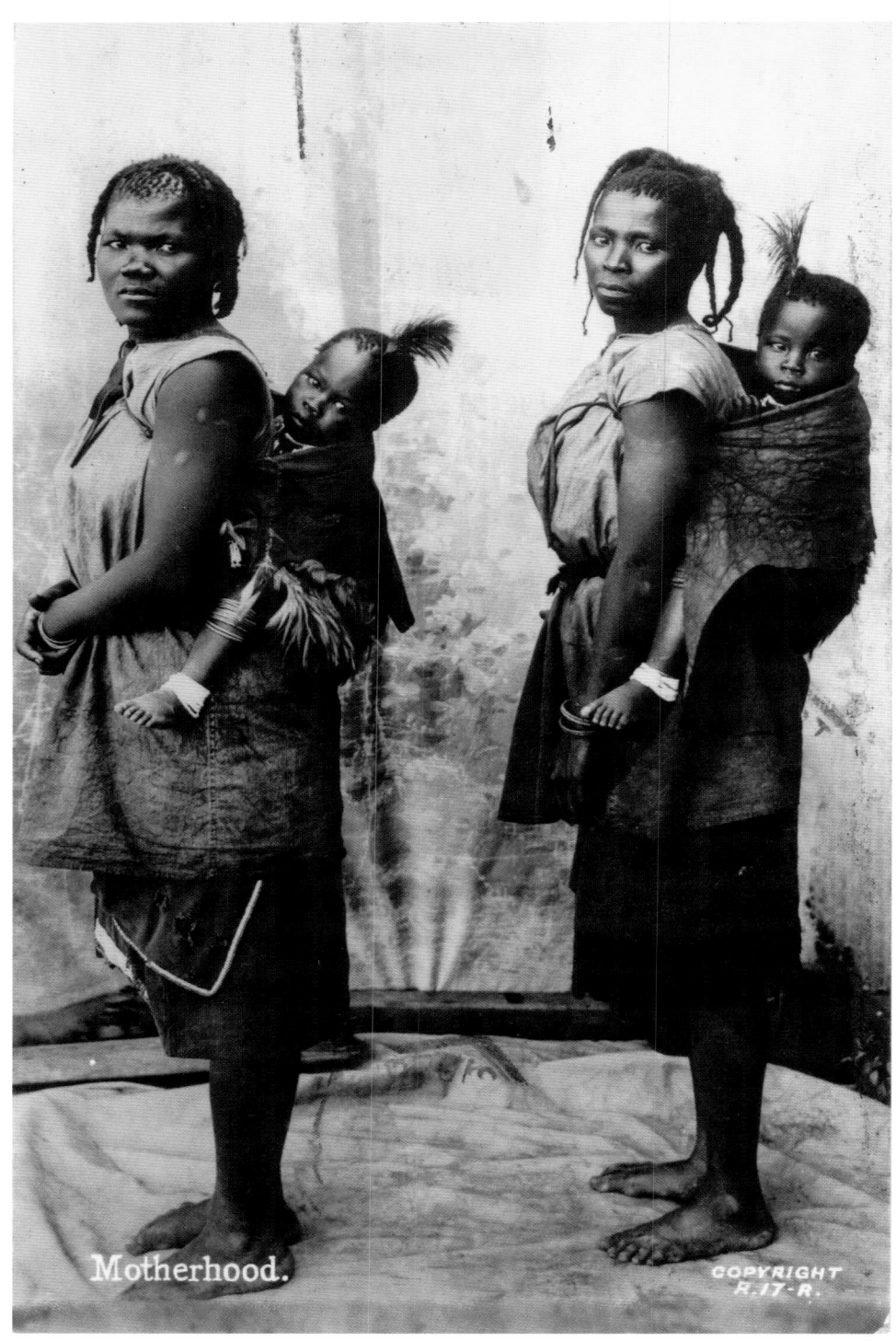

PLATE 79
Unknown photographer
Motherhood
Published by "SAPSCO" Real Photo, Box 5792,
Johannesburg, South Africa, c. 1910
Silver gelatin print, postcard
Hood Museum of Art: Purchased through
the Hood Museum of Art Acquisitions Fund;
2006.18.28

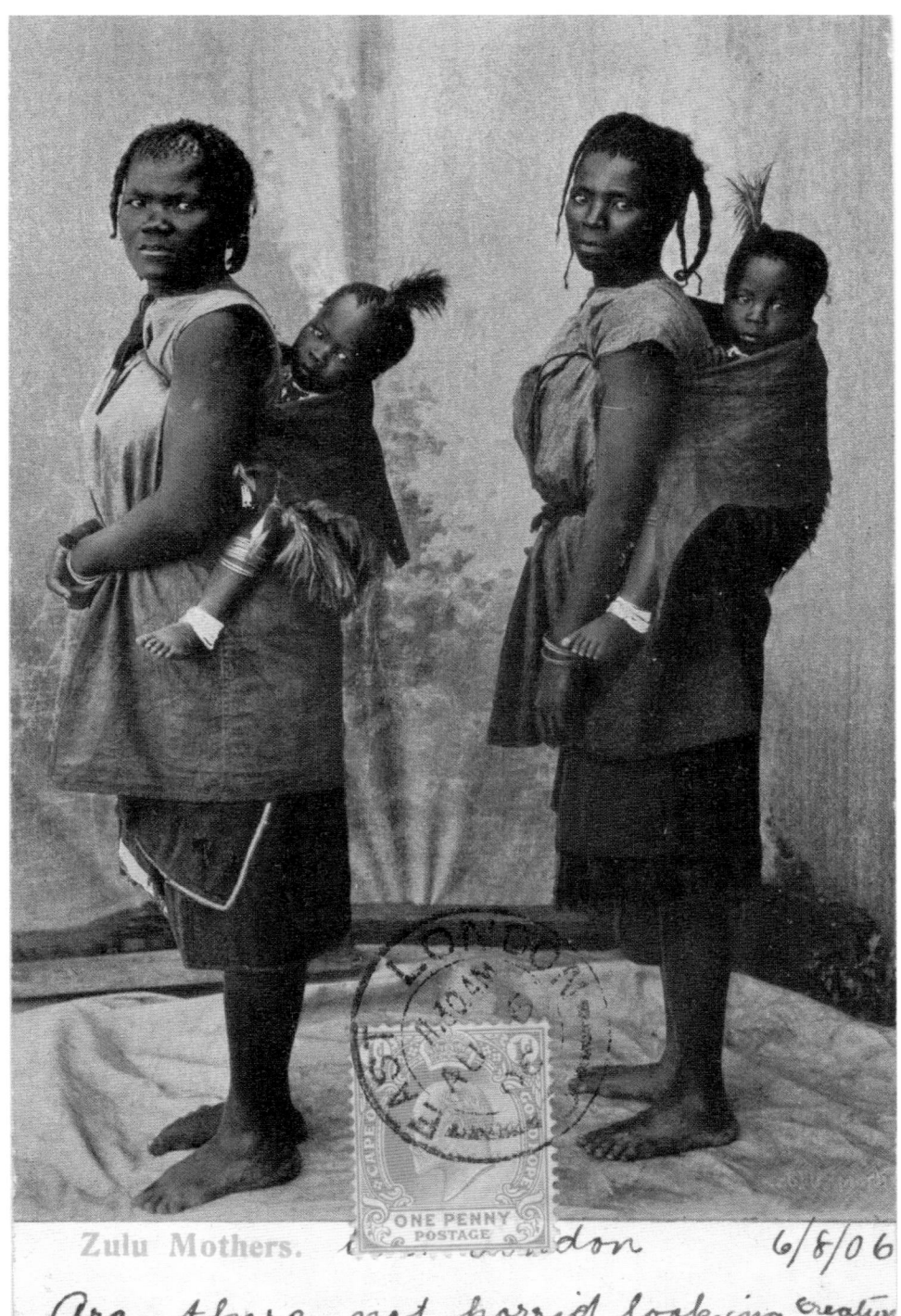

Zulu Mothers. London 6/8/06

Are these not horrid looking creatures

PLATE 80
Unknown photographer
Zulu Mothers, c. 1900
Published by R.A.T. & Co., Ltd. Cape Town,
South Africa, c. 1903, cancellation August 1906
Hand-tinted halftone print
Courtesy of Christraud Geary

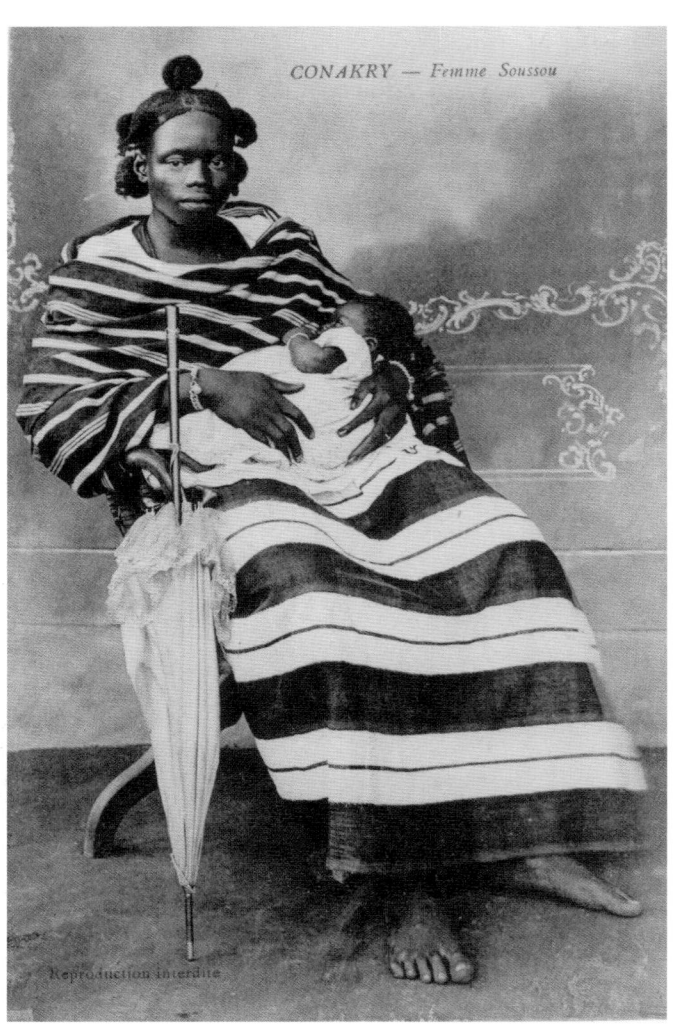

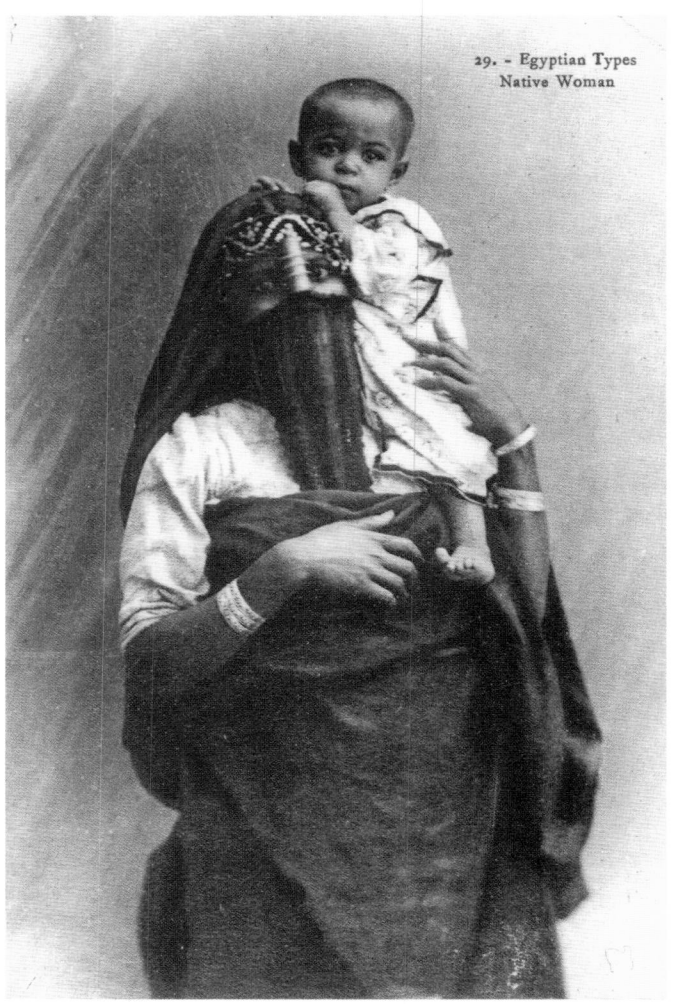

PLATE 81
A. James, Sierra Leonian? Guinean?
(active c. 1900–c. 1930)
CONAKRY—Femme Soussou
[Conakry—Susu Woman], c. 1910
Publisher unidentified, c. 1920
Collotype, postcard
Courtesy of Christraud Geary

PLATE 82
Zaslawky & Kalmanovitch
29. — Egyptian Types Native Woman
Published by P.C.M.J., Alexandria, Egypt-Paris,
France, early twentieth century
Collotype, postcard
Hood Museum of Art: Purchased through
the Hood Museum of Art Acquisitions Fund;
2006.18.25

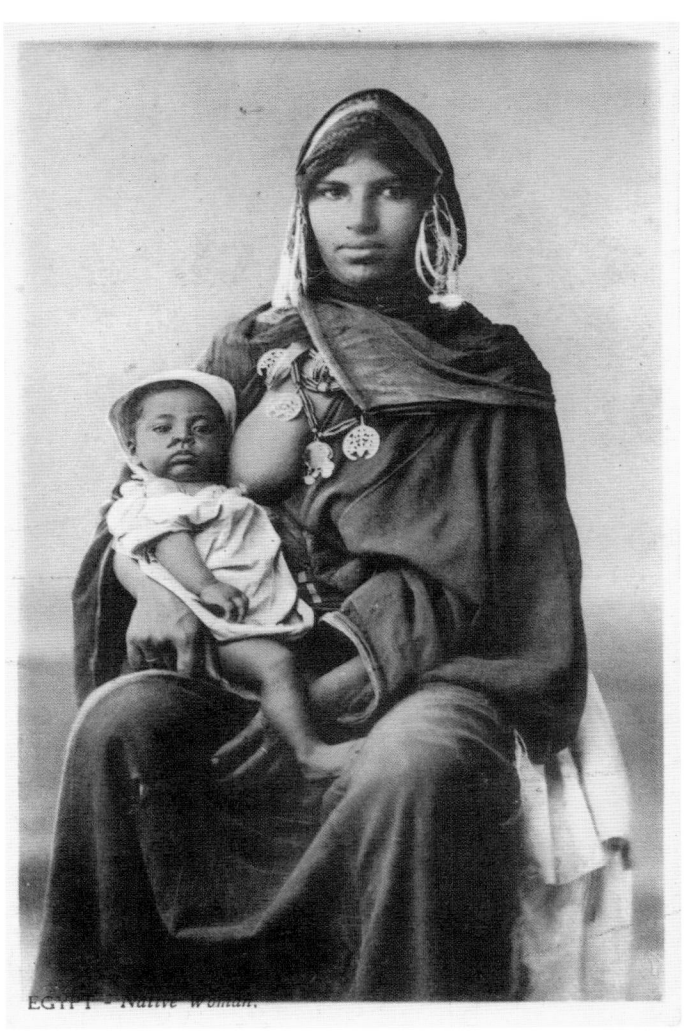

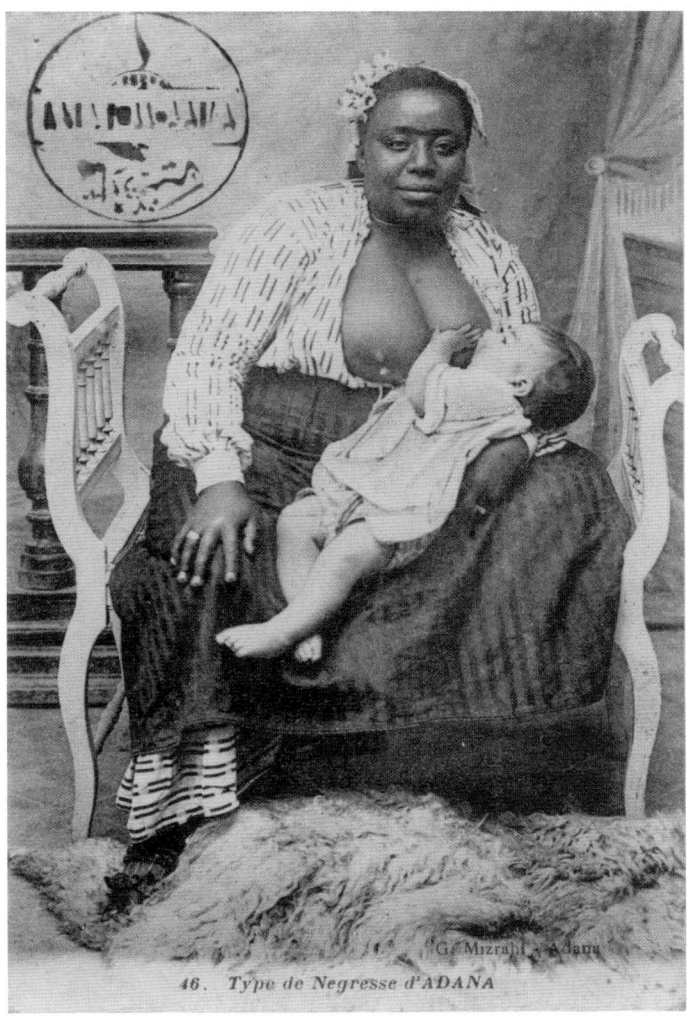

PLATE 83
Unknown photographer
EGYPT—Native Woman
Published by L. Scortzis et Co.—Cairo, Egypt,
#131, early twentieth century
Collotype, postcard
Hood Museum of Art: Purchased through
the Hood Museum of Art Acquisitions Fund;
2006.18.37

PLATE 84
G. Mizrahi, Adana (Turkey) (active c. 1900),
Turkish?
46. Type de Negresse d'ADANA [46. Type of Negro
woman of Adana], c. 1900
Published by Baudiniere, Paris, c. 1905
Collotype, postcard
Courtesy of Christraud Geary

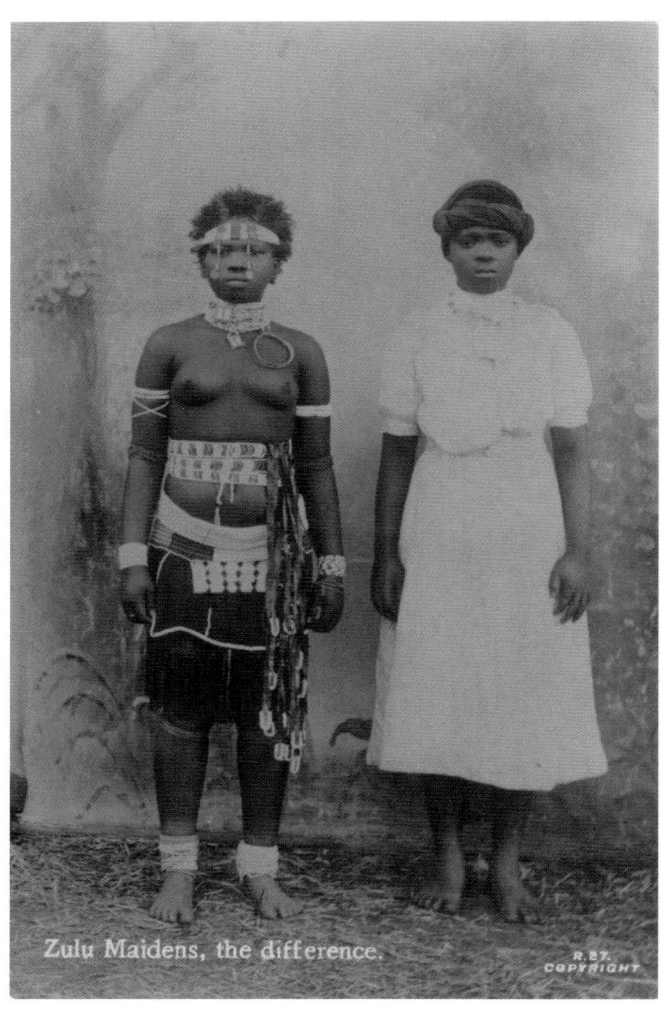

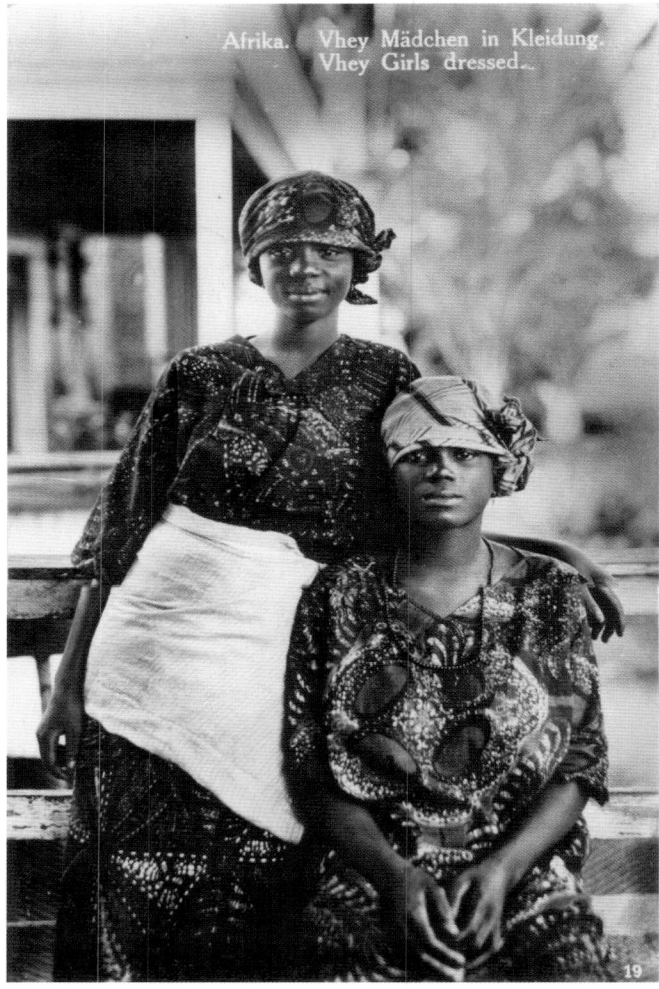

PLATE 85
Unknown photographer
Zulu Maidens, the difference, c. 1900
Published by "SAPSCO" Real Photo, Box 5792,
Johannesburg, South Africa, c. 1910
Silver gelatin print, postcard
Courtesy of Christraud Geary

PLATE 86
M. Dinklage Jr., German (active c. 1930)
Afrika. Vhey Mädchen in Kleidung,
Vhey Girls Dressed, c. 1930
Publisher unidentified, c. 1930
Silver gelatin print
Courtesy of Christraud Geary

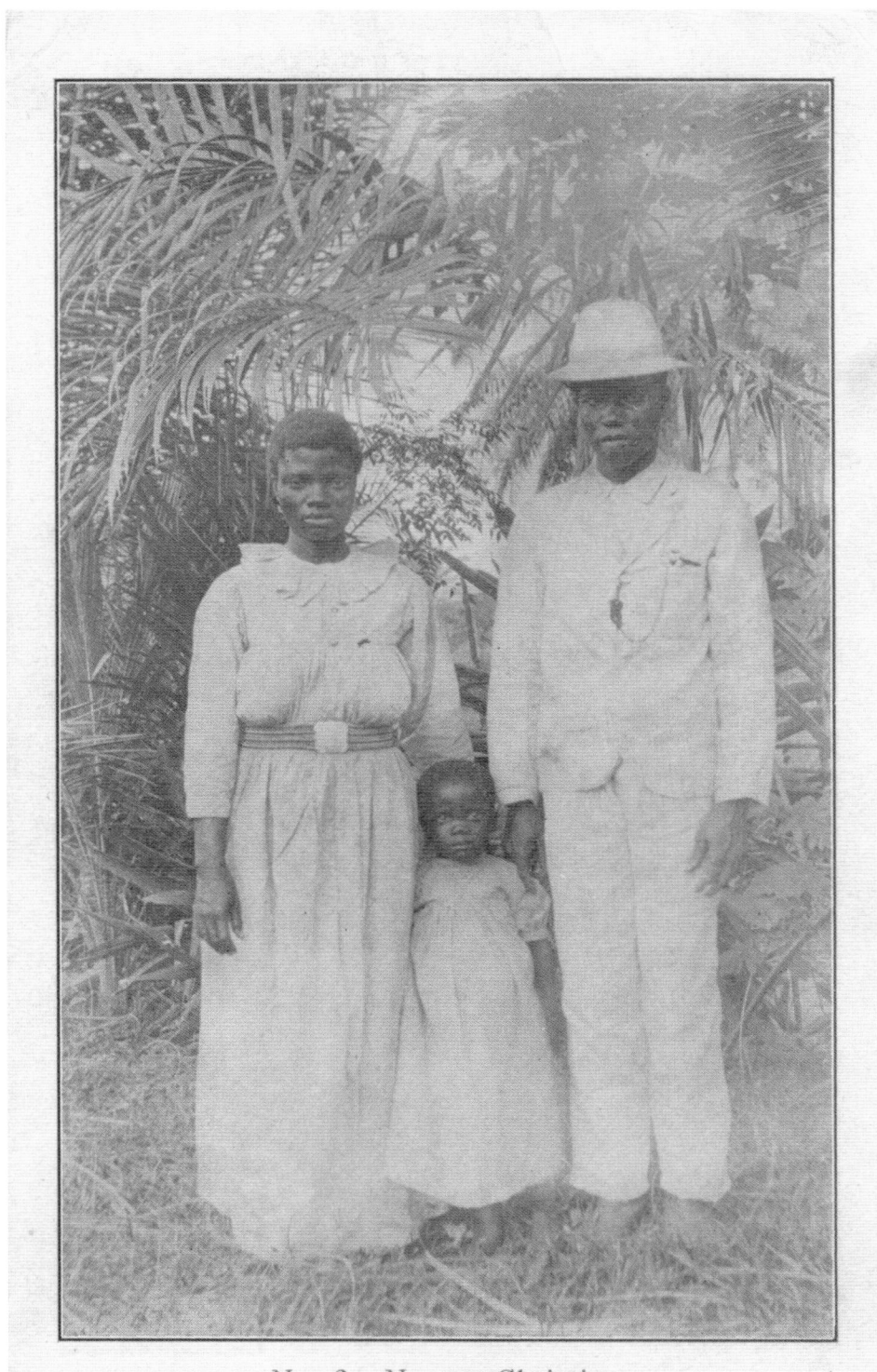

No. 2. Now a Christian.

PLATE 87
Unknown photographer
No. 2. Now a Christian, c. 1910
Published by the American Baptist Union,
Boston, Mass., U.S.A., c. 1910
Halftone print, postcard
Courtesy of Christraud Geary

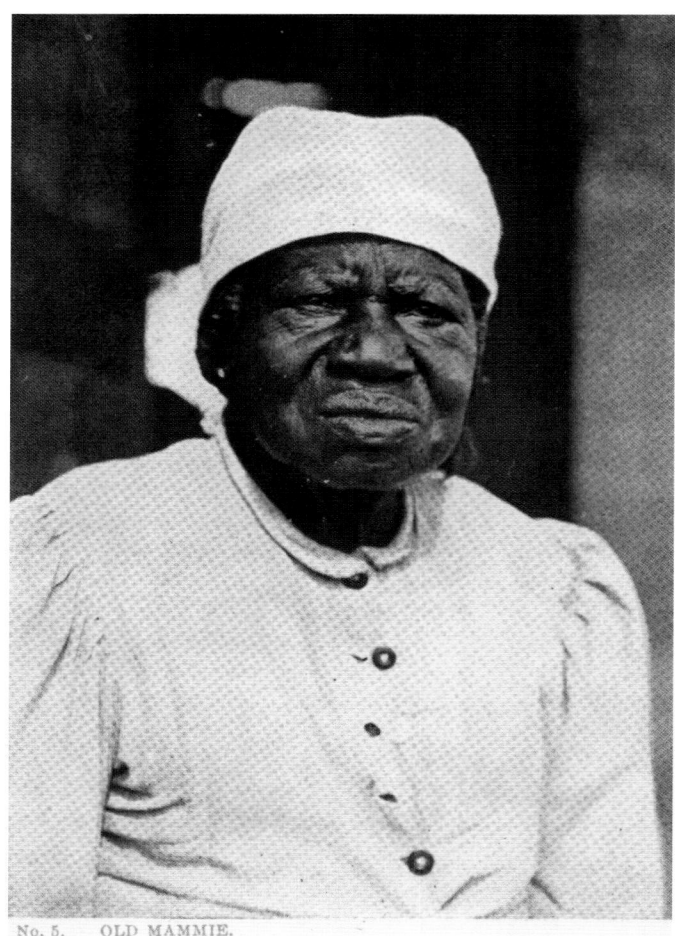

No. 5. OLD MAMMIE.

PLATE 88
Unknown photographer
No. 5. OLD MAMMIE, early twentieth century
Hand-tinted collotype, postcard
Hood Museum of Art: Purchased through
the Hood Museum of Art Acquisitions Fund;
2006.18.5

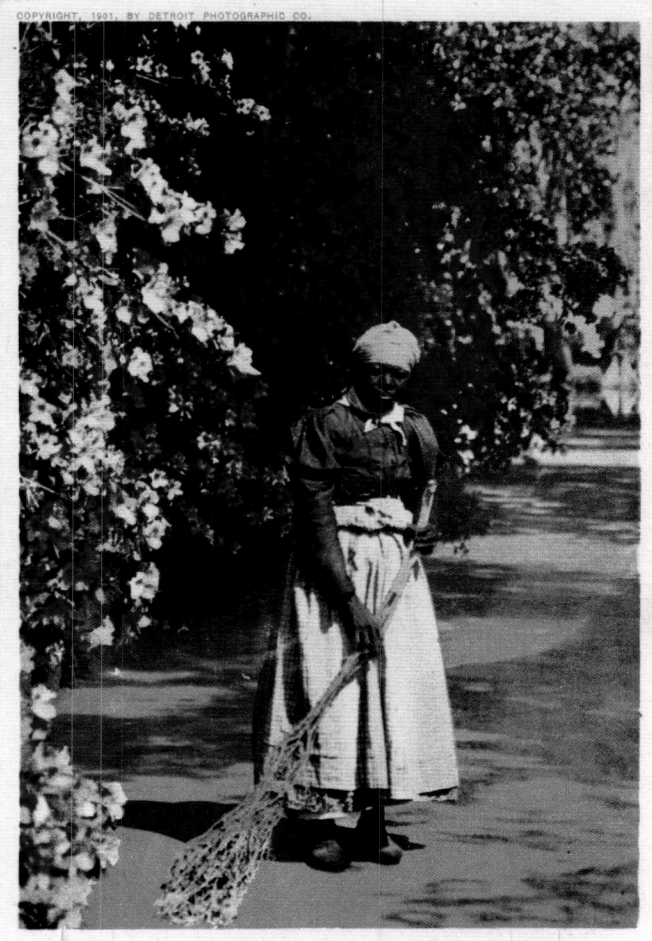

COPYRIGHT, 1901, BY DETROIT PHOTOGRAPHIC CO.

5779. AUNT PHOEBE, MAGNOLIA-ON-THE-ASHLEY, CHARLESTON, S. C.

PLATE 89
Unknown photographer
*5779. AUNT PHOEBE, MAGNOLIA-ON-THE-ASHLEY,
CHARLESTON, S. C.*, early twentieth century
Hand-tinted collotype, postcard
Hood Museum of Art: Anonymous gift;
2007.20.1

EXCHANGES: SENZENI MARASELA I*

It is difficult to negotiate being black and female outside the context of apartheid. I believe we are still victims as black women. I don't know what it was like to suffer under apartheid. I come from a black privileged background. I have certainly picked up the bill for it. I was educated in private schools all my life. Despicable efforts were made to socialize us as black women who spoke a bit of this, a bit of that, until we had no language of our own. Insecurity about my identity and that of a girl child without a solid mother figure makes up Senzeni Marasela. It is from this position that I respond to the rest of the world (plate 117).

Research has made me realize that my situation is not unique, however. Absent mothers are common in the lives of young black children. Unnamable forces for generations removed the black female figure from her role as caregiver. Many went off to raise children for other women. Others became hopeless alcoholics; still others suffered under the hands of men who were also victims of these unnamable forces. Some, like my mother, became suspended in a state of shock and waited patiently for the future to go away and leave them alone. We have very few visible heroines as black women.

* Artist statement for *Black Womanhood*, e-mail communication, May 16, 2007.

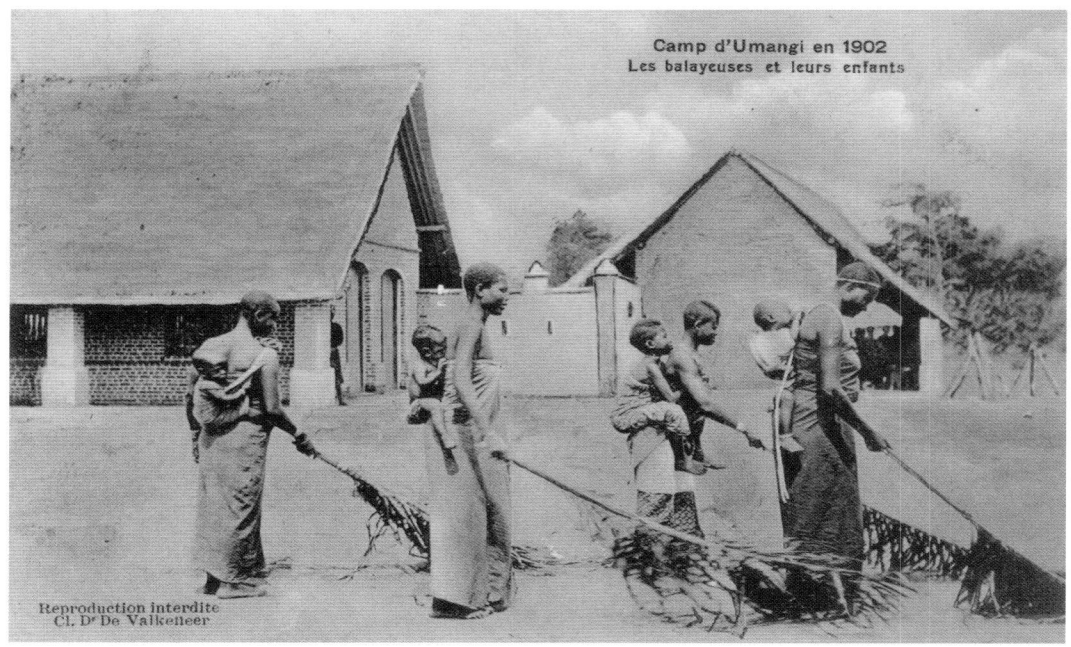

Camp d'Umangi en 1902
Les balayeuses et leurs enfants

Reproduction interdite
Cl. Dr De Valkeneer

PLATE 90
Dr. De Valkeneer, Belgian (active 1900)
*Camp d'Umangi en 1902, Les bayaleuse
et leurs enfants* [Camp Umangi in 1902,
The sweepers and their children], 1902
Published by Ligue nationale pour la
protection de l'enfance noire au
Congo Belge. c. 1910
Collotype, postcard
Courtesy of Christraud Geary

PLATE 91
Alex A. Accolatse, Togolese (1894–1950)
LOMÉ—Togo Native Bear [sic] Sellers,
c. 1920
Published by A. Accolatse, Togo, c. 1928
dated October 12, 1929
Collotype, postcard
Courtesy of Christraud Geary

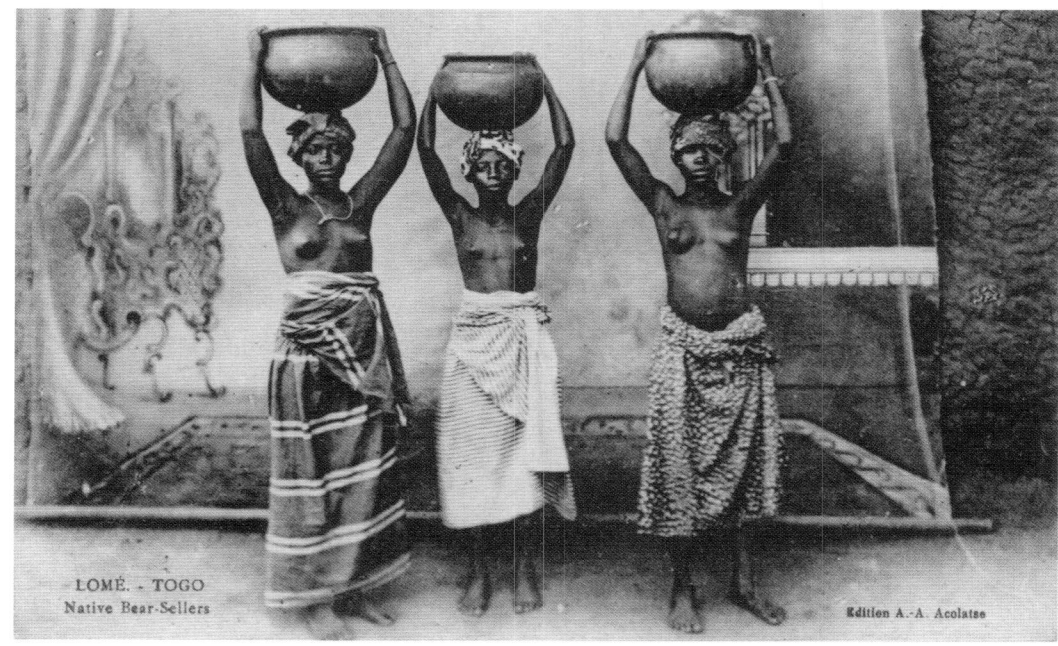

LOMÉ. - TOGO
Native Bear-Sellers

Edition A.-A. Acolatse

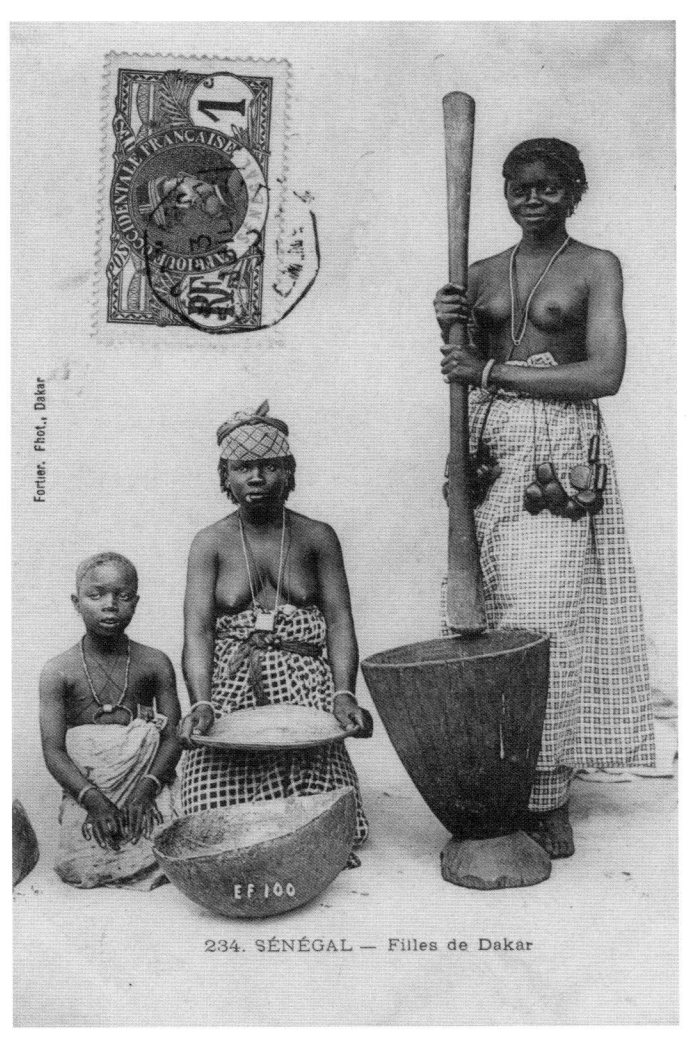

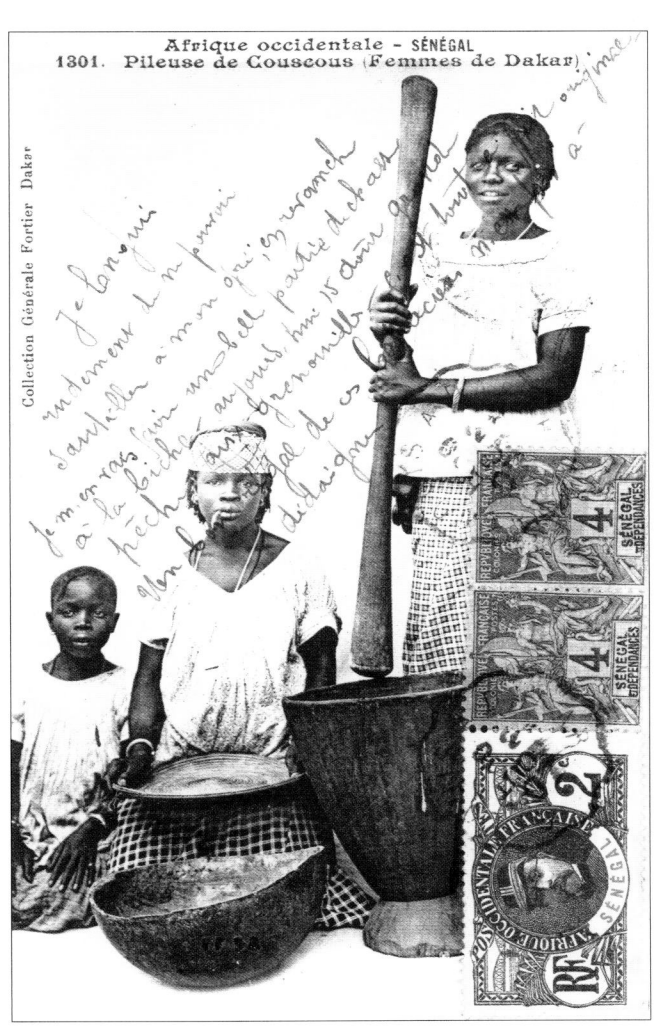

PLATE 92
François-Edmond Fortier?, French (1862–1928)
234. SÉNÉGAL—Filles de Dakar
[234. Senegal—Girls of Dakar], c. 1900
Published by Fortier, Phot., Dakar, Senegal,
c. 1902
Collotype, postcard
Courtesy of Christraud Geary

PLATE 93
François-Edmond Fortier?, French (1862–1928)
*Afrique occidentale—SÉNÉGAL, 1301. Pileuse
de Couscous (Femmes de Dakar)* [West Africa—
Senegal, 1301. Couscous pounders (Women of
Dakar)]
Published by Collection Générale Fortier,
Dakar, Senegal, c. 1900
Collotype, postcard
Hood Museum of Art: Purchased through
the Hood Museum of Art Acquisitions Fund;
2006.18.34

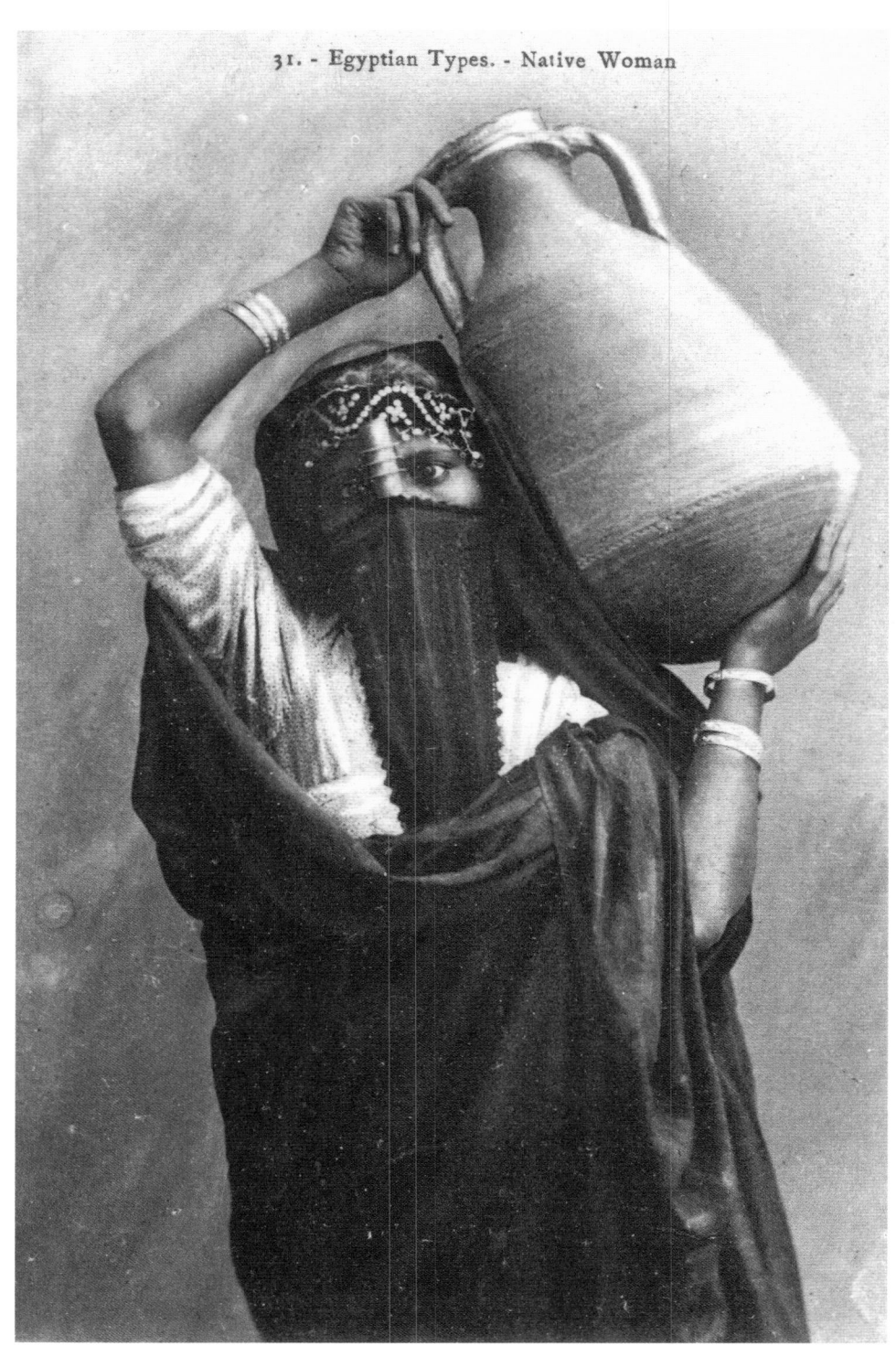

31. - Egyptian Types. - Native Woman

PLATE 94
Zaslawsky & Kalmanovitch, Alexandria
31. — Egyptian Types. — Native Woman
Published by P.C.M.J. Alexandria, Egypt-Paris,
France, early twentieth century
Collotype, postcard
Hood Museum of Art: Purchased through
the Hood Museum of Art Acquisitions Fund;
2006.18.24

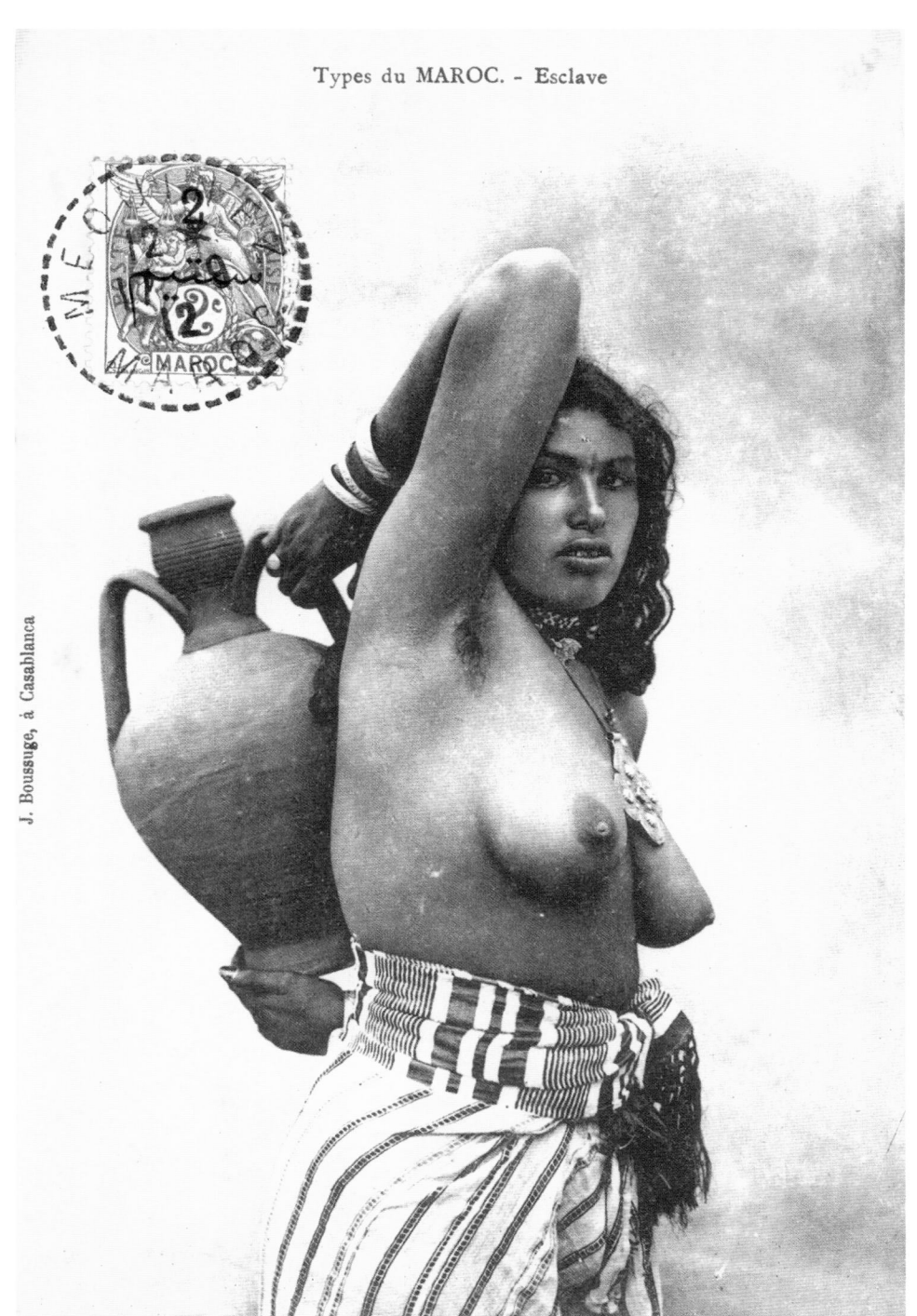

Types du MAROC. - Esclave

J. Boussuge, à Casablanca

PLATE 95
Unknown photographer
Types du MAROC. — Esclave [Moroccan types—
Slave]
Published by J. Boussuge, Casablanca, Morocco,
early twentieth century
Collotype, postcard
Hood Museum of Art: Purchased through
the Hood Museum of Art Acquisitions Fund;
2006.18.15

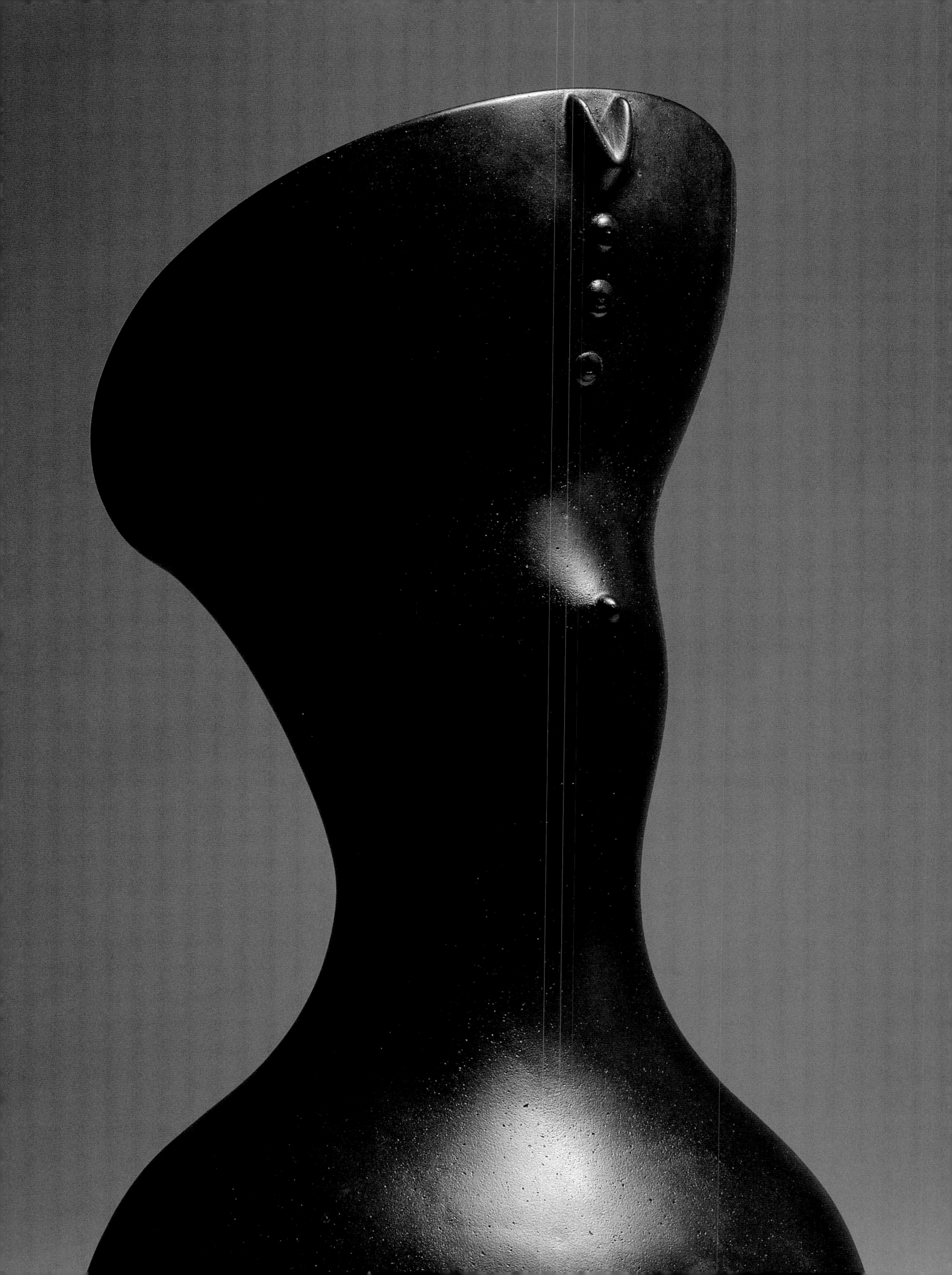

PART III | MEANING AND IDENTITY: PERSONAL JOURNEYS INTO BLACK WOMANHOOD

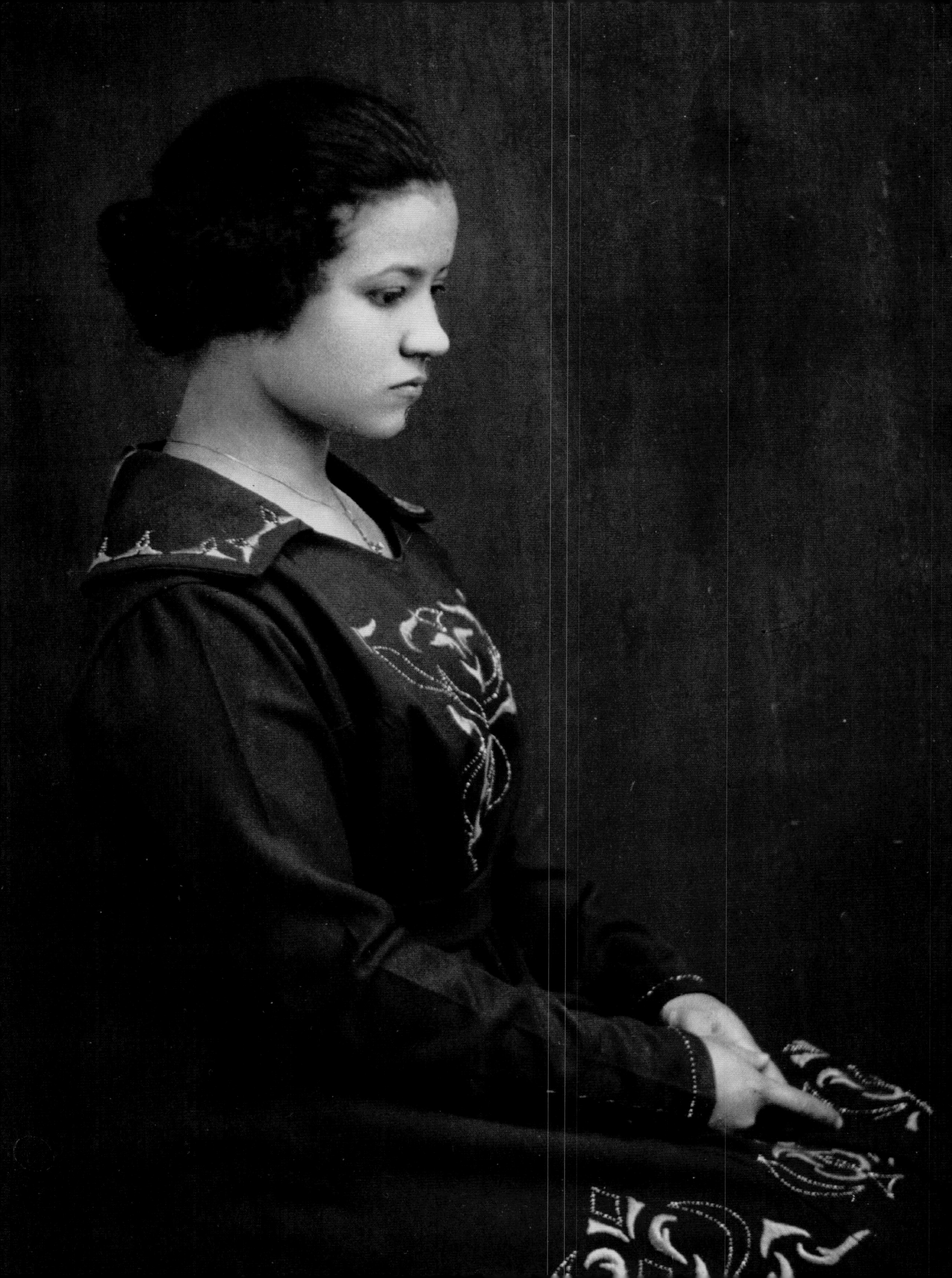

6 Picturing the New Negro Woman

Everything to this race is new and strange and inspiring. There is a quickening of its pulses and a glowing of its self-consciousness. Aha! I can rival that! I can aspire to that! I can honor my name and vindicate my race! Something like this, it strikes me, is the enthusiasm which stirs the genius of a young African in America; and the memory of past oppression and the fact of present attempted repression only serve to gather momentum for its irrepressible powers. . . . What a responsibility then to have the sole management of the primal lights and shadows!

—ANNA JULIA COOPER[1]

As we look at such politicized, artistic, and constructed images of African American women in this exhibition, it is possible to see "what a responsibility for their sole management" meant to black photographers and their female sitters in the first part of the twentieth century. They knew they had a responsibility to define, to redefine, the black woman's life and their culture.

The historical gaze has profoundly determined how the black female body is regarded in contemporary society. The interplay between the historical and the contemporary, between self-presentation and imposed representation, are all fundamental aspects of art-making practices. As an artist, photographer, educator, and African American woman, I too grapple with ongoing oppression associated with images of black women. Central to my work is a constant awareness that how the black female body is displayed affects how we all see and interpret the world. This essay examines a short but crucial period in the history of black visual culture, a time when beauty was seen as an inspiration for racial pride, self-empowerment, and employment amid racist imagery.

In *The Black Female Body: A Photographic History*, writer and photographer Carla Williams and I investigated the artistic and cultural history of photographs of African and African American women from the beginning of photography to the present.[2] In this and the following essay, we will look at images that circulated in America from the 1890s to the 1940s, a time when racial identity was posed and reconsidered in photography and when debates on racial uplift and beauty were at the forefront of black intellectual and nationalist thought.[3]

The photographs of that period transformed the visual representation of black America, both in the public realm of popular culture and within the intimacy of the family album. Even during photography's early years in the mid-nineteenth century, images of African American women could be divided into two categories: idealized glimpses of family members in romanticized or dramatic settings, and subjugated depictions of black women at work (plate 89), "mammies (plate 88; see also figures 5.1–5.3) or prostitutes." For the most part, the idealized

opposite FIGURE 6.11 Florestine Perrault Collins, American (1895–1987), *Self-portrait*, early 1920s, black and white photograph. Photograph courtesy of Arthe Anthony.

photographs were treasured and preserved in black family albums, while racist images were circulated on postcards, stereographs, and posters. Hence access to and interpretation of these images also were limited to two distinct audiences: the familial and the public. Photographs that visually realized the dreams and desires of their individual communities and captured a spirit of transformation stood in sharp contrast to the mass-produced images that reinforced widely held stereotypes that sought to diminish the humanity of African Americans.

All over the United States, "African Americans reinvented themselves, as more than a million souls removed themselves from the provinces to the metropole, from the periphery to the center, from South to North, from agriculture to industrial, from rural to urban, from the nineteenth century to the twentieth," writes Professor Henry Louis Gates Jr. "The greatest transformation of all, of course, was a 'new' Negro culture, the outcome of the exchange of traditional southern and northern black cultures and the resulting synthesis of the two."[4] The desire for personal images of family members offered skilled photographers a prominent place in their communities, and the portraits of race leaders and celebrities were in high demand.

The term "New Negro" came to represent a spirit of self-awareness, artistic consciousness, and racial pride in black communities after 1900 and was reflected in art, print, artifacts, photography, and film. In his essay "Rough Sketches: A Study of the Features of the New Negro Woman" in the Atlanta-based monthly journal *Voice of the Negro* in 1904, Atlanta artist and professor John Henry Adams Jr. accompanied his sketches that intended to define black femininity with this description: "An admirer of Fine Art, a performer on the violin and the piano, a sweet singer, a writer mostly given to essays, a lover of good books, and a home making girl, is Gussie. . . ."[5] In his drawings and his writings, Adams was attempting to construct an idealized image of the New Negro woman through a physical description of her body in performance. He placed the woman in a typically female role, empowered by beauty and creative activities.

The "New Negro" had its greatest effect on black culture in the 1920s, when most images disseminated in the wider public portrayed blacks as subordinate. A number of black women challenged these predominantly negative representations by visiting photography studios and constructing images that represented their real or desired lifestyles. For example, writer Gertrude Marlow describes an early formal photograph of businesswoman and banker Maggie Mitchell (Lena Walker) that "shows her with her hair parted down the middle, with a curl over each side of her forehead, standing stiffly erect amidst the stock props of a Victorian photographic studio. Her face is much too strong to be conventionally pretty, but she exudes a handsome, if solemn, presence."[6] In 1903, Walker founded the St. Luke Penny Savings Bank in Richmond, Virginia. She was photographed often and used portraiture to signify her personal wealth and the activities of the businesses she founded in the area. Such photographs offered an alternative to the demeaning, distorted, and polarizing images of "Mammy" and "Aunt Jemima," negative portrayals of black domestic workers produced during this time. Drawing on this theory in her writings on black women and beauty, Maxine Leeds Craig believes that "[w]hile black intellectuals were crafting and promoting an image of upstanding black womanhood, the white media generally offered two stock images: the hypersexual black woman and the asexual black woman workhorse, the 'mammy' . . . the image of the 'mammy,' distorted the meaning of work in black women's lives."[7]

The most pervasive and damaging stereotypes of black women domestic workers were the "Mammy" and the "Aunt Jemima," created for predominantly white audiences in the late nineteenth century. The image of the Aunt Jemima was created as an advertising character in the fall of 1889 by Chris Rutt, who was in partnership with Charles Underwood to promote a new self-rising flour made by their troubled flourmill. Rutt chose the name "Aunt Jemima" after he attended a blackface vaudeville production in which the popular song "Old Aunt Jemima" was performed, and by 1890 the name was copyrighted. Projecting a lazy, docile, and ready to serve attitude, the Aunt Jemima stereotype, a holdover from the Old South, hit the height of popularity in 1893, when the Davis Mill Company, which now owned the copyright, decided to hire an actual person to perform the role of Aunt Jemima at the World's Columbian Exposition in Chicago. They hired Nancy Green, a former slave and assistant to a prominent Chicago judge, to personify the demeaning and damaging stereotyped advertising image of Aunt Jemima, serving pancakes, singing songs, and telling stories of the Old South to visitors to the fair.

As historian Paula Giddings points out, in 1923 the Daughters of the Confederacy went too far when they petitioned Congress to authorize a statue in Washington, D.C., in memory of "Black Mammies."[8] Chandler Owen, co-editor of *The Messenger,* responded,

> They want to bring back memories of the slave days when black mammies toiled in the cotton fields, cleaned the houses, cared for the children, nursed them at their bosoms. . . . They want a memorial of the Southern white's good times gone. To the Southern bourbons these memories are like the photo of a choice and fond friend who had passed away. Though we cannot bring back the friends, we may often look upon and kiss the picture. We favor erecting a monument to the New Negro, who is carving a new monument in the hearts of our people. . . . We favor a monument to the Negro women who have risen above insult, assault, debauchery, prostitution, and abuse to which these unfortunate "black mammies" were subjected. Yes, we favor erecting a monument to these women, who have almost wiped out this chasm of caste, who have broken the cordon of chains and are now trying to throw them off. Let this "mammy" statue go. Let it fade away. . . . Let its white shaft point like a lofty mountain peak to a New Negro mother, no longer a "white man's woman," no longer the sex-enslaved black mammy of Dixie—but the apotheosis of triumphant Negro womanhood!"[9]

Despite protests like Owens's, which were published in the African American press, the legislation authorizing the construction of a monument to the "Faithful Colored Mammies of the South" passed the full Senate.[10] The legislation showed how the dominant culture maintained its power over the depiction and description of black women. But the act was never carried out, a victory that resulted from editorials denouncing the legislation that were published in the black press and from the opposition of black leaders, who demanded that the idea be abandoned.

Soon the New Negro Movement was the preeminent symbol of race consciousness dedicated to the notion that all men and women are created equal, and it offered the visual images to prove it. Through photographic portraiture, women began to define a visual group identity. The collaboration between photographer and client, artist and audience, is evident in early issues of *Crisis* magazine. *Crisis* editor W. E. B. Du Bois published photographs of black women of achievement, sometimes featuring them on the cover. These photographs helped construct and visualize a black middle class. Du Bois admitted his personal fascination with the medium of photography in his "Opinion" column in *Crisis*: "Why do not more young colored men and women take up photography as a career? The average white photographer does not know how to deal with colored skins and having neither sense of the delicate beauty or tone nor will to learn, he makes a horrible botch of portraying them. From the South especially the pictures that come to us, with few exceptions, make the heart ache."[11] He asserted in a reflexive essay written in 1951, titled "Editing the Crisis," that "Pictures of colored people were an innovation; and at that time it was the rule of most white papers never to publish a picture of a colored person except as a criminal and the colored papers published most pictures of celebrities who sometimes paid for the honor. . . ."[12]

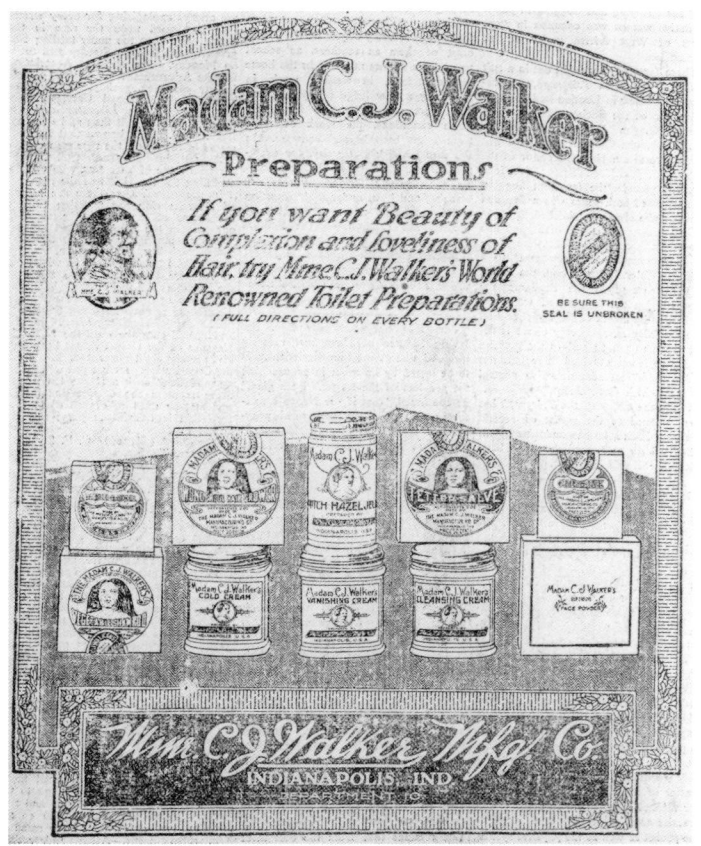

FIGURE 6.1 Advertisement for Madame C. J. Walker—Preparations, 1920, black and white photograph. Photograph courtesy of Library of Congress, Newspaper and Periodicals Reading Room, LC-DIG-PPMSCA-02902.

Between 1900 and 1930, African American photographers offered another space in which to view the black community. As art historian Camara Holloway explains,

> Producing photographs that glorified the black body and hailed black achievement was a transgressive act . . . the New Negro [imagery] destroyed the illusions required to justify segregation. . . . Blacks needed a means to affirm themselves, and the portrait as symbol provided a critical psychical armature upon which to build a valorized identity.[13]

A good number of black photographers and their subjects believed that defining their own identity and beauty through photography was a significant step in the fight against negative representations.

A few black women used these "transgressive" photographs to promote their work, both their businesses and social and civic activities. The black women's club movement that began around the turn of the twentieth century became an important political force, and the photographic image was a vehicle for exhibiting the clubs' collective power. Businesswoman and entrepreneur Madame C. J. Walker used her photographic portrait to illustrate her many successes in the beauty industry (figure 6.1). A photograph of her was featured in a *Pennsylvania Negro Business Directory* (figure 6.2).

> In her full-length directory photograph Madam Walker struck a . . . refined pose. . . . Reflecting her increased income and newly acquired status, she wore a dress with a delicate ivory lace bodice. A thick fabric belt cinched her waist, accentuating her full-figured, well-proportioned body. With her hands clasped behind her back, the only sign of her former life as a farm worker and washerwoman was the stumpy shape of her forearms, their muscles enlarged from years of twisting and squeezing soap through waterlogged sheets and tablecloths. But of course it was her hair that she wished to emphasize. Madam Walker had pinned her now healthy tresses into a carefully coifed crown, styled so that it gracefully swooped away from her face. When women saw her photo and heard her life story, they clamored to take her course and sit for her treatments.[14]

The photograph epitomized Walker's newfound wealth. Black women entertainers used similar images on record covers, sheet music, and promotional materials.

The black press played a central role in the promotion of beauty as a means of "racial pride." Photography was viewed as an art form and as a venue for popular culture. Many of the photographs of African American women reproduced in picture books, journals, and newspapers published for a black readership were designed to refute the destructive stereotyped images circulating among the wider public. Between 1892 and 1922, black presses around the country sought to combat the prevailing stereotypes and recognize and appreciate beauty within black culture. In the late 1890s, black newspapers published glamorous photographs of black women attending events, and as early as 1891 *The Appeal* sponsored a beauty contest titled "Who is the Most Beautiful Afro-American Woman?"[15] In 1914, *The New York Age* sponsored a national beauty contest, "The Chosen Fifteen Most Beautiful Women of the Negro Race in the United States," for which readers were asked to submit photographs. The editors promised to publish photographs every week, feature the "Chosen Fifteen" in a book and exhibition, and present them with an inscribed "gold bar pin."[16] One of the twelve "disinterested" contest judges was the noted black photographer C. M. Battey, whose photographs Du Bois used often on the cover and inside pages of *Crisis*.

Hundreds of photographs were submitted for the contest, which became so popular that an editor published letters from readers about it: "A correspondent, whose letter we are reproducing, has suggested . . . in an interesting manner his individual idea of the composition of the ideal type of beauty which will serve as a typical representation of the cosmopolite beauty of the Negro women of the United States."[17] A significant number of black American women participated, and photographic studios from around the country opened their doors to women

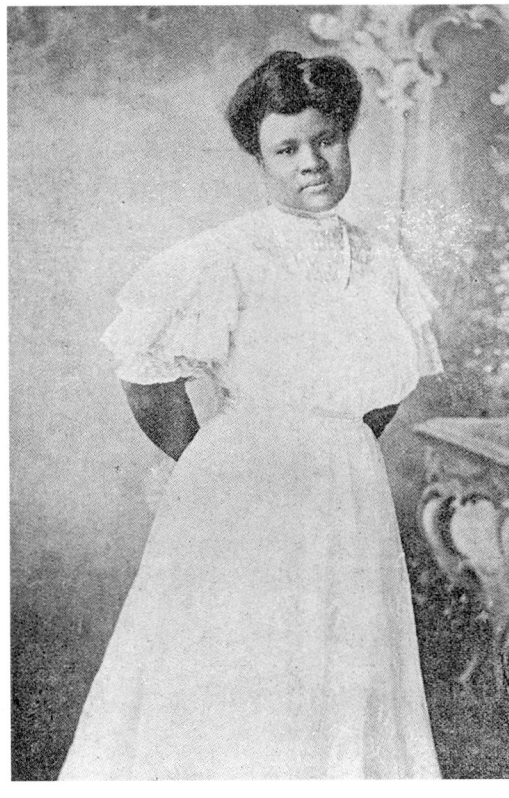

FIGURE 6.2 Unknown photographer, Madame C. J. Walker, date unknown, photograph reproduced from newspaper. Photograph courtesy of Library of Congress, Prints & Photographs Division, LCMS-44669-32.

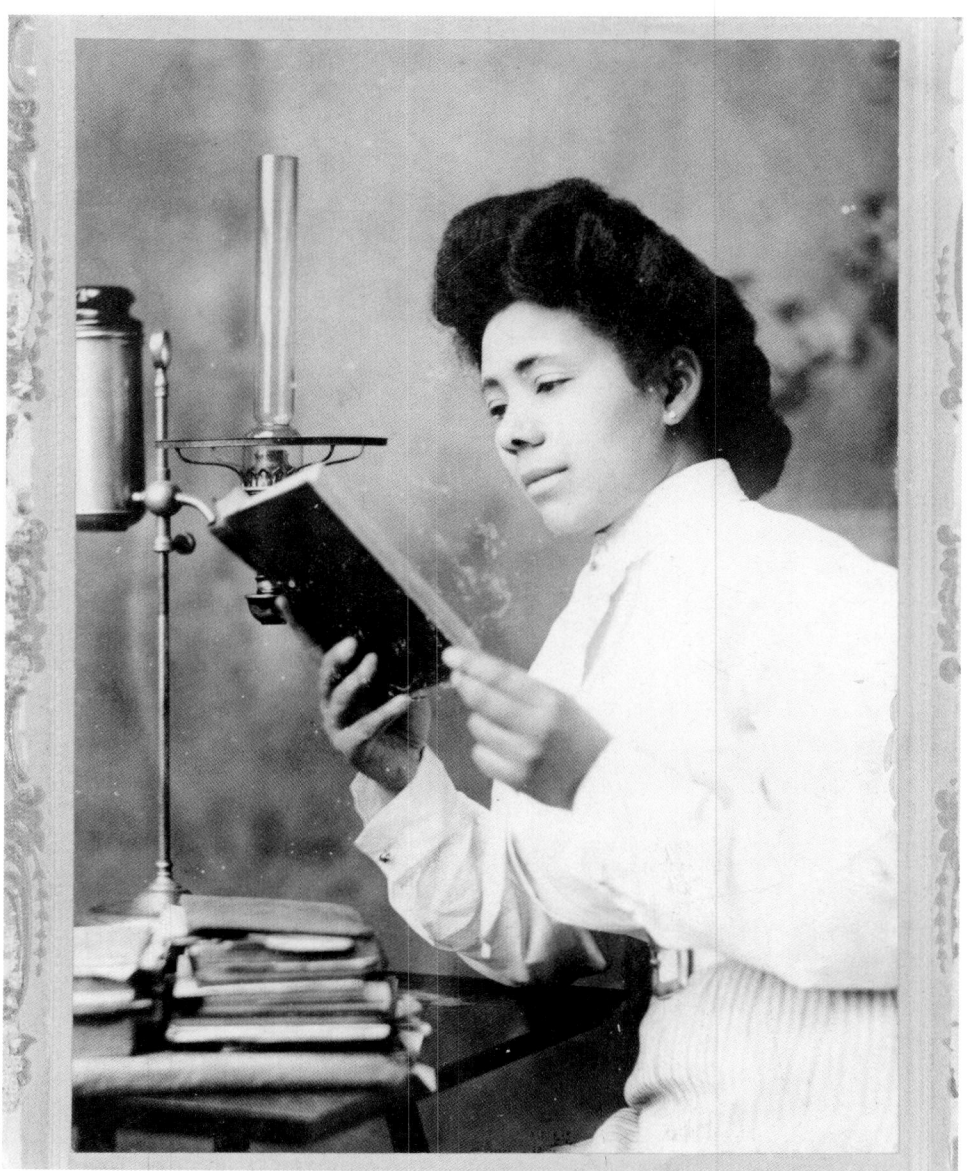

seeking to be portrayed in both Victorian and seductive poses. These constructed images offered the viewer and the judges multiple ways in which to view the black female subject. Sociologist Maxine Leeds Craig has observed that "the rhetoric and staging of black beauty contests were explicitly racial. In some cases, the rhetoric grew out of a deliberate effort to demonstrate the falsehood of white depictions of the black race."[18] In her eloquent writing on beauty, Craig shares how the black press played a critical role in promoting an African American notion of beauty and offered an opportunity to discuss the ramifications of white depictions of black culture.

From the 1890s to early decades of the twentieth century, reader participation beauty contests were extremely popular, circulation-boosting features for newspapers throughout the country. Photography studios and the Eastman

Company's new portable "Kodak" camera made it possible for members of the middle class to capture their own images in photographs. Newspapers took advantage of the widespread availability of snapshots by encouraging female readers to send in their photographs and be acclaimed as beauties.[19]

In the same way, the sitters themselves wanted to celebrate their beauty and achievements by conveying a sense of self-worth. Examining the photographic archives in dozens of libraries, I have come to see that black women at the turn of the century were concerned about how they were portrayed. The photograph did much more than record the presence of black women in America—it became a communal image of prestige and power of women who were beautiful, educated (figure 6.3), religious, employed, and exploring their dreams. The mirror image in photography became a metaphor for the mirror image of their ideals and their desire for racial uplift. The visual interpretation of the New Negro as self-conscious and race-conscious was intentional. Photographs served as evidence that black Americans were multifaceted, and they played an important role in making the black experience visible. In the South, photographers and their studio backdrops visually transformed black women tenant farmers into representations of educational advancement and economic and artistic success. In the North, Midwest, and West, photographers documented the newest residents of the cities—black migrant workers from the rural South and immigrants from the Caribbean—who forever changed the visual representation of their communities. And in 1900, Fannie Barrier Williams, Booker T. Washington, and N. B. Wood served as co-editors of *A New Negro for a New Century: An Accurate and Up-to-Date Record of the Upward Struggles of the Negro Race*, an essay about the changing self-image of black America.[20] The book included an essay by Williams titled "The Colored Woman and Her Part in Racial Regeneration," illustrated with portraits of successful black women. The "New Negro Woman" image was indeed concerned with racial uplift and improving the collective image.

The search for a new life proved to be a boon to photography, which was utilized by young black women heading out west as mail-order brides (figure 6.4). In his book about the black Americans moving west, William L. Katz asserts, "filled with hope, young candidates set out from Boston, Philadelphia, and New York. . . . Each sought her American dream, a new beginning. They hoped to find the thrill of love, the warmth of family, and a new life."[21] Photography played a key role in introducing mail-order brides to black miners in the West. Teenage girls and women modeled for local photographers and mailed their photographs to newspapers, women's organizations, and to the men themselves. A women's organization, the Busy Bee Club, helped the miners find brides. "Wedding-day photographs of mail-order brides show attractive young African American women. Some photos captured a bride's nervous smile or sad, worried eyes. Vulnerable young women never before married and thousands of miles from home and family wondered about their new lives as married women."[22] The West offered a new adventure that included different opportunities for young women, both life-threatening and life-fulfilling. By visiting photographic studios before

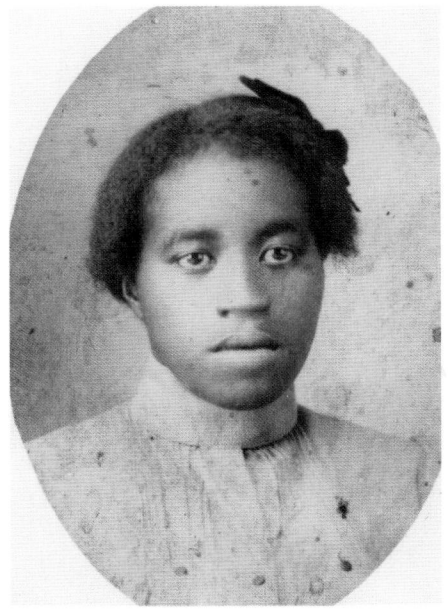

FIGURE 6.4 Unknown photographer, Grace Johnson, mail-order bride, date unknown, black and white photograph. Photograph courtesy of William Katz.

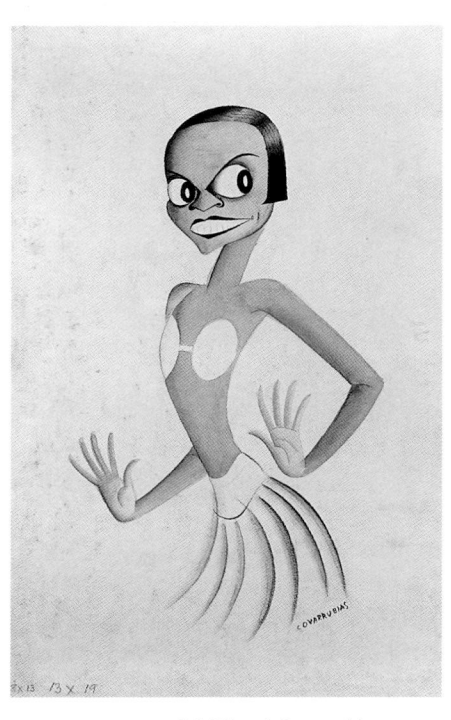

FIGURE 6.5 Unknown photographer, three African American women posed with studio prop automobile, 1905–1915, black and white photograph. Nannie Helen Burroughs collection. Photograph courtesy of Library of Congress Prints & Photographs Division, LC-USZ62-112102.

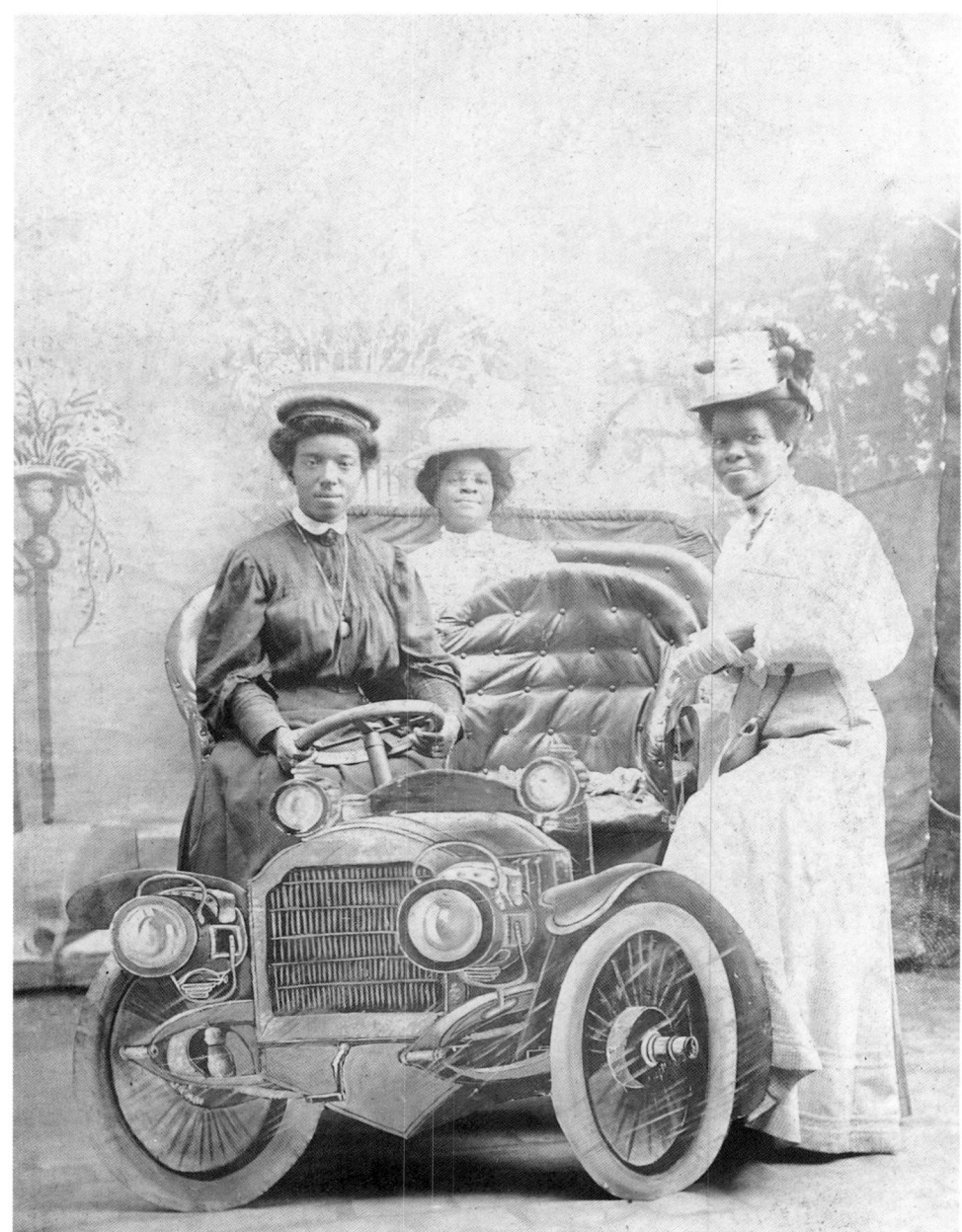

FIGURE 6.6 Miguel Covarrubias, Mexican (1904–1957), *Florence Mills*, 1925, drawing. Cartoon Drawings Library of Congress. Photograph courtesy of Condé Nast Publications and the Library of Congress, Prints & Photographs Division, LC-USZ62-92974.

they left home—standing in front of the camera with props like high-school diplomas, fancy dresses, hats, and automobiles (figure 6.5)—these women created a narrative that sparked the imagination of lonely miners. More and more, photographers began to record images of black women seeking new lives, new identities, new prospects, and new jobs.

Challenging the New Negro vision during this period was the popular cultural imagery that viewed African Americans as oddities and caricatures. The makers of these materials were obsessed with representing blacks as stereotyped symbols, updated for the 1920s. In the April 1927 issue of *Vogue* magazine, Mexican artist and caricaturist Miguel Covarrubius provided a disingenuous view of the New Negro, which was also published earlier in 1925 in *Vanity Fair* (figure 6.6). Petrine Archer-Straw writes,

> *Vogue's* depiction of the New Negro [was] a type that came straight out of white fantasies, with all the old traits of the savage and the erotic concealed beneath street-smart suiting. Of course, this "new negro" had nothing to do with the one the intellectuals around the Harlem Renaissance were busy defining. He was closer to an American Jim Dandy, an effete and overdressed travesty.[23]

The Covarrubias caricature ridiculed the New Negro movement by juxtaposing the dignified portraits produced by black artists and photographers, such as James Van Der Zee (figure 6.7), with the colorfully produced caricatures printed in mainstream media. The movers of the New Negro made a concerted effort to identify the "self" in visual images made by black photographers, a "self" that counters Covarrubias's and similar images of black men and women.

But even within the African American community, efforts to promote beauty contests within the framework of racial uplift were not without controversy. One reader suggested a type of Negro beauty that would be ideal. The letter was published on the front page of the *New York Age*. The ideal Negro beauty

> should have a well balanced and symmetrical head, full slender neck, the features clear cut, with the appearance of being chiseled rather than cast; the forehead broad and slightly expansive, a fine Negro nose with a trace of the Egyptian and a slight aquiline curve; the mouth fairly small but well proportioned and a slightly pointed, round, firm chin; the eyes should be large but slightly elongated; surmounted by a fine brow that is not too sharp, delicately arched, and last but not least, with the marvelous fine curving of eyelash of which the Negro race can be justly proud.[24]

The desire to focus on the ideal type of lighter-skin women often caused controversy among the readership. Another reader wrote a response to the outcome of the *Age's* 1914 contest. Isaac Fisher of the *Negro Farmer* appealed to artists and readers to

> select some definite race type or types—types that retain the features of the race in softened, chastened, refined outlines. And these types we are going to print often in our newspapers, use on our calendars, put on our Christmas cards, hang on the walls of our daughters' rooms, place in the students' rooms in

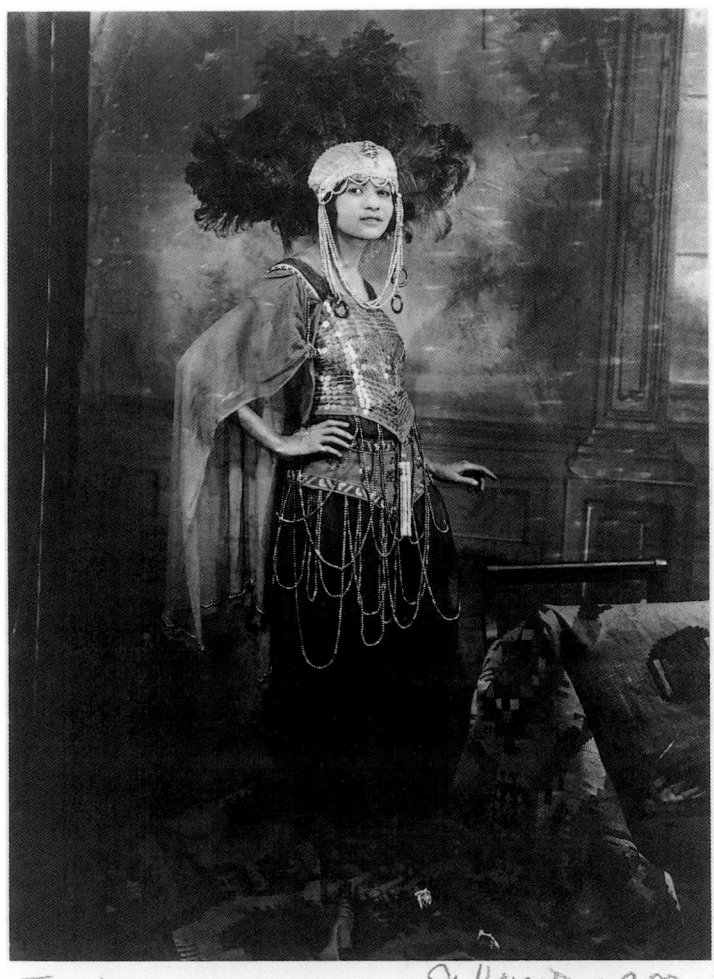

FIGURE 6.7 James Van Der Zee, American (1886–1983), *Dancer, Harlem*, 1925, gelatin silver print. Photograph courtesy of the Library of Congress, Prints & Photographs Division, LC-USZ62-104172 © Donna Van Der Zee.

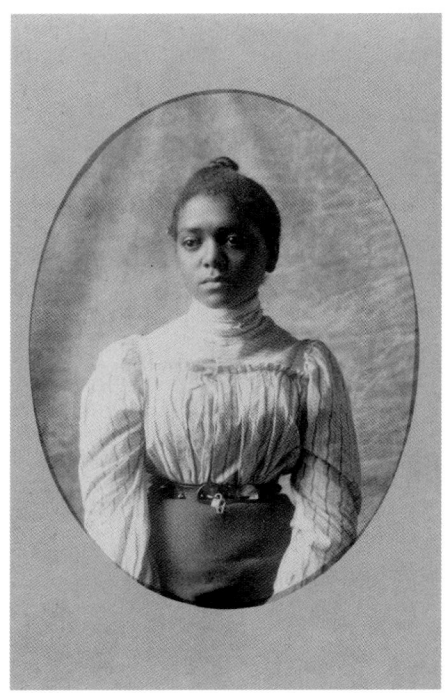

FIGURE 6.8 Unknown photographer, African American woman facing slightly left, 1899 or 1900, gelatin silver print. Du Bois albums of photographs of African Americans in Georgia exhibited at the Paris Exposition Universelle in 1900. Photograph courtesy of Library of Congress, Prints & Photographs Division, LC-USZ62-124728.

colleges, hang on the walls of our churches until a little colored girl, just becoming conscious of her youthful beauty, will go and stand before a picture of a beautiful girl type of her own race and decide to be like her.[25]

The competitions sponsored by newspapers and magazines did indeed portray black women as objects to be desired. But they also established a model for the later "black is beautiful" movement and offered a way to discuss the fundamentals of what might constitute black beauty.

Fisher separated class from color and urged African Americans who had access to the means of cultural production to do the same. Both Fisher and the editors of the Age sought to defeat racist caricatures of blacks. Neither perspective had an audience outside of African American communities for a long time to come.[26]

It has been argued that the "portrait photograph is the site of a complex series of interactions—aesthetic, cultural, ideological, sociological and psychological."[27] Such interactions can be found both in the public images published in newspapers and periodicals and in the personal photographs displayed in private homes. Black imagery in the 1920s was both performance and situated within the notion of the "real." Studio photographers painted elaborate backdrops, including interiors of libraries and broad staircases, for their clients; some stored clothing for their clients' use. With their Victorian poses and middle-class values, their images created a visual record of black women's aspirations and achievements. The notion of performance and the act of being photographed is based in the early history of human displays in world fairs and world expositions, which date back to the Greco-Roman period and became especially popular in the nineteenth and early twentieth centuries.[28]

A SHORT HISTORY OF THE BLACK BODY ON DISPLAY AT EXPOSITIONS

Two significant expositions brought widespread attention to black Americans: Chicago's Columbian Exposition of 1893 and Atlanta's Cotton States and International Exposition of 1895. Though no exhibit at the Chicago exposition featured a "representative" portrayal of African American life, there were midways where visitors could encounter seemingly realistic recreations of colonial African villages, complete with inhabitants. Shawn Michelle Smith writes that

at the many of the world's fairs, the geographical layout of buildings and exhibits was designed explicitly to reproduce this fantasy: Visitors to the 1893 Chicago Columbian Exposition were encouraged to walk through the Midway, with its native villages, toward the center of the fair, marked by its literally white, Greco-Roman buildings. . . . The "scientific" displays that drew evolutionary *evidence* of primitive savagery from the colonies ideologically reinforced, in turn, the virtues of European conquest, American imperialism, and racial segregation.[29] [emphasis added]

Photographs of "authentic" African women and men on postcards, cabinet cards, and in souvenir pamphlets were in turn sold to exposition visitors. Two postcard views of a young girl indicate the degree to which black women were treated without regard for their specific identities. In both images, the girl stands, wearing only jewelry, head wrap, and beaded belt, with fabric on the table beside her. In one view (plate 62a), labeled "A Pesseh Girl in Full Dress," she is shown from behind, leaning on a table. In another photograph (plate 63a), the same young woman is standing in a three-quarter frontal pose touching her breast and is identified as "A Kroo Virgin in Full Dress"; she looks directly into the camera. Her real identity did not matter; the goal was to reinforce a popular stereotype. There is an intriguing juxtaposition embedded in these two images: the "science" of ethnography and anthropometry claimed scientific status exactitude, with the plethora of photographs used to "prove" ethnicity, yet there is a distinct lack of accuracy—or even concern for accuracy—in these expositions. Additionally, another problematic detail, often overlooked, is the girl's ankles: she is in chains, which undercuts the notion that the subject is willing to be on display.

A number of black women had wanted to join the planning committee for the exposition, but their requests were rejected. The *New York Age* published an editorial criticizing their absence from the committee: "We object. We carry our objection so far that if the matter was left to our determination we would advise the race to have nothing whatever to do with the Columbian Exposition or the management of it."[30] Others voiced their disapproval of human displays of African women and men at the 1893 exposition by constructing what they considered positive alternatives to racial stereotyping. Ida B. Wells-Barnett (1862–1931), journalist and anti-lynching crusader, and abolitionist Frederick Douglass (1818–95), for example, published a pamphlet titled "The Reason Why the Colored American Is Not in the World's Columbian Exposition" in 1893. The small pamphlet focused on the racist displays and segregatory nature of the exposition.

One of the organizers of the largest exposition to date, W. E. B. Du Bois used photographic images at the Paris exposition that clearly showed his understanding of the power of photography. As a sociologist, Du Bois was most interested in showing the conditions and progress of black Americans since the end of slavery. He displayed the results of his own research on the black family and also offered a critical view of the new life of black women in Georgia. He included portraits of well-dressed, self-conscious young women, both students and leading members of the Atlanta community (figures 6.8 and 6.9). By presenting unidentified portraits that showed the diverse skin colors of black Americans, Du Bois used the power of photography to depict a reality rarely acknowledged at international expositions at that time. The portraits served as models for a new visualization of black women. Each had a political and visual agenda that relied on a photographic representation of the New Negro. The scholar, mother, sister, nursemaid, student, musician, homeowner, surrey driver, and even the *femme fatale* were all represented in the photographs in the Georgia exhibit.

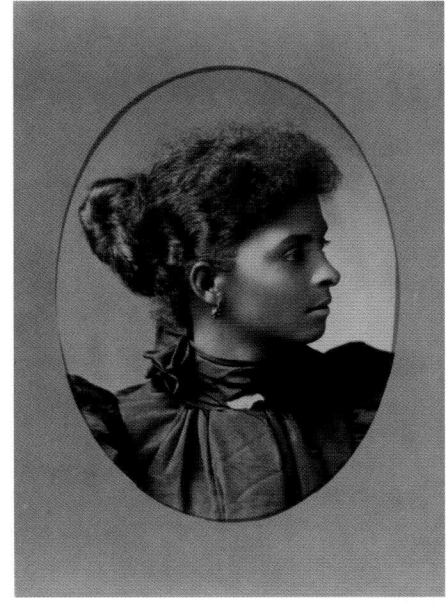

FIGURE 6.9 Unknown photographer, African American woman facing right, 1899 or 1900, gelatin silver print. Du Bois albums of photographs of African Americans in Georgia exhibited at the Paris Exposition Universelle in 1900. Photograph courtesy of Library of Congress, Prints & Photographs Division, LC-USZC4-10674.

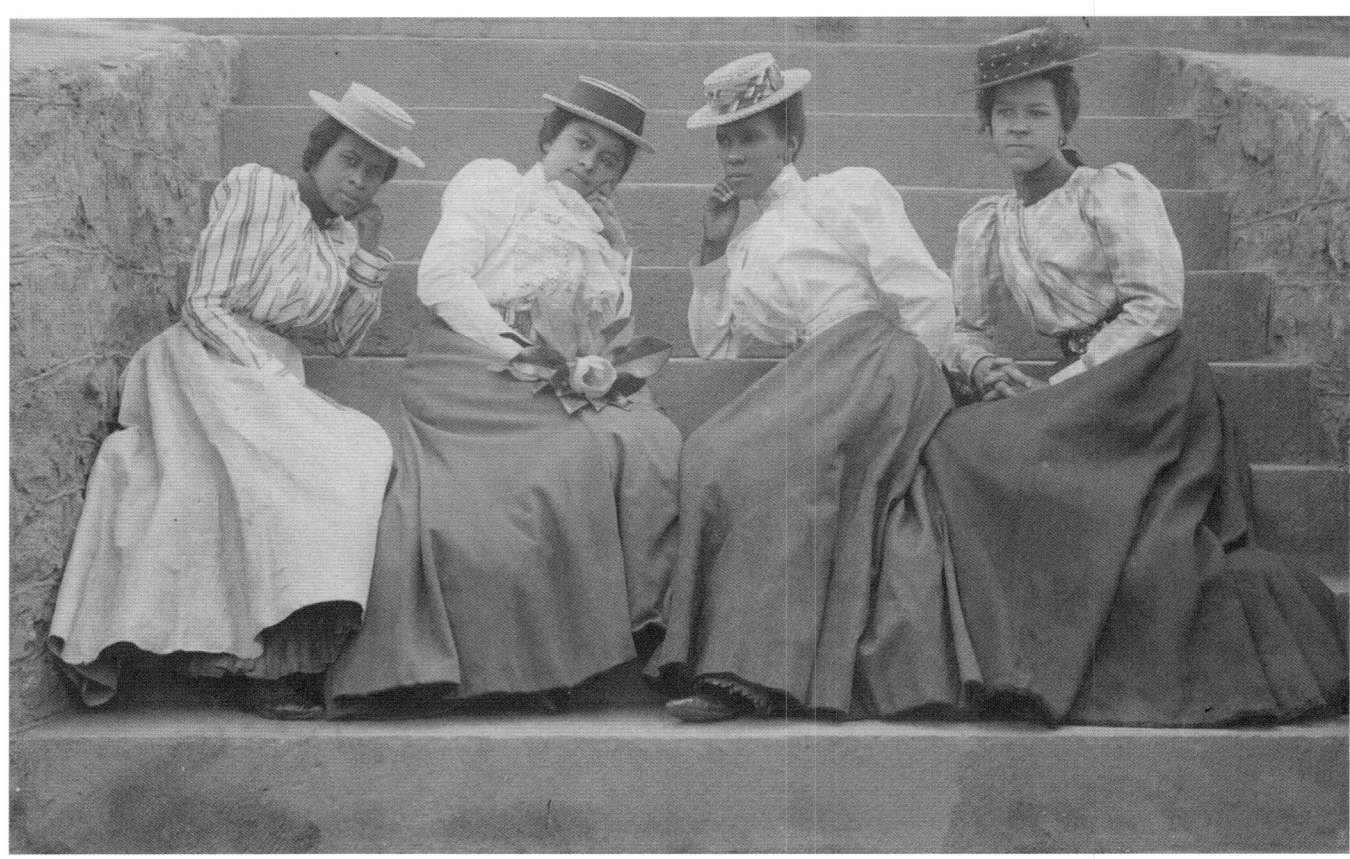

FIGURE 6.10 Thomas Askew, American (1850s–1914), four African American women seated on steps of building at Atlanta University, Georgia, 1899 or 1900, gelatin silver print. Du Bois albums of photographs of African Americans in Georgia exhibited at the Paris Exposition Universelle in 1900. Photograph courtesy of Library of Congress, Prints & Photographs Division, LC-DIG-PPMSCA-08778.

The New Negro woman's desire to present herself as part of a progressive community—a club woman, a businesswoman with middle-class status—is evident in these photographs. One of the photographers, Thomas Askew, was married to a seamstress, Mary Askew. Clothing was a key signifier for the New Negro and for his/her detractors as well. Portraits of young girls and women wearing lace scarves, portrait brooches, drop earrings, lockets, ostrich plume hats, bracelets with charms, and feather boas recast the black woman as a collector of fine clothing, preservers of ancestral mementoes, and enthusiastic participant in creating the image of the "New Woman."

A longtime activist on women's rights, educator, and first president of the National Association of Colored Women, Mary Church Terrell (1863–1954) wrote in support of the proposed Paris exposition. On October 18, 1899, she wrote to the organizers, "Dear Sir: The effort you are making to provide for a Negro Exhibit at the Paris Exhibit is laudable and should be encouraged by every man and woman identified with the race. . . ."[31] In an 1898 speech, her response to the notion of the oppositional gaze in this was "even the white people who think they know all about colored people and are perfectly just in their estimate of them are surprised when they have an ocular demonstration of the rapidity with which a large number of colored women has advanced."[32]

As fashion historian Joan Severa points out, at the end of the nineteenth century, "the New Woman took action and made certain that her dress allowed her to participate more fully in all aspects of life. This trend ensured that women had more physical freedom and that the new styles of clothing were accessible to the millions."[33] The New Negro woman was not excluded from this description. Du Bois's curatorial vision was both aesthetic and political; Thomas Askew's photographs of four black female students posed on the steps of a building on the campus of Atlanta University (figure 6.10) show this active participation in life. They are dressed in everyday walking dresses with leg-'o'-mutton sleeves and stylish straw hats. As was au courant in the late 1890s,[34] their hats are tilted and each woman is in a relaxed pose; the one on the far right wears drop earrings, another is holding a flower.

When we look at the photographs, we perceive a tension in the well-dressed students and residents of Georgia. The subjects' style of dress reveals the status of the sitters, either real or hoped for; we see them today as class-conscious individuals. Joanne Entwistle notes "this tension between clothes as revealing and clothes as concealing of identity,"[35] which I suggest is an important aspect of the photographs Du Bois commissioned.

In the configuration of cultural imperatives and possibilities that characterized the Harlem renaissance, the bourgeois African American woman found herself with the onerous task of endless "performing—and proving her identity to a mainstream public unwilling to believe in her existence."[36] W. E. B. Du Bois saw photography as crucial visual text. His discerning eye and his creation of a collective group portrait of African American women is evident in his selection of images in *Crisis* magazine.[37] I suggest that his use of photography was cultural work, which can be seen in his choices for the Paris project. In the *theater of desire* that was the photographer's studio, Du Bois recast the New Negroes as collectors of fine clothing and enthusiastic participants in preserving and creating the image of the New Negro woman. Du Bois's exhibit concentrated on African Americans in Georgia to reexamine common concepts of the southern black, then seen only as day laborer. Du Bois also wrote that "all art is propaganda";[38] thus he used the photographic image to promote the achievements as well as to draw attention to injustices.[39]

WOMEN IN *CRISIS*

Juxtaposing the notions of stereotyping and representing, Du Bois consciously used photographs of an idealized type of black woman on covers of *Crisis* to promote racial pride and create a visual taxonomy in which to read photographs of black people.[40] As Paula Giddings writes,

> Femininity was the talk of the twenties. . . . The emphasis was on glamour. . . .
> Particularly in the cities, Black women embraced the beauty ethos of the times. . . .
> All the major periodicals, including *Opportunity*, *The Crisis*, and the *Messenger*,
> featured attractive black women on their covers. . . . The January 1924 issue of
> the *Messenger* reflected the general thinking when it announced that from then

on it would "show in pictures as well as writing, Negro women who are unique, accomplished, beautiful, intelligent, industrious, talented and successful."[41]

The *Messenger*'s series of published photos was titled "Exalting Negro Womanhood." I agree with Nina Miller's assertion that these image campaigns were

> a key reason for the resiliently iconic status of contemporaneous bourgeois African American womanhood, a category that included the women of the renaissance intelligentsia: it was through the image of beautiful, genteel femininity that the race could most fully participate in a libidinally charged national culture and identity.[42]

The *Messenger* announced, "We are going to take them by states, displaying two or three pages of these women artistically arranged each month."[43] *Half Century Magazine, The New York Age,* and *The Chicago Defender* also published photographs depicting black women,[44] which were so important to these magazines and newspapers that they pleaded with their readers in editorials:

> Don't hesitate to send in your picture because you do not consider yourself unusually good looking. . . . We merely want to show the unbelievers of our own and other races that there are as many beautiful Colored women as there are beautiful women in other races.[45]

A writer to *Half Century* wrote that he found "the publication of numerous photographs of African American women 'helpful' in rebutting whites' claims that 'Colored' women were ugly."[46] This momentum followed through World War II as beauty contests and pageants flourished in black communities throughout the United States.

WOMEN IN PHOTOGRAPHY

The twentieth century also brought to light new images by black women photographers. The camera in the hands of women photographers at the turn of the century created a slightly different vision of their community. Photo historian Naomi Rosenblum writes,

> The gains that had been made during the previous quarter-century (1890–1915) were too significant to be obliterated. In fact, the perception arose that women's photographic accomplishments had become such an accepted fact that they no longer required special nurturing. Increasingly, women were being offered jobs in photography . . . growing numbers of women free-lanced as photographers . . . and by the 1930s several women had been active as journalists and portraitists.[47]

The *Cleveland Gazette* published in 1886 that a black woman, Fannie J. Thompson, of Memphis, Tennessee "devoted her school vacation to the study of photography."[48] Between 1900 and 1930,[49] the one hundred documented black

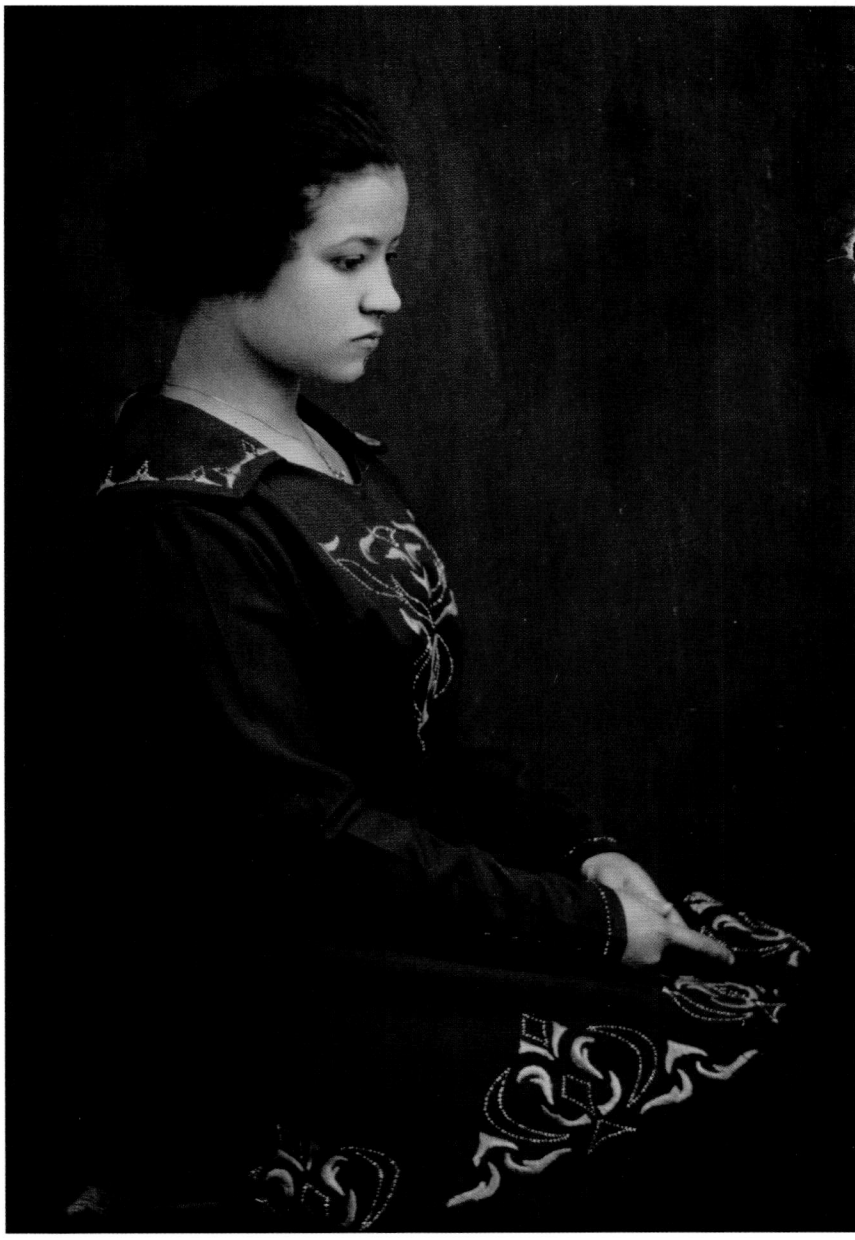

FIGURE 6.11 Florestine Perrault Collins, American (1895–1987), *Self-portrait*, early 1920s, black and white photograph. Photograph courtesy of Arthe Anthony.

female photographers working in this country made compelling portraits of their black subjects, many of them women. Although art photography was not the direction of New Orleans camera girl Florestine Perrault Collins (1895–1987) (figure 6.11), she experimented early in this genre with models, friends and family members who acquired qualities that suggest the transformative nature of photography, the photographer's sympathy, and her understanding for her subject.

Photographing families in Collins's neighborhood was crucial to her business. By reviewing her photographs of this period, it is clear that the sanctity of the American family was central for the well-being of the race. Collins owned and operated a studio there from 1920 to 1949, photographing families and visiting soldiers. One of the earliest female photographers to gain local prominence, she opened her first studio in the living room of her family home. In 1909, she began working as a photographer's assistant. Her biographer Arthe Anthony writes that her employers often left her alone in the studio. Collins remembered:

> I worked for a studio on Canal and St. Charles Streets. This man was so lazy that he would go out and want to go to a show. So he saw that it was to his advantage to teach me how to make pictures so that he could go and leave me in charge, which he did. . . . He saw that I was apt and learned easily. He left me in charge. . . . And that's how I began to pick it up, I began to learn. In fact, he started me doing the finishing part of the work, the developing, and the printing. . . . Then finally when he got pushed he started teaching me how to take pictures.[50]

According to Anthony, Collins, a "creole of color," would sometimes be mistaken for white. Collins would use this misidentification to her benefit; she knew that a black woman would not have had the opportunity to work as a photographer's assistant in the South. "If they thought that I was colored they probably wouldn't have allowed me to take pictures," she recalled.[51] Collins also worked for the Eastman Kodak Company as a developer. Later, she supported herself full-time as a photographer, often advertising her specialties in the city directory. On occasion, Collins and her brother Arthur Perrault (1900–1960) worked together in her portrait home/studio in the Treme area of New Orleans.[52] Collins's business flourished over the years. "People traveled from small towns to have quick-finished photos taken at Collins's studio," which was especially popular also among the New Orleans Treme community.[53]

CONCLUSION

What are we to make of these extraordinary images, so full of tension and irony, propaganda and art, implied and visual text? Imagery played a crucial role in highlighting the dreams and ideals of both the black middle class and the working poor by addressing social structures and aesthetic concerns. The photographs not only countered the negative black imagery typically promoted in popular culture, but they also documented a body of images of a vibrant family life and a growing middle class, transforming the subjugated black imagery and encouraging viewers to reexamine visual history as they learned it. The contemporary photographs in *Black Womanhood* do what only the finest photography can achieve: they create a new awareness and historical consciousness, exemplifying pride and determination that has the power to rewrite history.

Many of these images call on the viewer/reader to close the chapter on racial stereotyping in all artistic forms, inviting us to imagine the battle that awaited the black visual artist in the early years of the twentieth century. The fight, which had to begin with the creation of representational imagery of black American life, was a continuation of a battle fought in the previous century. In America, vernacular images—such as enslaved women and servant children—were the most frequently mass-produced images of black people. As a result, our perceptions of nineteenth-century black America are often based on images of the mammy, the primitive, or the exotic black woman. The exaggerated features and demeaning situations depicted by racist photographers have left an enduring negative impact that has continued to this day. As professor Ann Douglas writes,

> It is one thing to be in search of the *primitive* as white artists of the 1920s were; another thing to be told . . . that you are the primitive, the savage *id* of Freud's new psychoanalytic discourse, trailing clouds of barbaric, prehistoric, preliterate *folk* culture wherever you go.[54] (emphasis added)

In my view, the social context of these images sought to dominate and subjugate black people.

The work of many of the contemporary artists in this exhibition is changing and challenging the collective image. They are aware that images of black women were and still are caught in an awkward public space between the "real" and the "transformed." Drawing on photographs of black women from the past and contemporary images, the artists working with photography are noting what it means to be both in front of and behind the camera. Many of the contemporary artists in *Black Womanhood* are using family collections, photographers' archives, and public repositories to provide a visual conversation on this subject. Photography encouraged the visual in the New Negro movement, and the photographs of some artists today continue the visualization of new images and perspectives about the image of the black woman. ❧

1 Louise Daniel Hutchinson, *Anna Julia Cooper: A Voice from the South* (Washington, D.C.: Smithsonian Institution Press and the Anacostia Neighborhood Museum, 1981), 196.

2 Deborah Willis and Carla Williams, *The Black Female Body: A Photographic History* (Philadelphia: Temple University Press, 2002).

3 In her 1926 essay "I Am a Negro—and Beautiful," which was published on July 10 in *Negro World*, Amy Jacques Garvey exemplifies this ideology. At that time, Amy was the second wife of Universal Negro Improvement Association president Marcus Garvey, and her essay encouraged empowerment among black Americans through the notion of beauty.

4 Henry Louis Gates Jr., "New Negroes, Migration and Cultural Exchange," in *Jacob Lawrence: The Migration Series*, ed. Elizabeth Hutton Turner (Washington, D.C.: The Rappahannock Press in association with the Phillips Collection, 1993), 19.

5 John Henry Adams Jr., "Rough Sketches: A Study of the Features of the New Negro Woman," *Voice of the Negro* (August 1904), 446.

6 Gertrude Woodruff Marlow, *A Right Worthy Grand Mission: Maggie Lena Walker and the Quest for Black Economic Empowerment* (Washington D.C.: Howard University Press, 2003), 27.

7 Maxine Leeds Craig, *Ain't I a Beauty Queen: Black Women, Beauty and the Politics of Race* (New York: Oxford, 2002), 32.

8 Paula Giddings, *When and Where I Enter: The Impact of Black Women on Race and Sex in America* (New York: William Morrow and Company, 1984), 184.

9 Judith Wilson, "How the Invisible Woman Got Herself on the Cultural Map: Black Women Artists in California," in *Art/Women/California, 1950–2000: Parallels and Intersections*, ed. Diana Burgess Fuller and Daniela Salvioni (Berkeley: University of California Press, 2000), 330.

10 See Chandler Owen's "Black Mammies," in *The Messenger* (April 1923), 670; also cited in Giddings, *When and Where I Enter*.

11 W. E. B. Du Bois, "Opinion of W. E. B. Du Bois," *Crisis* (October 1923): 248–249.

12 Quoted in Sondra Kathryn Wilson, ed., *The Crisis Reader: Stories, Poetry, and Essays from the N.A.A.C.P.'s Crisis Magazine* (New York: The Modern Library, 1999), xxix.

13 Camara Dia Holloway, *Portraiture and the Harlem Renaissance: The Photographs of James L. Allen* (New Haven: Yale Art Gallery, 1999), 35.

14 A'Lelia Perry Bundles, *On Her Own Ground: The Life and Times of Madam C. J. Walker* (New York: Scribner, 2001), 96.

15 *Chicago Appeal*, January 31, 1891.

16 *New York Age*, September 17, 1914.

17 *New York Age*, August 6, 1914, 1.

18 Craig, *Ain't I a Beauty Queen*, 52.

19 Ibid., 48.

20 Booker T. Washington, N. B. Wood, and Fannie Barrier Williams, eds., *A New Negro for a New Century: An Accurate and Up-to-Date Record of the Upward Struggles of the Negro Race* (Chicago: American Publishing House, 1900).

21 William Loren Katz, ed., *Negro Population in the United Sates, 1790–1915* (New York: Arno Press and the New York Times, 1968), 35, 37.

22 Ibid., 35.

23 Petrine Archer-Straw, *Negrophilia: Avant-Garde Paris and Black Culture in the 1920s* (New York and London: Thames & Hudson, 2000), 27.

24 Quoted in Craig, *Ain't I a Beauty Queen*, 50.

25 "Isaac Fisher and the *Age* Beauty Contest," *New York Age*, October 4, 1914.

26 Craig, *Ain't I a Beauty Queen*, 52.

27 Graham Clarke, *The Photograph* (Oxford: Oxford University Press, 1997), 102.

28 France held national expositions every eleven years beginning in 1797, holding its first Exposition Universelle (international exposition) in Paris in 1855. But it wasn't until the 1867 Paris exposition that non-Europeans were included; that year also featured a photographic division, the largest French photographic display up to that time. By 1889 exposition organizers sought to attract visitors by creating a "village" displaying Senegalese men and women. In July of 1892, the city of Paris announced another international exposition to be held in 1900. The theme focused on "progress" and "the desire for the world to continue evolving" (Bronwyn A. E. Griffith, ed., *Ambassadors of Progress: American Women Photographers in Paris, 1900–1901* [Washington, D.C.: The Library of Congress in association with the Musee

d'Art Americain Giverny, France, 2001], 12). Forty-two nations planned to participate; the American contingent would include a group of African Americans.

29 Shawn Michelle Smith, *Photograph on the Color Line: W. E. B. Du Bois, Race, and Visual Culture* (Durham: Duke University Press, 2004), 14.

30 Robert William Rydell, *All the World's a Fair: America's International Expositions, 1876–1916* (Chicago: University of Chicago Press, 1984), 52.

31 Mary Church Terrell, "The Negro Exhibit at Paris," *The Colored American*, November 3, 1900, 8.

32 Quoted in Craig, *Ain't I a Beauty Queen*, 32.

33 Joan Severa, *Dressed for the Photographer: Ordinary Americans & Fashion, 1840–1900* (Kent: The Kent State University Press, 1995), 474.

34 Severa, *Dressed for the Photographer*, 443.

35 Joanne Entwistle, *The Fashioned Body* (Cambridge: Polity Press, 2000), 113.

36 Nina Miller, *Making Love Modern: The Intimate Public Worlds of New York's Literary Women* (New York: Oxford University Press, 1999), 182.

37 Anne Elizabeth Carroll argues that in each issue of *Crisis*, "women appear among the graduates in special issues, they are more commonly depicted, anonymously, on the covers, in glamour photographs and drawings. Though there are exceptions, then, men most often are used to show the business and financial success of African Americans, while women demonstrate their beauty and social achievements." *Word, Image, and the New Negro: Representation and Identity in the Harlem Renaissance* (Bloomington: Indiana University Press, 2005), 42.

38 Quoted in Wilson, *The Crisis Reader*, 323.

39 In a reflective editorial titled, "Editing the *Crisis*," W. E. B. Du Bois stated that with the use of photographs "we doubled the size of the tiny first issue in December 1910. We increased the number of pictures, trying two-color jobs on the cover in 1911 and three colors in 1912, 1917–1918. Our special education and children's numbers began in 1914. From time to time we issued special numbers on localities like Chicago and New Orleans; on 'Votes for Women' and the pageant 'Star of Ethiopia'" (quoted in Wilson, *The Crisis Reader*, xxix).

40 Daylanne English argues that "under Du Bois's editorship, the *Crisis* comprises a kind of eugenic 'family album,' a visual and literary blueprint for the ideal, modern black individual . . . [His] column functions to counter racist representations of African Americans by the white press; but given the predominantly black readership of the *Crisis*, such compulsive cataloging also serves to keep the 'family' updated on its members' activities." "W. E. B. Du Bois's Family *Crisis*," *American Literature* 72, no.2 (June 2000): 300.

41 Giddings, *When and Where I Enter*, 185.

42 Miller, *Making Love Modern*, 152.

43 Quoted in ibid., 153.

44 *Half Century Magazine* published an article using some of C. M. Battey's photographs titled "Types of Racial Beauty."

45 From "Who is the Prettiest Colored Girl in this Country?" and "Are You One of Those Perfect Types?" consecutively (*Half Century Magazine*, September 1921, 9).

46 *Half Century Magazine*, November 1921, 21.

47 Naomi Rosenblum, *A History of Women Photographers* (New York: Abbeville, 1994), 150.

48 *Cleveland Gazette*, May 22, 1866, p. 1, col. 1.

49 The 1890 census listed 2,201 female photographers, which included six Negro women photographers (Katz, *Negro Population in the United Sates, 1790–1915*, 527). The census of 1900 recorded seventeen black women photographers out of 3,587 women working in the field. United States Bureau of Census, *1900 Census Report* (Washington, D.C.: Government Printing Office, 1902), 547.

50 Quoted in Arthe Anthony, "Reading Visual Autobiographies: Reconstructing Women's Lives in a Creole of Color Community in New Orleans, 1900–1930," excerpt from the manuscript of a forthcoming book on Florentine Perrault Collins, 10.

51 Anthony, "Reading Visual Autobiographies," 11.

52 A number of women had their studios in their residences.

53 Coleman Warner, "Historic Studio Faces Demolition," *Times-Picayune*, June 24, 1995, p. A-8.

54 Ann Douglas, *Terrible Honesty: Mongrel Manhattan in the 1920s* (New York: Noonday Press, Farrar, Straus and Giroux, 1995), 98.

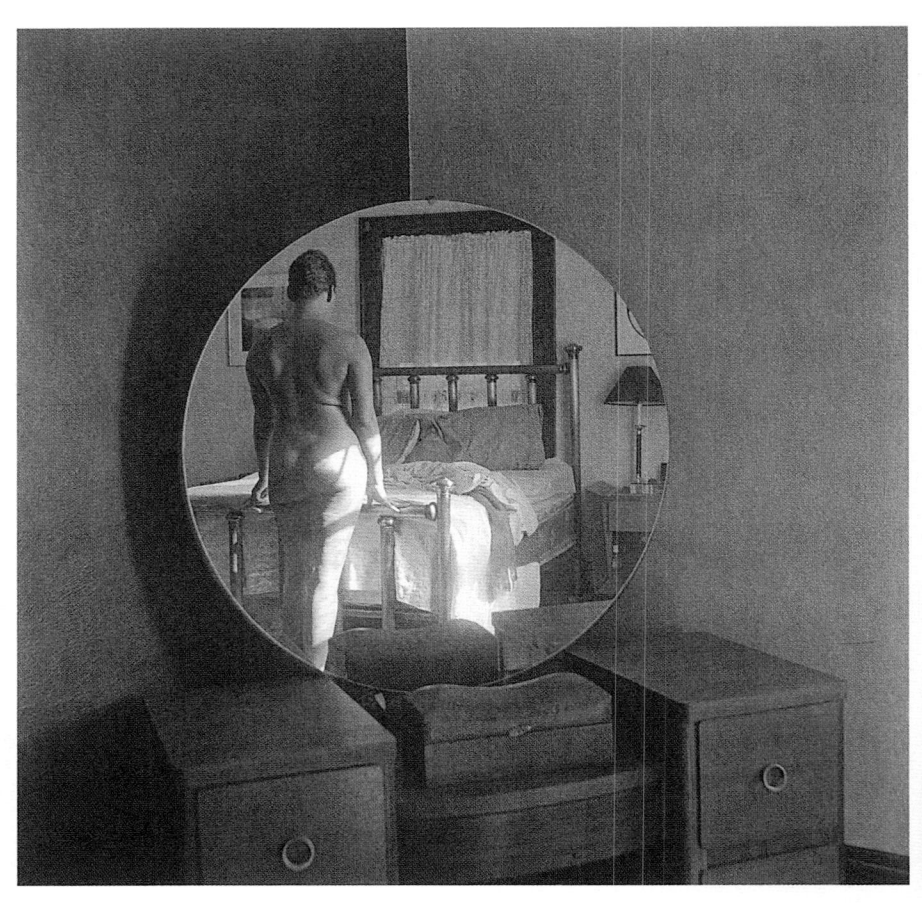

28/40

Carrie M. Weems, 2001

IT WAS CLEAR,
I WAS NOT MANET'S TYPE
PICASSO –– WHO HAD A WAY
WITH WOMEN –– ONLY USED ME
& DUCHAMP NEVER EVEN
CONSIDERED ME

7   The Women Who Posed:
Maudelle Bass and Florence Allen

Throughout art history, the artist's model has been the unsung, uncredited collaborator in countless works of art. Two African American women, Maudelle Bass Weston (1908–1989), a modern dancer and artist's model known professionally as Maudelle, and Florence "Flo" Allen (1912–1997), a professional artist's model and modeling teacher, posed for photographers, painters, and sculptors for more than fifty years in the San Francisco Bay Area.

Both Maudelle and Flo began their modeling careers around 1933, when the mainstream (i.e., non-black) image in the United States of African American women was the mammy, a large, dark-skinned, desexualized, loyal caretaker perpetuated by Hollywood and advertising, epitomized by the character of Aunt Jemima.[1] Though there were artists from the Harlem Renaissance through the New Negro period who actively sought to present a more complex picture of African American life and culture, Maudelle and Flo did not precisely fit the New Negro model of black womanhood and femininity, either—the usually light-skinned, middle-class pillar of the community and family. Neither woman embodied the favored roles or appearance set forth for middle-class African American women, as Deborah Willis describes in this volume. Through the figuring of their mostly nude bodies, Maudelle and Flo enacted and defined a new, modern definition of the black woman that moved beyond the discourse of slavery, sexual degradation, and stereotype, thereby anticipating black women's self-portraiture of the late twentieth and early twenty-first centuries, such as in the works of Renée Cox (plates 104 and 110), Carrie Mae Weems (figure 7.1), Fern Logan, and Myra Greene.

The difference between modeling and portraiture is critical to this discussion. Modeling is largely anonymous; the model is not so much meant to represent herself but rather to enact a posture or embody an ideal, such as of physical beauty. The motivation for the model, however, can be quite personal. In an article originally published in the journal *Raritan* in 1996, Elizabeth Hollander, a former art model, explains that "the model performs for a kind of inner mirror that allows one to feel on the inside how one looks on the outside."[2] Photography, of

opposite FIGURE 7.1 Carrie Mae Weems, American (born 1953), *Not Manet's Type*, 2001, offset photolithograph, published by Segura Publishing Company, Inc., Tempe, Arizona. Purchased through the Olivia H. Parker and John O. Parker 1958 Acquisition Fund, Hood Museum of Art; PR.2002.17.1

course, complicates this relationship, as the medium by its very nature tends more toward realism and individual recognition. For this reason, many professional artist's models prefer not to pose for photographic artists.[3] Posing as the model for a work of art, particularly a photograph, is a type of performance work in which the cultural body enacts a signifying role that communicates beyond the artist's capabilities and aspirations for the work; a model is, after all, not merely a prop but an active participant in the creative process. According to historian Hugh Kilmer, "[modeling] is performance brought to its most elemental, without external support of any kind: text, sounds, costume, or furniture."[4]

Models have traditionally been anonymous, as, in the West, the notion of "genius" attached to artistic creation elevates the artist above all other contributors to the artistic process. Perhaps the most famous identified model is Victorine Meurent, an artist who posed as the central figure in Edouard Manet's 1863 painting *Olympia*; lesser known but nevertheless identified is Laure, the Afro-Caribbean model for *Olympia*'s black attendant.[5] Beginning in the nineteenth century, artists' models were usually drawn from the working and lower classes, so their intentionality with regard to the artistic process must be filtered through an understanding of the economy of their labor. Unlike the majority of artists' models, Maudelle and Flo were often (though not consistently) identified by name—it was very uncommon in the 1930s and 1940s for models of any race to be identified, let alone recognized for their work. In the 1940s, African American painter and printmaker Eldzier Cortor (b. 1916) was one of the first artists to focus on nude black women subjects, and though one statuesque woman is clearly recognizable throughout much of his work, she remains unidentified. Cortor's reluctance to discuss his models exemplifies the difficulty of identifying these women and thoroughly evaluating their contributions.

Modernism is not a movement traditionally associated with African American cultural practice and precedents in African American Modernism are "not always congruent with canonical histories of European and American modernism," according to curator Helen Shannon.[6] Yet the cultural production of the Harlem Renaissance, for example, paralleled and informed the development of a European-based Modernism in the early twentieth century.[7] Maudelle's work bridges the discourses of Modernism, through her work with non-black artists, and the New Negro movement, in which "[b]lacks had to determine not only where the individual belonged in early twentieth-century American society, but also where a people who historically had been rejected from majority American society fit into contemporary culture."[8] Emerging out of both the New Negro period and the Modernist movement in art, Maudelle and Flo existed within a cultural framework as a bridge between the two extremes of representation for black women in the United States—the nineteenth century, in which black women had little or no control over their representations, and the late twentieth and early twenty-first centuries, in which their decisions about how they "choose" to be depicted call into question the primacy of agency as a defense against self-exploitation.

Living and working in California at a physical remove from black cultural centers such as Harlem or Chicago gave Maudelle and Flo a certain freedom for the kind of work they wanted to pursue. The history of blacks in California and in the arts in particular differs significantly from their Eastern counterparts, in that they were less exclusively informed by European practices and more influenced by indigenous cultures of the Americas. This geographic difference is crucial. Art historians Lizzetta LeFalle-Collins, Judith Wilson, and Kellie Jones have all written about black women artists in California, including Los Angeles sculptor Beulah Ecton Woodard (1895–1955), for whom Maudelle modeled, and Washington native Thelma Johnson Streat (1912–1959), "the first black woman to operate professionally as an artist while residing in California."[9] Woodard's belief that "accurate depiction of African costume and features could enhance African American pride"[10] dovetails with Maudelle's "dream to re-create through the medium of the African dance, the heritage of racial dignity lost to the Negroes through their century-old experience of slavery and oppression."[11]

Streat's father taught her to paint at age ten. In 1934, she enrolled in classes at the Portland Art Museum School[12] and the University of Oregon. Moving to San Francisco in the late 1930s, Streat worked on the Works Progress Administration's Federal Art Project (WPA-FAP) and assisted Mexican artist Diego Rivera on his mural for the Palace of Fine Arts at the Golden Gate International Exposition. Around 1946, Streat turned increasingly to interpretive dance, which came to be described as "interpretive" and "Afro-Primitive."[13] Often performing in front of her paintings and "miming with her body the painted forms,"[14] Streat "believed her dances to be the physical translation of the movement of her paintbrush."[15] Although there is much overlap in their time in California and no evidence exists that the two women ever met, Streat's work in dance and interest in folklore and other cultures aligns her practice with Maudelle's.

MAUDELLE

As I researched the representation of black women's bodies, a beautiful, strong-featured, naked, dark-skinned woman kept appearing in the work of various artists, including painters Abraham Baylinson, Nicolai Fechin, and Diego Rivera, sculptor Woodard, and Modernist photographers Johan Hagemeyer (figure 7.2), Sonia Noskowiak, Edward Weston (figure 7.3), Carl Van Vechten, Weegee, Manuel Alvarez Bravo, and Lola Alvarez Bravo.[16] Although sometimes she was unidentified and at other times her name was misspelled, I eventually learned her name was Maudelle Bass Weston.[17] Born in Early County, Georgia, Maudelle Bass moved to Los Angeles in 1933 to pursue her dance studies. Over the course of her career, she studied and performed throughout the United States and Mexico with the Lester Horton Dance Group, the Fowler School of African Culture, the American Ballet Theater, Arte Folklorico de Mexico, and with dancers and choreographers including Asadata Dafora and Pearl Primus, though she primarily performed her own choreography of African, Afro-Cuban, Balinese, Egyptian, Moroccan, and

Caribbean dances, based on her research and interpretation. This level of artistic control was highly unusual and posits a strategy of self-presentation that informed her modeling work.

Soon after Maudelle's relocation to Los Angeles, a friend encouraged her to model for artists. She posed regularly at venues including the Otis Art Institute, the Stendahl Art Galleries, and Los Angeles Junior College.[18] During these modeling sessions she often posed for artists whose own careers had already merited or would merit widespread attention. "She is now considered one of the best models in Southern California," enthused one reporter.[19] From all indications, she earned her living as a performing artist and model; there is no record of any other kind of employment in which she might have engaged. Using the opportunity of the sitting, she portrays an individual who does not conform to the expectations of a black woman in 1939—she is neither mammy nor New Negro representative, but an expressive artist representing herself as a living embodiment of the African history and culture she promoted in her dance and beyond.

An invitation to perform at a birthday party prompted her initial research into African dance customs. Maudelle wanted to choreograph an African dance, but none of her teachers felt they could adequately help her, so she started to conduct library research.[20] According to scholar Leah Creque-Harris, "[l]earning African dance from library research was not an uncommon methodology"[21] for dancers and choreographers, although Maudelle also learned the rhythms from Prince Modupe (Paris), a Nigerian prince, artist, and drummer. It proved to be a successful strategy; during a period when most black modern dancers had great difficulty securing audiences for their work, Maudelle worked continually. A 1938 newspaper profile further iterates Maudelle's role as cultural interpreter and evinces her awareness of that role:

> Maudelle will never consider a successful concert career alone the achievement of her aims. She wants more than anything else to teach the people themselves to dance. It is their lives, their frustrations and their hopes, that her own work expresses so vividly. But, she believes, that it is only by the participation of the people in the dance, that the dignity, the power of the African dance, can serve its real purpose as a medium of expression for the darker peoples of the world.
>
> She has gone back to primitive Africa for her inspiration. Nevertheless, she has not been content to transplant [identically] the African dances. The primitive movements, the patterns and the spirit—even the drums—are there. But the ideas she creates from this basic inspiration are her own, drawn from the life around her.[22]

Though Maudelle worked as a model, her own performance work and the relative recognition that came with it certainly were brought to bear on all of her sittings. Maudelle's selection of accomplished collaborators ultimately insured that her work would not be forgotten, though it is only through her modeling work that a consideration of her performing art can occur.[23] As dance historian John O. Perpener III has noted, "the careers of most African-American dancers

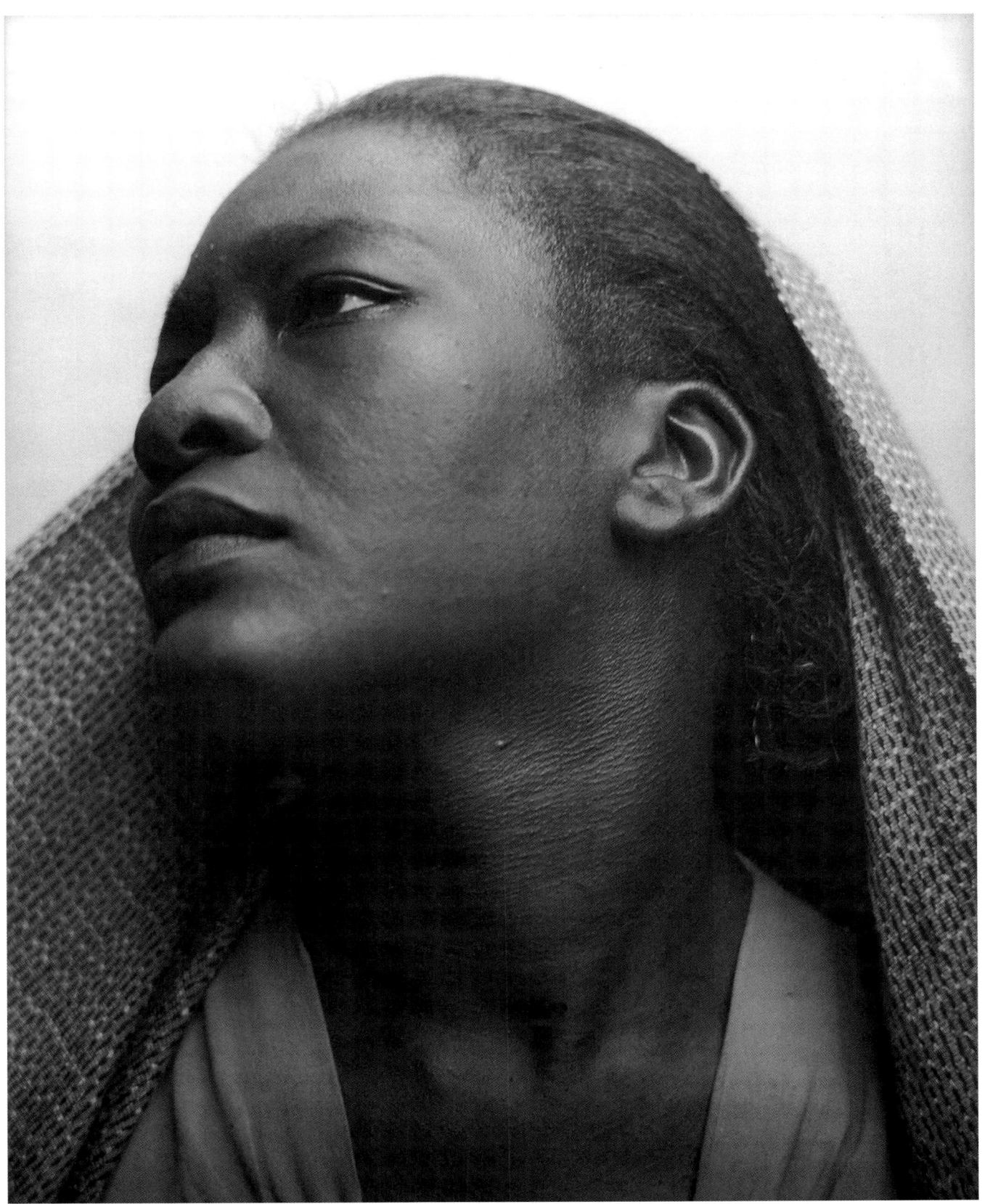

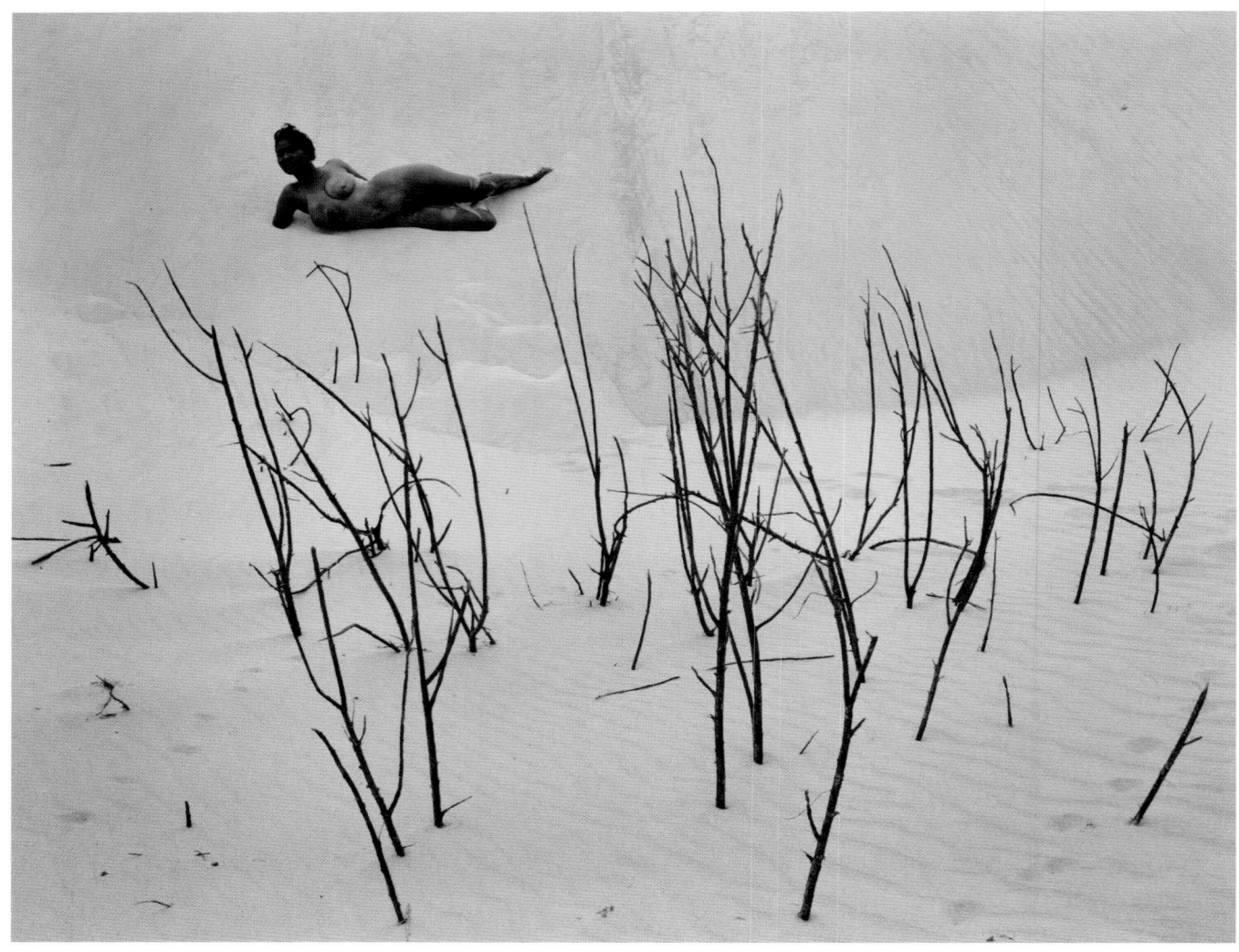

FIGURE 7.3 Edward Weston, American (1886–1958), *Nude on Dunes* (Maudelle Weston Oceano), 1939, black and white photograph. Photograph courtesy of the Center for Creative Photography, University of Arizona, N39-M-17, ©1981 Arizona Board of Regents.

were so poorly documented in dance history literature that questions concerning who was significant and who was not became moot."[24] Because there is no known visual documentation of her performances, Maudelle's modeling images assume an additional currency as representative of her artistic intent and work. Though the images are not a substitute for her performances, they can be understood as an artistic equivalent. The same power and strength she purportedly exhibited in her dance performances is evidenced in still visual media.

It is through her dual role as performing artist and model that Maudelle employed an expressive strategy that influenced the development of black women's representation in mid-twentieth-century art. Like many artists of her time and in subsequent generations, Maudelle clearly saw her image and her career as quite apart from the dominant modes of representation. According to Perpener, "all of the earliest black concert dance artists expressed concern about overcoming stereotypes and bringing attention to themselves as serious artists."[25] Significantly, Maudelle saw her two bodies of work as equivalent, moving fluidly between them. "Why not?" she once remarked. "When I don't have the urge to dance, I can always model!"[26] The figuring of Maudelle as a new, modern black woman—strong, independent, and culturally connected to her African origins—is significant. Maudelle's desire to learn and interpret African dance was in keeping with the *négritude* movement that, according to historian Nick Nesbitt, "mark[ed] a revalorization of Africa on the part of New World blacks, affirming an overwhelming pride in black heritage and culture."[27] Her work as an independent creative artist and her desire to help figure a new representation of black people emphasizing African cultural emulations were integral in the cultural transformations taking place.

FLORENCE ALLEN

I learned of Flo Allen purely by chance. I had been researching Maudelle for years, and inquiring at the San Francisco Art Institute's library where I knew Maudelle had posed,[28] I announced myself by going into my schpiel about researching an "African American artist's model." The librarian, Jeff Gunderson, lit up. "Flo Allen?" he responded. Until that point, no one had ever mentioned her name to me, nor had it appeared in any of my research. Florence Wysinger Allen, a third-generation Californian, hailed from Oakland and spent her entire career in the Bay Area. She posed for more than fifty years for artists including Diego Rivera, Mark Rothko, Roy DeForest, Richard Diebenkorn, Joan Brown, and Mark Adams—essentially a Who's Who of Bay Area artists. According to artist Beth Van Hoesen, "It's her coloring that is so beautiful, so special. She's always good to draw. Things happen."[29] The way in which Peter Steinhart describes her is telling of the way in which race was a positive factor in her appeal: "tall, strongly built, dark black, and had a loud and familiar informality that translated quickly into an air of command."[30] Race, however, did not define her career or her successes.

Flo began her modeling career quite by accident—she dropped by a painting class (Flo was never an artist herself), and the "next thing I knew, I was nude—except for my patent leather shoes and this little hat. From there on, it was complete show biz."[31] Despite her breezy manner regarding her early days, Flo began modeling to earn money and regarded modeling as a profession. She did not want to be confused with the topless dancers for which San Francisco was famous. Nudity was central in Allen's work: "you can't think with your clothes on," she once remarked of her preference for posing nude[32] (figure 7.4), which, significantly, also paid more—75 cents per hour versus 50 cents for clothed. She also noted that "clothes didn't really make that much difference" to the outcome of the work, since when she modeled in a swimsuit for students, "the little devils would just paint in the nipples and pubic hair. Now that's what I call artistic imagination!"[33] Allen was active in securing better rates of pay for artists' models, and in 1946 she became a founding member and later president of The Bay Area Models' Guild, a San Francisco-based union that is still active and the only sustained model's union in a U.S. metropolitan area.

FIGURE 7.4 Harry Bowden, American (1907–1965), *Florence Allen posing for a drawing class at CSFA, May 4, 1948,* 1948, black and white photograph. Courtesy of the Florence Allen papers, 1920–1997, in the Archives of American Art, Smithsonian Institution.

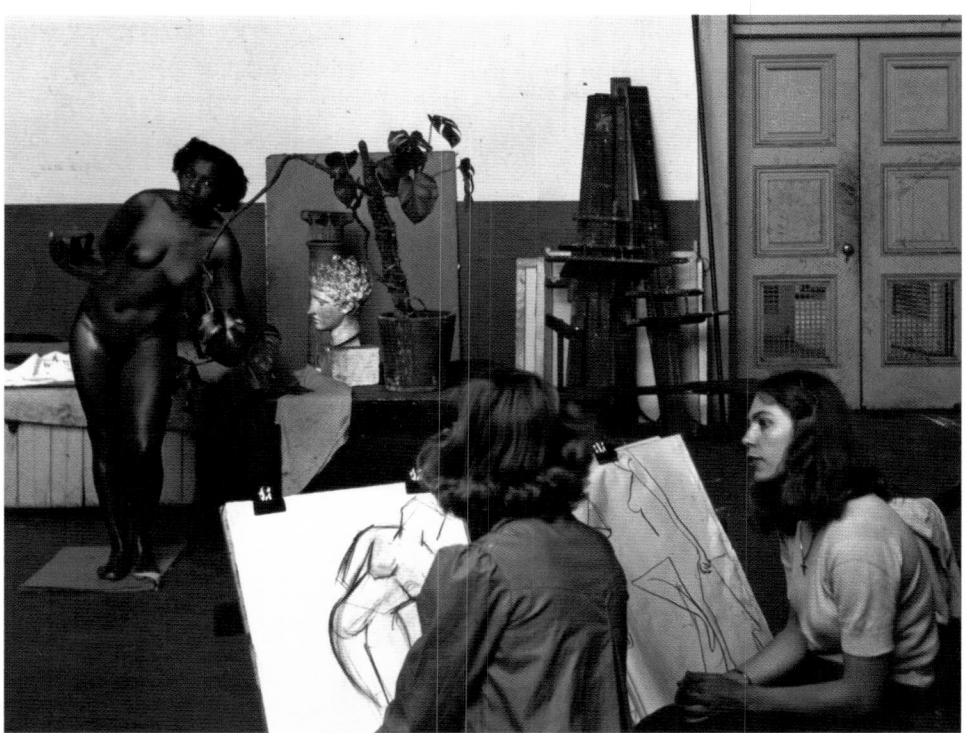

Like Maudelle, Flo did not conform to any conventions of black womanhood. Art historian Judith Wilson, who grew up in the Bay Area, recalls meeting Flo:

I remember being at the Spaghetti Factory one time with my parents—around 1964–67—and being surprised when this ebullient, dark-skinned woman spotted my dad and came over to our table. . . . What startled me was that Flo seemed so different from almost any other black woman I'd seen firsthand at that time. . . . Unlike my mom's middle-class black clubwomen friends, with their Doris Day "flips" and space helmet "bubble" hairdos, Flo's hair was pulled taut from her face and bound high on her head, ending in either some type of bun or ponytail. And, instead of the period's neatly tailored, Jackie Kennedy-style, A-line dresses, Flo wore something like a tunic-length, black knit sweater and black tights or capris—a costume that announced her boho free spirit and casual ease with her voluptuous body. I don't recall jewelry, but my impression of her as "flamboyant" makes me think she probably wore accessories that were as striking as her personality.

  After she'd left our table, I asked who she was and recall my dad answering "Flo Allen!" in tones that suggested her local celebrity or reputation as a "character." Either he or my mom explained she was an artists' model, something I knew involved the scandal of nudity.[34]

Flo, Maudelle, Streat, and Rivera all converged—though not simultaneously—at the Golden Gate International Exposition in 1939, which featured the Gay Way. This was a mile-long, circular amusement zone, which included a "Candid Camera booth," where visitors could come and photograph models.

It was there that Flo posed for one of the few photographic images of her modeling. Working in the 1970s on her never-published autobiography titled *Who's Nude*, Allen coined the term "newd" to distinguish her work from the "lewdness" of popular burlesque performers alongside whom she'd worked. After her early work at the exposition, Allen, like many artists' models, eschewed posing nude for photographers because they "can play awful tricks with it. The photographer can be ever so reputable and then put down the negative and someone superimposes it and you end up in one of those machines down at the terminal."[35] After retiring from modeling, Allen became the coordinator of models at the California College of Arts and Crafts and taught a model certification workshop in the school's extension program. "Know your body from stem to stern" was her motto/prerequisite for prospective models.[36] "There's an art to this business. There's a hell of a lot more to it than skin and bones. It's very difficult work. You find muscles you didn't know you had. Just when you think you're relaxed, the sweat starts running—and then you itch. The strain is tremendous."[37] So recognizable was she that in 1965 she was given a thirty-year career retrospective of her modeling work, and in 1987 the Stephen Wirtz Gallery in San Francisco mounted a benefit retrospective of her work.

CONCLUSION

"Florence Allen lives here. Genuflect when entering," read the sign at the top of the stairs upon entering Flo's apartment in 1967.[38] Hugely popular, well-respected, charismatic, and dynamic, Flo commanded respect from those who knew and worked with her; an artist friend made the sign that entreated visitors to "bow down" as they came near. As a black woman among mostly white artists, Flo positioned her career in a way that had little to do with racial constructions—she and the countless artists who drew, painted, or sculpted her saw in her an ideal physical type. That she was black was largely incidental. "This race business. . . . What a drag. When it really comes down to it, who belongs to what and to whom? . . . Let's face it, there are few pure Africans in America. This Duke's Mixture or mulligan has made no difference to me or to my real friends," she mused.[39]

Conversely, through her performances both as a dancer and as a model, Maudelle sought to advance an image of black women as strong, beautiful, powerful, and rooted to a tradition of dance and movement originating in Africa. Self-taught and tireless in her promotion of arts rooted in Africa, she forged an exceptional career for herself and in the process helped redefine black female sensuality and sexuality through her fearless celebration of her body.

Neither Maudelle's nor Flo's were easy or uncomplicated choices. As black artist's models beginning in the 1930s and 1940s they took off their clothes for (mostly) white men, but in doing so they were not pandering to stereotypes of black women's sexuality. As two very individual model bodies, Maudelle and Flo employed vastly different yet equally expressive strategies that radically influenced the development of black women's representation in twentieth-century American art. Though there is no direct evidence that either woman's work has influenced specific artists of younger generations (except for *this* author/artist; see plate 105), it is fair to say that the barriers through which they broke and the images they projected helped open the dialogue surrounding the representation of black women and their bodies. Would there be a Zanele Muholi (plate 122) or Renée Cox (plates 104 and 110) had there never been a Maudelle Bass or Florence Allen? It is altogether likely there would be. Our understanding of their work, however, requires an ability to place their images within an informed historical continuum to which Bass and Allen richly contributed, and we can hardly question the agency of contemporary models and performers without considering those who preceded them in their choices, especially when we have precious access to their thoughts and words regarding their work. Their legacies provide a glimpse into a period of the twentieth century in which two black female bodies came to represent an ideal, a fantasy, and ultimately themselves. 🦋

1 K. Sue Jewell, *From Mammy to Miss America and Beyond: Cultural Images and the Shaping of U.S. Social Policy* (London: Routledge, 1993).

2 Quoted in Helen Taylor, *Circling Dixie: Contemporary Southern Culture Through a Transatlantic Lens* (New Brunswick: Rutgers University Press, 2001), 3.

3 Anonymous, "The Art of Modeling," symposium discussion, The Bay Area Models Guild & Worth Ryder Gallery, University of California, Berkeley, June 24, 2004.

4 Quoted in Taylor, *Circling Dixie*, 3.

5 See Eunice Lipton, *Alias Olympia: A Woman's Search for Manet's Notorious Model & Her Own Desire* (Ithaca: Cornell University Press, 1999); Jill Berk Jiminez, ed., *Dictionary of Artists' Models* (London and Chicago: Fitzroy Dearborn Publishers, 2001).

6 Quoted in Lowery Stokes Sims, *Challenge of the Modern: African American Artists 1925–1945* (New York: The Studio Museum in Harlem, 2003), 6.

7 See Sims, *Challenge of the Modern*, 2003.

8 John O. Perpener III, *African-American Concert Dance: The Harlem Renaissance and Beyond* (Urbana and Chicago: University of Illinois Press, 2001), 9.

9 Judith Wilson, "How the Invisible Woman Got Herself on the Cultural Map: Black Women Artists in California," in *Art/Women/California, 1950–2000: Parallels and Intersections*, ed. Diana Burgess Fuller and Daniela Salvioni (Berkeley: University of California Press, 2002), 203.

10 Ibid., 209.

11 Lillian Jones, "Occupational Sketches of People in Interesting Work: Maudelle—African Dancer and Model," *The California Eagle* 59, no. 28, October 20, 1938, 1.

12 Now the Northwest College of Art.

13 The Guerrilla Girls, "Thelma Johnson Streat: Dancing on a Paintbrush," in *The Guerrilla Girls' Bedside Companion to the History of Western Art* (New York: Penguin Books, 1998), 83.

14 Ann Eden Gibson, *Abstract Expressionism: Other Politics* (New Haven and London: Yale University Press, 1997), 159.

15 The Guerrilla Girls, "Thelma Johnson Streat," 83.

16 There are more than fifty known extant images of Maudelle by different artists.

17 Amy Conger identifies Maudelle as Maudelle Weston. Maudelle Bass married Antiguan dancer and United Negro Improvement Association (UNIA) President George Weston in 1960, long after she posed for Edward Weston (no relation) and after she had stopped modeling. *Edward Weston: Photographs from the Collection of the Center for Creative Photography* (Tucson: Center for Creative Photography, the University of Arizona, 1992).

18 Jones, "Occupational Sketches of People in Interesting Work," 1.

19 Ibid.

20 Beverly A. Barber, "Pearl Primus: In Search of Her Roots, 1943–1970" (Ph.D. diss., Florida State University, 1984), 57.

21 Leah Creque-Harris, "The Representation of African Dance on the Concert Stage: From the Early Black Musical to Pearl Primus" (Ph.D. diss., Emory University, 1992), 51.

22 Jones, "Occupational Sketches of People in Interesting Work," 1.

23 In conversations with the author, several individuals who met Maudelle late in her life remember her particular concern with not having her earlier career eclipsed by that of her husband. One anecdote recounts how Maudelle pulled a handful of battered Edward Weston prints of her out of her handbag to share with a surprised visitor—their value to her was not as Weston vintage prints but rather as a record of her work.

24 Perpener, *African-American Concert Dance*, xi. Another notable dancer and artist's model was Edna Guy (1907–1982), who, though still relatively obscure, is today better known in dance circles than Maudelle. As a young girl growing up in Summit, New Jersey, Guy dreamed of becoming a modern dancer. Beginning in 1923, while a teenager, Guy began to write to her idol, the famed dancer Ruth St. Denis. Guy first met St. Denis after a concert in October 1922; she sent a note backstage during the intermission signed "Edna Guy, Colored Girl." After leaving Denishawn after six years having never danced with the company, Guy worked different odd jobs, including artist's model, while auditioning for shows for which she was routinely rejected. Guy didn't possess the fair-skinned complexion that was required of black show performers during this period. She did model, however, for artists including Miguel Covarrubias, for whom she posed nude for a group of photographs. Modeling was simply a way to make ends meet for Guy.

25 Perpener, *African-American Concert Dance*, 18.

26 This quote is from a newspaper article too closely trimmed to determine the original citation. Gregson Davis's personal papers, Chapel Hill, North Carolina.

27 Nick Nesbitt, "Negritude," Africana.com, http://www.africana.com/research/encarta/tt_242.asp, cited 09/19/2004.

28 In 1939, San Francisco Art Institute was the California School of Fine Arts. Though no evidence has yet surfaced that they knew one another, Maudelle and Flo posed there on the same days in 1939.

29 Quoted in Blake Green, "An Artist's Model Looks Back," *San Francisco Chronicle*, June 6, 1980, 28.

30 Peter Steinhart, *The Undressed Art: Why We Draw* (New York: Knopf, 2004), 123.

31 Quoted in Blake Green, "Flo Allen—First in the Art of Topless," *San Francisco Chronicle*, October 6, 1978, 29.

32 Quoted in Green, "An Artist's Model Looks Back," 28.

33 Ibid.

34 Judith Wilson, personal e-mail communication with Carla Williams, May 2005.

35 Quoted in Green, "An Artist's Model Looks Back," 29.

36 J. A. Pimsleur, "Flo Allen—Legendary Artist's Model," *San Francisco Chronicle*, June 18, 1997, A20.

37 Ibid.

38 Caroline Drewes, "The Legendary Flo Allen. . . ," *San Francisco Sunday Examiner and Chronicle*, March 19, 1967, 4.

39 Ibid.

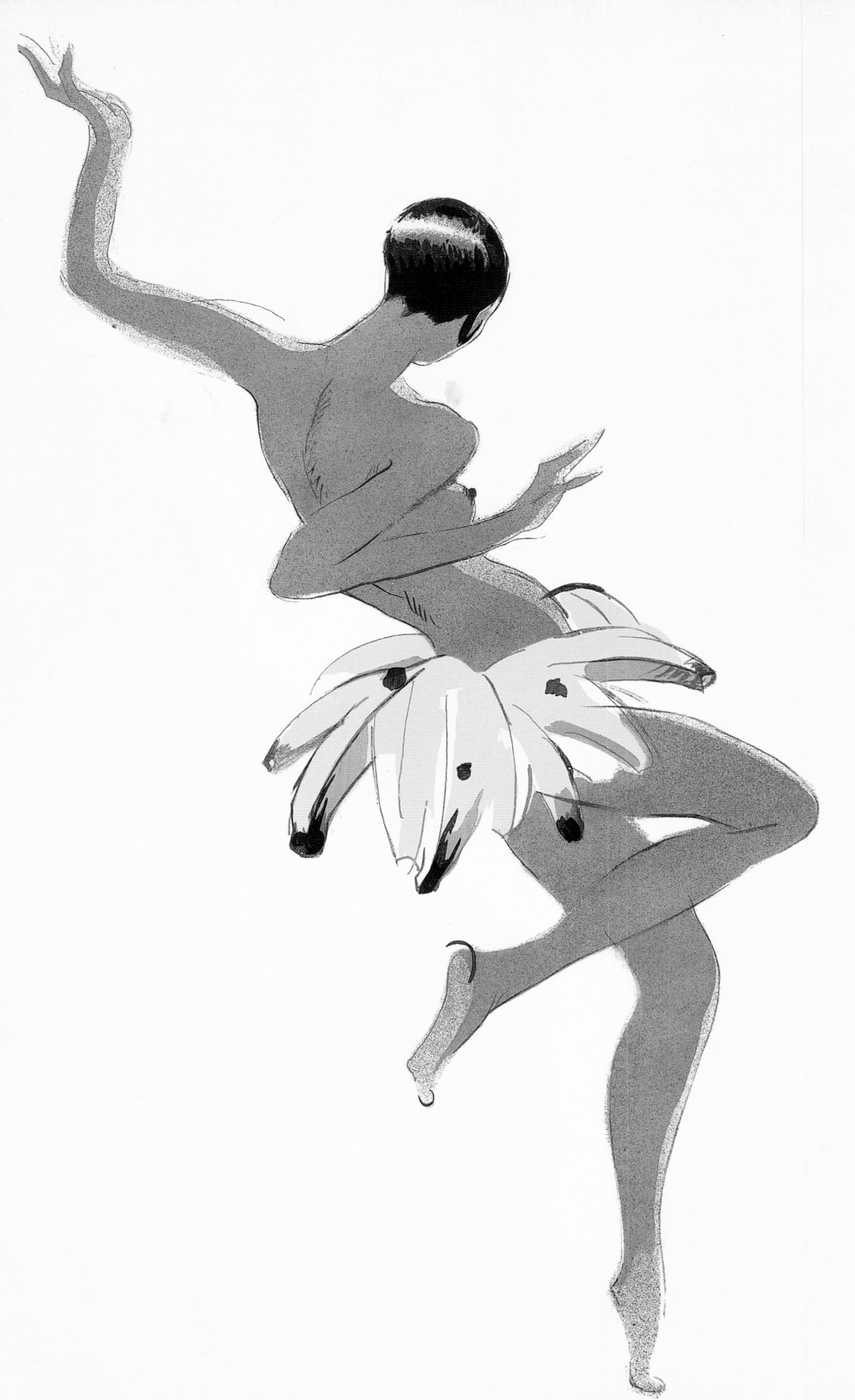

PAUL
COLIN

8   Housing and Homing the Black
    Female Body in France: Calixthe Beyala
    and the Legacy of Sarah Baartman
    and Josephine Baker

*Between. The legs. The Black woman comes to the New World with only the
body. And the space between. The European buys her not only for her strength
but also to service the Black man sexually—to keep him calm.*

— MARLENE N. PHILIP[1]

The necessity of protecting the boundaries and identity of the West informs its
different receptions of the black male and female body. If both the black woman
and black man exist within a sexualized and racialized regime of representation,
as Marlene N. Philip indicates, then the different positioning of black women
as sexual objects available to both black and white men entails and informs a
smoother circulation and reception of the black female body in the West. Indeed,
it is not accidental that the most famous and "invited over" traveling black bodies
in the history of French immigration—namely, Sarah Baartman (plate 45) and
Josephine Baker (plates 77 and 78)—are female. Nor is it coincidental that their
itineraries paralleled the trajectories of widely circulated images of African
women on colonial-era postcards sent to France.[2]

Sarah Baartman's itinerary is emblematic of the Western appropriation of
the black female body, a phenomenon that the colonial postcard dramatized after
the invention of photography in the first half of the nineteenth century. Like
Baartman, the colonial photographic subjects had little control over the trajectory
or the use of their images and bodies. Although Baartman supposedly entered in
a "contractual agreement" with the English surgeon who took her to London and
with her promoters,[3] her lack of foresight undermines any reading of agency into
these arrangements. Unaware of the fate of their portrait images, the colonial
photographic subjects in Africa were also ignorant of the larger ideological implications of their semi-nudity and poses, particularly the erotically and sexually
charged nature of these images when showcased out of context, their deployment
supporting racist and colonialist theses about primitiveness.

Unbeknownst to the photographic subjects, the editing and addition of
captions to some of these photographs expose the different agendas of the photographer and the photographic subjects.[4] For example, in a black-and-white and
a hand-colored postcard of the same two Zulu mothers (plates 79 and 80), the

opposite Paul Colin (1892–1985),
French. Josephine Baker in Banana
Skirt, from *Le Tumulte Noir*, 1929,
lithograph. Schomburg Center for
Research in Black Culture, Art and
Artifacts Division, New York Public
Library, Astor, Lenox and Tilden
Foundations. Photograph courtesy of
National Portrait Gallery © 2007
Estate of Paul Colin/Artists Rights
Society (ARS), New York/ADAGP, Paris

FIGURE 8.1 J. N. Alcobia (dates unknown), *Femmes Indigènes*, collotype, postcard, published by Maison Moura & Irmão, cancellation March 1920. Purchased through the Hood Museum of Art Acquisitions Fund; 2006.18.9.

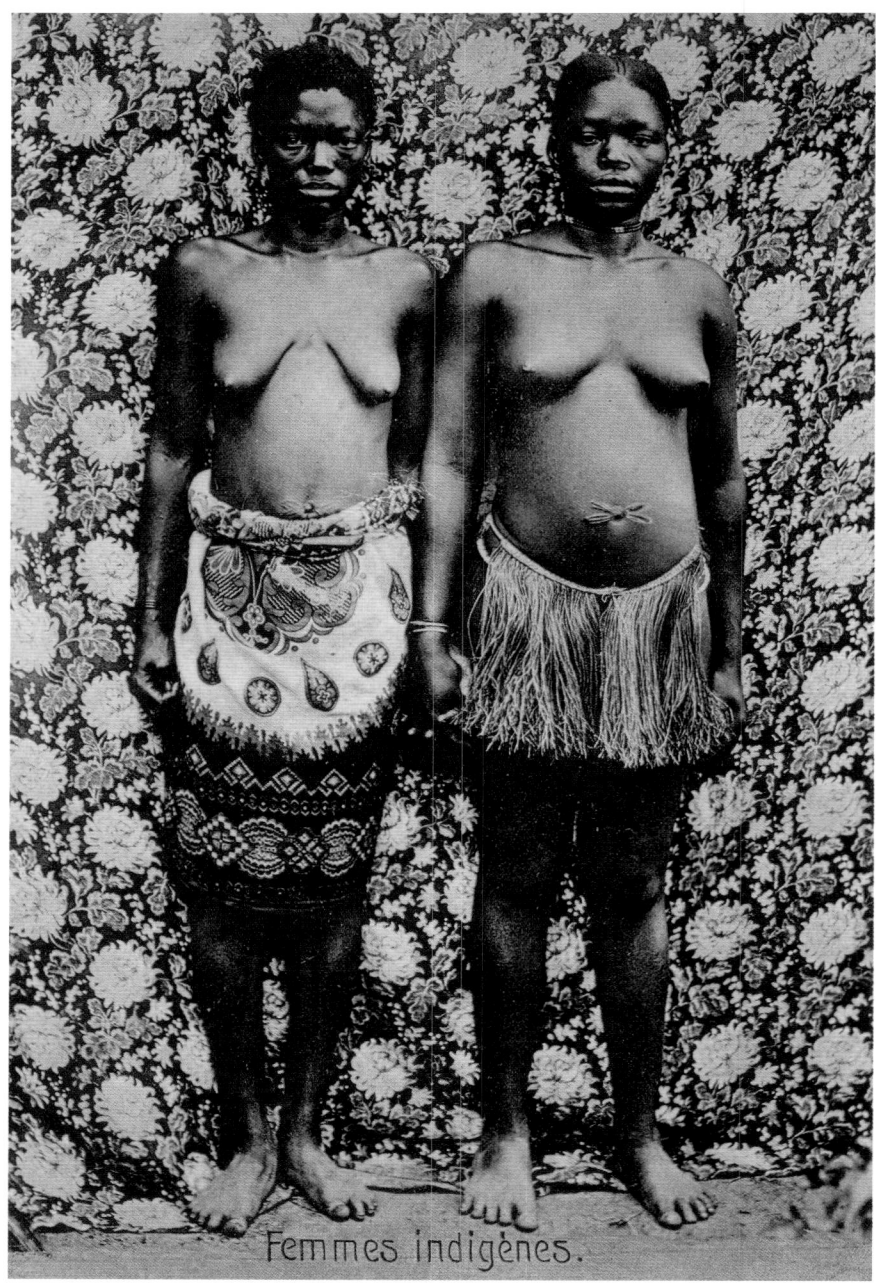

Femmes indigènes.

subjects' profile pose is similar to representations of ethnographic "types" that participated in the colonialist production and fixing of Otherness. On the colored postcard, the handwritten comment, "Are these not horrid looking creatures!" and the final version of this edited presentation of African womanhood conveyed important information about the subject's Otherness that was never provided to the photographic subject, yet was easily understood by European consumers. Similarly, the fate of Sarah Baartman as a naked body available to the Western gaze and to pursuits of "science"—an end Baartman never predicted and agreed to—calls the notion of "contractual agreement" into question.

Like Baartman, the African American performer Josephine Baker was a welcomed and popular black body on the European entertainment scene. Baker moved to Paris in 1925 and quickly rose to international fame with *La Revue Nègre*, hanging out with the likes of Picasso, Le Corbusier, and Hemingway. She toured Europe, playing into European audiences' fantasies of the black sexual primitive, a talent she also displayed in cinema with *La sirène des tropiques* (1927), *Zou Zou* (1934), and *Princesse Tam Tam* (1935). As an African American woman, Baker had already been exposed to racial politics in the United States. She thus comprehended the interface of race, gender, and sexuality in delineating the spaces of black womanhood in the West. Unlike Baartman, Baker possessed the foresight into and an astute awareness of the ideological repercussions of her staging of racial difference. She was able to profit from the sexualization of her own body by inhabiting, then manipulating the Western spaces in which she performed black womanhood. By 1927, Baker was the highest paid entertainer in Europe, the richest black woman in the world, and among the most photographed celebrities in Europe.

The resemblance between Josephine Baker's famous banana skirt, depicted in Paul Colin's lithograph of the artist (plate 78), and native clothes featured in colonial postcards (plate 50 and figure 8.1), ethnographic photographs (plate 54), and nineteenth-century sculpture from the Belgian Kongo (now Democratic Republic of Congo) (figure 8.2), suggests the ideological affiliations between the phenomenon of the colonial postcard and the black traveling bodies of Baker and Baartman. Baker's presence and survival on the French scene as a black female performer was made possible by the same craving for exoticism and Otherness that enabled and accompanied Baartman's European sojourn.

In the 1920s, European encounters with Otherness were repackaged as "primitivism," a new way to consume the Other under the cover of art and the intellectualized discourses of ethnography. Interest in primitivism quickly became part of the shaping of a sophisticated, open-minded, and modern European self.[5] During the first quarter of the twentieth century, the events of the Universal Exposition of 1900, colonial photography, Picasso's African-influenced paintings, and museum exhibitions of "*art primitif*" helped create the idea of a primitive black Africa and positioned Baker as a supplier of that idea and experience. Her performances of "*danse sauvage*" and her look of "*les sauvages*" fed into the allure of the primitive and exotic. Baker was all the more dependent on the "*sauvage*" look, which she needed to mark her African American body as an "authentic" African body. As an African American woman, she represented, for European audiences, a diluted version of Africanness, blackness, and Otherness that significantly reduced the alienation they anticipated they would experience.[6] Borrowing the "*sauvage*" look popularized by colonial-era photography and postcards as also demonstrated in museum displays of African sculpture, particularly in Paris at that time, Baker sexualized herself as a wild African, offering her audiences an intense encounter with the undiluted and unspoiled Otherness that the colonial photographs and African sculpture promised.

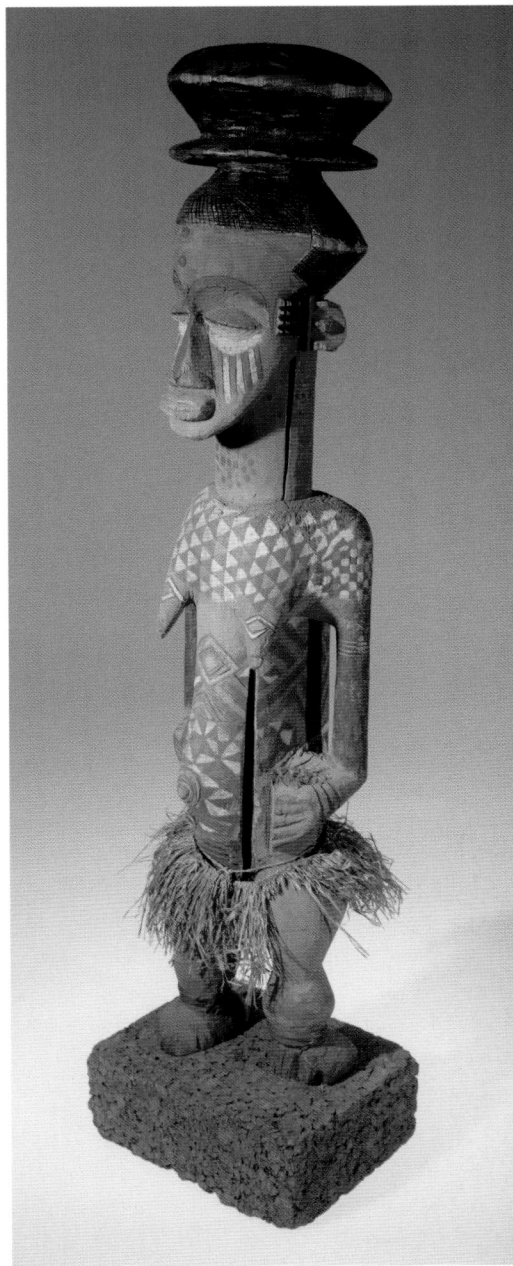

FIGURE 8.2 Unknown artist, Kuba peoples, Democratic Republic of Congo (former Belgian Congo), female figure, nineteenth century, wood. American Museum of Natural History, 90.0/5308. Photograph courtesy of American Museum of Natural History.

Colonial postcards laid the ideological foundation for the space and discursive slot that would house black womanhood in Europe. In fact, the erotic and sexual currency of the black African female body during the nineteenth century converted into an international passport that secured Baartman's and Baker's existence as travelers crisscrossing European space, ultimately housing and homing themselves in France. Baker in particular openly embraced France as home.[7]

The representation of black women as sexually available bodies in present-day European advertisements indicates that some of the same ideologies that enabled the mobility of Baartman and Baker in European society are still entrenched in current spatial politics and inform the spaces available for negotiating black womanhood in contemporary France. In Switzerland, a campaign for Chiquita bananas recycled the palatable image of Josephine Baker to sell bananas. The analogy between the consumption of bananas and the sexual enjoyment provided by the black female body perpetuates the colonial tradition of reducing the black female body to an exotic delicacy for Western palates.[8] A similar regime of representation of the black female body as a consumable product informs a magazine ad in *Lou* for lingerie and an ad for Benetton, a popular Italian clothing label (figure 8.3 and figure 5.8). The former taps into the colonial sexualization and eroticization of the African female body by luring customers with the promise of wild, uninhibited sex. The primitive look is achieved here with raffia skirts, much like those in colonial photography (plate 54 and figure 8.1), and the body posture, which evokes Josephine Baker's sexually charged *"danse sauvage."* The glossy look of the model's oiled skin further underscores her association with the highly polished surfaces of African sculptural representations of female beauty (plates 1, 5, 20, and 42), and the oiled skin of young African female initiates during dances performed in their coming-out rituals.

THE CALIXTHE BEYALA PHENOMENON

These racialized and sexualized regimes of representation inform my exploration in this essay of what I call the Calixthe Beyala phenomenon. Beyala, a prolific writer, moved from her native Cameroon to France in the mid-1980s and is today one of the very rare black African writers to make a very comfortable living from her writing. A controversial personality routinely discussed on African and Franco-African online discussion forums, Calixthe Beyala is embraced by Western audiences but disparaged by African readers, who accuse her of pandering to Western audiences with her stereotypical images of Africans and her pornographic exhibitions of African women in her novels.[9] Beyala's reception along racial lines evokes similarly mixed reviews of Baker's performances by the African American press. Film historian Charlene Regester documents the objections of "respectable" African American leaders to what they perceived as a degrading and debasing of the black female body.[10] In fact, Baker's sexually charged performances took place against the background of efforts by black women's clubs in the United States to challenge negative images of black womanhood through a de-sexualization and de-eroticization of the black female body.[11] Like Josephine Baker, Calixthe Beyala is unusually and highly visible on the French media scene, often appearing on television in a context where blacks and minorities are very much underrepresented. Since her arrival in France, the immigrant writer has quickly become one of the most recognized and welcomed black faces in France. This French hospitality extended to her subsequently allowed her to inscribe herself upon the French landscape.

In a gesture quite unusual for a postcolonial African writer, Beyala openly embraces France as home and declares herself to be fully French, particularly in *An Afro-French Woman's Letter to Her Compatriots*[12] and various media outlets, a posture of identity that recalls Josephine Baker's. By adopting French citizenship and working undercover as a courier for the Resistance during World War II, Baker both affirmed and enacted her belonging to the French nation. In her biography of Baker, Phyllis Rose argues that Josephine Baker had become "more French than the French."[13] Along the same lines, cultural anthropologist Benetta Jules-Rosette writes that the two versions of Baker's song *J'ai deux amours* ("I have two loves") capture her orientation towards France. The concluding refrain of the early version was "I have two loves; my country and Paris." In the mid-1930s, Baker changed this refrain to "My country is Paris."[14]

Beyala's embrace of France as home clashes with both postcolonial identity politics and the experiences of racialized immigrants in France. At the same time, this French hospitality begs the question of the relocation of the black female body to France. Which bodies are allowed in? Is the "in" body a docile body? Does housing and homing the black female body in France entail accepting and reinforcing racialized and sexualized regimes of representations? Or, to borrow from cultural theorist Stuart Hall's question, "Can a dominant regime of representation be challenged, contested or changed?"[15]

The how and why of the French space Calixthe Beyala inhabits have attracted critical scrutiny, often in the form of acerbic and non-constructive attacks, which sometimes fail to capture the complexity of the text and performance that Calixthe Beyala constitutes.[16] In a highly informative and perceptive article on Beyala's French television appearances, literary scholar Nicky Hitchcott refreshingly breaks the trend as she documents the relation of love and seduction between Beyala and the smitten French media, which embraces her as "an icon of African femininity in France."[17] Hitchcott's study of Beyala's television performances shows that the writer's sexualized and eroticized physical features always take center stage: the interviewers comment on her looks, the camera zooms in on her legs, and the erotic aspects of her novels are overemphasized. Hitchcott appropriately sees residues of Sarah Baartman and colonial fantasy here. Even more troubling for Hitchcott is Beyala's own complicity—she flirts with presenters and makes such outrageously racially and sexually charged declarations as "we fuck really well"[18] in reference to sexual practices among Africans.

But Hitchcott presents Beyala as a confused soul, "uncertain about how to position herself in the French public eye and within the French nation."[19] On the

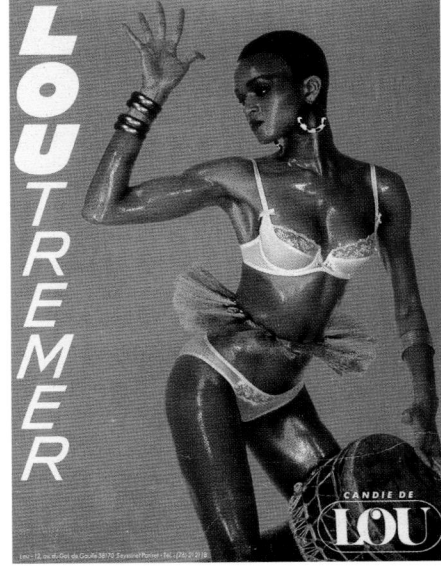

FIGURE 8.3 Unknown photographer, *Lou Tremer* (cover of *Lou* magazine), 1983. Photograph courtesy of Bibliothèque Forney, Ville de Paris.

other hand, I grant Beyala more agency and control in the fabrication and manipulation of these representations as well as in her deployment of the iconic black female body. Jules-Rosette approaches Josephine Baker from a similar vantage point and further reinforces my reading of Beyala and Baker together.[20] Jules-Rosette argues that Baker's "clever use of performative strategies of assimilation and doubling to surmount cultural barriers" are often overlooked.[21] She makes the relevant argument for my analysis of Beyala's performative image that Baker used race as "a series of costume changes."[22] Baker's use of native costumes as part of her act and her performances of different images of black womanhood, from "the animal-like stereotype of the exotic banana dancer" to the "all-too-human sophistication of a worldly Princesse Tam-Tam"[23] echo Beyala's performative identity practices.

I read Beyala against the background of the fetishization of the black female body in France, but I also attach her to a tradition of black female performers in France. While there are a number of studies on the representation and consumption of black female bodies, including Baker's and Baartman's,[24] fewer posit that these women gaze back at their spectators and actively deploy their bodies to achieve higher ends. Among such ends is the destabilization of hegemonic distributions and arrangements of space. When the colonized body, otherwise kept at bay, tactically lets itself into and settles in the dominant structure, it disrupts the self-production, perception, and projection of the metropolitan center as a mono-chromatic and mono-cultural body. As Smadar and Swedenburg write, "The savage is no longer out there but has invaded the home here and has fissured it in the process,"[25] particularly in their parody of the dreaded renegotiation of metropolitan space and identities as racialized populations setting up house in the heart of whiteness.

Beyala's August 2000 television appearance with host Philippe Bouvard offers such a moment of fracturing French identity. Following years of tactically working and performing herself into a place in the dominant structure of power where she is highly visible and audible, Beyala, now a recognized figure in France, came out on national French television and almost maliciously confronted the French spectators with a reconfigured Frenchness:

> I am more French than you are. I have a better knowledge of French culture than 90 percent of my [French] compatriots. So, am I an immigrant? I don't think so! Calling me an immigrant is almost an insult. I am not an immigrant to France. This is my home. It is my homeland. I love her. I live her and this is where I claim my rights. And let me add, Phillipe, that if I did not contend that much, I would not be a true French.[26]

The outspokenness of Beyala is in line with her recent political and social activism in France. Since the mid-1990s, the writer has been actively campaigning for the rights of minorities in France. Beyala is not a confused victim who has fallen prey to French neocolonial fantasies, as Hitchcott might contend. In her novels, beneath her tactical recycling of colonialist images of African women, she displays a sophisticated awareness and understanding of the sexualization of black women. My reading of Beyala as a text, side by side with the itineraries that she charts for her African female protagonists in her fictional novels set in France, further privileges the agency of the female performer over the authority of the (French) consumers of the spectacle of black womanhood that the writer both directs and stages herself in. I also emphasize her strategic deployment and reappropriation of the black female body as a space-clearing tool. Hers is the same tactic used also by contemporary black visual artists in the exhibition *Black Womanhood*.

Beyala's tactic has been to carve herself a space within the center of French culture, firmly anchoring herself in its heart. She then recuperates that space as a site of resistance. I use "tactic" here in Michel De Certeau's sense of the term, meaning subversive actions undertaken on the territory of the dominant:

> The space of a tactic is the space of the other. Thus it must play on and with a terrain imposed on it and organized by the law of a foreign power. It does not have the means to keep to itself, at a distance, in a position of withdrawal, foresight, and self-collection: it is a maneuver "within the enemy's field of vision,". . . and within enemy territory . . . it must vigilantly make use of the cracks that particular conjunctions open in the surveillance of the proprietary powers. It poaches in them. It creates surprises in them. It can be where it is least expected. It is a guileful ruse. In short, a tactic is an art of the weak.[27]

Calixthe Beyala and her writing are very much trivialized. Yet I would argue that her media performances and novels tactically invite that trivialization, which subsequently allows her to operate "within enemy territory." De Certeau's "art of the weak" is indeed the art of the trickster, a figure whose complexity and sharpness is better captured by Eshu, the mischievous trickster-god of Yoruba mythology in Nigeria. Eshu's geographical location at the crossroad makes him highly relevant to the tactics and spatial practices of Beyala and her migrant female protagonists. Eshu's liminal location allegorizes his propensity to change his form at will and deactivate different identities as the situation demands to confuse people and blend into any space. I will examine specifically Beyala's migrant female protagonists in her novel *Amours Sauvages* (1999) as trickster-tacticians who, like Beyala herself, perform themselves in and out of places. Of particular interest to me are their space-clearing tactics. Beyala's female protagonists reclaim the black female body from a colonized state to articulate cartographies of resistance, producing subversive geographies and oppositional spaces of belonging where the migrant black female body can home and centralize itself.

TACTICS OF INSERTION INTO DOMINANT SPACE

Eve-Marie, the narrator and main protagonist of *Amours Sauvages,* is a voluptuous prostitute turned writer. Like most of Beyala's migrant women from Africa, she is married to a French man, who gave her a way out of prostitution and into a

French home. The African women who populate Beyala's immigrant milieu are prostitutes, performers, domestic workers, mistresses, and partners of French men. Of course, these different activities and roles that Beyala proscribes for black women in France capitalize on the well-recognized racialized and sexualized economy of representation, stereotypes that have been inscribed upon them since at least the nineteenth century in colonial literature, photography, and ethnographic narratives, an economy within which these women still exist. These roles constitute points of insertion into France.

The alleged tameness and exotic/erotic currency of the black female body and the hospitality subsequently extended to it by French hosts often allow these women to move away from the peripheral, well-contained, and policed immigrant milieu, thereby enabling them to position themselves within non-immigrant French space, households, and homes. Thus, in *Amours Sauvages*, Eve-Marie preys on the desires of French men for the exotic black female body: "I auctioned away my enormous negress buttocks."[28] Pléthore, Eve-Marie's French husband, exhibits a fetishist obsession with the black female body. He insists on his wife keeping a plump body, so she overeats to the point of obesity. While drawing a portrait of Eve-Marie, Pléthore inscribes his fantasies for Sarah Baartman on his wife's body:

> He waved the drawing under my nose: "That's you, darling! You are gorgeous!" I was puzzled. This woman could have been me, or any Hottentot Venus. Pléthore insisted that she looked like me and was my portrait. From then on, he drew me everywhere . . . even while I lay naked on the couch. "Ah, Ah! we will be wealthy, beautiful and famous!" he said the day he managed to sell a rough sketch to a Jew from the Sentier who fantasized about negro behinds. . . . He was such a naïve imbecile that I almost bought him a Trivial Pursuit or a plastic car toy.[29]

Beyala's narrative material for this scene directly borrows from the archives of the visual history of the black female body in France, with Eve-Marie being a composite of Baartman and Baker while Paul Colin—the French artist who captured Baker's banana skirt performance in his hand-colored portfolio of lithographs, *Le Tumulte Noir* from 1927 (see plate 78)—resurfaces in her husband. The gap between Eve-Marie's self-perception and her husband's perception of her is illuminating. Eve-Marie's diagnosis of her husband's imbecility, unbeknownst to him, is a reversal of the gaze and further establishes her as an agent and not a victim. She is, like Calixthe Beyala, a producer, a stage manager, and, like Baker, an actress in her own spectacle of Otherness.

The sophistication Eve-Marie displays informs my reading of the symbolism of prostitution in the novel. The prostitute's relation to space is fluid. She is a streetwalker who enjoys geographical mobility and has access to different socio-economic spaces because her clientele spans diverse backgrounds. In fact, the practice of space that prostitution entails evokes De Certeau's tactic. For Beyala's prostitutes, social boundaries are porous, since these women have access to different strata of the population. They are often able to relocate to higher social classes, exchanging prostitution for middle-class or upper-class status and lifestyle. Beyala's protagonists Eve-Marie in *Amours Sauvages* and Aminata in the novel *Le Petit Prince de Belleville* (1992) follow such an itinerary. Through her marriage to Pléthore, Eve-Marie leaves prostitution for a new social status and realizes her ambition of respectability: "Now that I was happily married, I would have a decent burial."[30] Beyala herself, in an interview, states that Eve-Marie's itinerary as a prostitute is irrelevant. What matters, instead, is that she has reached her final destination, meaning her successful integration to French society:

> I have created Eve-Marie as an homage to those black women who leave Africa without luggage and who succeed in making the best out of that situation with very meager resources. Eve-Marie . . . symbolizes the majority of those black women. They don't all become prostitutes. Some of them do, but this is not their ultimate goal in life. Their goal is integration to a new civilization and securing a future.[31]

Calixthe Beyala's prostitutes are more than sex workers. Prostitution becomes an elastic notion that encompasses a number of performative roles and relations. The symbol of prostitution allegorizes Beyala's own position as a commodified and exoticized writer. In fact, Eve-Marie the prostitute is also a writer. Beyala thus suggests a resonance between the commodified black body and black writer, between prostitution as an economic venture and exoticism as a means of literary existence and survival. Beyala, for instance, has made a career of and cashed in on the abused, grotesque, and exoticized bodies of African women. Her novel *Femme Nue, Femme Noire* (*Nude Woman, Black Woman*) (2001), which she claims is the first African erotic novel, borders on the pornographic through its graphic and detailed descriptions of the sexual experimentations of the bisexual female protagonist. Thus, the merging between prostitution and literary exotic eroticism is tightened again. The book was an instant success, almost immediately translated into Italian and German. The writer's description in her novels of the "consumers" of black bodies as "*Blancs à Négresses*,"or "Negress-lovers,"[32] and "*névrosés de Négresses*," or "Negress-neurotics,"[33] is, in fact, a shot at the Otherness-craving readers to whom she caters.

Looking beyond Beyala's recreations of stereotypical representations, we need to focus on the structural and material conditions that fostered the problematic and limited options that Beyala charts for black African womanhood today. The African woman's body is a site for the writer to address the gendered postcolonial condition but also the collusion between African and Western forces on the body of the African woman.[34] In a sense, the West is a contributor to the disastrous conditions within the postcolony that force many African women to relocate to the West. The Western colonial and neocolonial tampering with the structures of colonized societies, including gender arrangements, largely contributed to those very conditions that turned home into an oppressive place for African women.[35] These same conditions obliquely allowed the West to subsequently position itself as the rescuing hand around the colonialist paradigm of "White men . . . saving Brown women from Brown men."[36] In the postcolonial context Beyala describes, white men are no longer saving brown women from brown men; instead, brown women are saving themselves from an agonizing postcolonial Africa via white men.[37]

Prostitution, then, as Beyala uses it, is a commentary on the interplay between the operations of global capitalism and both the field of cultural production and the circulation of exotic bodies as commodities. The exotic writer and body are subject to the laws of global capitalism; lacking a "proper locus," they exist on the terrain organized by these laws.[38] Of course, the French philosopher Michel Foucault would position these bodies as prisoners and products of the dominant system, through which cooperation produces docile bodies.[39] The itineraries and spatial practices of Beyala and Eve-Marie's character, however, contradict Foucault's repressive disciplinary model, restoring the Western-homed African woman as an agent-tactician—not a panopticon-situated subject. The prostitute and the exoticized writer are practitioners of De Certeau's "art of the weak," which allows disenfranchised people to "reappropriate the space organized by techniques of sociocultural production" through a variety of practices undetectable by the dominant group.[40] We know that such practices of identities as Eve-Marie, whom Beyala later declares in the interview to be as French as any French (in a gesture similar to the writer's and Josephine Baker's own in-your-face self-positioning as French), defy national articulations of identity that equate Frenchness with whiteness. Hence, such integrations can only be achieved tactically as clandestine subversive activities. The metaphor of prostitution is quite fitting, then, since prostitution is a clandestine activity.

Calixthe Beyala's skillful recuperation of the prostitute and the black body and her positioning of Eve-Marie as tactician who clandestinely lets herself into the dominant space and transforms it to accommodate her as home are further reinforced with the metaphor of the *maquis*. In Francophone Africa, *maquis* are clandestine or non-regulated informal restaurants that people sometimes open in their houses. Eve-Marie opens a *maquis* in the apartment she occupies with her French husband while her next-door neighbors are French xenophobes. The definition of the term "*maquis*" in the *Dictionary of Word Origins* provides further insights:

> The French word *maquis* literally means "undergrowth, scrub," and its use for the resistance fighters who opposed German occupation during World War II is an allusion to their hide-outs in scrubby country. It is a borrowing, via Corsica, of Italian *machia*. This originally meant "spot" (it came from Latin *macula*, "spot, stain,". . .), but was transferred metaphorically to a "bush or thicket seen from the distance as a spot on the hillside."[41]

That Eve-Marie the "prostitute" converges with Eve-Marie the "*maquisarde*" is therefore logical. The *maquis*, which uses guerilla tactics, is an "art of the weak" that entails a clandestine and subversive practice of space. As a spot on the landscape, the *maquis* stains the visual uniformity of the landscape and is a signifier of contamination and impurity. As such, the *maquis* allegorizes the transformation of the French ethno-racial landscape through the emergence of cartographies of resistance that sabotage the hegemonic/monochromatic production and perpetuation of France, Frenchness, and whiteness.

THE BLACK FEMALE BODY AS CARTOGRAPHY OF RESISTANCE

As a way of dramatizing the black female body as cartography of resistance, the female characters that populate Beyala's immigrant universes are often grotesque. Eve-Marie inscribes on the French landscape her large and pitch-dark body, which she dresses in loud colors and patterns. Beyala reproduces the colonial imagery of the grotesque African body, virtually superimposing her migrant African female protagonists with the body of Sarah Baartman (plate 45 and figure 1.1) and thus feeding into French narratives of the grotesque African body. The body of Baartman filled the Parisian scene and imagination almost two centuries before Beyala and her protagonists came to occupy the same space. Beyala's superimposition of contemporary bodies in France with nineteenth-century representations of black female bodies and spaces magnifies the persistence of colonialist ideologies of black womanhood today. As a matter of fact, the display of Baartman's body in the Musée de l'Homme and its delayed repatriation indicates that the spaces that black womanhood in contemporary France has to negotiate cannot be separated from the history of Sarah Baartman's encounter with Europe.

But Beyala reinvents the grotesque black traveling body as a resistant body. In her novels, the black and white female bodies occupy space differently. In opposition to the emaciated, almost invisible figures of white French women, the large black female body is forcibly a voracious consumer of space. Its imposing and noticeable presence entails a redistribution of space at the expense of white bodies. In Beyala's novels, the expanding cartography of blackness parallels a shrinking cartography of whiteness.

Beyala's images of the expanding African female body evoke the semiotics of the imposing body in some African cultures.[42] For example, the postcard in plate 50 features a young woman in a native dress of layered textiles. Like the layering of clothes and the big West African *boubous*, this dress practice produces imposing and charismatic bodies whose occupation of space mark them as important (plates 55, 56, and 57). The Nigerian artist Sokari Douglas Camp demonstrates this in her sculpture *Gelede From Top to Toe* (plate 96), which features the voluminous form of the layered female body.[43] The semiotics of the imposing body often mediated the relationship between the colonial photographer and the photographic subject, allowing the latter to exercise some degree of control over his/her image. The seated women in the two postcards in plates 55 and 56 have spread their legs to expand their occupation of space, thereby creating the image of importance for themselves but also for the expected African viewers—her intended audience—of the picture. The self-positioning of these women neutralizes the colonialist gazes of the photographer and colonialist audiences. Producing and imposing their bodies as charismatic bodies, the two women disable colonialist recuperations and reductive readings of their images.[44]

DECOMPOSING AND RECOMPOSING
VISUAL SIGNS OF BLACK WOMANHOOD

Besides producing France as a space both visually disharmonious and carnivalesque, the loud presence of the African body in Beyala's texts dramatizes the alterity of the new French nationals and the Africans' resistance to assimilation through such exaggerated features as Maimouna's "huge lips that could serve as seats"[45] in Beyala's *Comment Cuisiner son Mari a l'Africaine*[46] and Mlle Babylisse's "huge braids" from *Les Honneurs Perdus*.[47] The writer's isolation of and comments on specific parts of the black woman's body comprise a critical satire of ethnographic typing that illuminates the workings of the "science" of ethnography and anthropometry and their alliance with colonialist discourses. In the ethnographer's case, the use of corporeal fragmentation and exaggeration intensified racial differences to preserve the boundary of race. In her novels, Beyala constantly overemphasizes parts of the black woman's anatomy (buttocks, breasts, and lips), purposefully setting them apart from the rest of the body so that they emerge as additions or touch-ups. This intentional exaggeration is part of an emerging artistic and intellectual tactic of commenting on and subverting the colonial production, assemblage, and editing of the black female body and the recycling of stereotypical images of African and black women.

Like Beyala's purposeful exaggerations of those parts of the black female anatomy singled out by the colonial gaze, Renée Cox's *Hot-En-Tot* (plate 104) dramatizes the intensity of the colonial gaze on the breasts and buttocks as part of the Western racialized production of black womanhood. The flagrantly assembled bodies of Cox's *Hot-En-Tot* and Beyala's black female protagonists are direct appropriations of French impressions of Baartman and reenactments of Cuvier's dissection of her body. But these postcolonial reenactments of Cuvier's gestures are meant to break down the colonial visual code of black womanhood. Literary scholar Henry Louis Gates Jr.'s theory of "signifyin(g)"[48] encourages reading Cox's and Beyala's recycling of colonial visual discourses as decompositions and recompositions of racist visual signs of black womanhood. In *The Signifying Monkey* (1988), Gates presents "signifyin(g)" as a black vernacular rhetorical strategy that consists in revising meaning by "troping" the master tropes to reverse them. "Signifyin(g)" relies on such rhetorical devices as repetition, hyperbole, parody, metaphor, and doubling to allow the black cultural producer to "repeat and reverse simultaneously as he does in one deft discursive act."[49]

Beyala and Cox trope the master colonialist trope of the black female body through repetition with difference. The parody consists here in the fact that the new copy uses hyperbole in the form of repeated exaggerations of distinct body parts of black women to redirect the gaze of the viewers/readers back to the original producer of the image. The latter is thus reconfigured as a site of critical intervention. The repetition also reverses by uncovering and dramatizing the fabricated nature of the original image. The visible white thread that holds the breasts and buttocks of the *Hot-En-Tot* and Beyala's overtly flagrant and overemphatic repetitions of colonialist and racist clichés and her description of her African female protagonists along the lines of ethnographic "types" are rhetorical strategies that magnify the colonial thread running through the visual signs of black womanhood and the reduction of the black female body into fragmented sexual parts.

The Western colonizing gaze de-aestheticizes the black female body by approaching it through the prism of Western aesthetic ideals. For Beyala and Cox, "signifyin(g)" the black female body entails the rejection of Western beauty ideals as a prerequisite to embracing and reclaiming the black female body. Renée Cox's proud *Hot-En-Tot* and the voluptuous black female protagonists of Calixthe Beyala in her novels *Les honneurs perdus, Amours sauvages,* and *Assèze l'Africaine* are relocated into an Afrocentric regime of representation. This is a gesture of re-mapping the black female body, enacting its affiliation to and existence within African aesthetic ideals. Even in exile, as is the case with the diasporic bodies of Beyala and her female protagonists, the black female body proudly resists interpellation and transformation by Western space. Beyala's writing of France as a carnivalesque space and the defiant features of Renée Cox's *Hot-En-Tot* magnify the black female body inhabiting Western space without it being inhabited by Western space.

Cox and Beyala "signify" the colonial icon of Sarah Baartman into a postcolonial icon for Western constructions of Otherness. The colonial fixation on Sarah Baartman's exaggerated body parts and "grotesquerie" mirrors the production of the bare-chested African woman as a paradigm through the recurrent and predominant portrayal of topless African women on colonial postcards (plates 83 and 84). One set of postcards by the French colonial photographer François-Edmond Fortier magnifies the production of the bare-chested African woman as part of the colonial appropriation, rearrangement, and production of the black female body, with the same "Arab" woman posing clothed (plate 68) and then bare-chested (plate 69).[50] Two other postcards by Fortier feature three females—a child, an adolescent, and an adult—first wearing their usual, everyday clothing (plate 93) and then stripped of their blouses (plate 92). The Western blouses that the women probably wore to the photography studio do not fit the Western perception of the exotic African untouched by European civilization and culture. The second picture exposes the editing of African cultures and womanhood to produce a version of Africa—epitomized by topless black women—more palatable to Western audiences. In yet other postcards, the women are clearly posing in ways that emphasize their breasts (plates 91 and 95).

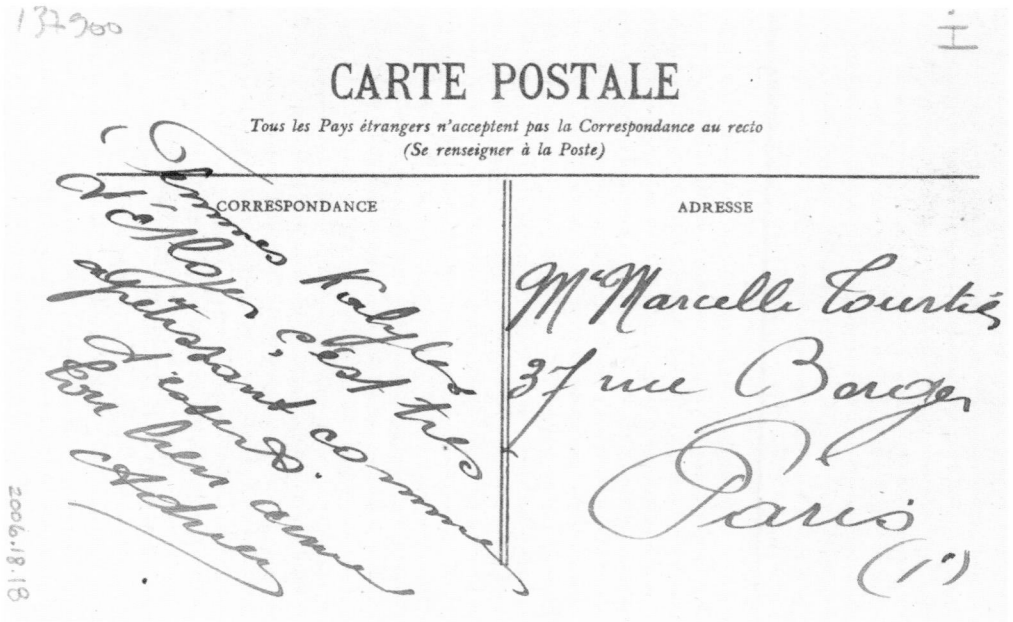

5111. - TYPES. - Femmes Kabyles - E. S.

These various colonial representations of black womanhood participated in the formation of Western consumers of the black female body and subsequently catered to the needs of these audiences, from fulfilling their fantasies to entertaining them. The captions about "types" on many colonial-era post-cards show the production and fixing of the native woman as a body perpetually available to serve the sexual desires of men. These fantasies of unlimited and total possession are revealed in their forcefulness with the merger between the bodies of the native woman and the prostitute. Many of these North African "type" postcards, like figure 8.4a, were depictions of women from the entertainment and prostitution quarters of Algeria. This conflation of the prostitute body with the racialized body participated in the pathologization of black womanhood in the nineteenth century.[51] Literary scholar T. Denean Sharpley-Whiting persuasively argues that this pathologization crystallized the ambivalent relationship that European males developed with the black female body. The European male psyche is torn between a desire to possess and know the mysterious black female body and the restrictive codes of social morality that police sexual behavior and construct racial sexual promiscuity as unlicensed sexual activity.[52] The black female body is then made to bear the marks of that thwarted desire through a "projection of the undesirable into the desired, yet feared

FIGURE 8.4 Unknown photographer, *5111.—TYPES. — Femmes Kabyles— E. S.* [5111.—Types. —Kabyle Women—E. S.], early twentieth century, collotype, postcard, a) *recto* and b) *in verso*. Purchased through the Hood Museum of Art Acquisitions Fund; 2006.18.18.

CARTE POSTALE

Tous les Pays étrangers n'acceptent pas la Correspondance au recto
(Se renseigner à la Poste)

CORRESPONDANCE   ADRESSE

object."[53] Hence, racialized women "came to represent that which the European male could not articulate without psychic crises: uninhibited sexuality. And uninhibited sexuality is presumably a characteristic of the prostitute."[54]

On the back of the postcard in figure 8.4b, the sender has written: "Kabyle women from Algeria. A very tasty dessert"![55] The comment reveals the sender's partaking of the "dessert," either in fact or in fantasy. This postcard reenacts the reception, commodification, and consumption of Baartman's body and image in England and France, but also of Baker, which the Sudanese artist Hassan Musa allegorizes in *Mission Paris-Afrique*, a caricature of French ethnographer Michel Leiris "verifying the authenticity of Josephine Baker's bananas" (figure 8.5). Leiris was among the French intellectuals who gravitated toward and formed the audience of black and African cultures and primitivism in 1920s Paris. Musa's positioning of Leiris in his painting—looking at Baker from behind, an angle from which Baartman is also viewed in figure 1.1—stresses the continuity between the audiences who saw Baartman and Baker and the repackaging of nineteenth-century ideologies of the black female body as primitivism in the twentieth century.

Musa's *Allégorie à la Banane* (plate 106) further resonates with Beyala's location of the African female body within a global economic circuit. Musa superimposes the painted image of Josephine Baker, based on the famous Walery photographs (see plate 77), on an economic map of Africa. In this work, Baker is leaving the African continent, following the westward movement of its natural resources. Musa, who like Beyala lives and works in France, teases out the relationship between the commodification of African female bodies—particularly as sexually charged commodities that entertain Western audiences—and the operations of global capitalism that plunder the human and natural resources of the continent. Josephine Baker's figurative journey into and out of Africa shows how the continent functions as one of her many black costumes, in this case the primitive and exotic black costume that Beyala inherits and cashes in on sixty years later.

Like Musa's *Allégorie*, the thematization of ethnic foodways in the novels of Calixthe Beyala constitutes a comment on her Western reception and canonization as an exotic writer, and the subsequent trivialization of her texts as exotic cuisine for Otherness-craving Western readers. For instance, Christian Charrière's favorable review of Beyala's *Les Honneurs Perdus* in *Le figaro Littéraire* describes the novel as "a very original and savory novel: this is a combination of caiman and fresh cream."[56] The culinary metaphor here, in Beyala's texts as in Musa's painting, "testifies to the commodification of non-Western cultural expressions and their availability for consumption if they are to succeed on the Western market."[57] The metaphor also speaks to the laws of supply and demand that regiment the circulation and hosting of black female bodies in France as exotic specialties and delicacies.

In *Colonial Desire*, Robert Young excavates and analyzes the coupling of race and sexuality in colonial discourses of race.[58] He concludes that desire for the Other was deeply embedded in theories of race. As such, the black female body

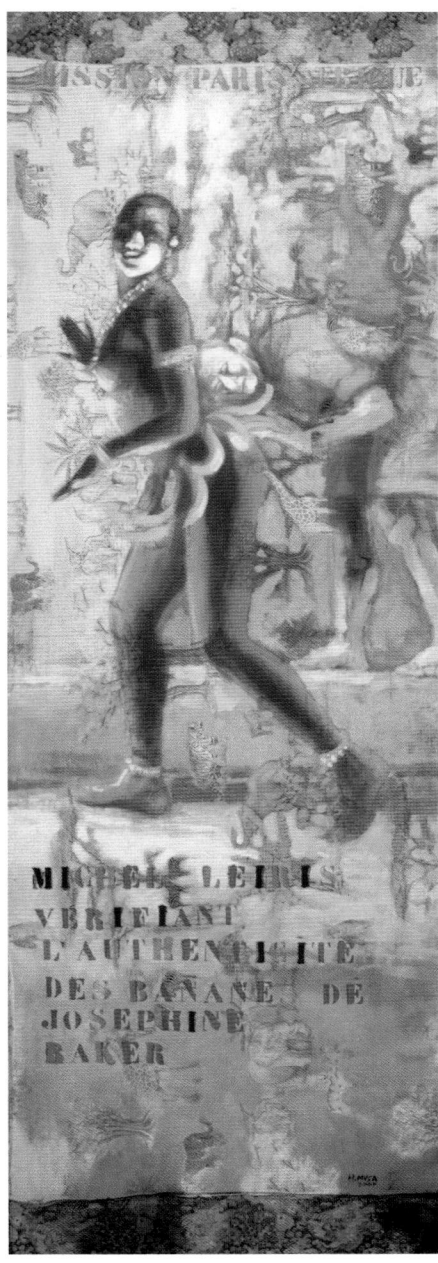

FIGURE 8.5 Hassan Musa, Sudanese (born 1951), *Mission Paris-Afrique* (detail), 2002, ink on textile. Photograph courtesy of Hassan Musa.

is a montage and collage that documents a history of the fantasies and neuroses of white male subjects. In sum, the black female body has become a history of white desire because it has functioned as a sublimated outlet of white libidinal energies, a function aptly conveyed in Musa's *Allégorie a la Banane* and Brett Berliner's reference to the African woman's body as the "metropolitan's ethno-erotic playground."[59] Thus, highlighting the different touch-ups to which the black female body has been constantly subjected, artists such as Beyala, Cox, and Musa document the repressions and expressions of white desire. Calixthe Beyala's novels, very much like Cox's photographs and Musa's paintings, uncover the black female body as a supplemented body in French philosopher Jacques Derrida's sense of the word, revising Jean-Jacques Rousseau's notion of the supplement as an inessential extra added to something complete in itself.[60] Derrida argues that to supplement something necessarily entails adding to it with the purpose of completing it, since what is complete in itself cannot be added to—the supplement can only occur when there is an original lack.[61] Whereas Derrida focuses on the supplementee as being constituted by lack, the collages of Beyala, Cox, and Musa redirect our gazes back to the supplementer. The lucid gaze of Cox's *Hot-En-Tot* and Musa's Josephine and the sarcastic gaze that Eve-Marie directs to both her husband and his fellow "negrified Whites" narrate the hollowness and lack of the white subject. The supplemented black body, then, (ful)fills the fantasies of the hollow white subject.

My reading of Beyala's tactical and skillful deployment of the exotic black female body as a site of resistance and re-territorialization is conducted against the background of a solid line of scholarship that vigorously exposes the commodification of Otherness. bell hooks's essay "Eating the Other" is an emblematic piece that offers a cohesive articulation of these concerns. Whereas I have been arguing that exoticism tactically destabilizes dominant identities, hooks is adamant that the commodification of racial, ethnic, and cultural differences is at the expense of the Other. hooks certainly has a point, but at the same time that she talks about the "cultural appropriation of the Other,"[62] the "exploitation of Otherness,"[63] and "consumer cannibalism,"[64] she overlooks the agency of the Other and the complex dynamics between consumer and supplier of consumed goods. In hooks's analysis, the Other's place within this chain is that of consumed goods supplied by white merchants to white consumers.

From my analysis of Beyala, and as visually demonstrated by Cox and Musa, it is apparent that critical tools relying on Manichean approaches fail to account for the complexity of the relationship between the different parties implicated in the marketplace. This complex interaction is a result of the spectrum of unstable and multiple positions each party occupies. Similarly, the exotic Other exists on the marketplace not as consumed goods only, but also as manufacturer, marketer, and supplier of these goods, as Schildkrout also demonstrates in her essay. The exotic Other is the Deleuzean "schizocapitalist subject," a "desirable product that produces desire."[65] This active role on the marketplace entails the production and channeling of flows of desire and the fabrication of authentic Otherness through the exaggeration and invention of difference. In Olu Oguibe's words, individuals marked as Other by dominant groups often "decide to play the Other."[66] I take his important observation one step further and interpret the notion of "playing the Other" as meaning both performing the Other and fooling another individual, in this case the dominant group or gullible consumer of Otherness. Along similar lines, Beyala's thematization of performance in her novels is a commentary on the shrewdness of the Other and the naïveté of the dominant group, thus reversing hooks's model of naïve exotic victims versus entrepreneurial white exploiters. Very much like Beyala, the performer who is conscious of both her audience's expectations and the rules of incorporation into the global literary circuit, her protagonists skillfully perform themselves in and out of situations and places.

Most of the criticisms of Calixthe Beyala, which target her writing of African womanhood, testify to both the politically and emotionally loaded nature of representations of the black female body in the postcolonial context. It also demonstrates the positioning of postcolonial cultural producers as "under-review respondents" to colonial representations. Stuart Hall has organized these postcolonial responses along three strategies: reversal of the stereotype, addition of positive images to the repertoire of negative representations, and contestation of the stereotype from within. This latter strategy, with which I associate Beyala, Cox, and Musa's work, is "more concerned with the forms of racial representation than with introducing a new content" and takes advantage of the "shifting, unstable character of meaning" to "make the stereotypes work against themselves."[67] While the African reception of Beyala indicates a postcolonial penchant for and legitimization of the two first strategies as counter-representational, I nonetheless contend that Beyala—like Cox and Musa—is a postcolonial respondent to colonial representations of African womanhood. Calixthe Beyala's evolution on the French scene and her images of black women urge us to consider the spaces of African womanhood in contemporary Europe in light of the history of the black body in France. Each in their own way, Beyala, Cox, and Musa deploy the black female body as a site to not only address the colonial past but also expose the continuation of the colonial production of the racialized female body. Their strategy of redirecting the gaze back to the producer and consumer of African womanhood is a necessary and long-called-for stage in the postcolonial deconstruction of the black female body. ❧

1 Marlene Nourbese Philip, *A Genealogy of Resistance and Other Essays* (Toronto: Mercury Press, 1999), 76.

2 See Malek Alloula, *The Colonial Harem* (Minneapolis: University of Minnesota Press, 1986), and Christraud M. Geary, *In and Out of Focus: Images from Central Africa, 1885–1960* (London: Philip Wilson, 2002), for a broader look at postcard representations throughout colonial Africa.

3 T. Denean Sharpley-Whiting, *Black Venus: Sexualized Savages, Primal Fears, and Primitive Narratives in French* (Durham: Duke University Press, 1999), 18.

4 See also Christaud Geary, "The Female Black Body, the Postcard, and the Archive" in this volume.

5 See Marianna Torgovnick, *Gone Primitive: Savage Intellects, Modern Lives* (Chicago: University of Chicago Press, 1990), and Petrine Archer-Straw, *Negrophilia: Avant-Garde Paris and Black Culture in the 1920s* (New York and London: Thames & Hudson, 2000).

6 The controversy over Baker's election as "Queen of the Colonies" for the 1931 French Colonial Exhibition illustrates how French audiences perceived her at this point. The Exhibition Committee was bombarded with letters complaining that she was a product of America and not of Africa. Her straightened hair was even used as evidence of her lack of authenticity. Other critics argued that she was too old by African standards anyway (Lynn Haney, *Naked at the Feast: A Biography of Josephine Baker* [New York: Robson Books, 1981], 185).

7 See the different autobiographies and biographies of Josephine Baker, including Joséphine Baker and Marcel Sauvage, *Les mémoires de Joséphine Baker* (Paris: Kra, 1947); Joséphine Baker and Jo Bouillon, *Joséphine* (Paris: Robert Laffont, 1976); Stephen Papich, *Remembering Josephine* (New York: Bobbs-Merrill, 1996); Phyllis Rose, *Jazz Cleopatra: Josephine Baker in Her Time* (New York: Vintage Books, 1989); J. C. Baker and C. Chase, *Josephine: The Hungry Heart* (New York: Random House, 1993); and Haney, *Naked at the Feast*.

8 See Kimberly Wallace-Sanders's essay in this volume, "The Body of a Myth: Embodying the Myth of the Black Mammy Figure in Visual Culture."

9 Beyala does not shy away from graphic descriptions of sexual scenes. Her latest novel *Femme nue, femme noire* is the first erotic African novel and has provoked quite a stir among African audiences. In her native Cameroon, she was labeled a "dangerous woman" for featuring a bisexual woman who engages in all types of unprotected sex in a context marked by AIDS.

10 Charlene Regester, "The Construction of an Image and the Deconstruction of a Star—Josephine Baker Racialized, Sexualized, and Politicized in the African-American Press, the Mainstream Press, and FBI files," *Popular Music and Society* 24 (2000): 47.

11 See also Darlene Clark Hine, "Rape and the Inner Lives of Black Women: Thoughts on the Culture of Dissemblance," in *Hine Sight: Black Women and the Reconstruction of American History* (Brooklyn: Carlson Publishing, 1994), and Deborah Willis, "Picturing the New Negro Woman," in this volume.

12 *Lettre d'une Afro-Française à ses compatriots*. All translations are mine unless noted otherwise.

13 Rose, *Jazz Cleopatra*, 162.

14 Bennetta Jules-Rosette, "Two Loves: Josephine Baker as Icon and Image," *Emergences* 10, no. 1 (2000): 63.

15 Stuart Hall, *Representation: Cultural Representations and Signifying Practices* (London: Sage, 1997), 269.

16 For a discussion of reductive readings of Beyala, see Ayo Abiétou Coly, "Court Poet and Wild Child: Two Readings of Calixthe Beyala's *Les Honneurs perdus*," *Nottingham French Studies* 43, no. 3 (Autumn 2004): 15–27.

17 Nicki Hitchcott, "Calixthe Beyala: Black Face(s) on French TV," *Modern and Contemporary France* 12, no. 4 (2004): 476.

18 "*On baise vraiment.*"

19 Hitchcott, "Calixthe Beyala," 479.

20 Jules-Rosette briefly mentions that Beyala appears to be drawing on Baker's larger public image in France. Like Baker, Beyala has adopted a Rainbow Tribe consisting of twelve children of different nationalities. The writer also had plans to open an international school in Cameroon, which recalls Baker's open university project (Jules Rosette, "Two Loves," 72).

21 Jules-Rosette, "Two Loves," 74.

22 Ibid., 65.

23 Ibid.

24 See Kimberly Wallace-Sanders, *Skin Deep, Spirit Strong: The Black Female Body in American Culture* (Ann Arbor: The University of Michigan Press, 2002); Deborah Willis and Carla Williams, *The Black Female Body: A Photographic History* (Philadelphia: Temple University Press, 2002); and Michael D. Harris, *Colored Pictures: Race and Visual Representation* (Chapel Hill: North Carolina Press, 2003).

25 Lavie Smadar and Ted Swedenburg, eds., *Displacement, Diaspora, and Geographies of Identity* (Durham: Duke University Press, 1996), 2.

26 "Bouvard des succès," *France 2* (26 August 2000).

27 Michel De Certeau, *The Practice of Everyday Life* (Berkeley: University of California Press, 1984), 37.

28 "Je vendais mon immense derrière de négresse a prix modérés." Calixthe Beyala, *Amours sauvages* (Paris: Albin Michel, 1999), 9.

29 "Il agita le dessin sous mon nez: 'C'est toi, ma chérie! T'es magnifique!' J'étais perplexe. Cette femme aurait put être moi ou n'importe quelle Venus hottentote, mais Pléthore disait qu'elle ne ressemblait et c'était moi. Dès lors, il me dessina partout . . . même couchée nue sur le canapé. 'Ah, ah! Nous serons riches, beaux et célèbres!' dit-il le jour où il reussit à fourguer un croquis à un juif du Sentier qui fantasmait sur le fessier négre. . . . Il était si naïvement imbécile qu'un peu plus, je lui aurais acheté un Trivial Pursuit ou une voiture en plastique" (Beyala, *Amours sauvages*, 123).

30 "Avec mon bonheur rangé de femme mariée je pouvais prétendre à un enterrement décent" (Beyala, *Amours sauvages*, 26).

31 "Le personage de Eve-Marie est un personage que j'ai crée a partir de la pensée des femmes noires globalement, qui partent de l'Afrique sans bagage et qui arrivent à s'adapter à la situation avec le peu de moyens qu'elles ont. Eve-Marie . . . est d'ailleurs le symbole de la majorité des femmes noires qui partent sans rien; toutes ne se prostituent pas, certaines le font. Mais ce n'est pas le but de leur vie; le but de leur vie est de s'intégrer à une nouvelle civilisation, de se créer un avenir" (quoted in Fanny Brochand, "Interview: Calixthe Beyala" (2000), http://delirium.lejournal.free.fr/interview_calixte_beyala.htm).

32 Calixthe Beyala, *Comment Cuisiner son Mari à l'Africaine* (Paris: Albin Michel, 2000), 67.

33 Calixthe Beyala, *Les honneurs perdus* (Paris: Albin Michel, 1996), 239.

34 See Ifi Amadiume, "African Women's Body Images in Postcolonial Discourse and Resistance to Neo-Crusaders," in this volume.

35 For a discussion of the impact of colonization on gender arrangements in African societies, see Filomena Chioma Steady, ed., *The Black Woman Cross-Culturally* (Boston: Schenkman, 1981); Ifi Amadiume, *Male Daughters, Female Husbands: Gender and Sex in an African Society* (London: Zed Books, 1987; 4th edition, 1994); Oyeronke Oyewumi, *The Invention of Women: Making Sense of Western Gender Discourses* (Minneapolis: University of Minnesota Press, 1997).

36 G. Spivak, "Can the Subaltern Speak?" in *Marxism and the Interpretation of Culture*, eds. Cary Nelson and Lawrence Grossberg (Basingstoke: Macmillan Education, 1988), 296.

37 For example, in Beyala's novel *Assèze l'Africaine* (Paris: Albin Michel, 1994), Assèze, the main protagonist, and a group of fellow migrant African women from impoverished backgrounds in Africa, work for a sweatshop in Paris. Alexandre, who is both the French husband of Assèze's sister and Assèze's lover, made a fortune importing expired milk to Africa. The writer exposes the forces of global capitalism and their implications in the underdevelopment of Africa and the fate of African women who are then forced to migrate to the West as cheap labor in sweatshops and/or commodifying and auctioning their exotic bodies to satisfy the demands of first-world male consumers. Similarly, a study of personal ads on the internet and in magazines show a heavy predominance of young African women looking exclusively for white Western men, often recycling colonial images of black womanhood to hook in Western consumers.

38 De Certeau, *The Practice of Everyday Life*, 37.

39 In this case, the reward of housing and homing the body becomes a disciplinary practice that produces the docile bodies of Beyala and her migrant African women. The housed and homed body is thus forcefully a docile one.

40 De Certeau, *The Practice of Everyday Life*, 37.

41 John Ayto, *Dictionary of Word Origins* (New York: Arcade, 1990), 337.

42 For a discussion of the political and symbolic aspects of clothing in Africa, see Hildi Hendrickson, ed., *Clothing and Difference: Embodying Colonial and Post-colonial Identities* (Durham: Duke University Press, 1996), and Jean Allman, ed., *Fashioning Africa: Power and the Politics of Dress* (Bloomington: Indiana University Press, 2004).

43 See Wallace-Sanders, "The Body of a Myth," in this volume, which discusses the same tactics found in American cultural contexts, and Geary, "The Black Female Body, the Postcard, and the Archives," in this volume, for a discussion of these tactics in African photography.

44 Geary makes a similar claim, arguing that some Central African communities subverted the photographer's intent and recuperated the photographic occasion as one of self-fashioning and self-projection (*In and Out of Focus*).

45 "Bouche si lippue qu'on pourrait en user comme d'un siege."

46 Beyala, *Comment Cuisiner*, 46.

47 "Enormes tresses" (Beyala, *Les honneurs perdus*, 36).

48 Henry Louis Gates Jr., *The Signifying Monkey: A Theory of African American Literary Criticism* (New York: Oxford, 1988).

49 Ibid., 52.

50 It should be noted that Fortier has featured this same young woman in various postcards and ethnic "type" scenarios.

51 Sanders Gilman, *Difference and Pathology: Stereotypes of Sexuality, Race, and Madness* (Ithaca: Cornell University Press, 1985).

52 See also Jan Nederveen Pieterse, *White on Black: Images of Africa and Blacks in Western Popular Culture* (New Haven: Yale University Press, 1992), 178–187; Iris Young, "Breasted Experience: The Look and the Feeling," in *The Politics of Women's Bodies*, ed. Rose Weitz (New York: Oxford University Press, 1998); Anne Laura Stoller, *Race and the Education of Desire: Foucault's History of Sexuality and the Colonial Order of Things* (Durham: Duke

University Press, 1995); and Anne Laura Stoller, *Carnal Knowledge and Imperial Power: Race and the Intimate in Colonial Rule* (Berkeley: University of California Press, 2002).

53 Sharpley-Whiting, *Black Venus: Sexualized Savages, Primal Fears, and Primitive Narratives in French*, 74.

54 Ibid.

55 "Femmes Kabyles d'Alger. C'est très appétissant comme dessert!"

56 "Une oeuvre tres originale et savoureuse: du caiman au piment et à la crème fraiche." Quoted in Pierrette Herzberger-Fofana, *Littérature feminine francophone d'Afrique noire* (Paris: L'Harmattan, 2000), 324.

57 Ayo Coly, "Court Poet and Wild Child: Two Readings of Calixthe Beyala's *Les Honneurs perdus*," *Nottingham French Studies* 43, no. 3 (Autumn 2004): 47.

58 Robert Young, *Colonial Desire: Hybridity in Theory, Culture, and Race* (London: Routledge, 1995).

59 Bret Berliner, *Ambivalent Desire: The Exotic Black Other in Jazz-Age France* (Boston: University of Massachusetts Press, 2002), 136.

60 Jean-Jacques Rousseau, *Essay on the Origins of Language and Writings Related to Music* (Hanover: Dartmouth College Press, 1998).

61 Jacques Derrida, *Of Grammatology* (Baltimore: The Johns Hopkins University Press, 1974).

62 bell hooks, *Black Looks: Race and Representation* (Boston: South End Press, 1990), 26.

63 Ibid., 28.

64 Ibid., 31.

65 Gilles Deleuze and Felix Guattari, *A Thousand Plateaux: Capitalism and Schizophrenia* (Minneapolis: University of Minnesota Press, 1987), 7.

66 Olu Oguibe, *The Culture Game* (Minneapolis: University of Minnesota Press, 2004), 21.

67 Hall, *Representation*, 274.

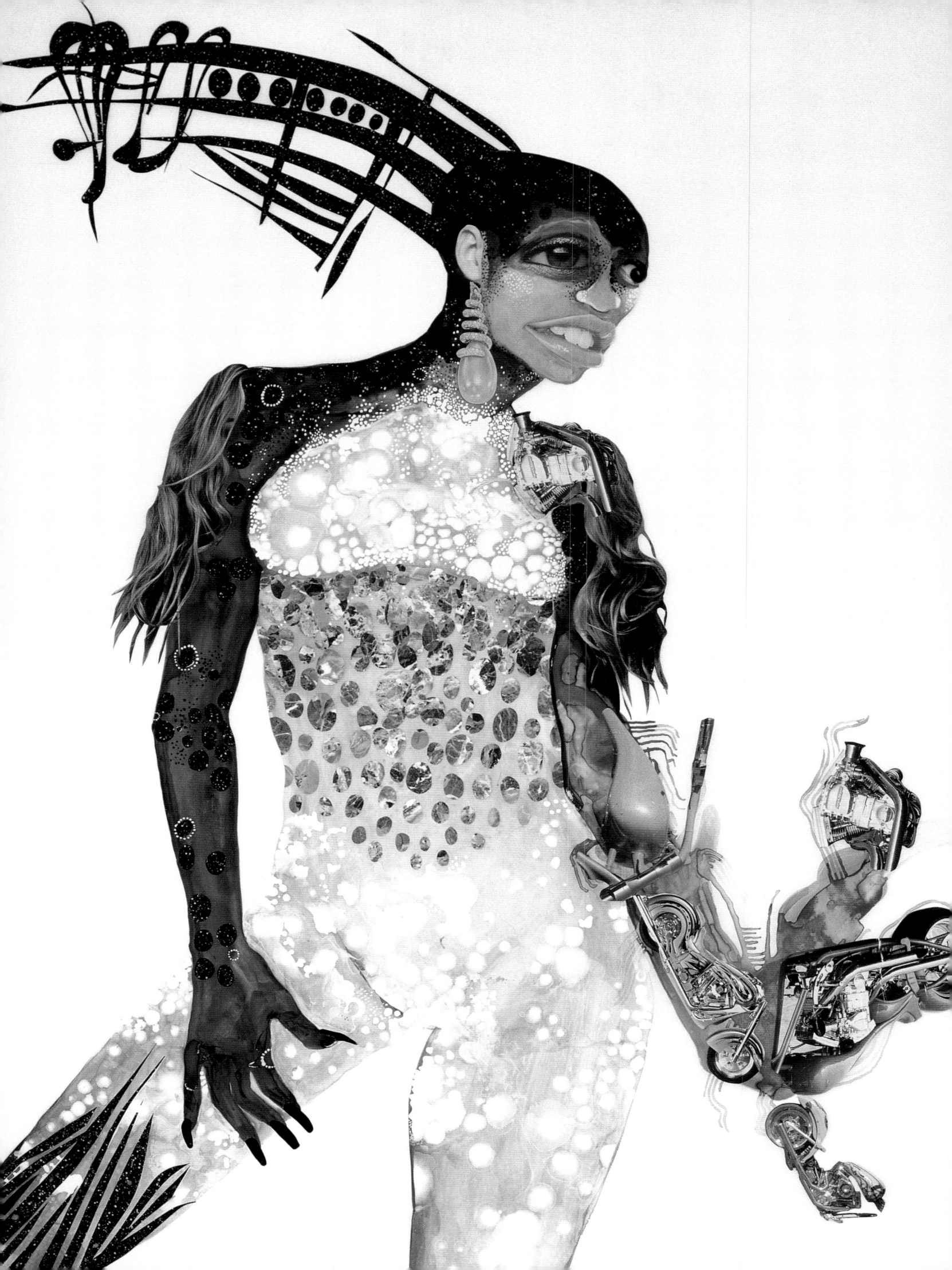

9   Decolonizing Black Bodies: Personal Journeys in the Contemporary Voice

In early European visual and literary representations, the African female body became "a symbol of the deceptive beauty and ultimate savagery of blackness."[1] These representations gave rise to a racist dialogue deeply entrenched in notions of gender and sexual difference, which Peter Erickson asserts created a trope for disrupted harmony,[2] especially in European perceptions of the Self and Other. African woman in early European depictions particularly represented "a body both desirable and repulsive, available and untouchable, productive and repro- ductive, beautiful and black."[3] In this essay, I examine various contemporary artists' techniques and tactics in confronting and decolonizing the dichotomous relationship between European cultural imagination and stereotypes of the black female body.

THE BLACK VENUS: SUBVERTING COLONIAL FIXATIONS ON RACE, SEX, AND THE BLACK FEMALE BODY

Initially, European artists depicted the African female body in religious texts as temptress, salacious queen, and seductive wife. Stemming from the troubled relationship between European expansionism, the Western cultural imagination, and its perception/reception of the African female body, these depictions soon evolved into widely recognizable icons of the "black Venus." Africa's women were therefore transformed by Western repulsion/attraction into beasts, nymphs, slaves, servants, and sexual commodities,[4] serving as a counterpoint to notions of virtuous and moral white womanhood. Many of these icons continue to be per- petuated—for both positive and negative means—in popular culture, but serve as particularly fertile grounds for the deconstruction of colonial and postcolonial narratives by contemporary African and African-descended artists.

In the last few decades, African and Diaspora artists have begun to disrupt Western-centric representations of the "Black Venus" figure and her sexually

opposite Wangechi Mutu, Kenyan (b. 1972), *Double Fuse* (detail), 2003. Ink and collage on mylar. Hood Museum of Art: Purchased through the Charles F. Venrick 1936 Fund; MIS.2003.38. Photograph by Jeffrey Nintzel

conflated "nature" by appropriating and strategically re-presenting some of the same historical stereotypes they are critiquing to create new, thought-provoking, and often confrontational images of an empowered and outspoken black female presence. For example, the U.S.-based Kenyan artist Wangechi Mutu employs the technique of physical exaggeration of the female body. This method recalls the physical exaggeration in early European allegories of Africa in which racist perceptions of African women's inflated behaviors and physical forms "evoked an immutable distance between Europe and Africa on which the development of racial slavery depended."[5] This distancing continues to define racial and sexual differences, which Mutu attempts to disrupt by alerting the viewer to the absurdity of both historical and contemporary racist ideologies conflating African female sexuality and complacency.[6] According to Mutu, her visually disturbing surrealistic collages of corporeal fragmentation and exaggeration

> question the relationship between resilience and compliance. I present the viewer with figures from palpable pop cultural sources while simultaneously frustrating an easy reading through meticulous altering and disfiguring of the original allegory. Borrowing from wildlife magazines . . . for example, parodies the travel catalogue image of exotic natives pictured in their beautiful land.[7]

Initially and from a distance, Mutu's figures appear to be beautiful, powerful, and sensual, like evocations of female superheroes from comic books and computer games. Upon closer inspection, however, the incongruity of shapes, sizes, textures, materials, and colors reveal bizarrely generated hybrid beings—part woman, part beast, part machine—whose missing and distorted features remind us of captured and mutilated prey, bionic creatures, or cloned misconstructions.

"My collages," Mutu notes, "reveal themes of loss, desire, morbid fantasy, and the injured body, drawing equally from African vernacular, modernist European collage styles and American mass culture . . . pillag[ing] glossy fashion and coffee table books on tribal Africa, for my material."[8] In the diptych *Double Fuse* (plate 108), Mutu has cut out body parts from photographs in women's fashion magazines and motor sports magazines—a dichotomous reference to the fetishism of male and female domains in Western popular culture. In these reassembled and pasted together collages, Mutu juxtaposes biological/artificial, human/machine, black/white, soft/hard, and feminine/masculine to reference the fragmentation, exploitation, and exaggeration of the sexualized black female body during the colonial era. Like Josephine Baker's exaggerated performance of African sexuality (plates 77 and 78), Mutu's art parodies more recent Western representations of the submissive, exotic, and marginally located native woman portrayed in *National Geographic*, in documentary films about Africa, and in contemporary fashion magazines. Noting the burden that cultural representation places upon women's bodies, Mutu asserts, "[f]emales carry the marks, language and nuances of their culture more than the male. Anything that is desired or despised," she adds, "is always placed on the female body."[9] Mutu's collages overturn that which is desired or despised.

Mutu recycles but also transforms the image of the sexualized black woman into reconstructed and dehumanized combatants, evoking the violence of fragmentation and displacement. Inscribing the skin of her female protagonists with African wildlife patterns, she recalls colonial attitudes about African women as beast-like sexual objects, whose parallels are found in contemporary popular culture and the mass media. From her larger *Creature* series, *Double Fuse* features two idealized female figures, menacing twins who tease out the boundaries between balance and disproportion, beauty and deformation. With these images, Mutu hopes

> to generate multiple, mutually contradictory impulses. Seductive source materials and recognizably feminine materials startlingly guide us toward a questioning on how photographic images depict women as simply erotic, and non-Europeans as primitive. I place myself and the viewer into a delicate position where we are reminded of our own involvement in the mechanisms that generate demeaning and fetishized images of people. Still I refuse to surrender to puritanical elements of "institutionalized feminism" with its demands for female virtue. Through the figures' flamboyance, satire, and deviance, my subjects transcend their predicament and become models for multitudes of manifestations.[10]

Covered in surrealistic patterns and marbled textures, the twin figures in *Double Fuse* resonate also with images and sculptural representations of young African female initiates, whose supple bodies have been painted and patterned with symbolic designs and scarification markings that signal their transformation from girlhood into womanhood, as described in chapters 1 and 2. Contrary to the vulnerable state of young female initiates, however, Mutu's figures are virtual "battlefields of obscene dynamics but rendered beautiful, chic and tantalizing."[11] In *Double Fuse*, she endows her heroic and enticing hybrid twins with machine-like arms, composed of motorcycle parts that become menacing weapons, which, as Tara McDowell astutely reminds us, evoke the words of cultural theorist Stuart Hall:

> Just as masculinity always constructs femininity as double—simultaneously Madonna and Whore—so racism constructs the black subject: noble savage and violent avenger. And in the doubling, fear and desire double for one another and play across the structure of otherness, complicating its politics.[12]

Complicating the politics of representation, Mutu's avenging twins—like Sokari Douglas Camp's *Gelede from Top to Toe* (plate 96) with her imposing body, commanding presence, and "missile" breasts—can defend, empower, and reconstitute themselves in whatever form best suits their own desires, fantasies, and goals.

Likewise, the Côte d'Ivoirian artist Emile Guebehi locates his methods of subversion in the strategic use of physical exaggeration. His eerily realistic sculptures of "ideal" African women (plate 103) palpably mimic Western iconic depictions of the sensual, voluptuous, and sexualized black female body that are especially reminiscent of colonial depictions of the "Black Venus" embodied in European depictions of Saartjie Baartman or nude anthropological "types." Guebehi also embeds his work, however, with references to traditional African art and iconography through his emphasis of the figure's breasts, hips, and buttocks — like female figures whose exaggerated physical forms serve as symbols of human and agricultural fertility. Yet his figures deny simplistic interpretations as metaphors of African or Western "ideals." Guebehi's life-sized figures are endowed with an almost satirical — if not directly challenging — presence and expression, reflecting larger issues in contemporary Côte d'Ivoirian life.

Since the end of colonial period, Guebehi has witnessed dramatic cultural changes in Côte d'Ivoire and the increasing tension between traditional and Westernized lifestyles. Focusing on the role of women in contemporary Côte d'Ivoire, his work addresses the power shifts within gendered domains, particularly women's struggle to balance life in the traditional roles and ideologies of West African patriarchal societies with competing and increasingly prevalent Western moral and sexual values. His commanding figures therefore speak to the rising empowerment of Côte d'Ivoirian women and the challenges that this introduces into their lives while disrupting the historical stereotype of the subservient/domesticated African woman, which has been written into the Western imagination. His sculptures indicate instead her transformation now into a strong, competent, and defiant force.

The South African artist Penny Siopis tackles the perpetuation of stereotypical icons and ideologies of the African woman by commenting upon the continued ethnographic and museological gaze that often denies — indeed, ignores — contemporary transformations of African womanhood. Siopis, who has long been interested in the contemporary and historical relationship between black and white women in South Africa, situates herself at the center of her investigations into the new possibilities of black and white South African female identities located within the post-apartheid context.[13] In the 1990s, Siopis began to incorporate objects from junk shops and ethnographic museums into her self-portraits. These objects are both a part of and outside of her personal history, the history of South Africa, and the cultural representations of its people.

In *Mask and Myself* (plate 123), for example, Siopis digs deeper into the constructs of identity created in the colonial and apartheid eras through her own white, female, South African body juxtaposed by objects representing the museological/anthropological gaze upon the black female body. In this photograph, she dons white gloves like those used in museums for handling art, denoting the special treatment given to the object. She also incorporates the ethnographic prop of a traditional African breastplate, like the Makonde example in plate 26. The breastplate in *Mask and Myself* not only reverses the male use of such female appendages to emulate African womanhood in male masquerades but also marks the artist's renegotiation of gender, sexuality, and identity. The mask does not erase racial differentiation; rather, it accentuates it by exposing the continual tensions between the politics of cultural presentation and representation, where black women continue to be treated as ethnographic specimen and anthropological curiosities.

DEFLATING MYTHS OF THE ODALISQUE

Ever since Titian's *Venus of Urbino* (1538), the icon of the reclining nude in Western art history has served as an unabashed promise of sexual availability. Historical representations of the reclining woman in Western art history, especially, have contributed lasting power to the politics of seduction and the promise of promiscuity. The odalisque figure of eighteenth- and nineteenth-century European painting finds its less sophisticated equivalents in ethnographic portraiture such as François-Edmond Fortier's composition of two young women strategically posed on a mattress, exuding allure and sexual availability (plate 75). Fortier's ethnographic "type" photograph borrows its composition almost directly from Orientalist compositions created fifty years earlier, as in Félix Jacques Moulin's two portrayals of boudoir scenes, both featuring a black female servant and an ostensibly north African odalisque. In one photograph, his subjects are clothed (figure 9.1), in another, nude (plate 76). Not surprisingly, both servant and prostitute are presented as sexual commodities, posed upon foreign and exotic import goods. In one photograph the subjects pose on a kilim rug that communicates their exotic nature, in another they are on a leopard skin, further implying their animalistic sexuality.

The nineteenth century, with its heightened goals of imperialism and colonialism, yielded a new—though fictionalized—"reality" of Africa, made possible

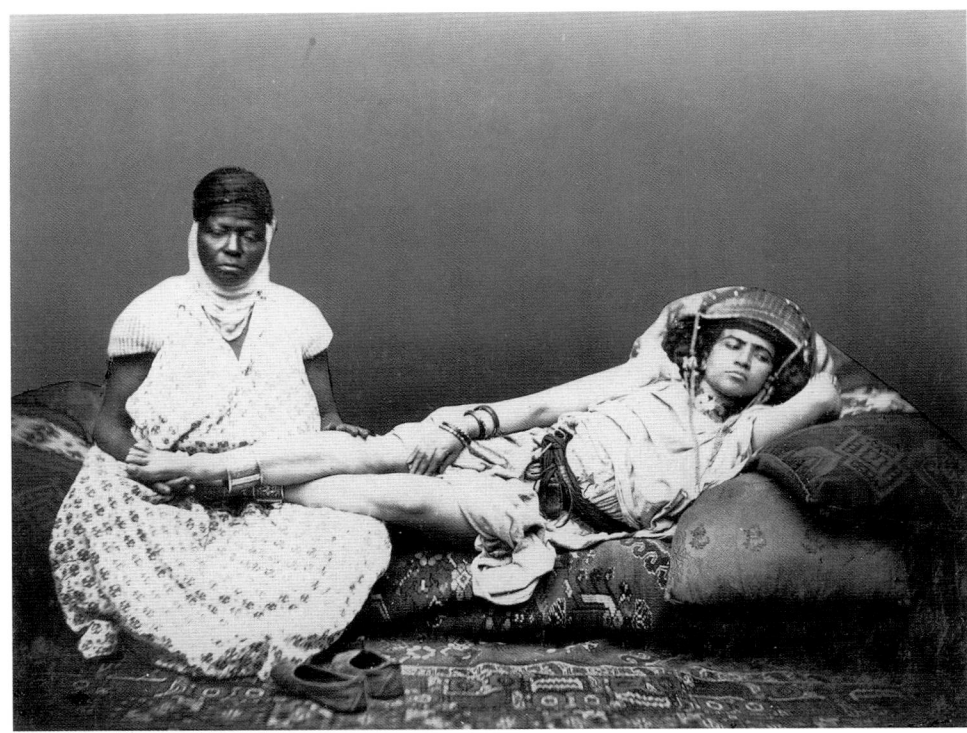

FIGURE 9.1 Félix Jacques Moulin, French (1802–after 1869, active Paris, 1840s–1850s), untitled (A Moorish Woman with Her Maid), about 1856, albumen silver print. The J. Paul Getty Museum, Los Angeles, California; 84.XO.431.31. Photograph courtesy of the J. Paul Getty Museum, Los Angeles, California.

through the medium of photography, which reinforced racist visual and ideological landscapes. As Houston A. Baker argues,

> At the nineteenth century birth of photography there was a grand illusion that reality could be taken in an objective frame. The perfect imitation of life was imaginable. But in the late twentieth century, we know there is no inside and outside of the frame to be clearly demarcated.[14]

Playing with Baker's "inside and outside of the frame," the U.S.-based Morrocan artist Lalla Essaydi uses contemporary understandings of photography as a *construction* rather than a *reality* to lead the viewer into questioning what is real and imagined, who is subject and object, and what defines Self and Other (plate 126). Essaydi is especially interested in those constructions of race and cultural identity that led to nineteenth-century clichés of the odalisque and the seduction of beauty epitomized by colonial representations of North African women, superimposed with romantic, Orientalist, and primitivist fantasies.

Essaydi is deeply aware of the impact that nineteenth-century Orientalist myths of North African "harems" and their accompanying visual "imitations of life" had in shaping rigid Western ideas about the implied sexuality of the (semi)veiled African bodies (figure 9.2; see also plates 69–76).

> I want the viewer to become aware of Orientalism as a projection of the sexual fantasies of Western male artists, in other words, as a voyeuristic tradition, but also to appreciate the authentic beauty of the culture being depicted. The world these artists encountered in North Africa was suffused with exquisite beauty—in the architecture, the decorative surfaces of the spaces, the fabric on furniture, or in women's clothing. I imagine this was all quite a contrast to the drabness of the European bourgeois culture of the time. It is this beauty I wish to reclaim. But to do so is tricky because within the context of Orientalism, such beauty is quite dangerous. It is what lures the viewer into accepting the fantasized slave status of the women in the paintings, in the harems, the slave markets, etc. In other words, how do we separate the beauty of the rooms, fabrics and so forth, from that of the women themselves, so seemingly passive and receptive, rather like the furniture or the welcoming spaces?[15]

Essaydi invites viewers to resist the stereotypes and ethnographic taxonomies embedded in these images, drawing attention instead to their own projected readings of the subject's identity, the real or imagined histories they convey, and the unbalanced relationship between reading foreign texts and bodies. Despite the serene quietude and sensuous beauty of her photographs, Essaydi quickly interrupts the Western gaze upon and consumption of the exotic and eroticized North African woman. For example, in *Femme du Maroc #23* (see plate 126) she replicates ethnographic conventions of posing for racial categorization (plates 53 a–c).[16] Conceptually, she borrows from Orientalist conventions of depicting the private and sexually enticing inner world of the North African "harem" or boudoir, replete with its African servant/slave and reclining odalisque surrounded by

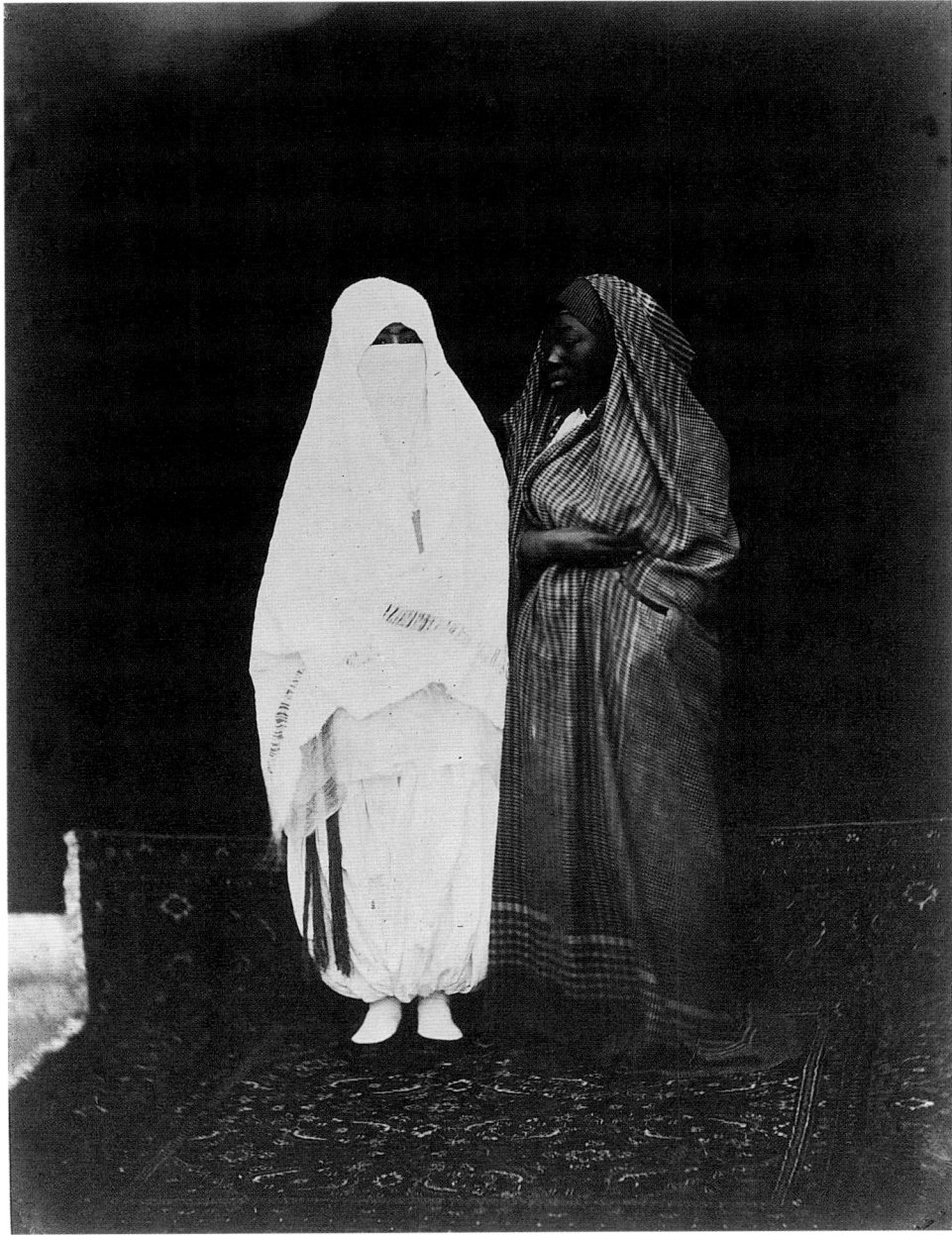

FIGURE 9.2 Félix Jacques Moulin, French (1802–after 1869, active Paris, 1840s–1850s), *Mauresque et négresse d'Alger (costume de ville)*, L'Algérie photographiée (tome 2): Province d'Alger, 1856–1857, albumen silver print. Cliché Bibliothèque nationale de France, Paris, Département: Estampes et photographie; FB-23901-23903. Photograph courtesy of Cliché Bibliothèque nationale de France, Paris.

sumptuous textiles. Unlike the multitudes of historic photographs that unabashedly present North African women in a racialized and sexualized context as a "type" (plates 71–75),[17] however, Essaydi conceals the subject's body from the Western gaze, blocking any hint of identity, sensuality, or sexual invitation with an all-engulfing, sumptuous white shroud. All that remains is the ambiguous sculptural presence of a woman, which most Western viewers easily interpret as a veiled Muslim woman—fully loaded with the baggage that goes along with this cliché. Upon the cloth, Essaydi inscribes her highly personal stream of consciousness in the painstaking process of henna painting, written in classic Arab calligraphy, an exclusively male art form used primarily for sacred Qu'ranic texts:[18]

I am dreaming and don't know how to talk about it. I am staring at the book and not sure what language I am supposed to speak. When a book is translated, it loses something in the process and what am I but generations of translations? I stand guilty outside and I stand guilty inside, profoundly buried in my translation, panting behind the words that are carried along by vital forces far greater than my own. I am a book that has no ending. Each page I write could be the first.[19]

A Moroccan of the Muslim faith, Essaydi often is identified only as an Arab artist. Her work *and* her identity, she exclaims, are as much grounded in the African continent and the Berber culture of Morocco[20] as in the Arab culture of North Africa and the Middle East.[21] Juggling her own sense of identity within the uncertain spaces of transnationalism, Essaydi is forced to question the very notion of place while also exploring new possibilities of artistic languages in which to speak as a woman in "translation" seen "through multiple lenses—as an artist, as Moroccan, as traditionalist, as liberal, as Muslim," and "caught somewhere between past and present" now "the East and the West."[22]

Essaydi's choice to speak in classic Arabic through the medium of henna painting is not incidental, as Berber and Arab women from North Africa use henna to inscribe symbolic motifs upon their bodies during important moments of womanhood, such as puberty, marriage (figure 9.3), conception, and the birth of her first child, "especially when that first born is male."[23] In henna painting—as in other Berber and African Muslim women's art forms, including pottery (plate 8), textiles, gourd containers (plate 11), and interior wall paintings—the interlaced or geometric designs sometimes incorporate also the symbol of *baraka*, a blessing for spiritual protective powers that can dispel disease and infertility.[24] In Morocco, henna is regarded as having *baraka*, and so women use it to guard against misfortune and the malevolent forces of the "evil eye"—which in the context of Western voyeurism takes on new meaning. There is no doubt that Essaydi's use of henna, as an artistic medium that privately expresses femininity, protection, and the intimate world of Muslim women, is at the core of her work.

Like the female form and space in *Femme du Maroc #23*, the henna-painted text is ambiguous, yet also highly personal and poetic. The fluid text reveals Essaydi's internalized narratives, ponderings, memories, and conflicts, which openly declare her complexity and individuality as a woman caught between two worlds. Her words and her act of calligraphic writing defy Muslim gender restrictions and regulations, but they also reject Western stereotypes of North African women, harems, and black female seduction by turning the focus away from the eroticized body and toward her own inner conflict with issues of multiple identities. As Essaydi explains,

in the absence of any specificity of place, the text itself becomes the world of the subjects—their thoughts, speech, work, clothing, shelter, and nomadic home. This text is of course incomplete. It involves the viewer as well as the writer in a continual process of reading and revising, of losing and finding its multiple and

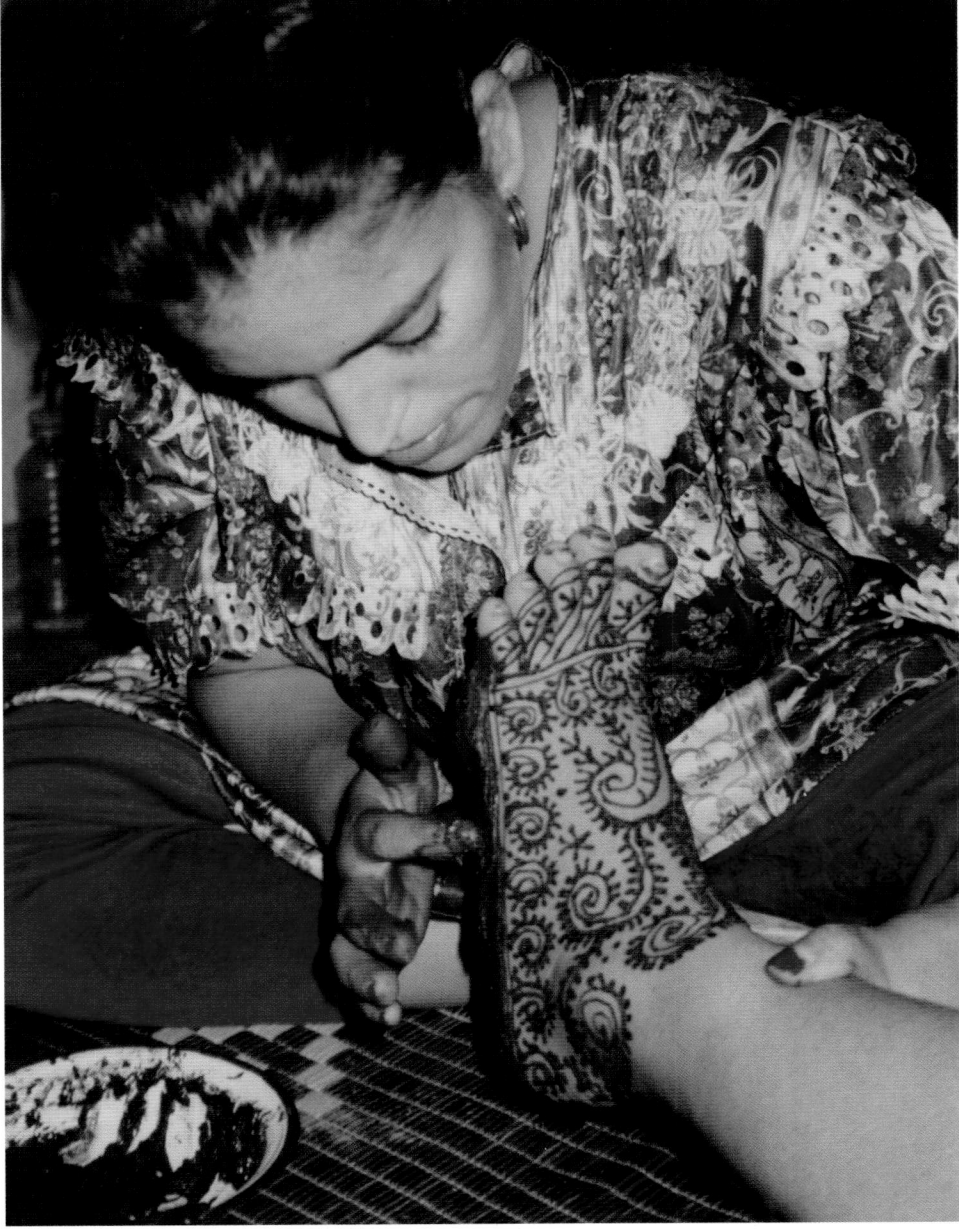

FIGURE 9.3 Khira Ouadderrou, *neggafa* (henna artist) from southern Morocco, 2001. Photograph by and courtesy of Cynthia Becker.

discontinuous threads. Similarly, the bodies of the women in the photographs can only be gathered and informed by multiple visual readings. Both are as elusive as "woman" herself—not simply because she is veiled or turns away—but because she is still in progress.[25]

If the viewer doesn't read Arabic, the narrative is indecipherable. As art historian Amanda Carlson has noted, Western "[a]udiences may miss the implications of these images if they are consumed by the voyeuristic tendencies that are actually being critiqued. . . . Writing implies a need for interpretation. It requires an investigation that is more rigorous than pure visual digestion."[26]

Unlike the female subjects in Orientalist works, Essaydi's subjects—

Moroccan friends, family, and acquaintances—are fully aware of her intentions and involved in her projects. They are willing participants in the emancipation of Moroccan women and their freedom to revise, edit, and rewrite the complex narratives of their own Arab/African identities after generations of translations and interpretations. In this manner, Essaydi's photographs transform myopic Western imaginings of Muslim women into complex layers of concealed identities, presenting herself *and* her subjects as confined yet also liberated, fluid yet rigid, elusive yet concrete.

Just as the Orientalist's "harem" fed into Western fantasies about North Africa's women during the nineteenth and early twentieth centuries, so too did primitivist ideologies about African women's promiscuity, which becomes an especially powerful site for deconstructing stereotypes of black women as sexual objects in the self-portraiture of the American photographer Carla Williams. "My self-portraits were initially informed by the history of portraits made by male photographers of their wives, lovers and muses. . . . Turning the camera on myself I sought to capture the intimacy of those unguarded moments."[27]

In many of her photographs, Williams attempts to divorce black nudity from a history of the colonial or ethnographic spectacle, inviting instead serious contemplation of beauty and sensuality.[28] Williams, like Essaydi, is keenly aware of the dangers of stereotypical translations of familiar icons. "I realized that my body could never be simply formal, or emotional, or personal. Most viewers would always see a black body regardless of my intent."[29] Nevertheless, as Williams points out, her own intentions of referencing historic portrayals in her art (plate 105) is "to suggest to the viewer that such precedents, while seemingly absurd and outdated, still contain a great deal of resonance and power with respect to the way that we read and respond to contemporary images of African American women."[30]

Borrowing the title *How to Read Character* from a late nineteenth-century book on phrenology and physiology, Williams creates large gilt-framed black-and-white photographs of fragmented and reconstituted body parts, which she then places next to photocopies of texts and images that reveal how history and its colonial sciences (anthropometry and physiognomy) have framed a visual language that "reads" racial and sexual characteristic onto the flesh. In plate 105 Williams juxtaposes and compares her own body—mapped and marked by strategically placed red dots—with an illustration of the choice cuts in a side of beef, blatantly subverting colonial ideologies about the categorization of race through the measurement of specific (choice) body parts. Further implicating this racist past, Williams's literal use of gilt frames around her body—as in Maud Sulter's photographic portraits of prominent black women (plate 99)—not only aestheticizes the black female body but also re-categorizes the ethnographic image into the refined world of the "fine" arts of the great Western "masters," not unlike the re-categorization of African sculpture from ethnographic "artifact" to "fine art" at the beginning of the twentieth century.

The Malian photographer Malick Sidibé also attempts to disrupt Western-centric politics of seduction by celebrating Malian women's newfound sense of self-discovery and self-reinvention, which emerged after independence from colonialism. Rejecting Western conventions of nude seduction, Sidibé explains that,

> in Mali, today, it is culturally not acceptable to show women completely nude; so [the models] wear *pagnes* [wrappers] and brassieres. I prefer them this way, not nude. When a woman's body is covered there is a certain mystery. When her body is covered with a *pagne*, a man becomes curious to know what it is concealing. It caresses her form; it conceals and reveals her at the same time. It is mysterious, pleasing, and tempting.[31]

As the artist emphasizes, the very fact that she is clothed heightens her desirability because her sexuality is implied through the hidden form, lines, and movement of her body underneath the textile.

> In Mali—essentially throughout Africa—the backside of a woman's body is most important. A woman's bottom as a symbol of her sexuality and her sex appeal is seen as being reflected through the rhythmic movement of her back and bottom. As such women use their backside to impress men. Malian women know this about their bodies, about themselves, and about Malian men, and they use this knowledge. . . . Movement, not nudity, is crucial to understanding the poetics of African women's bodies. It is a key to understanding women's sense of self, which they negotiate through their bodies . . . in how they learn to walk, move, dance, always aware (and utilizing!) the power of their bodies to communicate and convey a particular sense of self-assuredness.[32]

Sidibé's photographs of reclining women epitomize his formal study of the "poetics of African women's bodies" and the "Malian aesthetic of the concealed female body in motion."[33] This aesthetic, he asserts, is deeply grounded in Bamako's own history and in the contemporary renegotiations of self and identity liberated from both colonial legacies and restrictive traditional ideologies.

After Mali gained independence from France, Sidibé witnessed and photographically documented the nation's capital, Bamako, transform from a traditional city into a modern metropolis. While capturing the revolutionary emergence of a modern youth culture in the city's most popular nightclubs, in the streets of the bustling city, along the muddy shores of the Niger River, his own portrait studio became a safe haven for the renegotiation of modern Malian identity. "When modernism took hold of Bamako's youth," Sidibé explains, "men and women were eager to reinvent themselves as icons of modernity. Often, however, they did this at the risk of being caught by their traditionalist parents, who would send them away to re-education camps."[34] In his photo studio, however, Bamako's youth could safely play out their fantasies, emulating the exuberance of their newfound love for African American pop culture, music, and fashions.

For young girls, whose virtue, reputations, and marriagability were at stake, the public transformation into modernity was especially risky. Sidibé describes how young women would arrive at his studio with props and modern clothing hidden under their traditional wrappers (*pagnes*). Posing seductively (plate 111) or playfully—depending on the intended recipient of the portrait—Sidibé's subjects surrounded themselves with "props of modernity, such as Western handbags, shoes, radios, sewing machines, and even motorcycles," many of which he kept in his studio for just such purposes.[35] In the confines of the photo studio, Bamako's young women could play with and act out their own invented identities, searching for a desired self-image of modernity that they could not yet publicly express.

Sidibé notes that women's modesty is now less encumbered by traditionalist ideologies.[36] Their self-awareness and freedom to create and construct themselves in ever-changing ways is publicly acceptable, even palpable: "sometimes the women dress in contemporary fashion, for example, at work; sometimes they dress in traditional fashions, such as at weddings,"[37] all the while negotiating their way through the layered life of Mali's contemporary urban culture.

The ever-growing freedom of self-expression that Bamako's women are experiencing through dress, appearance, and body language also has given Sidibé greater artistic license to create photographs for himself rather than for his subjects. He now works with paid models, which allows him full control over the image and its intended message. Unlike his commissioned portraits (which were taken in a single shot), Sidibé creates hundreds of exposures of the same woman as in his series *Vue de Dos* (plate 112). Through minute gestural changes that perfect the harmony of form, line, and beauty, the photographer attempts to capture the fleeting essence of a woman's back in poetic motion, which according to both male and female citizens of Bamako with whom I spoke is her most important conveyor of beauty, sexuality, and self-confidence over which *she* maintains total control.

Alison Saar also takes up the iconic theme of the reclining nude in her sculpture *Caché* (plate 128), composed of a carved female figure lying nude on the floor, swathed in antique ceiling tin. Like aged skin, the salvaged tin emulates the unforgiving hands of time and experience that emboss the body with birthmarks, scars, stretch marks, and wrinkles. Yet the detailed and repetitious patterns evoke also the widespread practice of scarification in traditional African cultures—represented also in traditional African arts (see plates in part 1)—to mark women's belonging within the family and the larger community.[38]

The woman's long, straight hair evokes multiple cultural references. Composed of a dense mass of black wire stretched out on the floor away from her body, the figure's hair is pinned to the ground by a colossal ball of black wire. The sculpture's massive quantity of hair alludes to the accumulation of experience, to the passage of time—to all that it holds and keeps, which Saar uses as a symbol of her ancestry. The ball of hair/wire is strategically placed, lending itself to multiple readings and evoking questions: is it (the ball of hair, the passage of time, ancestry) rolling off and away from her, relieving her of its heavy burden, or is it pinning her down, paralyzing her as she tries to pull away?

Typically, Saar gives "anglosaxified" hair a dominant role in her sculptures, directly referencing the widespread practice among African American women of straightening their hair to change their self-image. The importance of hair in her work comments upon constructions of racial and cultural identity in America, including her own as a woman of mixed heritage. It also alludes to the importance of hair in African and African American cultures as a symbol of female beauty, ideal womanhood, and community. In African and African American cultures, hair and the grooming of hair are important signifiers of outer and inner ideals of beauty that soulfully, spiritually, intellectually, and physically reveal the accumulation of experience and wisdom that a woman gains from her social and cultural responsibilities. Visually extending this metaphor through the colossal ball weighing down the hair, *Caché* references also historic images of African and African American women and girls carrying heavy loads on their heads, such as pots or laundry baskets, further signifying the burden of responsibility to family and cultural heritage in American society today.[39]

Saar draws further upon visual clichés of the reclining female nude with its connection to historical images of the sexually available black woman. The figure's pose, however, a semi-fetal position, suggests a vulnerability that is anything but open and relaxed. With one hand poised on the ground, the figure appears to be ready to push up or away, further implicating the tensions between the relaxed reclining position and the action that has or is about to take place. Saar has titled this piece *Caché*, using the French word for "hidden" or "hiding place," which shrouds the sculpture with ambiguity. Enveloped in a metal but still malleable armored sheath, the figure indicates an unpacking, unloading, and distancing of oneself from the burden of history and heritage.

A QUESTION OF AFRICAN MOTHERHOOD

As historian Jennifer Morgan astutely describes of early European narratives about African womanhood, "the place of motherhood in the complex of savagery and race became central to the figure of the black woman. Unlike other monstrosities, the long-breasted woman—who, when depicted with her child, carried the full weight of productive savagery—maintained her place in the lexicon of conquest and exploration."[40] During the colonial era, Western media and popular culture continued to exploit the myopic image of the African mother carrying a child on her back (see plates 79 and 80) or the black Mammy with a white child on her lap (see plate 84) without considering the complexities of historical, cultural, political, or social circumstances on the experiences of black motherhood. In the postcolonial context, the ever-changing circumstances of black motherhood in contemporary life and the continued struggles of identities born out of painful experiences of black motherhood have become a fulcrum for critical counternarratives by African, African American, and Diaspora artists.

Descended from three generations of quilters, craftsmen, and artisans, Joyce J. Scott is a socially conscious artist propelled as much by the material world as by the cultural, social, and political legacy of her life and family, her memories and experiences of extensive travel around the world, and her scathing sense of humor and irony. In her beaded sculptures, Scott deliberately confronts class, racial, sexual, gender, and ethnic injustices toward black women by removing the stories embedded in her character's lives, which forces viewers to fill in the blanks through their own personal experiences, projections, and biases.

As an African American and female artist from a "blue collar, in fact in some cases, no collar" background,[41] Scott challenges the canon of the sculptural arts—a world historically dominated by male artists, monumentality, permanence, and grandeur—in her use of and "reinvention of the bead as a material of critical sculptural and emblematic import."[42] Scott infuses African sources into much of her work. As a jewelry maker, she carries a deep understanding of the history of beads used, for example, in the personal and body adornment of the Maasai of Kenya or the Zulu of South Africa. As a sculptor, she has mastered techniques of sculptural beadwork similar to that used in West and Central African art, particularly in the making of beaded regalia of Yoruba kings in Nigeria or Bamun sultans in Cameroon. And yet her sculptures are loaded with fierce interjections of American popular culture and African American satire, particularly the icon of the "Mammy" figure.

Scott's mother, textile artist Elizabeth Talford Scott, was a nanny to white children for many years, and as Morrison writes, "The artist bitterly recalls how her mother would later be abused by the children as they grew up and came to know racism."[43] Hence, the "Mammy/Nanny" figure from American literature and popular culture has served as a major icon in her politically charged and multidimensional sculptures. From 1986 to the early 1990s, Scott's black "Mammies" (see figure 5.11) sharply critiqued the contradictions involved in black women being praised as nurturing caretakers for other (white) women's children while also being shunned for their race. Scott, who "believes in messing with stereotypes, prodding the viewer to reassess,"[44] uses acerbic satire to reveal the oversimplification of complex histories of black motherhood in American visual and cultural stereotypes.

Scott's work exposes the surprisingly contemporary struggles of her "Mammy" persona with the slippage of racial and cultural identities, especially through her newest series of glass-skirted "Mammies." Referring to her new sculpture *Mammy under Undue Influence* (plate 116), which was created in response to the exhibition *Black Womanhood*, Scott notes that "this mammy speaks to the person trying to change herself from the core, so she might be whiter/prettier on the outside for society. The skirt is her skin as dressing, not so easily removed. Her desire to exchange her soul-self for a society-self shows how undue the influence is."[45] Her blouse buttons undone, revealing the European Venus inside, this powerful visual statement exposes Mammy's desire to anglicize herself according to Western standards of beauty—reminiscent, of course, of Venus de Milo and other European icons of beauty—and speaks also to the larger problematics of the de-Africanization of ideals of beauty in contemporary popular media and everyday life both in Africa and the West.

Scott's glass and beaded sculptures, which draw upon the craft movement with all of its presumed "low art" associations, connect her to black feminist artists such as Betye Saar and Faith Ringgold. Like her artistic predecessors, Scott uses the intimate, small-scale, and sensuous quality of glass and beads as a perfect tool to pull the viewer into the plight of her subjects, intentionally amusing, surprising, shocking, and challenging the viewer to think beyond the simplistic and stereotypical representations and understandings of black motherhood. As Scott exclaims, "I can't be complacent about the world I live in. . . . It's important to me to use art in a manner that incites people to look and then carry something home—even if it's subliminal—that might make a change in them."[46]

Like Scott, Senzeni Marasela uses the all-too-familiar mother and child icon to shatter the notion of the unfaltering presence of the African mother in her child's life, both in the colonial and post-colonial contexts. Growing up in South Africa in the 1980s toward the end of apartheid, Marasela spent much of her childhood separated from her mother, who like many other black women had to live away from their biological children as domestic workers for white families. The absence of a mother in Marasela's youth left memory gaps in an ambiguous past that she defines by her mother's intermittent presence. As the artist explains,

> I grew up with a schizophrenic mother. This experience informs my work of the last four years. It has been a journey of trying to patch together memories I have of her. Many rely on her medical reports, her bouts of insanity, and her constant absence in my childhood. Her condition also affected my sisters and brother. There was such an enormous difficulty in speaking about her that we almost excluded her in our conversations. We have learned that the many difficulties that she encountered were results of our past.[47]

As Colin Richards has noted, "[t]he comforts, the safety, the security we stereotypically associate with family privacy ring hollow" in Marasela's work,[48] who admits that "[m]y mother was never a place of comfort."[49] Despite the apparent calmness of Marasela's photographs, they nevertheless suggest the trauma of emptiness, separation, and anxiety, pervaded by absence of a maternal figure, such as in *Our Mother* (2002) (figure 9.4). In this triptych, Marasela captures an iconic African mother and child moment—or so it seems. But this is not a conventional representation; it is merely the shadow of a mother and child: the artist's mother carrying Marasela's son on her back, indicating the renegotiation of both women's identities as black South African women and mothers today. According to Marasela,

> Often my mother has said that she does not feel like she is a person who warrants any affection or attention from anyone else. She feels as though she is a *shadow*. What is also quite interesting is that we come from a society that does not expect women to have opinions about anything—even their own lives. Our role is clearly defined and our father is the head of the family and he expects himself to make all important decisions about the course of direction in our lives. When he can't,

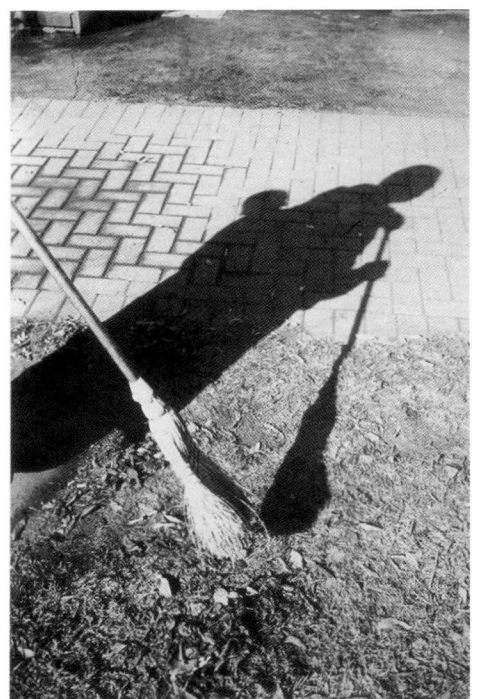
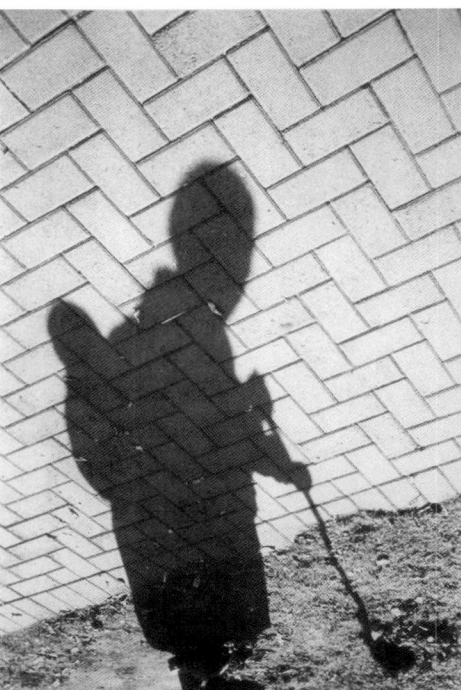
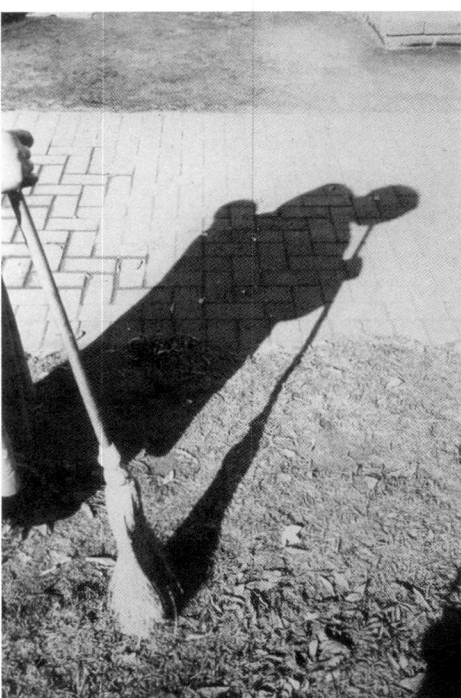

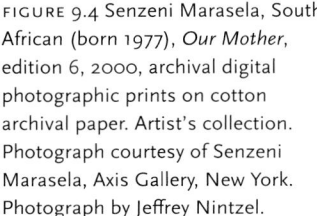

FIGURE 9.4 Senzeni Marasela, South African (born 1977), *Our Mother*, edition 6, 2000, archival digital photographic prints on cotton archival paper. Artist's collection. Photograph courtesy of Senzeni Marasela, Axis Gallery, New York. Photograph by Jeffrey Nintzel.

he feels castrated, I guess. This is not about my family alone but many others that are predominantly black and have ties to rural areas and their "culture." It is also interesting to look at how these silences are maintained and how her feelings of insignificance are true to many other black women, who feel that they are merely shadows, non-persons.[50]

The daughter of a policeman, Marasela was sent away as a girl to a Catholic school in a white Afrikaans suburb to shield her from witnessing or experiencing the horrors suffered by other black South Africans during apartheid. This, she notes, "robbed me of a chance to grow up being a proud black woman." Marasela speaks of her own guilt as the impetus behind much of her art. "By revisiting the past, by giving myself a place in it, I'll be able to forgive myself for my indifference."[51] Hence, Marasela directly confronts the elusive boundaries between private memory and public space, which for other black South Africans both during and after apartheid has been highly contested.

Marasela attempts to reconstruct memories of her mother through the manipulation of highly personal objects and imagery as mnemonic devices. These additionally serve as an avenue for confronting her own anger rooted in the past. In her more recent work, such as the *Theodorah Comes to Johannesburg* series, Marasela derives inspiration from her mother's personal histories or "her-stories." First dressing up her mother's old domestic "uniforms" with beading, embroidery, appliqué (plate 117a), lace, and doilies, Marasela then combines them with her own adorned childhood dresses or those of her young daughter Nikelwa (plate 117b), which she displays in installations together with haunting photographic self-portraits.

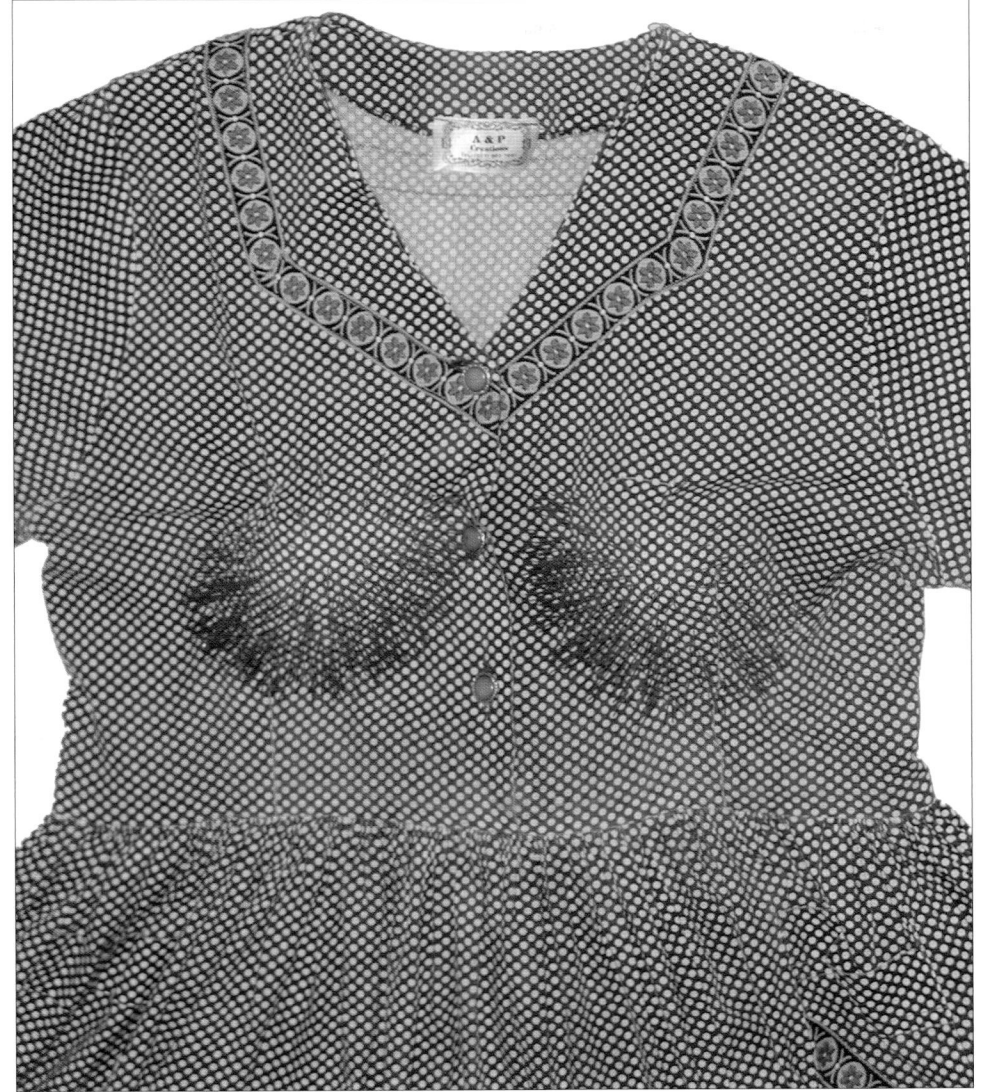

FIGURE 9.5 Senzeni Marasela, South African (born 1977), detail of plate 117, *Our Mother's Bosom*, from the *Theodorah Comes to Johannesburg Series*, 2007, cotton dress with appliqué and metal pins. Artist's collection. Photograph courtesy of Senzeni Marasela and Axis Gallery, New York.

Marasela's installation in *Black Womanhood* consists of a photographic diptych and two dresses. One photograph shows the artist inverted and prostrate in the shadows (plate 117c), wearing her mother's dress into which she has stuck numerous pins around the bosom area (figure 9.5). The image clearly evokes pain, not comfort, repugnance, not attraction, with the pins symbolizing the lack of a mother's nurturing and succor that the artist suffered as a child. The second photograph (plate 117d) shows a close-up of the artist's hands stitching another dress—the next step toward reconciliation with the past. Suspended from the ceiling and in front of the photographic diptych are two dresses: her mother's "domestic" garment (a symbol of South Africa's apartheid era) with the bust of pins and appliquéd hearts, and her daughter's blue denim dress, a symbol of South African modernity. Foreshadowing the inheritance of pain over generations of mother-and-child relationships, Marasela has stitched a message upon her daughter's dress:

I WAS TO DO THINGS THAT WOULD HURT ME MORE THAN THEM IT WAS DIFFI-
CULT TO STOP THE HOLES FROM GETTING BIGGER SO I WOULD NOT FILL THEM
WITH RESENTMENT RAGE AND REGRET OF MY EMPTINESS I LOATHED MY CHILD-
HOOD I ALMOST SUCCEEDED IN FORGETTING ABOUT HER ABSENCE AND HOW
GLARINGLY PRESENT IT WAS ON MANY OCCASIONS THAT SHOULD HAVE BEEN
IDEALLIC YOU STOLE MY DREAMS SO WHEN I STAGED REBELLIONS IT WAS TO
RECLAIM MY CHILDHOOD MY FANTASIES AND LEARN HOW TO WONDER ABOUT
SOMETHINGS OTHER THAN YOUR DEMONS I WAIT FOR THE DAY THAT YOU WILL
TAKE THEM DOWN BECAUSE THEY HAUNT US AND STEAL OUR TIME

As in much of Marasela's textile art, there is nothing dainty about the
stitched representations on the garments, which often include horrific images
or harsh narratives that convey her own and her mother's personal traumas,
haunted by loneliness, persecution, fear, lynching, and physical and psychological
abuse.[52] Excavating the memories and allowing the difficult subject matter of
abuse, oppression, and anger to resurface through her art, Marasela opens up
the dialogue about the silencing and erasure of unpleasant memories. The labor-
intensive, time-consuming process of working with textiles, needle, and thread,
on the other hand, helps Marasela reveal the internal psychological struggles of
both women as they come to grips with and reconstruct their own lives and memories within South Africa's charged history and begin the process of healing as
mother and daughter.

Presenting a very different picture of African motherhood is the American
photographer Fazal Sheikh, who in the 1990s created a series of portraits of East
African women and children. Sheikh uses these photographs to raise public
awareness about the collateral damage of war and armed civil conflicts that result
in humanitarian infractions against African women. In his series *A Camel for the
Son*, Sheikh juxtaposed serenely beautiful portraits of Somali mothers and their
children, survivors of the civil war and famine, with powerful narratives about the
trauma of refugee experiences. In his photograph *Amina Alio Abdi and her son
Mohammed* (plate 119), for example, Sheikh exposes the emotional predicament
of this Somali mother and her son, survivors of the cross-desert influx into the
feeding centers of Mandera, Kenya, in 1993:

> One afternoon a health care worker came to the feeding center to talk to the
> doctor about a family living in the camp. It was her job to identify families which
> were in need of the assistance the feeding center and hospital could offer. On
> this particular day, she had visited a family who already had a young boy at the
> feeding center; his mother brought him there every day. But when the health care
> worker visited the family she found that there was another child, an older sister,
> who was severely malnourished. When she asked the father why he had not sent
> his daughter to the center for treatment as well, he told her that it was because
> they needed their son to receive his portion without having to share it with his
> sister. The family had thought that their son's treatment would be reduced if they
> brought a second child, the daughter, to the center.[53]

In this portrait, Sheikh pulls the viewer into the image of Amina Alio Abdi through her tender, yet concerned, gaze upon her son, Mohammed, whose explicit expression alerts us to the child's fear and anguish. As in his other portraits from this series, Sheikh focuses on the emotions deeply etched into the faces of his subjects, supplementing the images with chilling narratives, sometimes collected directly from female refugees. Their stories reveal the harsh realities of human loss and the struggle for survival and dignity *within* the camp where enemy clan fighters crossed the border into Kenya to beat, rape, and humiliate the women, many who then suffered further persecution within their communities when they gave birth to the children of those who had raped them.[54]

Collaborating with his sitters in the construction of their portraits, Sheikh hopes to empower these African women, whose pleas for protection fell upon disinterested international ears. Unlike photojournalists, who candidly capture and exploit the disaster victims' moment of heightened emotional distress, Sheikh's sitters determine their own pose, dress, manner, and mood, and construct images of themselves that they want to present to the camera—and to the world, as they are fully informed and supportive of the public exposure their portraits will receive. As Sheikh notes, "Often the community would instruct the process and encourage renderings of those people and situations that they felt were relevant."[55] Sheikh's collaborative portraits therefore convey *part* of the story: the part that his subjects *want* to present of themselves, the part that highlights restoration, dignity, and healing without compromising the real consequences of their traumatic experiences.

FRAMING THE SOCIAL SELF AND OTHER THROUGH THE BLACK FEMALE BODY

Women's social roles often have been defined, determined, and depicted through images—whether in the traditional African or colonial contexts, certain materials and images have served very specific purposes of evoking associations in the viewer's mind that confirm expected ideologies. The emerging South African artist Nandipha Mntambo uses the recognizability of such icons and materials to disrupt the familiar and the expected in cultural memory.

> I have investigated notions of personal and cultural memory through the medium of cowhide. Through the use of the female form, I have investigated the broader themes of the "ideal female" and notions of femininity—about the quality of looking and behaving in the ways conventionally appropriate for a woman or girl. I have a particular interest in the subjective feelings we all have and impose on our everyday experiences. Residues of the experiences I have in my unconscious state filter into my creation of physical objects.[56]

Mntambo uses cowhide to create beautiful suspended encasings of the female form, such as in *Balandzeli* (plate 97), which play upon traditional South African cultural associations with cows and cowhide as symbols for manhood and the man's domain of life.[57] Mntambo's sculptures are beautiful and clearly feminine, while evoking culture-specific references to Zulu maternity aprons (plate 27). Yet they are also hairy, bestial, and evocative of traditional South African ideologies of manhood. As such, Mntambo's sculptures challenge the socially and culturally acceptable constructions of the female body, of femininity, and of beauty in South Africa.

> I have been preoccupied with questioning and unseating perceptions of desire, attraction, sexuality, sensuality and beauty; as all these are both subjective and ever changing. These aspects are interpreted in varying ways and cannot be condensed to one acceptable viewpoint. The subjective nature of individual interpretations and experiences, and how this influences life in general, has always been central to my production.[58]

To heighten the experience of illusion, Mntambo hangs her sculptures, which are made from casts of her own body, at a level that invites the viewer to step into or to imagine stepping into the hide, virtually becoming a part of the artwork and simultaneously occupying "a space or position that is not theirs."[59] Viewers are encouraged to imagine themselves in her skin, taking up the negative space of her absent body with all its cultural baggage and expectations, momentarily relocating the viewer's sense of self into that of the artist. Mntambo is both present and absent in her own body—a pivotal theme in the work of South African artist Berni Searle, who admits also that she is bound to representational traditions that have preceded her in her own negotiations of identity.

As Searle explains, "In many cases, my identity has been 'made' for me."[60] Yet by focusing on her own body located within her family legacy, she moves away from generic histories to reconstruct a "micro-history of the personal," a deliberate tactic that "reveals the radical insufficiencies of all identity."[61] "My work raises questions about attitudes towards race and gender," she notes, "and reflect[s] a desire to present myself in various ways to counter the image that has been imposed on me."[62]

In Searle's series *Colour Me* and *Discoloured*, history and identity reveal themselves as elusive and negotiable: perfect mechanisms to interrogate South African racial categories and the articulation of multiple—and often contradictory—identities around race and gender. "The self" she explains, "is explored as an ongoing process of construction in time and place. The presence and absence of the body in the work points to the idea that one's identity is not static, and constantly in a state of flux."[63]

Searle plays with the multiplicity of her own identities past and present by using the visual language of the nineteenth-century ethnographic gaze to disarm stereotypes of black womanhood, especially as they have played a role in South African politics, history, and visual culture. In *Traces* (plate 125), for example, Searle negotiates her own mixed or "coloured"[64] racial heritage by covering her nude body in a blanket of red, brown, and yellow spices that emulate skin colors, which "speaks in layers of both fantasy and reality."[65] Searle reflects upon her own (in)visibility in the politics of apartheid using her spice-covered skin "colour" to subvert racial content that determined intelligence, and ultimately defined also a person's "lacks" and "excesses" during the apartheid era.[66] But *Traces* also offers an escape from South Africa's oppressive skin politics, as her absent body leaves behind a negative silhouette. Hovering above images of scales and layers of aromatic spices, Searle's present/absent body protests the measuring of race in nineteenth-century and early twentieth-century anthropometry and physiognomy, which formed the basis of South African apartheid politics.

Searle's use of spices in the actual exhibition space evokes memories of fragrant exotic worlds and aromatic foreign foods, which celebrate the distinct culinary traditions of her culturally mixed family heritage.[67] The inclusion of the spices in both image and installation, however, serves as a powerful reminder of the global spice trade that brought white colonists and the slave trade to the Cape of Good Hope in the seventeenth century. This development eventually led to mixed marriages between local inhabitants and slaves and immigrants from other parts of Africa and the Indian Ocean, which produced children of mixed racial heritage, as in Searle's own family history.

During Searle's physical performances, which serve as the basis of her photographic installations, the spices act as irritants on her body. Through the spices she simultaneously references and *experiences* trauma and damage, reenacting the painful oppression suffered by slaves and later by blacks during colonialism and apartheid. The impermanence of the coloration of spices on her body, however, reveals also the superficiality of definitions of race and the resulting stereotypes, which deny the complexity of an individual's identities. "The ability to color oneself, on a range of levels, according to one's own agency and desire" allows Searle to assert her diverse identities, to reinvent and re-present the Self.[68]

Searle's photographic performances are as much about racial politics in South Africa as they are about sexuality and gender. Searle is very conscious of the possible (mis)interpretation of her body images as exotic when seen outside of South Africa, which could reinforce the very stereotypes she is trying to subvert. While many Western viewers might associate her nudity with sexuality, Searle uses it to evoke African women's exploitation of the power of their own nudity as a tactic of resistance to disarm colonial and Apartheid oppression. For example, in 1929 crowds of nude women took to the streets in anti-colonialist demonstrations in Eastern Nigeria. Another example occurred in 1990 when a group of black women in the South African town of Soweto stripped off their clothes as an act of resistance to male policemen who had been ordered to evacuate the informal settlement and an army of bulldozers that were going to destroy their fragile homes.

In *Stain*, Searle extends the metaphoric exploitation of one's own nude body to evoke also the history of violence and aggression against the African female body.[69] In South Africa, as elsewhere in Africa, rape has been a major risk for women caught in the midst of political conflict. During the apartheid era, women in war zones were often made to pay for the deeds of their absent husbands,

stain /steɪn/ v. & n. —v. 1 tr. & intr. discolour or be discoloured by the action of liquid sinking in. 2 tr. sully, blemish, spoil, damage (a reputation, character, etc.). 3 tr. colour (wood, glass, etc.) by a process other than painting or covering the surface. 4 tr. impregnate (a specimen) for microscopic examination with colouring matter that makes the structure visible by being deposited in some parts more than in others. 5 tr. print colours on (wallpaper). —n. 1 a discoloration, a spot or mark caused esp. by contact with foreign matter and not easily removed (a cloth covered with tea-stains). 2 a a blot or blemish. b damage to a reputation etc. (a stain on one's character). 3 a substance used in staining.

stain /steɪn/ v. & n. —v. 1 tr. & intr. discolour or be discoloured by the action of liquid sinking in. 2 tr. sully, blemish, spoil, damage (a reputation, character, etc.). 3 tr. colour (wood, glass, etc.) by a process other than painting or covering the surface. 4 tr. impregnate (a specimen) for microscopic examination with colouring matter that makes the structure visible by being deposited in some parts more than in others. 5 tr. print colours on (wallpaper). —n. 1 a discoloration, a spot or mark caused esp. by contact with foreign matter and not easily removed (a cloth covered with tea-stains). 2 a a blot or blemish. b damage to a reputation etc. (a stain on one's character). 3 a substance used in staining.

stain /steɪn/ v. & n. —v. 1 tr. & intr. discolour or be discoloured by the action of liquid sinking in. 2 tr. sully, blemish, spoil, damage (a reputation, character, etc.). 3 tr. colour (wood, glass, etc.) by a process other than painting or covering the surface. 4 tr. impregnate (a specimen) for microscopic examination with colouring matter that makes the structure visible by being deposited in some parts more than in others. 5 tr. print colours on (wallpaper). —n. 1 a discoloration, a spot or mark caused esp. by contact with foreign matter and not easily removed (a cloth covered with tea-stains). 2 a a blot or blemish. b damage to a reputation etc. (a stain on one's character). 3 a substance used in staining.

FIGURE 9.6 (detail of plate 124) Berni Searle, South African (b. 1964), *Stain*, from the *Discolored Series*, 5 panels, 2000, digital print with text. Hood Museum of Art: Purchased through the William B. Jaffe and Evelyn F. Jaffe Fund; PR.2002.67.1-5. Photograph by Jeffrey Nintzel. See plate 124, page 000.

brothers, and fathers through sexual torture and the violation of their bodies. In *Stain*, Searle magnifies those hidden parts of her body most commonly associated with tenderness and intimacy: the palms of her hands, the small of her back, the nape of her neck, the soles of her feet, and her belly. Upon closer inspection of the images, however, it is apparent that Searle has abruptly broken the promise of seduction and tenderness through the disturbing presence of purplish stains, made of Egyptian henna smeared on her body pressed up against a pane of glass. The appearance of swelling, distortion, and discoloration suggests bruising, abuse, violence, injury, and disease. Searle heightens the sense of violence conveyed by the photographs by including dictionary entries of the word "stain," circling specific meanings that, coupled with specific body parts, commit further violence upon the body (figure 9.6).

Zanele Muholi, an emerging South Africa artist also confronts the subject of violence to the female body in photographs that evolve around the lives and abuses that black gay women experience in South African townships. While some of her images highlight the pleasures and intimacy of the Gay/Lesbian/Bisexual/Transgender/Intersex (LGBTI) communities, many reveal the hate crimes and oppression directed toward them. As a gender and sexual rights activist, Muholi's work is without precedent in South Africa, where she has introduced a new and controversial perspective about gay women's sexuality into the national artistic landscape (plate 122), with its lack of black women openly portraying lesbian practices. Transgressing deep taboos about black female same-sex practices, she offers a radical break from stereotypical, male-dominated narratives about black female sexuality. She also disrupts the popular notion that lesbianism does not exist in African cultures.

Muholi's respectful relationship with LGBTI communities grants her entrance into their intimate spaces and provides the outsider with a sensitive and deeply personal glimpse into the challenges that black gay women face in South Africa. As Muholi explains, *Sex ID Crisis* and other works from this series of photographs

> document/constructs some of the key issues that confront our communities, including the lack of ownership many LGBTIs feel they have over their voices and space in the places they live, learn and work. The lack of visibility often results in crisis of sexual and gender identity, a closeted life and unemployment as some LGBTIs are forced out of school or work places because of their gender and sexual non-conformity in a society dominated by heterosexuality and patriarchy.[70]

In South Africa, where photography remains predominately a male art, Muholi's photographs evoke moments of women "living under siege"[71] in the first African nation to pass a Same Sex Civil Union bill. Hence she is carving out a public space for resistance to preconceptions about LGBTI communities while opening up greater dialogue about sexual and gender diversity. Her photographs empower her female subjects to reclaim the visual landscape after centuries of objectification through male fantasies about female sexuality.

TRAGIC IDENTITIES OF THE DISTANT BODY

In their preface to the exhibition catalogue *Distant Relatives/Relative Distance,*
curators Michael Stevenson and Joost Bosland assert,

> Artists with African connections living elsewhere in the world are, as a matter of
> course, negotiating their relative distance or closeness to the continent and
> these physical, cultural and ideological links manifest themselves on various lev-
> els. . . . The varied ways in which these artists respond to their relative distances
> from Africa encourage viewers to resist reductive assumptions around geograph-
> ical and national classifications. Their disparate aesthetic sensibilities, drawing
> on their different life histories and their fluid movements between capitals and
> continents, explode preconceptions that the adjectives of "contemporary" and
> "African" in any way limit or confine their art practice.[72]

Etiyé Dimma Poulsen defines herself as "a cultural hybrid,"[73] whose artwork
attempts to reconcile a fragmented identity. As an orphaned child, Poulsen was
transported from the once-familiar environment of a war-torn and famine-ridden
Ethiopian village into a small Danish town where her adopted family raised her. In
Scandinavia, she struggled to find language, belonging, and integration. Art
became her means of "reconstruct[ing] the complexity of an unspeakable experience,"[74] as well as an alternative means of expressing herself and her emotions.[75]
But when she later moved to France and then Belgium, Poulsen began to redis-
cover her African cultural heritage—which had been erased while growing up in
Denmark—through the vivid African communities she encountered in their cities.

> Growing up, I rarely thought of myself as black, even though I was constantly
> conscious of the fact that I was different from those around me. I perceived
> myself as human, not belonging to any nationality. My origins sacrificed, I was
> subjected to a very Western culture. I grew up listening to opera and classical
> music at home. . . . Of course, I am gradually becoming aware of my roots, my
> African side, and Ethiopian culture and arts, especially after moving to France.
> Living in Denmark, after my brothers and sisters left home, I was surrounded by
> Danish people all the time. When I arrived in France, I started to see more black
> people. It was like living a dream, I felt more "at home" in a way. It was like a rev-
> elation, a new kind of vision. I almost forgot who I was, how I looked . . . one
> could say that living in France started a kind of "return" to Africa for me.[76]

Clay, with its inherent connection to earth and land, became Poulsen's
medium of choice, reconnecting her with memories of Africa and its women.
Her technique of firing thinly layered clay on iron mesh produces "an exact copy
of the African soil, baked and torn apart by the sun."[77] Poulsen renders her
female figures tall, dignified, and proud (plate 102), yet they appear to be also
fragile, worn out, and cracked, as though "eroded from the years of harsh life and
perseverance"—like the women in her childhood village of Aroussi in the high-
lands of Ethiopia who struggle daily to keep their children alive.[78]

If you take a close look at the sculpture, you will be surprised to find that the expressions of the faces are actually generated by a cracked line which traces an eye or a wrinkle caused by the combustions and firing: it seems exactly through corrosion and fragmentation, the opposite—life—emerges![79]

Poulsen's regal sculptures help the artist reclaim her lost heritage, her mother, and her land, giving form to recollections that bring her closer to a sense of belonging in both Europe and Africa. Poulsen incorporates her own personal studies of African sculptural arts, especially Ethiopian art, into her sculptures, which emulate the archaic forms of terracotta fertility figures excavated from the scorched East African earth. But her figures possess also a certain contemporaneity in their simulation of the expansive corporeal presence of black *émigrées* living in European cities, their lower bodies wrapped in thick layers of colorfully patterned wrappers and cloths that explicitly—and proudly—announce their African heritage.

I still enjoy looking at African women in the streets and metro stations in Paris dressed in their "boubous" and their gracious bodies and beautiful black skin. African traditional sculpture moves me the same way. It is very gracious and very serene. This is very clear in the female figures.[80]

The poetic forms and spontaneous surfaces of her terracotta figures commemorate the beauty and perseverance of Africa's women, as she remembers them from her youth, whose lives are devoted to domestic labor, child rearing, toiling in the unforgiving fields, and—like Poulsen's mother before she died—selling produce at local markets to feed their children and make ends meet.

Also paying homage to Africa's women, Maud Sulter, a photographer and a poet of Scottish and Ghanaian descent, uncovers racist and sexist ideologies that led to the loss of history, particularly the erasure and silencing of the black female presence in Western history. As art historian Angela Rosenthal explains, Sulter

deals with the mysterious disappearance and erasure of a black presence in Europe, uncovering the destinies of people in the dark part of Europe's history, under slavery and the Holocaust, and shedding light on the life of the African and European diaspora. Yet the rhetoric of her art is subtle, highly ironic, and although polemical also always composed as poetic narrative. It is as if one was listening to the stories of the muse Calliope, in the ZABAT series impersonated by Sulter herself, who draws us into her spell, and simultaneously asks us to start searching for traces of a history, that has hitherto been silenced.[81]

ZABAT is a muse-series of nine large-scale Cibachrome works that Sulter produced in 1989 for the Rochdale Art Gallery (Greater Manchester, England), and that belongs in part to the Victoria and Albert Museum in London. Through this work, Rosenthal notes, Sulter establishes a poetic homage to black women artists.

The series finds a visual and aesthetic form to address the struggle with the dominant (white, male) arts establishment without getting caught up in limiting discourses about identity and institutional politics. The historical portraits each feature a prominent black woman artist, in the role of a muse, with different attributes and costumes of their choosing. For instance, the writer Alice Walker appears as Thalia, the comic muse; Ysaye Aria Barnwell, the singer of Sweet Honey in the Rock, is Polyhymnia, the muse of the sacred hymn, who is presenting a peacock egg in her left hand—symbolizing beginning and end; the visual artist Lubaina Himid appears as Urania, the "heavenly" muse of astronomy and astrology; and Clio is a portrait of Dorothea Smart. Performance artist Della Street enacts Terpsichore, the "joyful" Muse of Dance (plate 99). Resplendently dressed in shimmering pearl-white silk-dress that dramatically sets off her brown skin, and wearing a white aristocratic wig, Terpsichore evokes the Western portrait tradition depicting a white aristocratic woman with her black pages.[82] But here these figures are provocatively fused into one. Paintings in this tradition were popular in the seventeenth and eighteenth centuries in countries associated with the slave trade. Holland, England, and later, but to a lesser degree, in France, such paintings usually show white women with African pageboys. On rare occasions a black female slave or domestic servant appears.[83]

Sulter's *Terpsichore*, Rosenthal asserts, is neither slave nor servant. She is her own mistress, holding in her hand an attribute to Fool's Gold, which according to Sulter refers to the gold rush and the sugar trade. Sulter combines her photographs with poetry that evokes the history of slavery, abolitionism, emancipation, and modern life.[84] The poetic lines from *Terpsichore*, for example, reprimand the viewer to never forget one's own dark colonial history:

> For these things you have laid your dignity in the mud of history and we shall not forget. For sugar in your tea and a maid to sit for your portraits. For gold to wear at your bosom and a maid whose image you shall have painted out of your family portrait when the presence has become a trait not a gilding.[85]

The Muses' attributes refer also to other histories that witnessed the disavowment of black presence in the European culture, which literally has been erased. Sulter's *ZABAT* series participates in this process by seeking to counter cultural amnesia and marginalization in a way that literally relocates black women into the center of the pictorial stage. As such, Sulter exposes the sexist and racist presumptions of the Western portrait traditions, as they have existed throughout history.[86]

Also calling attention to cultural erasure and silencing, the artist cooperative IngridMwangiRobertHutter creates installation pieces that focus on the experiences of "hyphenated persons," as embodied by the Kenyan-German artist Ingrid Mwangi, who is regarded as a white person in Africa and a black person in Europe. Forced to deal with prejudices and alienation in both countries of her origin, Mwangi is in constant dialogue with herself and society, exploring, reinventing, and re-presenting her own corporeality according to her personal and the artists' collective experiences of self-discovery and self-reinvention.[87]

In *Dressed Like Queens* (plate 114), the IngridMwangiRobertHutter cooperative directly confronts racism, exoticism, and identity embedded in the persistent stereotyping they encounter in German daily life. This installation is comprised of three videos projected onto a triptych of large, hand-dyed red, brown, and green fabrics commissioned in Kenya. The central projection shows a pregnant woman, moving in a slow, majestic manner, who is flanked on each side by images of Mwangi, who emphatically narrates a text about African women—the metaphorical queens—whose clothes have been taken away from them. The narrative bears witness to the subjects' journey through difficult and troubled times, but whose strength, power, and insistence help them reclaim their rightful property and dignity. Mwangi's synthesized voice creates beastly sounds derived from discriminatory images in the Western perception of African savagery and brutal racial stereotypes, many recreated in Western historic images, comic strips, cartoons, and popular movies.

Encapsulating her own deep attachment to Africa and Europe, the Cameroonian photographer Angèle Etoundi Essamba, who lives in the Netherlands, aspires to unify and harmonize cultural differences and distances through the black female body.

> As a black woman living in a white world, I have chosen to picture the world in black and white. Otherness, identity/duality, modernity/tradition, mysticism/reality . . . are important issues which always come back in my photographs. I attempt to shape a world of unity [through the] meeting of forms, races, and cultures. I want to show that a dialogue exists between cultures.[88]

These themes are especially apparent in her work from the 1980s, in which she focused on the relationship between African women, ideologies, and cosmologies. In *Esprit 2* (figure 9.7), for example, she overlaps the profile of a young African woman with a traditional African mask representing female spiritual beauty, to demonstrate "the close and intimate relationship, the cohabitation of the mystic and the human, the interaction between the world of our ancestors and our world."[89] In the traditional African cultural context, women—and masks representing women—are often considered to be direct links to the world of deities, spirits, and ancestors. In *Esprit 2*, Essamba attempts to reestablish this connection for herself (and for other women), which she asserts can be so easily disrupted when living as an African in Europe.

In her more recent photographs, her black female subjects celebrate the diversity of their experiences of strength and individuality. As the artist notes, by "showing strong women, self assured dark women, who are fully aware of their beauty, sensuality, and strength, I want to break through the cliché image of the oppressed woman."[90] In *Noirs #211* (plate 113), Essamba captures the serene beauty of the sculptural form of a pregnant woman's belly, dramatically lit to heighten its sumptuous form. Like a Dutch still life, it is a "representation of the black body in its full maturity—ripe fruit, pregnant and fertile, dynamic, the Tree of Life. The pregnant body becomes a mental space reflecting fascinations, a

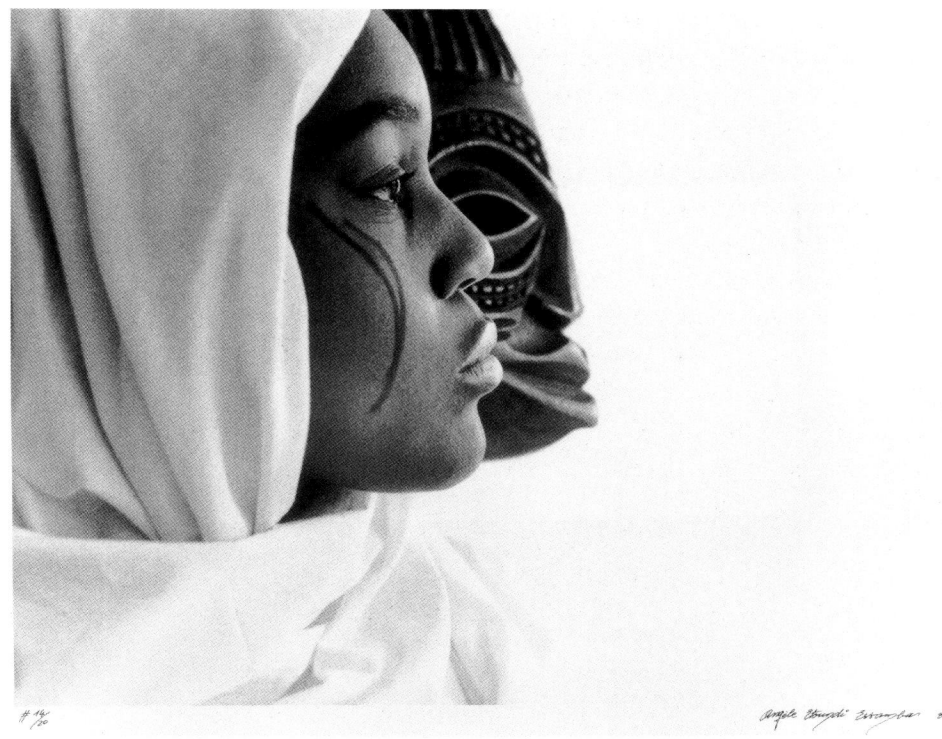

FIGURE 9.7 Angèle E. Essamba, Cameroonian (born 1962), *Esprit 2*, 1985, gelatin silver print. Hood Museum of Art: Purchased through the Alvin and Mary Bert Gutman 1940 Acquisition Fund; PH.2003.30.3. Photograph by Jeffrey Nintzel.

space for contemplation."[91] Dark drapery obscures the subject's "blackness," diverting the viewer's attention away from her race (which played such an important role in historical definitions of sexuality) and refocusing it on the contemplation of beauty, strength, and hope for new life.

In the work of the U.S.-based, Cuban-born artist Maria Magdalena Campos-Pons, the challenge of living "elsewhere in the world" creates an open-ended investigation into history and memory and an examination of their roles in the formation of her own continually evolving identity as a black woman living in the globalized world. Campos-Pons notes that when she entered art school in Cuba she became

> aware of the absence of female black artists in the history of Cuban art. I took that as an opportunity and also a privilege, as my mission or role to fulfill. That has been my driving force. I have had the privilege to tell the stories that I have wanted to talk about. I don't know if I am a writer who detoured to visual arts because I am a storyteller, but [my work] is more about a collective story that I try to tell using my body as a device [to be] anybody, as a [representation of] separation, uprooting, and the anguish of it; of exile—forced or voluntary—and the anguish of it; of displacement due to political, economical, or personal reasons. I don't want to call it tragedy, these journeys and their implications. I try to be as metaphorical as possible, because I don't want [my art works] to be read as my personal stories. They are not. They are only reflections; I use the power of language to reflect and comment upon [them].[92]

Consequently her art evolves around women's histories in slavery, migration, fragmentation, and journeys across oceans, which for her carry memories of Africa, Cuba, Europe, and America in a constant cycle of translation, renewal, and self-discovery.[93]

Campos-Pons centrally locates her body, fragmented and then reconstructed—both actually and metaphorically—in framed twenty-four-by-twelve-inch Polaroid photographs (plates 115, 120, and 121). She is simultaneously in one and many places, each body fragment occupying its own territory but together becoming the sum of all its parts. Her body—and her person—yearn for but do not always find belonging in one place; yet she finds comfort in the plurality of place: a consequence of her hybrid identity. Campos-Pons notes that while she was growing up in Cuba,

> Africa was my backyard . . . Africa was my mother, my grandmother, my uncle. It was everything that I knew, and that was a very rare feeling but almost a displaced feeling. When I arrived in Africa [in my forties], I was writing "can you ever return to a place you never left but where you have never been before?" At the same time, Cuba is very European and when I am in Europe I feel very much at home . . . when I am in Paris, I think "Havana!" All this sense of overlap and juxtaposition, [causes] hybridity and fragmentation—a disparity of elements and culture. It is flamboyant to some extent. But Cuba is a very flamboyant place. It is exuberant in nature and by cultural construct. It is exuberant in the way that it thinks about itself: it is this tiny little island with pretensions that are much, much larger than what it actually is. Cuba takes up a lot of space in the imagination![94]

Using her body, Campos-Pons performs this imagined space that is Cuba—"larger than what it actually is"—where many things and cultures come together to form its multiple identities.

> Cuba is very hybrid. It is very mysterious. It is very mulatto; it is a melting pot for real. It is a Mesoamerican culture with indigenous tradition, an African culture, and a Hispanic culture that merged, in a way, I think . . . like Brazil. This kind of interrelationship—interweaving of culture—takes a stronghold to define and to construct what the culture is.[95]

In answer to this line of inquiry, Campos-Pons inscribes newly negotiated identities upon her own black female body. Like the transnational experience, her body accepts and rejects, maintains and transforms, deconstructs and reconstructs blackness, femininity, and sexuality—based on her own terms rather than those imposed on her. Her body becomes a repository for both memory and its renegotiation—along with all the pain, imagination, and dreaming that this entails.

In her self-portraiture, Campos-Pons adorns her body in colors, symbols, objects, and textures that recall her youthful memories of African cultural elements in Cuba, while also reliving her actual experiences of being and traveling in the world today. These visual narratives are physical transformations that echo not only her own continual process of questioning and redefining the boundaries of her layered identities (as a Cuban, a black woman, and a transnational artist) but also of the subversive methods that other black women in the world use to overcome their boundaries, such as in *Bim Bim Lady Dakar Swatch* (plate 121):

> "Bim Bim Lady" refers to what I witnessed in my visits to the market in Dakar, Senegal, where the ladies sell numbers of very salacious and erotic items. I found it very intriguing and powerful that we make all kinds of misconceived readings of the need to spread our Western feminist parameters of freedom, sexuality, etc. to the "oppressed/repressed" veiled Muslim women. Then you arrive in Dakar, as in my case, and find the most provocative, determined women. The Bim Bim are lingerie made out of African beads, full of imagination and lust. The fabric in my photo is usually intended for use around the hips in a well-choreographed night dance, I was told. In any case, I left the market with new knowledge and a few good items.
>
> Of course it is not my intention to imply a reading of freedom and western feminism only as an equation of sexual eroticism or lust. I just found my personal reading [of these women] very revealing and intriguing, especially the implication of the subversive component under apparent standards of submission. My take [on these ladies] is only partially fragmentary and without the deep understanding behind their social-political circumstances.
>
> In my interpretation, I go back and further press the issue, placing the intended fabric in a unlike function. So I am celebrating the sense of adventure and power of the beautiful and resilient ladies under their veil working the market from sunrise to sunset in the dusty roads of Dakar.[96]

Unlike the veiled "Bim Bim" ladies of Dakar, Campos-Pons bares herself to the world. And yet like the strength hidden under their veils, Campos-Pons remains guarded and in control, distancing herself from and resisting the viewer's familiarity through tactics of visual subversion: eyes closed, back to the viewer, corporeal fragmentation, such as in two works from *When I Am Not Here/Estoy Allá* (plate 115 and 120), presenting only parts of the whole. As she asserts, this is a selfhood inscribed by one's own choosing. It is liberating and creates a vast realm of self-(re)discovery. By questioning "the history and code of representation" of black womanhood through her own body,[97] Campos-Pons negotiates for herself a new territory of hybridity. This new territory is a place, she exclaims, where she hopes there will be "more kindness and more tolerance . . . to recognize the [importance of] plurality" in ideologies of black womanhood.[98]

CONCLUSION

Western iconographies of race and sexuality have consistently cast black women as simplistic stereotypes, such as the "Hottentot Venus," the "Sable Venus," the "odalisque," "Mammy," and more. As Janell Hobson has pointed out, "struggles for black female subjectivity constantly grate against [these] distorted images of the dominant culture." And consequently, artists seeking new feminist aesthetics of the black female body have had to take up "an oppositional stance" to subvert ideologies of "the black body grotesque."[99]

The contemporary artists in *Black Womanhood* have crossed multiple boundaries to decolonize these injurious meanings inscribed and enacted upon the black female body. And as their statements and artwork indicate, the very same clichés that oppressed, misrepresented, and objectified black womanhood throughout history now serve as some of their most effective tools in disarming the racist ideologies that they embody. These artists' provocative and defiant objectives remove Western-centric ideologies of black womanhood from an obstinate racialized position, placing them instead into a critical discourse about the disputability and mutability of both historical and contemporary "truths," revealing the complex and multiple identities of black women throughout time and (trans)cultural contexts. The joining together of these diverse artistic voices in writing a new chapter of visual history demands that the dominant culture steps back and considers its own role and choices in the construction, questioning, or shattering of their "own fictions of self"[100] as well as in the fictions of difference and otherness that divide and distance rather than unite. ❧

1 Jennifer L. Morgan, "'Some Could Suckle over Their Shoulder': Male Travelers, Female Bodies, and the Gendering of Racial Ideology, 1500–1770," *The William and Mary Quarterly*, 3rd series, 54, no. 1 (January 1997): 169.

2 Peter Erickson, "Representation of Black and Blackness in the Renaissance," *Criticism* 35: 514–515; Morgan, "'Some Could Suckle over Their Shoulder,'" 169,

3 Morgan, "'Some Could Suckle over Their Shoulder,'" 170.

4 Perhaps the most widely known examples of such iconic figures include the black nymphs in Hieronymus Bosch's *Garden of Earthly Delights* (circa 1510); the black slave/servant in Edouard Manet's *Olympia* (1863); the harem women in Delacroix's *Women of Algiers* (1834); and countless other Orientalist depictions in the nineteenth century. For a treatise on the representation of blacks in Western art history, see Jean Vercoutter, Jean Devisse, Amadou-Mahtar M'Bow, Michel Mollat, Frank M. Snowden, and the Menil Foundation, *The Image of the Black in Western Art* (Cambridge: Harvard University Press and Houston: Menil Foundation, 1976).

5 Morgan, "'Some Could Suckle over Their Shoulder,'" 191.

6 See Lauri Firstenberg, "Perverse Anthropology: The Photomontage of Wangechi Mutu," in *Looking Both Ways: Art of the Contemporary African Diaspora*, ed. Laurie Farrell (New York: Museum for African Art and Gent: Snoeck Publishers, 2003), 137–143, for a discussion with the artist about her work.

7 Wangechi Mutu, artist's statement for the exhibition *Creatures by Wangechi Mutu*, Jamaica Center for Arts and Learning, Jamaica, New York, February 1, 2003– April 12, 2003.

8 Ibid.

9 Quoted in Merrily Kerr, "Wangechi Mutu's Extreme Makeovers," *Art on Paper* 8, no. 6 (July/August 2004). As of February 16, 2007, available at http://www.akrylic.com/ articles/44/1/Wangechi-Mutus-Extreme-Makeovers/Art-On-Paper-Vol. 8-No-6-JulyAugust-2004.html.

10 Mutu, artist's statement for the exhibition *Creatures by Wangechi Mutu*.

11 Erika Dalya Muhammad, "Body Politic," *Art Review* 2, no. 6 (2004): 61–63.

12 Quoted in Tara MacDowell, "New Works: Wangechi Mutu" (San Francisco: San Francisco Museum of Modern Art, 2006).

13 See Annie E. Coombes, "Gender, 'Race,' Ethnicity in Art Practice in Post-Apartheid South Africa: Annie E. Coombes and Penny Siopis in Conversation," *Feminist Review* 55 (Spring 1997): 110–129, for an interview with Siopis about her new work after the end of apartheid.

14 Houston A. Baker Jr., "Islands of Identity: Inside the Pictures of Carrie Mae Weems," in *These Islands: South Carolina and Georgia by Carrie Mae Weems* (Tuscaloosa: University of Alabama Sarah Moody Gallery of Art, 1995), 15.

15 Lalla Essaydi, artist's statement sent by e-mail communication to Barbara Thompson, October 6, 2006.

16 See Christaud M. Geary, "The Female Black Body, the Postcard, and the Archive," in this volume.

17 See Geary, "The Female Black Body, the Postcard, and the Archive," in this volume, for a discussion of this racist convention also in other parts of Africa.

18 For a larger discussion of Essaydi's subversive use of classic Arabic calligraphy on woman's body, clothing, and the ground she walks on to describe the internal world of the female experience, see Susan Denker, "Lalla A. Essaydi: Converging Territories," *Nka, Journal of Contemporary African Art* 19 (Summer 2004): 86–87.

19 Excerpt from written text on Essaydi's cloths. Translation provided by the artist.

20 The Berber peoples, who are ethnically, culturally, and linguistically distinct from Arabs, consider themselves the indigenous inhabitants of northern Africa.

21 Essaydi, personal communication with Barbara Thompson, 2006.

22 Essaydi, artist's statement for the exhibition *Converging Territories* at the Lawrence Miller Gallery, New York, quoted in Amanda Carlson, *Converging Territories*, ed. Laurence Miller (New York: powerHouse Books, 2005), 27.

23 Essaydi, artist's statement for the exhibition *Converging Territories*.

24 The henna designs are often comprised of series of lozenges, rows of triangular motifs often surrounding squares or rectangles, and zigzags. Sometimes the lozenges are spiked with five projections to denote the concept of *baraka*, which is expressed also in the gesture or depiction of an outstretched hand to invoke the symbolism of five, or *khamsa*. This latter symbol is apparent in the way that the diamond, zigzag, and triangular patterns are often grouped in fives in Berber women's body arts.

25 Essaydi, artist's notes on new series of work, *Femmes du Maroc*, 2005, sent by the artist in an e-mail to Barbara Thompson, October 27, 2006.

26 Amanda Carlson, "Leaving One's Mark: The Photography of Lalla Essaydi," in *Converging Territories*, ed. Laurence Miller (New York: powerHouse Books, 2005), 5.

27 Carla Williams, artist's statement, 2002, quoted in Janell Hobson, "The 'Batty' Politic: Toward an Aesthetic of the Black Female Body," *Hypatia* 18, no. 4 (Fall 2003): 98.

28 Hobson, "The 'Batty' Politic," 98.

29 Carla Williams, artist's statement, 2002, quoted in Hobson, "The 'Batty' Politic," 98.

30 Ibid.

31 Malick Sidibé, personal communication with Barbara Thompson, August 26, 2006.

32 Ibid.

33 Ibid.

34 Ibid.

35 Ibid.

36 Ibid.

37 Ibid.

38 See Thompson, "The African Female Body in the Cultural Imagination," and Ifi Amadiume, "African Women's Body Images in Postcolonial Discourse and Resistance to Neo-Crusaders," both in this volume. See also Mary Nooter Roberts, *Body Politics: The Female Image in Luba Art and the Sculpture of Alison Saar* (Los Angeles: UCLA Fowler Museum of Cultural History, 2000).

39 See Jessica Dallow and Barbara C. Matilsky, *Family Legacies: The Art of Betye, Lezley, and Alison Saar* (Chapel Hill: Ackland Art Museum and Seattle: University of Washington Press, 2005), for a discussion of Saar's work in conjunction with African American cultural symbolism.

40 Morgan, "'Some Could Suckle over Their Shoulder,'" 179.

41 Joyce J. Scott, quoted in Leslie King-Hammond, "Acting Up and Out: Artistry in the Life of Joyce Jane Scott," in *Joyce J. Scott Kickin' It with the Old Masters*

(Baltimore: Baltimore Museum of Art and Maryland Institute, College of Art, 2000), 11.

42 King-Hammond, "Acting Up and Out: Artistry in the Life of Joyce Jane Scott," 10.

43 Scott, quoted by Keith Morrison, "Pin-Pricked Deities: The Art of Joyce Scott," in King-Hammond et al., *Joyce J. Scott Kickin' It with the Old Masters*, 68.

44 Scott quoted in King-Hammond, "Acting Up and Out: Artistry in the Life of Joyce Jane Scott," 13.

45 Joyce J. Scott, personal e-mail communication with Barbara Thompson, May 16, 2007.

46 Joyce J. Scott, quoted in King Hammond et al., *Joyce J. Scott Kickin' It with the Old Masters*, 54.

47 Artist statement for *Black Womanhood*, personal e-mail communication, May 16, 2007.

48 Colin Richards, "Senzeni Marasela," in *10 Years 100 Artists: Art in a Democratic South Africa* (Cape Town: Bell-Roberts Publishing, 2004), 230.

49 Ibid.

50 Ibid.

51 Senzeni Marasela, personal communication with Lisa Brittan and Gary Van Wyk, 2006.

52 When Marasela's mother was institutionalized for clinical depression for a period of two years off and on, the hospital staff recorded the therapy sessions, many of which recalled unpleasant memories of physical and sexual abuse that her mother had suffered, presumable by an "uncle," who was never confronted with the matter by those who knew about it. Marasela's mother has since forgotten these memories due to her illness.

53 Fazal Sheik, *A Camel for the Son* (Rotterdam: Netherlands Photo Institute, 2001), 49.

54 Sheikh, *A Camel for the Son*, 16. The United Nations High Commission for Refugees estimates that between 1993 and 1999, almost 8,000 women were raped in and around the refugee camps of Kenya's northeastern desert. Similar abuses currently being experienced by women in Darfur, Sudan, reveal the continued failure on the part of the international community to protect women against humanitarian abuses in times of conflict.

55 Fazal Sheikh, personal communication with Barbara Thompson, 2003.

56 Nandipha Mntambo, artist's statement for MAFA thesis proposal at Cape Town University, Michaelis School of Fine Art, Cape Town, 2006.

57 See my essay "The African Female Body in the Cultural Imagination," in this volume, in which I discuss cow symbolism in the Zulu culture.

58 Mntambo, artist's statement for MAFA thesis proposal at Cape Town University, Michaelis School of Fine Art.

59 Ibid.

60 Quoted in Rory Bester, "Floating Free," in *Berni Searle* (Cape Town: Bell-Roberts Publishing, 2003), 10.

61 Liese Van der Watt, "Identity's Lack, Identity's Excess: Two Works by Berni Searle and Minette Vári," in *A Decade of Democracy*, ed. Emma Bedfors (Cape Town: South African National Gallery, 2004), 120.

62 Quoted in Sue Williamson, "Berni Searle," *ArtThrob*, http://www.artthrob.co.za/00may/artbio.html, 2000.

63 Ibid.

64 In apartheid South Africa, the term "coloured" referred to people of mixed racial heritage, who were classified into seven genetic subgroups as determined by invasive tests and measurements of their physical features.

65 Tracy Murinik, "Berni Searle," *Nka, Journal of Contemporary African Art* 13/14 (Spring/Summer 2001): 77–78.

66 See Van der Watt, "Identity's Lack, Identity's Excess," for a discussion of the ways in which Searle's work plays with issues of lack and excess.

67 One of Searle's maternal great-grandfathers came from Mauritius as a cook, the other from Saudi Arabia, bringing with them distinct culinary traditions that became part of Searle's family life (Van der Watt, "Tracing Berni Searle," *African Arts* 37, no. 4 [Winter 2004]: 77).

68 Murinik, "Berni Searle," 78. See also Bester, "Floating Free."

69 Coombes, "Gender, 'Race,' Ethnicity in Art Practice in Post-Apartheid South Africa," 187.

70 Zanele Muholi, artist's statement for *Visual Sexualities*, a mini-exhibition held in conjunction with the Gender and Visuality Workshop, University of the Western Cape, Library Atrium, August 26–September 10, 2004.

71 Pumla Dineo Gqola, quoted in Gabi Ngcobo, "Zanele Muholi," *ArtThrob*, http://www.artthrob.co.za/06dec/artbio.html, undated.

72 Michael Stevenson and Joost Bosland, *Distant Relatives/Relative Distance* (Cape Town: Michael Stevenson Gallery, 2006), 12.

73 Quoted in Florence Alexis, "Creativity and the Hybrid Subject: Etiyé Dimma Poulsen, the Artist in Her Own Words," in *Gendered Visions: The Art of Contemporary Africana Women Artists*, ed. Salah M. Hassan (Trenton: Africa World Press, 1997), 58.

74 Quoted in Alexis, "Creativity and the Hybrid Subject," 53.

75 Ibid., 60.

76 Quoted in ibid., 58–59.

77 Quoted in ibid., 53.

78 Ibid., 55.

79 Quoted in ibid., 60.

80 Quoted in ibid., 60–61.

81 Angela Rosenthal, personal e-mail communication with Barbara Thompson, February 27, 2007.

82 Maud Sulter states that "'Della Street' . . . had created that costume as part of a dance performance, installation-type piece called 'The Quizzing Glass.' It was dealing with the relationships between women within the power imbalance of a slave/mistress situation" (http://www.vam.ac.uk/vastatic/microsites/photography/story.php?storyid= pho52&row=2).

83 Rosenthal, personal e-mail communication with Barbara Thompson, February 27, 2007. See David Dabydeen, *Hogarth's Blacks: Images of Blacks in Eighteenth Century English Art* (Athens: University of Georgia Press, 1987), 21–36, and Kim Hall, *Things of Darkness: Economies of Race and Gender in Early Modern England* (Ithaca: Cornell University Press, 1995), 240–53.

84 Maud Sulter, personal communication with Angela Rosenthal, 2007.

85 Quoted in Maud Sulter, *ZABAT: Poetics of a Family Tree* (Hebden Bridge: Urban Fox Press, 1989); see under entry for *Terpsichore*.

86 Rosenthal, personal e-mail communication with Barbara Thompson, February 27, 2007.

87 Berthold Schmitt and Bernd Schulz, eds., *Your Own Soul: Ingrid Mwangi* (Heidelberg: Kehrer, 2003). See also Simon Njami, "Memory in the Skin: The Work of Ingrid Mwangi," in *Looking Both Ways*.

88 Artist statement, personal e-mail communication with Barbara Thompson, November 16, 2006.

89 Artist statement, personal e-mail communication with Barbara Thompson, November 16, 2006.

90 Quoted in Mirjam Westen, "Noirs: Angèle Etoundi Essamba," in *Noirs* (Arnhem: Museum voor Moderne Kunst, 2001), 3.

91 Artist statement, personal e-mail communication with Barbara Thompson, November 16, 2006.

92 Campos-Pons, in an interview with Barbara Thompson, December 8, 2006.

93 Campos-Pons's grandfather was transported as a slave to Cuba to work on the Vega sugar plantation, where her family was still living and working while she was growing up.

94 Campos-Pons, in an interview with Barbara Thompson, December 8, 2006.

95 Ibid.

96 Campos-Pons, personal e-mail communication with Barbara Thompson, January 21, 2007.

97 Campos-Pons, in an interview with Barbara Thompson, December 8, 2006.

98 Ibid.

99 Hobson, "The 'Batty' Politic," 87–89.

100 Shannon Fitzgerald and Tumelo Mosaka, eds., *A Fiction of Authenticity: Contemporary Africa Abroad* (St. Louis: Contemporary Art Museum, 2003), 45.

PLATES

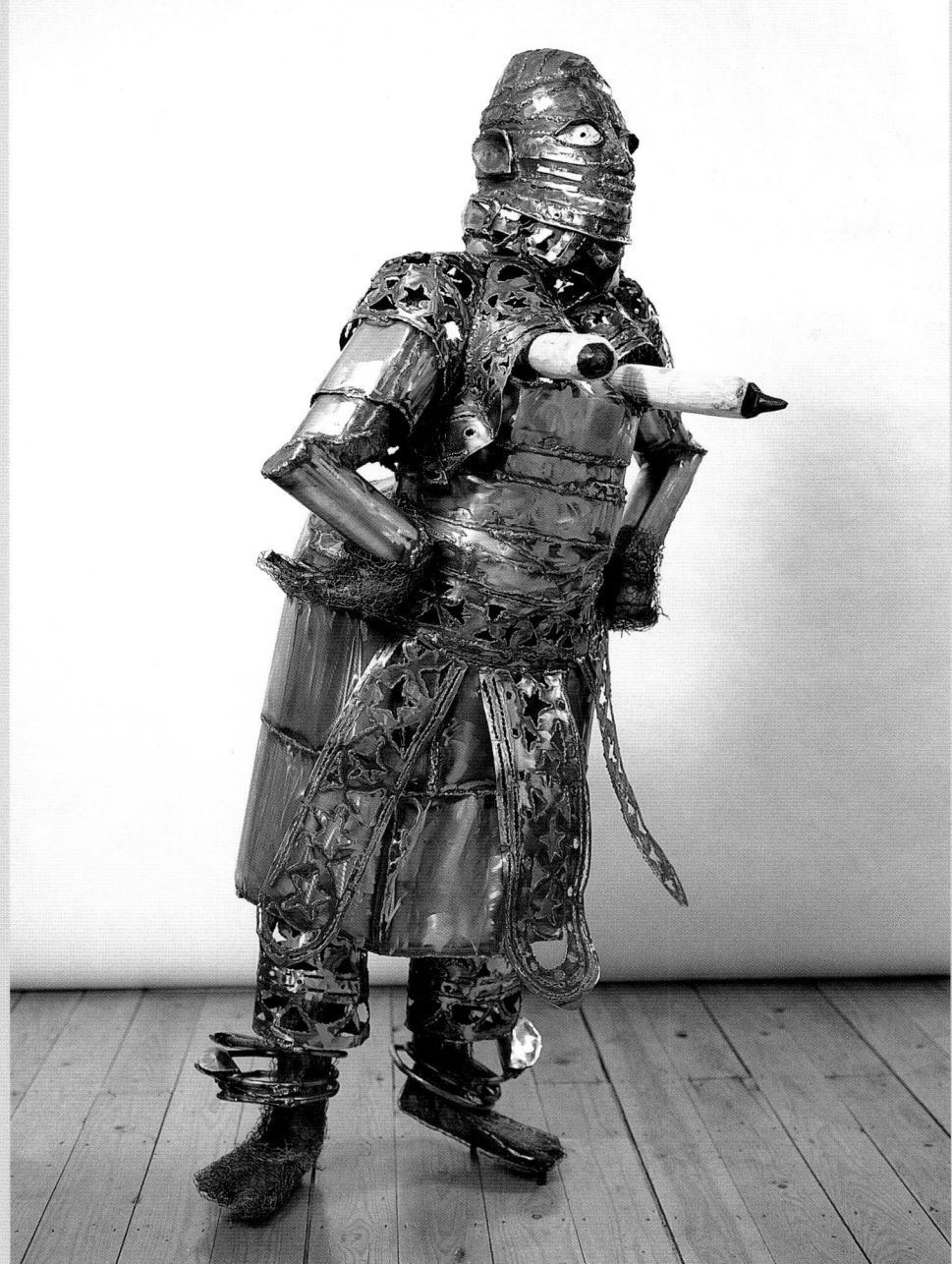

PLATE 96
Sokari Douglas Camp, Nigerian-British (b. 1958)
Gelede from Top to Toe, 1995
Steel, wood, chicken wire, paint
Private Collection, managed by
Citigroup Private Bank
Photograph courtesy of Sokari Douglas Camp
© 2007 Artists Rights Society (ARS),
New York/DACS, London

EXCHANGES: SOKARI DOUGLAS CAMP II*

Gelede from Top to Toe is a challenge. The structure has the look of a female but I was making a portrait of a man trying to be a woman. I do not think it is my idea of a beautiful Nigerian/Yoruba woman, but her missile breasts demand to be noticed whether you are male or female. Masquerades have dual sexuality because the performers are men who sometimes play women. There are masquerades of males, but their figure, through their costume, is made to both look pregnant and seem as if they have an erection all on the same form. These are enticing elements that go beyond beauty. I cannot say that *gelede* is a powerful representation of Nigerian women because the masquerade was created as a satire of powerful domineering women. But the sculpture celebrates that we are something to face and the breasts on *Gelede from Top to Toe* are like missiles.

* Sokari Douglas Camp, personal communication
with Barbara Thompson, January 14, 2007.

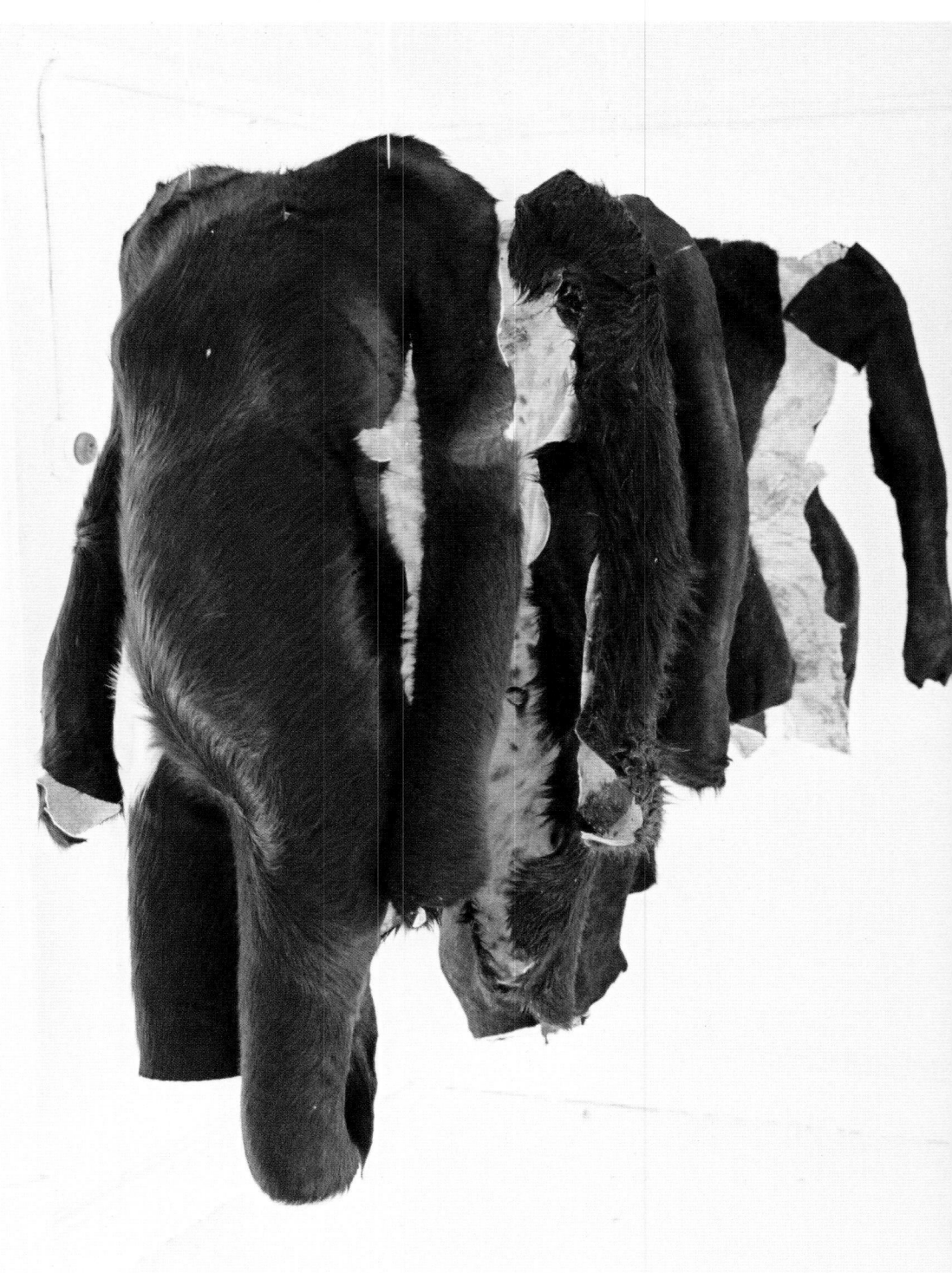

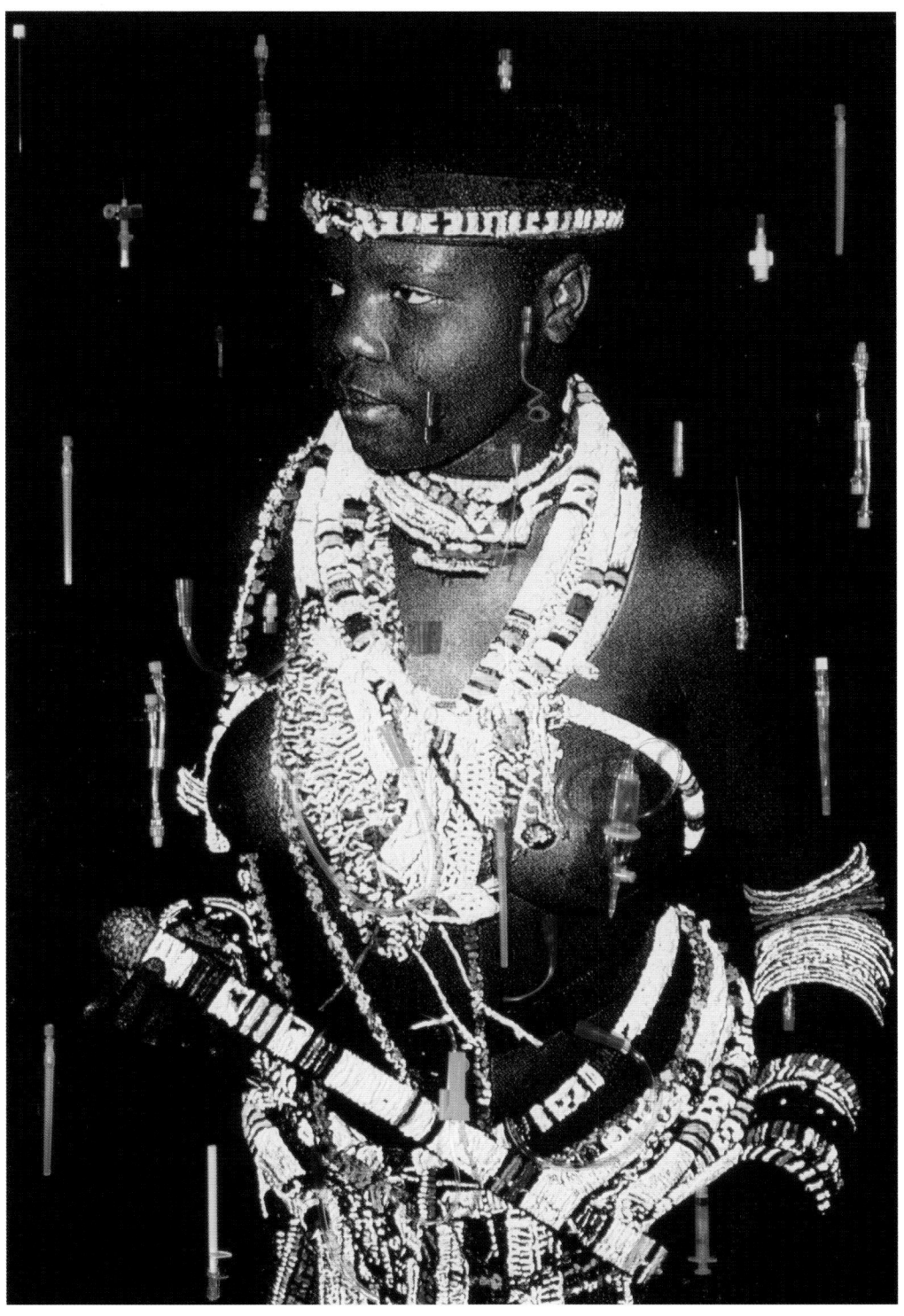

PLATE 98
Penny Siopis, South African (b. 1953)
South Africa Postcard 3, 1994
Laminated photocopy, oil paint,
plastic medical objects
Artist collection
Photograph courtesy of Penny Siopis
and Axis Gallery, New York

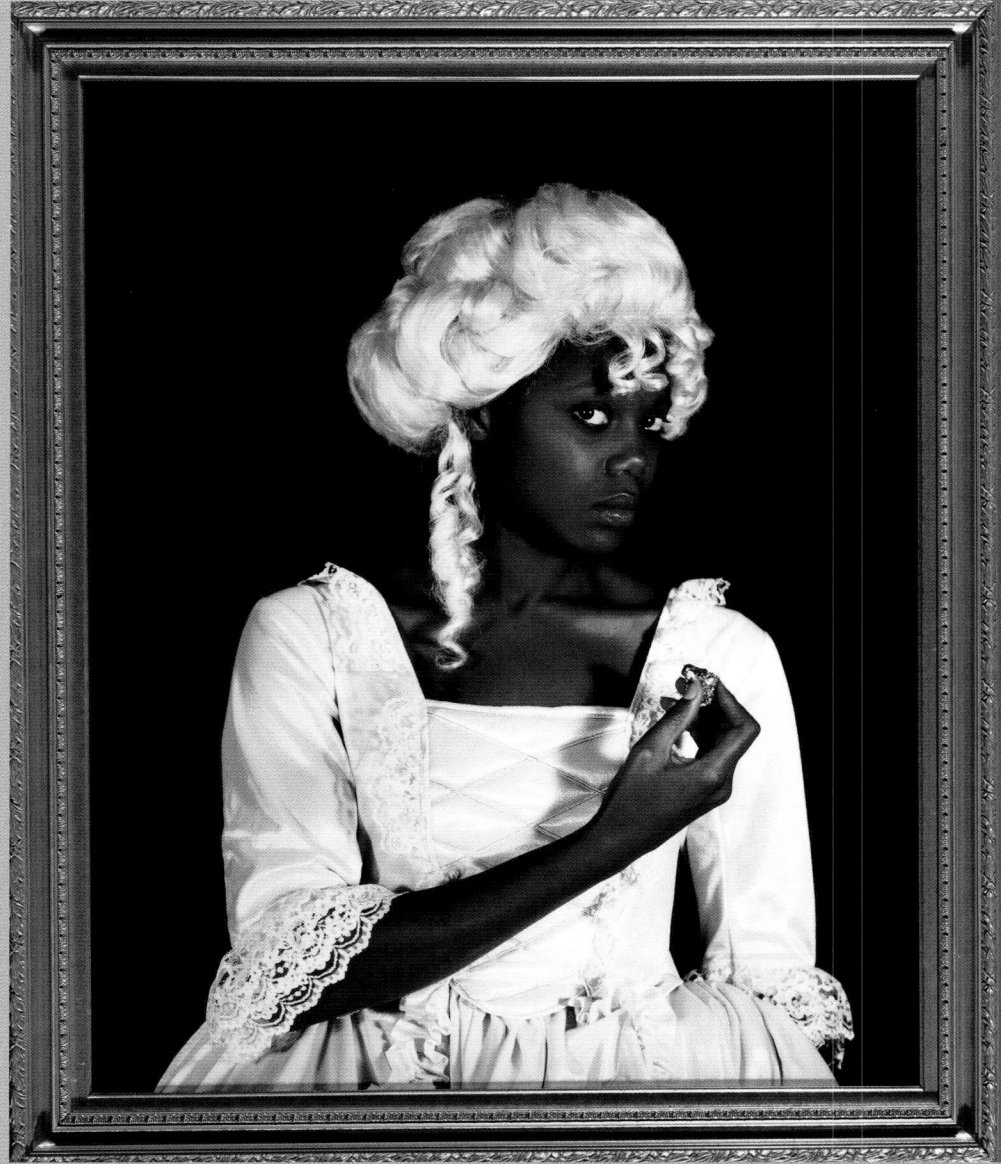

PLATE 99
Maud Sulter, Scottish (b. 1960)
Terpsichore, 1989
Dye destructions print
Arts Council Collection, London
Photograph courtesy of Maud Sulter
and the Arts Council Collection,
London

EXCHANGES: MAUD SULTER*

This whole notion of the disappeared, I think, is something that runs through my work. I'm very interested in absence and presence in the way that particularly black women's experience and black women's contribution to culture are so often erased and marginalized. So that it's important for me as an individual, and obviously as a black woman artist, to put black women back in the center of the frame—both literally within the photographic image, but also within the cultural institutions where our work operates.

* From http://www.vam.ac.uk/vastatic/ microsites/photography/story.php?storyid=ph052&row=3

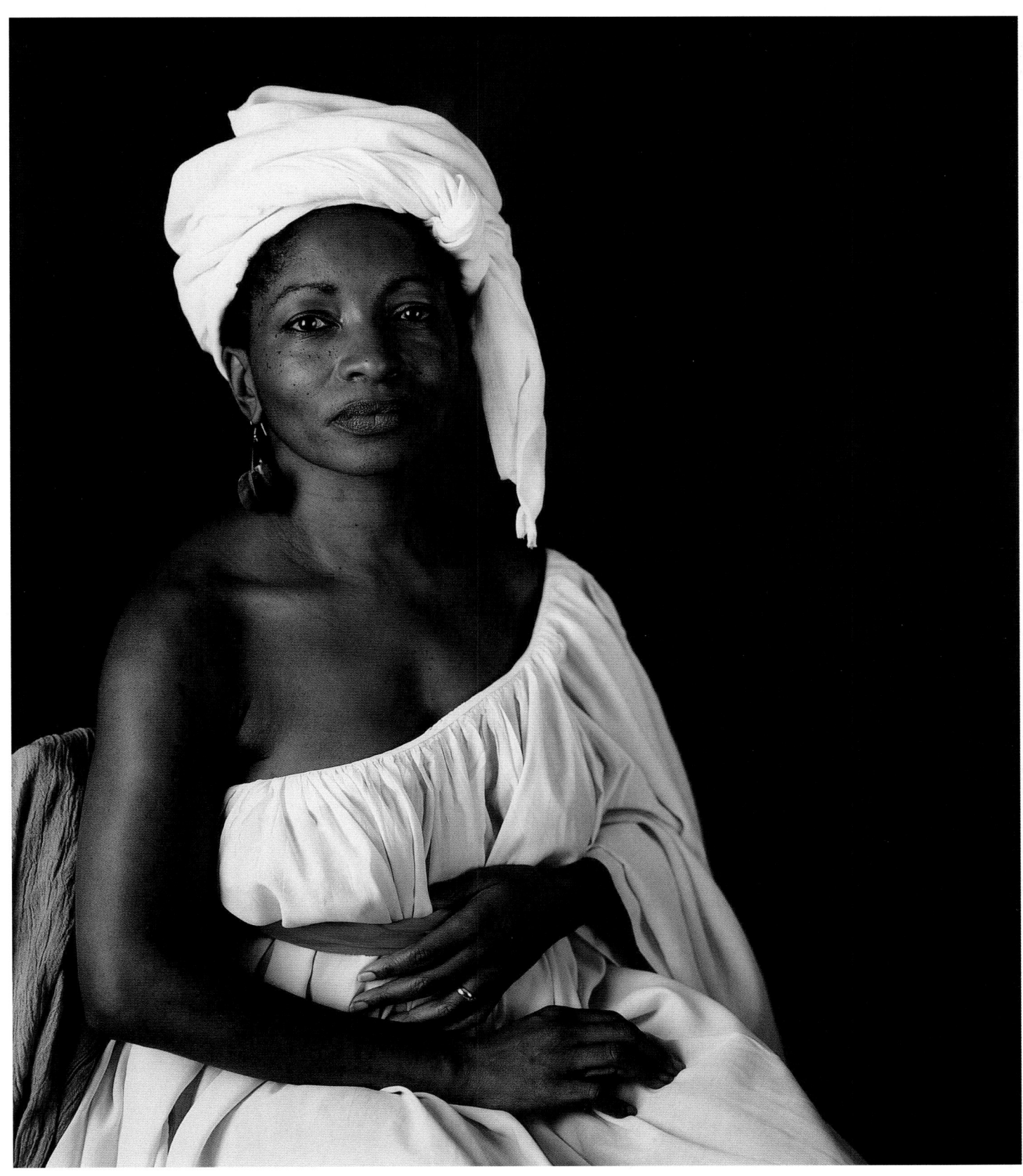

PLATE 100
Maud Sulter, Scottish (b. 1960)
Bonnie Greer, b. 1948, 2002
Polaroid photograph
Angela Rosenthal Collection
Photograph by Jeffrey Nintzel

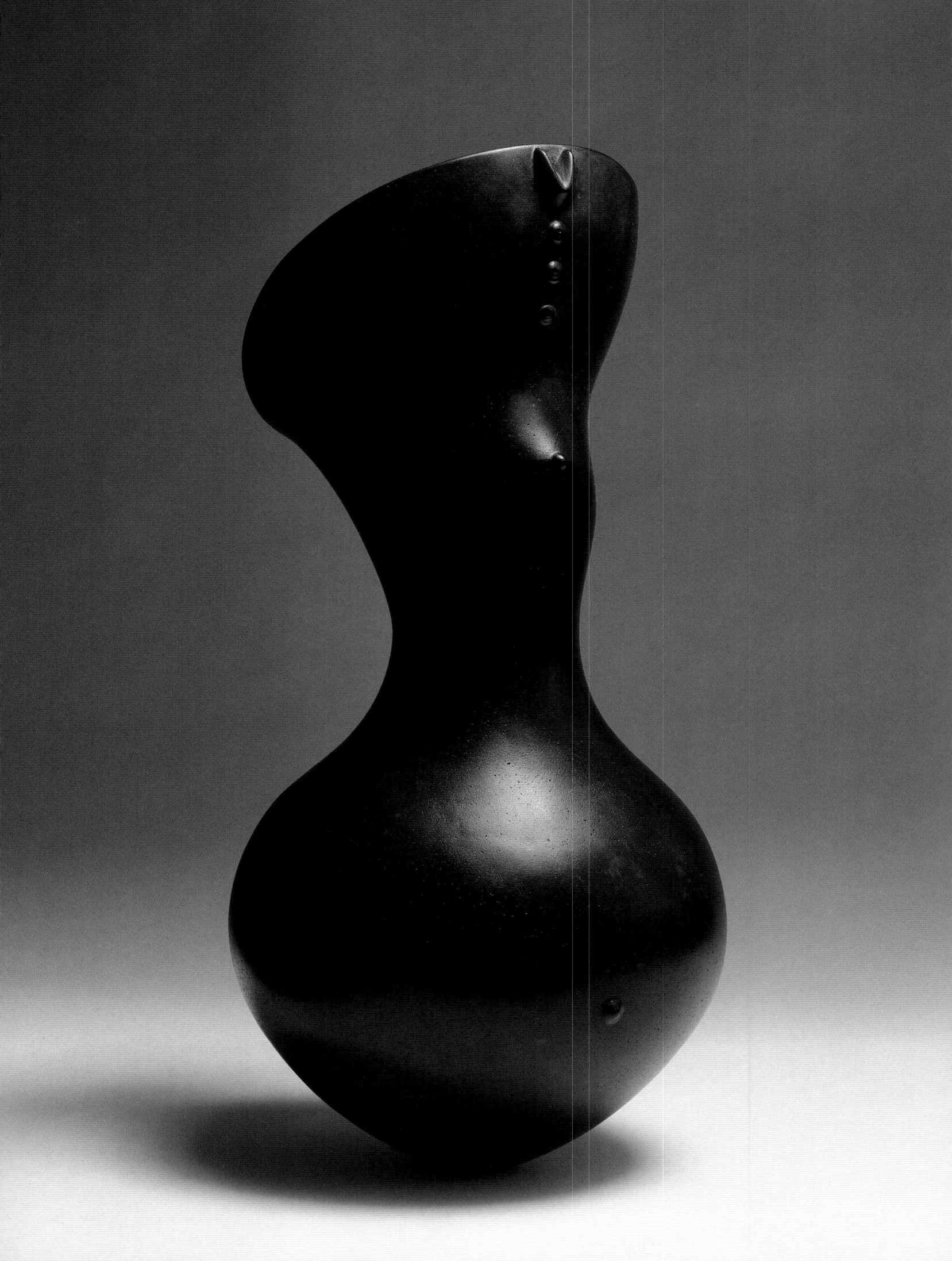

opposite PLATE 101
Magdalene Odundo, Kenyan (b. 1950)
Untitled, 2003
Blackened terracotta
Hood Museum of Art: Purchased through
the William B. Jaffe and Evelyn A. Jaffe-Hall
Fund and the Claire and Richard P. Morse
1953 Fund; c.2003.50
Photograph by Jeffrey Nintzel

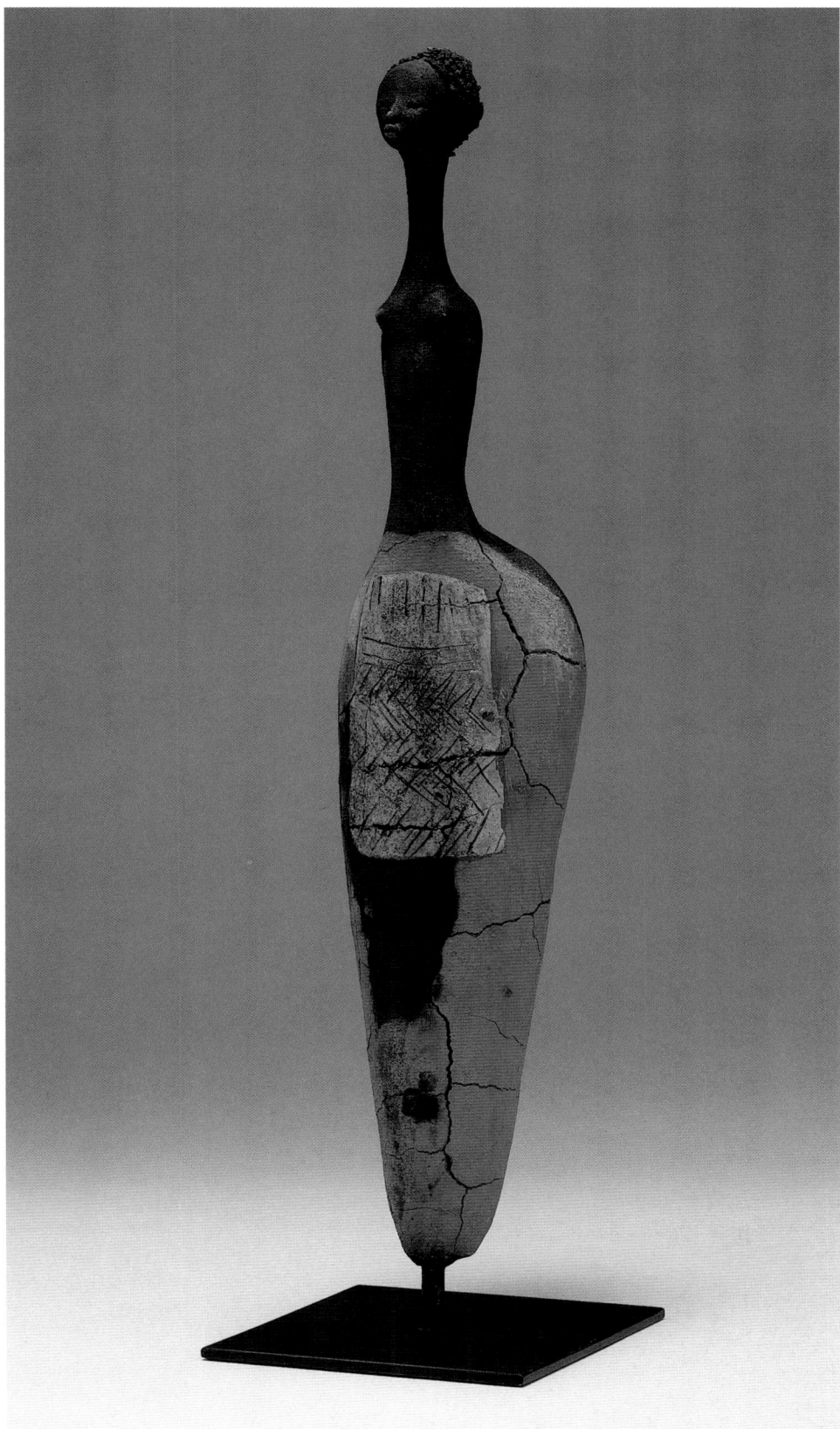

PLATE 102
Etiyé Dimma Poulsen, Ethiopian-Danish
(b. 1968)
Woman in Orange Cloth, 2006
Ceramic, mixed media
Hood Museum of Art: Purchased through
the Charles J. and Opel Zimmerman
1923 Fund; 2006.22
Photograph by Jeffrey Nintzel

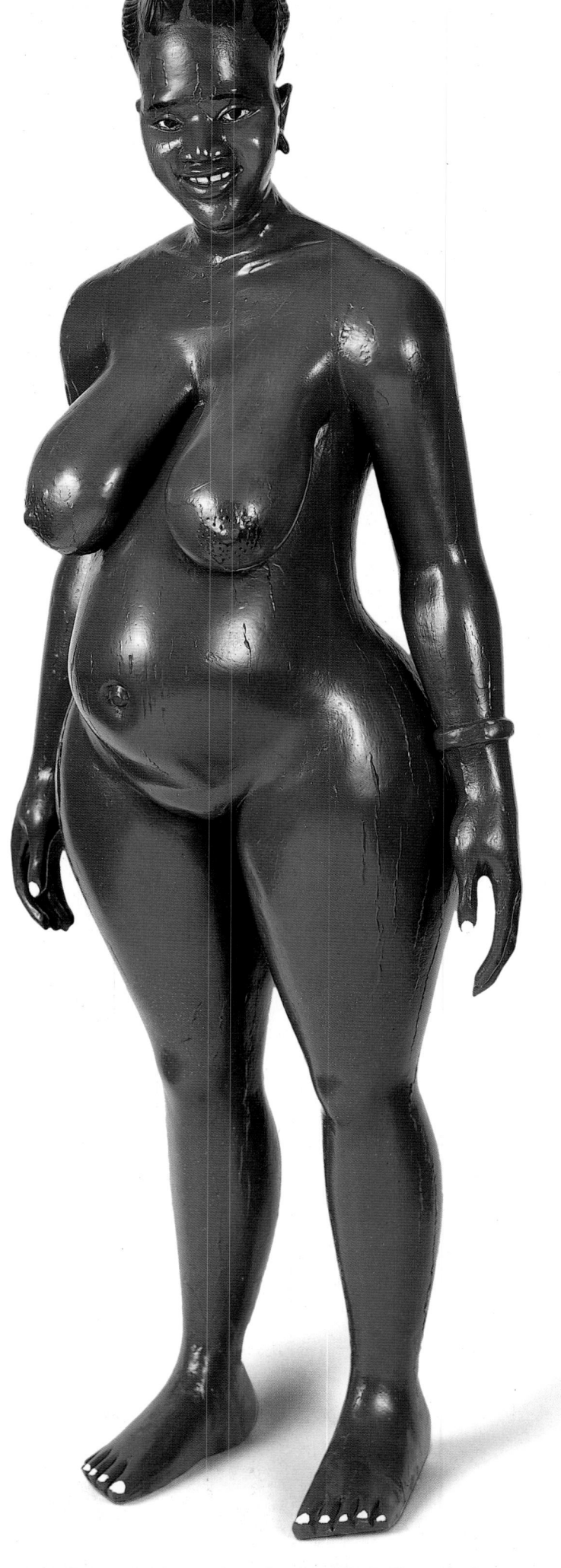

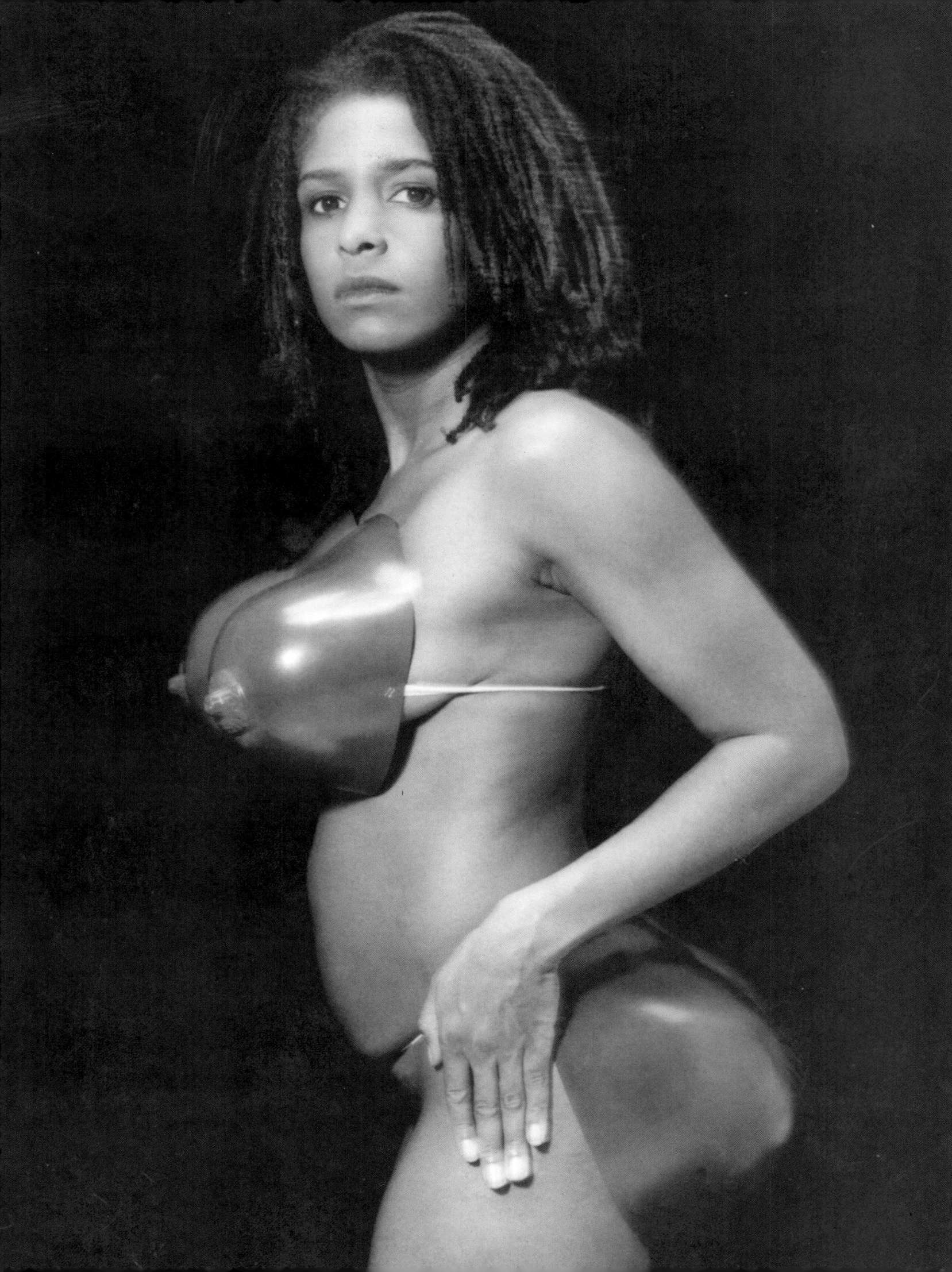

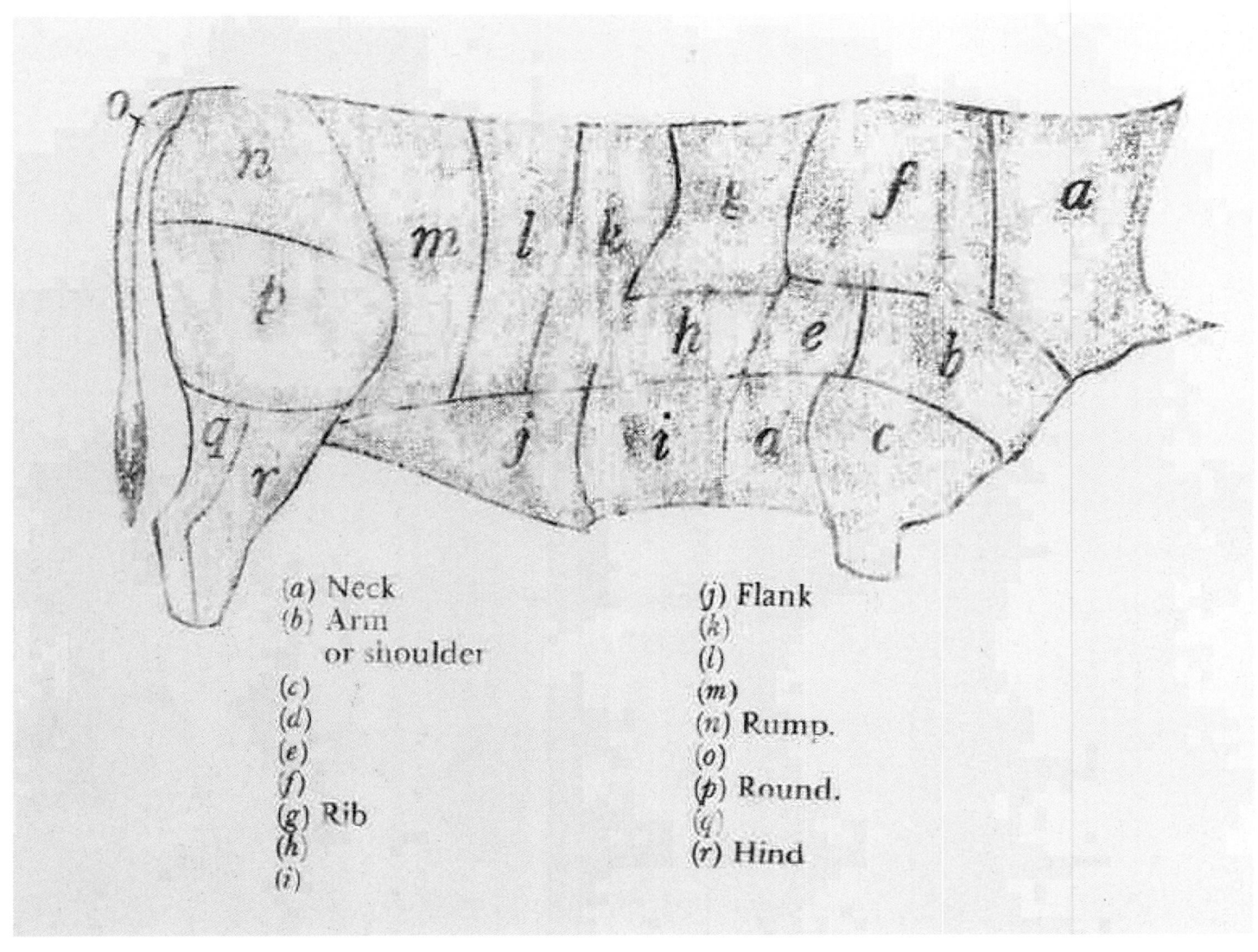

(a) Neck
(b) Arm
    or shoulder
(c)
(d)
(e)
(f)
(g) Rib
(h)
(i)

(j) Flank
(k)
(l)
(m)
(n) Rump.
(o)
(p) Round.
(q)
(r) Hind

PLATE 105
Carla Williams, American (b. 1965)
Untitled from *How To Read Character*, 1990–1991
Gelatin silver print, photocopy transfer
Deborah Willis Collection
Photograph courtesy of Carla Williams

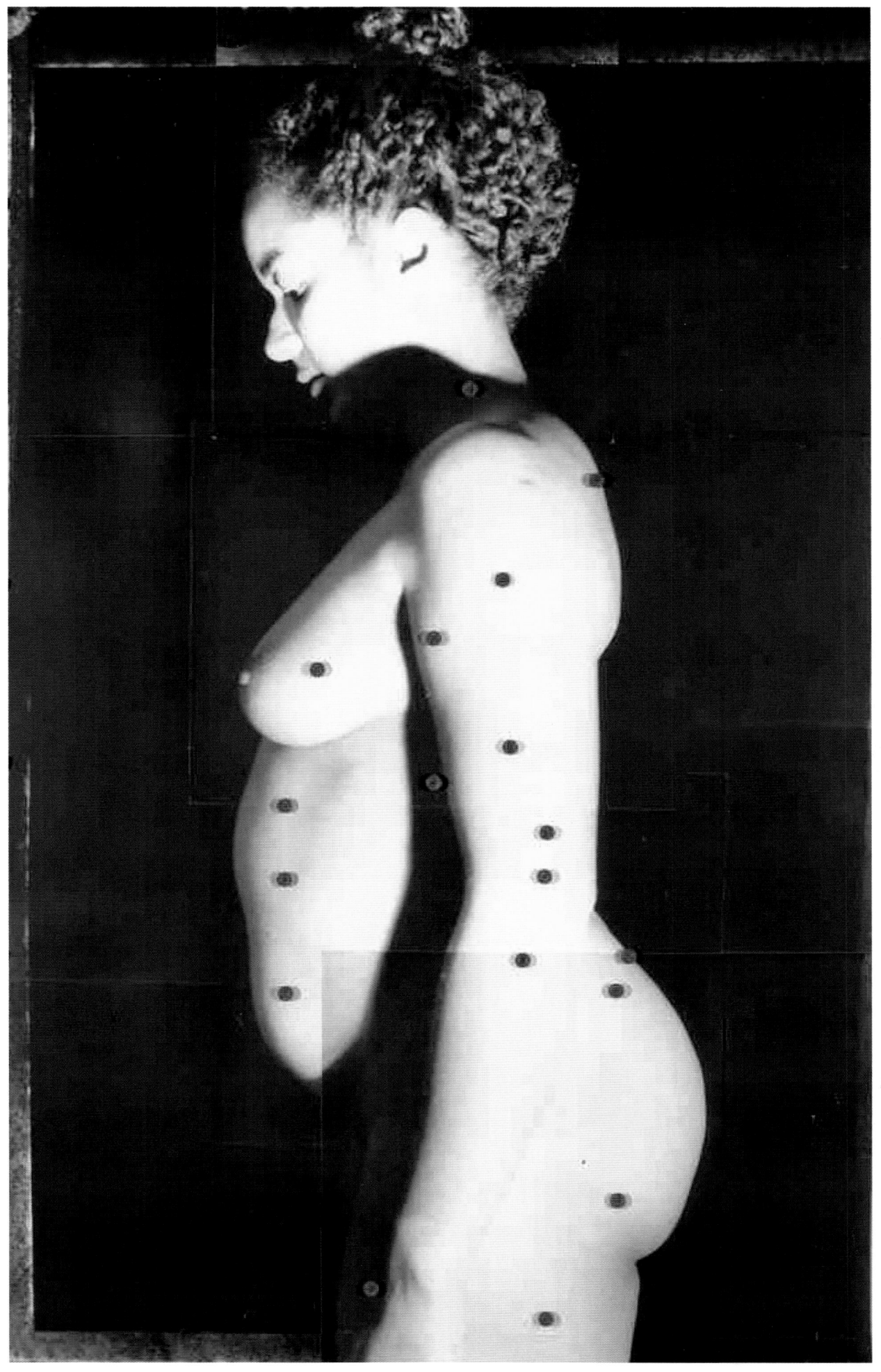

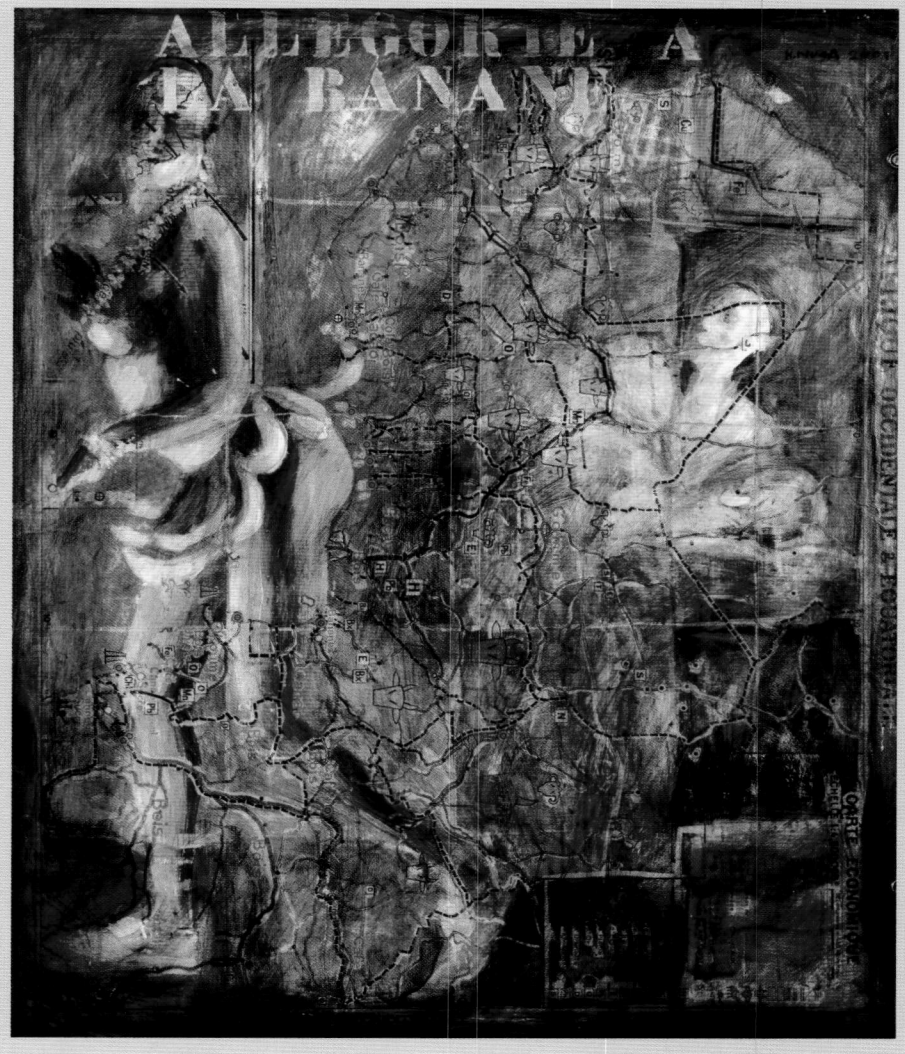

EXCHANGES: HASSAN MUSA, PART II*

Maps are images. They are handmade interpretative images; living images reflecting life changes. As with images, maps are naturally false representations of reality. As cultural objects, I think no map is innocent because people usually draw maps to mark the limits of the land under their control—or the lands they want to control. All the great wars were conducted around maps and millions of people died because someone sent them to defend or attack a line on a map. All this history makes maps look more obscene than the conventional folkloric images of obscenity.

There is something pornographic about maps. It has to do with the pretention of maps to show reality. Pornographic images tend to expose what is supposed to be "the real thing" about sexual behavior while only showing their conformity to one-dimensional and commercially codified norms for a complex human behavior. Saartje Baartman was exposed in a cage to Londoners and Parisians

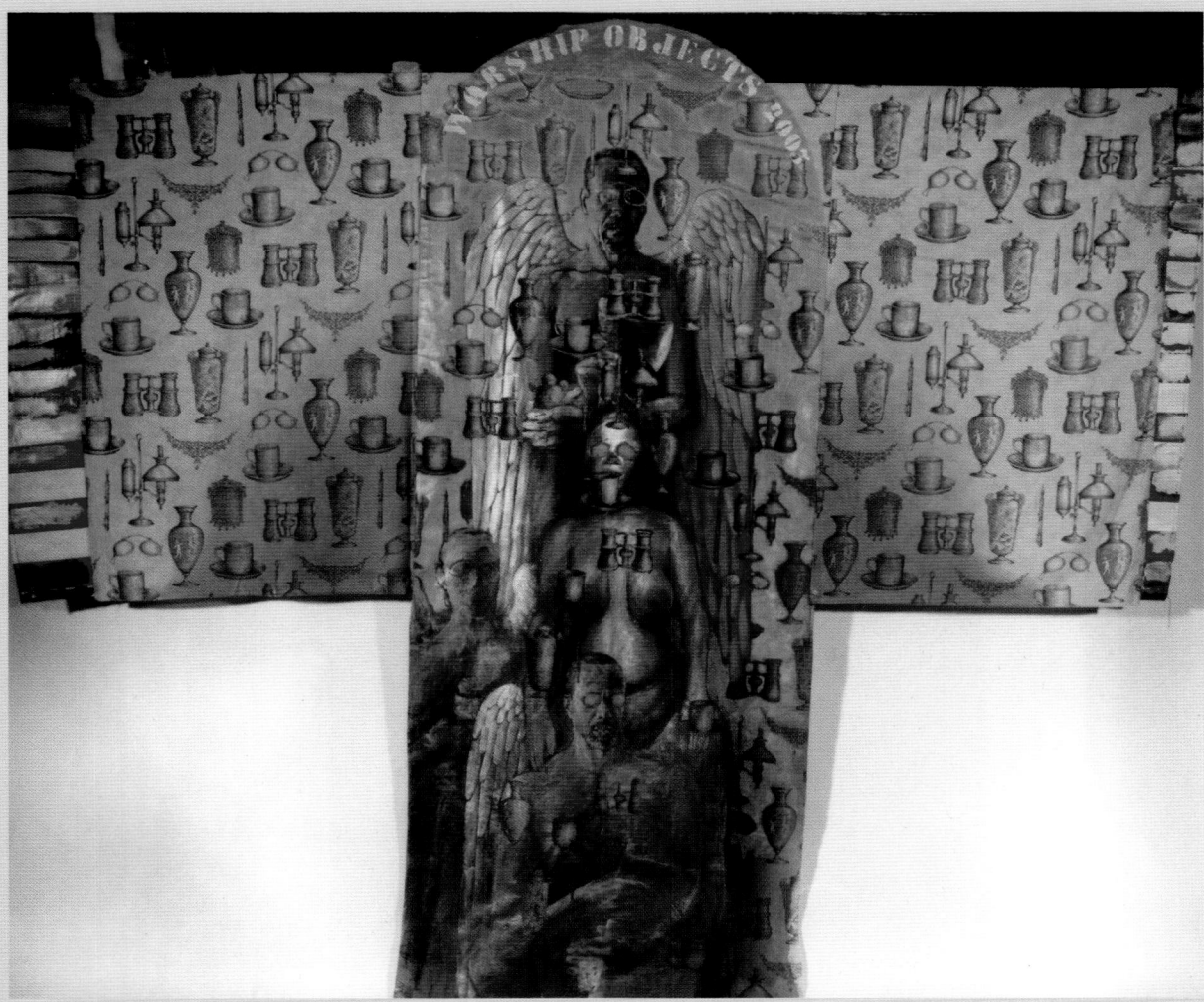

who paid to see her sexual organs. She never had a choice about exposing herself as an African sex symbol. A state of deep misunderstanding should have isolated her from her European audience but she was unable to understand the spell of *"l'art nègre"* that might have enchanted her European audience. When one considers this from Josephine Baker's point of view, one may find that Baker, the artist, positioned herself deliberately in this attitude of *"l'art nègre."*

I use maps in my paintings (plate 106) the same way I use printed fabrics (plate 107). When I take a piece of cloth with sunflower patterns and paint on it, the order of the sunflower patterns works as a map that enables me to reach the image of a Van Gogh lost somewhere in the fabric's visual story. The difference between a map and a fabric with sunflower patterns is that the map patterns are loaded with precious political references. I picked the first maps from my school garbage. Maps of the twentieth-century world (Soviet Union, French colonies, etc.) were thrown away because they were considered outdated. I always appreciated maps. When I was a child, I used to draw geographical maps for my classmates who were not very good in drawing. I enjoyed drawing and coloring maps. This practice represented—for the child I was—an opportunity to project my dreams far away from my small home town. In this perspective, maps were magical objects.

* Hassan Musa, personal e-mail communication with Barbara Thompson, November 25, 2006.

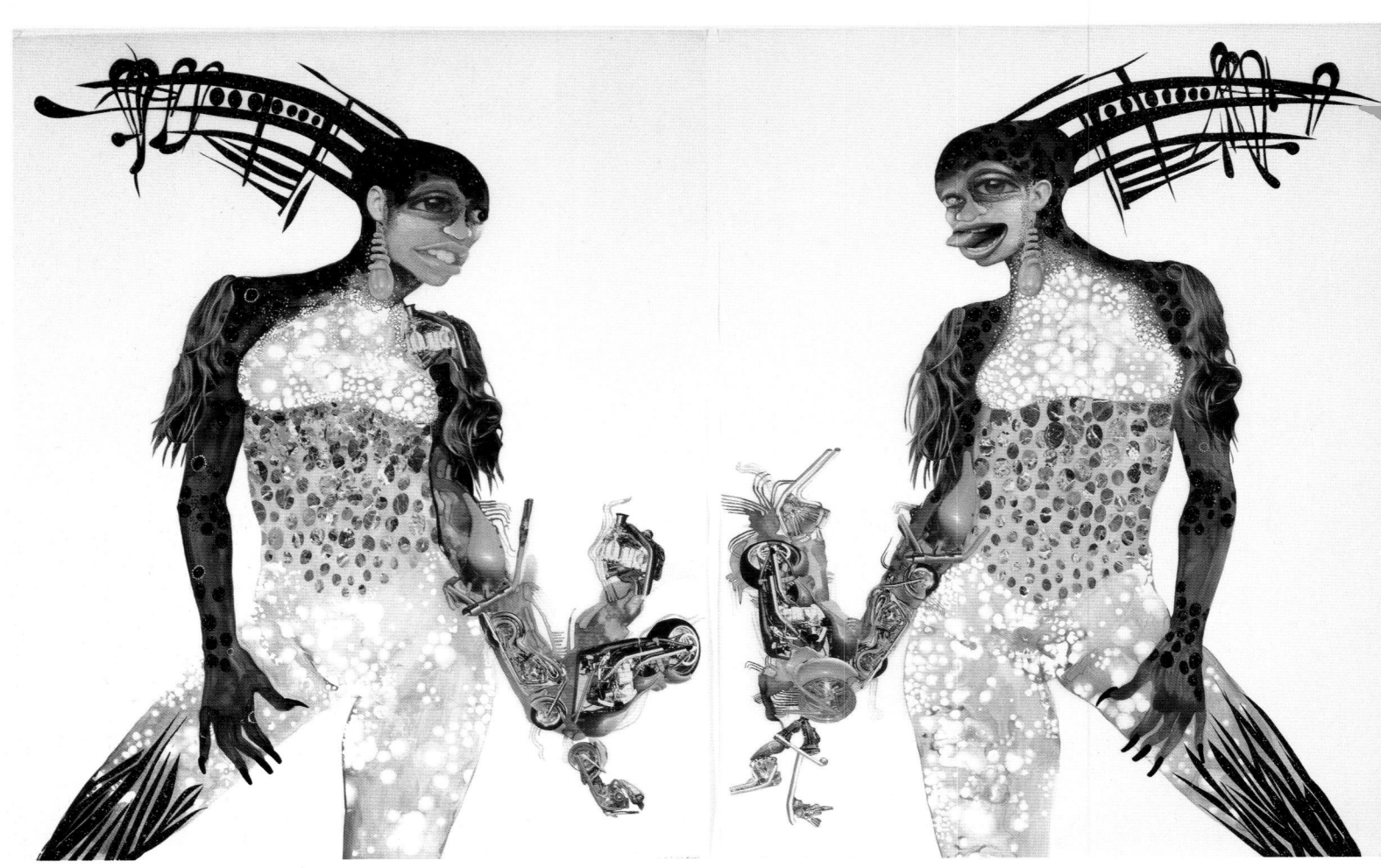

PLATE 108
Wangechi Mutu, Kenyan (b. 1972)
Double Fuse, 2003
Ink and collage on Mylar
Hood Museum of Art: Purchased
through the Charles F. Venrick
1936 Fund; MIS.2003.38
Photograph by Jeffrey Nintzel

EXCHANGES: WANGECHI MUTU*

Violent incidences are often fastened to images of privilege in my drawings (plate 108). Images of altered or slightly mutilated bodies with diseased skin sometimes look like bizarre and colorful fabric costumes. There is this tiny percentage of people who live like emperors because elsewhere blood is being shed. Women's bodies are particularly vulnerable to the whims of changing movements, governments, and social norms. They're like sensitive charts—they indicate how a society feels about itself. It's also disturbing how women attack themselves in search of a perfect image, and to assuage the imperfections that surround them.

I'm fascinated by stereotypes. We become like deer in the headlights when we're exposed to them. I don't believe attacking stereotypes head-on is an effective solution—they seem to get more power from this type of attention. I'm fascinated by how we come to a collective consensus as to what a stereotype is, and, even further, on how to use it against one another. So few things are really what they're rumored to be, and yet we use them to form opinions constantly. "Civilized behavior," "primitive art," "democratic nations"—they're all volatile and nebulous definitions. I suppose you could say that I mine stereotypes for their weak foundation and produce figures that are distillations of my own issues, beliefs, perceptions, and personal stereotypes.

* Excerpts from an interview with Laurie Ann Farrell, editor, in *Looking Both Ways: Art of the Contemporary African Diaspora* (New York: Museum for African Art and Gent: Snoeck Publishers, 2003), 142–143.

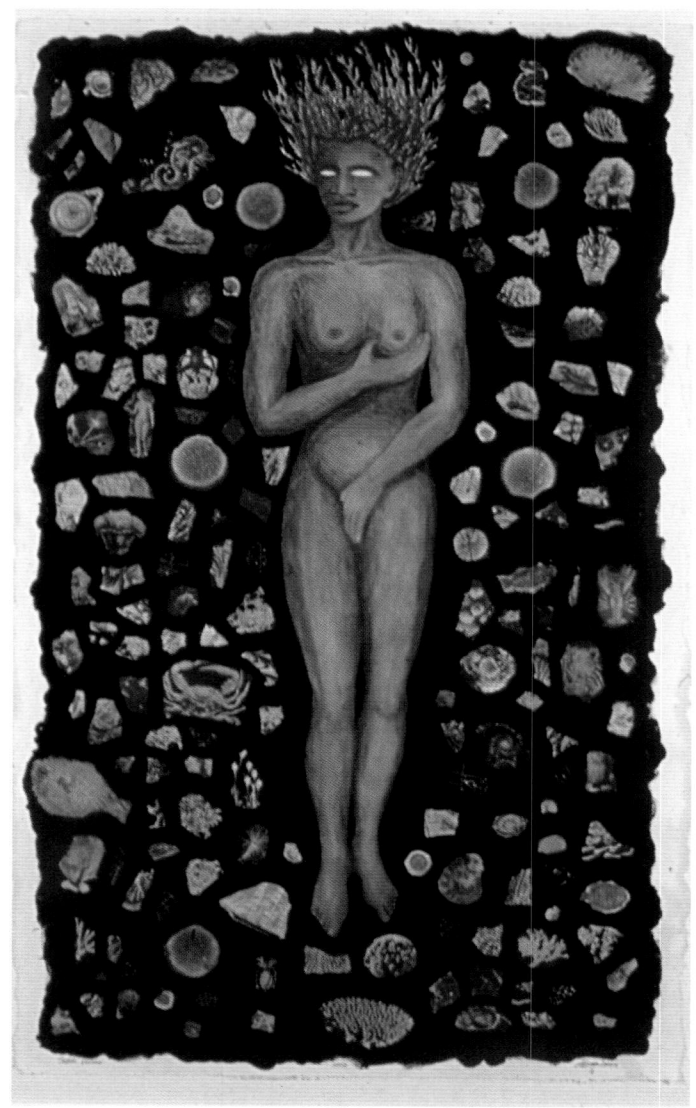

PLATE 109
Alison Saar, American (b. 1956)
Sable Venus, 2003
Mixed media on paper
Bonnie Rabin Collection
Photograph courtesy of
Phyllis Kind Gallery, New York

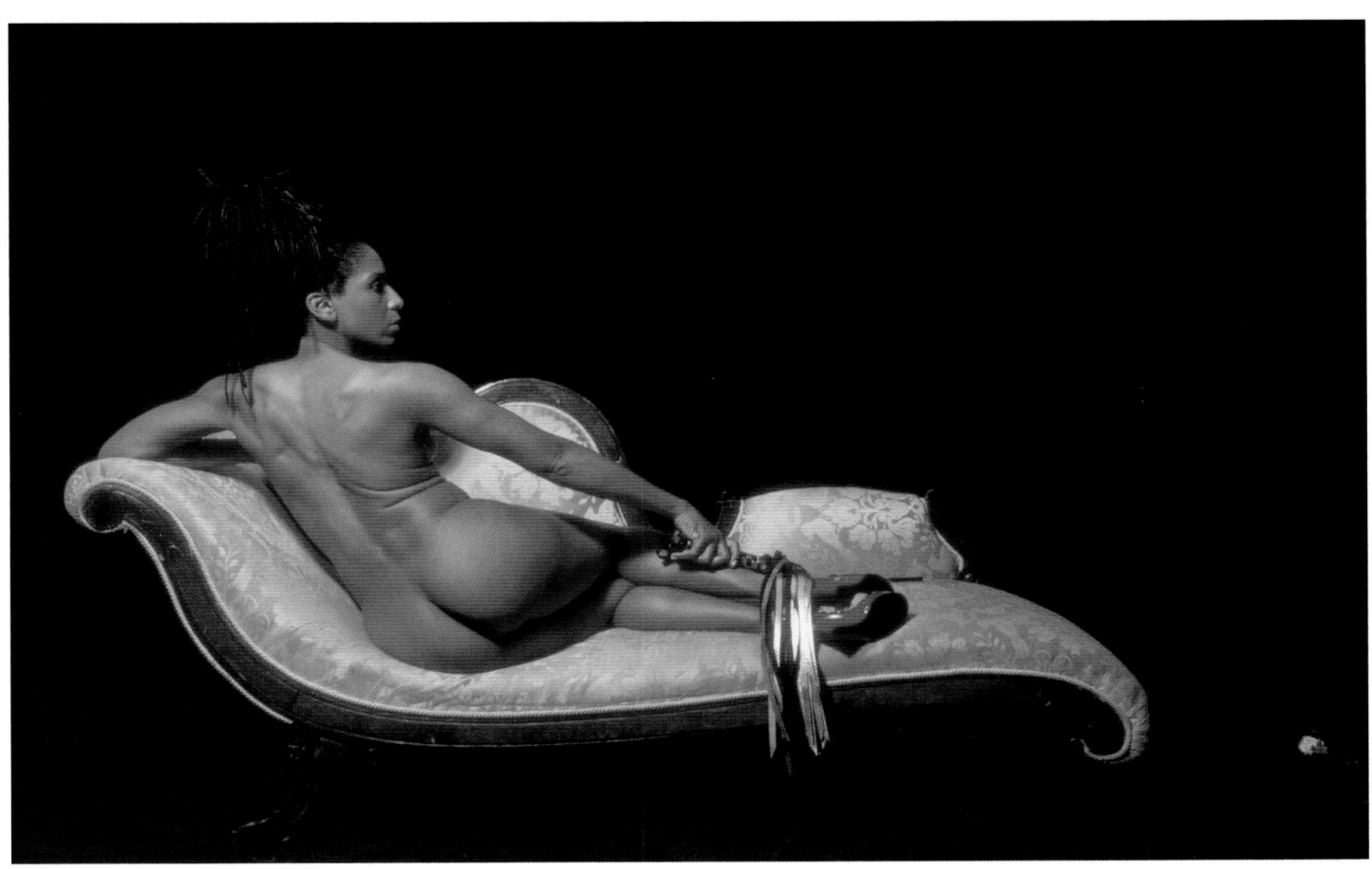

PLATE 110
Renée Cox, American (b. 1957)
Baby Back, 2001
Archival digital "C" print
Artist's collection
Photograph courtesy of Robert Miller Gallery,
New York © Renée Cox
Courtesy Robert Miller Gallery, New York

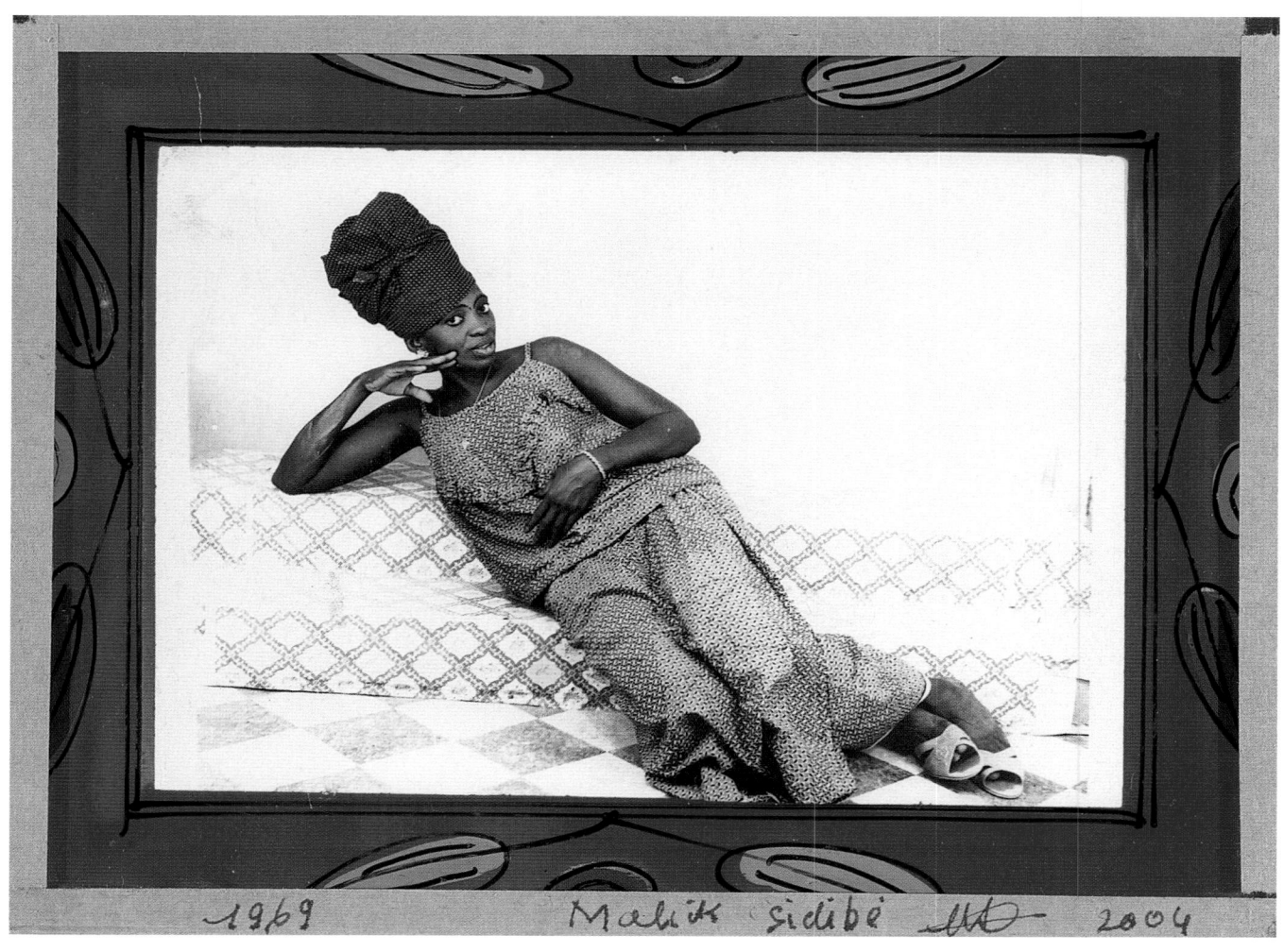

PLATE 111
Malick Sidibé, Malian (b. 1936)
Untitled (Reclining woman), 1969
Gelatin silver print, painted glass frame
Hood Museum of Art: Purchased through
the Hood Museum of Art Acquisition Fund;
2005.19
Photograph by Jeffrey Nintzel

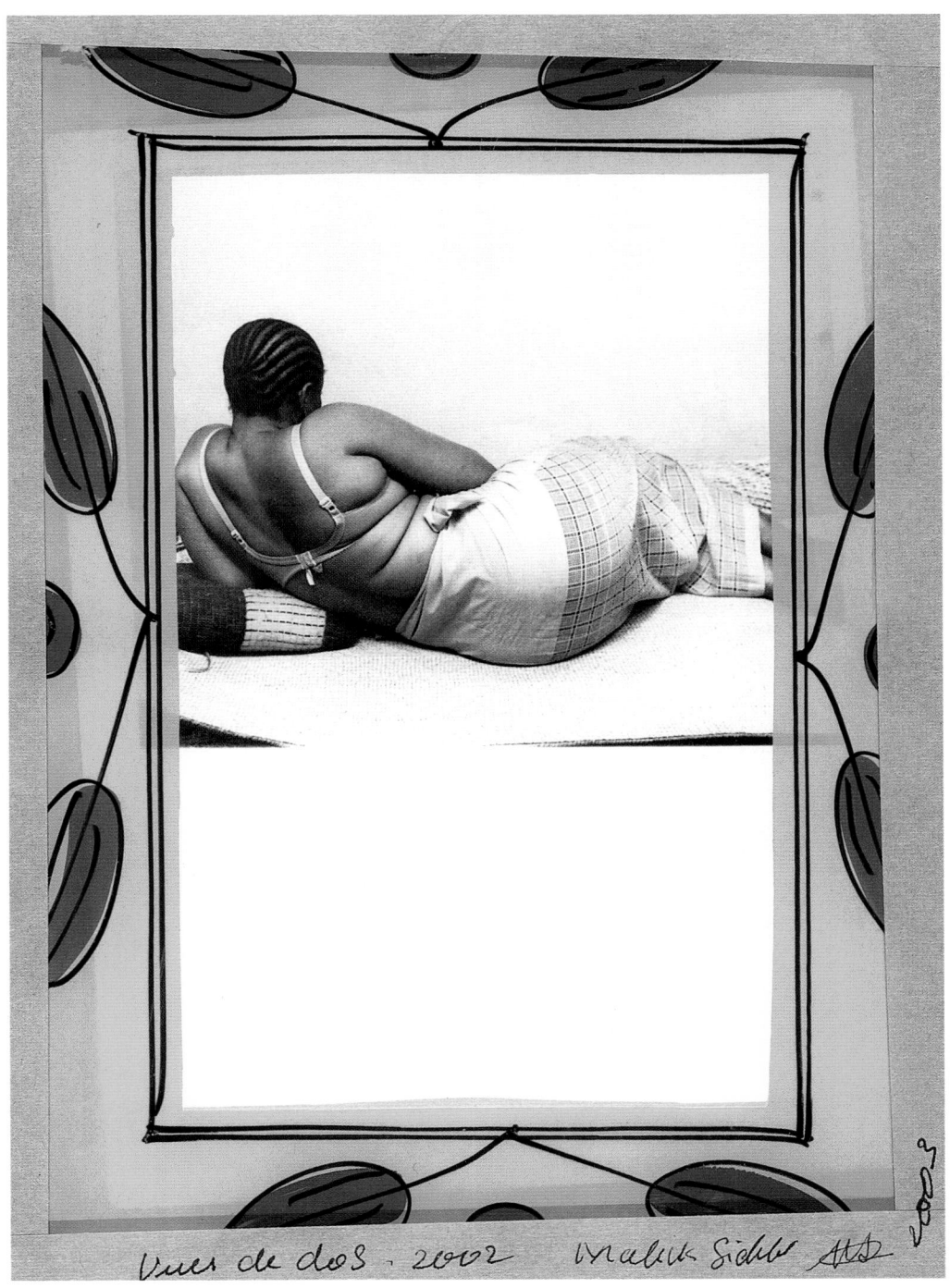

Vues de dos. 2002   Malick Sidibé

PLATE 112
Malick Sidibé, Malian (b. 1936)
Vues de Dos, 2002
Gelatin silver print, glass, cardboard, tape, and string
Hood Museum of Art: Purchased through
the Olivia H. Parker and John O. Parker '58
Acquisition Fund; PH.2003.36
Photograph by Jeffrey Nintzel

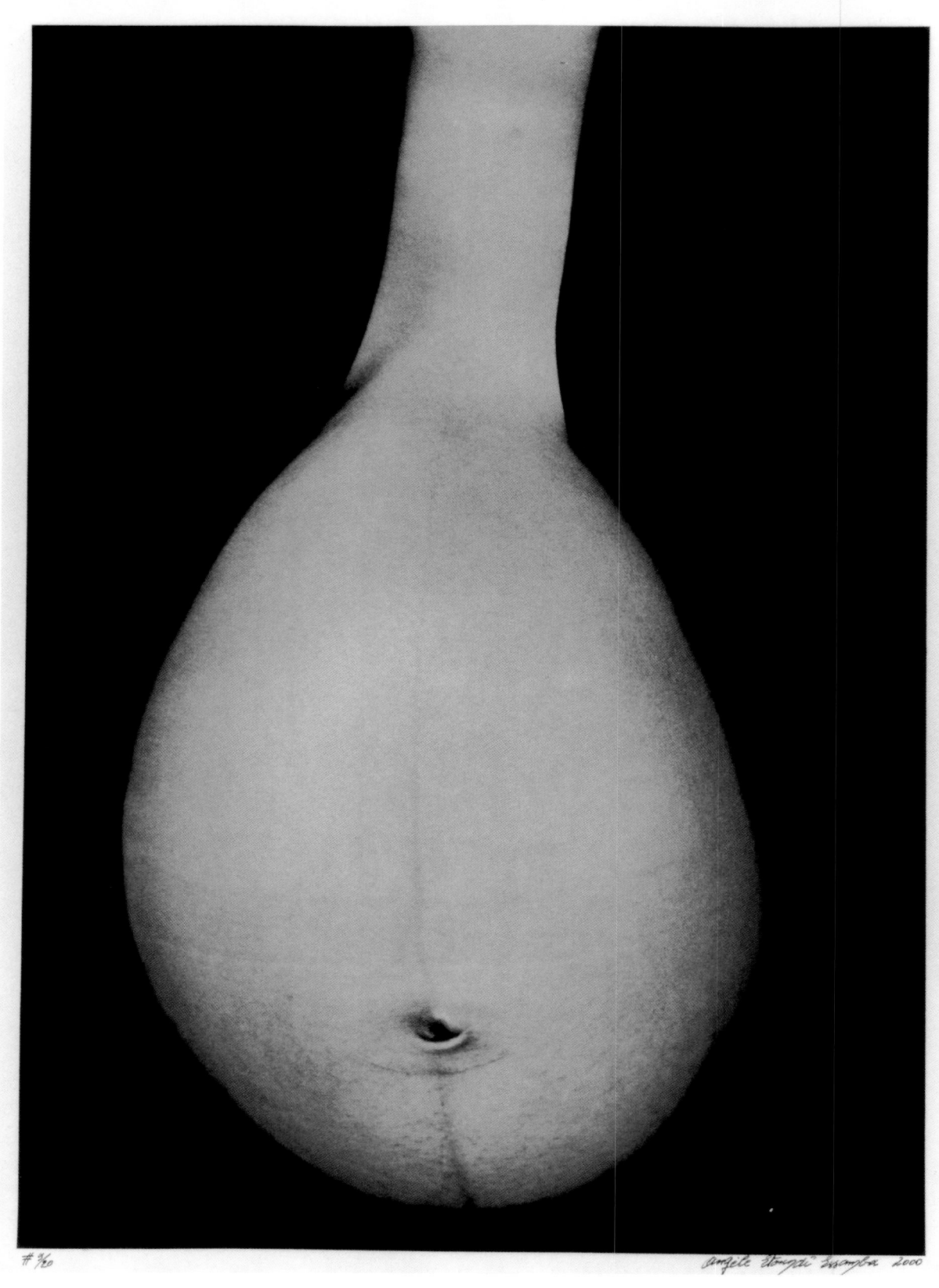

#3/80

Angèle Essamba Essamba 2000

PLATE 113
Angèle E. Essamba, Cameroonian (b. 1962)
Noirs #211, 2000
Gelatin silver print
Hood Museum of Art: Purchased through the
Alvin and Mary Bert Gutman 1940 Acquisition
Fund; PH.2003.30.1
Photograph by Jeffrey Nintzel

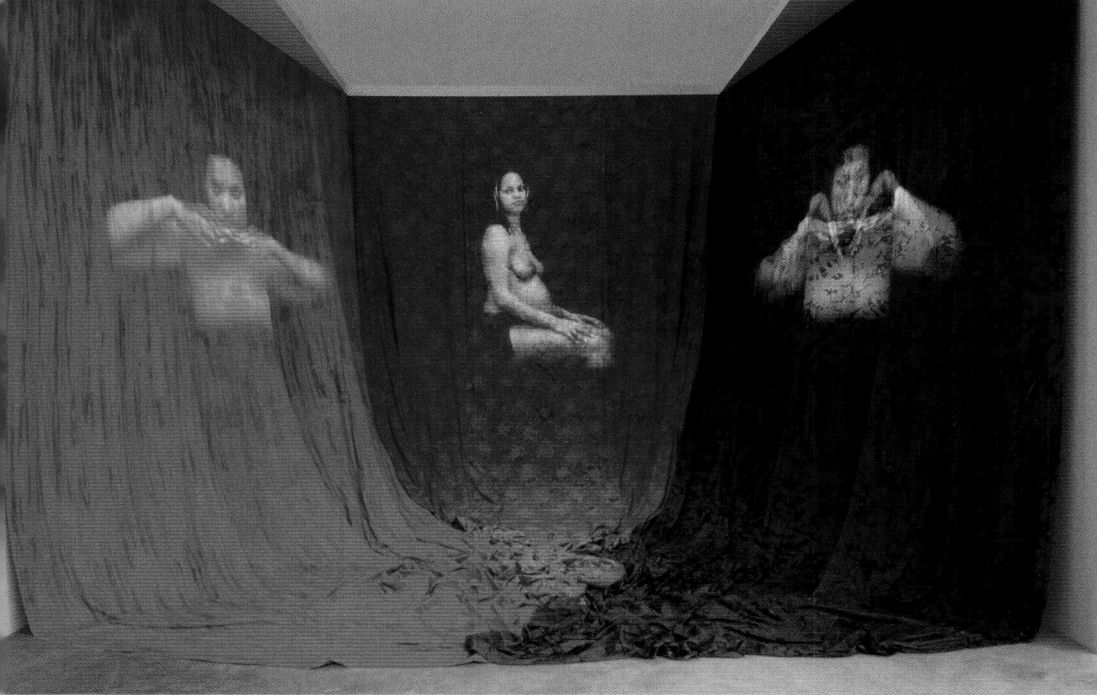

PLATE 114
IngridMwangiRobertHutter,
comprised of Ingrid Mwangi, Kenyan-German
(b. 1975), and Robert Hutter, German (1964)
Dressed Like Queens, 2003
3 video projections on hand-dyed fabrics,
3 DVD/Pal, sound
Artist's collection
Photograph courtesy of Ingrid Mwangi
and Robert Hutter

EXCHANGES: INGRID MWANGI (OF THE INGRIDMWANGIROBERTHUTTER COLLECTIVE) II*

From the beginning it was a very negative image of Africa and Africans that was spread by the European con-
querors in order to justify slavery and colonialism. Bringing to mind the history of distortion and falsification
arising from the ideology of racism, we should question whether centuries of the established attitude has not
left its mark upon us all, influencing relations between African people and people from Western societies on all
different levels of interaction, be it of political, economical, or social nature. Until today, there have not been
sufficient official apologies for the history of events that has taken place in Africa. Let us not forget that it was
only recently that the last regime of white-minority rule in Africa was officially ended. This does not mean that
the mentality of the people who lived within that system has been changed overnight.

The continuing reports of racist behavior throughout Europe and America make it obvious that we have
not overcome the history that began as the need to suppress and exploit a whole culture to satisfy the economical and power-hungry needs of another.

To go one step further: Could it be that the negative image of Africa is in fact being kept alive through the
use of a new system of one-sided information, wrong interpretation and judgment, and this in order to achieve
new justification for the imbalance?

My attempt is to find an authentic expression of Self, which reflects the lives of women of African heritage today. The piece has ritualistic qualities, of a kind one has not come across, as they are newly constructed from individual histories. I act out a body and voice performance titled *Reclaimed* in dialogue with the
installation, picking up on the idea of dressing as an act of communication and an expression of identity. The
performance incorporates painting on the skin, using red Kenyan earth to mark certain parts of my body in
simple self-invented patterns. Finally, I engage in an expressive and personal way of singing and using my
voice, to reflect the power and beauty I feel when "thinking African."

* Excerpt from artist statement in Ingrid Mwangi and Robert Hutter, "Redressing,"
Dressed Like Queens, 2003. http://www. ingridmwangi.de/mh/text_Statments1.html.

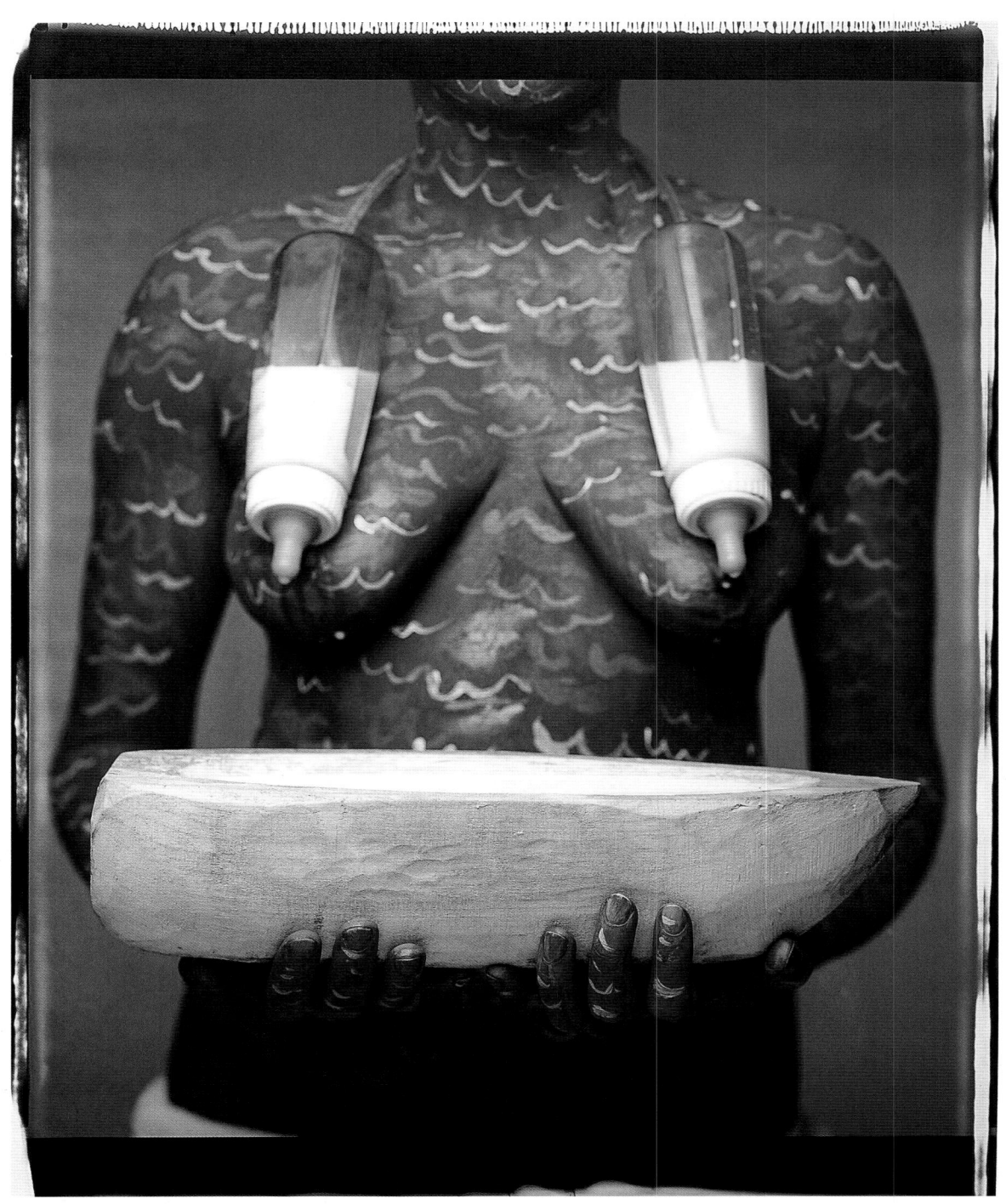

PLATE 115
Maria Magdalena Campos-Pons, Cuban (b. 1959)
When I Am Not Here/Estoy Allá, 1994
Polaroid photograph
Artist's collection
Photograph courtesy of Maria Magdalena
Campos-Pons and Howard Yezerski
Gallery, Boston

opposite PLATE 116
Joyce J. Scott, American (b. 1948)
Mammy under Undue Influence, 2007
Blown, caste and lampworked glass,
beadwork (peyote stitch)
Hood Museum of Art: Purchased
through the Virginia and Preston T.
Kelsey '58 Fund; 2007.51
Photograph by Jeffrey Nintzel

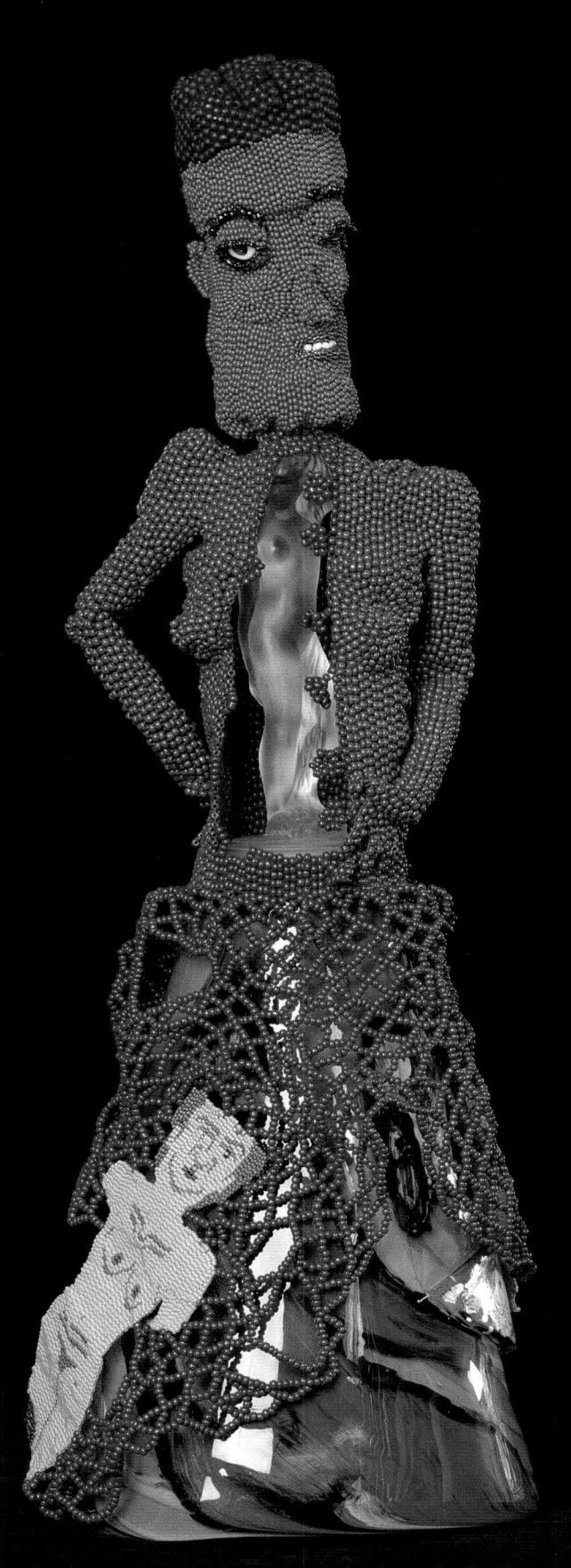

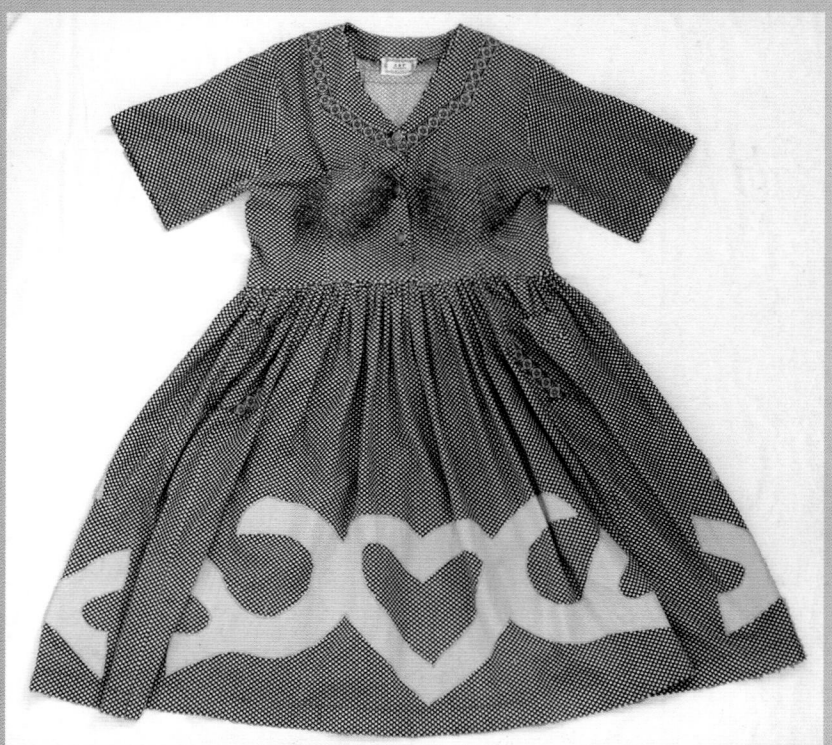 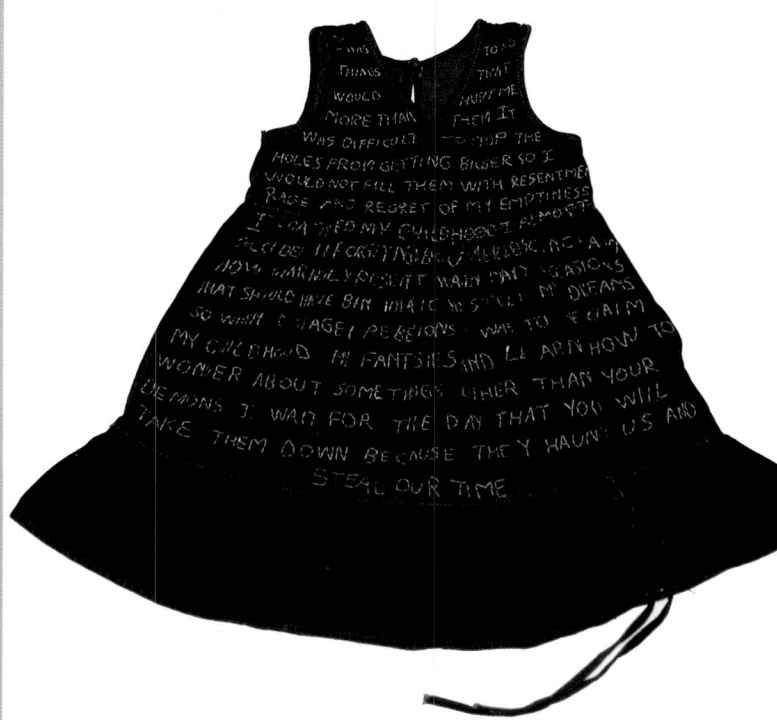

EXCHANGES: SENZENI MARASELA II*

Sewing is important to me. First because it is tied up with the earliest memories I have of our mother. She used to sit for hours while we growing up sewing buttons and undone hems. Sewing, I believe, is a form of meditation. For me it offers redemption for the disruptive anger I felt towards my mother as a young woman.

I believe that my persona, Theodorah, who is created in the image of my mother, fights through my work. She attempts with every stitch I make to bury and reconcile with her past. This is because outside of the frames of my needlework she has a muzzled voice. She is a nonentity. I see my work as a departure toward liberating Theodorah instead of casting in shadow her abilities to love and feel. For me, I read Theodorah in context, which is something that rarely happens when we look at black female's lives. While we do take responsibility for who we are, the rest of the world must take responsibility for shaping what we are now.

* Artist statement for *Black Womanhood*, e-mail communication, May 16, 2007.

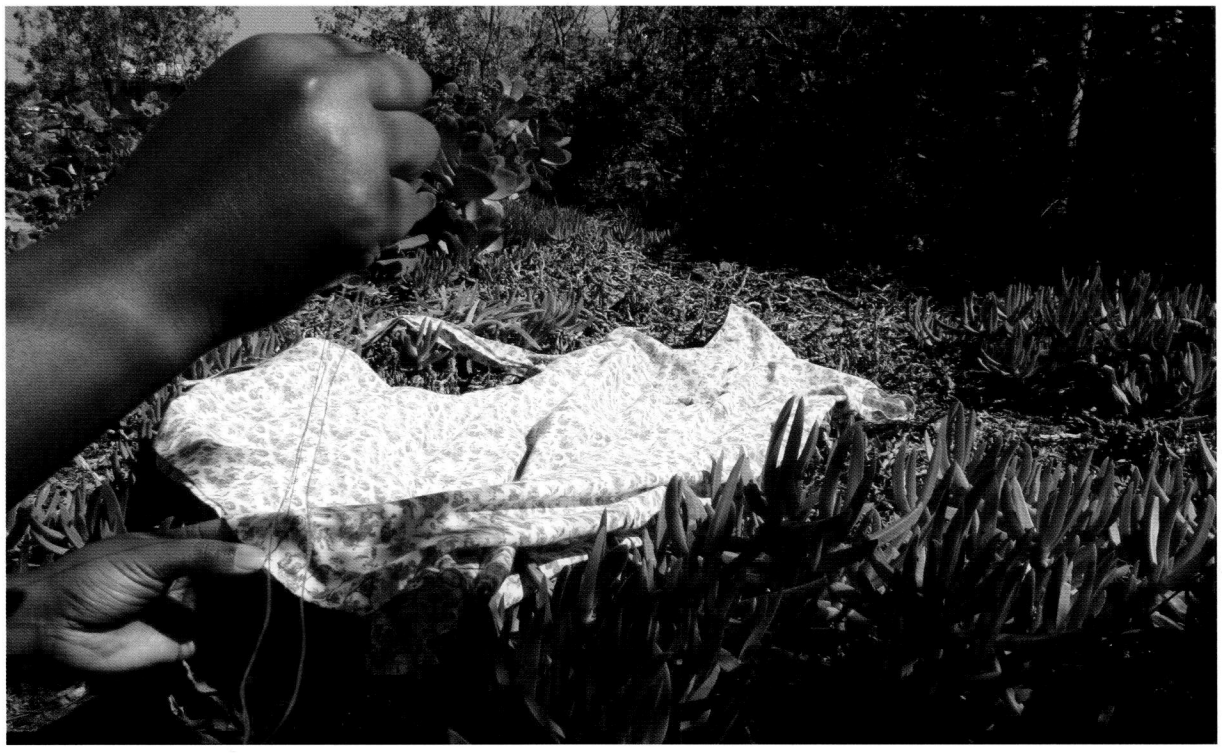

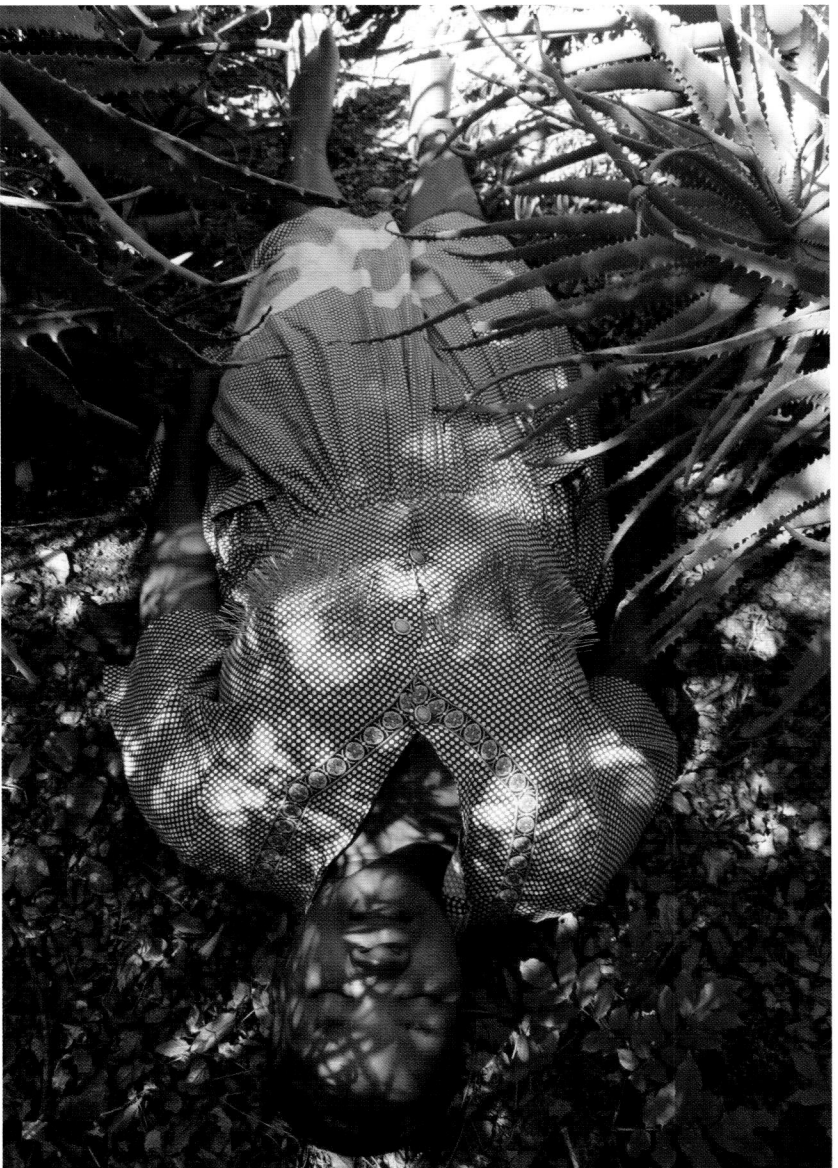

PLATE 117
Senzeni Marasela, South African (b. 1977)
Installation pieces from the *Theodorah Comes to Johannesburg Series*, comprised of

opposite left
a. *Our Mother's Bosom*, 2007
Cotton dress with appliqué and metal pins

opposite right
b. *Theodorah, Senzeni and Nikelwa*, 2006
Denim dress with needlepoint lettering

above
c. *Theodorah, Senzeni and Nikelwa (iv)*
Digital print on archival paper

left
d. *Theodorah, Senzeni and Nikelwa (v)*
Digital print on archival paper

Artist's collection
Photograph courtesy of Senzeni Marasela
and Axis Gallery, New York

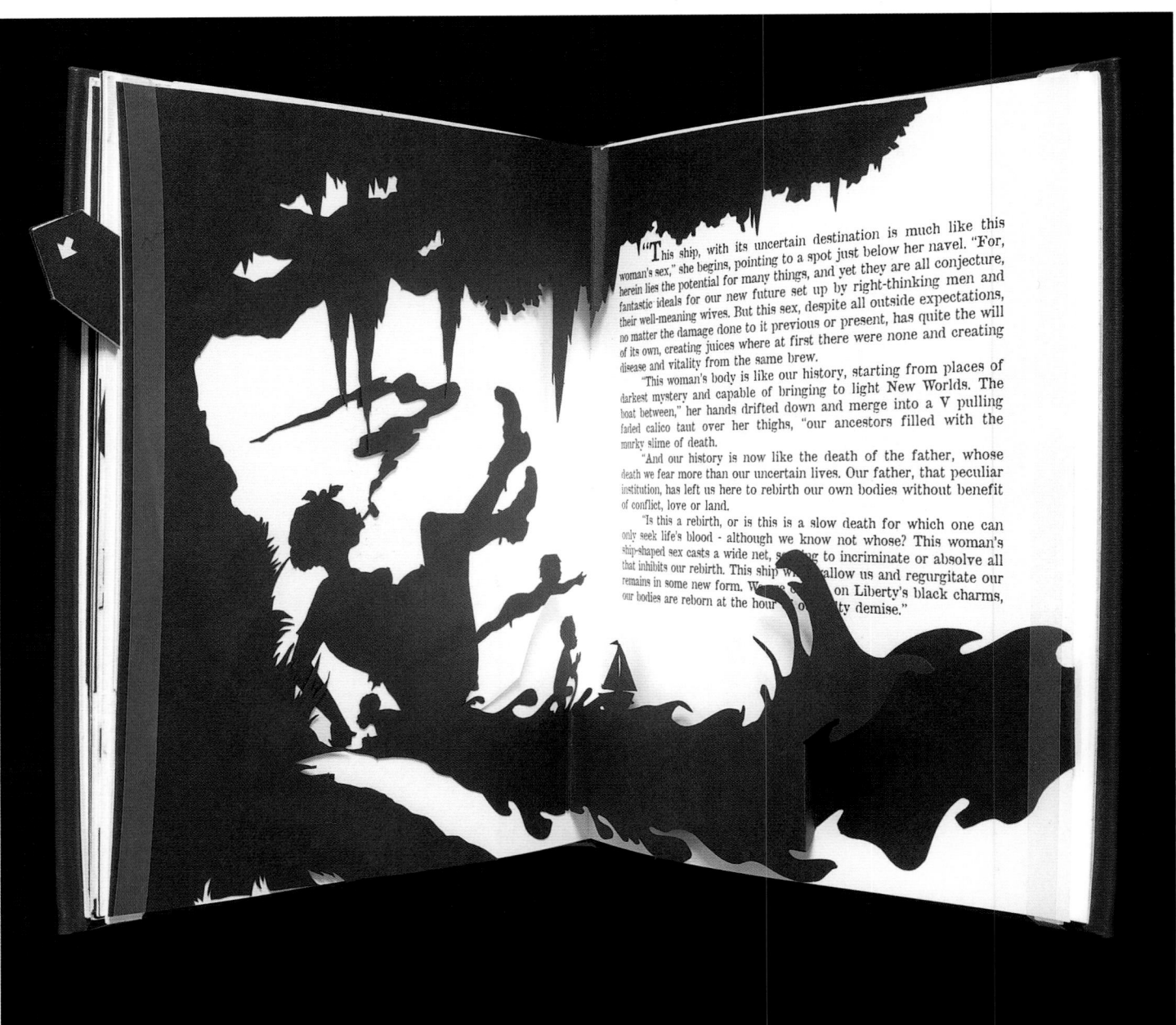

The text visible within the artwork reads:

"This ship, with its uncertain destination is much like this woman's sex," she begins, pointing to a spot just below her navel. "For, herein lies the potential for many things, and yet they are all conjecture, fantastic ideals for our new future set up by right-thinking men and their well-meaning wives. But this sex, despite all outside expectations, no matter the damage done to it previous or present, has quite the will of its own, creating juices where at first there were none and creating disease and vitality from the same brew.

"This woman's body is like our history, starting from places of darkest mystery and capable of bringing to light New Worlds. The boat between," her hands drifted down and merge into a V pulling faded calico taut over her thighs, "our ancestors filled with the murky slime of death.

"And our history is now like the death of the father, whose death we fear more than our uncertain lives. Our father, that peculiar institution, has left us here to rebirth our own bodies without benefit of conflict, love or land.

"Is this a rebirth, or is this a slow death for which one can only seek life's blood - although we know not whose? This woman's ship-shaped sex casts a wide net, se__ng to incriminate or absolve all that inhibits our rebirth. This ship w___ __allow us and regurgitate our remains in some new form. W____ ___ on Liberty's black charms, our bodies are reborn at the hour __ ___ty demise."

PLATE 118
Kara Elizabeth Walker, American (b. 1969)
Freedom: A Fable; A Curious Interpretation of the Wit of a Negress in Troubled Times, 1997
Paper
Hood Museum of Art: Gift of the Director of the Hood Museum of Art; MIS.997.53
Photograph by Jeffrey Nintzel

opposite PLATE 119
Fazal Sheikh, American (b. 1965)
Amina Alio Abdi and her son Mohammed, feeding center, Somali refugee camp, Mandera, Kenya, 1993–2002
Toned gelatin silver print
Hood Museum of Art: Purchased through the Alvin and Mary Bert Gutman 1940 Acquisition Fund; PH.2003.2
Photograph by Jeffrey Nintzel

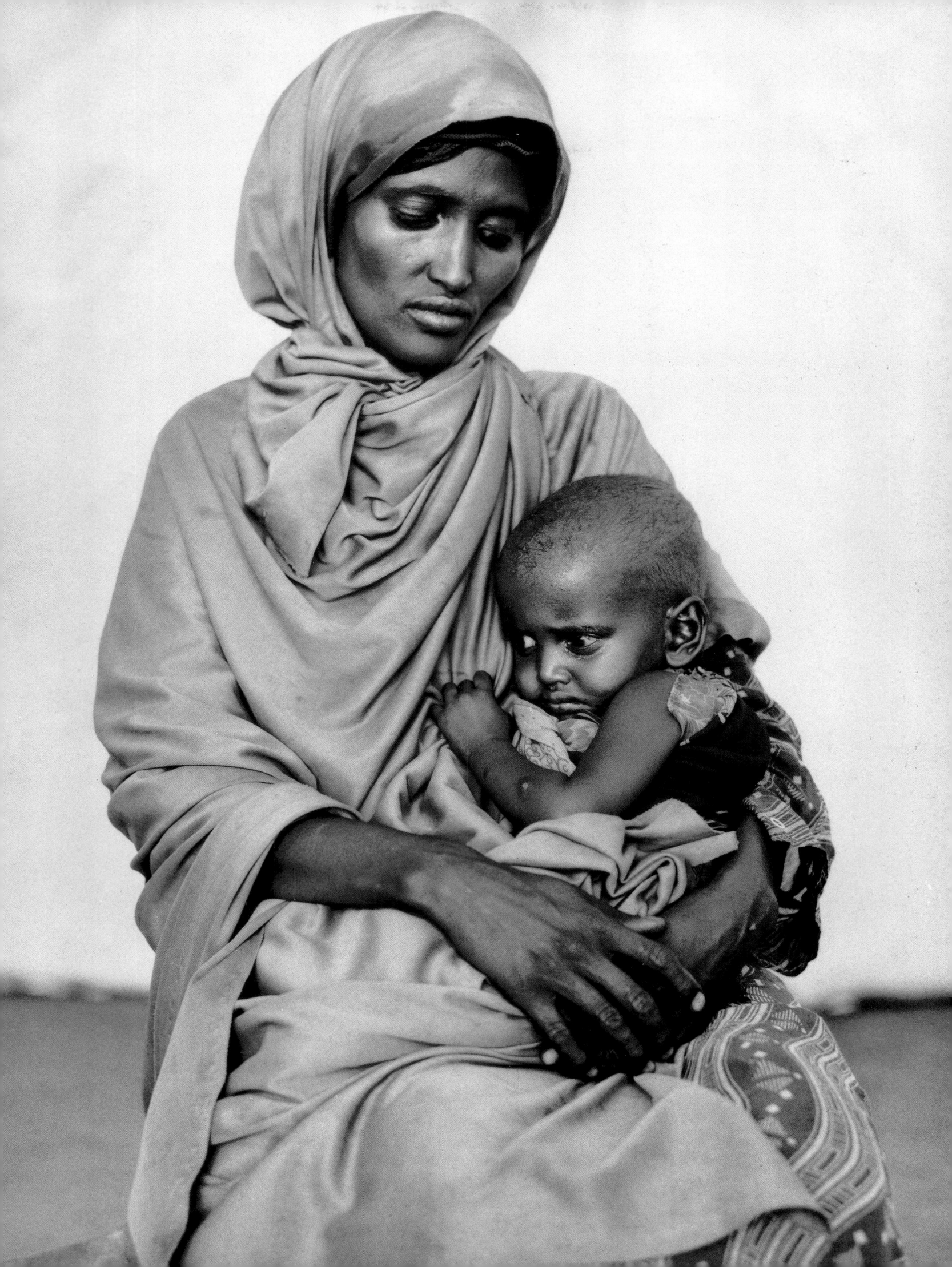

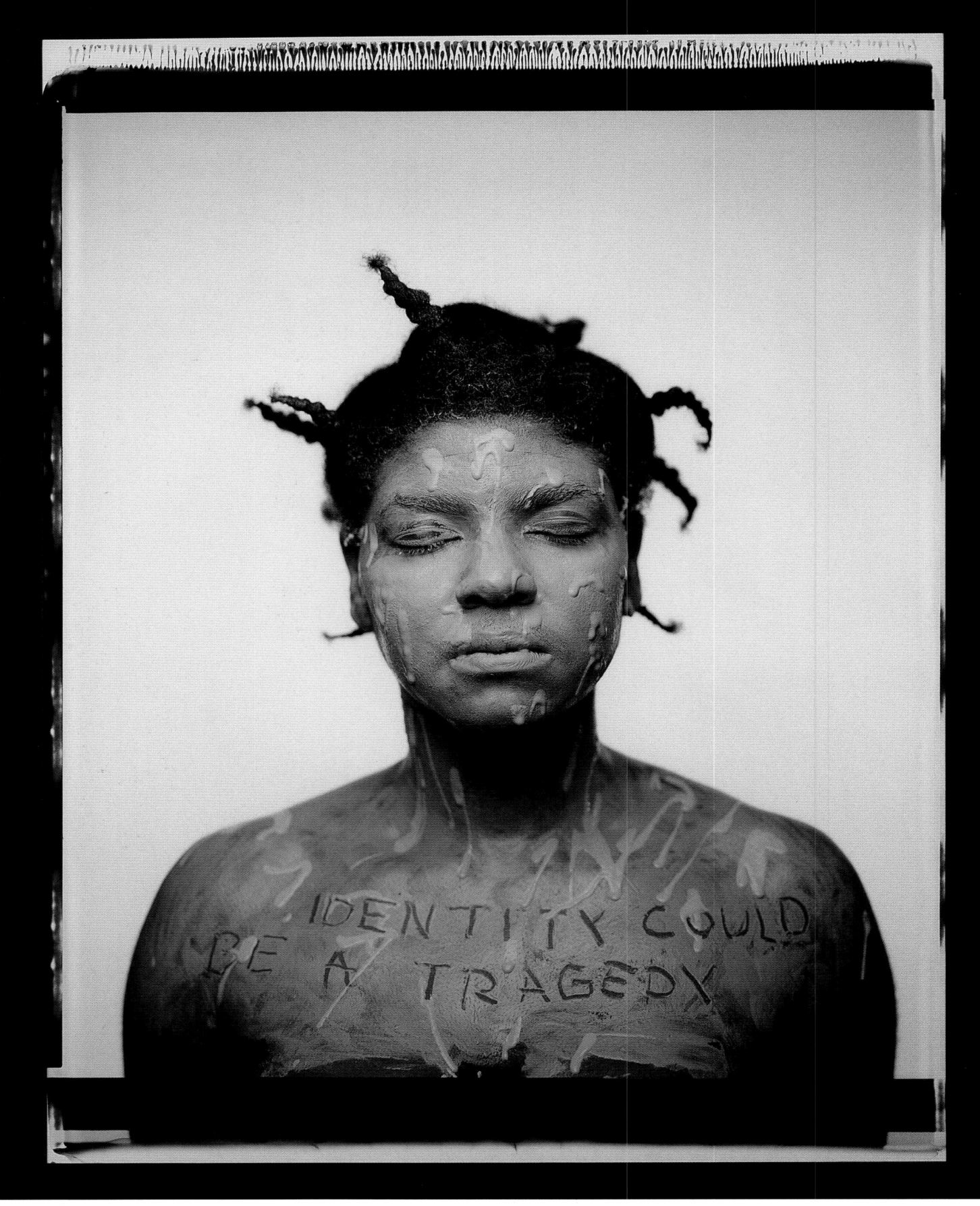

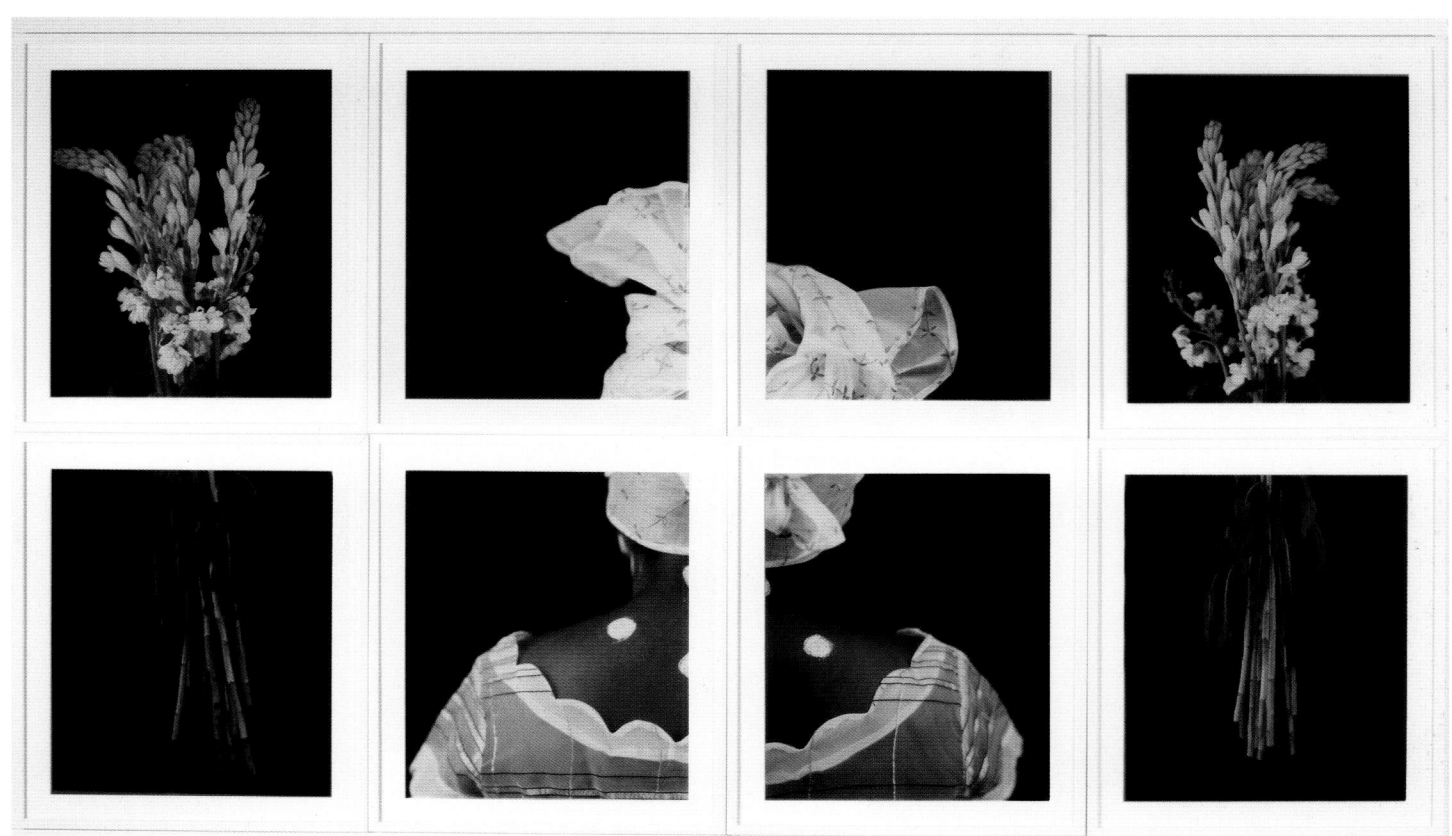

PLATE 121
Maria Magdalena Campos-Pons, Cuban (b. 1959)
Bim Bim Lady Dakar Swatch, 2006
Polaroid photograph
Bernice Steinbaum Gallery, Miami
Photograph courtesy of Maria Magdalena
Campos-Pons and Bernice Steinbaum Gallery,
Miami

opposite PLATE 120
Maria Magdalena Campos-Pons, Cuban (b. 1959)
When I Am Not Here/Estoy Allá, 1996
Polaroid photograph
Artist's collection
Photograph courtesy of Maria Magdalena
Campos-Pons and Howard Yezerski Gallery,
Boston

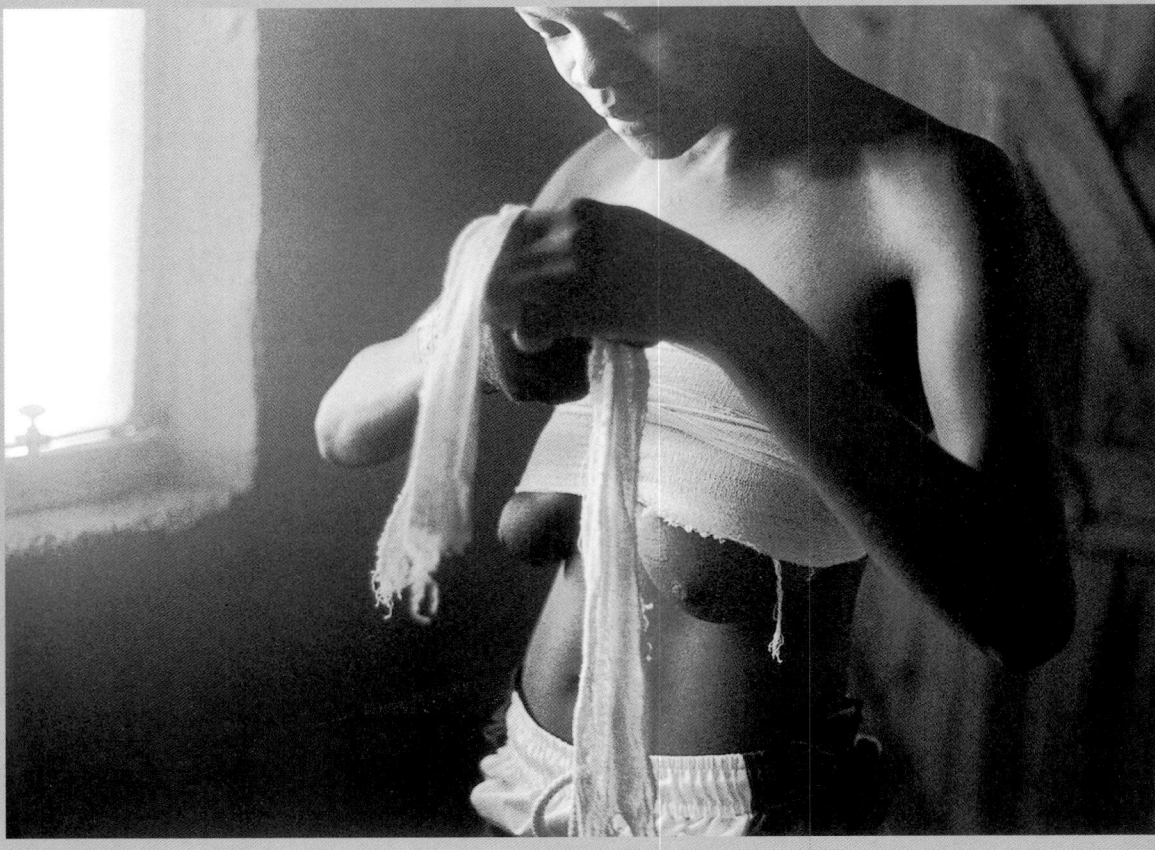

PLATE 122
Zanele Muholi, South African (b. 1972)
Sex ID Crisis, 2003
Gelatin silver print
Hood Museum of Art: Purchased through
the Hood Museum of Art Acquisitions
Fund; 2006.42
Photograph by Jeffrey Nintzel

EXCHANGES: ZANELE MUHOLI*

This is a time for a visual state of emergence. The preservation and mapping of our herstories is the only way for us black lesbians to be visible. The textualization of our cultures is not sufficient but historicizing is not impassable. It is for this reason that I embark on what I call visual activism. My work (plate 122) is about observing and taking action. I take pictures of myself and other women to heal from my past. It is personal issues that make me do what I do, for I have been raped more than 50 times by just listening to what women who have confessed and confirmed their love for other women have been through.

I have seen people speaking and capturing images of lesbians on our behalf, as if we are incapable and mute. I have witnessed this at Gay Pride events, at academic conferences, in the so-called women's movement forums. Research opened my eyes even wider than the lens, and it made me feel autonomous. I refused to become subject matter for others and to be silenced. Many have exiled our female African bodies: by colonizers, by researchers, by men. Sarah Baartman became a spectacle for Europeans, and she died in a foreign land. She was never given a chance to speak for herself. It is for this reason that I say No, not yet another black body.

* Artist statement, undated, ArtThrob, http://www.artthrob.co.za/06dec/artbio.html.

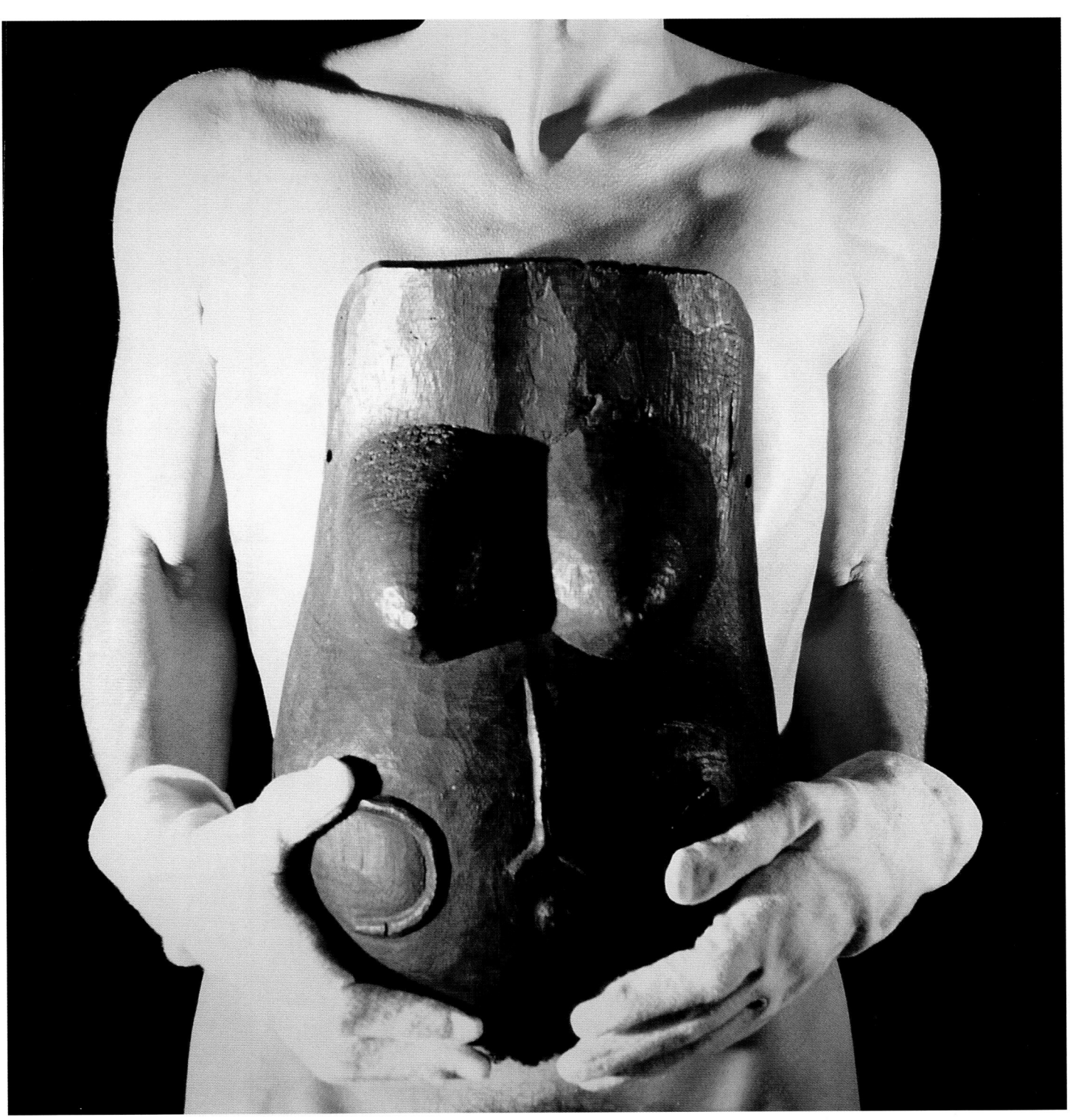

PLATE 123
Penny Siopis, South African (b. 1953)
Mask and Myself, 1994
Cibachrome
Jerome Stern collection
Photograph courtesy of Penny Siopis and
Jerome Stern
Photograph by Bruce White

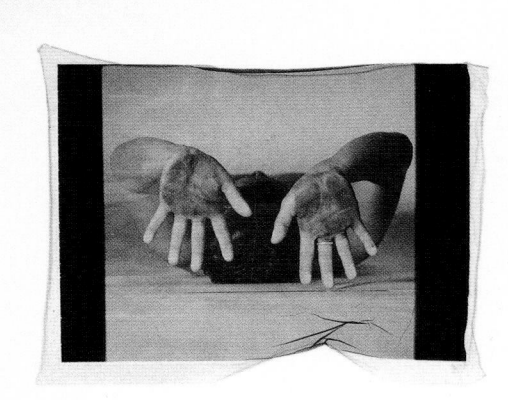

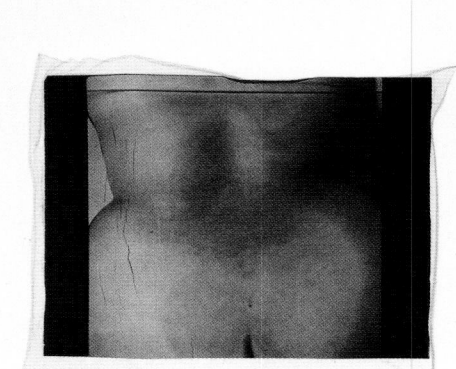

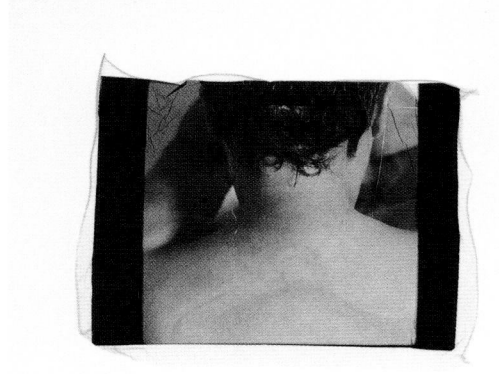

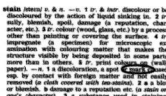

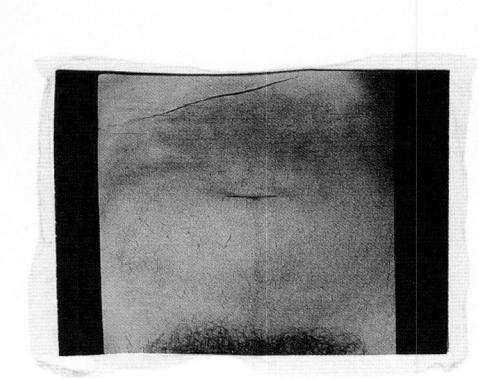

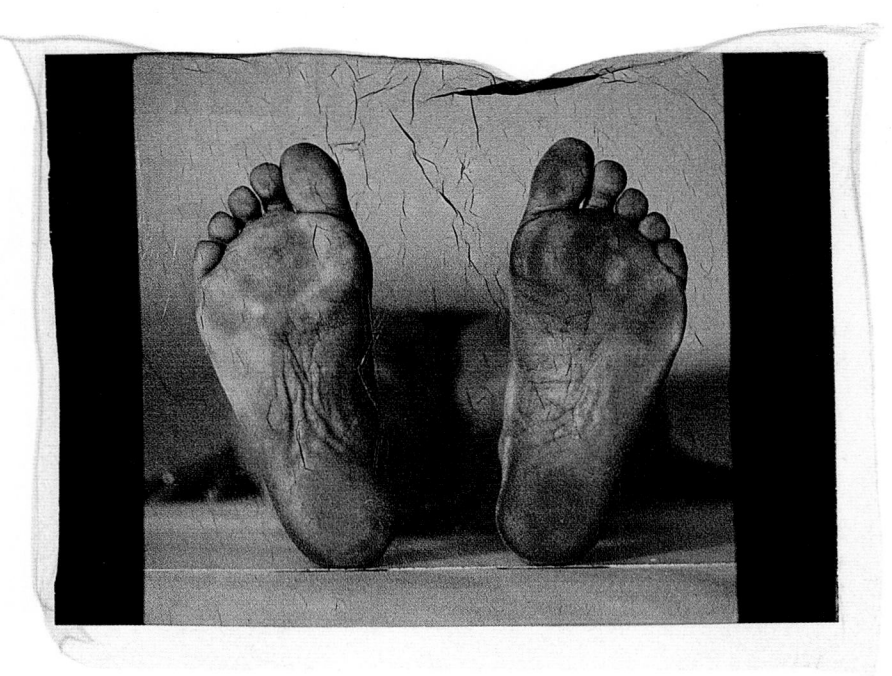

stain /stem/ *v. & n.* —*v.* **1** *tr. & intr.* discolour or be
discoloured by the action of liquid sinking in. **2** *tr.*
sully, blemish, spoil, damage (a reputation, character, etc.). **3** *tr.* colour (wood, glass, etc.) by a process
other than painting or covering the surface. **4** *tr.*
impregnate (a specimen) for microscopic examination with colouring matter that makes the
structure visible by being deposited in some parts
more than in others. **5** *tr.* print colours on (wallpaper). —*n.* **1** a discoloration, a spot or mark caused
esp. by contact with foreign matter and not easily
removed (*a cloth covered with tea-stains*). **2 a** a blot
or blemish. **b** damage to a reputation etc. (*a stain on
one's character*). **3** a substance used in staining.

PLATE 124
Berni Searle, South African (b. 1964)
Stain, from the *Discolored Series*, 5 panels, 2000
Digital print with text
Hood Museum of Art: Purchased through
the William B. Jaffe and Evelyn F. Jaffe Fund;
PR.2002.67.1–5
Photograph by Jeffrey Nintzel

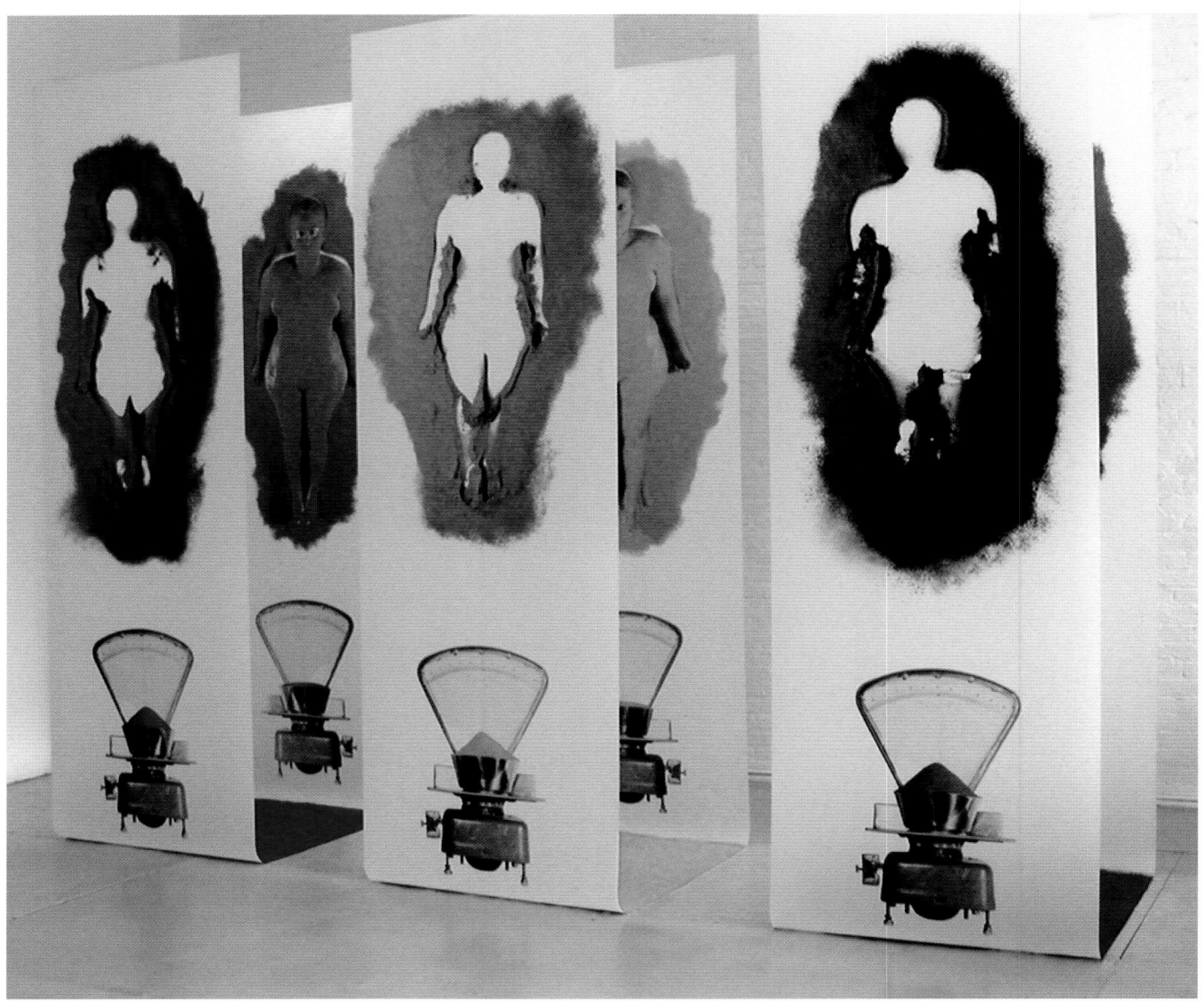

PLATE 125
Berni Searle, South African (b. 1964)
Traces (from the *Colour Me Series*), 1999
Digital print on tracing paper, spices
Artist's collection
Photograph courtesy of Berni Searle
and Axis Gallery

pages 347–349 PLATE 126
Lalla Essaydi, Moroccan (b. 1956)
Les Femmes du Maroc # 23a–c, 2005
Chromogenic print
Hood Museum of Art: Purchased through
the Robert J. Strasenburgh II 1942 Fund;
2006.76.1, 2006.76.2, 2006.76.3
Photograph courtesy of Edwynn Houk Gallery,
New York

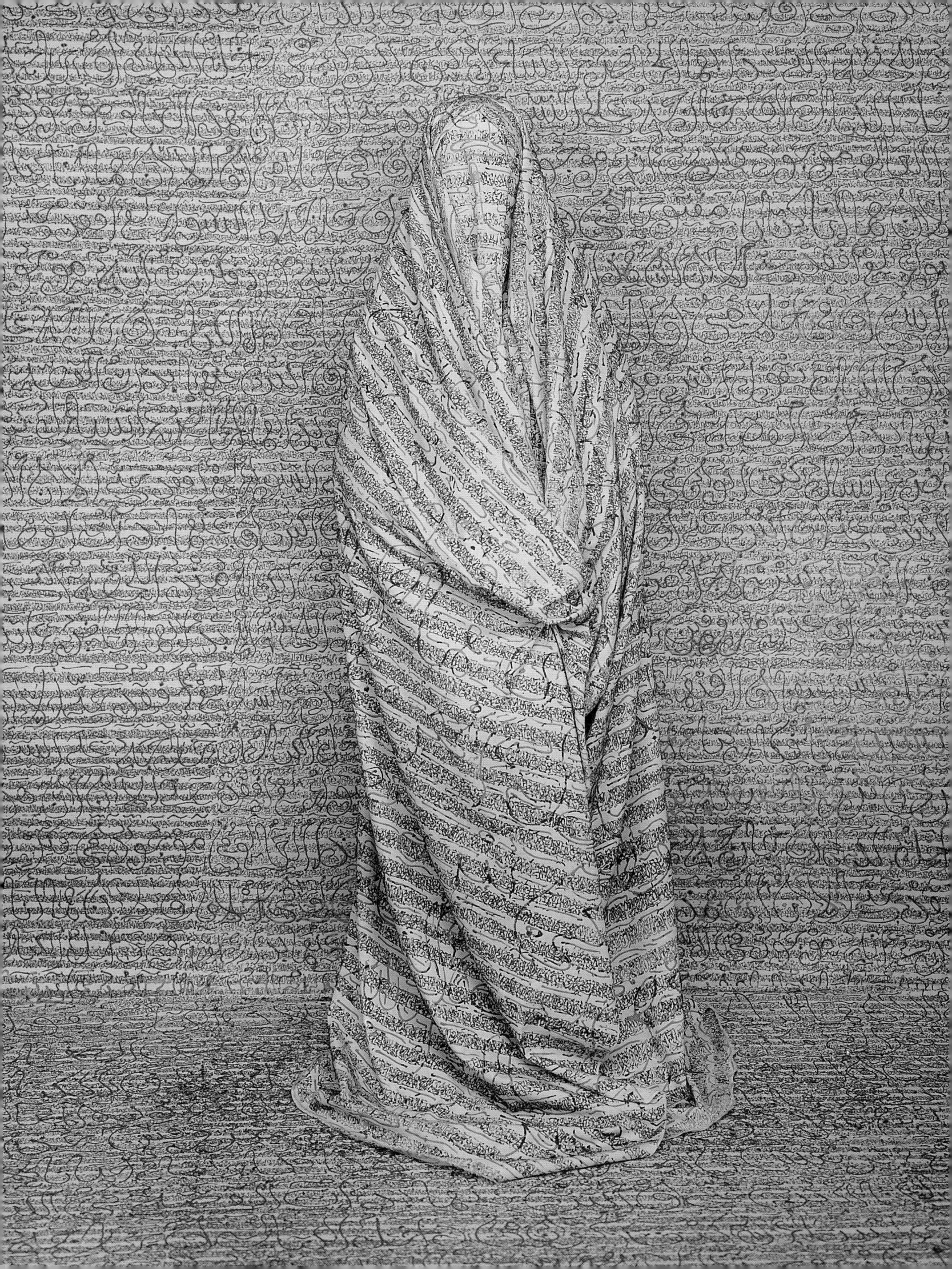

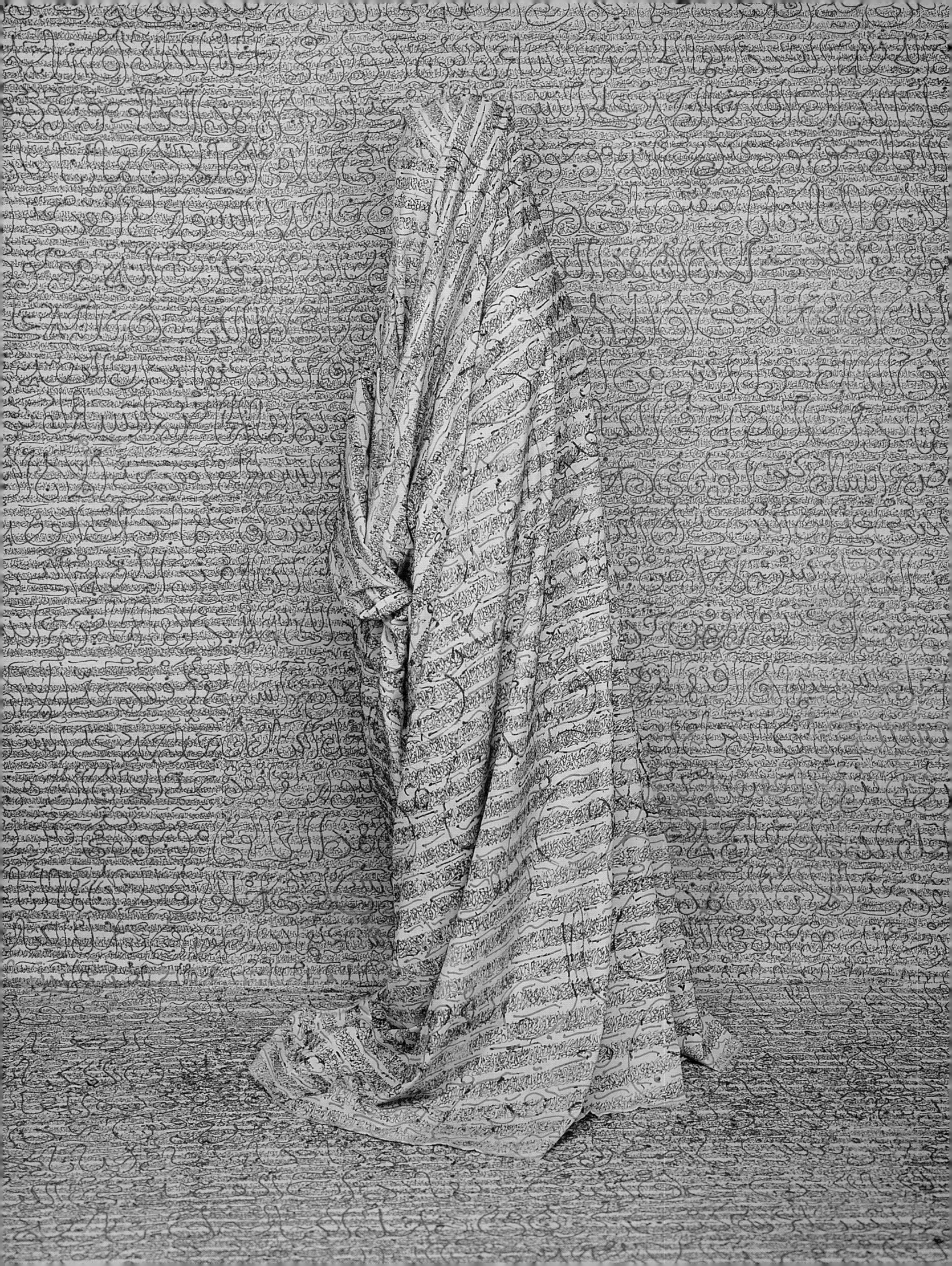

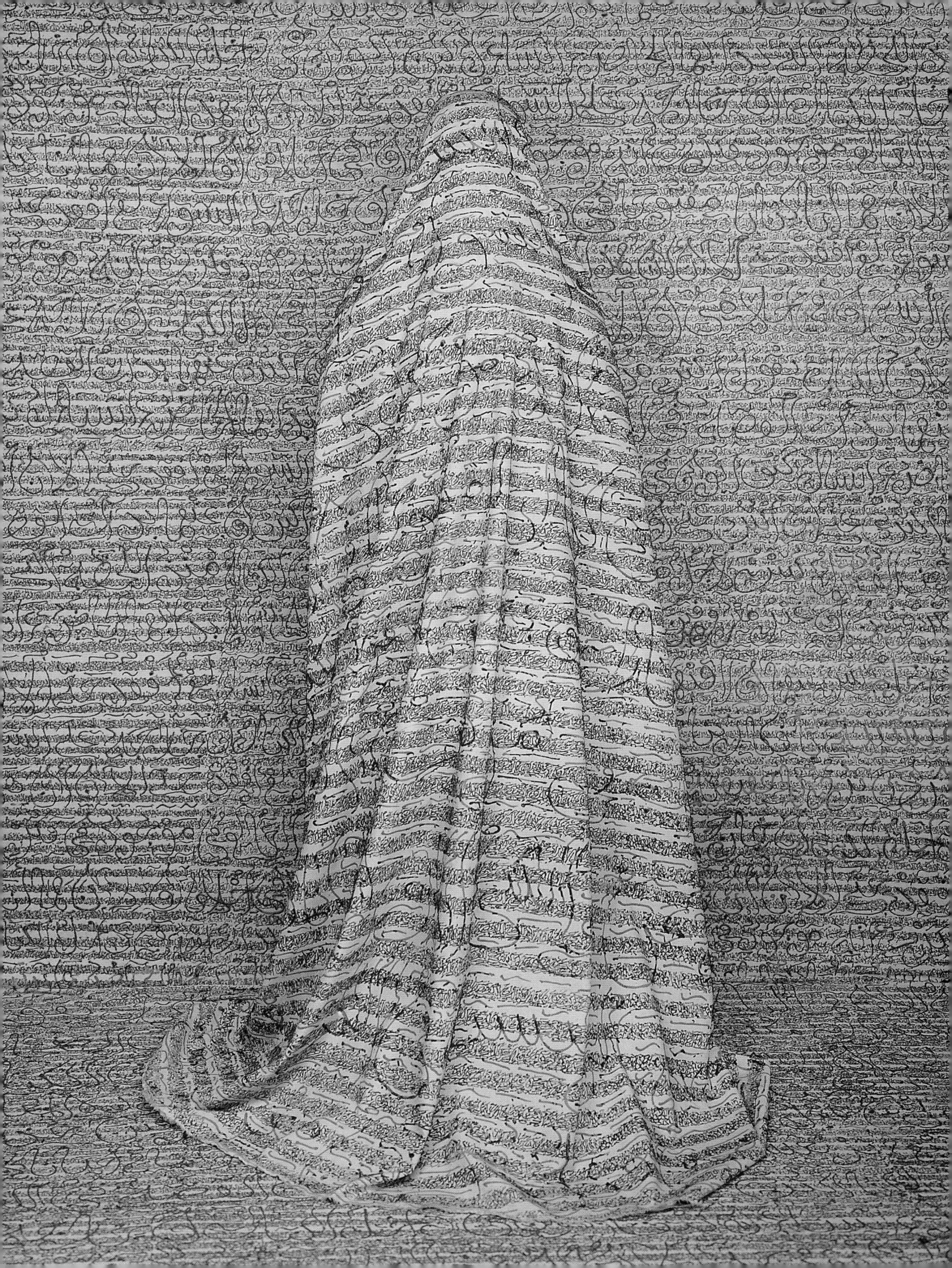

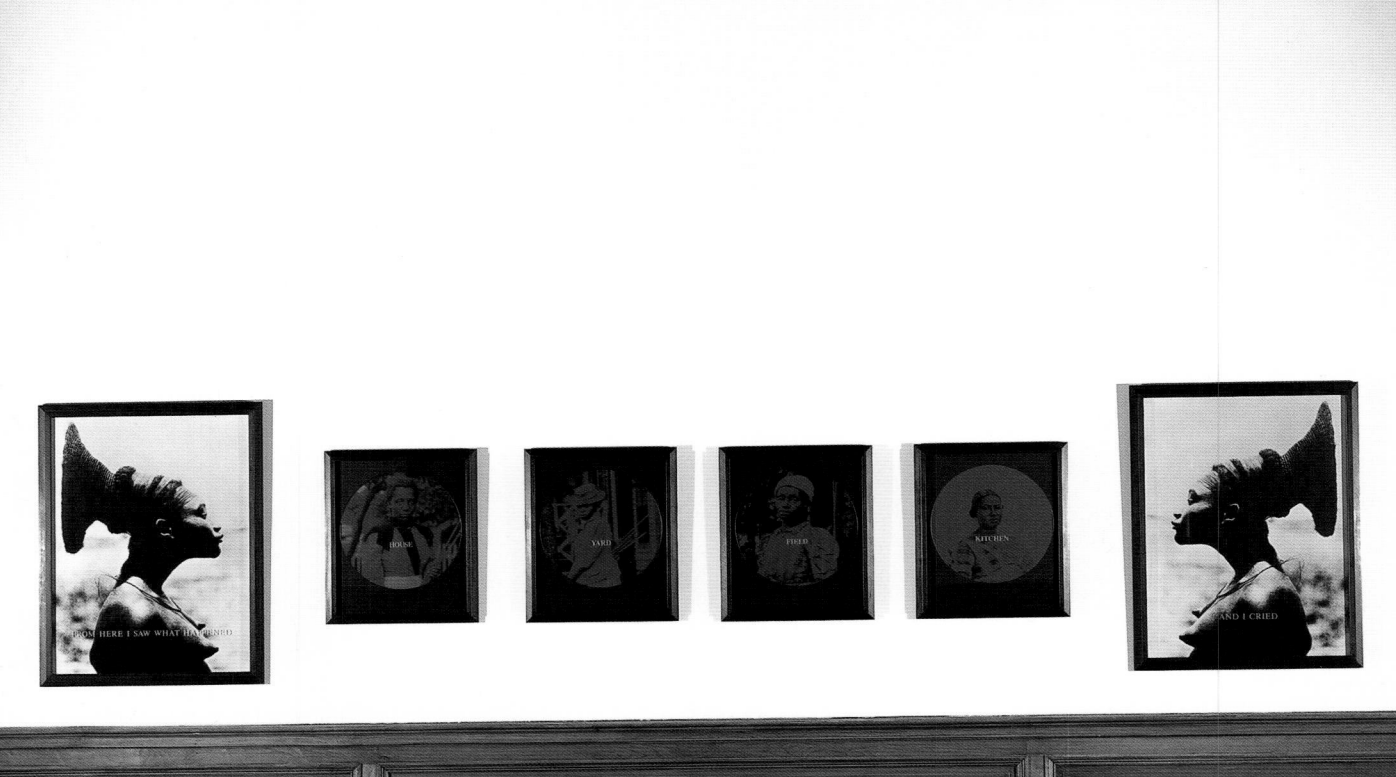
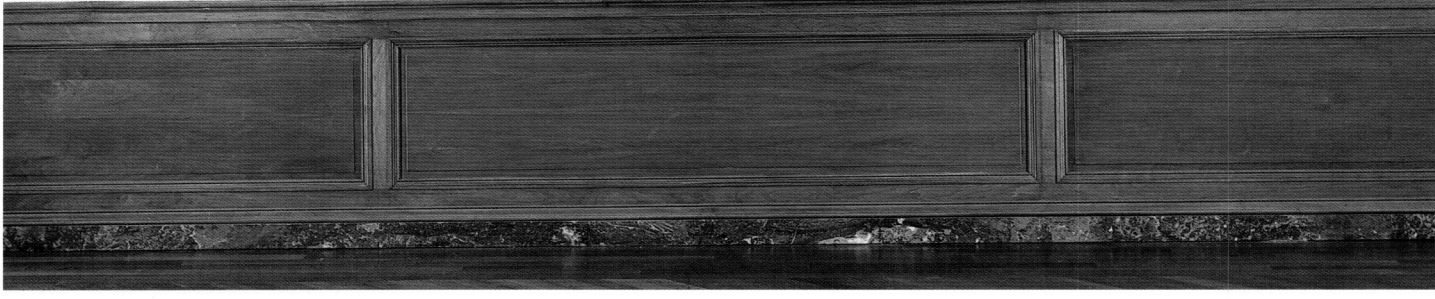

PLATE 127
Carrie Mae Weems, American (b. 1953)
Untitled (*From Here I Saw What Happened
And I Cried*), 1995–1996
Chromogenic color prints and
sand-blasted glass
The Baltimore Museum of Art: Collectors Circle
Fund for Art by African Americans, and Edward
Joseph Gallagher III Memorial Fund;
BMA 2002.30a–b, 2002.31a–d
Photograph courtesy of
The Baltimore Museum of Art

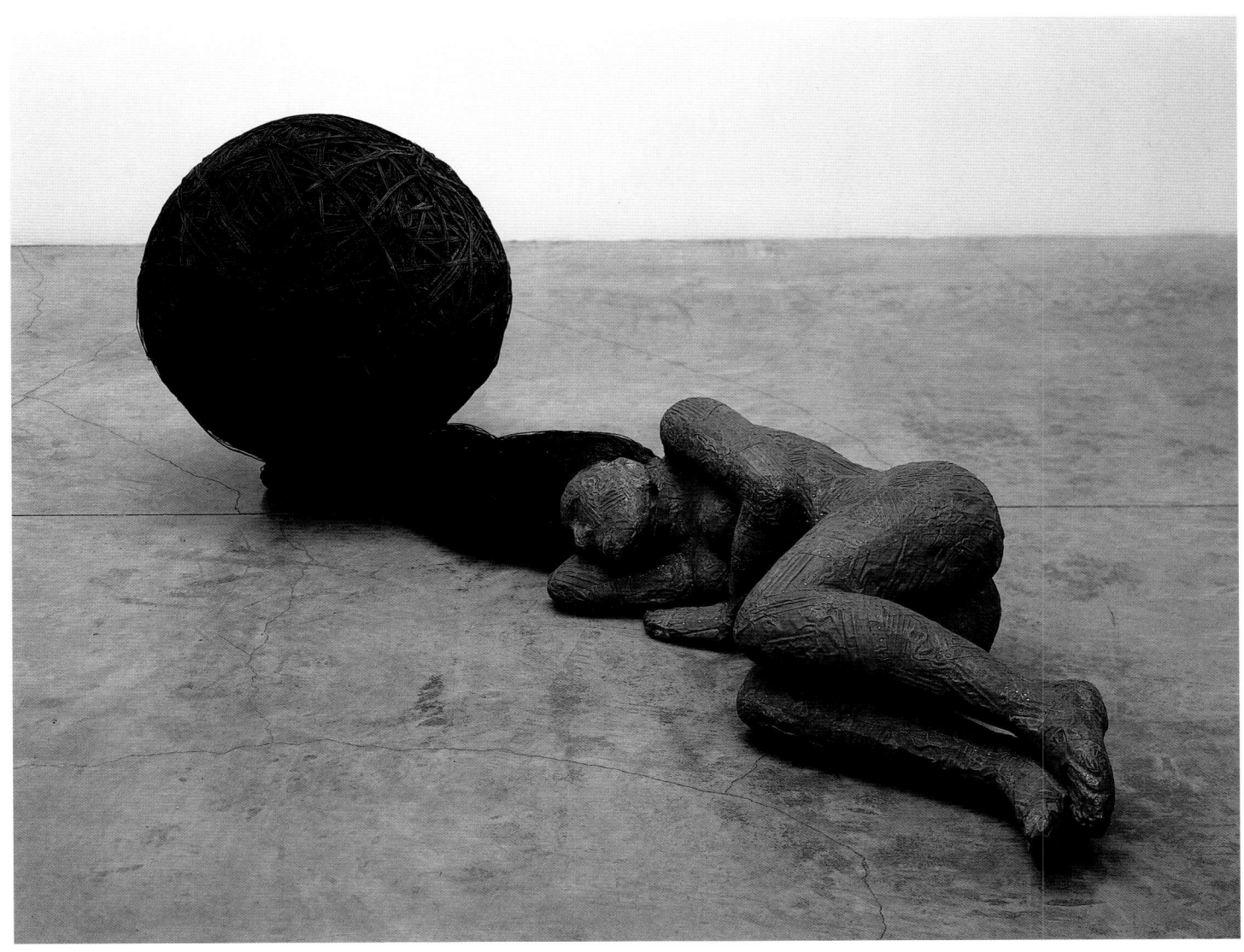

PLATE 128
Alison Saar, American (b. 1956)
Caché, 2006
Wood, ceiling tin, and wire
Hood Museum of Art: Purchased through
the Virginia and Preston T. Kelsey 1958 Fund;
2006.32
Photograph courtesy of Alison Saar and
LA Louver Gallery, Venice, California

Artists

MARIA MAGDALENA CAMPOS-PONS was born in Matanzas, Cuba, in 1959. She studied at the National School of Art and the Higher Institute of Art in Havana, Cuba, before moving to Boston and receiving an M.A. in Painting and Media Arts in 1988 at the Massachusetts College of Art. She continues to live and work in Massachusetts. Campos-Pons's migration to the United States, as well as her familial history that can be traced from Africa to Cuba and then America, inspires her self-referential art, which often combines various media including sound, written text, video, lighting effects, and photography. In her work, Campos-Pons explores the intersection of art and autobiography, using the themes of memory, matriarchy, domestic labor, race, femininity, and heritage. Her work reflects upon migratory experiences of black Africans in the Atlantic world and the transcultural experiences of African people from historical and contemporary periods of diasporic groups. Campos-Pons has held solo shows at the Indianapolis Museum of Art (Indiana); Museum of Modern Art (Salvador, Bahia, Brazil); and the MIT List Visual Arts Center (Cambridge, Massachusetts), as well as group shows at venues including the biennials in Seville, Spain, Venice, Italy, and Johannesburg, South Africa; Museum of the African Diaspora (San Francisco, California); and the Museum of Contemporary Art (Brisbane, Australia). Campos-Pons has received numerous awards and fellowships, including the Louis Comfort Tiffany Foundation Grant and fellowships from Radcliffe College at Harvard and the New England Foundation for the Arts. Her work is featured in many international collections, including the Fogg Museum at Harvard University (Cambridge, Massachusetts); National Museum of Fine Arts (Havana, Cuba); and the Victoria and Albert Museum (London).

RENÉE COX was born in Colgate, Jamaica, in 1960, but she was raised in New York, where she became interested in fashion photography and film. She returned to school in 1992 to do independent studies at the Whitney Museum of American Art and obtain an M.F.A. at the School of Visual Art in New York. Shortly afterwards, Cox began to create critical photographs that examined and reinterpreted Eurocentric visual and artistic histories. Cox's controversial works insert black subjects, most often including her own nude body, into famous art historical and pop culture imagery to expose racial and sexual taboos. In Cox's 1996 revised version of da Vinci's *The Last Supper,* for example, she portrays a nude, female Christ surrounded by black disciples and a white Judas. Whether Cox photographs herself as a superhero rescuing "Uncle Ben" and "Aunt Jemima" from their respective food labels, or photographs community members back in Jamaica, her subjects are alert and aware of the audience's gaze. In this way, Cox reminds the viewer that it is her agency as the artist that gives the audience access to the body and reinserts a black presence into hegemonic visual and cultural histories. Cox has been a part of solo and group exhibitions at venues including the Whitney Museum of American Art (New York); University Art Museum at University of California (Berkeley); and the Brooklyn Museum (New York). She has also been guest lecturer and professor at various New York City area universities and colleges and was recipient of the New Foundation for the Arts, Artists Fellowship Award, as well as Artist-in-Residence at Light Works in Syracuse, N.Y.

SOKARI DOUGLAS CAMP was born in the Kalabari town of Buguma in southern Nigeria in 1958. She left Nigeria in 1979 to study art in the United States at the California College of Arts and Crafts. The following year, she moved to England to pursue a B.A. and M.A. at the Central School of Art and Design and the Royal College of Art in London. While Douglas Camp is a British citizen and continues to live and work in London, the imagery of her African culture is strongly evident in her art. Douglas Camp employs her life-size and at times moving sculptures to question the adoption and display of African masking traditions in Western museums devoid of context, movement, and action. Her sculpture has more generally approached the themes of diaspora and cross-cultural dialogue by manipulating

Western visual icons to question strict definitions of nationality and cultural belonging. Douglas Camp has held solo and group exhibitions at the Museum of Mankind (London); National Museum of African Art (Washington, D.C.); New Museum of Contemporary Art (New York); and the Dakar (Senegal) and Havanna (Cuba) biennials. Douglas Camp has been awarded the Saatchi and Saatchi Award, a British Council Commonwealth Fellowship, and was the 2006 Honorary Fellow of University of the Arts, London. Her works can be found in the permanent collections of institutions such as the American Museum of Natural History (New York); British Museum (London); Minneapolis Museum of Art (Minnesota); and the Glenbow Museum (Calgary, Canada).

ANGÈLE ETOUNDI ESSAMBA was born in Douala, Cameroon, in 1962 but moved to Paris at the age of nine, where she later received her Baccalaureat in Philosophy. In 1982, she moved to Amsterdam and studied photography at the Fotovaschool, putting up her first exhibition in 1984. Essamba continues to live and work in Amsterdam as a photographer, dancer, poet, and designer. Essamba photographs primarily black women using images of highly individualized subjects to challenge Eurocentric expectations of Africans. Her photographs reflect her personal view of the body and its physical beauty separate from exoticized or romantic depictions. Her relatively traditional and formal photography training in the Netherlands is evident in the careful attention to form and contrast. Using precise and controlled photographic composition, Essamba places her subjects in dynamic poses that suggest strength and pride while emphasizing the sensual qualities of the body to give her subjects back their own beauty and agency. Her work has been featured in solo and group exhibitions at international venues including the Afrika Museum (Berg en Dal, Netherlands); Phila-delphia Museum of Arts (Pennsylvania); Museum of Modern Art (Arnhem, Nether-lands); National Museum of Yaoundé (Cameroon); and UNESCO. Her art was also selected for biennials in Venice, Havanna, South Africa, and Dakar. In 1996, she was awarded the Prix Spécial Afrique at the Festival des Trois Continents, Nantes (France), for her 1995 suite of black and white photographs, *White Line.*

Born in 1965, the Moroccan artist **LALLA ASSIA ESSAYDI** lived also in Saudi Arabia for many years and studied art in Paris in the early 1990s before moving to the United States. She received her B.F.A. from Tufts University in 1999 and her M.F.A. from Boston's School of the Museum of Fine Arts in 2003. A photographer, painter, and installation artist, Essaydi now lives and teaches in New York City and Boston. She confronts viewers with clichés of Muslim women that stem from loaded nineteenth-century Orientalist paintings and romantic narratives about North African "harems." Her art expresses the complex balance of tradition and modernity in the Islamic world but also addresses the more general themes of exposure, vulnerability, voyeurism, and confrontation in the Western fascination with the exotic. Essaydi has exhibited in solo shows at venues including the Danish Center for Culture and Development (Copenhagen), Williams College Museum of Art (Williamstown, Massachusetts); Chicago Art Institute (Illinois); and various international photography festivals. She is represented in a number of collections, including the Fries Museum (Leeuwarden, Nether-lands); Museum of Fine Arts (Houston, Texas); Kresge Art Museum, University of Michigan (East Lansing, Michigan); and the Columbus Museum of Art (Ohio).

EMILE GUEBEHI was born in 1937 in the village of Anomo in Côte d'Ivoire but now lives and works in Abidjan. On the advice of a healer in his village, Guebehi took up wood carving in 1966. Impressed with his initial work, Guebehi's local community agreed to relocate him to the village of Songbo Dagbé on the well-traveled road into the city of Abidjan. Soon, the artist and his younger brother were being commissioned by surrounding communities to create commemorative carvings, which were exhibited publicly to record and celebrate a community's cultural heritage. More recently, Guebehi has been creating coconut palm wood sculptures of individ-ual human figures and group scenes based on specific village themes and daily experiences. Guebehi's recent sculptural work, which is only now emerging on the American contemporary art scene, has been featured at the Museum of Fine Arts, Houston (Texas), Abidjan National Museum, Musée d'Art Moderne et Contemporain (Geneva), and the Saatchi & Saatchi Gallery (London).

Now based in Johannesburg, South Africa, **SENZENI MARASELA** was born in 1977, raised in a white Afrikaans suburb, and attended Catholic school as a child. Influenced by her social marginalization and sheltered upbringing, when Marasela later pursued a B.F.A. from the University of the Witwatersrand in Johannesburg, she began to revisit apartheid-era histories that were often concealed from the public as well as personal familial histories that she herself did not know. Using photography, photo-transfers, silkscreens, handicrafts, and everyday found objects, Marasela illuminates issues such as the continued impact of colonialism and the place of women in male-dominated South African culture, revealing how private and public remembrance can determine the presence or absence of memory. Marasela has exhibited widely within South Africa and is an emerging artist in Europe and North America. She has had solo and group exhibitions at the Johannesburg Art Gallery and the National Art Gallery of Namibia (Windhoek), and in 2005 was the South African representative for the Beijing biennial in China. In 2000, she was the "Fresh Artist in Residence" at the South African National Gallery in Cape Town and was a visiting artist at the Kokkola Fine Arts Academy of Vasa, Finland, in 2001. Marasela's works are in the permanent collections of the South African National Gallery (Cape Town) and Wellesley College Davis Museum and Cultural Center (Wellesley, Massachusetts).

Born in Pretoria, South Africa, in 1982, **NANDIPHA MNTAMBO** has a B.A. in Fine Arts from the Michaelis School of Fine Arts at the University of Cape Town and is currently an M.A. candidate at the same institution. Mntambo's art is born out of a deep concern with materiality, using discarded and unexpected materials. Mntambo works primarily with raw cowhides, which she prepares, tans, and then molds on her own body and pre-fabricated forms to create floating sculptures that mimic the shape of the human body. The visceral aspects of the hair, fat, and odor that are part of the hide's organic nature and the addition of materials such as animal bones and glass beads create a multifarious attraction and repulsion to Mntambo's sculptures. Mntambo's nascent career in South Africa is giving way to growing international interest. She has exhibited work in solo and group shows in South Africa at the Johannesburg Art Gallery, South African National Gallery (Cape Town), and the University of Cape Town, as well as abroad at the Centro Atlantico de Arte Moderne (Canary Islands, Spain). Mntambo has work in permanent collections both at the South African National Gallery (Cape Town) and at the Johannesburg National Gallery (South Africa). She was the recipient of the Curatorial Fellowship for the Brett Kebble Art Awards in 2005 as well as the Mellon Meyers Fellowship in 2003.

ZANELE MUHOLI, an artist and activist, was born in Umlazi, Durban, in 1972 and now lives in Johannesburg, South Africa. In 2002, she co-founded the Forum for the Empowerment of Women (FEW), a networking, empowerment, and support organization for black lesbians. Her photography and reporting for *Behind the Mask,* an online magazine of lesbian and gay issues in Africa, encouraged her to pursue professional photographic training, which she completed in 2004 at the Market Photo Workshop in Newtown, South Africa. Muholi's photography came to national attention in 2004 with her first solo exhibition, *Visual Sexuality,* at Johannesburg Art Gallery. Since then, she has gained renown for her frank and intimate photographs of the lives of black lesbian women from Africa, which challenge the history of the portrayal of black women's bodies in documentary photography. As an activist and photographer, she portrays the women she photographs as complex individuals with voices, encouraging viewers to question their own social norms and breaking from

any stereotypical narratives about black female sexuality. An emerging artist, Muholi has held solo exhibitions at the Johannesburg Art Gallery (South Africa) and the Vienna Kunsthalle (Austria) and has participated in group exhibitions at the Centro Atlantico de Arte Modern (Canary Islands, Spain) and the South African National Gallery (Cape Town). She was the recipient of the 2005 Tollman Award for the Visual Arts and the LGBTI Arts and Culture Award and was the first recipient of the Bhp Billiton/University of Witwatersrand Visual Arts Fellowship. Muholi's work has appeared in numerous gay and feminist publications and is featured in the permanent collection of the South African National Gallery (Cape Town).

HASSAN MUSA was born in 1951 in Sudan and graduated from the College of Fine and Applied Arts of Khartoum, Sudan, with a diploma in painting in 1976. In the late 1970s, he attended Montpellier University, France, for his doctoral studies in fine art and art history. Musa, who lives and works in Domessargues in the south of France, works in various media and is an accomplished calligrapher and a performance artist. He regularly contributes to several Sudanese and Western periodicals and has been a vocal critic of what he sees as the reactionary art of the earlier generation of Sudanese modernist artists known as the Khartoum School. His work focuses on the critical appropriation of Western masterpieces and visual icons in what some call postmodern versions of history paintings. These paintings are often executed in textile ink on printed cloth, consciously blending the designs of the fabric with Musa's own artistic themes and drawing attention to art practices outside of Western-sanctioned aesthetics. By juxtaposing and satirizing well-known icons from art history and pop culture, Musa creates a powerful criticism of Western capitalism and the monolithic narratives of Western art history as a whole. Musa's art has been shown in solo exhibitions at the Whitechapel Art Gallery (London); Malmö Konsthall (Sweden); and Under a Different Sky (Copenhagen, Denmark), as well as recent group exhibitions at venues including the

Venice Biennale, Museum Kunst Palast (Dusseldorf, Germany), and the Museum for African Art (New York).

Currently living in Brooklyn, New York, WANGECHI MUTU was born in Nairobi, Kenya, in 1972, where she was raised before leaving to study in Great Britain and the United States. Trained as a sculptor, painter, and anthropologist, Mutu received her B.F.A. from Cooper Union in 1996 and an M.F.A. from Yale University in 2000. She creates mixed media collages, piecing together magazine imagery, photographs, paint, and other found materials to create grotesquely exaggerated or marred human figures. Often evoking plastic surgery, eating disorders, genocide, and social Darwinism, Mutu's art examines implicit ideologies tied to and layered upon the female body, especially by exploring competing and paradoxical notions of femininity and cultural identity in colonial histories, in African and Western politics, and in the growth of global commodification. Mutu's art has been exhibited in solo and group exhibitions internationally at the San Francisco Museum of Modern Art (California); Tate Modern (London); Kunstpalast Dusseldorf (Germany); and the Centre Pompidou (Paris). Her work has been featured in the Gwangju biennial in South Korea and the Johannesburg biennial in South Africa. Her art is in the permanent collections of institutions such as the Museum of Contemporary Art (Los Angeles, California); Whitney Museum of American Art (New York); Museum of Contemporary Art (Chicago, Illinois); and the Saatchi Gallery (London). She has lectured and taught at universities throughout the United States and has been awarded fellowships and residencies at Yale University (New Haven, Connecticut), the Studio Museum Harlem (New York), and the Jamaica Center for the Arts Fellowship (Queens, New York).

Born in Kenya in 1975 to a German mother and a Kenyan father, INGRID MWANGI moved fifteen years later with her mother and brothers from Nairobi to Germany. She attended the University of Fine Arts in Saarbrucken, Germany, where she studied until 1996 with Ulrike Rosenbach, a renowned German video artist and former student of Joseph Beuys. Promoting Buey's methodology, Rosenbach encouraged Mwangi to use body art and performance as a means of investigating and collapsing stereotypical narratives of race, gender, and sexuality. The artist now lives, works, and teaches in Ludwigshafen, Germany. She is married to fellow German artist **ROBERT HUTTER**, who was born in Germany in 1964. Together they have formed the artist collective IngridMwangiRobertHutter, which seeks to make art that uses video, installation, performance, and photography to explore issues of race and cultural heritage as well as Western clichés about African appearances. Utilizing their corporeality as determined by body, skin, hair, and voice, the IngridMwangiRobertHutter collective explores the relationship between violence, memory, and identity. Their extensive exhibition history includes shows at venues such as the Center of Contemporary Art of East Africa (Nairobi, Kenya); Museum for African Art (New York); and the Kunsthalle Lophem (Belgium), as well as the Elizabeth A. Sackler Center for Feminist Art at the Brooklyn Museum (New York); the Dak'art biennial (Senegal), and numerous international video and arts festivals.

Born in Nairobi, Kenya, in 1950, **MAGDALENE ODUNDO** was educated in Kenya and India before moving to England in 1971 to obtain a B.A. in graphic design at the West Surrey College of Art and Design. She turned to pottery in the mid-1970s, traveling to Africa to study the techniques of female potters in Nigeria and Kenya and visiting the well-known female potters of San Ildefonso, New Mexico. She returned to London to complete a master's degree at the Royal College of Art. She is now professor of ceramics at the Surrey Institute of Art and Design University College in Farnham (England). Odundo works in the traditional African technique of hand-built pottery, using coils of clay to mold her vessels into human-like forms that defy rational symmetry, often pushing the limits of gravity while maintaining beauty, balance, and form. While Odundo's work has obvious corollaries in African traditions of anthropomorphic ceramics and sculpture

as well as blackened ware, she also derives much of the form and method of her work from global ceramic and sculptural traditions, ranging from Greco-Roman antiquities to European and American modernist sculpture. Odundo has had solo exhibitions in venues including the Samuel P. Harn Museum of Art (Gainesville, Florida); National Museum of African Art, Smithsonian Institution (Washington, D.C.); and the Museum fur Kunst und Gewerbe (Hamburg, Germany); as well as group shows at the Museum of Mankind (London); Metropolitan Museum of Art (New York); and the Los Angeles County Museum of Art (California). Odundo's art is represented in various international collections including the British Museum (London); Brooklyn Museum (New York); and the Museum of Fine Arts, Houston (Texas).

ETIYÉ DIMMA POULSEN was born in Aroussi, a rural village in Ethiopia, but was orphaned by the age of two. She was adopted by a Danish friend of the family and spent her childhood moving from Ethiopia to Tanzania and Kenya before finally settling with her adoptive father in Denmark. Her artistic skills were recognized by friends and family from a young age. She began painting at the age of fourteen to express emotions obscured by language barriers. Poulsen studied art and art history on the island of Amager, outside of Copenhagen, and taught creative arts in youth programs before moving to France in 1991. She relocated her studio in 1993 to Antwerp, Belgium, where she presently lives and works. Originally trained as a painter, Poulsen began experimenting in the early 1990s with firing iron mesh forms coated with a thin layer of clay. These profoundly personal figures, like Poulsen's own life, are born out of circumstance and chance. Poulsen has participated in international solo and group exhibitions at the Världskulturmuseet (Göteborg, Sweden); Alliance Française (Addis Ababa, Ethiopia); Dak'art biennial (Senegal); and the Herbert F. Johnson Museum of Art at Cornell University (Ithaca, New York). Her work is represented in the National Museum of African Art, Smithsonian Institution (Washington, D.C.), and the Hans

Bogatzke Collection of Contemporary African Art (Herdecke, Germany).

ALISON SAAR was born in Los Angeles, California, in 1956 to the well-known African American artist Betye Saar and to Richard Saar, an art conservator. She received a B.A. in art and art history at Scripps College in 1978 and an M.F.A. from the Otis Art Institute of the Parsons School of Design in Los Angeles in 1981. Saar's studies of African, Latin American, and Caribbean art and religion as well as her interest in issues of social identity have informed her work both aesthetically and theoretically. In the 1980s, Saar began making sculptures and room installations that focused on issues surrounding the African diaspora as well as the sexual stereotypes and voyeurism that often surround the black female body in European and American art. These issues continue to be a theme in Saar's work. The feminized sculptures she creates embody the power, fertility, and strength of women, often echoing themes found in the traditional arts of Africa and its Diaspora. Her work is unique in its combination of found materials—soil, wood, hair, wax, and tin—and diverse cultural references. Saar's work has been featured in solo and group exhibitions at the Whitney Museum Biennial (New York); The White House (Washington, D.C.); Metropolitan Museum of Art (New York); and the J. Paul Getty Museum (Los Angeles). Saar's art is held in the collections of many of these museums as well as the Hirshhorn Sculpture Garden (Washington, D.C.); Walker Art Center (Minneapolis); and the Whitney Museum of American Art (New York). She has received numerous awards, including grants and residencies from the Guggenheim Foundation, the National Endowment for the Arts, the Studio Museum Harlem, and the Washington Project for the Arts.

Born in Baltimore, Maryland, in 1948, **JOYCE J. SCOTT** is a sculptor, jeweler, printmaker, installation artist, performance artist, and educator. She received a B.F.A. from the Maryland Institute College of Art and an M.F.A. in crafts from Institute Allende in Mexico with further specialized study at the Rochester Institute of Technology in New York and Haystack Mountain School of Crafts in Maine. Following three generations of basketmakers, quilters, and wood, metal, and clay workers in her family, Scott employs weaving, quilting, beadwork, and glass in her artwork. Scott draws also on creative traditions from her Scottish, Native American, and African heritage, referencing historical events as well as contemporary pop culture in artistic commentaries about racism, sexism, and violence. The technical skill, intricate beauty, and satirical inferences of her art entice the viewer to confront the provocative and sometimes harsh social realities of her subject matter. Scott has exhibited her work at solo shows in numerous institutions such as the San Francisco Art Institute (California); Corcoran Gallery of Art (Washington, D.C.); and the Center for Contemporary Arts (St. Louis, Missouri), as well as at group shows in museums such as the New York Historical Society (New York); Bronx Museum (New York); and the Museum of Fine Art, Boston (Massachusetts). Her awards include the Louis Comfort Tiffany Foundation Award, a fellowship from the National Endowment for the Arts, and an appointment as an American Crafts Council Fellow in New York. Scott's work is in the permanent collections of such institutions as the Stedelijk Museum-Hertogenbosch (Netherlands); Baltimore Museum of Art (Maryland); and the Detroit Institute of Art (Michigan).

BERNI SEARLE was born in 1964 in Cape Town, South Africa, where she continues to live and work. She studied at the Michaelis School of Fine Art at the University of Cape Town, completing her undergraduate degree in 1987 and her M.F.A. degree in 1995. Searle uses photo-based media, installation, and video to encourage viewers to think about the politics of race and gender and to question arbitrary categories of race or nationalism. Recently, Searle has used the language and representations of ethnography to draw attention to the biased and permanent nature of documenting history and the role of visual culture in justifying perceived differences between people. Her work demonstrates how the artist can intervene in historical stereotypes by

uprooting fixed notions of identity. Searle has exhibited at numerous venues in South Africa and internationally, including solo and group shows at the South African National Gallery (Cape Town); Canberra Gallery (Australia); Kunsthalle Vienna (Austria); and the National Museum of African Art, Smithsonian Institution (Washington, D.C.). Her work is held at many of these museums as well as the permanent collection of the Australian Parliament and the Buhl Foundation (New York). In addition to being featured at biennials in Venice, Dakar, Shanghai, and Cairo, Searle was the recipient of a UNESCO award and the Standard Bank Young Artist award. She has completed residencies at the Canberra Institute of Arts (Australia); the Institute of Visual Arts at the University of Wisconsin (Milwaukee, Minnesota); and the Civitella Ranieri Fellowship for artist residency at Umbria, Italy.

Born in 1965 in New York City of American, Kenyan, and Pakistani heritage, photographer, writer, and activist **FAZAL SHEIKH** is currently based in Switzerland. Since graduating with a B.A. from Princeton University in 1987, he has worked with displaced communities in East Africa, Pakistan, Afghanistan, Brazil, Cuba, and India. Sheikh's interest in photographing refugee communities began after he visited Kenya in 1992 on a Fulbright Fellowship in the Arts to photograph the refugee camps near the border of Somalia. Since then, Sheikh has used his photography to raise public awareness of the less publicized stories of inequities, infractions, and the consequences of persecution, particularly among refugee populations. Using the slow and deliberate process of large-format portrait photography, Sheikh creates compelling images of individually named refugees, at times allowing the images to speak for themselves, at times providing testimonials from his subjects. His work has been featured internationally in solo shows in the United Nations (New York); the Museum of Contemporary Art (Moscow); and the Art Institute of Chicago (Illinois); and in group shows including the Berlin Photography biennial (Germany); Corcoran Museum of Art (Washington,

D.C.); Tate Modern (London); and the BildMuseet (Umea, Sweden). Sheikh has won many awards, including the 2005 MacArthur Fellowship, the Recontres d'Arles Le Prix Dialogue de l'Humanité, and a National Endowment for the Arts Fellowship in Photography. His photos are featured in public and private collections worldwide, including the Los Angeles County Museum of Art (California); Fondation Henri Cartier-Bresson (Paris); and the Museum of Kenya (Nairobi).

Born in 1935 in the village of Soloba, Mali, **MALICK SIDIBÉ** demonstrated a gift in art from an early age. Impressed by his drawing skills, Sidibé's tutors encouraged him to enlist at the École des Artisans Soudanais (now the Institut National des Arts in Bamako), where in 1955 he was singled out by the French photographer Gerard Gillat to work in his photo studio in Bamako. By 1962, Sidibé opened his own photography studio, becoming one of the founding fathers of contemporary Malian photography. Sidibé began first as an industrial and documentary photographer, but in the late 1970s he became more interested in studio portraiture. He carefully posed and lighted his subject against simple textile backgrounds, accompanied by props that communicated the subjects' personal connection to traditional and contemporary Malian life. Long celebrated in his home country of Mali and around Africa, Sidibé found critical acclaim in Europe and America in the early 1990s. Since then, his work has been featured in solo exhibitions in international institutions such as the Galleria Nazionale d'Arte Moderna (Rome); Museum of World Cultures (Berlin); and the Museum of Contemporary Art (Chicago, Illinois); as well as group exhibitions at the Istanbul biennial; the Harvard University Art Museums (Cambridge, Massachusetts); and Museum of the African Diaspora (San Francisco, California). His work is in the permanent collections of such institutions as the Metropolitan Museum of Art (New York); the San Francisco Museum of Modern Art (California); the International Center of Photography (New York); and the Seattle Art Museum (Washington). In 2002, Sidibé was awarded the Hasselblad

Foundation International Award in Photography, and in 2007 he won the lifetime achievement award at the 52nd Venice Biennial.

Born in Vryburg, South Africa, in 1953, **PENNY SIOPIS** studied Fine Arts at Rhodes University and Portsmouth Polytechnic before becoming lecturer at the Natal Technikon in Durban. Since moving to Johannesburg in 1984, she has been lecturing in the Department of Fine Arts, University of Witwatersrand, where she is currently Associate Professor in Fine Arts and chairperson of the department's governing committee. Siopis has exhibited extensively in South Africa, where she is best known for her "banquet" paintings and ironical history paintings from the 1980s, which focus on questions of race and gender representation in public history. During the 1990s, she extended her already eclectic range of media to include monumental installations, film, and video, which intersect biography and autobiography in narrating aspects of South African history through film. She has exhibited her work at the South African National Art Gallery (Cape Town); Museum Bochum (Germany); Cantor Arts Center at Stanford (San Francisco, California); and the British Council Student Centre, London. Her work has been featured also in the 1993 Venice Biennale (Italy); the 1995 Johannesburg Biennale (South Africa); and the Sixth Havana Biennale (Cuba) in 1997, and is in the collections of Chase Manhattan Bank (New York); Durban Art Gallery (South Africa); the Johannesburg Art Gallery (South Africa); South African National Gallery, Cape Town (South Africa); and the Pretoria Art Museum (South Africa).

MAUD SULTER is a poet, historian, teacher, and artist born in Glasgow, Scotland, in 1960 to Scottish and Ghanaian parents. Her Scottish grandfather was an amateur photographer who infrequently published his work, and it was through his images that Sulter originally became interested in photography. Sulter utilizes various media in her work, including photography, sound recordings, performance, and text, to focus on the critical re-examination of established histories, especially with those narratives that address slavery, the persecution of minorities, and black cultural heritage. Sulter is particularly interested in the erasure of black women's contributions to culture and uses her photography to make these women visible by putting them back into the cultural institutions in which their presence has often been marginalized. Sulter's work has been in a variety of solo and group shows throughout the United Kingdom and can be seen in the Victoria and Albert Museum (London); the National Portrait Gallery (Edinburgh); the New Hall ArtCollection at the University of Cambridge (England); and the Scottish Parliament (United Kingdom). She was awarded the British Telecom New Contemporaries Award 1990 and the Momart Fellowship at the Tate Gallery of Liverpool in 1990.

KARA WALKER was born in 1969 in Stockton, California, where her father served as a studio art professor. When the family relocated to Atlanta, Georgia, she experienced the culture shock of moving from a liberal, academic environment to what Walker saw as a conservative and socially inflexible environment. During her childhood, Walker defined and expressed herself through her artwork and went on to receive a B.F.A. in painting and printmaking from the Atlanta College of Art in 1991 and an M.F.A. in painting and printmaking from the Rhode Island School of Design in 1994. Walker currently lives in New York, where she is on the faculty of the M.F.A. program at Columbia University. She is best known for her use of black-paper silhouettes to create ambiguous satires, sharp visual narratives, and panoramic friezes that address the history of American slavery and racism while disrupting any simplistic dichotomies of good/bad, right/wrong, or black/white that a viewer might bring to the work. Walker has had solo exhibitions at the Museum of Modern Art (New York); San Francisco Museum of Modern Art (California); Deutsche Guggenheim Museum (Berlin, Germany); and the Tate Liverpool (England); and has exhibited in many group shows, including the Whitney, Istanbul, and São Paulo biennials. Walker received an Art Matters fellowship and is one of the youngest recipients ever to be given a John D. and Catherine T. MacArthur Foundation Achievement Award. Her work is featured in many public and private collections, including the Art Institute of Chicago (Illinois); Corcoran Gallery of Art (Washington, D.C.); Museum voor Modern Kunst (Arnhem, Netherlands); and the Walker Art Center (Minneapolis).

CARRIE MAE WEEMS was born in Portland, Oregon, in 1953. She earned a B.F.A. from California Institute of the Arts, Valencia, in 1981, and an M.F.A. from the University of California, San Diego, in 1984. She also pursued graduate studies in Folklore at the University of California—Berkeley, and in 1999 was presented with an honorary doctorate from the California College of Arts and Crafts, Oakland. One of the nation's most accomplished African American photographers, Weems often combines written texts, banners, commemorative plates, sound, sculpture, and narrative tableaux in her photographic installations. Devoutly committed to radical social change and the examination of issues of racism, classism, and sexism, Weems often uses nineteenth- and early twentieth-century images of Africans and African Americans to critique photography's complicity in constructions of race, class, gender, and sexuality. Weems has exhibited her work extensively at institutions such as the Boston University Art Gallery (Massachusetts); Whitney Museum of American Art (New York); Künstlerhaus Bethanien (Berlin, Germany); Moderna Museet (Stockholm, Sweden); and the National Museum of Women in the Arts (Washington, D.C.). Weems has also exhibited at the Dakar (Senegal), Johannesburg (South Africa), and Florence (Italy) biennials and has received numerous awards and residencies, including the Alpert Award for the Visual Arts and the National Endowment for the Arts Visual Arts Grant. Weems continues to teach in colleges and universities throughout the country.

CARLA WILLIAMS, an artist, writer, and activist, was born in 1965 in Los Angeles, California. She received her Bachelor of Arts in art and archaeology and visual arts at Princeton University in New Jersey in 1986. She continued her education at the

University of New Mexico in Albuquerque and received her Master of Arts in 1998 and an M.F.A. with a concentration in photography in 1996. When Williams started making nude self-portraits in the mid-1980s, she realized that she could not avoid a politicized reading of the black female body, entrenched as it is in the long visual and cultural histories that have shaped stereotypical imagery. Williams continues to make self-portraits for her own private consumption that allow her to envision a vibrant and self-defined sensuality, occasionally sharing this work through her website and through exhibitions. Her work has been featured in solo and group shows at the Center for Contemporary Arts (Santa Fe, New Mexico); Detroit Institute of the Arts (Michigan); and Studio Museum Harlem (New York); and is in the permanent collections of the University of New Mexico at Albuquerque Art Museum and the Princeton University Art Museum (New Jersey). Williams has served as a Rockefeller Fellow at Stanford University and is co-author of *The Black Female Body* and co-editor with Deborah Willis of *They Called Her Hottentot: The Art, Science and Fiction of Sarah Baartman.*

Contributors

IFI AMADIUME is a Nigerian poet and Professor of Religion, African and African American Studies, and Women's Studies at Dartmouth College, where she teaches courses on indigenous religions of Africa, women in African religions, and African studies. She received her Ph.D. at the University of London in 1983 in social anthropology and has taught in African studies at the University of Nigeria and The School of Oriental and African Studies, England. Amadiume's research interests include issues in gender, society, and culture in Africa, specifically matriarchy, women's organizations, and women's roles in African and diasporic indigenous religions. Her pioneering work in African feminist discourses includes *Male Daughters, Female Husbands: Gender and Sex in an African Society,* which was selected among the one hundred best books by African authors in the twentieth century; *African Matriarchal Foundations: The Igbo Case; Reinventing Africa: Matriarchy, Religion and Culture; Daughters of the Goddess, Daughters of Imperialsim;* and *The Politics of Memory: Truth, Healing and Social Justice* (co-edited with Abdullahi An Na'im).

AYO ABIÉTOU COLY received her Ph.D. at the Pennsylvania State University in comparative literature and women's studies and is currently Assistant Professor of Comparative Literature and African Studies at Dartmouth College. She has taught also at the University of Notre Dame and Pennsylvania State University, with research and teaching interests in Francophone African cinema and African women literary writers, gender identities and politics in Africa, postcolonial theory, colonial and postcolonial masculinities, and human rights. She has published in *The Literary Griot, Research in African Literatures, Nottingham French Studies,* and *The Canadian Review of Comparative Literature.* Her forthcoming publications include "Male Wives, Female Husbands: Immigration and the Geography of Home and Gender" and "Human Rights or Humanizing Rights: (Re)Claiming The Circumcised African Woman," and a book titled *Out of Their Fathers' House, at the Crossroads of Roots and Routes: Expatriate African Women Writers and the (Re)location of Home.* She has served as chair and organizer of the seminars "Humanists, Humanitarians and Other Travelers: Postcolonial and Postmodern Encounters with Otherness," "Re-Imagining the U.S.-Eurocenter," "New Directions in African Cinema," and "Narratives of Postcolonial Homecoming," among others, for various American Comparative Literature Association Annual Meetings and was organizer also of the African film series "Black Gazes, Whites Cameras."

Prior to her appointment as curator of African and Oceanic Art at the Museum of Fine Arts in Boston, **CHRISTRAUD GEARY** was curator of the photographic archives of the National Museum of African Art, Smithsonian Institution, for thirteen years. Geary, who studied at the University of Mainz and received her doctorate in Cultural Anthropology and African Studies from the University of Frankfurt, has conducted field research in Cameroon, Senegal, Nigeria, Kenya, Tanzania, Zimbabwe, and South Africa. Her research and curatorial interests have focused on the history of photography in Africa and African art, published in *Images from Bamum: German Colonial Photography at the Court of King Njoya; Seydou Keita, Photographer: Portraits from Bamako, Mali; Delivering Views: Distant Cultures in Early Postcards; South Africa, 1936–1949: Photographs by Constance Stuart Larrabee;* and *In and Out of Focus: Images from Central Africa, 1885–1960.* She has also taught at Wellesley College, Tufts University Institute of Anthropology, and Universität Münster, Germany.

Prior to her appointment as Chief Curator at the Museum for African Art in New York in 2005, **ENID SCHILDKROUT,** who received her Ph.D. in social anthropology from Cambridge University in 1970, was Curator at the American Museum of Natural History for three decades, where she also served as chair of the anthropology department from 1997 to 2002. Drawing heavily on museum collections and her fieldwork throughout the African continent, her research focuses on changing cultures of

Africa, the construction of ethnicities and transnational migrations in Africa, interpretation of material culture and African art, ecotourism, and its influence on African societies. She is best known for her seminal work on the Mangbetu culture in *African Reflections: Art from Northeastern Zaire* (co-curated with Curtis A. Keim) and *The Scramble for Art in Central Africa*. She has written extensively on Mangbetu arts in *Africa: The Art of a Continent, Unpacking Culture: Art and Commodity in Colonial and Postcolonial Worlds,* and numerous peer reviewed journals.

BARBARA THOMPSON, Curator of African, Oceanic, and Native American Collections at the Hood Museum of Art, received her Ph.D. in African art history at the University of Iowa, where she also served as Adjunct Professor of Art History. Her research interests include African women's arts, African ceramics, traditional East African healing arts, and contemporary African art. She has curated numerous exhibitions of African art, including *Beyond Beauty: The Arts of African Women* (Grinter Gallery, University of Florida, 1995); *A Sense of Common Ground: Excerpts, The Photography of Fazal Sheikh* (Hood Museum of Art, 2003); *Crossing Currents: The Synergy of Jean Michel Basquiat and Ouattara Watts* (Hood Museum of Art, 2003); *A Point of View: Africa on Display?* (Hood Museum of Art, 2003–4); and Fred Wilson's site-specific project *So Much Trouble in The World—Believe It or Not!* (Hood Museum of Art, 2005). She has published in *African Arts; Ceramics: Art and Perspectives;* and *Ceramics Technical* and contributed essays to *Hair in African Art; Kulte, Künstler, Könige in Afrika; The Interrelatedness of Music, Religion and Ritual in African Performance Practice;* and *Intermedia: Enacting the Liminal.*

KIMBERLY WALLACE-SANDERS received her Ph.D. in American studies from Boston University in 1996 and is Associate Professor of the Graduate Institute of Liberal Arts and Women's Studies at Emory University. She teaches courses on race and representations of the female body in American culture, representations of ethnicity, race, and gender in American culture and identity, advertising stereotypes, and African American material culture, and contemporary feminism. Her publications include the edited volume *Skin Deep, Spirit Strong: Critical Essays on the Black Female Body in American Culture,* which was nominated for the 2003 NAACP Image Award for Literature, and most recently, *Mammy: A Century of Race, Gender and Southern Memory.* Her research also appears in *American Quarterly, Initiatives, SAGE: A Scholarly Black Woman's Journal,* the *Oxford Companion to African American Literature,* and *Burning Down the House: Recycling Domesticity.*

CARLA WILLIAMS is a writer and photographer who lives and works in San Francisco, California. She received her M.F.A. in photography at the University of New Mexico, Albuquerque, in 1996. She has served as artist in residence at the Helene Wurlitzer Foundation Taos, New Mexico, in 2005; as Rockefeller Fellow at the Humanities Center, Stanford University, 2002–2003; and artist in residence at Light Work in Syracuse, New York, in 1997. Her art has been featured in *Here and Now* (de Saisset Museum, Santa Clara University 2005); *The African Effect: Kara Walker and Carla Williams* (Center for Contemporary Arts, Santa Fe 2004); *Reflections in Black: A History Deconstructed,* and *Treatment: Women's Bodies in Medical Science and Art* (Dinnerware Gallery Tucson 1999). She has published also in *They Called Her Hottentot: The Art, Science and Fiction of*

Sarah Baartman (co-edited with Deborah Willis), *Photography* (with Therese Mulligan); *The Black Female Body: A Photographic History* (with Deborah Willis); *Thurgood Marshall;* and *Photography from 1839 to Today: George Eastman House, Rochester, NY,* now titled *1000 Photo Icons.*

DEBORAH WILLIS is Professor of Photography at the College of Arts and Sciences, Africana Studies at the Tish School of the Arts, New York University. She has been chosen as 2005 Guggenheim Fellow and Fletcher Fellow, 2000 MacArthur Fellow, and was the 1996 recipient of the Anonymous Was a Woman Foundation award. Willis has pursued a dual professional career as an art photographer and as one of the nation's leading historians of African American photography and curator of African American culture. Her art work has been included in *A Sense of Place* (Frick, University of Pittsburgh, 2005); *Regarding Beauty* (University of Wisconsin, 2003); *Embracing Eatonville* (Light Works, 2003–4); *HairStories* (Scottsdale Contemporary Art Museum, 2003–4); *Re/Righting History: Counternarratives by Contemporary African-American Artists* (Katonah Museum of Art, 1999); *Memorable Histories and Historic Memories* (Bowdoin College Museum of Art, 1998); and *Cultural Baggage* (Rice University, 1995), among others. Her notable projects include *The Black Female Body: A Photographic History* (with Carla Williams); *A Small Nation of People: W.E.B. DuBois and the Photographs from the Paris Exposition; Reflections in Black: A History of Black Photographers—1840 to the Present; Visual Journal: Photography in Harlem and D.C. in the Thirties and Forties; Picturing Us: African American Identity in Photography;* and *VANDERZEE: The Portraits of James VanDerZee.*

Bibliography

Abrahams, Yvette. "Images of Sara Bartman: Sexuality, Race and Gender in Early Nineteenth-Century Britain." In *Nation, Empire, Colony: Historicizing Gender and Race*. Eds. Ruth Roach Pierson and Nupur Chaudhuri. Bloomington and Indianapolis: Indiana University Press, 1998. 220–236.

Adams, John Henry Jr. "Rough Sketches: A Study of the Features of the New Negro Woman." *Voice of the Negro* (August 1904): 323–326.

Alexis, Florence. "Creativity and the Hybrid Subject: Etiye Dimma Poulsen, the Artist in Her Own Words." In *Gendered Visions: The Art of Contemporary Africana Women Artists*. Ed. Salah M. Hassan. Trenton: Africa World Press, 1997. 53–61, 103.

Allman, Jean, ed. *Fashioning Africa: Power and the Politics of Dress*. Bloomington: Indiana University Press, 2004.

Alloula, Malek. *The Colonial Harem*. Minneapolis: University of Minnesota Press, 1986.

Altick, Richard. *The Shows of London*. Cambridge: Harvard University Press, 1978.

Amadiume, Ifi. *Male Daughters, Female Husbands: Gender and Sex in an African Society*. London: Zed Books, 1987; 4th edition, 1994.

———. "The mouth that spoke a falsehood will later speak the truth: going home to the field in Eastern Nigeria." In *Gendered Fields: Women, Men & Ethnography*. Eds. Diana Bell, Patricia Caplan, Wazir Jahan, and Abdul Karim. London: Routledge, 1993. 182–198.

———. *Reinventing Africa: Matriarchy, Religion and Culture*. London: Zed Books, 1997.

———. "Bodies, Choices, Globalizing NeoColonial Enchantments: African Matriarchs and Mammy Water." *Meridians: feminism, race, transnationalism* 2, no. 2 (2002): 41–66.

———. "Sexuality, African Religio-Cultural Traditions and Modernity: Expanding the Lens." Africa Regional Sexuality Resource Center 2006 (http://www.arsrc.org/index.htm).

Angelou, Maya. *And Still I Rise*. New York: Random House, Inc., 1978. Available at http://www.poets.org.

Anthony, Arthe. "Reading Visual Autobiographies: Reconstructing Women's Lives in a Creole of Color Community in New Orleans, 1900–1930." From the manuscript of a forthcoming book.

Archer-Straw, Petrine. *Negrophilia: Avant-Garde Paris and Black Culture in the 1920s*. New York and London: Thames & Hudson, 2000.

Atkinson, Brenda and Candice Breitz, eds. *Grey Areas: Representation, Identity and Politics in Contemporary South African Art*. Johannesburg: Chalkham Hill Press, 1999.

"Are You One of Those Perfect Types?" *Half Century Magazine* (September 1921): 9.

Aronson, Lisa. "African Women in the Visual Arts." *Signs: Journal of Woman in Culture and Society* 16, no. 3 (1991): 550–574.

"The Art of Modeling." Symposium discussion. The Bay Area Models Guild & Worth Ryder Gallery, University of California, Berkeley, June 24, 2004.

Ayto, John. *Dictionary of Word Origins*. New York: Arcade, 1990.

Baker, Houston A. Jr. "Islands of Identity: Inside the Pictures of Carrie Mae Weems." In *These Islands: South Carolina and Georgia by Carrie Mae Weems*. Tuscaloosa: University of Alabama Sarah Moody Gallery of Art, 1995. 14–19.

Baker, J. C., and C. Chase. *Josephine: The Hungry Heart*. New York: Random House, 1993.

Baker, Joséphine, and Jo Bouillon. *Joséphine*. Paris: Robert Laffont, 1976.

Baker, Joséphine, and Marcel Sauvage. *Les mémoires de Joséphine Baker*. Paris: Kra, 1947.

Bal, Mieke. *Double Exposure: The Subject of Cultural Analysis*. London: Routledge, 1996.

Barber, Beverly A. "Pearl Primus: In Search of Her Roots, 1943–1970." Ph.D. dissertation, Florida State University, 1984.

Baschet, Eric. *Africa 1900: A Continent Emerges*. Vaduz and Zug: Jeunesse Verlagsanstalt and Swan Productions, 1989.

Bascom, William. *African Arts in Cultural Perspective*. New York: Norton, 1973.

Basden, George T. *Niger Ibos*. London: Frank Cass & Co. Ltd., 1938. Reprint, New York: Barnes and Noble, 1966.

———. *Among the Ibos of Nigeria*. London: Frank Cass & Co. Ltd., 1921. Reprint, London: Cass 1966.

Bell, Brendan, and Ian Calder, eds. *Ubumba: Aspects of Indigenous Ceramics in KwaZulu-Natal*. Pietermaritzburg: Tatham Art Gallery, 1998.

Bell, Claire. *In/Sight: African Photographers from 1940–the Present*. New York: Guggenheim Museum, 1996.

Benet, Stephan Vincent. *John Brown's Body*. New York: Rhinehart and Company, 1927.

Berger, John. *Ways of Seeing*. London: British Broadcasting Corporations and New York: Penguin Books. 1972. Reprint, London: British Broadcasting Corporation and New York: Penguin Books, 1977.

Berliner, Brett. *Ambivalent Desire: The Exotic Black Other in Jazz-Age France*. Boston: University of Massachusetts Press, 2002.

Berns, Marla. "Ga'anda Scarification: A Model for Art and Identity." In *Marks of Civilization*, ed. Arnold Rubin. Los Angeles: University of California—Los Angeles Museum of Cultural History, 1988. 57–76.

———. "Ceramic Clues: Art History in the Gongola Valley." *African Arts* 22, no. 2 (February 1989): 48–59, 102–103.

Bester, Rory. "Floating Free." In *Berni Searle*. Cape Town: Bell-Roberts Publishing, 2003.

Beyala, Calixthe. *C'est le soleil qui m'a brûlée*. Paris: Stock, 1987.

———. *Tu t'appelleras Tanga*. Paris: Stock, 1988.

———. *Le petit prince de Belleville*. Paris: Albin Michel, 1992.

———. *Assèze l'Africaine*. Paris: Albin Michel, 1994.

———. *Les honneurs perdus*. Paris: Albin Michel, 1996.

———. *Amours sauvages*. Paris: Albin Michel, 1999.

———. *Comment cuisiner son mari à l'africaine*. Paris: Albin Michel, 2000.

———. *Lettre d'une Afro-Française à ses compatriotes*. Paris: Mango, 2000.

———. *Femme nue, femme noire*. Paris: Albin Michel, 2001.

Birnbaum, Martin. "The Long-Headed Mangbetus." *Natural History* 43 (1939): 73–83.

Bourgeois, Arthur P. "Yaka Masks and Sexual Imagery." *African Arts* 15, no. 2 (February 1982): 47–50, 87.

Brochand, Fanny. "Interview: Calixthe Beyala." http://delirium.lejournal.free.fr/interview_calixte_beyala.htm. 2000.

Brown, Karen McCarthy. "Mama Lola and the Ezilis: Themes of Mothering and Loving in Haitian Vodou." In *Unspoken Worlds: Women's Religious Lives*. Eds. Nancy Falk and Rita Gross. Belmont: Wadsworth Pub. Co., 1989; 2nd ed. 235–245.

———. *Mama Lola*. Los Angeles and Berkeley: University of California Press, 1991.

Bovin, Mette. *Nomads Who Cultivate Beauty: Wodaabe Dances and Visual Arts in Niger*. Uppsala: Nordiska Afrikainstitutet, 2001.

Bullington, Judy. "Thelma Johnson Streat and Cultural Synthesis on the West Coast." *American Art* 19, no. 2 (Summer 2005): 92–107.

Bundles, A'Lelia Perry. *On Her Own Ground: The Life and Times of Madam C. J. Walker*. New York: Scribner, 2001.

Capel, Anne K., and Glenn E. Markoe, eds. *Mistress of the House, Mistress of Heaven: Women in Ancient Egypt*. New York: Hudson Hills Press, 1996.

Carlson, Amanda. "Leaving One's Mark: The Photography of Lalla Essaydi." In *Converging Territories*. Ed. Laurence Miller. New York: powerHouse Books, 2005.

Carroll, Anne Elizabeth. *Word, Image, and the New Negro: Representation and Identity in the Harlem Renaissance*. Bloomington: Indiana University Press, 2005.

Chambers, Robert, ed. *The Book of Days: A Miscellany of Popular Antiquities*, 2 vols. London and Edinburgh: W. and R. Chambers, 1864.

Chicago Appeal. "Beauty Contest." January 31, 1891.

Clarke, Graham. *The Photograph*. Oxford: Oxford University Press, 1997.

Coleman, Evelyn. *The Collector's Encyclopedia of Dolls*. New York: Crown, 1971.

Collins, Patricia Hill. *Black Sexual Politics: African Americans, Gender, and the New Racism*. New York: Routledge, 2004.

Coly, Ayo Abiétou. "Neither Here nor There: Calixthe Beyala's Collapsing Homes." *Research in African Literatures* 33, no. 2 (2002): 34–45.

———. "Court Poet and Wild Child: Two Readings of Calixthe Beyala's *Les Honneurs perdus*." *Nottingham French Studies* 43, no. 3 (Autumn 2004): 15–27.

Conger, Amy. *Edward Weston: Photographs from the Collection of the Center for Creative Photography*. Tucson: Center for Creative Photography, University of Arizona. 1992.

Coombes, Annie E. "Gender, 'Race,' Ethnicity in Art Practice in Post-Apartheid South Africa: Annie E. Coombes and Penny Siopis in Conversation." *Feminist Review* 55 (Spring 1997): 110–129.

———. "Skin Deep/Bodies of Evidence: The Work of Berni Searle." In *Authentic/Ex-Centric: Conceptualism in Contemporary African Art*. Ithaca, N.Y.: Forum for African Arts Prince Claus Fund Library, 2001. 178–201, 244–245.

Corbey, Raymond. "Alterity: The Colonial Nude." *Critique of Anthropology* 8, no. 3 (1988): 75–92.

———. *Wildheid en beschaving: De Europese verbeelding van Afrika*. Baarn: Ambo, 1989.

Craig, Maxine Leeds. *Ain't I a Beauty Queen: Black Women, Beauty and the Politics of Race*. New York: Oxford, 2002.

Creque-Harris, Leah. "The Representation of African Dance on the Concert Stage: From the Early Black Musical to Pearl Primus." Ph.D. diss. Emory University, 1992.

Dabydeen, David. *Hogarth's Blacks: Images of Blacks in Eighteenth Century English Art*, Athens: University of Georgia Press, 1987.

Dallow, Jessica, and Barbara C. Matilsky. *Family Legacies: The Art of Betye Lezley and Alison Saar*. Chapel Hill: Ackland Art Museum and Seattle: University of Washington Press, 2005.

David, Philippe. *Inventaire générale des cartes postales Fortier*. 3 vols. Saint-Julien-du-Sault: Fostier, 1986–88.

Davison, Patricia. "South Africa Beer Pots." *African Arts* 18, no. 3 (May 1985): 74–77, 98.

De Certeau, Michel. *The Practice of Everyday Life*. Berkeley: University of California Press, 1984.

"Deep and Personal Expression: The Art of Thelma Johnson Streat." Wall label, March 7–July 6, 2003, Portland Museum of Art.

Deleuze, Gilles, and Felix Guattari. *A Thousand Plateaux: Capitalism and Schizophrenia*. Minneapolis: University of Minnesota Press, 1987.

DeMott, Barbara. *Dogon Masks: A Structural Study of Form and Meaning*. Ann Arbor: UMI Research Press, 1982.

Denker, Susan. "Lalla A. Essaydi: Converging Territories." *Nka, Journal of Contemporary African Art* 19 (Summer 2004): 86–87.

Derrida, Jacques. *Of Grammatology*. Baltimore: The Johns Hopkins University Press, 1974.

Dill, Bonnie Thornton. "Across the Boundaries of Race and Class: An Exploration of the Relationship between Work and Family among Black Female Domestic Servants." Ph.D. diss. New York University, 1979.

Douglas, Ann. *Terrible Honesty: Mongrel Manhattan in the 1920s*. New York: Noonday Press, Farrar, Straus and Giroux, 1995.

Drewal, Henry John. "Mami Wata Shrines: Exotica and the Construction of Self." In *African Material Culture*. Eds. Mary Jo Arnoldi, Christraud M. Geary, and Kris L. Hardin. Bloomington and Indianapolis: Indiana University Press, 1996. 308–333.

Drewal, Henry John, and Margaret Thompson Drewal. *Gelede: Art and Female Power Among the Yoruba*. Bloomington: Indiana University Press, 1983.

Drewes, Caroline. "The Legendary Flo Allen." *San Francisco Sunday Examiner and Chronicle*, March 19, 1967, 4.

Drysdale, Isabel. *Scenes in Georgia*. Philadelphia: American Sunday School Union, 1827.

Du Bois, W. E. B. "Opinion of W. E. B. Du Bois." *Crisis* (October 1923): 248–249.

———. "Criteria of Negro Art." In *The Crisis Reader: Stories, Poetry, and Essays from the N.A.A.C.P.'s Crisis Magazine*. Ed. Sondra Kathryn Wilson. New York: The Modern Library, 1999.

Dürr, P., Steven Grant, B. Sivan, and E. Tompapa. *Images de Guinée*. Conakry: Editions Imprimerie Mission Catholique, 1991.

Edwards, Elisabeth. "Photographic 'Types': The Pursuit of Method." In *Picturing Cultures: Historical Photographs in Anthropological Inquiry*. Ed. Joanna Cohan Scherer. Special Issue of *Visual Anthropology* 3, no. 2–3 (1990): 235–258.

Eliot, Thomas Stearns. "Tradition and the Individual Talent." In *The Sacred Wood*. London: Methune, 1920. Bartleby.com, 1996. On-line edition published 1996 by Bartleby.com, Inc. Available as of November 10, 2006, at www.bartleby.com/200/.

English, Daylanne. "W. E. B. Du Bois's Family Crisis." *American Literature* 72, no.2 (June 2000): 291–319.

Entwistle, Joanne. *The Fashioned Body*. Cambridge: Polity Press, 2000.

Enwezor, Okui. "Reframing the Black Subject: Ideology and Fantasy in Contemporary South African Art." In *Contemporary Art from South Africa*. Ed. Hope Marith. Oslo: Riksutstillinger, 1997.

———. "Reframing the Black Subject: Ideology and Fantasy in Contemporary South African Representation." *Third Text* 40 (Autumn 1997): 21–40.

———. *The Short Century: Independence and Liberation in Africa, 1945–1994*. Munich: Prestel, 2001.

Erickson, Peter. "Representations of Blacks and Blackness in the Renaissance." *Criticism* 35 (1993): 514–515.

Evans-Pritchard, E. E. "A Contribution to the Study of Zande Culture." *Africa* 30 (1960): 309–324.

———. "A Further Contribution to the Study of Zande Culture." *Africa* 33 (1963): 183–197.

———. "A Final Contribution to the Study of Zande Culture." *Africa* 35 (1965): 21–29.

———. *The Azande: History and Political Institutions*. Oxford: Clarendon Press, 1971.

Ezra, Kate. *Mother and Child in African Sculpture*. New York: The African American Institute, 1986.

Fagg, William. *Yoruba Sculpture of West Africa*. New York: Alfred A. Knopf, 1982.

Fall, N'Goné and Jean Loup Pivin, eds. *An Anthology of African Art: The Twentieth Century*. New York: Distributed Art Publishers, Inc. and Paris: Revue Noire Éditions, African Contemporary Art, 2002.

Farrell, Laurie Ann, ed. *Looking Both Ways: Art of the Contemporary African Diaspora*. New York: Museum for African Art and Gent: Snoeck Publishers, 2003.

"Finds the Beauty Contest Helpful." *Half Century Magazine* (November 1921): 21.

Firstenberg, Lauri. "Perverse Anthropology: The Photomontage of Wangechi Mutu." In *Looking Both Ways: Art of the Contemporary African Diaspora*. Ed. Laurie Ann Farrell. New York: Museum for African Art and Gent: Snoeck Publishers, 2003. 137–143.

Fitzgerald, Shannon and Tumelo Mosaka, eds. *A Fiction of Authenticity: Contemporary Africa Abroad*. St. Louis: Contemporary Art Museum, 2003.

Flandrau, Grace. *Then I Saw the Congo*. New York: Harcourt, Brace, and Co., 1929.

Gaither, E. Barry. "Imagining Identity and African American Art, or, It's Me You See!" In *Convergence, 8 Photographers*. Ed. Deborah Willis. Boston: Photographer Resource Center, Boston University, 1990. 8.

Gates, Henry Louis Jr. *The Signifying Monkey: A Theory of African American Literary Criticism*. New York: Oxford, 1988.

———. "New Negroes, Migration and Cultural Exchange." In *Jacob Lawrence: The Migration Series*. Eds. Lawrence, Jacob, Elizabeth Hutton Turner, and Lonnie G. Bunch. Washington, D.C.: The Rappahannock Press in association with the Phillips Collection, 1993. Introduction.

———. "The Body Politic." In *Thirteen Ways of Looking at a Black Man*. New York: Random House, 1997.

Geary, Christraud M. "Different Visions? Postcards from Africa by European and African Photographers and Sponsors." In *Delivering Views: Distant Cultures in Early Postcards*. Eds. Christraud M. Geary and Virginia-Lee Webb. Washington, D.C.: Smithsonian Institution Press, 1998. 147–177.

———. "Nineteenth-Century Images of the Mangbetu in Explorers' Accounts." In *The Scramble for Art in Central Africa*. Eds. Enid Schildkrout and Curtis A. Keim. London and New York: Cambridge University Press, 1998. 133–168.

———. *In and Out of Focus: Images from Central Africa, 1885–1960*. London: Philip Wilson, 2002.

Geary, Christraud M., and Virginia-Lee Webb, eds. *Delivering Views: Distant Cultures in Early Postcards*. Washington, D.C.: Smithsonian Institution Press, 1998.

Gibson, Ann Eden. *Abstract Expressionism: Other Politics*. New Haven and London: Yale University Press, 1997.

Giddings, Paula. *When and Where I Enter: The Impact of Black Women on Race and Sex in America.* New York: William Morrow and Company, 1984.

Gilman, Sanders. *Difference and Pathology: Stereotypes of Sexuality, Race, and Madness.* Ithaca: Cornell University Press.

Gips, Terry. "Joyce Scott's Mammy/Nanny Series." *Feminist Studies* 22, no. 2 (Summer 1996): 310–320.

Glaze, Anita. "Woman Power and Art in a Senufo Village." *African Arts* 8, no. 3 (Spring 1975): 24–29, 64–68, 90–91.

Gleason, Judith, and Elisa Mereghetti Tesser. *Becoming a Woman in Okrika* (film). New York: Filmmakers Library, 1990.

——— and Chief Allison Ibubuya. "My Year Reached, We Heard Ourselves Singing: Dawn Songs of Girls Becoming Women in Ogbogbo, Okrika, Rivers State, Nigeria, January 1990." *Research In African Literatures* 22, no. 3 (Fall 1991): 135–148.

Golden, Thelma. "Some Thoughts on Carrie Mae Weems." In *Carrie Mae Weems: Recent Works, 1992–1998.* New York: George Brazilier Publisher, in association with Everson Museum of Art, Syracuse, New York, 1998. 29–34.

Gore, Charles, and Joseph Nevadomsky. "Practice and Agency in Mammy Wata Worship in Southern Nigeria." *African Arts* 30, no. 2 (Spring 1997): 60–69, 95.

Green, Blake. "Flo Allen—First in the Art of Topless." *San Francisco Chronicle,* October 6, 1978, 29.

———. "An Artist's Model Looks Back." *San Francisco Chronicle,* June 6, 1980, 28.

Gregson Davis papers. Chapel Hill, North Carolina.

Griffith, Bronwyn A. E., ed. *Ambassadors of Progress; American Women Photographers in Paris, 1900–1901.* Washington, D. C.: The Library of Congress in association with the Musée d'Art Americain Giverny, France, 2001.

The Guerrilla Girls. "Thelma Johnson Streat: Dancing on a Paintbrush." In *The Guerrilla Girls' Bedside Companion to the History of Western Art.* New York: Penguin Books, 1998. 83.

Haardt, Georges-Marie, and Louis Audouin-Dubreuil. *La Croisière noire. Expédition Citroën Centre-Afrique.* Paris: Librarie Plon, 1927.

Haardt de la Baume, Caroline. *Alexandre Iacovleff, L'Artiste Voyageur.* Paris: Flammarion, 2000.

Hackett, Rosalind. *Art and Religion in Africa.* Leicester: Leicester University Press, 1996.

Hall, Kim. *Things of Darkness: Economies of Race and Gender in Early Modern England.* Ithaca: Cornell University Press, 1995.

Hall, Stuart. *Representation: Cultural Representations and Signifying Practices.* London: Sage, 1997.

Haney, Lynn. *Naked at the Feast: A Biography of Josephine Baker.* New York: Robson Books, 1981.

Harris, Joel Chandler. *Uncle Remus, His Songs and His Sayings: The Folk-lore of the Old Plantation.* New York: D. Appleton and Company, 1881.

———. *The Chronicles of Aunt Minervy Ann.* New York: Scribner, 1899.

Harris, Michael D. *Colored Pictures: Race and Visual Representation.* Chapel Hill: North Carolina Press, 2003.

Harris, Trudier. *From Mammies to Militants.* Philadelphia: Temple University Press, 1982.

Hassan, Salah M., ed. *Gendered Visions: The Art of Contemporary Africana Women Artists.* Trenton: Africa World Press, 1997.

Hendrickson, Hildi, ed. *Clothing and Difference: Embodying Colonial and Post-colonial Identities.* Durham: Duke University Press, 1996.

Herzberger-Fofana, Pierrette. *Littérature feminine francophone d'Afrique noire.* Paris: L'Harmattan, 2000.

Hine, Darlene Clark. "Rape and the Inner Lives of Black Women: Thoughts on the Culture of Dissemblance." In *Hine Sight: Black Women and the Reconstruction of American History.* Brooklyn: Carlson Publishing, 1994.

———. "Introduction." In *The Face of Our Past.* Eds. Kathleen Thompson and Hilary Mac Austin. Bloomington: University of Indiana Press, 1999. xi.

Hitchcott, Nicki. "Calixthe Beyala: Black Face(s) on French TV." *Modern and Contemporary France* 12, no. 4 (2004): 473–482.

Hobson, Janell. "The "Batty" Politic: Toward an Aesthetic of the Black Female Body," in *Hypatia* 18, no. 4 (Fall 2003): 87–105.

Hollander, Elizabeth. "On the Pedestal: Notes on Being an Artists' Model." *Raritan* 6, no. 1 (1996): 26–37.

Holloway, Camara Dia. *Portraiture and the Harlem Renaissance: The Photographs of James L. Allen.* New Haven: Yale Art Gallery, 1999.

hooks, bell. *Black Looks: Race and Representation.* Boston: South End Press, 1990.

———. "Selling Hot Pussy: Representations of Black Female Sexuality in the Cultural Marketplace." In *The Politics of Women's Bodies.* Ed. Rose Weitz. New York: Oxford University Press, 1998.

Hutchinson, Louise Daniel. *Anna Julia Cooper: A Voice from the South.* Washington, D.C.: Smithsonian Press and the Anacostia Neighborhood Museum, 1981.

Hutereau, Armand. *Notes sur la vie familiale et juridique de quelques populations du Congo belge.* Tervuren: Musée du Congo Belge, 1909.

Iacovleff, Alexandre. *Dessins et peintures d'Afrique, Croquis et notes de voyage.* Paris: Éditions Lucien Vogel, 1927.

Impy, Oliver, and Arthur MacGregor, eds. *The Origins of Museums: The Cabinets of Curiosities in Sixteenth- and Seventeenth-Century Europe.* 2nd ed. London: House of Stratus, 2001.

Jell-Bahlsen, Sabine. "Eze Mmiri di Egwu, The Water Monarch Is Awesome: Reconsidering the Mammy Water Myths." In *Queens, Queen Mothers, Priestesses and Power: Case Studies in African Gender.* Ed. Flora Kaplan. New York: New York Academy of Sciences, 1997. 103–134.

Jewell, K. Sue. *From Mammy to Miss America and Beyond: Cultural Images and the Shaping of U.S. Social Policy.* London: Routledge, 1993.

Jiminez, Jill Berk, ed. *Dictionary of Artists' Models.* London and Chicago: Fitzroy Dearborn Publishers, 2001.

Jones, G.I. *The Art of Eastern Nigeria.* Cambridge: Cambridge University Press, 1984.

King-Hammond, Leslie. 2000. "Acting Up and Out: Artistry in the Life of Joyce Jane Scott." In *Joyce J. Scott Kickin' It with the Old Masters.* Baltimore: Baltimore Museum of Art and Maryland Institute, College of Art, 2000. 8–13.

Kresge Art Center and Maude Wahlman. *Ceremonial Art of West Africa: From the Victor Du Bois Collection. An Exhibition at the Kresge Art Center Gallery, September 30–November 4.* East Lansing: The Kresge Art Center Gallery, Michigan State University, 1979.

Larkin, Brian, and Birgit Meyer. "Pentecostalism, Islam & Culture: New Religious Movements in West Africa." In *Themes in West Africa's History.* Ed. Emmanuel Kwaku Akyeampong. Athens: Ohio University; Oxford: James Currey; and Accra: Woeli Pub. Services, 2006. 286–312.

Leusinger, Elsy. *The Art of Black Africa.* New York: Graphic Society Ltd, 1972.

Jones, Lillian. "Occupational Sketches of People in Interesting Work: Maudelle—African Dancer and Model." *California Eagle* 59, no. 28 (October 20, 1938): 1.

Jules-Rosette, Bennetta. "Two Loves: Josephine Baker as Icon and Image." *Emergences* 10, no. 1 (2000): 55–77.

Junker, Wilhelm. *Travels in Africa during the Years 1875–1878.* A. H. Keane, translator. London: Chapman and Hall, 1890.

Kaplan, Flora S., ed. *Queens, Queen Mothers, Priestesses, and Power: Case Studies in African Gender.* New York: New York Academy of Sciences, 1997.

Katz, William Loren, ed. *Negro Population in the United Sates, 1790–1915.* New York: Arno Press and the New York Times, 1968.

Keim, Curtis A. "Precolonial Mangbetu Rule: Political and Economic Factors in Nineteenth-Century Mangbetu History (Northeast Zaire)." Ph.D. diss. Indiana University, 1979.

Kilmer, Hugh. "Figure Modeling: A Radical Performing Art." In *Perspectives on Figure Drawing.* Unpublished, 1996.

Kerels, Henri. *Arts et métiers Congolais: douze gravures originales en couleurs.* Brussels: Les Editions de Belgique, 1937.

Kerr, Merrily. "Wangechi Mutu's Extreme Makeovers." *Art on Paper* 8, no. 6 (July/August 2004). As of February 16, 2007, available at http://www.akrylic. com/articles/44/1/Wangechi-Mutus-Extreme-Makeovers/Art-On-Paper-Vol8-No-6-JulyAugust-2004.html.

Labelle, Marie Louise. *Beads of Life: Eastern and Southern African Beadwork from Canadian Collections.* Gatineau: Canadian Museum of Civilization, 2005.

Lacan, Jacques. *The Four Fundamental Concepts of Psycho-Analysis.* Ed. Jacques Alain Miller, translated from French by Alan Sheridan. New York: Norton, 1978.

Lagamma, Alisa. "The Metropolitan Museum of Art, New York." *African Arts* 34, no. 2 (Summer 2001): 72–77.

Lam, Wilfredo, and Musée Dapper. *Lam Métis.* Paris: Edition Dapper, 2001.

Lang, Herbert. "Famous Ivory Treasures of a Negro King." *American Museum Journal* 18, no. 7 (1918): 527–552.

———. Fieldnotes, Department of Anthropology. New York: American Museum of Natural History, 1910.

Lavitt, Wendy. *Knopf Collectors Guide to American Antiques: Dolls.* New York: Knopf, 1983.

———. *American Folk Dolls.* New York: Knopf, 1982.

Lipton, Eunice. *Alias Olympia: A Woman's Search for Manet's Notorious Model & Her Own Desire.* Ithaca: Cornell University Press, 1999.

MacDougall, David. *The Corporeal Image: Film, Ethnography, and the Senses.* Princeton and Oxford: Princeton University Press, 2006.

MacDowell, Tara. *New Works: Wangechi Mutu.* San Francisco: San Francisco Museum of Modern Art, 2006.

Mack, John. "Art, Culture and Tribute among the Azande." In *African Reflections: Art from Northeastern Zaire.* Eds. Enid Schildkrout and Curtis A. Keim. New York and Seattle: American Museum of Natural History and University of Washington Press, 1990. 217–233.

MacKethan, Lucinda. "Plantation Fiction." In *The History of Southern Literature.* Ed. Louis Rubin. Baton Rouge: Louisiana University Press, 1985. 209–218.

Marlow, Gertrude Woodruff. *A Right Worthy Grand Mission: Maggie Lena Walker and the Quest for Black Economic Empowerment.* Washington D.C.: Howard University Press, 2003.

Marshall, Paule. "The Negro Woman in Literature." *Freedomways* 6 (1966): 21.

Maseko, Zola. *Life and Times of Sara Baartman* (film). New York: First Run/Icarus Films, 1998.

Maudelle and George Weston papers. Schomburg Center for Research in Black Culture, New York Public Library.

Mbembe, Achille. "Regard d'Afrique sur l'image et imaginaire coloniale." In *Images et colonies.* Ed. Pascal Blanchard and Armelle Chatelier. Paris: ACHAC and SYROS, 1993. 133–137.

Mbiti, John S. *African Religions and Philosophy.* New York: Praeger, 1969.

McGreal, Chris. "Coming Home." *The Guardian,* 21/02/2002, London: Guardian News and Media Limited, 2002.

Miller, Nina. *Making Love Modern: The Intimate Public Worlds of New York's Literary Women.* New York: Oxford University Press, 1999.

Mitchell, Margaret. *Gone with the Wind.* New York: Macmillan Company, 1935.

Monti, Nicolas. *Africa Then: Photographs 1840–1918.* New York: Alfred A. Knopf, 1987.

Morgan, Jennifer L. "'Some Could Suckle over Their Shoulder': Male Travelers, Female Bodies, and the Gendering of Racial Ideology, 1500–1770." *The William and Mary Quarterly,* 3rd Ser., 54, no. 1 (January 1997): 167–192.

Morgan, Jo Ann. "Mammy the Huckster." *American Art* (Spring 1995): 87–107.

Morton, Patricia. *Distorted Images: The Historical Assault on Afro-American Women.* Westport: Praeger, 1991.

Mshana, Fadhili S. "Art and Identity among the Zaramo of Tanzania." Ph.D. diss. State University of New York, 1999.

Mudimbe, Valentin Y. *The Invention of Africa: Gnosis, Philosophy, and the Order of Knowledge.* Bloomington: Indiana University Press, 1988.

Muhammad, Erika Dalya. "Body Politic." *Art Review* 2, no. 6 (2004): 61–63.

Murinik, Tracy. "Berni Searle." *Nka, Journal of Contemporary African Art* 13/14 (Spring/Summer 2001): 74–79.

Musée Municipal de Boulougne-Billancourt. *Coloniales 1920–1940.* Paris: Graphireal, 1989.

Mwangi, Ingrid, and Robert Hutter. "Redressing." Statement to the video installation *Dressed Like Queens.* 2003. http://www.ingridmwangi.de/mh/text_Statments1.html.

Nesbitt, Nick. "Negritude." 2004. As of 9/19/2004, available at Africana.com, http://www.africana.com/research/encarta/tt_242.asp.

Negri, Eve de. *Nigerian Body Adornment*. Lagos: Nigeria Magazine, 1976.

New York Age. August 6, 1914, 1.

———. "Last Week of Beauty Contest." September 17, 1914, 1.

———. "Isaac Fisher and the *Age* Beauty Contest." October 4, 1914.

Ngcobo, Gabi. "Zanele Muholi." ArtThrob, undated. http://www.artthrob.co.za/06dec/artbio.html.

Njami, Simon. "Memory in the Skin: The Work of Ingrid Mwangi." In *Looking Both Ways: Art of the Contemporary African Diaspora*. Ed. Laurie Ann Farrell. New York: Museum for African Art and Gent: Snoeck Publishers, 2003. 145–152.

———, ed. *Africa Remix*. Ostfildern: Hatje Cantz and New York: D.A.P., 2005.

Nwapa, Flora. *Efuru*. London: Heinemann, 1966.

———. *One Is Enough*. Enugu: Tana Press, 1981; reprint, Trenton: Africa World Press, 1995.

———. *Women Are Different*. Enugu: Tana Press, 1986; Trenton: Africa World Press, 1992.

———. "Priestesses and Power Among the Riverine Igbo." In *Queens, Queen Mothers, Priestesses and Power: Case Studies in African Gender*. Ed. Flora S. Kaplan. New York: New York Academy of Sciences, 1997. 415–424.

Oguibe, Olu. *The Culture Game*. Minneapolis: University of Minnesota Press, 2004.

Ommer, Uwe. *Black Ladies*. Cologne and New York: Taschen, 1995.

Onwurah, Ngozi. *And Still I Rise* (film). New York: Women Make Movies, 1993.

———. *Monday's Girls* (film). San Francisco: California Newsreel, 1993.

Owen, Chandler. "Black Mammies." In *The Messenger*, April 1923, 670. Cited in Paula Giddings, *When and Where I Enter: The Impact of Black Women on Race and Sex in America*. New York: William Morrow and Company, 1984.

Oyewumi, Oyeronke. *The Invention of Women: Making Sense of Western Gender Discourses*. Minneapolis: University of Minnesota Press, 1997.

Page, Thomas Nelson. *Social Life in Old Virginia Before the War*. New York: C. Scribner's Sons, 1897.

Papich, Stephen. *Remembering Josephine*. New York: Bobbs-Merrill, 1976.

Parkhurst, Jesse. "The Role of the Black Mammy in the Plantation Household." *Journal of Negro History* 23 (1938): 25.

Perpener, John O. III. *African-American Concert Dance: The Harlem Renaissance and Beyond*. Urbana and Chicago: University of Illinois Press, 2001.

Philip, Marlene Nourbese. *A Genealogy of Resistance and Other Essays*. Toronto: Mercury Press, 1999.

Phillips, Ruth B. *Representing Women: Sande Masquerades of the Mende of Sierra Leone*. Los Angeles: UCLA Fowler Museum of Cultural History, 1995.

Piché, Thomas Jr. "Reading Carrie Mae Weems." In *Carrie Mae Weems: Recent Works, 1992–1998*. New York: George Braziller Publisher, in association with Everson Museum of Art, Syracuse, New York, 1998. 9–27.

Pieterse, Jan Nederveen. *White on Black: Images of Africa and Blacks in Western Popular Culture*. New Haven: Yale University Press, 1992.

Pimsleur, J. A. "Flo Allen—Legendary Artist's Model." *San Francisco Chronicle*, June 18, 1997, A20.

Prochaska, David. "The Archive of *Algérie Imaginaire*." *History and Anthropology* 4 (1990): 373–420.

Quanchi, Max, and Max Shekleton. "Disorderly Categories in Picture Postcards from Colonial Papua and New Guinea." *History of Photography* 25, no. 4 (Winter 2001): 315–333.

Ray, Benjamin C. *African Religions: Symbol, Ritual, and Community*. Upper Saddle River: Prentice Hall, 2000. 2nd ed.

Regester, Charlene. "The Construction of an Image and the Deconstruction of a Star—Josephine Baker Racialized, Sexualized, and Politicized in the African-American Press, the Mainstream Press, and FBI Files." *Popular Music and Society* 24 (2000): 31–84.

Richards, Colin. "About Face: Aspects of Art History and Identity in South African Visual Culture." *Third Text* 16/17 (Autumn/Winter 1991): 101–133.

———. "Senzeni Marasela." In *10 Years 100 Artists: Art in a Democratic South Africa*. Cape Town: Bell-Roberts Publishing, 2004. 230–231.

Roberts, Mary Nooter. *Body Politics: The Female Image in Luba Art and the Sculpture of Alison Saar*. Los Angeles: UCLA Fowler Museum of Cultural History, 2000.

Rollins, Judith. *Between Women*. Philadelphia: Temple University Press, 1985.

Rose, Phyllis. *Jazz Cleopatra: Josephine Baker in Her Time*. New York: Vintage Books, 1989.

Rosenblum, Naomi. *A History of Women Photographers*. New York: Abbeville, 1994.

Ross, Doran H., and Timothy F. Garrard. *Akan Transformations*. Los Angeles: Regents of the University of California, 1983.

Rousseau, Jean-Jacques. *Essay on the Origin of Languages and Writings Related to Music*. Trans. and ed. John T. Scott. Hanover: University Press of New England, 1998.

Rydell, Robert William. *All the World's a Fair: America's International Expositions, 1876–1916*. Chicago: University of Chicago Press, 1984.

———. *World of Fairs: The Century-of-Progress Expositions*. Chicago: University of Chicago Press, 1993.

——— and Nancy E. Gwinn, eds. *Fair Representations: World's Fairs and the Modern World Century-of-Progress Expositions*. Amsterdam: VU University Press, 1994.

Salmons, Jill. "Mammy Wata." *African Arts* 10, no. 3 (April 1997): 8–15, 87.

Scheinberg, Alfred L. *She: Images of the Woman in Black African Art*. New York: Germans Van Eck Gallery, 1983.

Schiebinger, Londa. *Nature's Body: Gender in the Making of Modern Science*. Boston: Beacon Press, 1993.

Schildkrout, Enid. "The Spectacle of Africa through the Lens of Herbert Lang." *African Arts* 24, no. 4 (1991): 70–85, 100.

———. "Gender and Sexuality in Mangbetu Art." In *Unpacking Culture: Art and Commodity in Colonial and Postcolonial Worlds*. Eds. Ruth Phillips and Christopher B. Steiner. Berkeley: University of California Press, 1999. 197–213.

———. "L'art Mangbetu: l'invention d'une tra-dition." In *Du Musée colonial au musée des cultures du monde. Actes du colloque organise par le musée national des Arts d'Afrique et d'Oceanie et le Centre Georges Pompidou, 3–6 juin 1998*. Ed. Dominique Taffin. Paris: Maisonneuve et Larose, 2000. 109–125.

Schildkrout, Enid, Jill Hellman, and Curtis A. Keim. "Mangbetu Pottery: Tradition and Innovation in Northeast Zaire." *African Arts* 22, no. 2 (1989): 38–47.

———. and Curtis A. Keim. *African Reflections: Art from Northeastern Zaire*. New York and Seattle: American Museum of Natural History and University of Washington Press, 1990.

———, eds. *The Scramble for Art in Central Africa*. Cambridge and New York: Cambridge University Press, 1998.

Schmitt, Berthold, and Bernd Schulz, ed. *Your Own Soul: Ingrid Mwangi*. Heidelberg: Kehrer, 2003.

Schneider, Jürg, Ute Röschenthaler, and Berhard Gardi, eds. *Fotofieber: Bilder aus West- und Zentralafrika, Die Reisen von Carl Passavant 1883–1885*. Basel: Christoph Merian Verlag, 2005.

Schweinfurth, Georg A. *The Heart of Africa: Three Years' Travels and Adventures in the Unexplored Regions of Central Africa from 1868 to 1871*. 2 vols. New York: Harper and Bros., 1874.

———. *Artes Africanae: Illustrations and Descriptions of Productions of the Industrial Arts of Central African Tribes*. Leipzig: F. A. Brockhaus, 1875.

Scott, Joyce J. *Fearless Beadwork: Handwriting and Drawings from Hell*. Rochester: Visual Studies Workshop, 1994.

Severa, Joan. *Dressed for the Photographer: Ordinary Americans & Fashion, 1840–1900*. Kent: The Kent State University Press, 1995.

Sharpley-Whiting, T. Denean. *Black Venus: Sexualized Savages, Primal Fears, and Primitive Narratives in French*. Durham: Duke University Press, 1999.

Shaw, Thomas MacDonald. "Beauty and Art." In *Fulani Matrix of Beauty and Art in the Djolof Region of Senegal*. Lewiston: Edwin Mellen Press, 1994. 47–84.

Sheikh, Fazal. *A Camel for the Son*. Rotterdam: Netherlands Photo Institute, 2001.

Sieber, Roy, ed. *Hair in Africa Art and Life*. Munich: Prestel Verlag, 2000.

——— and Roslyn Adele Walker. *African Art in the Cycle of Life*. Washington, D.C.: Smithsonian Institute Press, 1987.

Sims, Lowery Stokes. *Challenge of the Modern: African American Artists 1925–1945*. Acknowledgements. New York: The Studio Museum in Harlem, 2003.

Smadar, Lavie, and Ted Swedenburg, eds. *Displacement, Diaspora, and Geographies of Identity*. Durham: Duke University Press, 1996.

Smith, Shawn Michelle. *Photograph on the Color Line: W.E.B. Du Bois, Race, and Visual Culture*. Durham: Duke University Press, 2004.

Sneider, Betty. "Body Decorations in Mozambique." *African Arts* 6, no. 2 (Winter 1973): 26–31, 92.

Spivak, G. "Can the Subaltern Speak?" In *Marxism and the Interpretation of Culture*. Eds. Cary Nelson and Lawrence Grossberg. Basingstoke: Macmillan Education, 1988. 271–313.

Steady, Filomena Chioma, ed. *The Black Woman Cross-Culturally*. Boston: Schenkman.

Steinhart, Peter. 2004. *The Undressed Art: Why We Draw*. New York: Knopf, 1981.

Stevenson, Michael, and Joost Bosland, *Distant Relatives/Relative Distance*, Cape Town: Michael Stevenson Gallery, 2006.

Stocking, George W., ed. *Bones, Bodies, Behavior*. Madison: University of Wisconsin Press, 1988.

Stoller, Anne Laura. *Race and the Education of Desire: Foucault's History of Sexuality and the Colonial Order of Things*. Durham: Duke University Press, 1995.

———. *Carnal Knowledge and Imperial Power: Race and the Intimate in Colonial Rule*. Berkeley: University of California Press, 2002.

Stowe, Harriet Beecher. *Uncle Tom's Cabin, or, Life among the Lowly*. Boston: John P. Jewett & Company and Cleveland: Jewett, Proctor & Worthington, 1852.

Sulter, Maud. *ZABAT: Poetics of a Family Tree*. Hebden Bridge: Urban Fox Press, 1989.

Swantz, Marja-Liisa. *Ritual and Symbol in Transitional Zaramo Society*. Uppsala: Scandinavian Institute of African Studies, 1986.

Taylor, Helen. *Circling Dixie: Contemporary Southern Culture through a Transatlantic Lens*. New Brunswick: Rutgers University Press, 2001.

Taylor, Pegi. "A View from the Platform." In *Dictionary of Artists' Models*. Ed. Jill Berk Jiminez. London and Chicago: Fitzroy Dearborn Publishers, 2001. 3.

Terrell, Mary Church. "The Negro Exhibit at Paris." *The Colored American*, November 3, 1900, 8.

Thompson, Barbara. "The African Collection at the Hood Museum of Art." *African Arts* 37, no. 2 (Summer 2004): 14–33, 93n.

Thompson, Robert Farris. "Abatan: A Master Potter of the Egbado Yoruba." In *Tradition and Creativity*. Ed. Daniel Biebuyck. Berkeley: University of California Press, 1969. 120–182.

Torgovnick, Marianna. *Gone Primitive: Savage Intellects, Modern Lives*. Chicago: University of Chicago Press, 1990.

Turner, Patricia. *Ceramic Uncles and Celluloid Mammies*. New York: Anchor Books, 1994.

Tyre, Peg "Shocking the Jocks," *Newsweek*, March 8, 2004. http:// msnbc.msn.com/ id/4409142/.

United States Bureau of Census. *1900 Census Report*. Washington, D.C.: Government Printing Office, 1902.

Van der Watt, Liese. "Identity's Lack, Identity's Excess: Two Works by Berni Searle and Minette Vári." In *A Decade of Democracy*. Ed. Emma Bedfors. Cape Town: South African National Gallery, 2004. 120–127.

———. "Tracing Berni Searle." *African Arts* 37, no. 4 (Winter 2004): 74–79, 96.

Van Kerckhoven, Guillaume-François. "L'expédition Vankerckhoven." *Belgique coloniale* 2 (1896): 26–49.

Van Overbergh, Cyrille, and Eduard De Jonghe. *Les Mangbetu*. Brussels: Institut International de Bibliographie, Albert de Wit, 1909.

Vansina, Jan. "Reconstructing the Past." In *African Reflections: Art from Northeastern Zaire*. Eds. Enid Schildkrout and Curtis Keim. New York and Seattle: American Museum of Natural History and University of Washington Press, 1990. 69–88.

Vercoutter, Jean, Jean Devisse, Amadou-Mahtar M'Bow, Michel Mollat, Frank M. Snowden, and the Menil Foundation. *The Image of the Black in Western Art.* Cambridge: Harvard University Press and Houston: Menil Foundation, 1976.

Vogel, Susan Mullin. "Baule Scarification: The Mark of Civilization." In *Marks of Civilization: Artistic Transformations of the Human Body.* Ed. Arnold Rubin. Los Angeles: Museum of Cultural History, University of California—Los Angeles, 1988. 97–106.

———. *Africa Explores: 20th Century African Art.* New York: Center for African Art and Munich: Prestel Verlag, 1991.

Walker, Roslyn A. *African Women/African Art: An Exhibition of African Art Illustrating the Different Roles of Women in African Society.* New York: The African-American Institute, 1976.

Wallace-Sanders, Kimberly. "A Peculiar Motherhood: The Black Mammy Figure in American Literature and Popular Iconography." Ph.D. diss. Boston University, 1995.

———. *Mammy: A Century of Race, Gender and Southern Memory.* Ann Arbor: University of Michigan Press, 2006.

Wallace-Sanders, Kimberly, ed. *Skin Deep, Spirit Strong: The Black Female Body in American Culture.* Ann Arbor: The University of Michigan Press, 2002.

Wardwell, Allen. *African Sculpture.* Philadelphia: University of Pennsylvania Press, 1986.

———, Alfred L. Scheinberg, Maureen A. Zarember, and Tambaran Gallery. *Woman Eternal: The Female Image in African Art.* New York: Tambaran Gallery, 1991.

Warner, Coleman. "Historic studio faces demolition." In *The Times-Picayune,* June 24, 1995, A-8.

Wembah-Rashid, J. A. R. "Isinyago and Midimu: Masked Dancers of Tanzania and Mozambique." *African Arts* 4, no. 2 (Winter 1971): 38–44.

Wendl, Tobias. "'Observers are Worried': Fotokulissen aus Ghana." *Snap me one: Studiofotografen in Afrika.* Ed. Tobias Wendl and Heike Behrend. München: Prestel Verlag, 1998. 29–35.

Wesemael, Pieter van. *Architecture of Instruction and Delight: A Socio-historical Analysis of World Exhibitions as a Didactic Phenomenon (1798–1851–1970).* Rotterdam: Uitgeverij, 2001.

Westen, Mirjam. "Noirs: Angèle Etoundi Essamba." In *Noirs.* Arnhem: Museum voor Moderne Kunst, 2001. 3–4.

White, Deborah Gray. *Aren't I a Woman?* New York: Norton Books, 1985.

"Who is the Prettiest Colored Girl in this Country?" *Half Century Magazine* (September 1921): 9.

Wicker, Kathleen O'Brien, and Kofi Asare Opoku. *Priesthood and Ritual in Ghana: Abidjan Mami Water Shrine* (film). Upland: GerberMedia, 1994.

———. *Priesthood and Ritual in Ghana: Moree Mamme Water* (film). Upland: GerberMedia, 1996.

Williams, Fannie Barrier. "The Colored Woman and Her Part in Racial Regeneration." In *A New Negro for a New Century: An Accurate and Up-to-Date Record of the Upward Struggles of the Negro Race.* Ed. Booker T. Washington, N. B. Wood, and Fannie Barrier Williams, Chicago: American Publishing House, 1900.

Williamson, Sue. "Berni Searle." In *ArtThrob,* http://www.artthrob.co.za/ 00may/artbio.html, 2000.

———. "Should I Stay or Should I Go: The Ceaseless Dilemma of the Artists of Island Africa." In *Looking Both Ways: Art of the Contemporary African Diaspora.* Ed. Laurie Ann Farrell. New York: Museum for African Art and Gent: Snoeck Publishers, 2003. 10–11.

Willis, Deborah, and Carla Williams. *The Black Female Body: A Photographic History.* Philadelphia: Temple University Press, 2002.

———. *They Called Her Hottentot: The Art, Science and Fiction of Sarah Baartman* (Philadelphia: Temple University Press, 2006).

Willis, Liz. "*Uli* Painting and the Igbo World View." *African Arts* 22 (1988–89): 62–67, 104.

Wilson, Judith. 2002. "How the Invisible Woman Got Herself on the Cultural Map: Black Women Artists in California." In *Art/Women/California, 1950–2000: Parallels and Intersections.* Eds. Diana Burgess Fuller and Daniela Salvioni. Berkeley: University of California Press, 2002, 201–216.

Wilson, Sondra Kathryn, ed. *The Crisis Reader: Stories, Poetry, and Essays from the N.A.A.C.P.'s Crisis Magazine.* New York: The Modern Library, 1999.

———. "Black Mammies." In *The Messenger Reader.* New York: Modern Library, 2000. 330.

Women and Power: The Feminine Spirit in African Art, Selections from the Museum of Art and Archaeology. Columbia, Missouri: Museum of Art and Archaeology, 1990.

Woody, Howard. "International Postcards. Their History, Production, and Distribution (Circa 1895–1915)." In *Delivering Views: Distant Cultures in Early Postcards.* Eds. Christraud M. Geary and Virginia-Lee Webb. Washington, D.C.: Smithsonian Institution Press, 1998. 13–45.

Young, Iris Marion. 1998. "Breasted Experience: The Look and the Feeling." In *The Politics of Women's Bodies.* Ed. Rose Weitz, New York: Oxford University Press, 1998.

Young, Robert. *Colonial Desire: Hybridity in Theory, Culture, and Race.* London: Routledge, 1995.

Index

Mangbetu, 6 pl. 15, 6 pl. 53b, 24 pl. 15,
        70 pl. 46, 71–91, 81 f. 3.5, 82 f. 3.6, 87 f.
        3.7, 92 n. 9, 106, pl. 12, 107 pl. 13, 108
        pl. 14, 109 pl. 15, 140 pl. 53b, 182 pl. 46,
        188–89 pl. 53a–c
manhood, 38–40, 51, 297–98
Mano, 50
maquis, 268–69
Marasela, Senzeni, 219, 293–96, 295 f. 9.5,
        310 n. 52, 336, 353
        Our Mother, 293–94, 294 f. 9.4
        Theodorah Comes to Johannesburg,
        295 f. 9.5, 336–37 pl. 117
Marlow, Gertrude, 228
marriage
        as responsibility of women, 41, 62
        mail-order brides, 233–34, 233 f. 6.4,
        234 f. 6.5
        marriagability, 35, 289
        preparing for, 35, 40, 44, 55
        rituals of, 40, 55, 60–61, 286
Marshall, Paule, 163, 177
Martinet, Aaron, 28 f. 1.1
mask
        gelede, 52, 96, 97
        men's, 32
        women's, 32, 35, 50, 304
masquerade
        female, 51
        funerary, 32
        gelede, 52, 97, 313
        initiation, 32, 148
        Makonde, 38
        male, 32, 34, 282
        masqueraders, 32, 34, 148, 199 pl. 65
        ritual, 32
        Sande Society, 32, 51
maternal, 30, 52, 65, 163, 165, 169, 173
maternity, 21, 29, 42, 52, 82, 163, 169, 176,
        178, 298
        and clothing, 44
matriarchy, 49, 67
matriarch, 49, 56, 61
matriarchal, 49, 50, 62, 66
matrilineal, 39
Matubani and body painting, 76, 77 f. 3.4
maturity, 35, 42, 127, 304
mbari
        for Ala, 60 f. 2.9
        for Mammy Water, 64 f. 2.11
Mbembe, Achille, 158–59
Mbiti, John, 42
mbubu. See *ebubu*
Mbunza, 71, 72, 72 f. 3.1, 73–75, 78
McClure's, 168
McDowell, Tara, 281
Mende, 32, 50, 95 pl. 1
menstruation, 39, 41, 90, 97
Mereghetti Tesser, Elisa, 61
Messenger, 229, 239–40

Meurent, Victorine and Edouard Manet's
        Olympia, 248, 309 n. 4
Mills, Florence in *Vanity Fair*, 234 f. 6.6, 235
missionary, 49, 58, 63, 147–49
Mitchell, Maggie. See Maggie Lena Walker
Mitchell, Margaret, 165–66, 179 n. 8
Mizrahi, G., 170–72, 215 pl. 84
Mntambo, Nandipha, 120, 297–98, 353
        Balandzeli, 297, 314 pl. 97
        model
        artist's model, 233, 241, 247–48, 250,
        253–55, 289–90
model's union, 253
modeling, 85, 247–48, 250, 252, 255
        poses, 53, 55–56, 80, 85, 143–44, 147,
        150–52, 155, 168, 171, 231–32, 236,
        259–60, 283, 291, 297
        women as, 85, 151, 160 n. 6
Modernism, 73, 248, 289
modesty, 50, 73, 290
Monti, Nicolas, 143
morality, 27, 50, 272
Moree, 66
Morgan, Jennifer, 291
Morgan, JoAnn, 177–78
Mosaka, Tumelo, 17
Moses, Monday, 63
motherhood
        and femininity, 169
        and sexuality, 169
        postcards of, 149, 212 pl. 79, 213 pl. 80, 214
        pl. 81/82, 215 pl. 83/84, 217 pl. 87, 220
        pl. 90
        black, 163–64, 173, 291–93, 296
        chiefly, 32
        in African arts, 43, 52
        mock, 39
        role of women, 41–42
Moulin, Félix Jacques, 207 pl. 76, 283, 283 f.
        9.1, 285 f. 9.2
Muholi, Zanele, 256, 300, 342, 353–54
        Sex ID Crisis, 300, 342 pl. 122
mukudj, 32, 47 n. 21, 99 pl. 4
        and coiffure, 32
Musa, Hassan, 209, 273–75, 324–25, 354
        Allégorie à la Banane, 273–74, 324 pl. 106
        Mission Paris-Afrique, 273 f. 8.5
        Worship Objects, 325 pl. 107
music, 63, 80, 127, 289
        songs, 39, 52, 62–63, 97, 229
        women's songs, 62–63
musical instruments, 72, 86, 88
        harp, 83, 86–88, 93 n. 47
Muslim, 209, 285–86, 288, 307
Mutu, Wangechi, 280–81, 327, 354
        Double Fuse, 278 pl. 108, 281, 326 pl. 108
mwali, 39, 39 f. 1.7, 40
mwana hiti, 39, 39 f. 1.7, 47, 110 pl. 16, 111 pl.
        17, 112 pl. 18
mwana sesere, 39

Mwangi, Ingrid. See
        IngridMwangiRobertHutter cooperative
myth, 60, 64, 91, 163–64, 173, 177

N'gamsa, 35
Nalengbe, 75
nanny, 165, 175, 292
National Association of Colored Women, 238
National Geographic, 83, 280
Ndiaye, Demba, 153
neck rings, 50
nedjombine, 75
negbe, 79, 84
neggefa. See henna
négritude, 253
Nenzima, 75–76, 76 f. 3.3, 84
Nesbitt, Nick, 253
Netlaang, 41
New Negro,
        image of the, 228–31, 232 f. 6.3, 233–35,
        235 f. 6.7, 237–39, 243, 247
New York Age, The, 231, 235, 237, 240
Ngbaka, 87
Niam-Niam, 87–88, 93 n. 47
Niangara, 84
Nigerian postcards of women, 158 f. 4.15, 159,
        186 pl. 50, 261, 269
njorowe, 38, 119 pl. 26
Nka, 17
nkanda, 38
nkpu, 60, 61
Nnobi, 54–57, 59–61, 63, 68 n. 14/19
        See also Nwajiuba Ojukwuisiana na Nnobi
        Women's Council, 58 f. 2.8
Nobosodrou, 70 pl. 46, 83, 90, 182 pl. 46
North African ethnographic types, 284–85
        and postcards, 203 pl. 70/71, 204 pl. 73,
        283 f. 9.1, 285 f. 9.2
Nupe, 116 pl. 23
nurturance, 21, 29–30, 51
nurturing, 32, 40, 52, 148, 292, 295
Nwajiuba Ojukwuisiana na Nnobi, 54,
        54 f. 2.2, 55–57, 57 f. 2.7, 58, 58 f. 2.8,
        59–61, 63, 69 n. 19
        and comportment, 55–56
        and clothing, 56, 56 f. 2.5
Nzakara, 87

O'Brien Wicker, Kathleen, 65–66
obi, 55
occult, 64–65
odalisque, 283–84, 307
Odundo, Magdalene, 6 pl. 101, 89–90,
        224 pl. 101, 354
        Untitled, 89, 318 pl. 101
Ofili, Chris, 17
Ogowe Lambarene postcard, 153, 154 f. 4.11
Oguibe, Olu, 275
Okondo, 74, 75 f. 3.2, 76 f. 3.3, 84, 91
Okrika, 61, 63